AND THE SEA WILL TELL

AND THE SEA WILL TELL

VINCENT BUGLIOSI

with Bruce B. Henderson

W. W. NORTON & COMPANY

NEW YORK   LONDON

For legal reasons, some of the names in this book have been changed.

For information about permission to reproduce selections from this
book, write to Permissions, W. W. Norton & Company, Inc.,
500 Fifth Avenue, New York, NY 10110

Manufacturing by R. R. Donnelley, Harrisonburg
Book design by Lovedog Studio
Cartography by Jacques Chazaud
Production manager: Amanda Morrison

Library of Congress Cataloging-in-Publication Data

Bugliosi, Vincent.
And the sea will tell / by Vincent Bugliosi with Bruce B. Henderson.
p. cm.
1. Henderson, Bruce B., 1946–. II. Title.
PS3552.U393A82   1991
813'.54—dc20   90–37457

ISBN-13: 978-0-393-32796-0 (pbk.)
ISBN-10: 0-393-32796-5 (pbk.)

W. W. Norton & Company, Inc.
500 Fifth Avenue, New York, N.Y. 10110
www.wwnorton.com

W. W. Norton & Company Ltd.
Castle House, 75/76 Wells Street, London W1T 3QT

2 3 4 5 6 7 8 9 0

TO MY MOTHER:

*No sweeter or more wonderful
woman ever lived.*

VB

I WISH TO ACKNOWLEDGE Frank Cooper, Wayne Alexander, Esq., Charlie Flowers, and finally, Robby Wald, without whom this book would not have been written.

—VB

CONTENTS

An ocean is forever asking questions,
And writing them aloud along the shore.

—EDWIN ARLINGTON ROBINSON

PALMYRA ISLAND

I had a foreboding feeling about the island. It was more than just the fact that it was a ghost-type island. It was more than that. It seemed to be an unfriendly place to be. I've been on a number of atolls, but Palmyra was different. I can't put my finger on specifically why. But it was not an island that I enjoyed being on. I think other people have had difficulties on that island.

—South Pacific yachtsman

AT ONCE BEAUTIFUL AND forbidding, this uninhabited tropical atoll is off the well-traveled path of the trade winds. Situated dead center in the Pacific Ocean, Palmyra was discovered by accident only in the nineteenth century. If one were to search the high seas for a setting that would lend itself to impenetrable mystery, this lonely outpost would not disappoint.

From afar, Palmyra is seductive: tall coconut trees and stretches of beach are enveloped by a coral reef and the brilliant shallows of the tropical ocean.

Once ashore, however, one finds that the vegetation that looks so lush and inviting from a distance is impassable except with a machete. Hordes of land crabs claim squatter's rights to much of the island. The beaches are not sandy, but rocky, and surrounded by coral as sharp as a surgeon's scalpel, capable of shredding the ribs of the sturdiest vessel. Only a narrow passage in the reef on the southwestern side allows access to a lagoon populated by schools of colorful fish, temptingly meaty but poisonous to eat. And it doesn't take long to notice in the crystalline waters the menacing gray shadows of nature's most perfect eating machines. *Sharks.* There is, finally, no escape from the blazing sun and stifling humidity.

Only the most adventuresome, or desperate, would plan an extended stay here. This is the true story of two men and two women who did. One married couple, two lovers. Four lives forever changed on an island that never wanted company. Each of the visitors sought escape from the world, but for very different reasons, their destinies intersecting on this deserted atoll. Not all of them would leave alive. The mystery shrouding their fate would be as dark and chilling as the ocean floor deep beneath Palmyra Island.

BOOK ONE
THE CRIME

CHAPTER 1

IT HAD RAINED DURING the night, one of those warm tropical showers that leaves the air heavy and sweet. A steady breeze born far out at sea touched the shore at sunrise, rustling the coconut palms. The clouds, like the folks around these parts in no hurry to move on, scattered slowly as the sun rose out of the ocean and washed the sky with bold streaks of light. A few arcs of rainbow loitered above, offering promise for the new day.

Hawaii's locals make a clear distinction between themselves and haoles, the sunburned tourists from the mainland. It is less a term of contempt than bemused pity. On the scenically spectacular island of Maui, most of these visitors pick up their rental cars at Kahului Airport and drive directly to Kaanapali Beach on the western coast, where they stay in glitzy resort hotels, down premixed Mai Tais served by waitresses in synthetic grass skirts, and tap their toes to the canned melodies of Don Ho. Haoles just don't know any better.

The real soul of Maui is manifest on the south shore, with its endless stretches of blinding white beaches. The sun-bleached dunes roll up to wide verdant fields of pineapple and sugar cane. Herds of cattle graze contentedly on the grassy slopes of the West Maui mountains. Majestic Haleakala, the highest point on the island, is a two-mile-high peak topped with a massive volcanic crater, a dramatic reminder that this is a land of sudden, violent change.

At Maalaea Bay boat harbor, Charlie, the winch operator, was working a squeaky crank that unwound a cable still wet from the rain. "Never thought I'd live to see the day this old gal went back in the water," he offered to anyone within earshot as he controlled the speed with which a trailer bearing a thirty-foot wooden sail-boat rolled down a launching ramp.

Boat launchings were hardly uncommon hereabouts, but a small crowd of locals had gathered to watch this particular one. These folks and a few hundred other kindred souls lived aboard boats in the bay. Most were dreamers who collected sea charts, atlases, and books about faraway places, yearning to pull up anchor and sail away, just like the excited young couple whose boat was now the center of attention. But few would do so.

Tall, shirtless Buck Duane Walker walked with long strides next to the trailer as it carried his boat toward the water. Thirty-six years old, he still had the athletic swagger of a younger man. His face and torso were deeply tanned, his shock of hair sun-streaked. He could have been just another aging surfer, but his glittery cobalt eyes darted quickly back and forth, as if he feared discovery.

A smiling strawberry blonde on the deck of the boat gave off a completely different air. Jennifer Jenkins, wearing cutoff chinos and a pastel halter top, also looked younger than her age, twenty-eight. She was five-four and, in truth, not the type to win a beauty contest. But she radiated an appealing apple-fresh quality. Neither coyness nor guile seemed hidden beneath her open, happy-go-lucky nature. Jennifer clutched a magnum of champagne for the traditional christening, but because people walked barefoot around the ramp area, she did not intend to smash it on the bow the way she'd seen it done in old newsreels of ship launchings. Instead, she planned to pop the cork with appropriate fanfare, baptize the deck with only a splash of bubbly, and drink the rest with Buck.

When they'd bought this boat four months before, it was mast-less and unrigged. Since sinking at its anchorage here in Maalaea Bay years earlier, the *Margaret* had earned a rep as a hard-luck boat. In lifting the submerged vessel from the harbor depths, a salvage crane had accidentally snapped her mast, and no one had bothered to replace it. After sitting on wooden blocks for two years, the boat was sold for four hundred dollars to a young married couple with ambitious plans for restoration. They fiberglassed over the cracked wooden planks of her hull, then painstakingly stripped and refin-ished the woodwork inside the cabin. Eventually, however, they became dispirited by the hard work that still remained to be done and sold the boat and trailer for $2,260—nearly all of the money Jennifer and Buck had been able to scrape up.

While Buck dedicated himself to the challenge of mending their sorry-looking vessel, Jennifer kept her assistant manager's job at a seafront bar favored by locals in Wailuku, Club Ginzo, so they had income to buy materials and supplies for the boat. Not being mechanically gifted or knowledgeable, Buck did not find the work easy. His only previous boat-repair experience had been helping his dad build some houseboats. But he had checked out library books on yacht design, construction, and repair. Setting up a portable generator so he'd have light for night work, he busied himself round the clock. He began by patching new cracks in the fiberglass and painting the hull. Manufactured masts were prohibitively expensive, so he joined together three forty-foot Douglas fir two-by-sixes to make a homemade mast and bolted it to the boat's frame from under the deck. Following one book's explicit instructions on how to secure the mast above deck, he fashioned a forestay, a backstay, two upper shrouds, and four lower shrouds to brace the mast. Working daily on the battered *Margaret*, he was pleased to see that the effort toughened him physically for what he jokingly called "the sailor's arduous life." He had little idea just how arduous it would prove to be.

Jennifer's shift ended at midnight. After work on hot, muggy nights, she'd take a couple of cold beers from the bar cooler down to Buck at the dock. They'd sit side by side on their beached boat, planning a life together, smooching in the moonlight.

Ignoring the warning of sailing folklore that renaming a boat is bad luck, they called their little vessel the *Iola*, a name Jennifer had suggested. "In Hawaiian, *iola* means 'to life,'" she had explained to Buck, who thought it an ideal choice. Finding a new life was the aim of all their effort. He had responded with a toast: "To the *Iola*. May she sail the seven seas and never more see the bottom of the ocean."

This morning, the *Iola* was finally ready for launching. She'd never be mistaken for an America's Cup entry, but the improvement over her previous condition was significant. "What a marvelous transformation we've wrought!" crowed Buck. She was thirty feet long on deck with nine feet of beam. Her hull was freshly painted an azure blue. Her secondhand sails, crisscrossed with stitched repairs, lay along the foredeck, ruffled by the breeze even though tied down to the jerry-built stanchions. The *Iola's* deep keel was made of cast iron, ensuring that the vessel would not list too severely at sea, even under full sail in a strong wind. This characteristic was ideal for novice sailors like Jennifer and Buck. Both had gone only day sailing; Jennifer had never even steered a boat by herself.

"Slow down, Charlie!" Buck suddenly yelled.

On deck, Jennifer beamed like a new mom. She would release the last of the lines that secured the *Iola* to the trailer when the boat hit the water—another minute or so. And then, in a day or two, she and Buck would be on their way.

Someone might well have described Jennifer as a hippie, and she would not have objected. Much about the Establishment seemed hypocritical and otherwise distasteful to her. Just six months earlier, the Vice President of the United States had resigned after pleading "no contest" to charges of tax evasion. And impeachment hearings against President Nixon were scheduled to begin in a few weeks. Jennifer and her generation had come of age in an era of political malfeasance at the highest levels and during a widely unpopular war in Vietnam, a period of conflict that sapped the nation's collective spirit and caused her and many of her peers to reject some of the older generation's values. "Make love, not war" sounded right on the mark to her.

Although Buck would join Jennifer in condemning government officials, the police, and virtually anyone else in power, his rhetoric had a coarser edge. She deplored, but he threatened. Indeed, the tattoos on his arms suggested something more than the trendy espousal of love and peace. On the left, a heart encircled with a ribbon stretched across his biceps, and his first name rippled in bold letters on his muscular forearm. There was nothing overtly sinister in the designs, not like a pirate's skull and crossbones, but they were crudely drawn and the skin beneath the indelible ink was scarred. They were exactly what they looked like: the kind of homemade tattoos that angry and bored men behind bars give one another.

Jennifer and Buck had met two years earlier in Hilo, the major town on Hawaii's Big Island. It had been an accidental meeting, crossing paths, as they did, in an apartment complex courtyard filled with blooming hibiscus. They exchanged hellos and friendly glances, and Jennifer, in a long green granny dress, tossed her mane of reddish-gold curls and kept walking. Buck, captivated, wheeled around and caught up with her. Later, he told her he'd made a split-second decision not to let her big dreamy eyes and bright pretty smile get away. That afternoon they shared some red wine under a palm tree in a nearby park, listening to the traditional music of a live band celebrating a Hawaiian holiday in honor of an ancient Polynesian king.

The sun dipped early that day behind a bank of pinkish clouds, and light died from the sky. The glowing sunset, the pulsating music, and the natural chemistry between them combined with a few hits off a joint to make Jennifer feel giddy with sensual delight. Buck leaned over and kissed her lips.

"You got an old man?" he asked.

She smiled playfully. "Nope."

They kissed again, this time more passionately.

Lying in each other's arms that night and talking in the hushed tones of new lovers, they discovered they had both ended up in Hawaii for not dissimilar reasons. She had arrived three years earlier to work for her uncle, who was recuperating from a near-fatal heart attack and needed help running his Kaneohe Bay resort. Buck had come to the islands to help his father build a cabin on the Big Island. Their unplanned tryst seemed like fate. They dubbed Roberta Flack's "The First Time Ever I Saw Your Face" their song, and soon were living together in the one-room cabin Buck and his father had built in Mountain View, an isolated mountainous area twenty miles southwest of Hilo. It wasn't much of a cabin—Jennifer thought it looked like an outlaw's hideout—and they had no electricity or indoor plumbing. But they moved in thrift-store furniture, she sewed lacy curtains, and it became home. A wood-burning stove warmed them on chilly mornings. Jennifer looked forward each morning to taking a mug of steaming coffee outside and strolling among the wild orchids and ferns as the golden sunshine poured through the treetops. She enjoyed leading a simple life, valuing friends and her man above material consumption. Here it was possible to live life more peacefully, more thoughtfully than she'd been able to in the anxious urban canyons of Los Angeles or the tensely electric atmosphere of New York. They talked marriage, and even went so far as to have blood tests, but getting a piece of paper that declared them a "legal" couple never ranked as a high priority.

Unfortunately, it soon became urgent that they depart their sylvan mountain hideaway. In fact, they had no choice but to leave Hawaii entirely. Against her advice, Buck had gone into business with an ex-con pal who was a big-time drug dealer in California. Buck had been arrested in Hilo selling several thousand dollars' worth of MDA (methylene dimethoxyamphetamine), a wicked combination of speed and a potent LSD-type hallucinogen, to a federal undercover narcotics agent; Jennifer had been arrested too, and both were facing federal charges. Worse, this was the second time Buck had sold MDA, shipped to him by his California connection, to a narc, so he faced two counts. Already on parole from a California state prison, where he'd served time for an armed robbery conviction, Buck's main fear was being sent back to San Quentin as a parole violator and having to finish a five-to-life sentence at one of the toughest prisons in the country.

If they were going to have a life together, it would have to be far removed from civilization—from courts and prisons and authorities. A few weeks ago, they had flown over to Honolulu and checked out books about Pacific islands from the main library. Buck thought one little island neither of them had ever heard of, called Palmyra, looked particularly promising. It sounded like a real Robinson Crusoe setting, with a protected lagoon, an unlimited supply of coconuts and fish, and balmy weather year-round. Best of all, it was uninhabited. No police, no prosecutors, no narcs, no arrest warrants. Of course, that also meant no grocery stores, no repair shops, no doctors, no help of any kind. They would have to fend for themselves.

Suddenly, there was a thud as their sailboat slipped on the trailer and tilted sharply to one side.

"Jen, hold on!"

Buck's warning came too late. Losing her footing, Jennifer fell and nearly rolled off the deck to the concrete below. But Buck was there to save her, his powerful arms reaching up and helping her down.

Out of inexperience, Buck had used nylon ropes to secure the boat to the trailer. They stretched, of course, so the hull slipped, causing the support blocks beneath it to topple. The wind cable had slipped only momentarily, but the boat had instantly lurched forward.

Frightening as it was for Jennifer, the mishap should have caused only a minor delay in the launching. But when the boat tipped to the side, two steel support beams angling up from the trailer pierced the hull below the waterline. And there the *Iola* sat, skewered like a pig at a luau.

Buck, livid at the disastrous sight before him, clenched his fists and spun furiously on the open-mouthed winch operator.

For a moment, Jennifer was sure Buck would attack fat, red-faced Charlie, even though everyone standing there could see it hadn't been his fault. But Buck didn't completely lose it. He took a step or two toward the man, then shouted a curse and bolted for the parking lot and his old pickup, without even glancing toward Jennifer.

She felt absurd standing before the stunned onlookers still holding the bottle of champagne, which somehow had not broken. "Baby, it's okay," she called to the man she loved. "We can patch the holes . . ." Her voice trailed off. Everyone was looking at her.

She was struck, at that instant, with the thought that, for once, they should have heeded conventional wisdom. They should not have changed the boat's name. *Bad luck will follow us wherever we go.*

CHAPTER 2

THAT SAME SPRING OF 1974, an eye-catchingly beautiful sail-boat named the *Sea Wind* was docked more than two thousand miles away at a San Diego marina. This thirty-eight-foot two-masted ketch, obviously maintained with exquisite care, was the pride and joy of Malcolm "Mac" Graham III, at forty-three a man more at home on a boat than on any landlocked place he'd ever lived.

Wiping his hands on an oily rag, Mac leaned over and flipped a switch. He jerked hard on a starter cord, and the generator's motor started on the first try. The engine sounded like new again. The valve job had done the trick.

As always on warm days aboard his boat, Mac was shirtless and barefoot, wearing nothing but swim trunks. In his weathered broad face, faint squint lines highlighted alert gray-blue eyes. Like his boat, Mac was sturdily constructed. Two inches shy of six feet, his squarish body was bronzed by years of working in the sun. He had a craftsman's long, supple fingers but the short-cropped hair of a Marine drill instructor. Mac was not all rawhide, though. Quick to smile and offer a friendly handshake, he was basically the eternal optimist—cheery, hearty, always willing to lend a helping hand. Mac's philosophy was that those who bring sunshine into the lives of others cannot keep it from themselves. Lots of folks in marinas around the globe were happy to count Mac Graham a friend.

In the fourteen years he'd owned the *Sea Wind*, Mac had sanded and painted virtually every plank of its hull, deck, and cabin. Recently, he'd completed a major remodeling that began with his ripping off the top and sides of the cabin and gutting the interior. Typically, he drew his own plans and did all the work himself, because he didn't trust anyone else to do as good a job. He bought only the finest materials and took his time, attentive to the most minute detail.

Though he'd earned an 84 average in two years at General Motors Institute, a Flint, Michigan, engineering school operated by the automotive giant, Mac rebelled at a future of being cloistered in an office forty hours a week slaving over automotive designs, and he withdrew before graduating. Deciding in college that he wanted to be a sailor—not one of those beer-guzzling weekend hobbyists, but a real blue-water sailor capable of matching his skills against the untamed forces of the sea—he moved to the West Coast to be closer to his dream, and found work in the marinas that dot California's shoreline. Mac seldom stayed long at any job, though in no time his employers came to appreciate his abilities as a naturally gifted "hands-on" engineer, intuitively creative and fascinated with all things mechanical. On a boat, you name it, Mac could do it. It was on land, caught up in the workaday world of landlubbers, that he seemed as out of place as a guest wearing sneakers at a society ball.

The overhaul of the *Sea Wind* had taken two years. When finished, the new cabin was nearly ten feet longer than the original and gave the boat a unique silhouette. Mac had installed the latest gear, including a powerful shortwave transceiver radio and a state-of-the-art automatic pilot system. In the galley, he installed a battery-powered refrigerator with a small freezer section, a shipboard luxury rarely seen except in the priciest of yachts. In the forecastle, Mac had built a snug little workshop with an elaborate workbench. Also aboard was a Zodiac rubber dinghy with a nine-horsepower Evinrude, and a "hard" (wooden) dinghy which sported its own small Sea Gull motor. The *Sea Wind* was an enviably well-outfitted, one-of-a-kind cruising boat, distinctive in both looks and seagoing efficiency.

Mac had survived several life-threatening experiences in tempestuous seas, but his passion for sailing remained undiminished. The sea had an almost hypnotic hold over him. Like the wise, aged fisherman in *The Old Man and the Sea*, Mac thought of the sea as a woman who could give or withhold great favors, and his romance with her was never dampened by any momentary ill disposition she might express. Meeting the challenge of the sea head-on could be hard and dangerous work, to be sure, but there was a thrill of accomplishment when he had survived the test. It was the joy of being alive. Mac did not always articulate his innermost thoughts, but he had memorized a poem that aptly summed up his feelings:

They stood upon the dock
as the ships went out to sea.
The wind took their sails
and left the land a memory.
Leaving those on shore to wonder
why the sailor goes.
All to wonder, what the sailor knows.

Mac had known he was born for the sea ever since he first sailed with his father off the coast of New England. The memories of those crisp, windswept mornings remained heartbreakingly clear. He would still picture his late father, tall at the helm, his patrician head with aquiline nose facing into the wind, fondly reminiscing about sailing with his own father. "Four generations of Grahams have owned boats, son. You probably will, too." It isn't often that a ten-year-old boy fully understands his destiny. But young Mac had.

When Mac was twenty-eight, an uncle died, leaving him $100,000 in stocks and bonds—and an equal amount to Mac's only sibling, a younger sister. There was money in the family tree; Mac's paternal grandfather had been a successful Wall Street investor. With his inheritance in hand, Mac didn't have to think twice. He began a long search, combing marinas for his ideal boat. He knew what he *didn't* want. He loathed the new fiberglass construction that was sweeping the boat-building industry after World War II. Sure, it took less upkeep than a wooden-hulled boat. Plastic flowers are less trouble than real flowers, too. He found what he wanted in the *Sea Wind*, a pristine ketch with fore-and-aft rigging, and wooden, like his father's boat. Built in 1947, the *Sea Wind* was so handsomely constructed, with closely spaced heavy oak framing and extra-thick inch-and-a-quarter planking on her hull, one admirer remarked that "she looked like she had been carved out of a single block of wood." From the moment he saw the "For Sale" sign hanging on her in the San Diego marina one summer day back in 1960, Mac was hooked. The *Sea Wind* had an ineffable grace. He even liked the name, which suggested to him a life of sailing the high seas as free as the capricious wind. Under the bowsprit was a gilded figurehead of a woman, a guardian angel protectively leading the way for vessel and crew. He forked over $20,000 for the *Sea Wind*. He left most of the remainder of his inheritance (and later, the assets from a $120,000 trust set up by his late grandfather) in conservative investments that, coupled with odd jobs as the need arose, gave him the financial freedom to sail the world's oceans whenever he had the urge.

A woman appeared from below deck. "I thought this would taste good," she said, handing Mac a cold beer.

Mac thanked his wife and took a long swig.

Thirteen years earlier, Mac had the *Sea Wind* docked at Underwood's Marina in San Diego and was busy making modifications on the boat. He was something of a ladies' man back then but had never been married or even engaged. One night coming out of a beachfront bar, he and a buddy came upon a car stalled in commuter traffic. The driver was Eleanor LaVerne Edington, a single, tiny-waisted blonde with an hourglass figure and pinup good looks. Always the gentleman, Mac got her car going and invited her back to the bar for a drink. She was accustomed to getting her share of such offers from men, and usually she turned them down. But she liked what she saw in this outdoorsy-looking man with kind eyes, so she accepted. A steady relationship soon began. Before long, Mac was endearingly calling her Muffin, then simply Muff. A year later he proposed marriage to her, and once again she said yes.

They weren't married immediately because Mac had plans to sail the *Sea Wind* around the world. He dearly loved Muff and wanted to spend the rest of his life with her, but right then his main concern was celestial navigation, which he'd studied in a night class but had never actually put to use in the middle of the ocean. Getting himself lost was one thing, but he didn't want to drag Muff along for what might be a frightening experience.

Muff didn't disagree, because she had never sailed for great distances and had her own trepidations about going to sea. Mac put an ad in the newspaper and recruited two fellows who were willing to crew for him and share expenses. His plan was for Muff to join him later. "If we make it to Tahiti," he told her, "you can fly down and we'll get married there. We'll make the rest of the cruise our honeymoon." Muff couldn't figure out how the two crewmen would fit into a romantic vacation on a boat whose living space was about the size of an average kitchen. But she understood early on that to be part of Mac's life meant that she would have to, want to, accept his way of life. When Mac was at the helm of the *Sea Wind*, facing a cleansing breeze and open sea, she could see he was as content as a young boy smiling through a dream. Watching from the dock with a flood of tears, she tried to remind herself of this as he sailed away on his great round-the-world adventure, leaving her behind.

Two weeks later, Mac called from Mexico. They had hit a terrible storm off Baja that had sunk several boats. After taking a pounding at sea for eleven days and nights, a damaged *Sea Wind* limped into safe harbor. Mac couldn't get his hands on some of the parts he needed to repair the boat, so he read Muff a list and asked her to bring them down from San Diego. By the time she arrived, Mac's two crewmen had quit. After their close call in the storm, neither had the stomach for continuing the voyage. Mac signed on Muff as his crew of one. They were married in August 1961, in La Paz, at the foot of Baja California. Mac was thirty, Muff twenty-eight. "Little Muff and I are one," Mac wrote to his parents. "Our marriage has made two people complete, and very happy."

Muff, who was fair-skinned, burned easily in the sun and was still self-conscious about the galaxy of freckles that covered her face in the summer. A shade over five feet tall, she was fine-boned, with delicate features. Rosy-red lipstick was the only makeup she wore on a regular basis. Her teeth were gleaming white. That a few were a tad awry did not mar an enchanting smile that caused her nose to wrinkle slightly. Her liquid brown eyes reflected happiness, love, hurt, or fear with vivid clarity. As a child, Muff found she could never get away with fibbing—her mother always read the truth in her eyes. More reserved than Mac, she didn't take to strangers right away. Muff felt comfortable with people only after she came to know and trust them.

Now forty-one, Muff was worried about the extra ten to fifteen pounds she carried around her hips these days. Mac had told her again and again to forget it—"I love every curve and every ounce"—but still she was always signing on for the latest fad diet to promise a svelter stern.

Muff liked watching her husband putter around the boat, as he'd been doing for the better part of this Saturday morning. Those tasks made him a contented man. "Sounds a lot better," she offered over the purring of the generator engine.

"The valves were loaded with carbon and the bushings were shot."

He shut down the engine and began putting away his tools, carefully wiping each one with a clean cloth, then putting it in its proper place in his toolbox.

"I'm going shopping," she said, reaching for her handbag and rummaging inside. She pulled out a stack of coupons she'd clipped from the newspaper. "A market in Chula Vista is advertising green beans at twenty-five cents a can."

Muff's job was to stock the *Sea Wind*'s pantry in preparation for their upcoming voyage to the tropics. It was no easy assignment, since Mac wanted to be gone for two years. Some goods she'd already purchased—canned vegetables, fruits, juices, and meats— were stored in the garage of her widowed mother's home in an older section of San Diego. Also in the garage—kept in a chest freezer—were frozen roasts, chickens, and hams, to be moved to the *Sea Wind*'s own freezer just prior to departure. Items taken for granted at home could be impossible to find or outrageously expensive in remote parts of the world.

Mac took another sip of beer and grinned teasingly. "You're going to drive thirty miles round-trip to save a few bucks on green beans? You'll almost burn that much in gas."

"We *do* have a Volkswagen." Though she smiled back, there was an edge to her words.

"You all right?"

"I guess so." She looked at him with heavy sadness.

He sat down next to her on a bench seat in the cockpit of the boat.

"You still don't want to go." It was a statement, not a question.

Muff didn't respond. Her silence—and those revealing eyes—said it all.

He placed a consoling hand on her leg. "My offer stands. I mean that."

"I don't want you to go without me." She rested her head on his broad shoulder, warm from the sun. She was unable to look him in the face.

"Muff, if you want to stay home, you should."

She smiled and shook her head. She knew she could not stay behind. Her place was to be with him.

"I'd better go before they raise the price on the green beans." She looked up perkily and planted a kiss on his cheek.

Mac was not fooled. "Are you coming tonight?" he asked.

"Where?"

"Remember? With Marie and Jamie to Hal Horton's house. He's the guy who knows all about that island in the Pacific."

She tried not to let her disappointment show. She loved their good friends the Jamiesons. Marie was a real character, and Jamie was a sweetheart. They had met back in 1966 when they docked next to each other at Underwood's Marina. The four of them always had so much fun together. Right now, though, the last thing Muff wanted to do was spend a night hearing about some deserted island Mac had ideas about visiting.

"We have to leave by six."

"Okay. I'll be back by then." It would at least be fun to see Marie and Jamie, she had decided.

Leaving the *Sea Wind*, Muff walked past boats being readied to shove off for an afternoon sail, the kind of recreational boating she secretly wished would satisfy her husband.

When she reached the parking lot, she pulled out a bottle of yellow pills from her purse. Her doctor had promised they would help. She gulped one tranquilizer and willed it to work quickly.

Alone in the car, Muff felt a chill that had nothing to do with the weather.

"I WAS BASED on Palmyra for almost two years. January '42 to '44." Hal Horton, sipping his cocktail, pointed a beefy finger at the map of the Pacific spread out on the dining-room table and kept talking. "It's that little speck about a thousand miles south of Hawaii. I swear, it's like one of those South Pacific movie islands. Right out in the middle of *goddamn* nowhere. And uninhabited. That is, except for a few ghosts, maybe."

The paunchy former Navy officer went on without missing a beat. "Once, one of our patrol planes went down near the island. We searched and searched but didn't find so much as a bolt or piece of metal. It was weird. Like they'd dropped off the edge of the earth. Another time, a plane took off from the runway, climbed to a couple hundred feet, and turned in the wrong direction. They were supposed to go north and they went south instead. It was broad daylight. We never could figure it out. There were two men aboard that plane. We never saw them again. We had some very bad luck on the island. Old salts in the Pacific called it the Palmyra Curse."

Muff winced.

Hal made another round of drinks at the wet bar.

Fascinated, Mac flipped through one of his host's old Navy photo albums. He learned there had been five thousand men and a few nurses stationed on Palmyra during World War II. The island had been a naval air facility, with several PBY seaplanes and a dozen or so SBD dive-bombers based there, primarily for long-range patrol. The single enemy action of the war occurred less than three weeks after the surprise attack on Pearl Harbor. A lone Japanese submarine surfaced three thousand yards offshore and began firing its deck guns at a dredge operating in the island's lagoon. A five-inch-gun battery on the island chased off the would-be raider. After that, the Empire of the Rising Sun expressed no interest in the isolated atoll.

"Pan Am had used it before the war for refueling its Clipper service to Samoa," Hal went on. "Most of the structures went up after Pearl Harbor, though. We even built a hospital on one end of the island. It was a good location for an emergency airfield, because so many aircraft were heading south out of Hawaii to other island chains. Problem was, Palmyra—with its islets, lagoons, and reefs forming a perfect horseshoe—is very small. You can fly over it at ten thousand feet and not see it if there are a few clouds in the sky. Once we heard a plane overhead trying to find us, but he crashed in the drink before he could find the runway. We didn't get to the poor guy fast enough. Sharks found him first."

"Oh, my God," Muff said, making eye contact with Marie.

"This Palmyra doesn't sound like such a wonderful place to me," Marie said loyally.

"How deep is the channel?" Mac asked, ignoring the women.

"Fifteen feet," Hal answered. "Plenty big enough for a sailboat. We used to get medium-sized cargo ships inside the lagoon. We built a loading dock for them. The West Lagoon, which is the main lagoon, is over three quarters of a mile long and over a half mile wide."

"I bet there're lots of places to explore," Mac said with boyish anticipation.

"Oh, yeah," Hal agreed. "Machine-gun bunkers, underground tunnels and storage areas—the works. I heard that the Navy left a lot of stuff behind when they pulled up stakes after the war. It was cheaper than shipping it all back. You'd find all kinds of relics, I bet."

"Sounds like it's worth spending some time there," Mac said.

"There's nothing there anymore in the way of docking facilities or usable equipment, I'm sure," Hal cautioned. "You'll have to bring everything with you."

"Our boat is very well-equipped," Mac said.

"Best-equipped I've ever seen," Jamie concurred.

Mac and Muff left that night with a stack of material on Palmyra, including a letter from an Army officer to a college professor planning a trip to Palmyra. "I can assure you it will be an experience that you will long remember," the military man wrote in 1963. "You will have plenty of animal, insect, fish, and bird companions, and after a while you become very friendly with them." Attached to the letter was a detailed three-page list of items to take to Palmyra, from "partner" and "well-equipped first-aid kit" to "pistol and ammunition." The letter concluded: "It's a place where you can remove yourself from the many problems of the world."

That was exactly what Mac wanted to hear. Although San Diego was more unspoiled and picturesque than most large cities, it still suffered from increasing traffic and crime. Reports of violent muggings, rapes, and shootings were alarmingly more frequent. Smog, a harbinger of urban blight, was becoming a concern, too. He sensed that his world lay somewhere out *there*, on the vast windswept bowl of the ocean, not here in a mushrooming city of half a million people jostling for space.

Muff, by contrast, would have loved life in a rambling, ranch-style home, complete with backyard pool, in this coastal city with its clean beaches and bustling shopping malls. She would have liked to have children, too. But even though Mac talked often in the earlier years of their marriage about raising a family, sailing had always stood in the way. Muff was reconciled to the inevitable. Was any life perfect?

She doubted she was capable of loving a man more than she loved Mac. She found him dashing and intelligent, and he seemed to love her deeply. She was still committed to the decision she'd made early in their marriage in accepting Mac's way of life. There was that rapt, yearning gaze that appeared in his eyes only when he talked about sailing. She had never asked him to choose between her and his other love. He deserved both. And anyway, she wasn't entirely sure which he would choose.

A few weeks after the visit to Horton's, Mac finished his Pacific itinerary. The *Sea Wind* would depart San Diego for Hawaii, dock there a month or so, and then set sail for Palmyra. If the island was everything Mac fantasized it to be, he intended to stay from six months to a year. Then they would continue on to Tahiti and other fabled islands throughout the South Pacific.

Mac gave notice to his employer, Triple A South, a ship repair business at Underwood's Marina. Recommended for the job by Jamie Jamieson, Mac had so delighted the owner with his mechanical prowess that he'd been promoted to a supervisory position within weeks. That had been almost a year ago, and now Mac had succumbed to that familiar longing to leave job and hearth behind, and set sail.

As their departure date approached, Muff felt increasingly apprehensive about the voyage. Internalizing her fears, she suffered from insomnia, heart palpitations, and stomach pains. Her doctor didn't find these symptoms disturbing—just indications of a bad case of nerves.

She did not have Mac's good memories of the sea. On their nearly six-year round-the-world honeymoon cruise a decade earlier, they had endured a horrendous typhoon in the South Pacific, a perilous journey through the Red Sea, and a close call with a marauding pirate ship in the Mediterranean. Living with the constant fear of bad weather and high seas, they had been drained by the tension that comes with sailing a small boat in a very big, very unpredictable ocean. She did not want to go through any of it again. But if something happened to Mac sailing alone, she would never be able to forgive herself for not being at his side.

"This trip will be easier than the world cruise," Mac assured her. "We'll only be gone two years. We can take it slow and easy. Honey, we'll have a great time."

"I hope so," Muff said, forcing a smile. "I don't know why I have such a funny feeling about this trip."

CHAPTER 3

A CAR CRUISED SLOWLY THROUGH the parking lot at Keehi Lagoon harbor, adjacent to Honolulu International Airport. Hundreds of pleasure boats bobbed gently alongside long rows of docks. Catamarans and trimarans, ketches and schooners, cutters and sloops, playthings of the young and old, the rich and not-so-rich, the adventurous and the lazy. For some, a boat was a way of life. For others, a brief weekend escape. For the owners of one boat temporarily moored here, Buck and Jennifer, an escape of an altogether different kind was planned.

The rental car braked to a halt and a man of medium height, thirtyish, jumped out from the driver's side. He wore a sober button-down dress shirt and plain suit slacks. From the breast pocket of his shirt, he drew a crinkled snapshot of a sailboat. He glanced at it, double-checking, then set off at a run toward a line of moored boats. "Stay here," he called back over his shoulder.

Inside the car, the older woman didn't know what her son had seen that made him move so quickly. It was probably another wild-goose chase. They'd had plenty of them these past few days. A number of people thought they recognized the *Iola* from the snapshot, but none had known or admitted where it or Jennifer might be now. Sarah "Sunny" Jenkins pondered whether she and her son, Ted, would find her daughter in time.

Arriving from California four days earlier, they had started their search on the Big Island at Jennifer's last address, the ramshackle cabin in the volcanic mountains outside Hilo. They found someone who told them Jennifer and her boyfriend had moved to Maui to restore and refit an old sailboat they had bought there. Sunny and Ted immediately caught a flight to Maui, and after a two-day search, they learned from a long-haired fellow working on a boat at Maalaea Bay that the couple from the *Iola* had finally managed to get their boat launched and had sailed over to Oahu. Undeterred, Sunny and Ted headed there, but as their flight circled Honolulu, Sunny's heart sank at the myriad small boats that jammed the waterways and harbors as far as she could see. How in the world were they ever going to find *one* boat in that horde? She stiffened her resolve. They had absolutely no choice but to try. After Jennifer's last letter, Sunny had relayed the unnerving news to Ted, and they had agreed that Jennifer must be talked out of this insane notion of sailing off with Buck Walker.

Sunny, her thick, chestnut hair shot with gray, was a handsome and self-possessed woman. Almost always, she showed the world a brightly sunny disposition—true to her nickname. Right now, though, she allowed herself to look worried and downcast. The *Iola* could have sailed days before.

Ted approached the car, his shirt wet through at the armpits and plastered to his chest. Runnels of sweat ran down his face.

Sunny rolled her window down, and a humid, hot breeze invaded the air-conditioned comfort of the car.

"I found her, Mom."

"Oh, Teddy, thank God." Sunny could hardly catch her breath.

"She'll be right up. It was pure luck. I saw just enough of the boat to see this thing sticking out"—Ted pointed to the picture of the boat and a bowsprit that was visible—"and I remembered the guy on Maui saying not many boats had it."

"How does she look?"

"Fine. She couldn't believe we were here." A look of concern crossed his face. "Mom, let's keep in mind what we talked about. Okay?"

Sunny nodded grimly. She just prayed their plan would work.

WHEN EVERYONE met for dinner that night at a waterfront restaurant, Sunny covertly inspected her daughter's boyfriend from across the table. She was struck by the length of his sandy hair, worn in shaggy hippie style. His large luminous eyes met hers unhesitatingly, and he carried himself with confidence and laid-back macho poise. Big and muscular, he exuded a natural élan. Sunny could see Jennifer falling for him. At the moment, Jennifer seemed content to do the talking for them both.

"So, Buck patched up the holes in the hull and we finally got her in the water," Jennifer was explaining between bites, "about, what—" She looked at Buck.

"Three, four weeks ago," he said.

"And I quit my job and we sailed over from Maui," Jennifer continued. "We were going to buy a ship-to-shore radio with the money you sent, Mom, but we decided against it. We needed to store up on stuff like sugar and flour. I'll be baking a lot. And we'll be catching lots of fish."

"You don't have a radio?" Sunny asked with deceptive calm.

Jennifer blithely shook her head.

"Two-way radios are expensive," Buck said, then smiled easily. "Besides, there's no one on shore we want to talk to that badly."

Did he mean to give offense, Sunny wondered, or was he just thoughtless?

You silly, stupid kids. The words were on the tip of Sunny's tongue. *How can you think of sailing out into the middle of the ocean without a radio? What happens if you need help?* But she kept quiet; she and Ted had agreed that confrontations and recriminations with Jennifer would be counterproductive.

Jennifer had been easy to raise as a child. They had lived in a third-floor walkup apartment in the Washington Heights section of New York City. Jennifer, a good-natured and animated young-ster, made friends easily. Sunny divorced Jennifer's father when the little girl was ten. With Ted off to school at Syracuse University in upstate New York, mother and daughter moved to Toronto, and that was where the trouble had started. By her third year of high school, Jennifer was cutting class to shoot pool with some friends. Her game improved; her grades went downhill. Sunny could do nothing with her. Eventually, there was an ultimatum from the principal: Jennifer could drop out voluntarily or carry the stigma of being flunked. "People in our family do not quit school," her Uncle Buddy told her. "Dropping out would be the worst decision of your life," her brother warned. But drop out she did, promising everyone she would re-enroll the following fall. That summer, mother and daughter moved to Los Angeles, and true to her word, Jennifer was back in school that September. She took things more seriously the second time around, earning As and Bs while working as a night clerk at a discount department store. After graduating the following June, she enrolled in junior college, majoring in psychology. A year later, she moved into her own apartment in the San Fernando Valley section of Los Angeles, but Sunny continued to see her regularly. Then, shortly after earning her junior college degree, Jennifer moved to Hawaii in 1969 to help Uncle Buddy run his Oahu resort, Ulu Ma Village, an authentic sixteenth-century Hawaiian village he had bought in Honolulu, taken down board by board, trucked across the island to Kaneohe Bay, and reassembled on seashore land he owned there. It was a bar and restaurant, and after Uncle Buddy made arrangements for tour buses to stop, business took off. Jennifer worked tables and handled bookkeeping and accounting.

After all these years on the islands, Jennifer's suntan was darker, her hair shorter and lighter, but to Sunny everything else about her seemed much the same. Still, she couldn't be sure she really knew her daughter these days. A few visits scattered over half a decade had revealed little of what was actually going on in her daughter's life. Take this drug-charge business—was Jennifer, like so many young people, heavily involved in drugs? She had long defended her regular use of marijuana (she was convicted in Hawaii in 1970 for illegal possession) as no different from a businessman's downing his daily martini after a hard day at the office. In her last letter, Jennifer had dismissed the drug charges against Buck and her as "trumped-up."

After dinner, Ted asked for the check and looked squarely at Buck. "Jenny wrote us about your legal problems. Is there anything we can do to help?"

"I don't think so," Buck said in a low voice.

Ted waited for more.

Jennifer broke the silence. "Buck was arrested on a charge of selling MDA. It's a drug, Mom, but it's not like heroin. More like grass. Anyway, I'd gone into town with Buck. He was arrested in the parking lot of Penney's. I was a few blocks away at a Laundromat, doing the wash. But they still ended up filing a charge against me for selling MDA, too. It isn't fair. None of it." (While Jennifer had had no problem telling her mother and brother about her earlier run-in with the law over marijuana—she was indignant rather than ashamed—she had *not* told them of her arrests and subsequent petty theft convictions in Hawaii in 1969 and 1973 for shoplifting. *Those* types of things one did not tell Mom.)

Jennifer honestly believed that Buck had been entrapped, and told her mother and brother so. But she left out certain facts that others would find damaging. She didn't mention that Buck was packing a powerful handgun (a 9mm pistol) at the time of his arrest—necessary protection, he subsequently explained to Jennifer, against being ripped off by another dealer. In addition, before these aborted MDA sales there had been Buck's attempts at growing marijuana—hundreds of plants out behind their cabin.

Jennifer had told Buck at the time that he was crazy to grow so much marijuana. Yes, she *liked* grass, liked the heady, warm sensation, liked the kind of cosmic euphoria she felt, liked listening to the Stones when she was loaded and hearing notes and harmonies she'd never noticed before, liked making love while suspended in a totally sensual dimension. It was a loving, accepting high, not destructive in any way, never a downer, and there were no hangovers. (She also liked Quaaludes enough to trade grass for the tablets whenever possible. "Ludes" caused her to tingle all over and feel very sensual.) She'd have been happy for him to grow just enough grass for their own use, but Buck wanted the heavy bread that came from dealing.

He'd gone whole hog, and they'd been ripped off just before harvest time—every single plant uprooted one night and taken away. Infuriated and hungry for revenge, Buck replanted, put out booby traps (some loaded with live rounds), and started keeping a loaded shotgun and revolver nearby. They'd had a huge argument about the firearms. When Jennifer insisted that he not bring them in the cabin, he'd finally relented, stowing them just outside the door.

"Buck has a court hearing tomorrow, but he's not going," Jennifer continued. "But the lawyer says that if Buck goes and pleads guilty to one count of selling MDA, they'll drop the other charge against him and the phony charge they have against me."

"Buck's going to jump bail?" Ted asked.

Jennifer nodded cheerfully.

Ted's thoughts raced. "Buck, did I hear correctly? If you show up in court tomorrow and plead guilty to one count, the charges against Jennifer will be dropped?"

"That's what the lawyer says," Buck answered flatly.

"Will you be taken into custody?"

"No. They'll give me a sentencing date for the drug charge," Buck said, giving no more than he was asked.

"Our lawyer says they'll let him remain out on bail until he's sentenced," Jennifer added. "But after he does his federal time on the MDA charge, California will extradite him and revoke his parole from San Quentin. I don't want him to go back there. That place turns people into *animals*."

She couldn't possibly share with them all the horror stories Buck had told her about the notorious prison. He had witnessed stabbings, beatings, stompings, shootings, and stranglings. An inmate could get killed for not paying back a pack of cigarettes. A guy had to be mean and tough twenty-four hours a day in order to survive. "If you gave in to them," Buck had told her, "they'd make a punk out of you." He explained explicitly what that meant. Buck said that he'd rather die than go back to San Quentin. The terror in his eyes whenever he recalled his time there finally convinced Jennifer that they had no choice but to flee from Hawaii and the MDA charge.

"Buck paid for his mistake," Jennifer told her mother and brother. "He was only a teenager and the gun wasn't even loaded, but they called it armed robbery and sent him to San Quentin."

Jennifer still remembered the first time Buck told her about his prison record—they had just started living together. When she asked him what he had done and he answered, "Armed robbery," she'd been shocked. She'd despised guns and violence of any kind, even in movies or on television. She hadn't known what to say to him. Despite his tenderness with her, did he harbor a hidden streak of violence? Buck had kept quiet for a moment, as if he under-stood her feelings. When he finally added that the gun wasn't loaded, that somehow helped. "I just hung out with the wrong people at an impressionable age," he explained. Since she had already fallen deeply in love with Buck, she dismissed his some-what shady past with the thought that everyone is entitled to a mistake or two. She'd certainly made a few herself, and had fudged the line on some laws she didn't respect.

Ted wanted to keep the logic clear and irrefutable in what he was about to say. "Buck, if just by showing up in court tomorrow and pleading guilty to one of the charges you'll get Jennifer cleared, why don't you do it? I'll go with you."

Walker didn't take long thinking about it. "Okay. This is my problem anyway."

"It's *our* problem," Jennifer said resolutely, as if affirming where her first allegiance lay at this table.

After Sunny and Ted returned to their hotel and Jennifer and Buck went back to the *Iola*, Ted began to think that he was mak-ing the best of a bad situation. He would go to court with Walker to ensure that the charge against his sister would be dropped. That settled, he and his mother would get Jennifer alone and try their damnedest to talk her out of running away with Buck.

Ted found it difficult to understand his sister's behavior. Actu-ally, they had so little in common and so many years separated them that each might as well have been raised an only child. He was eight years old when his baby sister was born. When their mother and father divorced, it had been more traumatic for Jen-nifer than for Ted, who had cut himself off emotionally from his troubled father years earlier. Jack Jenkins, a warehouseman on the Lower East Side of Manhattan, never beat his children, but he cru-elly neglected them; he would come home too drunk to do any-thing but pass out in his chair in the living room. Ted had lost all respect for his father and, in college, had chosen the path taken by his mother's brother, Uncle Buddy, who had made a sizable fortune in sales before going into the resort business. The month Ted grad-uated from Syracuse with a business degree, he married his college sweetheart, Donna, and they moved to the West Coast, where he began his own sales career. Within ten years, Ted was running his own educational book sales firm, and he and his wife were raising six children in their suburban home thirty miles from San Francisco.

The last time he'd spent any time with Jennifer was a couple of years earlier when she and two girlfriends had "crashed" at his place, camping out for a month in sleeping bags on the living-room floor. Ted, busy as usual at work, was out of the house early every morning and not back until well after nightfall. Donna, stuck at home all day, bore the brunt of the intrusion. "Jennifer and her friends are flower children," she whispered to Ted late one night in bed. "No bras and lots of pot. I don't have *anything* in common with them. They think we're horribly straight." Ted had smiled at that. "We are," he said. One Sunday evening just before the three visitors left, he and Jennifer stood on a bluff overlooking the woods behind the house and compared their differing philosophies of life.

"I see life as kind of a river," Jennifer had said. "I'm just flowing along with the current, going wherever the river takes me and enjoying the trip."

"Suppose you don't like where the current takes you?"

"Then I let the current take me someplace else."

Ted thought about that for a few moments. He wished they could agree on *something*. "Each of us is in control of his own fate. We can make our lives better or we can make them worse."

The sun had gone down and a chill was coming on, but neither made a move to return to the house.

Jennifer explained that she didn't want to be like most people, "locked into a role" defined by their families' expectations and their social milieu. "Life, then, becomes a stage where people simply act out predetermined roles." She wanted to write her own role, her own lines, unshackled from the will of others. "I want to define my own dimensions," she told her brother.

Of course, Ted knew that lots of young people like Jennifer were leading unconventional lives and taking other chances. Besides using a variety of recreational drugs, many were hitting the streets to protest the unpopular war or running off to Canada to dodge the draft. More couples than ever were openly living together without getting married. Values were changing, and much of society had been caught up in the vortex of experimentation and dissent. He'd done none of it himself—he'd never even tried a joint, not once. He'd been too busy making a living and raising a family for such silliness. Nonetheless, he did feel uncomfortably straight sometimes—particularly around his baby sister. She seemed so certain she had found the right approach to life.

Jennifer smiled almost forgivingly. She had voted for McGovern. Ted had voted for Nixon. What could she possibly say that would bridge such a gap?

"Look, Teddy, I know my life-style isn't for you. You've got six kids to support. You need to get from one point to another, regardless of which way the river is flowing. But I like the river. And for good or for bad, I want to experience it." Remorse, Jennifer had decided, was better than regret.

JENNIFER HAD been genuinely pleased that her mother and brother had showed up in Hawaii. Though these days she rarely agreed with their priorities or politics, she dearly loved them both. Their purpose in coming was no mystery. So she wasn't surprised when they invited her to join them at their hotel the following afternoon. Alone, without Buck.

When she got there, Jennifer had to smile. Both Mom and Ted seemed so *prepared*. They looked like two neophyte actors waiting nervously for the curtain to go up, fearful of blowing their lines.

"Jennifer, I'd like you to come back with me and take over my mail-order business," her mother began. "I could train you and retire."

Jennifer was touched. There was a time a few years ago when she would have jumped at the chance to be her own boss and run her own business, but not now.

"Mom, it's a wonderful offer. I really appreciate it. But I'm committed. For months I've been working with one thing in mind—getting our boat ready so we can leave Hawaii. I've been putting money into it. Buck's been working on the boat. This is something we've decided to do, and we're going to do it. I can't change that course. I can't desert Buck. He'd probably go without me, but I don't think he could make it alone. He needs me."

He needs me. Sunny knew she'd hear those words sooner or later. Since Jennifer had been a little girl, she'd responded to anything or anyone who needed her. A stray dog, an injured sparrow, a neighborhood kid who fell and scratched his knee. It was no accident that Jennifer's boyfriends had always been losers. She went for men who had two strikes against them, not those born on third base, because she had an overpowering desire to be needed. Maybe it all began in her childhood, when she would have liked to do something to help her father stay sober, but was powerless to do so. Sunny said nothing.

"Jennifer, there are some legal ramifications that need to be addressed," Ted said dispassionately. "Though there's no longer a charge against you—"

"By the way," Jennifer interrupted, "thanks for going to court with Buck this morning. It's a relief to have my charge dropped." Buck's sentencing had been set for the summer.

"Jennifer, if you leave with Buck, you could find yourself facing new charges," Ted said. "Like aiding and abetting a fugitive."

Jennifer considered. "If I were his wife, they couldn't charge me with helping him, could they?"

Ted's opening salvo had backfired. He didn't want to give Jennifer reason to marry Buck Walker. "There's something else to consider," he said, hurrying on. "Even if they don't charge you with anything, you would be living the life of a fugitive. Buck could never come back, and neither could you. Are you willing to abandon your family, leave this country with him on a sailboat, and stay away the rest of your life?"

"I'm *not* abandoning my family," Jennifer said with conviction. "It's not like I'm dropping off the face of the earth. Anyway, Buck has promised it won't be forever. In a few years, he'll come back and turn himself in. He thinks they'll go easier on him if he can show that he hasn't gotten into any trouble since he left." Even Jennifer had a hard time with that last part. She couldn't picture Buck actually turning himself in, as he had solemnly promised her one night when they lay cuddled together in their bunk on the *Iola*. But this was a problem to be faced down the road.

"Don't you think they'll *find* you?" Sunny asked, unable to keep her voice from rising. "There's no way you can run from this. The government's got planes and ships to hunt down fugitives. They've got the FBI."

Jennifer stayed calm. She respected her mother's right to be upset. "Our plan is to find a secluded spot, off the beaten path, kind of an island paradise," Jennifer explained. Buck had warned her not to name the island they had picked out. She fully agreed because she wasn't convinced that her mother or her brother would keep quiet if the FBI showed up on the doorstep with a fugitive warrant for Buck. "He'll change his name and we'll start over," she continued. "I'll be fine and he'll be fine and we'll be happy. I love Buck and he loves me. I know you think my love for him is blind. But that's not so. I know what I'm getting into."

"It's not that love is blind, sweetheart. It's just that it sometimes refuses to believe what it sees. You're certainly intelligent and perceptive enough to realize that going off with Buck is a great risk. But you've talked yourself into believing there's no risk at all, just oodles of love and living happily ever after."

"Mom, I'm sorry. I'm going with him."

Sunny sat there like a carved figure, holding her chin in one hand, beaten and frightened, wondering how Jennifer could be deaf to the sense in what they were saying. This wasn't at all like her daughter. *Have I lost her? Is Buck Walker controlling her?*

Ted realized it was time for his ace in the hole. A friend of his, a deputy district attorney in California, had agreed to run Buck Walker's name through the state computerized system for criminal records. The result was a lengthy rap sheet, beginning with Buck's first arrest at age twelve, his escape from a juvenile detention home the following year, and two incidents of joyriding the year after that. The list included two more escapes from juvenile hall, another joyriding charge, and an arrest for grand theft auto, all before his sixteenth birthday. As Walker grew, so did the gravity of his criminal activities. Charges piled one on top of another and revealed a past riddled with much more than everyday hell-raising: robbery (age sixteen), two burglaries (age seventeen), and the armed robbery conviction at age eighteen that had earned him a sentence of five years to life in San Quentin. Seven months after his 1961 parole from state prison, he was at it again, arrested for a Los Angeles burglary. Incredibly, all that information was contained on only the first two pages of Walker's rap sheet, and there were two more pages left. It wasn't as if Buck had made one foolish mistake and paid his debt to society. He had been breaking the law throughout his life. Ted didn't want Jennifer to know he was checking up on Buck, so he did not mention the rap sheet. Still, there was something he was determined to tell her, because it was scary enough to make most people think twice about having anything at all to do with Buck, let alone going off to sea with him.

"Jen, did Buck tell you that seven years ago he was committed to a mental hospital for the criminally insane?"

Jennifer defiantly folded her arms in front of her, unmistakable body language for digging in. "Sure. He was just faking it so he wouldn't have to go back to San Quentin."

The answer was so quick, so sure, that Ted Jenkins realized right then that nothing he or his mother could say would deter Jennifer from going to the ends of the earth with Buck Walker. Buck had preempted them by presenting his version of his disturbing past, and Jennifer was intractable. Though Jennifer felt that now and then Buck tried to improve on the truth, she believed he was essentially honest, and had told her the truth about his past.

Ted briskly gathered up his papers and tapped them on the table until the edges were perfectly aligned, then slipped them back into his briefcase. He glanced up at Jennifer, at the tight little smile on her face, and tried not to feel annoyed as well as defeated. He hoped she knew what the hell she was doing.

Though she'd said little, Sunny was emotionally drained. She sighed deeply. Taking off her glasses, she rubbed fatigue-reddened eyes. Like her son, she'd saved her strongest argument for last.

"Jennifer, I've been having these terrible nightmares. They're always the same. You're on a boat and a huge wave crashes over you. The boat goes over and you are drowning. All I can think is, *Jennifer is drowning, Jennifer is drowning.* When I wake up, I'm so upset I can't get back to sleep. Sweetheart, if you go out on the ocean in that little boat, I don't think you'll ever come back."

Jennifer leaned forward and comfortingly clasped her mother's arm. "I love you for caring so much about me, Mom. But everything is going to be all right." And so she believed. She was happier with Buck than she had ever been with a man. They would make it. It might take some work, a good dose of luck, and the right push from life's river, but she was lost in love with her man, and that was all that mattered.

THE NEXT day, Sunny and Ted hugged and kissed each other goodbye at the Honolulu airport and agreed they'd done their best. Sunny boarded a plane for Los Angeles, and her son went to another departure gate to catch a San Francisco flight.

Once in the air, Sunny looked out the window at the vast blue sea stretching over the curve of the horizon. She couldn't bear the thought of Jennifer down there somewhere on a tiny sailboat, a mere speck in a watery void. She yanked down the shade, blocking the view.

Even if their little boat did not sink on the long sailing trip, Sunny worried about ex-con Buck Walker. His surface charm was probably a tool of survival. Who knew what he was capable of doing? If Jennifer got on his nerves in the middle of the ocean, and he had a short fuse . . .

Sunny said a prayer she was to repeat countless times, but she placed little faith in divine intervention. Her nightmares were so terrifyingly real. She felt the deep pain of loss, as if she had truly seen her daughter alive for the last time.

A WEEK later, Sunny received a greeting card in the mail. On the front was a drawing of a sailboat skimming the sea and the words *Today's cares can soon vanish.* The message concluded inside—*into the bright hopes of tomorrow.* Enclosed was a handwritten note:

Dear Mom,

In reevaluating my position, as you asked me to do, I find I cannot alter my course.

The upcoming experience is going to be good for me. I'll do things that I've long been ready to do but didn't because I conveniently found enough diversions to scatter my energies elsewhere, accomplishing little or nothing. Now there will be things which *must* be done to live our lives—food to be grown, bread to be baked, things to be learned about self-sufficiency.

I have great respect for your intuitions. But when emotions are overrun with apprehension and fear of the great unknown, sometimes intuitions become more dramatic than what is real. Those who ventured to America from the old country went into the unknown in search of something better. Many who set out never reached their goal, but many who remained at home did not survive either. Some who reached their haven found it to be another hell. Others found a better life for themselves.

I feel we will reach our goal. Whether I'll be totally content with my life there remains to be seen, but that I will become a more self-sufficient, able person, I have few doubts.

I'm glad that you and Teddy came over. It was so nice to spend time together. I love you both.

All my love,
Jennifer

CHAPTER 4

MARIE JAMIESON WAS AMAZED by her friend.

After a hurried and somewhat confusing call in midmorning, Muff had appeared on the Jamiesons' front porch as edgy and heavy-laden as a refugee. In her arms she held a box that pushed against her chin. Shopping bags hung from her wrists. As usual, she was trying to do too much at once, but the strain visible on her face was not, in Marie's view, fully explained by the physical load she was carrying.

Half amused, half concerned, Marie helped her good friend bring in the rest of the accumulation of stuff that could not be taken to sea on the upcoming voyage. She was astonished that it covered the large utility table in the family room and the tiled counters that ringed the kitchen as well.

This kind of pack-rat behavior, as Muff's friends knew, was indulged by Mac most of the time. He loved to tell people about the time he'd tried to change his wife's ways. Because the bow of their sailboat was lower in the water than the stern, he had *ordered* her to throw out some of her hoard. Next time he looked, the stern was lower than the bow. Muff had simply shifted everything to the back. Mac would howl with laughter when he told the story, and Muff would smile shyly. Maybe she'd heard him retell it enough.

This morning, after making some coffee, Marie was touched to see Muff going through some of the odds and ends, as if she couldn't bear to part with it all. Some boxes held old magazines, newspapers, and other junk that didn't have obvious value or a personal connection. Others were filled with knickknacks from their cruise around the world. In one ratty old suitcase, there was nothing but a collection of rather ordinary seashells. Muff showed how she had painstakingly cleaned and polished each one; they all brought back a memory of her shared life with Mac.

Scattered throughout were authentic treasures of a comfortable, tasteful life—delicate bone china from England, signature lead crystal stemware and serving bowls, a complete dinner service of sterling silver, and a Tiffany platter.

Unable to resist, Marie picked up one of the brilliantly shining dinner knives and noticed an unusual design on the handle.

"That's Mac's family crest," Muff said.

"Honey, I feel a little nervous keeping things this valuable. I mean, these are family heirlooms. Shouldn't someone else have them?"

Marie and Muff loved making each other laugh, and Marie's laugh—so big and so hearty for one so petite—would sometimes surprise even her best friends. But there was no way to work a laugh into what was now taking place.

"Don't worry about it," Muff said. "I've kept just enough nice things on board for our special dinners once a week. We do the whole formal bit when we're cruising, you know, with white linen and silver candelabra. I even make Mac put on a white shirt, if you can believe it." Her laugh was brittle. Her mind seemed to wander. "Of course, if anything *does* happen, all of this stuff should go to Mac's family." She paused. "I guess I could leave it with my mom, but she's pretty well along in years."

Marie knew Muff wasn't looking forward to the trip, and she instinctively wanted to grab Muff in a big bear hug and tell her not to go on this crazy adventure. She felt protective of her kindhearted, unassuming, but quietly courageous friend, as she often did. The truth was, though, that Muff was in some ways less in need of protection than her self-confidently macho husband. Mac had a tendency to trust the wrong person, as he had done recently in a phony stock deal. Muff had told him to steer clear; that she didn't trust the guy, who, sure enough, took him for several thousand dollars.

Marie wouldn't say this to just anybody, but she was convinced that Muff had an unusual ability to receive "vibes" from people, maybe even sense something about to happen. It could be eerie, as if she had been born with invisible antennae on the lookout for trouble. Just for fun, Marie had occasionally tested Muff's ability to guess what someone was thinking or anticipate a phone call. Muff was correct so often that Marie couldn't scoff at the notion of ESP.

Swiftly but nervously, as if she'd been putting it off, Muff reached down into one of the boxes on the kitchen counter and pulled out a finely molded Italian religious figurine, evidently the Virgin Mary in her characteristic blue shawl. Her eyes were closed, in adoration or in secret pain. There was an ugly crack in the ceramic forehead.

Muff hesitated, gingerly holding the figurine. "Here, I want you to have this," she said, thrusting it into Marie's hands. "It's . . . something we got in Italy on our honeymoon cruise."

"Oh, Muff, I couldn't. This must—".

"Please. Please!"

"But if it reminds you of—"

"Marie," she said quietly, "you don't understand. I never want it in my sight again. If you want to, just throw it out. I don't want anything to do with it."

Marie was flabbergasted. Muff was shaking, hardly able to catch her breath.

"Look at her," Muff said finally. "Look at what's happened to her. . . . Don't you see? *The hole in her head,*" Muff said, referring to a deep gash. She covered her face with her hands and began crying uncontrollably.

Marie put down the statuette and grabbed her friend tightly around the shoulders. The hysteria was catching. Marie found herself crying, too, completely overwhelmed with a sense of dread and loss.

"I'm . . . not coming back," Muff moaned.

"Oh, Muff, you can't—"

"Mac and I—we'll never see you again."

"Honey, if you feel that way, you can't go! Stay here. Mac will understand. He wouldn't want to put you through this kind of misery."

Muff stiffened immediately and stepped back from Marie's embrace. Trying to force a brave smile, she snatched a paper towel from the kitchen rack and awkwardly dabbed at her eyes. She laughed, and Marie joined in. They shared a sense of the ridiculous, and the tension broke.

"No," Muff said. "My place is with Mac. He wants to go. He has to go. So do I. Right?"

Marie felt cold chills.

"Look, Muff, no one *has* to do anything. Mac, of all people, should understand that." Muff just smiled at her. "Come stay with us while he's gone. He can find a crew, take his big trip and explore his dumb island, and come home and tell us all about it. I promise, we'll look at every one of his damn slides."

Setting her lips grimly, Muff shook her head slowly. "Just one more cruise. That's what he . . . we promised each other."

Marie tried to object, but Muff stopped her with a quick peck on the cheek and a casual hug.

"Got to run," she said. "Thanks for keeping this stuff for us. Love you."

Later that night, Marie burst into tears while she was telling her husband about the incident.

Jamie always tried to see the rational side of things. It was his nature. "She's just upset. You know how she hates long cruises. Muff is a homebody."

"No, it was more than that." Marie gestured toward the bags and boxes, which were still lying around the kitchen, untouched. "She was terrified."

"That's awfully strong—"

"Jamie, I know Muff. She was saying goodbye."

"Well, of course—"

"No, Jamie," Marie said haltingly. "Muff was telling me goodbye for . . . forever."

NOT EVERYONE took Muff's foreboding so seriously.

Her best friend, Billy Bunch, rendezvoused with Muff one evening in front of the San Diego May Company for a last window-shopping excursion before the sail.

Billy and Muff had known each other since 1952, when they met at the Y pool, where each swam laps after work. It turned out that both worked at General Dynamics, one of Southern California's giant aerospace employers. In fact, they were assigned to the very same project: the T-29 jet trainer line. Muff worked in the blueprint department; Billy was an electrician. They hit it off right away, even though Billy, twenty-eight, was married, and Muff, twenty, was still single. Muff was the responsible, serious one, while Billy tended to be more carefree and happy-go-lucky.

After wearing themselves out dashing in and out of stores along the well-lit boulevard and gasping at the prices, they treated themselves to cookies and coffee.

It was then Muff confided her fears to Billy.

"Been to your fortune-teller?" Billy chided gently.

She knew Muff went occasionally to a spiritualist and took seriously the old Gypsy lady's predictions. Billy didn't put stock in such prophecies, but she tried not to be *too* judgmental. She and Muff had the kind of frank and open friendship where each could say anything without fearing a putdown.

"I went to her last week because I've had these strange feelings, and I wanted to see what she had to say. Before I'd even told her how I really felt, she got this worried look and told me something terrible will happen to us if we go."

"Oh, go on and have a good time. She's been wrong before, hasn't she?"

"Yeah. But I just don't want to leave. I really don't."

Billy knew there was more to Muff's desire not to make the trip. Several times, she'd expressed concern about leaving her mother for so long.

Twice-widowed Rose King, in her early eighties, lived in San Diego, as did Muff's older sister, Peggy Faulkner, also a widow. The oldest sister, Dorothy Young, was married and lived in nearby La Mesa. Her mother wasn't really sickly, just elderly, but Muff feared something might happen to her before she and Mac returned.

Billy knew Muff had never forgiven herself for being at sea with Mac on their world cruise when her stepfather died of cancer and her mother needed her so desperately. (Muff's father, a mechanic, died when the family lived in Pueblo, Colorado. Still a schoolgirl at the time, Muff, with her two sisters and mother, moved to San

Diego. Her stepfather, George King, hadn't entered the picture until after she was grown and living on her own.) For Muff, blue-water sailing meant not only being away from home, but also being apart from her loved ones and friends when they needed her, and she them.

"Look, I know you're worried about your mother," Billy said, still trying to deflect her friend's concerns on the eve of their departure. "But she has Peggy and Dorothy. And anyway, she's pretty darn healthy. Don't worry about her. You have your own life to live."

Muff nodded distractedly.

Billy laughed and playfully poked her friend's arm. "Hey, worry about me. With you gone, who the heck am I gonna find to beat at tennis?"

Muff cracked up.

There's that sweet smile, Billy thought with satisfaction. Sometimes, her friend was just too nice for her own good.

CHAPTER 5

AT SUNRISE ON JUNE 1, 1974, the *Iola* departed Port Allen on the southern shore of Kauai, the first island of the Hawaiian chain to rise from the smoking seas millions of years ago.

Long before Jennifer and Buck lost sight of the cloud-draped peak of mile-high Mount Kawaikini, they picked up the northeast trades and were heading southward at a good clip.

The sense of being alone on the sea with the man she loved, feeling young and healthy and free, soaking in the brilliant sun and cooled by ocean spray, was exhilarating to Jennifer. Their future was now in their hands, not the law's, and they were heading for a faraway adventure that held new and thrilling possibilities.

Her pleasant reverie came to an end in a few hours when the

wind fell and they were dead in the water, just bobbing on the waves. They discussed starting the outboard engine attached to the stern, but decided not to. What fuel they'd brought had to last. They'd just wait it out.

Experienced sailors would have been shocked to see three dogs traveling aboard the *Iola*. Sailboats rarely carry even one dog. Jennifer owned a small ball-of-fluff mutt, Puffer, named because of the way she panted happily after playing. When she'd decided to bring Puffer along on the voyage, Buck had countered that he was going to bring his two dogs; Sista, a brindle-colored part-Lab bitch, and Popolo ("black" in Hawaiian), a male pit bull. Buck's dogs were big, clumsy, and hopelessly dumb, and Popolo had a mean streak. Jennifer had tried to talk Buck out of bringing them. "Sure, I'll leave them if you leave Puffer," he had said stubbornly. There was no way she could leave her little Puffer, who was as responsive to her moods as a confidante, so all three dogs and 150 pounds of dog food were along for the ride. To keep the dogs from being washed overboard, Buck had picked up eighty feet of netting at a fishing supply house and secured it to the lifelines from bow to stern.

The wind picked up again early that first afternoon, and Buck hoisted the mainsail. But at nightfall, when the wind tapered off, he lowered the main and put up the smaller jib, which gave the *Iola* about two knots.

The slow-moving boat's rolling motion became more uncomfortable, causing Buck to feel queasy, but they didn't know how to respond. Neither realized that they were "under-canvasing," a common mistake of novices, who tend not to put up enough sail. Experienced sailors would have stayed with more sail in an effort to squeeze out more speed, which would have diminished the wallowing effect. Buck went below to nap. In the close quarters, he became even more nauseated.

Jennifer, less affected, remained at the helm alone. The night was soundless except for the uneasy creaking of the booms and gaffs. Her biggest fear was colliding with another ship in the inky blackness. A big ship would have radar, though. *Wouldn't it?* But suppose it wasn't working or the operator was snoozing? She kept a sharp lookout for lights or looming shadows in the night.

Buck unsteadily came up on deck and relieved her for a couple of hours, manning the helm until one in the morning, when he called for Jennifer to take over. At sunrise, they switched places again, and she promptly fell exhausted into the bunk. She wondered, before going to sleep, if every day of the voyage would seem as long as the first one.

Buck had often fantasized about sailing around the world. But he found the reality of being on a small boat at sea much more enervating than his dream. His seasickness worsened the second day, and he ended up spending most of the first week in bed.

Alone at the helm, Jennifer elected not to struggle with the mainsail—it took more brute strength than she could summon—but to stay with the jib. That kept them going slowly, bobbing laboriously through the waves.

Buck was depressed even before they started, and now he was the grumpiest she'd ever seen him. She knew it wasn't just the nausea from the undulating sea or his fugitive status (*that* curiously never fazed him), but the recent death of his father in a construction accident. She tried to respond to Buck's emotional needs. When he wanted to talk about his father, they talked. When Buck wanted to be alone—which was most of the time—she respected his silence.

Buck idolized his father, describing him at various times as "the most dominant figure in my life" and "the most fascinating man I ever knew. I was like a wart on his nose, never tiring of watching him." Buck would say that in his father's approval he soared, while his disapproval "was bone-crushing." In Buck's eyes, there simply was no positive human characteristic his father did not possess. He was "handsome, intelligent, had extraordinary logical ability, and no one could possibly resist his charm."

Jennifer had met Wesley Walker on several occasions. Her perception of him was markedly different from Buck's. To Jennifer, Buck's father was a wanderer, a dreamer, a loser. (He was also a rigid disciplinarian, quite the opposite of Buck's complaisant, overly protective mother, Ginger.) He also had an insensitive streak that she'd found disturbing. When Buck was in the fifth grade, a bully had chased him home from school. He complained to his father, but was told to figure out a *physical* way to deal with the threat by himself. Buck's solution was to hide a length of two-by-four in the bushes halfway between school and home. When the bully chased him the next day, Buck stopped for the board and clubbed the surprised bully into submission. That evening, when the other kid's parents appeared at the Walker house to complain about their son's injuries, Wesley Walker ordered them off his property. Then he put his arm around his son and congratulated him. "Dad taught me two lessons that time," Buck explained to Jennifer. "To think for myself, and it never hurts to carry a big club." Another maxim he told his son to live by? "Try always to be straight with yourself, however much you may con the world."

Ailing in the *Iola*'s cabin, Buck tried to suppress his nausea with food. An experienced sailor had advised him that keeping something in his stomach when seasick would prevent the dry heaves. So he started every morning with a pot of tea, biscuits with honey, and generous helpings of oatmeal. He dumped spoonful after spoonful of sugar in the hot cereal, hoping it would give him energy. After eating, however, he promptly went out to the railing and—as old salts say—fed the fish. Then he'd go back to bed for an hour or so before wobbling back into the galley to make another meal for himself from their precious hoard.

Jennifer had spent more than a thousand dollars—virtually all of their money—stocking up on supplies for the trip. She had concentrated on the basics, like rice and soybeans and flour and sugar, shopping for bargains and making purchases in large enough quantities to get discount prices—such as a fifty-pound sack of red beans, which she knew to be a good source of protein. They had packed away a lot of canned goods, too—peaches, applesauce, pineapples, plums, green beans, carrots, creamed corn, and meat products like Spam and chili. Also, dried goods like fruits and nuts and grain for baking, all kept in plastic bags to keep out the moisture. And six dozen eggs, each one covered with Vaseline and turned periodically so they wouldn't go bad. They'd brought along thirty gallons of fresh water, a few cans of powdered orange drink, and two half-gallon jugs of vegetable oil for cooking.

Every available storage space in the *Iola*'s cramped cabin was full of goods, making it difficult to move around. In fact, when Jennifer and Buck were below at the same time, one of them had to turn sideways to allow the other to pass.

The *Iola*'s companionway steps into the cabin landed right in the center of the boat. The galley had a two-burner stove on gimbals (designed to remain level even when the boat was not), atop which sat a stained tin coffeepot, a single cabinet, and a tiny metal sink where the dishes were washed sparingly with bottled water. On the port side was a narrow bunk with a foam-rubber cushion covered in black Naugahyde. When Jennifer and Buck slept together, they did so on their sides, spoon-in-spoon style, as there was no room for assuming other positions. The hub of activity for Buck and Jennifer centered around the circular drop-leaf table in the cabin's galley, on each side of which were built-in benches. It was here that they not only ate their meals, but spent virtually all their time below unless they were working in the galley or sleeping. The burled table served as chess table and navigation station, too.

The boat's quarters were tight, but homey. Jennifer had sewn magnolia-print curtains, which covered the portholes and several of the open storage bins. There were other touches that revealed a woman's hand. Two miniature cattleya orchids, potted. A hanging macramé. A tattered Raggedy Ann doll. The scent of peppermint soap.

Buck and Jennifer were planning to rendezvous on Palmyra with their friend Richard "Dickie" Taylor and his brother, Carlos, at the end of August. They'd all become acquainted at Maalaea Bay when Dickie was outfitting his thirty-two-foot sailboat beside the dry-docked *Iola*.

Before leaving for Palmyra, Buck had worked out a business deal with the Taylor brothers that they hoped would make them all rich. From seeds they would take with them, Buck and Jennifer would grow a large crop of marijuana on Palmyra, far away from cops and rip-off artists. Dickie and Carlos were to handle the distribution end of the business, smuggling the dope into Hawaii and selling it for big profits. As part of the deal, they would bring supplies with them to Palmyra in late August.

Since that first day out of Port Allen, the *Iola*'s mainsail had not been raised. Jennifer had managed with only the jib up. On deck, she vigilantly kept the boat headed due south, while Buck stayed below in the bunk reading spy novels, and eating. She told Buck he might feel better if he came up on deck for some fresh air, but he claimed he was too tired. She began to wonder how much of his alleged seasickness was a cover for laziness. He was out of his element, okay, but so was she. Why wouldn't he at least try to help?

One night, when Jennifer could no longer keep her eyes open at the helm, she tried tying the wheel in place so it wouldn't turn. It seemed to work. She took a final look in all directions. There were no lights. Still, she knew it would be chancy. But maybe she could go down and close her eyes for a few minutes.

When she went below, Buck was awake, sitting on the bunk cleaning his handgun—a .22-caliber revolver—while smoking a thin marijuana cigarette.

The sight of the gun made her uneasy. It brought back memories of their biggest argument at Mountain View. When she had put her foot down and told him she did not want him bringing guns into their cabin, he'd ordered her to shut up. She ended up running outside and jumping in her van, an old bread truck with pink butterflies painted over the grille. He'd peppered rocks at the van as she pulled away. When she returned a few days later, Buck was ready to promise not to bring guns into the house again, but he did not apologize. Not for yelling, not for telling her to shut up, not for the rock throwing. In fact, Jennifer had never to this day heard Buck ever say to her, or to anyone else for that matter, "I'm sorry." Not once. There were people like that.

"I still don't like having guns aboard," she said resignedly, taking a hit off the joint. Before leaving Hawaii, Buck had made a persuasive argument for bringing weapons on the trip, explaining that they needed protection from pirates and other bad types they might be unlucky enough to encounter on the open seas. She had reluctantly agreed, and had even acquiesced when Buck insisted she take target practice. (She had surprised herself by hitting the tree on both her attempts.)

He smiled, but mechanically, without humor or warmth. The scraggly beard he'd been growing made him look surly. He seemed to savor the weight of the gun in his hand. "Remember what I said, Jen. A person would be crazy to sail the high seas these days without protection."

The .22 was his two-by-four in the bushes.

"I was sitting here thinking about Jake," Buck went on, dabbing a spot of oil on a soft cloth.

Jennifer, exhausted, collapsed at the galley table. She felt resentment rising. Buck had goofed off below all day, eating, resting, reading. And now he was primed to talk, while she hungered for sleep.

"You remember Jake?"

"Yeah."

Jake, as she'd heard often, had been Buck's favorite teacher at San Quentin.

Although Buck had dropped out of school in the seventh grade, he had taken various courses in prison and become a serious reader of a wide range of books, from detective novels to more challenging works like Will Durant's *The World of Philosophy* and Ayn Rand's *Atlas Shrugged*, a novel that portrayed a world in which his father, Buck believed, would have succeeded. Buck's favorite biblical book was the story of Job, with which he identified strongly, given his interpretation of the circumstances of his life. In prison, Buck once met notorious "Red Light Bandit" Caryl Chessman, the convicted kidnapper and rapist. Buck, who dreamed of being a published writer, had read Chessman's well-received book, *Cell 2455, Death Row*, and admired his fellow prisoner's gift for compelling narrative. In their only conversation, the two cons discussed books they found important and provocative. About the time Chessman went to his death in San Quentin's gas chamber, Buck received his high school diploma by mail.

Buck was pushing the rag down the barrel of the revolver with a rod. "In World War Two, Jake was an Army major. One time he was ordered to reconnoiter around an enemy-held Pacific island with a squad of men."

Jennifer was so tired she had to fight to keep her eyes open, and here was Buck telling her some war story.

"Early in the mission, they captured a Japanese sentry. They couldn't spare men to return him to their own lines, and they obviously couldn't take the prisoner with them on their mission."

Buck was now wiping the trigger mechanism with a clean corner of the rag. "So, Jake ordered his sergeant to shoot the prisoner. The sergeant refused. Jake admitted to me it was probably an illegal order. Still, he said he didn't believe in issuing an order that he wasn't prepared to carry out himself. He thought about it a long time. It was important to get the information they'd been sent for. On the other hand, shooting the prisoner seemed tantamount to . . . murder."

Jennifer perked up. "Jake called the mission off and took the prisoner back, right?" He was, after all, Buck's hero.

"No." Buck spoke without emotion as he loaded his .22. "He shot him and completed the mission. As Jake pointed out, millions of words have been written about morality over thousands of years. But in the end, it comes down to a very personal decision."

Jennifer said nothing for a long time. From the way Buck talked, next to his father, Jake had had more influence on him than anyone. It amazed Jennifer that Jake had tried to make a strong moral argument to his class of convicted criminals for killing the man, and she was troubled that Buck had accepted the reasoning so readily.

Jennifer slept only sporadically that night. She popped up anxiously every half hour to make sure the wheel was still tied in position and to ease her fear that a ship might bear down on them in the night. Buck slept soundly.

The ocean voyage was draining her stamina. Her face and shoulders were burned from the sun. Her once-shiny hair was caked with salt. Her hands were ugly dishpan-raw. Her arm muscles ached from pulling on the sails and lines, and her legs were stiff from sitting so long at the helm.

Each day, she hoped Buck would find his sea legs, but the incessant rocking of the boat seemed too much for him. He was sick most of the time and even put off the crucial task of bringing the twenty-horsepower Mercury outboard motor inside where it wouldn't be ruined by the constant dampness.

She had been forewarned that most wooden boats leak to a

degree. But the *Iola*, elderly and often repaired, leaked a hell of a lot. It made matters worse that her hull had been fiberglassed by the previous owners, who must have thought they were sealing the leaks for good. Actually, the only proper repair of a wooden hull is recaulking the leaking planks, but that is a bigger job than slapping on a coat of fiberglass. Everything looked fine while the *Iola* sat in the harbor, but in ocean sailing, wooden planks tend to work back and forth, causing the *Iola's* fiberglass to crack immediately. This exposed the old leaks and allowed seawater to soak through the hull. Too, the cabin's forward hatch let in water, even though they kept it shut as tightly as possible. Everything in the bow stayed soaked. Because of all the leaking they had to start the generator and run the pump daily to keep down the water level in the bilge.

At dusk one evening, alone at the helm as usual, Jennifer saw they were heading toward ominous dark clouds lying low and heavy over the water. Suddenly, with no additional warning, a squall with near-gale-force gusts hit the *Iola*. The air and rain were bone-chilling cold. Clad only in shorts and T-shirt, Jennifer found herself shivering uncontrollably.

Buck rushed topside and leaped on the cabin top to close the air vent, which was letting in rainwater. Jumping back down to the wet deck, he lost his grip on the boom and slipped. He landed headfirst, striking his face on a metal stanchion.

Jennifer heard the sickening thud and wheeled to see Buck, semiconscious, rolling off the deck toward the churning ocean. It was a disaster she had feared all along.

She had pleaded with Buck to wear a lifeline whenever he came topside in inclement weather, but he'd always resisted. "If I go overboard, just throw me a flotation pillow and I'll swim back to the boat." But what if he was *unconscious*?

The netting for the dogs saved his life. Jennifer quickly tied down the wheel and rushed over, but it was a full minute before he was alert enough to respond so she could help him out of the netting and back onto the deck. Feeling woozy, Buck went below to lie on the bunk. One eye swelled angrily.

Jennifer did what she always did when the seas got rough, only this time with no help from Buck. She reefed the jib—rolling up some sail so as to catch less wind—and put the stern into the wind to prevent the boat from heeling over too steeply.

She hurried below and donned a vinyl foul-weather parka, thick pants, and rubber-soled deck shoes, then returned to the helm, where she strapped on a chest harness connected to a safety line that would keep her tethered to the *Iola* if she was swept overboard.

The next instant, she was caught full in the face by sea spray from the raging waters. When she choked and gasped for breath, the wind smothered her mouth with a blast of air. It was like sticking her head out the window of a fast-moving car. She couldn't breathe—she was suffocating! She swung away from the fierce wind, coughing, spitting out salt water. Her eyes stung; her feet and hands were wet and freezing. "*Buck*," she cried out. The roiling sea rose vertiginously high, causing the *Iola* to swing wildly into the wind and tipping the vessel over at a crazy angle. Terror and amazement blanched Jennifer's face as blinding billows of water burst upon the little boat. Over the maelstrom of howling wind and crashing seas, she cried out: "*Buck . . . goddammit!*"

Buck, tossed from his bunk, struggled topside and grabbed the wheel. Straining desperately, with Jennifer huddled next to him, he slowly got the *Iola* turned downwind, straightening the *Iola* out. Minutes later, the squall dissipated completely, and the sky was as clear as black Baccarat crystal. The moon lay on the horizon like a lighthouse beacon, their course lying perpendicular to the path of its rippling reflection.

They hugged each other long and hard, and Buck went back below to rest, Jennifer taking over the helm. She blew on her numbed red hands and vigorously rubbed them together.

The isolation of being stuck on a leaky sailboat in the middle of the ocean was beginning to wear on both of the lovers. They found it unexpectedly and oppressively claustrophobic. Here they were upon the open expanses of the world's largest ocean, yet they were feeling uncomfortably hemmed in. And with never the slightest break in the ruler-straight line of the distant horizon, all they could see in any direction—today, yesterday, tomorrow—was water, the vast, impervious Pacific Ocean. The creaking confines of the sailboat became their entire world. Their isolation together was complete.

Day after day, they saw neither land, ship, nor plane. It was as if they had fallen off the earth into an endless waste of water, just as the maps of medieval Europe had predicted. The problems of the world no longer mattered. They were on their own either to conquer the elements or succumb.

The finality of Jennifer's action in sailing off with Buck to a deserted isle had finally hit home. "*Are you willing to abandon your family, leave this country with him on a sailboat, and stay away the rest of your life?*" Her brother Ted's words flooded her head. Though at the time she had denied that she was deserting anyone or anything, she saw now that she was doing just that. She had left civilization behind. She couldn't phone her mother and say, "You're right, Mom, I want to come home and take over your business." Nor could she change her mind and turn back. Buck would be caught and returned to prison. On the other hand, they didn't know for sure what they would find once—or *if*—they reached their destination, yet they planned to make this place their home. And they had all of thirty dollars between them. The die was irrevocably cast. Jennifer wondered why she had never foreseen the consequences of her actions.

To compound her fears and anxieties, Buck, without explanation, began to retreat into himself. For one thing, they hadn't made love since leaving Hawaii a week before, an unusually long abstinence for them.

Buck was the most adventuresome lover she had ever known. It was as if he'd created sexy scenarios in his mind during his years in prison and whenever he felt randy, wanted to act out every one of them. "Turn over this way." "Let's try it like this." "You know what I've always wanted to do?" He was *summa cum laude* in eroticism.

Had they not been alone on a sailboat in the middle of the ocean, his lack of attention would have caused Jennifer to wonder if he was being unfaithful again. She still felt a stab of betrayal when she thought of Gina Allen, the coquettish girlfriend of Mike, whose Hilo roofing business had employed Jennifer at the time she met Buck. The work—carrying loads of roofing materials up and down ladders—was far too strenuous for Jennifer, and Buck later took over helping Mike. The two couples often got together, and Jennifer always sensed that Gina had tarted herself up for Buck. One night at Mike's place after he'd passed out from too much booze and grass, Gina suggested that the three survivors climb in the backyard hot tub. Buck thought it was a great idea and began undressing. The next thing Jennifer knew, Buck and Gina were naked, necking playfully. Buck summoned Jennifer to join them, making it obvious what he had in mind. Shocked and upset, Jennifer stormed out, slamming the door behind her. When Buck came home the next morning, she asked nothing about the night before and he volunteered no details. She had not wanted to know then, or later, when Buck spent late nights in Hilo. To be fair, he had never promised Jennifer a monogamous life together. Just the opposite, in fact, as he bemoaned having been denied so many experiences for too many years behind bars. He needed to be free to act on his urges, he told her. At least he was being honest about it. Jennifer tried to overlook Buck's occasional liaisons, hoping he'd get it out of his system. Yet it hurt whenever she sensed, as women so often can, that another woman had been in her man's arms.

But Jennifer had to face a much worse problem after a week at sea. *She and Buck had no idea where they were.* Months before they left, Jennifer had volunteered to be the navigator. She knew that finding a little island represented on the chart by a dot in the middle of the Pacific Ocean wasn't going to be a cinch. She'd heard that even the most experienced ocean navigators could miss that small a target. It wasn't like hitting the Hawaiian Islands with their several good-sized mountains and busy lanes of sea traffic.

She had learned everything she knew about the complex subject of celestial navigation from books—like a paperback guide called *Ten Easy Steps to Navigation*, which she had brought along. She had never taken a sight or worked out an actual navigation problem until this trip, so Jennifer had no reason to trust her navigating. The positions she plotted on the map fluctuated wildly—one day, according to her calculations, they had sailed three hundred miles south. "Wow, we're making great time," exclaimed

Buck, who was only too willing to believe such good fortune. But the next day, *they had gone seven hundred miles to the east!* Jennifer knew that in optimum conditions, given the *Iola's* slow speed, they couldn't go more than fifty or sixty miles in twenty-four hours. Clearly, her calculations stank—and they did not change the *Iola's* course based on them. They just kept heading in the direction the compass pointed to for due south.

Nevertheless, she doggedly followed the same routine each morning. She tied the wheel down, surveyed the horizon, and went below, tuning the AM-FM transistor radio to the international channel that gives the soft tick-ticking of Greenwich Mean Time. The seconds ticked off until a melodic recorded female voice said: "At the tone, Mean Time will be twenty-one hours and ten minutes." In three or four seconds, a louder tick signaled the minute mark. At exactly that moment, Jennifer started the stopwatch and went topside. Dutifully following the step-by-step instructions in her how-to book, she raised the sextant and looked into the eyepiece that reflected, through a tiny oval mirror, the line of the horizon in relation to the position of the sun. Once fixed on that point, she checked the corresponding scale of numbers on the bottom of the sextant, which gave her the angle between the horizon and the sun. Jennifer would then go back below and use the navigation book to translate the sextant's number into a formula based on several factors, including the season of the year and the exact time of day. Finally, she drew a "line of position" on a chart of the central Pacific. "Of course," the book offered helpfully, "this is not a line of position as much as a curve or circle of position. What you are measuring is the geographical position of the sun at the time of your sighting." Right.

Four hours later, she repeated the process. She extended the first line of position until it met on the chart with the latest one. Where the two lines crossed was supposed to be their current position. But every time Jennifer saw the haywire result of her careful work staring up at her, she felt like throwing the sextant and book overboard.

They were lost.

She fought to push back her feelings of desperation. She *could* figure out this problem. She *had* to. She'd taken math in college, she had confidence in her analytical abilities. She was a capable woman, not a helpless damsel in distress. She went back to the celestial navigation book again and again, trying to find her mistake, but the solution continued to elude her.

On their tenth morning at sea, with Buck on deck at the helm, Jennifer had no sooner awakened than the realization stunned her. *North, not south!* She reached for her navigation book. Somehow, she had assumed all this time that she was supposed to be using the logarithm for south latitude. That's where they were headed. But she woke up realizing that was wrong. They were *north* of the equator.

Her novice's mistake had been understandable. As her guide confirmed, the *north* logarithm was for use above the equator, where they were. She excitedly spread out the chart and did some quick figuring, using the previous day's sightings. The position she came up with looked probable, unlike her others, but she wanted to be certain. Three hours later, after two new sightings, Jennifer pointed to a spot on the chart and proudly told Buck: "That's where we are—halfway to Palmyra."

Buck hugged and kissed her. His relief was obvious, and it occurred to Jennifer that he'd been more worried about the uncertainty of their position than his sense of machismo had permitted him to let on. But they weren't home free, yet. From her library research, Jennifer knew that Palmyra's low-slung islets could only be seen from within six to eight miles, making it easy even for the most deadeye navigator to miss the atoll completely.

It wasn't long before Jennifer discovered a new worry: running out of food if and when they found Palmyra. Take the sugar supply. She had planned to use it only for baking, since neither she nor Buck used it in coffee or tea or on cereal. But Buck was now being extravagant with the sugar, feeling it might help him regain his energy. And he was imploring Jennifer to bake, because bread and biscuits would be likely to settle his stomach. The supplies were dwindling at an alarming rate. As for her own diet, Jennifer drank cups of black coffee morning and afternoon and ate one light meal a day, usually in the evening. A year or so before she met Buck, she had put on a lot of weight—ballooning to 170 pounds. To take off fifty pounds, she had cut down to one meal a day and become a vegetarian. She still seldom ate meat. Planning to supplement their food en route to Palmyra with fish, and once on the island, to eat fish as the mainstay of their diet, they had brought along fishing poles, reels, hooks, lines of various test weights, even a spear gun. But so far, they hadn't managed a single catch, other than a bony little flying fish that sacrificed itself by crash-landing on the deck. So much for their dreams of fresh mahi-mahi or tuna or bluefin along the way. Although Jennifer had only fished a couple of times in her life, Buck had claimed to be an expert angler. She hoped his inability to catch anything so far wasn't an indicator of things to come on their "island paradise."

Thirteen days into the trip, Jennifer was down below calculating their position when Buck yelled for her to come topside. At last he had begun to feel better and had been spending more time on deck helping sail the boat.

On deck, she found him struggling with a line. From the frenetic splashing in the water, this was obviously a big catch. She was overjoyed at the thought of fresh fish for dinner. But this fish had other ideas. Suddenly, it made a lurch under the boat, but Buck, lightning-fast, bent over the stern and jerked on the line. His powerful arm hoisted the wildly thrashing, silvery body into the air. With a net, he swooped aboard a tuna weighing thirty pounds at least. Laughing, he grasped it by its gaping mouth.

"Goddamn!" he shouted with pride.

But his exhilaration was short-lived. "Fuck! The hook's in my thumb."

"Oh, no." Jennifer gasped, stiffening.

Somehow, Buck managed to wrest the tuna off the hook. It dropped to the deck, flip-flopping helplessly.

Coolly and deliberately, Buck pushed the hook through his thumb until the curved end with the barb was visible on the other side.

Jennifer felt faint.

"Get the file," he said evenly.

"Oh, God!"

"You've got to file down the barb," he said. The beads of sweat popping out on his forehead belied his calm voice.

Bravely controlling her own squeamishness, Jennifer tried, but every time she moved the file across the barb, Buck's whole body tightened. Clenching his teeth, he took it stoically at first. But soon he began to moan, softly. Jennifer trembled as she scraped metal against metal, making more blood flow.

"Try doing it with your eyes open, Jen." Somehow, he'd managed a wisecrack.

"I just can't . . . hurt you like this," she stammered, turning away.

Without a word, Buck grasped the eye of the hook with pliers and snapped it off. He took a deep breath and yanked out the bloody hook.

A relieved Jennifer dabbed antiseptic on the wound and dressed it quickly.

She now understood what she had heard about ocean cruising being "days of boredom punctuated by moments of sheer terror." She also felt she knew a little bit more about Buck. For all his self-pity and fecklessness on the trip so far, he could be very composed and self-sufficient when necessary. He was a survivor.

The next day, they had a memorable moment of a very different kind; in a flurry of cheerful splashing, the sea around the *Iola* became alive with porpoises.

Chattering like squirrels, playfully vying with each other to be seen and heard, the smiling mammals raced in front of the bow, aimed their blunt snouts skyward, and jumped several feet into the air, flashing their white underbellies in a precisely choreographed aquatic ballet.

Beautiful as this welcoming visit was, the performance of the porpoises reminded Jennifer that she and Buck and the *Iola* were intruders. This huge, unpredictable expanse, teeming with secret and dangerous life, was another world. They would be outsiders, always.

At the sight of the porpoises, Puffer and Buck's two big hounds went crazy. They barked and barked, but the porpoises seemed to fly even higher. Jennifer and Buck, who seldom wore clothes on pleasant days, stood naked and smiling under the warm sun. The scent of the sea about them, they lovingly held hands.

"Look at us," Jennifer said. "We're as brown as berries." By now, any patches of angry red burn had turned to tan. Buck's thick neck and powerful shoulders were almost mahogany; her softer skin was a glowing nut-brown. The beard he'd started since being at sea was coming in a reddish blond, and she playfully stroked his stubble, happily surprised at how soft it was already getting.

They laughed and kissed, as if they'd just found each other again.

A diffuse lemon sunlight filled the air. This was the kind of balmy and beautiful day that made Jennifer enjoy being on a sailboat in the middle of the ocean. She hoped it was a sign things were beginning to get better.

That evening, the sunset was unusually brilliant, more chromatically various and luminescent than any fireworks display.

"Know what you're seeing?" Buck asked smugly as the sun touched the dark horizon line of the ocean.

"A sunset, dummy," Jennifer sensed some sort of challenge.

"Actually, it's a mirage."

She was skeptical and not really interested. Beauty needed no explanation. It just was.

"Well, listen up and you can learn something from old Buck. The setting sun actually dips below the horizon a couple of minutes before you lose sight of its image. It has to do with curving light rays. I'm serious, Jen."

Jennifer shrugged. "Prettiest mirage I've ever seen."

The pale-blue scrim of the sky merged with lush oranges and brooding violet, until finally, in the last hushed moments of sunlight, the impeccably white cirrus clouds in the high distance blushed pink.

In the stillness, Buck said, "Red sky at night, sailor's delight."

Jennifer knew the rest. "Red sky in the morning, sailor's warning." The famous old saw was suddenly a special shared moment.

They went below and made salty, sweaty love. Beneath their

urgent cries, few sounds disturbed the ocean silence. Water lapped softly against the bow, the sails and shrouds occasionally flapped in the light evening breeze, and the little *Iola* nosed steadily southward.

For Jennifer, life seemed so peaceful, and safe, at that moment.

The next morning, they awoke to a sunrise as red as fresh blood.

JENNIFER TOOK the responsibility of keeping the *Iola*'s log. She really liked the idea of recording their experiences in her own words. For whom? Themselves? Posterity? She didn't think about that aspect very deeply. She just went through the daily exercise with determined regularity, much like a young girl keeping a diary no one would ever see.

> *June 14. 120 miles from our destination. Raised main sail for about 6 hrs. Made good time.*
>
> *June 15. Believe we have hit the doldrums—becalmed with light squalls. Little progress made. Under jib—self steering. Bathed in rain. Barely able to get a fix through all the clouds.*
>
> *June 16. Still becalmed. Gray skies, no sun to fix so far. Drifting southwest—periodical rainsqualls. Glimpses of sunshine gave us a fix. Still not much progress.*
>
> *June 17. Got up enough wind to raise the main sail—put up the larger jib too. Progress is still very slow. Buck ran out of tobacco and is miserable. Baking cornbread.*

On the morning of June 19, Jennifer made an exciting discovery. Barely containing her glee, she approached Buck to make a serious announcement. "If this wind holds true," she said, and paused dramatically, "we should be . . . sighting Palmyra off the port bow around three o'clock this afternoon!" She fairly whooped.

"You sure?" Buck asked in disbelief.

"According to my calculations." She grinned.

She'd come a long way with her navigating. Now working with

the correct logarithm, she felt confident she was accurately tracking their position. The chart showed them to be within twenty miles of Palmyra, and she was certain that's where they really were.

Even so, when she caught sight of the island while peering from the bow a few hours later, she found herself almost in a state of shock. She felt tingly all over and couldn't stop laughing, even as she screamed out, "Land ho! Land ho!" They'd actually made it!

Buck squinted at the horizon, then joined in excitedly. "You did it, Jen baby! Samarand at last!" He liked using an early name for Palmyra he'd picked up in one of the books.

"Whaddaya know," she marveled. It was just about the greatest success of her life. And she'd done it all by herself.

"Incredible!" Buck yelled. "Columbus could have used you!"

"I *did* say it would be today. Didn't I?" She sounded as if she couldn't believe it herself.

She was a navigator now, a *real* oceangoing navigator. She had achieved something amazing.

It had been nineteen days since she and Buck left Hawaii. Along with Jennifer's log, they'd kept count on a calendar illustrated with a picture of an old whaling boat. To be sure, they certainly hadn't broken any speed records, but then the *Iola* was no world-class racer. The plan, of necessity, was slow and steady progress toward their destination. But they'd done it, and even the dogs got caught up in the moment, barking merrily.

Jennifer darted below and brought up two glasses of straight dark rum. She and Buck sat contentedly on deck, their legs dangling over the side. As a light wind pushed them through the gentle seas directly toward their destination, they gazed raptly at the slit of land on the horizon.

"To our island," Buck said with feeling.

They clinked glasses and drank to their good fortune. Only now, with the end in sight, did Jennifer allow herself to admit how easily they could have failed.

When they approached close enough, they altered course to come around well west of the island to a narrow channel indicated on the chart. Entering the island's lagoon was not going to be easy, thanks to Buck's laziness. He had neglected for so long to bring their motor inside that salt water and humidity had caused it to freeze up. They would have to sail through the narrow channel, hemmed in on both sides by treacherous reefs, without power.

But Jennifer did not want to give in to a downer. Eagerly taking up the binoculars, she saw surf breaking over the hidden reef and a sparkling white beach beckoning on the north shore. What had seemed undefined bushiness from a distance now became visible as well-defined coconut trees—*thousands* of them. They made a dark, thick barrier, and their fronds waved almost helplessly, idiotically. Jennifer, not knowing why, found them unsettling.

June 19. LAND HO! At 4:15 P.M. we spotted Palmyra off our port side. Wind very light—unable to make landfall before dark. Headed east. Strong winds all night. Then becalmed.

June 20. Spotted Palmyra again this morning, dead west. Winds very light. Very frustrating—rainsqualls and enough wind to get us just about where we were yesterday at this time. But then the wind ceased. So near and yet so far!

Not only were they frustrated to be so close yet unable to reach the lagoon, they were also fearful of going aground on a submerged reef. To play it safe, they headed away from the island just before nightfall, drifting a little out to sea. They could have made it into waters shallow enough for an anchorage, but the unseen jagged coral reefs might rip apart the boat's hull. To enter the lagoon, they had to ease through the channel. With the outboard motor fouled, they were dependent on a fortuitous shift in the wind.

June 21. Though winds were light last night and are brisk today, we're having trouble relocating our island.

June 22. Couldn't find her. Lowered all sails last night—no wind thru today. Reading. Took sights.

June 23. Fair trade winds. Hoisted all sails and went in pursuit of our island. Re-LAND HO at 12:30, giving us plenty of time to gain anchorage. For entry, we're hoping for a SE wind. We are off SW shore. Saw a light on island at night. Possibly another boat?

Jennifer, out of kindness or prudence, did not mention the obvious: if Buck had done his job, they would already be ashore. And he didn't bring it up, even to apologize, but the unacknowledged tension built.

June 24. So nice to wake up and have the island right there in front of us.

Nice, but infuriating. Palmyra lay before them, close enough to swim to, yet the necessary wind did not rise off the bow. Suppose a southeast wind blew only rarely in this region? What would they do in that case? The current was no help; it always flowed out of the channel to the ocean rather than inward.

June 25. Another day of reading. Strong NE winds continue.
June 26. Buck caught two big fish this morning. Soaked them in brine and hung them out to dry. Will use for bait. A family of manta rays came scouting their dinner. Still NE trades. Still waiting and reading.

But when they awakened on the morning of June 27, a wind was blowing steadily southeast. Excitedly, they tumbled out of bed, hoisted sail, and got under way. From the description of Palmyra in the Pacific sailing guide, they knew they had to line up with the two poles at either end of the channel to hit a straight course down the middle. But as Buck took the wheel and tried to do so, the wind suddenly died and the *Iola* came to a halt, subject now to the mercy of the outflowing current. Minutes later, as the *Iola* drifted backward, there was a sudden bump followed by a harsh scrunching sound from beneath the boat. The fragile *Iola* had gone aground on a coral head.

Reacting quickly, Buck lowered the sails.

Jennifer tried to keep her cool. She kept looking at the island, tantalizingly near. If they did begin to sink, she thought, at least they could lower the dinghy and row to shore. They'd be saved, but they could well end up losing most or all of their supplies.

Buck, at his best when disaster loomed, dived over the side to check beneath the boat. He saw right away that, luckily, it was the solid iron part of the *Iola*'s keel that rested on the coral. There was no readily apparent damage to the hull itself. He went up to fill his lungs again, then swam back down to check the other side of the boat, and ran smack into the cold staring eyes of a sleek, implacable shark at least six feet long. The sound of his heart thudded in his ears. He kicked hard to break the surface and scrambled up the side of the *Iola*.

Jennifer looked bewildered.

"Friendly shark," he gulped, still trembling.

"Uh-huh. How do you know it's friendly?"

"He invited me to dinner."

She didn't laugh at his joke, in case he'd be encouraged to show off by jumping in again. "Don't you go back down there."

The warning proved unnecessary. Just then she spotted two motorized dinghies coming out of the channel, one behind the other. "We've got company."

The strangers in the boats headed directly for the *Iola*, then cut their engines and bobbed in the water about twenty yards away.

"Ahoy," a darkly tanned older man yelled from the lead boat. "Need some help?" In the other, a skinny middle-aged man and a teenage boy watched without expression.

"*Please*," Jennifer shouted. Buck hung back, suddenly sullen at the presence of others on the island.

"Take it you're without power?"

"Motor's frozen."

"Want us to pull you off the coral?" Their would-be rescuer saw that Jennifer was the designated liaison.

"Yes. Thank you."

The powerboats moved into position and the men tossed over lines to Buck, who silently secured them to the *Iola*'s bow. In no time, they were pulled free and the dinghies were towing them through the narrow channel at a steady clip.

Jennifer stood on deck, craning her neck eagerly for a good look at the island close up. As they entered the lagoon, her first vivid impression was of all the lush surrounding greenery. The waters of the lagoon sparkled emerald and blue, rimmed by thin strips of blinding white sand and lumps of greenish coral. Clearly visible in the crystalline shallows, schools of colorful fish darted by, and the noisy chatter of birds rose in the distance. From this vantage, the army of coconut trees now towered over the jewel-like setting like sternly forbidding sentinels, an impenetrable host.

"Remember, my name's Roy Allen," Buck growled under his breath. "Don't slip up."

Back in Hilo, Buck had persuaded Gina Allen to give him her husband's identity papers, including his birth certificate. In fact, the real Roy A. Allen had little use for them. A professional rodeo cowboy, he had been kicked in the head by a bull five years earlier and had since been confined to a Tennessee Veterans Administration hospital in a ward reserved for patients with little hope of recovery. Buck had used the ID to get a passport in the name of Roy Allen.

Buck's warning reminded Jennifer that no matter how serene their new home looked as they neared the shore, their existence here would never be free of worry and suspicion.

"Okay, *Roy*," she answered resignedly. "But what are you going to do about that big ole 'Buck' tattoo on your arm?"

He glared at her and stalked away.

CHAPTER 6

MIDWAY BETWEEN SAN DIEGO and Hawaii, the *Sea Wind* hit seas so rough that Mac and Muff couldn't see over the tops of the waves. That night, Muff lost a pot of stew off the stove when the boat abruptly heeled, painfully scorching her hand. It took an hour to clean up the mess as the boat kept lurching. "Why is it every time we go to sea," she wailed, "it's lousy, lousy, lousy?"

But unflappable Mac thought the trip was going quite well. The favorable winds increased their speed, and there'd been no equipment failures or breakdowns. Even in such heavy weather, he was invigorated by fast, flawless sailing. The days were mostly steel-gray, but Mac's vision of the adventures that lay ahead brought a silver lining to any overcast. He whistled a lot these days. The tune he was stuck on was an old favorite: "The High and the Mighty," the title tune for a 1950s movie about macho pilot John Wayne bravely pulling an airliner through a crisis.

Each night, comfortable and snug in his bunk (and with the automatic-pilot steering device keeping the *Sea Wind* on course, which could be verified by periodically checking the compass in the cabin), Mac would turn the light switch off, and by the soft glow of a kerosene lantern, read *An Island to Myself*, the true story of a man who had lived alone on a tropical island. If only his Muff, sleeping fitfully in her own bunk nearby, could share in his excitement. . . .

On May 25, 1974, at the height of Hawaii's famously idyllic spring, they arrived off the western shore of the massive Big Island. They had sailed more than two thousand miles in only eighteen days, one of the *Sea Wind*'s best legs ever.

Dropping sail, they proceeded under power through the narrow channel of Hilo's Radar Bay, glimpsing the varicolored bright blossoms whose riotous profusion gave the island one of its nicknames, the Garden Island. The docking area could barely accommodate a mere dozen boats, but Mac spotted a suitable anchorage adjacent to the concrete quay.

They moored next to a sailboat owned by Curtis Shoemaker. A short, sinewy man in his mid-fifties with a bronzed, weather-beaten face that looked as if it had been fashioned with a blunt instrument, Shoemaker had been sailing since his days as a Sea Scout in Hawaii in the 1930s. Now a telephone repairman, he lived in Waimea, a mountainous outback about forty-five miles northwest of Hilo, and was an avid ham radio operator.

Mac and Muff instantly hit it off with Shoemaker and his wife, Momi. They frequently visited back and forth. When the two women went shopping one afternoon, Curt checked out Mac's two-way radio and liked what he saw, deeming it a first-class setup. He suggested that they establish a radio communications link with each other as long as Mac and Muff were on Palmyra.

"You could get in real trouble on an island like that all by your-self," Shoemaker cautioned. "It might be a good idea to keep regular contact with the outside world." He explained that he had a high-powered radio at his mountaintop home and that they could fix a predetermined schedule for communication.

Mac was never one to admit he might someday need emergency aid, but he liked the idea that his and Muff's relatives and friends could get word to them in their secluded paradise via Curt's radio.

While in port, Mac undertook some essential last-minute fix-it projects. After Hilo, there would be no other ports of call for a long time. They would have to rely entirely on the supplies and equipment they took to Palmyra.

More than one friend had teased Mac and Muff about the large supply of medicine they stashed on the *Sea Wind*. But in far corners of the world they couldn't call the family doctor or visit the corner drugstore, so they carried their own floating pharmacy, complete with pages of typed instructions and recommended dosages. A former *Sea Wind* crewman was responsible for the instructions and the plethora of drugs, such as Pyribenzamine, Aralen, sulfadiazine, and the like. A medical doctor, he had signed on for the world cruise in 1961 and left behind his black bag when he and his fellow crewman deserted Mac in Mexico.

Neatly put away in the storage areas were enough tools and spare parts for Mac to open his own boat repair shop. He had everything from pipe fittings and bits to bolt cutters and deck fittings. He had not just one electric drill, but four. There was an electric generator and 1,100-watt portable alternator. And, as the hardware store ads say, much, much more.

Muff was equally well outfitted for her considerable chores as cook and all-around boatwife, challenging roles aboard a small boat at sea for months at a time. She had a full arsenal of pots and pans for cooking and baking, as well as some convenience gadgets which, because of battery drain, are not often found on boats, such as an ice crusher, food processor, blender, electric mixer, and pressure cooker.

There was also a permanent maritime reference collection aboard the *Sea Wind*. Titles like *The American Practical Navigator, Dictionary of Fishes, Medical Emergencies in Pleasure Boating*, and *Pacific*

Islands Yearbook revealed the scope of the couple's readiness for a self-reliant life at sea.

And there were weapons aboard, as well. Mac had a .30-caliber Marlin rifle, a small derringer, and a powerful handgun, the latter kept below deck in a special hiding place beside his bunk. Even lying there, he could slide back a panel in a cabinet, revealing the narrow shelf upon which lay the handgun, one of the most potent ever built, the Colt .357 magnum, capable of blowing the arm off an intruder. Of course, Mac was a man comfortable with guns, having learned how to handle them during a brief Army stint in the 1950s. Muff, as anyone who knew her would suspect, was leery of firearms, but she had come to accept the need to have them aboard after a terrifying incident on their round-the-world cruise.

It had happened after they cleared the Straits of Gibraltar and were cruising off the coast of Morocco after dark. Mac was especially vigilant at the helm that night because pirates in trawlers had reportedly been ramming sailboats in the area, boarding them, stealing everything of value and killing everyone aboard, then scuttling the boats. Suddenly from the darkness, Mac had heard the sounds of a large ship's engine. To his horror, the outline of a trawler headed directly toward him. When he quickly shifted the *Sea Wind*'s course, the trawler followed suit. Mac saw that the two craft were headed for collision. He raced below, grabbed his rifle, and flipped the switch for the two powerful spotlights mounted halfway up the front mast. Yelling to sleep-dazed Muff, he scrambled back topside and stood directly under the spreader lights' white beams as Muff scampered in the shadows to take the helm. Mac snapped up the rifle, aiming at an unmoving shadowy figure on the bridge of the mysterious trawler. Illuminated like a frog about to be gigged, Mac knew his actions could be clearly seen from the trawler. If it did not change course within moments, the *Sea Wind* would surely be rammed, perhaps even sunk. But before that happened, Mac intended to shoot. *He's going to get us but I'm going to get him, too,* Mac thought as he slipped his index finger inside the trigger guard. Time seemed to freeze as the two vessels silently converged. How close could he let them come before he had to fire? Was the other man drawing a bead upon him? Then, in the next instant, the trawler veered sharply away, only narrowly missing the *Sea Wind*. Someone, in this eyeball-to-eyeball confrontation, had blinked. It hadn't been Mac.

They survived that threat, Mac came to believe, for two reasons: he had the right instincts when it counted, and they had the proper equipment aboard—in this case, bright spotlights and a handy rifle. The incident reinforced Mac's confident belief that a person made his own luck, as well as his conviction that ocean sailing was not for the weak or ill-prepared. Despite his close call and others he and Muff had experienced, Mac did not doubt his ability to survive whatever challenge their new adventure would offer. However severe.

June 4, 1974

Dearest Mother,

We're staying in Hawaii until we have a full moon for the trip. When we do leave, we'll be going to Palmyra. We've heard a lot about how the island used to be, but really don't know what to expect now. I'll give Mac six months (or even less) there and he will be ready to leave. You know how changeable he is. Anyway, after Palmyra I can write you and you will be able to write us, as the next places he wants to go have mail service. I hate it being like this, each of us having to worry if the other one is well and safe.

Your loving daughter,
Muff

June 24, 1974

Dear Jamie and Marie:

I was down the whole trip from San Diego to Hawaii, thinking about leaving our friends. I still get lumpy in the throat when I think of all of you.

We're all stored up and ready to leave for Palmyra, and we even have a full moon. Mac is afraid we might miss it—such a small place in such a big ocean. I pray we have a good trip there.

Till later, take care of yourselves. Will write when I can.

Love,
Mac and Muff

THEIR RITUAL of leaving port hadn't changed over the years. Muff dutifully played the supporting role assigned to her. Mac was captain and she was the crew.

On this clear blue morning, just as the last threads of sunrise disappeared from the sky, they went through the exercise as they had hundreds of times before. He'd already rechecked every item of equipment, using a mental checklist that was ingrained in his memory by now. No airline pilot in the world was more careful in his preflight than Mac was in preparing the *Sea Wind* for sea.

Today, as always, he waited until everything was just as he wanted, peered out through the bobbing craft in Hilo harbor to visualize his course to the big blue, and smiled a self-satisfied grin.

Gruffly, assuming a pose that landlubbers could dismiss as pompously theatrical, Mac spoke over his shoulder. "Muff, let's do it." Perhaps he was playing a bit to Shoemaker, who stood on the wharf ready to release the boat's lines.

Muff was standing just inside the companionway, poised beside the ignition switch. "Okay, honey."

In the cockpit, Mac turned the key. "Hit it."

She flipped the switch. Mac pushed the starter button and the engine caught right away. Letting the engine idle so the oil would thin out and properly lubricate all the parts, he weighed anchor. He then waved to Shoemaker, who untied all lines but one, a stern line. As Mac pulled in the lines, he dropped them into perfect loops on the deck.

When he was satisfied with the pitch of the engine, Mac cut the suspense by announcing for all to hear: "Casting off!"

Shoemaker dropped the last stern line and Muff gathered it in. The *Sea Wind* was on her own.

As unruly squads of sea gulls mewed and wheeled overhead, Mac engaged the engine and they began creeping forward. Behind them, the faint sounds of Hilo's bustling early-morning traffic became ever more faint, a steady hum of civilization they did not expect to hear again for a long time. Low in the sky, the rising sun was blinding. It washed over the huge Chinese banyan trees that lined the bayfront drive and guarded the verdant acres of Lili-uokalani Gardens. But these features of the landscape rapidly grew indistinct.

Despite herself, Muff sensed immediately that the reality of being under way would drain away some of her fears and misgivings. They were on familiar territory and Mac was in full command. She had done her part, and she'd continue to do her part. She was determined not to misstep or fall a millisecond behind. Sailing depended so much on proper balance and timing. Mac needed her, but every minute of the day, he was the skipper, and she needed him even more.

Her husband sat at the helm, his back straight as a board, his brown hand resting on the wheel, sharp eyes glancing 180 degrees to take best advantage of any eventuality. He felt the morning sun warm on his leathery neck, the refreshingly cool spray of water from the offshore wind on his face.

As they edged their way through the Radar Bay channel, Muff took over the steering and Mac upped sail with practiced efficiency. First the mizzen, then the main and jibs. They all billowed out instantly in the gusting breeze, snapping the halyards musically against the masts.

Back at the helm, Mac looked up at the sails. It was a move as automatic and unconscious as that of a cautious driver checking the rearview mirror. The wind was fresh and steady, and all the sails were taut and full. He shifted the engine into neutral. He would allow it to idle awhile longer before shutting it down, but they were under sail now, and for Mac, there was no feeling like it in the world.

Charged, now fully alive, the beautiful craft surged forward, heading out the channel into the open sea, straining anxiously to fly upon the rolling surface.

Mac and Muff went about the steady work of joining forces with wind and water. Breezes rose and fell and shifted, but slowly even the tip of mighty Mauna Loa peak, rising more than thirteen thousand feet above sea level, sank into the shimmering sea behind them.

When Muff brought cups of piping hot coffee, they sat together in the cockpit, Mac at the helm, enjoying the radiance of early morning. The day passed without incident. Long before sunset, they were alone upon the watery bowl of visible ocean. No other craft could be seen. They moved across a bright, unruffled sea.

As the air cooled, then became chill, a powerful northeasterly began to blow, urging them strongly and precisely in the direction of Palmyra Island.

Mac, at last, had what he wanted. They were heading into the unknown, and he was exuberant.

CHAPTER 7

THOUGH DESIGNATED AN ISLAND on some charts of the Pacific, Palmyra is in fact an atoll, the very rim of a steep-faced volcanic peak in a gigantic underwater range whose mountains, hidden deep within the ocean, are among the world's highest. Unlike actual islands, atolls are virtually flat, with no hills or mountains. Palmyra's highest elevation is only six feet above sea level.

A horseshoe curve of more than a dozen islets are spaced like jewels on a long necklace surrounding a protected lagoon—the old volcano crater—a configuration common to atolls. Each islet is composed of hard sand and constantly growing coral, carpeted with a dense growth of shrubs and coconut palms.

For centuries this ancient atoll lay undiscovered, six degrees north of the equator, near the zone where the northeast and southeast trade winds meet and tussle.

On the night of June 13, 1798, Edmond Fanning, an intrepid American sea captain, was sailing his ship, the *Betsey*, northwestward toward home from a trading trip to the Orient. Fanning, a well-known sailor of fortune, had already discovered a Pacific island that now bore his name. Suddenly, struck in his cabin by a compelling premonition of danger, Fanning hurried on deck and briskly ordered the helmsman to heave to in the darkness. Astonishingly, the first dim light of early dawn disclosed a low reef, dead ahead. Fanning's ship would surely have foundered there had he not trusted his mariner's sixth sense. With heady relief, the *Betsey's* crew upped sail and carefully rounded the reef on its northern flank. Fanning climbed aloft to the crow's nest high atop the mainmast. Through his spyglass, he saw a small, unprepossessing island on the opposite side of the reef. This is the first recorded view of Palmyra, and the *Betsey's* brush with destruction became the first omen of danger to be associated with the island.

The island was officially christened when a second ship chanced by and gained credit for the actual discovery, Fanning having failed to make a timely report of his finding. On November 6, 1802, a Manila-bound American ship, the *Palmyra*, was thrown off course in heavy seas and pushed near the island by the elements. When the weather cleared, the crew went exploring ashore, and occupied themselves on the atoll for about a week. It took nearly four years for a dispatch from the *Palmyra's* skipper, Captain Sawle, to be relayed from one vessel to another and finally reach home with the news:

> New island, 05° 52' North, 162° 06' West, with two lagoons, the westmost of which is 20 fathoms deep, lies out of the track of most navigators passing from America to Asia or Asia to America.

Fourteen years later, a Spanish pirate ship, the *Esperanza*, kept a grim appointment with destiny in the waters off Palmyra. Sailing with a rich cargo of gold and silver artifacts stolen from Inca temples in northern Peru, the vessel was attacked by another ship, and a bloody battle ensued. Surviving *Esperanza* crew members managed to sail her off with the treasure intact, but soon wrecked on submerged coral reef. As the ship sank, the pirates successfully transferred their treasure and provisions to the nearby deserted atoll: Palmyra. The following year the stranded men built rafts, split into two groups and, after hiding their treasure, sailed off in opposite directions for help. It is known that one raft sank. An American whaler found and rescued its only survivor, seaman James Hines, who soon died of pneumonia. None of the crew members on the other raft was ever heard from; it is assumed all died at sea. And since no one has ever reported finding the Inca cache on Palmyra, it might still rest there, a collection of Mesoamerican objects several times more valuable in today's art market than the gold and silver would be as precious metals.

The litany of disasters had scarcely begun. In late 1855, word reached Tahiti that another ship, a whaler, had wrecked on Palmyra's treacherous reefs, but an attempt to find the missing ship and her crew was unsuccessful.

In 1862, Hawaii's King Kamehameha IV granted a petition from two subjects of his, Zenas Bent and J. B. Wilkinson, for authorization to take possession of Palmyra under the Hawaiian flag. Bent and Wilkinson treated the island as virtually their own, building a rudimentary house, planting a vegetable garden, and leaving "a white man and four Hawaiians" there to "gather and cure *biche de mer*," an edible sea slug prized in the Orient. Later that year, Bent sold his interest in Palmyra to Wilkinson, who in turn willed his proprietary interest in the property to his Hawaiian wife. Palmyra was included among the other Hawaiian Islands when they were annexed to the United States by act of Congress in 1898.

In 1911, Judge Henry E. Cooper of Honolulu purchased Palmyra for $750 from the heirs of Wilkinson's widow. He kept Palmyra and adjacent properties until 1922, when he sold off all but one islet for $15,000. The old judge apparently believed a rumor that the treasure of the *Esperanza* was buried under a banyan tree on that islet—called Home Island. The new owner of the remainder of Palmyra, Leslie Fullard-Leo, a South African diamond miner turned building contractor, had heard about Palmyra shortly after moving to Honolulu and thought it likely to be a peaceful refuge far removed from the rigors of civilization. But Fullard-Leo visited his uninhabited island only twice in seventeen years. When he died, Palmyra was inherited by his three sons, who also rarely visit it. Home Island has passed on to Judge Cooper's descendants.

The Fullard-Leo family was forced into a legal skirmish with the U.S. government to keep Palmyra. In anticipation of the expected Pacific war, Palmyra was declared a "prohibited defense area" by an Executive Order dated December 19, 1940, and assigned to the jurisdiction of the Navy Department, which constructed a naval base there for five thousand servicemen. The Fullard-Leos resisted in four federal court battles. The clincher came in 1946, when the U.S. Ninth Circuit Court of Appeals declared the brothers' title to Palmyra Island valid. The court held that since both occupancy and claim of title to Palmyra by Bent, Wilkinson, and their heirs (buttressed by regular payment of property taxes) existed long prior to U.S. annexation of Hawaii, and were honored by the Hawaiian government, Palmyra was in fact privately owned, even though it is a "possession" of the United States. Soon after the circuit court's decision, the Navy swiftly pulled out, abandoning buildings, gun emplacements, and empty ammunition dumps.

Since Palmyra's status as private property had been affirmed, visitors like Mac, Muff, Buck, and Jennifer needed permission from the owners to spend any time there, but the Fullard-Leos, who live in Honolulu, had learned long ago that it was impossible to keep uninvited guests off their island. Sensitive to what South Sea sailors had long called the Palmyra Curse, her owners took out substantial liability insurance to protect them from a host of calamities that might occur to visitors on their island, and hoped for the best.

JUNE 27, 1974

AS THE *Iola* was towed into the lagoon, Jennifer was struck with the feeling that time had come to a halt on Palmyra. The lagoon, smooth as a mirror and so clear one could make out the coral configurations on its bottom, was flanked on three sides by miniature islands, each overgrown with tall coconut trees marching down to the waterline. The island was as pristine as she had hoped.

But Palmyra, though uninhabited, was not, as she and Buck had hoped, a deserted island.

On the north side of the lagoon they moored the *Iola* between two other boats at a line of steel-reinforced wooden pilings (four, in all) that boaters call "dolphins." Scarcely fifteen yards of water separated the *Iola* from shore, and the boats on each side of it were around twenty yards distant. Jennifer and Buck, with a cargo of excited dogs, rowed their dinghy the short distance to the beach, where the pent-up animals went crazy and gamboled madly, barking and yapping and running around in circles.

As Jennifer planted her feet on solid ground for the first time in twenty-eight days, the earth seemed to be shifting under her. She was ecstatic to be off the boat and safe after an ocean voyage of a thousand miles. From where she stood, she could smell the earthiness, the fertile greenery of the jungle. It pulsed with hidden life.

Jennifer, her eyes moist with happiness, hugged Buck tightly. The warm, bright sun enhanced the specialness of the moment.

They were soon introducing themselves to the other people on the island. One of the neighboring boats was the *Poseidon*, a forty-eight-foot ketch owned by Jack Wheeler. He and his lively teenage son, Steve, had manned one of the dinghies that towed the *Iola*. Also aboard Wheeler's boat were his wife, Lee, and their attractive daughter, Sharon. The other boat was the *Caroline*, a forty-four-foot motor-sailer with twin diesel engines that was on a charter out of Honolulu and skippered by Larry Briggs, who had been in the other dinghy.

"How was your trip?" someone asked.

"*Long*," Jennifer said, smiling. "Took us nineteen days from Port Allen. And we sat outside the channel here for over a week, waiting for the wind to shift so we could sail in."

"Sorry to hear that," Jack Wheeler said. "Welcome to Palmyra anyhow."

Wheeler, fiftyish, was a wiry man with long sideburns and horn-rimmed glasses that rested near the end of his nose. He volunteered to take Jennifer and Buck on a tour of the island, "seeing as how I'm kinda the unofficial mayor of this place." There was the hint of unspoken challenge in his tone.

As they began walking, Wheeler explained that they were on the biggest islet—Cooper Island.

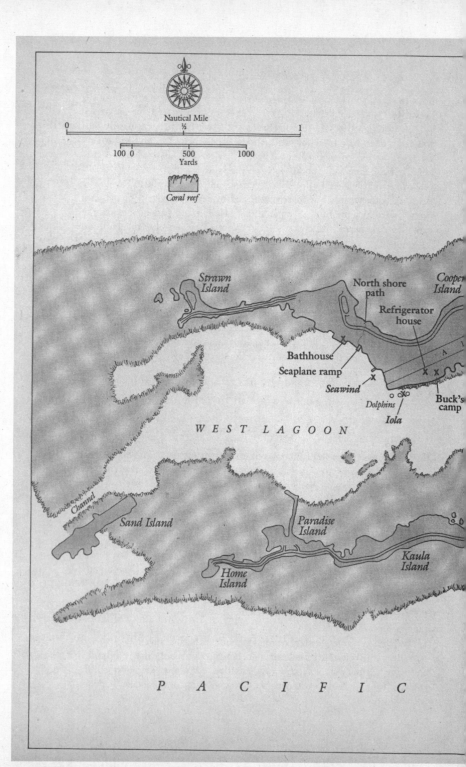

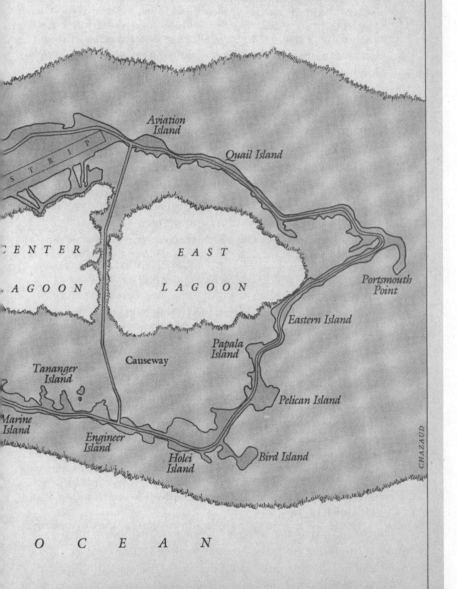

PALMYRA
ISLAND

STRIP

Aviation
Island

Quail Island

CENTER

LAGOON

EAST

LAGOON

Portsmouth
Point

Eastern Island

Papala
Island

Causeway

Tananger
Island

Pelican Island

Marine
Island

Engineer
Island

Holei
Island

Bird Island

CHAZAUD

O C E A N

"Named for an old judge, I'm told. All these islets were connected together by the Seabees during the war. The road that hooked them up is now gone in lots of places. The causeway through the lagoon is pretty broken down, too. Best thing to do if you want to get around to the other side of the lagoon is to take a dinghy right across."

Just before they entered the jungle, Wheeler pointed out a clearing adjacent to his boat. "We have a nice fireplace there for outdoor cooking. You'll have to try some of the wife's smoked fish."

Wheeler smiled knowingly. "Now, you know about the poisonous fish?"

"Poisonous?" Jennifer said, her expression tightening. She looked at Buck for his reaction, but he disguised his surprise. They had both been counting on a diet rich in fish.

"Yeah. Ciguatera is what I'm talking about. The fish carry a toxin produced by a certain kind of algae here. You also see it in Hawaii and the Caribbean. Even Florida. But there are a few varieties of fish that are edible, and tasty, too. Papio are excellent eating, and they're all over the place. Mullet are good, too, but leave the red snapper alone. They're good eating back home, but you'll get mighty sick if you eat them here. We had a cat with us on a trip here some years back. We'd feed her a piece of fish and then watch to see if she threw up. If she kept it down, we figured it was all right."

Jennifer was appalled by this apparent insensitivity. "Weren't you worried about killing the cat?"

"Naw. Cats are different. If people and dogs eat something that's poisonous, they can get real sick, even die. A cat will just puke."

As far as sea life was concerned, Jennifer told Wheeler what was uppermost in her mind: Buck's scary run-in with the shark.

Wheeler nodded sagely. "They're as thick as fleas on a hound. The lagoon's a breeding ground for blacktip sharks. They're one of the most aggressive sharks in the Pacific. Get up to six feet long. Be careful about taking a dip."

"Don't worry," Jennifer said with a shudder. She had no intention of even wading in the picturesque lagoon. Its peaceful aspect was all illusion, she thought. Part of the dream had soured.

Wheeler led them inland along a narrow trail that had obviously been painstakingly chopped through the brush. What had looked like feathery greenery from the sea was actually quite a formidable hedgerow. Soon they came upon a strip of steaming-hot, pock-marked asphalt. Jennifer was jolted to realize that the pavement was alive with squirming, squawking birds, thousands of them. Buck's dogs charged for the grounded birds as Jennifer scooped a fright-ened Puffer into her arms.

There was a great explosion of shrieks and flapping as the black-and-white terns rose in protest, hovering in squadrons ten or twelve feet in the air. Jennifer could now see why the birds refused to leave. The asphalt below them was covered with nests of help-less baby chicks.

"Buck!" Jennifer hollered.

Before Buck could react, Popolo, the pit bull, gripped a full-size tern in his jaws. Buck cuffed the dog on his head, and it dropped the bird. The bird flapped once or twice, then lay still. It had been bitten nearly in two.

"Oh, Popolo," Jennifer said scoldingly. "Look what you've done." Puffer's whining seemed to echo her distress.

"Your dog that hungry?" Wheeler asked, not kindly.

"Nope," Buck said, with eyes narrowed. "Just that ornery."

Buck put his dogs on a length of rope he'd brought along and tied them to a coconut tree.

The tour resumed. "This is an old military airstrip," Wheeler explained. "It was built back in the early forties. The damn thing's a mile long, though you can't tell now because of all the vegeta-tion taking over. Those birds nest all the way down it."

The three of them worked their way across the crowded run-way, all—but especially Jennifer—walking gingerly to keep from stepping on eggs and chicks. Occasionally, an angry parent would dive-bomb the trio, brushing their heads at top speed.

"We've eaten some of the eggs," Wheeler said, his voice nearly drowned out by the whoosh-whooshing of the frantic birds. "Kinda fishy-tasting, but not bad. To make sure they're fresh, what you do is mark off a twenty-by-twenty-foot area here on the run-way, clear it of eggs, and come back the next day. Any eggs inside the marked area are fresh ones."

When they reached the other side of the runway, the racket calmed down. Wheeler led the way along another jungle footpath.

It was like walking in a huge greenhouse. The humidity and heat had become stifling. Jennifer was breathing with difficulty from the excitement and exertion. Buck dripped with sweat.

"Is it always this hot?" he asked.

"Never varies more than a few degrees, day or night." Wheeler smiled dryly. "Even the rain is warm." He enjoyed having the edge on these newcomers. It was the kind of authoritarian attitude Buck and Jennifer had hoped to leave behind.

There were only a few feet of visibility through the vegetation in any direction. The occasional chatter of brightly colored birds darting from tree to tree in the green canopy above was the only evidence of life, but Jennifer sensed that scores of unseen creatures were lurking out of sight, watching silently.

They came to a wide clearing that had recently been cut out of the underbrush. An old warehouse stood at the edge of the forest. Inside they found a dilapidated road grader, a ten-wheeler military truck, and an old boat with the letters "U.S.A.F." on both sides of its hull. All showed the effects of more than three decades of neglect in a tropical climate, as well as vandalism.

"In the eleven years since we were last here, there's been a lot of wanton destruction," Wheeler said. "Look at all the slashed tires. And bullet holes."

Jennifer was troubled by the jagged holes in the metal. Who would get their kicks shooting up an old truck? Whoever these trigger-happy cowboys were, she didn't want them coming back while she and Buck were living here.

"You'd think sailing people would be a better sort," Wheeler reflected.

He went over to the rescue launch. "They call this a drop boat because the Air Force would drop it into the water from a plane. It was equipped to take care of survivors who had to wait for a rescue. You know, fresh water, canned foods, first-aid gear, life jackets, that kind of thing. It was still running when I was here years ago and we used to play around with it in the lagoon. One time I used it for a real rescue. A Japanese trawler was tooting its whistle like crazy just outside the channel. I took the rescue boat out. One of the fishermen had been impaled by a swordfish."

"What happened to him?" Jennifer asked in horror.

"Poor fella didn't make it." He turned away.

Jennifer's uneasy feeling about Palmyra was growing stronger. The lagoon was postcard-quality but full of sharks. Catching fish was apparently a snap, but some of them were poisonous. Though the island, from a distance, suggested the fertile South Seas paradise created by the genius of Gauguin, the empty, crumbling structures and rusting hardware left by the military from a time gone by gave a ghostly feel to the place.

"This is my third trip," Wheeler said. "First time was back in '57."

They had stopped under the shade of a tree for relief from the broiling sun. Jennifer tried to fan herself with a palm frond, but the splintery leaves couldn't capture and push much air. Buck was too uncomfortable to interact much with the others. Wheeler, utterly at home on Palmyra, seemed oblivious to the sultry, unyielding heat, although his tan cotton shirt, drenched with perspiration, stuck to his back like the wrapper of a melting Hershey bar.

"I had a job with Scripps, the oceanography institute, during the international geophysical year," Wheeler chattered on. "The wife and I spent fifteen months here. I was taking upper-air weather observations, monitoring the tide, stuff like that. We like it here. It kinda grows on you. There's lots of exploring to do. The wife and I and the kids found an underground bunker once. Enough goodies to open a war surplus store."

"You sure know your way around," Buck said, wiping sweat from his eyes. Jennifer sensed he might be trying to set the older man up. But for what?

"Yeah." Wheeler grinned widely. "Like I told you, I call myself the unofficial mayor of Palmyra. We know the Fullard-Leos, the owners. Say, how long you guys staying?"

"Awhile," Buck said cautiously. He looked exhausted, but he was on full alert.

"Well—what did you say your name was?"

"Roy Allen. And my wife is Jennifer."

"We were thinking of planting a garden," Jennifer interjected. "Maybe live off the land for awhile."

Wheeler thought about that for a moment. "If you folks are planning to stay, you should write the owners for permission, seeing as how it's private land and all. I'm here as their representative this trip. They want me to get the airstrip in shape so planes can land. I don't know, though. All those birds are a real problem, if you ask me. But my son and I are doing what we can to clear the strip."

"I'll give you a hand," Buck said. He had decided how to play the hand fate had dealt them. Who knew? If he ingratiated himself with this officious "old bore," as he would later refer to Wheeler, a situation might arise where he could use Wheeler's help.

Wheeler seemed to consider Buck's hefty shoulders and taut muscular arms. "A couple more strong arms would be good," he agreed. "We start around dawn and knock off before the hottest part of the day."

"Sounds like a good plan," Buck said.

Rested, they resumed the tour, but Wheeler soon stopped under a palm tree and rummaged around for something. "Here's another good thing to know," he intoned, still coming on strong. "See this here coconut? It's the beginning of a new tree. Sends out a little sprout on the top when it's ready to start growing." He pointed out the burgeoning root. "At the same time, the insides of it change." He slipped his machete from its sheath on his belt and hacked open the coconut's husk by making parallel gashes, then stripped off the sections between. Then he cracked the inner nut with one blow, revealing a white pudding-like substance. "The milk on the inside turns solid. It's called spoonmeat. It's supposed to be the new tree's food." He cut the spongy stuff in two and gave the halves to Jennifer and Buck. "Go ahead," he urged. "Try it." The offer sounded more like a challenge than a gift.

Jennifer compliantly bit into her piece and was rewarded with a pleasantly cool sweetness. "Oh, yes. That's delicious," she said, inwardly laughing at the charge this old-timer beachcomber so obviously got from disclosing the lore of life on a tropical island.

Buck just grunted.

Wheeler beamed. "And it can be fried or baked. Comes out

tasting somewhere in between squash and yams. I'm going to leave the rest of the coconut here. We'll come back in a few minutes and check on it." He made this announcement with an odd expression.

Once again, they moved on and Wheeler continued to lecture enthusiastically. He demonstrated how to cut out the heart of a palm tree by slicing the trunk in two right below the lowest fronds. He praised it as great for salad, as if this were not generally known.

"The owners don't like us to cut mature trees down," he explained. "So we look for the small ones coming up that are two or three feet high. I wouldn't even call them trees yet. It's okay to thin them out. Most of them wouldn't grow up anyway because they're so close together.

"Now, if you want to do some exploring by yourselves later on, there's a barracks out yonder," he said, stopping to point to a section of jungle indistinguishable from the rest. "Still has odds and ends of furniture and stuff. And there's a path through the trees that takes you out on the island's north shore, where you'll find more old buildings, concrete ammo dumps, gun-battery housings, and machinery all over the place left by the Navy. There's a few drums of old gas, too. It works fine. You can help yourselves."

That got Buck's attention. "We can use it for a little generator we've got," he said.

"Hey, if you've got a portable generator, you'll want to know about the ice cream parlor. It's back this way." Wheeler once again forged ahead, explaining en route exactly how they could make "ice cream" from coconuts.

Soon they spied a flat-roofed concrete bunker nestled in the undergrowth. Next to one outside wall sat an outmoded refrigerator with an extension cord snaking inside the building through a barred window. Inside the small freezer section of the refrigerator was a container of coconut ice cream. "The wife just made it this morning," Wheeler explained. "Have a taste."

Jennifer dipped a finger into the frosty, rich mixture and licked it clean. It sure wasn't Baskin Robbins, but it was good.

Buck declined. He was tiring of this road show.

"Not sure what the Navy used this building for," Wheeler spouted on, "but I keep my generator inside. Feel free to use the fridge. Cools your beer, keeps your ice cream and fish, even makes ice cubes. Guess you'll inherit the fridge when we leave. You can hook up your own generator to it and be in business. Now," he paused dramatically, "let me show you the bathtub."

"*Bathtub?*" Jennifer practically screeched.

"A freshwater bath at that," Wheeler said triumphantly. "The military left behind a big tank that collects rainwater. The water is no good for drinking 'cause of all the algae that's growing inside the tank. But it sure feels good."

"A real bath sounds like heaven," she said.

On their way to the bathtub, they passed by the tree under which Wheeler had left the coconut shell, and Jennifer was flabbergasted. In the short period of time they'd been gone, the shell had filled completely with small crabs fighting with comic ferocity over the remnants of the coconut meat.

"Hermit crabs," Wheeler explained. "They're the garbagemen of the island. Them and the rats, they clean up everything."

"I haven't seen any rats," Jennifer said, hoping against hope. Her love of small animals didn't extend to rodents.

"You leave food out, you'll see 'em," Wheeler promised. "Big ole wharf rats. Compliments of the U.S. Navy."

The image made Jennifer's skin crawl, and she began to watch more carefully where she stepped.

Arriving back at the lagoon, they encountered an old wharf and a barnlike warehouse. At the front was a dock where wartime supply ships had unloaded cargo. Behind the warehouse, there was a twelve-thousand-gallon water tank. "It doesn't have a top on it anymore," Wheeler noted. "With all the rain showers we get around here, we don't have to worry about it getting empty."

Someone had set up an old four-legged porcelain bathtub with a hose running off a tap from the tank.

"Guess you guys will want to be getting your towels," Wheeler said, grinning like a schoolboy.

"I can hardly wait," Jennifer said. She had to give him credit. He had saved the best for last.

But when she and Buck skipped off to the *Iola*, their plan for an immediate bath was postponed by another offer. A crewman on the *Caroline* hollered an invitation for a drink. On board, they downed rum mixed with coconut milk, accepted (and smoked) a joint from one of the younger crewmen, and swapped sea stories with their hosts. Briggs and his crew were shepherding a group of amateur radio operators who, like obsessed Boy Scouts, spent their every waking hour ashore tinkering with their transmitters and receivers. The next destination was nearby Kingman Reef, which occasionally bared a strip of sand a foot or two out of the water. "The radio boys want to set a record for establishing the most remote radio station in the world," the charter skipper explained, rolling his eyes skyward to show what he thought of the idea.

An hour or so later, Jennifer gathered their soap and towels, and taking Buck's hand, headed for the bathtub. They were merrily tipsy, and the cool bathwater added to their delight. Between deep soulful kisses, they splashed each other like kids running under a sprinkler on a summer day, and returned to the boat feeling tinglingly clean, refreshed, and optimistic.

Back aboard the *Iola*, Buck fiddled with the outboard motor while Jennifer began cooking a hunk of fish Jack Wheeler had brought over for them. They had it for dinner that night. The fresh fish was tender and delicious. After a poignantly lovely sunset, they wordlessly went below and made love by candlelight. Their floating cocoon rocked gently to their shared rhythm.

Later, Buck read aloud to Jennifer from a book she had brought along, Euell Gibbons's account of purposeful beachcombing. He sensibly chose the chapter covering all the useful products derived from coconuts. Delectable possibilities seemed endless, but ice cream still topped Jennifer's list.

They slept well that night. Jennifer no longer had to jump up every hour or so to monitor their course. Tied up to the dolphin in the placid lagoon, she felt they were safe at last.

The next morning, without prodding, Buck left early to help Jack Wheeler. When he returned several hours later, he was flushed and sweaty, and trudged off to take a bath. When he came back, Jennifer was taking some biscuits out of the oven.

"How'd the work go?" she asked, really wondering how he had gotten along with Mr. Wheeler.

"Okay, but I think nature is gonna win the battle."

"Even if they fix it up, how can a plane land with all the birds on the runway?"

Buck shrugged indifferently. "Jack was talking this morning about having to poison them."

"*Poison* them?" she said. The idea was unthinkable.

"Wheeler told me he has enough poison in one of the sheds to kill an army. He said they'd have to burn the nests and crush the eggs, too."

Buck's voice was so steady that Jennifer couldn't tell whether he was opposed to the idea or not.

"Kill all those birds so a damn plane can land?" she said angrily. "For what? Probably so they can put in a golf course and fancy restaurant and hotel."

"Yeah, it stinks."

"They've already killed and wrecked enough things in this world in order to make money."

"Fucking-A right!" Buck chortled. He seemed to be enjoying Jennifer's display of righteous indignation.

"We can stage a sit-in on the runway so they can't land."

"In all that bird poop?" he said, cracking a smile.

"It's not funny," she said. "Don't laugh." Then she laughed.

"Who's laughing?" Buck said, laughing.

He kissed her. "You're beautiful when you're mad," he whispered as he took her in his arms.

June 29. Buck went to help Jack Wheeler and son in clearing runway. We're hoping to improve PR with the Wheelers and maybe get them to recommend to the owner that we stay on officially as caretakers—so I'll bake an extra loaf of bread for them. Made some grated coconut ice milk sherbert and froze it in ice box. What a luxury.

Buck and Jennifer's effort to ingratiate themselves with Jack Wheeler took a nose dive the next day when Popolo bit his son. At Jennifer's suggestion, Buck had tied up his dogs, because

Wheeler obviously didn't approve of their running loose. Unfortunately, young Wheeler had run past Popolo within the reach of his chain, and the dog had nipped him on the thigh. Though the youth's skin was broken, rabies was no threat, since no Pacific island (including Hawaii) has ever recorded a case. Even so, the Wheelers were upset.

On June 30, a couple hours after sunset, the *Caroline*, with her complement of ham radio operators, departed Palmyra, reducing the island's population to seven. By then, the fallout from the dog incident had dissipated. Buck was back helping Wheeler and his son clear the runway.

The following morning, Jennifer and Buck resumed their exploration of Palmyra, taking the dinghy directly across the lagoon from Cooper to Home Island. When they neared shore, they got caught up on a sandbar in about two feet of water.

Buck gave Jennifer the oars and got out. He pushed several times until the dinghy came free.

Jennifer saw the fast-moving shadows in the clear water before he did. She screamed.

In an instant, three sharks, flashing swiftly and silently through the water like menacing torpedoes, had converged on Buck from different directions.

Now aware of the danger, Buck yelped and jumped into the dinghy so hard Jennifer thought his feet might go through its wooden bottom. The small boat rocked precariously. Worried about being spilled out into the water, a distracted Jennifer lost her grip on one of the oars and it floated out of reach.

All three sharks were now circling the dinghy, as if desperately trying to pick up a lost scent. Her heart was thudding in her ears.

"Get us out of here, Buck! Now!"

With the single oar, he rowed them crookedly to shore.

Long after the sharks disappeared, Jennifer couldn't shake the incident. She had thought that sharks wouldn't attack unless they saw or smelled blood. Wrong. No sooner had Buck stepped into the water than these aggressive creatures had homed in on him. And the way they had circled the dinghy afterward . . . With a chill,

Jennifer thought it was as if they knew dinner was inside the boat. She resolved to never step foot in the lagoon, so picturesque, but teeming with danger.

The next afternoon, Jennifer spotted from the deck of the *Iola* a two-masted sailboat anchored just outside the channel. "Looks like we're due for a population explosion tomorrow," she cracked to Buck.

Actually, two boats glided into the lagoon the following day, July 2. First in was the double-masted boat she'd seen; its name, *Sea Wind*, now legible on the stern.

Buck rowed out to greet the new arrivals, sizing up their boat along the way. He recognized her as a ketch with unusually graceful lines. A middle-aged couple were bringing her in, the man concentrating at the bow but directing a blond woman at the helm.

As they drew near, Buck shouted, "There's an extra space over by us. Can I help you get in?" He was suddenly all smiles and hospitality, as if he'd usurped the mayoralty of Palmyra.

"Thanks just the same," the man yelled back. "We're looking for more privacy." He and the woman kept up their work.

Miffed, Buck rowed back to shore, where Jennifer and Wheeler were watching.

"Looks like he knows what he's doing," Wheeler said levelly, spitting out a twig he'd been chewing. "Boy, what a beauty of a boat. He'll probably put in at the little cove up the way. It's deep enough. Only problem is, without the dolphins to tie on to, it will take a lot of securing so they don't drag anchor and end up beached when the wind comes up."

An hour later, the island's newest visitors came traipsing down a jungle path toward the *Iola*. They all amiably introduced themselves. Jennifer thought Mac Graham looked the part of a storybook adventurer, with his military-style haircut, dark aviator glasses, knife-edge khaki shorts, and bare brown chest. He dismissed their sail from Hawaii—only *seven* days—as if it had been child's play.

"How many people are here?" he asked unhappily.

"Too many," Buck said, agreeing with the implication. "Hell of a note. We came here to play Adam and Eve on a deserted island."

Mac laughed. "We had the same idea." He took a pack of Marl-boros from his waistband and couldn't help but notice that Buck stared with the pale intensity of a helpless addict. "Like a smoke?" Mac asked obligingly, offering the open pack.

"Sure," Buck eagerly replied. He snatched out two cigarettes at once.

Jennifer smiled knowingly. There went Buck's typically ineffective plan to give up smoking when his tobacco ran out. One day en route to Palmyra he had even broken open a Lipton tea bag and rolled an ersatz cigarette. Since they'd reached Palmyra, he'd been desperate for a fellow smoker with a supply to share.

In this first sociable encounter, Mac did most of the talking. He acted so open and friendly that Jennifer had liked him immediately. It was apparent how thrilled he was to see his goal, Palmyra. His vibrant smile, expressive eyes, and quick sense of humor contrasted sharply with Jennifer's first impression of his wife, who seemed reticent, shy, perhaps even standoffish. Clearly, the woman stood in her husband's shadow.

Only a couple of hours later, the *Journeyer*, a sleek forty-five-foot cutter owned and sailed by Bernard and Evelyn Leonard, moored next to the *Iola*.

"Four boats," Wheeler grumbled to Jennifer. "Most I've ever seen here at one time. This must be the most popular vacation spot of the year."

Unspoken was the resentment practically everyone felt toward everyone else. Certainly, Wheeler, Buck, and Mac each believed, at some irrational level, that the others were intruding upon *his* territory. There was gridlock in Paradise.

CHAPTER 8

AS WHEELER HAD GUESSED, Mac and Muff had slipped the *Sea Wind* into the small cove, where the curvature of the shore afforded them the privacy they coveted. Mac tied the boat stern-first to two trees near the water, then dropped an anchor well off the bow. That would have been enough to satisfy most skippers, but Mac was extra careful with his beloved boat. He ran another line off the port bow and sank a second anchor in the shallow reef there. Eventually a squall, not an uncommon occurrence in the equatorial regions of the Pacific, would probably blow across the lagoon, and he wanted rock-steady protection against going aground.

Muff and Mac wrote their first letters from Palmyra two days later and gave them to Jack Wheeler to mail in Hawaii, where he and his family headed on the morning of July 6. These were the first of many letters that would keep relatives and friends back home eagerly awaiting the next entertaining installment of life on an enviably tropical and serene, if not deserted, Pacific island.

July 4, 1974

Dear Mother,

It is now just past midnight and at eight o'clock I was still working on the mooring and anchor lines. The temperature is 88 degrees, relative humidity 90 percent. There's a light breeze.

The island is beautiful beyond my wildest hope. Everything is exciting and I'm anxious to be off exploring. I hope to find some peace and quiet—where a man can sit at leisure.

Palmyra is everything I ever hoped for—and more.

Love,

Mac

Muff's first letter home—to her mother and two sisters in San Diego—expressed a different view.

July 4, 1974

Dear Mother, Peg and Dot,

Mac had to practically push me out of Hilo harbor. I didn't want to leave. We had a good sail down until we arrived off Palmyra. When we were ten miles away, a huge storm hit. It was like one of those Hollywood studio gales, where someone turns the fan on, only it was for real and I was terrified. We waited it out until the next morning.

There are a lot of poisonous fish here, red snapper for one, sharks and manta rays in the lagoon. It's incredible the amount of birds nesting here, mostly on an old runway. They cover it entirely. It is never quiet for a minute, not even at night. You'd think you were in Disneyland on the jungle safari ride.

A couple on a boat here had lived on Palmyra for a while about 15 years ago. Then, things and buildings and equipment on the island were still intact. Now it is falling down and what hasn't fallen down, vandals have torn down and destroyed. There are beds, mattresses, a fire engine, trucks, jeeps, all left over from the military. But everything is stripped like at a junkyard. It's sickening.

The other local inhabitants are land crabs, coconut crabs, hermit crabs, rats, tiny lizards, spiders, ants, roaches that fly and some that don't, mosquitoes, flies, and you-name-it. If it's creepy and crawly, it's here. This place is really a jungle.

Mac is thrilled to be here at last. But I already miss all of you and our friends.

Love,
Muff

Nonetheless, Muff dutifully joined Mac in setting up housekeeping in earnest. As she reorganized the galley for life in port, he hooked up the boat's power source to their large generator and serviced the *Sea Wind*'s engine. To make more living space on the *Sea Wind*, they removed the sails and carefully folded them. Mac lugged them to a nearby storage shed and, using a block and tackle, suspended them from a rafter, well out of the reach of rodents.

He hacked away the brush near the boat, then set to work building a makeshift dock with lumber scavenged on the island. That completed, he ran a rope from the dock to the boat ladder at the *Sea Wind*'s stern. They could now pull either one of their two dinghies back and forth to shore without always having to bother with a motor or oars.

Aboard the *Sea Wind*, Muff tied canvas awnings from the shrouds to cover the deck area and provide shade from the blazing sun.

One morning that first week, Mac declared that they needed a break. He persuaded her, despite her uneasiness about the jungle and its creeping things, to do some exploring with him before the day got too hot.

As they worked their way down a well-worn winding path, Muff realized how serious Mac was about exploring the island. "Most people stay on the trails," he said, taking out his machete. "But not me." He began hacking at what looked like an impassable wall of vines, shoots, and fronds.

Muff watched passively for a few minutes, then wandered alone up the path. She came across an enclave of old buildings that had been all but swallowed up by the jungle. Peeking into the crumbling shells of the structures, she had the strong feeling that strange, tragic things had happened on and around this island. Was it just her imagination?

Walking on, she was soon surrounded by a panoply of violent-hued flowers. She recognized wild morning glory, thick with deep-purple and carnelian red blossoms. Poinsettia, growing in abundance and tall as trees, were in full bloom, the showy scarlet bracts setting off the tiny yellow flowers. From behind the veil of forest echoed the calls of unseen, unfamiliar birds. Small sudden movements teased the periphery of her vision.

It wasn't long before Muff became aware that she could no longer hear Mac at work behind her. She quickly headed back, but when she came to a sharp curve in the trail she didn't recognize, she realized she had taken a wrong turn somewhere. She wheeled around.

"Mac. Where are you?"

There was no answer.

"Mac!" Her loudest shout sounded weak, ineffectual, all but absorbed by the unrelenting jungle.

She felt everything closing in on her. But she held on to the knowledge that the lagoon and the *Sea Wind* were just on the other side of a wall of vegetation in front of her. Or were they? Was the lagoon actually in the other direction? Now, the trails and the palm trees, *everything*, all looked alike to her. Where could Mac be? The jungle had devoured him without a trace.

Suddenly, she heard a commotion nearby. Midway up the ninety-foot-high trees she caught a glimpse of several blue-footed boobies clumsily trying to take flight.

Common in the Pacific, the appealing gull-like boobies have a white chest, gray wings, and a pretty dappling of blues and oranges around their eyes. These nesting birds, disturbed by Muff, had panicked.

As she watched, they flew directly into a leafy barrier. She couldn't imagine they could get through, and they didn't. But they continued to beat themselves against the thick foliage, squawking in fear. *My God, they're going to beat themselves to death*, she thought, realizing with shock that she was the aggressor here.

Muff hurried down the trail, hoping the birds would calm down when she was gone, and give up their suicidal escape attempt.

Suddenly, there was scurrying at her feet. She looked down to find a fat brown rat staring up at her, its tiny nose quivering in the air as if trying to place her scent.

She screamed, and jumped back. The rat held its ground without flinching, still regarding her with beady eyes. Then it went back to chewing on part of a coconut shell.

She heard chopping off in the distance.

"Mac!" she yelled desperately.

"Over here," came his unconcerned reply.

She finally found him, standing on a fresh trail he had fashioned.

Dripping with sweat, he was grinning widely at his accomplishment.

"I got scared, I couldn't find you." She sounded accusing, but Mac didn't bite.

He wiped his sweaty brow with a wet forearm. "Honey, you can't get lost on a two-hundred-acre island."

"*I* can."

"Then stay closer."

"I almost stepped on a big rat." Muff felt she deserved more sympathy.

"Well, they won't hurt you. They're not sewer rats like you find in the city. They're coconut rats. You know, honey, vegetarians. I think they're kinda cute."

At the end of Mac's trail was a concrete bunker that had been concealed in dense foliage. It was obvious that no one had been inside for decades. Mac was amazed and delighted to find forty untouched drums of aviation gas stored there, a trove for the outboard motor on their Zodiac dinghy.

"These things are heavy," Muff remarked, rather than praising his find. "How are you going to get them back to the boat?"

Mac pushed over a drum and nudged it with his foot. "I can do it." He didn't have an easy time rolling the drum all the way down the narrow trail back to the lagoon, but he managed, as Muff followed.

After a brief rest, Mac said he was going back for another drum, but Muff decided to wait for him. Just then he spied a foot-wide land crab lumbering along the beach. They loved crab. He threw a palm frond on the crab and trapped it beneath his foot.

Muff looked away, squeamish because she knew what came next.

With no hesitation, Mac reached down and snapped off the big meaty claw. He lifted his foot and let the amputee continue on its way.

Muff understood that snapping off the large claw would not kill a crab, which would eventually regenerate another. But she still felt it was a form of maiming, and probably painful. She'd never been able to do it herself.

Mac gave her the claw and headed back to his private fuel depot.

To keep the succulent meat fresh, Muff left the claw inside a large shell lying at the edge of the lagoon. She knelt down nearby, leaned over, and soaked her hair. Feeling refreshed, she sat back against a tree trunk and shut her eyes. Now that she was in sight of the *Sea Wind*, she felt she could relax.

Soon, a light splashing sound got her attention, and she opened her eyes to see a big moray eel trying to steal the crab leg. The eel's head had broken the surface of the water as it flailed at the shell. Its small yellow eyes and the row of sharp tiny teeth in its gaping mouth aimed for the tasty meat. Muff gasped in horror and leaped up, just as Mac reappeared.

"Look!" she screamed. "I put the crab leg—"

She watched dumbfounded as Mac calmly unsheathed his machete, walked over to the struggling eel, and with one firm swing decapitated it.

"Ready for dinner?" Mac casually asked, holding up the prized claw.

THE NEXT day, Mac set out on another mission, having drafted Muff again as a reluctant companion. *Wheeler asked for it*, Mac had convinced himself. Frequently, the *mayor* had talked about all the "good stuff" he'd found here, and bragged that he had hidden it so well "over by the East Lagoon" that no one would ever find it. This was just the sort of challenge Mac found irresistible. If Wheeler had really wanted to keep the stuff, Mac reasoned, he should have been cagey enough to take it with him. "Finders keepers," he told Muff. And to the victors in life go life's spoils.

There were two natural lagoons at Palmyra. During the war, the Navy had divided the eastern one with a cement causeway, creating Center Lagoon and East Lagoon. The *Sea Wind* lay at anchor in West Lagoon, as did the other boats tied up at the dolphins. East Lagoon was on the far side of the causeway, which, at the extremes of tide, lay as deep as two feet underwater. They motored eastward across Center Lagoon in their Zodiac, got out in two or three feet of water, and lifted the dinghy over the causeway. At the far side of East Lagoon, they landed on Papala Island, a slender islet about one hundred yards long.

Of the sixteen islets that form the broken horseshoe shape of Palmyra, Cooper, where the boats were moored and the old runway was located, is by far the largest. In addition to Papala and Cooper, the other islets are Strawn, Aviation, Quail, Eastern, Pelican, Bird, Holei, Engineer, Tananger, Marine, Kaula, Paradise, Home, and Sand. With the exception of Sand, which was adjacent to the channel entrance, all had been joined by the road built by the industrious Seabees. They had also built a narrow cement causeway through the lagoon to allow quicker access (by foot) between the islets on opposite sides of the lagoon. Seven of the islets lined East Lagoon; in places, some were not much wider than the road.

Mac and Muff carried the Zodiac up the beach and found a safe place to leave it.

From Papala, it was a short walk to the atoll's leeward side. They found an ocean beach of coarse sand and simmering, unmoving air. The absence of any breeze made the heat and humidity seem even more stifling. Feeling an asthmatic tightness in her chest, Muff could breathe only with difficulty. In no time, she and Mac both were basting in their own sweat.

After a quick and cursory search, Mac decided Wheeler's treasure was nowhere around there.

Back on Papala's lagoon side with its light breeze, Muff found a shady place to catch her breath while Mac walked south to the next islet, Pelican. The connecting road, broken up and submerged occasionally, was just barely passable.

Pelican was more densely overgrown. Rising to the challenge, Mac hacked away with his machete and soon uncovered an empty bunker and a concrete gun emplacement. It looked like a defensive position constructed in anticipation of an invasion. The find gave him renewed energy, and he turned to assault another wall of shrubbery, hacking and slashing, finding his rhythm. Two swipes with the whistling blade, then a small step forward. Hack, hack, step. Hack, hack, step. Wheeler's taunt drove him on. "You'll never find it." *Ha, ha. Never.*

Half an hour later, ankle-deep in fetid swampy waters, a drained Mac stopped and wearily looked around. Another bunker lay shrouded in vegetation. Was this it? More hacking . . . and then he cleared the open doorway, took one look inside, and grinned like a Cheshire cat.

He felt certain he'd found the hidden treasure, though it certainly didn't live up to Jack's constant bragging. In fact, the only things Mac took back with him that day were a ball of copper wire, a decrepit but intriguing oak water keg, and a clear glass Japanese fishing ball for Muff. But Mac Graham the adventurer had found what he was searching for, and there was satisfaction enough in that.

Palmyra was a puzzle, a welcome challenge, and he was equal to it. A man was free here to do . . . just about anything. The possibilities of the place seemed to unfold endlessly.

CHAPTER 9

JENNIFER CLIMBED INTO THE *Iola's* dinghy, rowed the fifty feet or so to the *Journeyer*, and shouted hello.

Bernard Leonard peered down haughtily at her from the deck of his sailboat. He was a reed-thin fellow fond of wearing white Bermudas and long socks rolled down to mid-calf below two of the knobbiest knees in the Pacific. Buck always imagined a little plastic propeller spinning from the top of a peculiar beanie Leonard wore on his high-domed head. Leonard told Jennifer he was a high school math teacher on summer vacation. From their few conversations, she'd decided that he was one of those people who greatly enjoy the sound of their own voice. She could picture him droning on self-centeredly to a roomful of captive, drowsy teenagers. His wife, Evelyn, was sometimes friendly, then suddenly distant. She and Jennifer had rendezvoused ashore a few times so that their lap-sized dogs could play together. Puffer was crazy about the Leonards' pooch, Windy.

"More coconut butter," Jennifer announced, grasping the *Journeyer*'s ladder to keep the dinghy from bumping the side.

"We so much enjoyed your last batch," said Bernard Leonard courteously. "Did you by chance remember to bring Euell Gibbons?"

"Yep. Got it right here." Evelyn had asked to borrow the book so she could read up on preparing some coconut dishes.

Leonard reached down to get the book and jar of butter from Jennifer. "I've some books for you," he said. "I'll bring them by tomorrow."

Jennifer was reading more than she ever had in her life. At least a book a week, sometimes two. It was terrific to have this influx of new titles. All yachties looked forward to trading books with other boats.

She pushed off and went back to the *Iola* for Buck, who had wanted to avoid Bernard Leonard. "Lord Leonard has a petty mind and an overbearing sense of his own importance," Buck had complained.

Jennifer thought Buck was being too harshly critical. "He's one of our *few* neighbors," she pointed out. "We should make an effort to get along."

Besides, the couple on the *Journeyer* were among the few people they might barter with for food, an increasingly important consideration to Jennifer, who watched nervously as the food supply on the *Iola* continued to dwindle. This was made all the more critical because Buck was turning out to be not much of a fisherman, routinely returning to the *Iola* empty-handed.

Buck took over the rowing for the longer trip to the *Sea Wind*, about two hundred yards up the western shore of Cooper Island. As usual, he was shirtless. His uniform of the day consisted of a pair of shorts and flip-flop sandals.

Jennifer made a mental note to try to remember to call him Roy in front of the Grahams. A week earlier, Buck had blown a fuse when he read her entries in the log. "I've told you, I don't want 'Buck' in writing. Use 'Roy'!" "Why don't you tell people that Buck is your nickname," she said. "You're not exactly hiding the tattoo." But Buck would have none of it. In an effort to keep the peace, Jennifer started referring to him as B in her entries, but he didn't like that any better. Her final compromise was to call him R in the log. When she imagined she was writing a B without closing the bottom loop, it seemed less contrived. She couldn't understand Buck's sensitivity about his name. No one was looking for him on Palmyra.

She had not yet seen the Grahams' boat close up. Anchored alone in the protected cove, the *Sea Wind* looked like a blue blood, sleek and proud. The sturdy dock and landing Mac had built seemingly overnight were entirely fitting, Jennifer thought. This boat merited that kind of respect.

Jennifer could see Mac on deck. She waved at him. "Coconut butter," she said, holding up a container.

He waved back cheerfully. "I've got a couple papio for you."

"Great."

It wasn't the first time Mac had shared a catch with Jennifer and Buck. He had a much better track record catching fish than Buck did, because the motor on his Zodiac made it possible to troll in the lagoon. The darting movements of the lure in the water quickly attracted fish. A hearty meal from out of the lagoon waters was the best gift anyone could give them these days, and Jennifer was grateful.

"Come aboard," Mac offered, as Buck aimed the dinghy with powerful and precise strokes.

The Grahams had been at Palmyra more than a week now. The two couples had run into each other ashore a few times and chatted amiably each time. Mac had done them a big favor a few days earlier by coming over in his Zodiac to help turn the *Iola* around to better protect her stern from the wind that occasionally whipped across the lagoon. Jennifer and Buck spent most of their on-deck time in the stern's cockpit.

But Jennifer knew that the Grahams and the Leonards had been socializing even more frequently, getting together regularly for dinner, becoming real buddy-buddy. That made sense. It wasn't just because of the age difference between the Grahams and Buck and her (Mac and Muff were forty-three and forty-one, Buck and Jennifer thirty-six and twenty-eight); the Leonards, closer to the same age as Mac and Muff, undoubtedly held many ideas and values in common with them, including some that Jennifer and Buck had in recent years rejected. Too, she figured that the older couples considered her and Buck the have-nots of Palmyra, as well as not up to the mark in social refinement.

Although sunset was approaching and Jennifer and Buck had planned to bathe before dark, they did not turn down Mac's invitation. For one thing, they'd heard tantalizing descriptions of the *Sea Wind* from others who'd been aboard her, and were frankly curious. Once on deck, Jennifer was dazzled by the boat, understanding that no superlatives could adequately describe its showcase quality.

Mac ushered them below. Entering the *Sea Wind*'s snug, wood-paneled cabin was like walking into a warm embrace. Muff greeted them shyly and poured chilled white wine into long-stemmed globlets, which she set on a table inlaid with foreign coins and lacquered to a smooth and mirror-bright finish. When Jennifer admired this galley table, Muff explained that they had collected the coins in many ports of call on their world cruise some years earlier.

Jennifer was astonished by the plush carpeting and rich furnishings. Most sailboats are fitted out in utilitarian fashion, but the interior of the *Sea Wind* was elegant, and the decorative appointments around the cabin, which included many objects of tribal art from their travels, added an air of worldly sophistication.

Jennifer noticed right away that every household object was resting in its assigned place. Each pot or pan had its own enclosure in the galley. The chess set was on a special made-to-fit shelf, as was the two-way radio. Small, caring touches by a couple who took pride in their home on the water were evident everywhere.

When an official tour was suggested, it was clear Mac had ushered admiring visitors around countless times before and that doing it again was no chore. They started out in the bow, where Mac showed off his workshop.

Buck was obviously impressed with the collection of tools, which included a metalworking lathe for making screws and other metal parts. Mac even had an acetylene torch, which he used for making new fittings and repairing riggings.

From bow to stern, the tour took twenty minutes, ending with a technical inspection of the *Sea Wind*'s auxiliary engine, a powerful inboard that riveted Buck's attention but meant little to Jennifer. Along the way, Mac had pointed out all the detailed work he'd done himself in the past few years, especially the woodwork he had fashioned by hand.

"Everything is so beautiful," Jennifer sighed when they had returned to the living quarters. "And comfy."

"We rough it some by living aboard a boat," Mac said, "but there's no reason for our life to be *too* rough."

Jennifer admired the refrigerator and its small freezer compartment. "Don't the lights and refrigerator drain your batteries?" she asked.

Mac explained that when the *Sea Wind* was in a port like San Diego they ran everything—including electrical lighting and the "freezer"—off shore power. "We just *plug* in," he said breezily. At sea, or in a remote location like Palmyra, they ran their utilities off four heavy-duty marine batteries—recharged every couple of days by their top-of-the-line gas-powered generator. Sometimes, during long periods at sea, they conserved battery power by using kerosene lamps for light.

Jennifer and Buck relaxed on a settee while Mac and Muff sat across from them in matching overstuffed chairs. This was almost like a sudden trip home, far from the daily inconvenience of Palmyra and the *Iola*. Mac segued from talking about the virtues of the *Sea Wind* to recalling highlights of their round-the-world cruise. Jennifer and Buck felt like favored guests that night—their hosts were so cordial and entertaining. Mac, a natural spinner of yarns, mesmerized them, leaping up or moving around to illustrate his points. He broke out a fifth of Jamaican rum, Muff opened a can of pineapple juice as mixer, and the four drank together like the best of friends. When it began to grow dark, Muff switched on a shaded table lamp, just as if they were in her living room in San Diego, and the soft glow of the light filled the cabin. She slowly began to open up, joining her husband in recounting their adventures. Once, when Mac found himself standing next to Muff, he casually put his arm around her and drew her nearer. Jennifer could see he was a man who was confident of himself and sure of the love of his wife.

"So, what are your plans?" Mac abruptly asked.

"We're going to be staying," Jennifer answered innocently.

Mac and Muff were silent, but their reaction was clearly written on their faces.

"We don't know for how long," Buck added, amused.

"Two friends are going to be joining us the end of August," Jennifer continued. "They're bringing provisions. We have to make do until then. We're supplementing our stores with what we can trade for and what we can find on land. I'm trying to get a vegetable garden going. What about you guys? How long are you going to stay?"

"A year anyway," Mac said without hesitation. "We brought enough provisions."

More than enough, Jennifer thought, by the look of the chock-full shelves.

As the evening wore down and Jennifer and Buck were leaving, Mac gave Buck a tin of tobacco and a package of papers so he could roll his own cigarettes.

"Mac, you don't know what you've done," said Jennifer, smiling. "You've got a friend for life now."

JULY 16, 1974

ON HER TWENTY-EIGHTH birthday, Jennifer woke up alone and lingered in the bunk, wondering what her mother was doing at that moment. If she had been at home, a chocolate cake would be baking in the oven, and her mother would be whipping up vanilla butter icing, Jennifer's favorite.

She was by herself now because Buck had moved off the *Iola* the day before. It had been a purely practical decision. He was too tall to stand completely upright in the *Iola*'s cabin; this way they could both have more elbow room. And she sure enjoyed not sharing the boat with Buck's two big dogs, especially since she usually got stuck cleaning up after them. He had originally asked her to move ashore with him, but there was no way she would sleep on or near the ground, what with all the land crabs and rats crawling around.

Buck had set up a livable camp. He'd found an old cot and mattress for his tent in one of the abandoned buildings, and had a lantern and Coleman stove. The food, though, remained on the *Iola*, where he and Jennifer prepared and shared their meals. She had hoped that with Buck living ashore, she could exercise tighter control over their supplies. But it wasn't working out that way. Buck indifferently continued to chow down like a famished wolf, and her nagging did no good. She couldn't fathom why he didn't seem to appreciate the seriousness of running out of supplies. What were they going to do? Their food stores were already lower than they should have been when they arrived on Palmyra, and with each passing day the situation was growing worse.

Aside from this irritation, however, Jennifer was not unhappy with Buck and did not consider their living apart a true separation. When they wanted to spend the night together, they did.

Soon after Jennifer dressed, the Leonards came by to announce they were leaving that morning. Bernard brought her more books, and Evelyn was carrying a small jar of cooking oil, a sack of flour, and some rice pudding.

Jennifer was touched—and surprised—by Evelyn's generosity. Just a few days earlier, the older woman had flatly refused to barter, explaining that after a long cruise, they didn't have enough food left on the *Journeyer* to give or trade away.

Evelyn asked to take Jennifer's picture before they departed. She posed on the *Iola*'s bow—a sunnily smiling, dimpled birthday girl in flowery shorts and a bikini top—cradling Puffer in her arms. She looked happy.

The Leonards were soon on their way. As the *Journeyer* nosed out into the lagoon under power, Bernard waved broadly. "Goodbye, Jennifer," he hollered. "Have a happy birthday and a wonderful year."

"Thank you, Bernie. Have a good trip."

He wasn't really a bad guy, she thought. A little stuffy and self-important, but not the hopeless jerk Buck made him out to be.

July 16. Journeyer *left today. Bernie and Evelyn brought by books, oil, and rice pudding, which I devoured entirely, though made some halfhearted effort to save 1/2 for R—then 1/4, then lost out to my appetite for something sweet, and just ate it all up. Later, R came by and started to make my birthday cake. I went down to his camp, read and relaxed while Mac delivered my present—he had retrieved our anchor which we lost when we got hung up on the reef the day we arrived. R invited Mac and Muff to partake of cake and coffee at 6:00, which they accepted. When I returned, we cleaned and filleted fish. We had fried fish patties for dinner. After bathing, we moved a very pretty cake down to R's camp and Mac and Muff arrived at 6 sharp with more presents—some roasted soy nuts and a sweet-smelling sachet. All sang "Happy Birthday" to me and I blew out the one big candle atop my cake after making a wish. Talked awhile, then Mac and Muff bid goodnite. After which, R and I smoked some hash and had an exquisite fuck—all and all, a very fine birthday.*

Jennifer didn't have to think twice about her birthday wish. It was often on her mind. *Please let everything work out all right for Buck and me.*

She didn't tell anyone, of course, because she desperately wanted her wish to come true.

CHAPTER 10

MUFF DID NOT WANT to upset her elderly mother by mentioning her own problems and worries when she wrote home on July 13, 1974, three days before the Leonards departed. But in spite of her good intentions, her gnawing concern about life on Palmyra broke through in every paragraph.

Dearest Mother,

Three boats are here now, but one, the *Journeyer*, is leaving and will take this letter with them. That leaves us alone with a hippie couple who plan to stay here and live off the land. It's just our luck that they decided to roost in Palmyra.

Mac has cleared the land around us and set up a little camp ashore that we use as an outdoor patio area. We found an old table, chairs, bench, and platforms to set the furniture on. This other couple, Roy and Jennifer, got one of the good chairs. I had pulled it closer to our area, then forgot it. The next day I saw him walking around our place and when I checked, the chair was gone. As Mac says, finders keepers, I guess.

Right near our camp, Mac has set up a workshop with a long workbench and we are really setting up house. We've done a little exploring. The other day, Mac found a building on the other side of the lagoon. He came back to get me and we took flashlights. It appeared to be a hospital and Mac thinks a communications center, too. Inside was spooky to me, but Mac went right in like he'd been there a hundred times.

Most of the island is junglelike and the birds carry on so you'd think you were in Africa, the deepest, darkest part. You need a machete to cut your way through and to clear away all the thick spiderwebs.

Roy and Jennifer have run out of sugar, cigarettes, and I

don't know what. They have bartered with other boats. Next they will ask us. I pray they won't. Roy has a chain saw that he uses to cut down trees so they can get to the coconuts easier. It makes Mac furious.

To top it off they have three dogs. This island is no place for dogs. She has a house-type dog (very sweet, named Puffer) and he has a Lab and pit bull which is trained to hunt. They don't have enough food for them. The two big dogs are already roaming out of hunger, looking for anything they can find to eat. What a mess. Why did we have to arrive at the same time?

Such is life six degrees from the equator.

Please write to Curt Shoemaker, the radio operator in Hawaii I told you about. He can pass word to us about how you are doing. (Hope your arthritis is better.)

Love,

Muff

Mac was exploring the interior of the island during the hottest part of the day, cutting his way through dense undergrowth with his machete, when he badly misjudged a powerful swipe at one branch. The blade easily severed the branch and flew into Mac's left leg, slicing through to the bone just below the knee. Blood poured down into his sock and sneaker.

Mac swiftly tied his bandanna, wet from sweat, around the cut. He was grimly calm, but realized he had to get back to the *Sea Wind*. Fast.

He considered the trail he'd just blazed, but it meandered too much. A straight line through the jungle would be quicker. He began chopping in that direction, handling the machete with renewed respect.

A few minutes later he had to stop to tighten the tourniquet. The bleeding had not even slowed. Just how much blood could he lose before he felt faint? Already, a weariness from all the exertion in the hot sun had settled in his limbs, and he felt himself moving at a dreamlike, slow speed, as exhausted as a runner at the end of a marathon. But he didn't dare stop to rest because he was losing

more blood all the time. It would do no good to yell for help, anyway, because no one was close enough to hear him.

He soon faced a growth of thick wild grass nearly his height.
Hacking through it in the stifling heat and humidity would require
energy he didn't have.

He turned away, searching for an easier way. Within minutes, he
was back at the barricade of tall grass. He cursed himself for not
carrying a compass. The sun was no help because high clouds had
sailed in with the afternoon breeze and veiled the sky. He tried to
reorient himself, unable to believe he was so confused. "*You can't
get lost on a tiny island*," he had told Muff. Now *he* was lost. As
his strength and self-confidence ebbed dangerously, he finally
chanced upon the runway, where the assembled birds greeted him
with a squawking cacophony that sounded like beautiful music to
his ears.

It wasn't far now.

Pulling the dinghy alongside the *Sea Wind*, he yelled for Muff.
She popped up from below, took one look at his bloody leg, and
let out an anguished cry.

"It's not as bad as it looks," he assured her, climbing aboard. "I
cut myself with the damn machete. We need to clean it."

Muff, who had taken advanced first aid, focused on the task at
hand. She cleaned the deep wound with cold fresh water, then
dripped searing peroxide into the cut. Mac barely flinched. "It's got
to have stitches," she pronounced briskly. "I'll get the sutures."

"Better bring some antibiotics."

The sutures had not been unpacked since Mac put them in the
first-aid kit before their honeymoon cruise—thirteen years ago.
Packed separately in foil, each length of thread was still usable, but
the needle had become too dull. Instead of stitching, Muff sprinkled a powdered sulfa drug on the wound, and closed it as completely as possible with butterfly bandages.

"It's a long way to a doctor or hospital," Muff said. "Please be
more careful, honey."

Grunting noncommittally, he swallowed an antibiotic pill and
went right to bed, obviously worn out from the ordeal. That night,

Muff set the alarm clock, and woke him at two o'clock for a second dose.

Unable to go back to sleep, she went topside. On the familiar deck, she nearly stumbled in the darkness. There was no moon and the stars must have been hidden by overcast.

She awkwardly groped her way to the stern and sat down to think. Looking out toward what she knew was the jungle, she could see nothing. The darkness was literally blackness. It was as if she had stepped into a closet and shut the door behind her. She couldn't remember ever being in such a dark place.

There wasn't any kind of sustained pastel dusk at Palmyra. Nighttime fell as if someone had dropped a curtain. Mac said the sudden darkness was explained by their proximity to the equator. Muff found it eerie.

Mac spent most of the next day in bed, alternately sleeping and reading. This was the first time since they had arrived at Palmyra that Muff had seen him taking it easy during the day. It took an injury, and perhaps some wounded pride, to keep him down.

In the evening, Muff prepared a special dinner. She thawed out two steaks, put them on the hibachi, and baked potatoes topped with some of Jennifer's coconut butter. She chilled a special bottle of champagne she'd been saving since San Diego, and they feasted.

The next day, Mac felt much better, though he would have to continue the antibiotics regimen for a week longer.

After this brief respite, Muff worried again, for she knew he would soon be back exploring the rugged island he saw as his domain.

When will he tire of this godforsaken place? She desperately wanted to help her man live out his dream, but she didn't know how much longer she could stand it here.

CHAPTER 11

IGNORING THE GENTLE RAINFALL, Jennifer scraped more
soil into the shovel and tossed it into a makeshift wheelbarrow.

Rain here was nothing like the gray, ugly torrents she'd experienced in New York, or California's winter downpours. On Palmyra, showers were not at all depressing. They were warm and
refreshing, something to look forward to as pure pleasure. They also
meant renewed supplies of life-saving fresh water. Usually, as now,
the sun still beamed during the showers.

Digging for scarce dirt had become a regular chore. Jennifer
never would have guessed the difficulty of gathering garden soil on
a coral atoll. It could only be found beneath trees and shrubs, but
even there it was never more than a few inches deep. The natural
flora thrived despite the lack of soil, undoubtedly because of the
rich nutrients from the island's abundant bird guano and decayed
vegetation.

She wheeled her cargo toward the cement structure they were
now calling the Refrigerator House. These days, the dilapidated
refrigerator was powered by their own portable generator. In the
time it took her to traverse those fifty yards or so, the rain stopped.

Buck, wearing only shorts and sunglasses, was on the roof of the
building, spreading out the previous load of dirt. His sinewy muscles were slick from the warm rain, and Jennifer appraised him
with a long look. She adored him.

Strange as it might seem, growing a roof garden made sense, as
they had learned the hard way when they first moved a batch of
vegetable and marijuana seedlings ashore. They'd left the tender little plants in paper cups filled with dirt on a broken-down picnic
table. During the night, many of the shoots had been eaten, presumably by crabs and rats. After taking the remaining plants back
to the boat, they searched for a spot that would be out of reach of

the marauders. Eventually, they decided to plant atop the roof of the Refrigerator House.

Buck had built a rickety ladder and rigged a five-gallon bucket on a length of rope for hauling the soil they collected.

"We've got enough here now to plant a few rows," he said.

Jennifer came back to reality. She knew what he had in mind. "The vegetables come first. We can't eat dope."

He chuckled good-naturedly. "Speak for yourself."

Jennifer hoped that growing their own tomatoes, cucumbers, peas, carrots, and lettuce would eventually ease the long-term food situation. But it would not solve their immediate problem. The plants wouldn't start producing for months, and as of now, they scarcely had one month's worth of food left on the *Iola*.

"How much more dirt you figure we need?" she asked.

"Eighty, maybe ninety wheelbarrow loads."

She groaned. Her back was already killing her, and she knew how hard dirt was to come by on this coral reef. "That'll take at least a week if we work five or six hours a day." She had no hope whatsoever that Buck would be so energetic.

She and Buck had already discussed what they would do if Dickie and Carlos didn't show up with provisions next month, as scheduled. Before Jack Wheeler left the island, she had asked him if food was available at the nearest island shown on the chart, Washington Island, some 120 miles to the southeast. Wheeler said yes, that there were some Gilbertese natives living there, but that Washington was a "reef island," meaning there was no channel, and in order to get ashore, a boat had to fight both the breaking surf and the dangerous coral reefs surrounding the island. The nearest island that could be reached where food could be purchased was Fanning, 175 miles to the southeast. Fanning, he explained, had a few hundred permanent residents, a general store, and, like Palmyra, a protected lagoon. But Wheeler had warned her that Fanning would be too difficult a voyage for a sailboat without a motor because they would be going against the wind. Instead, he suggested American Samoa, a much easier sail, he said, because of favorable winds and currents the whole way. "*Samoa*," Jennifer had said incredulously. "That's way south, isn't it?" Wheeler confirmed it was more than a thousand miles south of Palmyra, but he nevertheless recommended it over Fanning. Jennifer couldn't imagine a two-thousand-mile round trip to go grocery shopping.

They would try for Fanning, even though they wouldn't be able to buy much with their very limited funds. But Mac had expressed an interest in buying their portable generator, the same model he'd meant to get before leaving home. She knew he would give them a fair price. Also, Jennifer hoped she and Buck could find some kind of temporary work on Fanning and earn money to buy additional supplies. She planned to stock up on the staples—flour, sugar, rice, beans. Also, they wanted to buy an outboard motor they could use on both the *Iola* and their dinghy, so they could troll for fish in the lagoon. Those supplies would keep them going until the following spring, when the vegetable garden would be producing. That was her master plan, anyway, while Buck was more concerned about getting the marijuana crop going. He was planning for their smuggling operation with the Taylor brothers to make them rich by springtime.

While Buck was thinking big, Jennifer's attention was focused on basic day-to-day survival, for her the most unappealing aspect of life on Palmyra. She spent the majority of her time gathering and preparing food, like a woman in a third-world village. Making a batch of coconut butter took hours, beginning with collecting ripe coconuts—most of those on the ground had rotted—then grinding, blending, and cooking them. She and Buck had found a single banana tree on an islet across the lagoon, and they would row all the way over for just two or three bananas. Washing clothes and drying them in the humid air took half a day. Feeding the dogs—Jennifer prepared mullet and coconuts for them to supplement the shrinking supply of dog food—cleaning the boat, working on the garden . . . the chores seemed never-ending. "Paradise sure is exhausting," she groaned to Buck. "We're practically alone on a tropical island in the middle of nowhere, and I'm busier than a streetwalker when the fleet's in."

"Let's pretend I'm a horny sailor, huh?"

July 22. Carried loads of dirt in A.M.—after five trips I was ready to pass out. Another boat came in, the Shearwater *from Portland, Oregon. Two guys—Don Stevens and Bill Larson—on board. Have toured South Pacific, heading back home by way of Hawaii. R rowed out and helped moor them where Journeyer had been. More fish for dinner.*

July 23. Rainy day. Put up batch of sourdough starter. Also planted some m seeds. R came over and both of us stayed on boat and read. Mac brought over a good group of books—1984, a Harold Robbins, some Zane Grey, and another Agatha Christie. We gave them some books we'd already read.

Another old favorite for dinner—papio and coconut cake, some baked in shell, some fried. In the evening, the two guys on Shearwater *invited us to their boat. We were treated to rum and Cokes and cocktail peanuts. Made a deal to trade magazines and books next day. They gave R two packs of South Sea cigarettes. Don showed me his ship's log, full of pictures of Tonga, Fiji, etc. A very enjoyable evening.*

Everyone on the island was invited to a potluck dinner at Buck's camp on the evening of July 25.

Jennifer had cooked most of the afternoon, preparing garlic bread, an apricot nut loaf, and a coconut pudding pie, using flour and sugar donated by the *Shearwater*. Mac and Muff brought steamed potatoes and carrots, the last of the produce they'd bought in Hawaii.

Mac was impressed with how neatly the camp had been fixed up and outfitted since their visit on Jennifer's birthday.

Muff observed that Roy had finally made an effort to trim his undisciplined beard and long hair. "He looked powerful," she would later write to Bernard and Evelyn Leonard. "How I think Jack London might have looked." His improved appearance was not sufficient, however, to dispel her growing contempt for the big man with ugly tattoos. "I don't appreciate his bumming," Muff wrote in the same letter. "Roy wanted more cigarette papers and tobacco so he came over the other night to get some from Mac. They need so much of everything. Well, I guess the only way to look at it—when we run out of things to give them, we'll just have to leave Palmyra. That's fine with me."

Muff observed some young sprouts in paper cups and asked what they were growing. Without hesitation, Buck replied, "Marijuana." She thought he enjoyed waiting for her reaction.

"And vegetables, too," Jennifer quickly added.

Bill Larson from the *Shearwater* came to the party alone, bringing a bottle of rum and a canned ham. His shipmate, Don Stevens, had stayed in bed with a painful ear infection. A concerned Mac asked if they had any penicillin aboard and, when Larson answered no, went back to the *Sea Wind* and got some of the wonder drug for Stevens.

Buck had set up a record player in his tent, so while they ate outside next to a campfire, they listened to an album of love songs by assorted 1960s pop artists. Larson left early, taking a plate of food and Mac's gift of pills for his sick friend. Mac and Buck adjourned to the tent for a game of chess.

Jennifer played chess too, and was quite good. In fact, Mac, looking for chess action that morning, had come over to the *Iola* and taken Jennifer back to the *Sea Wind*. She beat him in the first game, apparently surprising both of the Grahams. Mac asked for a rematch and, to his relief, convincingly beat her the next two games. He was, Jennifer realized, a tournament-caliber player. But tonight, instead of watching the men play, as she would have liked, she stayed at the campfire to chat with Muff, who seemed downcast.

From the first day they met, Jennifer had considered Muff inhibited. The conversation as they sat around the fire caught her by surprise.

"I never wanted to come here," Muff said in a low, almost conspiratorial tone that wouldn't carry to the tent. "I don't see why Mac had to just pick up and leave."

Muff stared blankly at the fire, which still radiated warmth from the flameless embers. "We had a wonderful life in San Diego. Lots of friends, really good people. Everything was so nice."

Jennifer nodded, but said nothing. She couldn't believe Muff was opening up like this and confiding in her.

"My mother and two sisters live in San Diego. It was important for me to spend time with my mother."

Jennifer put a thick branch on the fire.

Muff wondered if she sounded pathetic or silly. Why was she trusting this aimless hippie with her innermost feelings? She didn't particularly respect Jennifer. Not her judgment, not her life-style, not her choice of men. But . . . she was the only other woman on Palmyra.

"I keep trying to get him to leave," Muff said, deciding to continue on. "He tells me to relax and enjoy myself. But I can't. He says he's here to discover something, but he doesn't know what. Neither do I." There was no bitterness in her voice, just unhappiness and bewilderment.

"Mac's an adventurer," Jennifer offered. She felt she had to comfort Muff somehow.

"Yes, he is. He loves living like this. He wanted to get out of the big city so badly. It got so he hated to read the paper in the morning. All the stories about rising crime convinced him it wasn't safe to walk down the street in broad daylight. And he was sick of all the congestion and cars and wanted to get away. But believe it or not"—she laughed—"I wish I was back home in the rat race."

"Well, I'm kinda glad to be out of the rat race," Jennifer said, "but this place does have its drawbacks."

Drawbacks, Muff thought derisively. "Sometimes I find myself wondering what will become of us," she sighed.

That struck a chord in Jennifer, but she was in no position to confide in Muff. She couldn't talk about Buck's fugitive status or share her many good reasons for worrying about the future. She and Muff were on this unyielding atoll for the same reason. Each was here because of her love for her man. But Jennifer's need for secrecy meant that this fleeting opportunity for them to understand each other was lost.

"I know what you mean," Jennifer said lamely. "I really do, Muff."

SINCE THE *Shearwater* was going to depart soon, letters home were written on July 30. Larson and Stevens would mail them from Hawaii.

Mac wrote his sister in Seattle.

Dear Kit,

We have been busy since arriving on Palmyra. I just finished making screens for the three hatches to keep the bugs outside where they belong.

I have told you about the other couple, Roy and Jennifer, who arrived a week before us to "their" deserted island to live the "survival life" indefinitely. I am not really upset at other people being on the island, but Muff is. Roy and Jennifer are really not our type, but to dissect them would take another letter.

The sharks are a major disappointment. There are lots of places I can take the Zodiac at high tide, but I am forever having to get out in shallow water to pull it along. I do so with machete in hand to chase off the inevitable feisty blacktip sharks. They come in all sizes. Two to four feet long in knee-deep water—and up to six feet long in deeper parts of the lagoon. I think I will have to learn how to handle them. For now, Muff refuses to get her feet wet.

It is now 3:00 A.M. and Muff is sleeping. A few raindrops are splattering through the mosquito netting, and I can see the star-filled sky. I love it here. It's not San Diego. It's not Seattle. It's not civilization. We're going to stay until we tire of it or the supplies run out.

Love,
Mac and Muff

Jennifer, still not revealing where she was, wrote her mother.

Dear Mom,

Because I never know for sure whether my letters find their way to you, I take every opportunity to write. Just so you know, so far I've written two prior letters to you and one to Teddy, which went out on boats that left here earlier. And I can't even get any mail back from you! Well, no one ever said Paradise would be easy.

In case you didn't get my other letters, let me repeat that we made it to our destination. It was a long, wet trip but I'm safe now. We are on a pretty atoll that has a lagoon and everything. We are eating lots of coconuts and fish, and working at getting a vegetable garden going. It's a hard life here, but I'm surviving.

I think of you often, and wonder when we'll next see each other. I thought of you on my birthday, and missed my chocolate cake with butter icing. Buck baked a cake for me—a real valiant effort.

Hope all is well with you. Give my love to Teddy and the rest of the family. Till next time.

All my love,
Jennifer

Muff wrote the Jamiesons.

Dear Marie and Jamie,

The hippie couple, Jennifer and Roy, have been busy trying to get their garden going. But some of what they're growing is to smoke, not to eat. They plan to stay here as long as they can. I sure wish we hadn't picked a time to come here and stay just when they did. I'd just rather their type weren't here. They are supposed to have some friends (two guys) coming down on a boat to bring them supplies, as they are nearly out of everything. Jennifer has been after the boats that come in for extra food. It really makes me mad—their mooching. They came down here to live off the land so why don't they do it and stop asking for things?

Well, I wish you could fly out to Palmyra for a visit. You don't know how much I miss you.

Till later,
Muff

AUGUST 1, 1974

LARSON AND Stevens sailed away feeling sorry for both of the women they had met on Palmyra. In different ways, each seemed lost, even miserable.

The sailors had enjoyed Mac's company. He was such a capable, friendly guy you couldn't help liking and admiring him.

But neither of them had thought much of Jennifer's old man—whatever his name was. Larson had challenged him once about the tattoo on his arm. "So is your name Roy or Buck?" When Jennifer's lover just glared back hotly, Larson gathered it would be wise to drop the matter.

As Palmyra sank below the horizon, Larson told his shipmate, "I think that guy—Roy or Buck or whatever the hell his name is—is volatile. *Real* volatile."

CHAPTER 12

WEDNESDAY, AUGUST 7, 1974

THE *SEA WIND*'S TWO-WAY radio crackled with interference. Mac was on the 20-meter band at 14285 kilohertz. It was almost fifteen minutes past his scheduled 7:00 P.M. contact with Curt Shoemaker, but all Mac could hear over the speaker was static heavy as artillery fire.

He kept fiddling with the frequency knob.

"It's never been this bad before," said Muff, standing next to him. "Are you sure this is the right day?"

"It's Wednesday night."

"Maybe something's wrong with the radio."

"I think it's atmospheric."

Then, as if someone in authority had declared a cease-fire in the heavens, the airwaves suddenly cleared and they heard a voice they recognized through the small metal speaker. "—VXV. Repeat, KH61HG calling W7VXV."

"It's *Curt*," Muff said with relief, keenly aware of how cut off Palmyra was from the rest of the world.

Mac depressed the transmit button. "This is W7VXV," he said

evenly into the microphone. "We hear you loud and clear, Curt. Over."

Mac was broadcasting illegally, using the call letters of an inactive ham operator Curt knew in Hawaii. Typically, Mac would have arranged to earn his own FCC license before leaving San Diego if he'd known they were going to be making regular radio contact with anyone. But for now, this would do. Curt had cautioned him not to mention the *Sea Wind*'s location. Federal communications authorities might overhear by chance, and broadcasting without a license is a crime.

"Aloha," Shoemaker said. "We have some traffic for you."

Letters from home!

"Momi will read them."

The velvety voice of Curt's wife came over the radio. "We do want to hear about what's going on with you," Momi said, "but Curt says I should read the traffic first."

First was a card from Muff's mother who said how happy she was to receive the letters Mac and Muff had sent out with the Wheelers and Leonards. She told her daughter not to worry about her. She was doing fine.

Next was a short note from Mac's sister. Kit gave chatty news about their mother, herself, and her three sons.

"Thanks for the news from home," Mac said. "It really means a lot to both of us." He could see that Muff was holding back tears. "By the way, did you get any messages for the other couple here? You know, Roy and Jennifer. They're still waiting to hear word about their resupply mission."

When Mac learned that Jennifer and Buck were anxious to confirm the arrival date of their friends bringing supplies, he had instantly volunteered to relay messages to their friends through Shoemaker, prompting Buck and Jennifer to write to the Taylor brothers. The Leonards had taken the letter three weeks before.

"Negative," Curt said. "No word on this end."

For the next fifteen minutes, Mac and Muff took turns chatting about their life on the island. Curt promised to send postcards to their mothers with the news that they were doing okay. Finally, they all said good night. "Oh yes," Shoemaker said before they signed off. He went on to say that President Nixon was reported to be on the verge of announcing his resignation.

That bit of news from home sent Mac and Muff to bed saddened for their President, and for their country.

MUFF AND Mac had been halfway down the path to the bathhouse when she realized they'd forgotten the shampoo. Mac volunteered to go back and get it, and Muff headed to the bath alone.

Not far along the path she came face to face with Buck's glowering pit bull.

The dog growled from deep within its throat, then suddenly leaped toward her. Muff screamed, simultaneously jumping back. The dog landed stiff-legged in front of her, baring sharp yellowed teeth, tensed to spring again.

Maybe it was her imagination, she thought, but the dog seemed to be more than mindlessly angry. He seemed *hungry*.

The other big dog, the Lab, ran out of the bushes barking. And then the little one Jennifer called Puffer, who'd always been so friendly, appeared on the scene, yapping.

But it was the now silent pit bull that Muff watched warily. She remembered reading somewhere that an excited dog that made no sound was probably preparing to attack. Eyes darting, she spied a rusted length of pipe a few feet away. When the heavily breathing pit bull gave no signs of backing off, she inched her way toward the possible weapon.

She grasped the pipe and was ready to protect herself just as Buck and Jennifer started yelling from the bath area. They were speaking in a language she didn't understand or recognize. But the pit bull stepped back a few feet.

When Muff took this opportunity to retreat backward, the pit bull charged with hackles raised.

Muff screamed, swinging the pipe in a wide arc in front of her.

"*Kapu!*" Buck yelled again.

The dog halted the charge and retreated.

By the time Jennifer and Buck came down the trail from the bathhouse, Mac had rejoined Muff. "You've got to do something about those dogs," Mac spat angrily. "They're a menace."

"Tell them *kapu,*" Jennifer explained. "Roy trained them in Hawaiian. That means 'no.'"

"You're out of luck if you don't know Hawaiian?" Muff shot back angrily, startling Jennifer.

Buck had not taken part in this conversation. He had casually walked past Mac and Muff and headed down the path, followed by his pets.

"If one of those damn dogs ever bites one of us," Mac muttered between clenched teeth, "I'll shoot it."

"Suits me," said a still-shaken Muff.

Jennifer ran to catch up with Buck as Mac and Muff headed toward the bathhouse.

"Tell them you're sorry," Jennifer said.

Buck acted as if he hadn't heard her. He said he was on his way to cut down some more trees for coconuts. Mac had already let Buck know a couple of times he did not think it was right for him to down the trees with his chain saw.

"Are you *trying* to make them mad?"

"They don't own this goddamn island!" Buck snapped.

Jennifer knew better than to try to make Buck see reason right now. She knew not to hassle him when he was like this. He was usually quiet and controlled, but if challenged, he could become furious in no time.

The previous day, for example, she'd innocently asked him why he'd started going around without his dental bridge. The gap where two top front teeth were missing made him look like some skid row wino. He had flared up: "I don't have to impress anyone!" At times, he *liked* coming across mean. She figured he'd learned this tactic in prison, as a warning not to mess with him. "If you look bad, no one will fuck with you," he had once told her.

Though Buck had never struck her, he'd admitted that he'd hit his ex-wife during their marriage. She would scream and throw things at him, he explained, so he'd slap her. Jennifer had made her reaction to his therapy clear, early on. "A man gets one chance to hit me. Then I'm gone. Hit me, lose me." Buck had never hit her, but Jennifer had never thrown anything at him. She sensed that if someone fed his anger, Buck could become uncontrollably violent, a dynamo of rage.

Living on Palmyra—far out of reach of the authorities—had not served to relax Buck. On the contrary, his frustrations and pent-up hostilities had inexplicably been exacerbated, perhaps by the trying conditions of their daily life. She tried to remain tolerant and understanding, aware she was becoming increasingly taut herself.

But Jennifer wasn't giving up.

Their food situation was a continuing cause for concern, yet it wasn't as if they were going to starve to death. They still had some supplies left, and there was always fish, coconuts, and crabs. She had created a salad recipe using some leafy plants that grew in abundance on the runway. She thought her "Runway Salad" was delicious when served with a dressing of coconut milk, a kind of equatorial *nouvelle cuisine.* They were bored with the restricted diet, but they *were* eating. And if they didn't hear from the Taylor brothers soon, they could sail to Fanning for more supplies.

Physically, Jennifer felt healthy and in good shape from all the manual work, and she could even allow herself some optimism about the future.

And after all, they *had* achieved their main goal in coming here: Buck was still a free man.

AUGUST 13, 1974

MUFF FELT languid, as was often the case these days. The unremitting summer heat in the depths of the tropics was draining her limited store of stamina. A tree sloth would leave her in a cloud of dust.

She was trying to lose weight, hoping she would thereby gain more energy and be more attractive. Her latest dieting effort called for drinking a glass of cider vinegar each morning. Some slick women's mag she had brought with her claimed this would curb the appetite and take inches off. Muff had packed four gallon jugs of vinegar for the trip and was religiously downing the recommended dosage every morning, but so far she hadn't shed a pound. As a reminder of her goal, she kept a calorie chart on the wall in the galley. But, especially when she was feeling out of sorts, she sneaked food when Mac wasn't around. These days, that happened more and more often.

She couldn't stand looking at herself in a mirror anymore. When she was younger, she'd been justifiably proud of her figure. "I used to have cheesecake legs," she had told Mac's sister a few months earlier. "Now I have cottage-cheese thighs."

She had been lying in the bunk around midday for almost an hour, exhausted, but unable to fall asleep. At first, the whine of a chain saw had kept her awake. Since the only one on the island belonged to Roy, she wasn't surprised when she went up on deck and spotted him west of their anchorage, near an old seaplane ramp, hunched over, chopping down another big coconut tree.

Mac was ashore—as usual. Muff hoped he would avoid a confrontation with Roy. Let him cut the blasted trees down. Who cared? She sensed Roy was threatened by Mac, the man he could never be. Her husband was honest, capable, and energetic, while Roy had his own sly methods of getting what he wanted. As when he copped the chair she'd put aside . . . and now, destroying a tree to get coconuts rather than shinnying up. But Roy was always quick to seek Mac's help, and Mac was always willing to give it.

When the sawing stopped, Muff made another attempt to sleep, but failed.

Honestly, she didn't understand where Mac got all his energy. Since they'd come to Palmyra, he'd been getting up around sunrise, his favorite part of the day on the island. In all the years of their marriage, she'd never seen him so eager to start the day—usually, he slept late.

Now, she stayed in her bunk later than Mac, took a nap or two in the day when he was out working or exploring, and still she was the first in bed every night. The island life that invigorated him debilitated her. It wasn't fair.

She shut her eyes to try again, but opened them as soon as she heard the sound of a boat engine that wasn't the Zodiac. There were new voices, too. As she got up, it occurred to her that it must be Jennifer and Roy's friends arriving with their supplies.

She went up on deck. There was an unfamiliar sailboat motoring into the lagoon, heading for the dolphins. She could see a bearded, long-haired young man standing on the bow.

Great, Muff thought. *Just what we need on this island. More useless hippies preaching about self-reliance and begging us to feed them.*

CHAPTER 13

TOLOA, THE BOAT THAT pulled into the Palmyra lagoon on August 13 as Muff was trying to nap, was a well-kept twenty-nine-foot sloop with two men aboard. They were definitely not hippies, and neither knew Jennifer and Buck.

The long-haired fellow was Thomas Wolfe, a pensive twenty-six-year-old chemical engineer from San Diego. He had lived for three years on a sailboat docked at Underwood's Marina, where Mac had berthed the *Sea Wind,* but had never met the Grahams. He had taken a year's leave of absence from his job with a pesticides company so that he could sail the Pacific and end up in New Zealand, which he'd always wanted to visit. He'd delivered a boat to Hawaii for a San Diego yachtsman who had sold it to someone on the Big Island. There, Wolfe sought a ride to the South Seas, and found it aboard the *Toloa,* next to which, coincidentally, he had docked in Hilo.

Norman Sanders, the *Toloa's* owner, had until recently been a geology professor at the University of California at Santa Barbara. A burly man with graying mutton chops and an Old Testament salt-and-pepper beard, Sanders showed more verve and intensity than many of his students. He had fallen into disfavor with the school administration for his confrontational tactics against what he considered to be the treacherous evils of big business. One of his campaigns had been directed against offshore oil drilling. To dramatize his opposition, he once sat in a strategically anchored rowboat in the Santa Barbara Channel for four days to stall placement of an oil-drilling platform. His self-published book, *Stop It!*, offered a step-by-step blueprint to other no-growth proponents on how to convince elected officials to halt development projects. After seven years of employment without a single pay raise, the outspoken Sanders failed to gain tenure at the university. Disgusted, he declared himself an expatriate and planned forthwith to move to Australia. His wife, Jill, and their little girl had sailed with him from San Diego to Hawaii, but at Hilo, the long-suffering seasick woman declared that she wasn't going to sail one more nautical mile. With daughter in hand, she caught the next flight to Sydney. So the former professor found himself in need of a crewman to help him sail the rest of the way to Australia.

For Sanders and Wolfe, the voyage to Palmyra had been uneventful. The sea had been blessedly calm, and the wind steady. The greatest excitement on the way down had sprung from their regular arguments over environmental matters. Sanders accused Wolfe of working hand in hand with the "enemy polluters." Wolfe usually countered that pesticides are necessary to human progress and Sanders was living in a fantasy world. They would become irked with each other and not talk for a few hours, then happily go at it again the next day.

One thing they had agreed on was stopping at Palmyra. A former Fullbright scholar, Sanders specialized in coastal geomorphology, or the study of coastal regions and the forces of nature that influence them. The prospect of visiting an island largely untouched by civilization was professionally appealing to him.

"I can't believe this island isn't going to have at least a few hippies living off the land," Wolfe joked.

"No, it'll be deserted," Sanders insisted. "Everything I've read says so."

Gliding into the placid lagoon under power, they saw one boat moored across the lagoon and a second boat—a ketch—anchored in a cove a few hundred yards to the west. They were steering the

Toloa toward a dilapidated wharf when a rugged-looking man called to them from a dinghy he was rowing their way.

"You don't want to tie up there," he shouted. "Too many rats around the dock. Best place is next to my boat. I'll give you a hand."

When they were secured to a dolphin, the man in the dinghy came aboard. Barefoot, he was bronzed from the sun, with shoulder-length hair and a full beard, and wore nothing but dirty cutoffs. He introduced himself as Roy, then asked: "You guys have any dope?"

Sanders shook his head and Wolfe said, "Sorry."

"That's okay," the visitor said. "I have my own. It's getting down to the dregs, though." He took a small plastic bag from his pocket and began rolling a joint of mostly seeds and stems.

Wolfe moved away to finish stowing the sails. As he passed Sanders, who was within earshot of Buck, he cracked pianissimo, "So much for your deserted island, Norm."

The air was soon filled with the pungent odor of marijuana.

THE NEXT morning, the newcomers gathered their fishing gear and went ashore to meet "Roy."

Warning them about poisonous fish in the lagoon, he'd offered to show them his favorite fishing spot and teach them which types of fish were safe to eat.

As Wolfe and Sanders approached the clearing where Roy had promised to meet them, they saw Jennifer, whom they'd also met the previous day, digging with a shovel as her boyfriend worked nearby.

The young woman's New York accent had surprised Wolfe, who had come across few New Yorkers sailing in the Pacific. Just as he was about to ask her how she'd ended up on Palmyra, a pit bull came charging out of nowhere, racing furiously toward them.

The two men halted, expecting the dog to stop and take a defensive stand. When the animal kept on and came within reach, Wolfe considered kicking it in the head but decided against such a drastic move in front of its owners. Surely the dog would stop, either on its own or in response to a command. Jennifer finally shrieked, but it was too late. The dog bowled Wolfe over as it bit into his midriff.

"Popolo, *kapu*!" Jennifer screamed. "*Kapu!*"

The pit bull backed away with a piece of torn shirt in its mouth, chewing greedily like a hyena snapping up a bit of offal.

As Wolfe stood up, he could see that the bite was deep. "Goddamn dog!" he shouted. "If that sucker ever comes near me again, I'll kill it."

"Good," Buck said, looking up coolly from his work. "We'd have some fresh meat around here."

Not only are the dogs pitifully hungry, Wolfe thought, but so are the people. Did this Roy fellow with the "Buck" tattoo care that little about his dog, or was he simply refusing to accept responsibility for its aggressive behavior? Whatever the case, he vowed to prepare himself for the next time the pit bull came around.

Wolfe returned to the *Toloa* to clean and bandage his stomach wound, then he joined Sanders again for their delayed fishing expedition.

Wolfe and Sanders followed Buck to Strawn Island, where they fished unsuccessfully for about an hour. Sanders gave up then and went off to study some nearby coral formations. He did not hear their odd guide say that he was going to try shooting a fish. In fact, Sanders didn't even know the man was packing a gun.

At the sharp reports—*bang, bang, bang*—Sanders instinctively dived for cover behind a tree trunk. He immediately thought, *Is this scary-looking doper trying to kill us?*

To his immense relief, he heard Wolfe shout excitedly: "You got one!"

Wolfe hadn't believed their guide could hit a fish with a bullet, but Roy was good with his .22-caliber revolver. He was less adept at logic. Even a gravely wounded fish doesn't wait around to be speared for dinner. The mullet thrashed on the surface for a few seconds, then submerged and disappeared.

Sanders waited for his heaving chest to subside before stepping out from behind the tree. He didn't want the guys to know that the unexpected gunfire had terrified him as much as it did.

After returning from fishing with Buck, Wolfe and Sanders returned to the *Toloa* for lunch. Wolfe then went back ashore for a bath, taking his machete along.

As he walked down the trail to the bathing area, he heard a dog bark. An ugly black muzzle poked through some nearby brush, as if trying to pick up his scent. He drew the machete from the sheath at his side.

The pit bull trotted into the clearing and bared his teeth in a hideous grin.

Wolfe stood his ground. "My turn, Rover," he said between clenched teeth as he tightened his grip on the machete. This time, he would fight offense with offense.

But the pit bull did not advance toward him. It was as if it knew better than to attack now. Nonchalantly, it lifted a leg against a tree, then turned its back on Wolfe and sauntered away.

A little disappointed, Wolfe slipped the machete back into its sheath and continued on. He came across Jennifer, still digging, this time near a concrete blockhouse.

"Exploring?" she asked, leaning on the stock of the shovel. "It won't take you long to realize you're seeing the same thing. Over and over."

"You mean like jungle and more jungle?"

Jennifer smiled. "And birds and more birds."

"What are you digging for?"

"Dirt." She giggled at his expression. "For real. There's a serious shortage of it around here. We're trying to get a garden going. The crabs aren't helping matters. They eat anything they can reach, so we're fixing up a place on the roof."

"A roof garden—just like in New York. You *from* there? Manhattan maybe?"

"Originally, yeah," she answered, "but I haven't lived there in years. This paradise is home now." The last line was delivered sarcastically.

"Guess you and your boyfriend thought you'd be alone here."

"Just like Tarzan and Jane. 'Course, Mac and Muff thought they'd be alone, too." She brushed back a wisp of damp hair from her forehead, less like Jane than an overworked Pearl Buck heroine.

In discussing the Grahams with Jennifer, Wolfe got the impression there was friction between the two couples, but did not press the point.

"Say, how's your flour and sugar supply?" Jennifer asked.

"We've got plenty. We don't bake much."

"If you give me some, I'll bake bread for you and keep a loaf for myself. Buck and I are almost out."

"His name Roy or Buck?"

"Well—Buck's a nickname."

Wolfe could see that she and her boyfriend were woefully ill-prepared and having a hard time of it on Palmyra. He agreed to give her some flour and sugar even though he and Sanders didn't need any of her baking, since they still had several loaves of bread they'd bought in Hawaii.

"We're thinking of sailing to Fanning to buy supplies," Jennifer said.

"*Sailing?* It's upwind the whole way. You'd better count on using your engine."

"Can't. It doesn't work."

"You'd take a helluva pounding against the wind."

Wolfe didn't tell Jennifer, but he would not have sailed anywhere on the rickety-looking *Iola*. The rigging, he'd noticed, was rusted telephone cable. The mast was inexpertly homemade, likely to snap in a bad storm. The spars looked spindly. And the boat obviously leaked, because he heard the noisy bilge pump running off and on. If it leaked while moored in the lagoon, what would happen when they tried to sail upwind against the trades? If her mast broke in the rough seas, they would drift downwind with little chance of being rescued, since no commercial freighters took that route. They might float helplessly for weeks, even months, until they starved or died of thirst under the burning sun.

"Maybe we won't have to go," Jennifer said. "Some friends in an Islander 32 are coming down in a couple of weeks."

"An Islander's a good boat." Hearing that made Wolfe feel better. The boat was a new fiberglass craft designed especially for the rigors of ocean sailing. The hippies would be all right once they got resupplied.

Later that afternoon, Wolfe and Sanders visited the *Sea Wind*. Wolfe in particular hit it off with Mac and Muff. He could see that the Grahams were a well-prepared, experienced yachting couple with an absolutely magnificent boat, a queen of the seas compared with Buck and Jennifer's garbage scow.

As Mac gave his traditional boat tour, Wolfe thought, *Jesus Christ, this isn't a boat, it's some kind of damned museum.* He listened politely as Mac pointed out various design features and pieces of equipment, but he was most impressed by the evidence provided by his own eyes. On the many long ocean voyages he'd made, he learned that the brass went first in the pernicious salt spray, then the wood. But here an antique sextant gleamed brightly in its velvet-lined rack, the compass and the flare pistol glistened. The varnish on the wood surfaces looked fresh, and had been waxed recently. He'd never seen anything like it except in pictures of the great yachts of multimillionaires who had salaried crews to keep every last fitting polished.

Mac took Wolfe ashore to show off his neatly arranged workshop. On a bench sat the old rusty outboard motor from the *Iola*. "I'm trying to fix it for them," Mac explained, "but it might be hopeless." In a garage next to his workshop, he boyishly asked Wolfe to admire a 1940s fire engine with tires gone flat. Behind it against a nearby wall were stacked numerous boxes of rat poison.

"Like to go fishing?" Mac asked.

"Sure. Haven't caught a thing since we got here."

"We'll take care of that."

The two of them took off in the Zodiac. They zipped across the lagoon to Mac's favorite fishing spot near the channel entrance. Wolfe, seeing his line knotted, dropped his hook and leader over the side. He was working at untangling the line when he landed his first fish. Catching a fish on an unbaited hook astonished him. After the hapless expedition with Roy that morning, Wolfe had assumed that the fishing around Palmyra was poor. Actually, the finny creatures were lining up to get caught.

It was close to sunset before they finally started to head back to the *Sea Wind*, laden with about fifty pounds of edible fish. Mac whistled most of the way in the gathering darkness, looking, Wolfe thought, the picture of perfect contentment, the confident male animal in control of his territory.

Back at the *Sea Wind*, Muff invited Wolfe and Sanders for dinner. She broiled some of that afternoon's catch, fixed steamed rice, and put together a salad from a small palm Mac had cut fresh that afternoon.

When Wolfe told his story about being bitten by the dog, the Grahams were frankly disgusted. It was clear from the conversation that Muff hated sharing the island with the other couple. And both she and her husband were especially leery of Roy.

"He doesn't say anything to me anymore," Muff said, "even when I say hello."

"He sure doesn't talk much," Wolfe agreed. He was reminded of the phrase "keeping his own counsel." That described Roy. So did "tightly wound."

"And those missing front teeth," she went on, "make him look—creepy."

Wolfe saw Muff give a slight shudder.

AUGUST 16, 1974

ON THEIR fourth and last full day on the island, Wolfe and Sanders joined the Grahams for a fascinating exploration of Palmyra's outer islets. The party marveled at the variegated formations, chatted playfully, and caught dozens of small crabs, a fine pretext for a going-away feast aboard the *Sea Wind* that night.

When they returned from the excursion after dark, Wolfe and Sanders walked back toward their boat in order to clean up. They dawdled along the way, stopping at a few old buildings and searching with flashlights for keepsakes of their stay. When Wolfe stepped into the shed where the old fire truck was parked, he noticed right away that the rat poison was gone. Every last box of it.

Normally, Wolfe wouldn't have thought twice about the missing poison. There were enough unwanted rodents on Palmyra to justify spreading some around. But after hearing Muff go on and on about Roy the previous night—well, her paranoia was contagious. The Grahams had so many things on the *Sea Wind* that Roy and Jennifer went without. Most important, good food and plenty of it.

From his occasional work with pesticides, Wolfe knew that this particular poison, warfarin, would be fatal to humans. It had been mixed with cornmeal, shaped into cubes. A few cubes crushed up and mixed in food might never be detected. It was odorless, tasteless, and effective in very low dosages. Not that the poison would kill anyone immediately. Rather, death would be an extremely painful, drawn-out affair lasting up to a week, during which the victim would be hemorrhaging internally and frequently vomiting.

Wolfe said nothing to Sanders. As they walked the rest of the way to the *Toloa*, he forced himself to deduce a logical explanation for the disappearance of the poison. Maybe, after hearing Wolfe's story the night before, Mac had sprinkled it around the island to waste a certain pit bull. That thought was reassuring.

At the *Sea Wind's* anchorage an hour later, Wolfe took Mac aside. He didn't want Muff to hear because she was already frightened enough. "You know, the rat poison is gone."

Mac blinked, but that was all.

Wolfe couldn't read him. A crazy thought flashed up: *Is it actually Jennifer and Roy who should worry?* Nevertheless, he added, "Be careful."

"I'll keep that in mind," Mac said. His voice was level and calm.

Aboard the *Sea Wind*, Muff was already busily at work on dinner, a 1950s Betty Crocker come to life. She had cracked all the crab, a laborious job.

Mac handed Wolfe and Sanders crystal tumblers brimming with bourbon over ice. "Seems like you just got here," he said warmly. "What's your next stop?"

"Apia," Sanders answered.

"Western Samoa, huh? Muff and I especially liked Pago Pago in American Samoa. What time you shoving off tomorrow?"

"Late morning."

"We'll give you a hand with the lines."

"That'd be great," Sanders said.

Muff sat down with a cocktail of her own. She had added the crab to a pot of rice and left it simmering. A ham was baking in the oven. "I sure wish you fellows would stay longer," she said plaintively.

The table had been set with sterling flatware. Muff served dinner on hand-painted china sold in chi-chi sporting boutiques—each plate decorated with a different type of ocean fish. The meal was scrumptious. Afterward, it was obvious no one wanted to say good night. Mac served after-dinner cognac in snifters.

"You guys have a gun?" Wolfe asked abruptly, without thinking. He wasn't sure why he asked, because he knew almost every cruising boat was armed.

"Oh, yeah," Mac answered. He went to the front of the cabin, opened a cabinet door above a bunk, and came back with his two handguns. He put the .357 magnum on the table in front of Wolfe, and next to it placed a small two-shot .38-caliber derringer.

It was the derringer that Wolfe picked up, because he'd never seen one. The weapon fit nicely into the palm of his hand. He held it for a few seconds, then put it down and looked at Mac. "It would be so easy for someone to just disappear here. You guys watch yourselves."

Wolfe understood that Mac and Muff weren't the only ones taking chances. He and Sanders had thousands of miles of unpredictable ocean to cross before they could truly relax. Deep-water sailing was risky business. The Grahams lived with a different kind of risk—being on a nearly deserted island where they could expect no help in an emergency. Jennifer and Roy, too, were living precariously. What would happen if they ran out of food and realized their boat couldn't make it to another island?

"I'm tougher than him," Mac blurted out, bolting down the remaining cognac in his glass.

Everyone in the cabin knew what he meant.

"If he tries to get me," Mac said jauntily, waving the big revolver like a Dodge City gunslinger, "I'll get him first."

It sounded like more than a promise. It sounded like a dare.

AUGUST 17, 1974

ABOUT NINE o'clock the following morning, Sanders returned from shore with a Buck knife. "I traded Roy for it," he explained, sliding the knife from its leather sheath to reveal a broken blade. "These knives have a lifetime guarantee. All I have to do is mail it in and they'll send me a new one."

"What'd you give him?" Wolfe asked.

"Just a large can of chili. He said he was starved for meat."

"Jennifer brought over a loaf of bread," Wolfe said. "I didn't want to take it but she insisted. It was pretty pathetic-looking. I threw it away."

Wolfe didn't tell his shipmate that he thought of the missing rat poison when Jennifer presented her small, hard loaf of bread, though he had a difficult time picturing the friendly woman stirring such a witch's brew.

Clearly, it was time to get out of here. Although Palmyra exerted some sort of primal attraction, Wolfe no longer wanted to be a part of the dangerously strained atmosphere. There was a curious tension in the air, like the oppressive sense of heat before a storm.

At noontime, Mac and Muff came alongside in their Zodiac, and Muff handed Wolfe a bundle of letters to mail in Samoa. With Mac's help, Wolfe slipped the *Toloa*'s mooring lines off the dolphins.

Sanders put the auxiliary engine into reverse, and the *Toloa* backed into the center of the lagoon. He shifted into forward and they motored toward the channel.

Wolfe waved to Jennifer, who waved back from the deck of the *Iola*. She seemed listless. Roy was nowhere to be seen.

Mac and Muff escorted the *Toloa* down the channel as if she were a departing ocean liner. As he felt the roll of the open sea, Wolfe cranked up the main and jib.

Pulling up at the reef near the entrance to the channel, Mac and Muff climbed on top of a big rock and stood there, waving. Wolfe and Sanders returned their farewell salute. Soon, the wind filled their sails and the *Toloa* sped southward.

Mac, Muff, Jennifer, and Buck were now alone on Palmyra.

CHAPTER 14

LATE ON THE AFTERNOON of August 17, long after he'd lost sight of Palmyra, Tom Wolfe went below to write a friend in California. The letter would not be mailed for days—not until he reached Samoa—but Wolfe wanted to put his feelings into words while his impressions were fresh.

"We sailed 1,000 miles to a tropical island named Palmyra," he began. "It has plenty of room, an abundant supply of water and coconuts, and good fishing. It's really a beautiful setting, right out of a South Pacific movie, with a lagoon, palm trees, beaches, coral reefs. But living there are two couples who are close to war. It's amazing. I mean, we came to paradise and found resentment and distrust. Isn't that a sad commentary on the world we live in?"

ONE OF the letters Muff had given Wolfe to mail was addressed to the Leonards on Kauai.

August 16, 1974

Dear Evelyn and Bernard,

On August 13th another boat arrived en route to Samoa. The dogs attacked one of the fellows from the boat, biting him on the stomach. We wanted to go out and shoot or poison the dogs but didn't.

These guys who are leaving tomorrow and taking this letter

with them said they felt tension the minute they stepped ashore and started walking around. I think this place is evil. Mac cut his leg again with the machete, this time while killing a pesky sand shark that was interested in nibbling on his toes. I can't believe how he's had so many injuries here and hardly any in six years of cruising around the world.

Hope we'll see you someday soon.

Love,

Mac and Muff

Another of Muff's letters was sent to Mac's mother, with a carbon copy to his sister.

August 16, 1974

Dear Mother and Kit,

Well, life continues to be full of excitement on this practically deserted island. I'll fill you in.

August 10: Cloudy in the morning but turned gorgeous. Mac exploring. I'm cleaning cupboards. The books and everything else are going moldy from the humidity.

August 11: I could not start the generator, so Mac had to work on it. I cleaned the cabin top and decks and have discovered a menagerie of lizards, which swim out to the boat from shore. I'm afraid they will be coming inside the cabin. I'm getting so jumpy from seeing so many lizards that I won't move anything unless I jiggle it first to see if something will run out from under it.

Mac finally got the generator going. Seems it was the fuel pump. I pray nothing will happen to it as we use it to power everything, including the two-way radio. Without it, we wouldn't be able to talk to Curt and Momi, as our batteries wouldn't hold out for long.

The hippie couple brought some mullet fish by. The mullet are delicious—taste like trout. Mullets are vegetarians, so they won't bite a hook or go after bait. You have to catch them in a net.

August 12: I finished cleaning the cupboards this morning

and made some delicious pancakes from scratch, using soya flour my mother gave me (and three eggs) and boy, they were good. Mac said they were the best I ever made. The cases of food that have been in the cockpit all this time have now been merged with the supplies down below. We will supplement our diet with fish, coconuts, and palm hearts, which are very good, either raw or fried.

Roy came over to get Mac to help him with his generator. Mac fixed it. There was an icebox left here and the couple have a Sears generator, so they plugged the icebox into the generator and keep fish and coconuts and she makes coconut ice cream. They also have vegetable seedlings they are going to plant in this garden they are making on the roof of a cement blockhouse. I wonder how successful it will be. They plan to stay here and live off the land. I wish they would sail away, but no such luck. They are expecting friends with supplies.

Wind very strong from the southeast, up to 20 knots in our little cove, so it must really be blowing outside. Looks like rain. Mac is reading and resting. The only time he rests is when he is recuperating from his wounds. He came back this afternoon with his second machete wound in three weeks. He was mad at himself for doing it again.

On Kit's copy, Muff wrote an additional handwritten note.

I just wish that couple would leave with their damn dogs. They've attacked two people. Now I don't walk around without a big stick. I just know the hippie couple will never leave, though.
Love,
M and M

After the *Toloa* left, the weather broke. It rained hard for two solid days.

Jennifer put out buckets to collect drinking water, then sequestered herself in the *Iola*'s stuffy cabin, reading Michener's

Drifters between naps. During the deluge, she left the boat only once, to gather coconuts to grind into several servings for Puffer. She was determined to make the last sack of commercial dog food last as long as possible.

The weather got even worse the night of August 19. Jennifer awoke with a start sometime after midnight. The boat was tossing in the howling wind. As she came to in the dark, she thought they were at sea again. The lagoon had never been this choppy. The mooring lines must have snapped and the boat must have drifted out of the channel into the ocean!

Jennifer vaulted from the bunk and stumbled through the pitch-black cabin, banging her knee painfully on something unseen before reaching the steps that led to the deck. When she gained topside, she was relieved to see that the boat was in fact still safely tied to the dolphin. She stood for a moment in the drenching wind, amazed at the intensity of the gale. The coconut trees rattled insanely. She hurried back below.

In the morning, after very little sleep, Jennifer was delighted to find that the storm had passed and the sun was shining brightly again in a clear teal-blue sky.

Buck showed up in the afternoon. He went right to the galley without saying anything.

"What are you doing?" she asked, following him.

"Making cookies."

"We have so little flour left. Why don't you have a coconut instead?"

"I'm tired of coconuts, Jen. And I'm fucking hungry."

August 20. Transferred dirt to roof. Gave R a haircut. Soybeans for dinner. And a beautiful sunset.

August 21. Very calm day—no wind. Dug 5 loads of dirt. Wrote another note to Dickie. Will have Mac relay via ham radio to Curt Shoemaker if we don't hear something soon. Rowed out to channel, fishing. No luck at all. Loaded up on some sprouted coconuts.

August 22. Today was a day of good news and bad news. The

good news was that Dickie and Carlos finally sent word via Mac that they'd be down. The bad news was that they would not be able to make it until the end of October.

Mac had written down Curt Shoemaker's message in full: "We have been delayed by unforeseen circumstances, but hope to see you in October. We've enjoyed your letters very much. Of interest is the fact that bird eggs are considered superior eating to chicken eggs in many European countries. Hopefully, we will bring everything you need. We promise to bring a turkey for Thanksgiving dinner. See you. Richard Taylor."

October was a long way off, given their low supplies. Rough trip or not, sailing to Fanning for food was their only option, and Jennifer and Buck immediately began to make preparations for their departure.

The first thing Jennifer did was remind Mac of his offer to buy their portable generator.

August 23. Mac gave us $50 for the generator. I started cleaning up and hauling things not needed to shore. R took motor off compost shredder and converted it to bilge pump, in case manual pump breaks down.

August 24. Made further strides in getting the boat seaworthy, tho hardly looks it at a cursory glance. R started in on front hatch—he's going to fiberglass it watertight. Mac passed final death sentence on our poor old outboard. It's too far gone to be fixed. So ends our day—no dinner other than a coconut milkshake.

August 25. Not what I consider a very high energy day—but then we haven't been eating very high energy foods lately. Collected 19 sprouted coconuts and R husked some for the trip. I resumed trying to get the boat stowed and orderly but another day is needed to finish the job. For the first time in 3 days, we'll have something other than coconut for dinner—beans. Maybe we'll generate more energy tomorrow.

August 26. Got a few things accomplished today. Between R and me, we must have gathered 20-plus sprouted coconuts. Started charging the batteries. Mac brought by Fanning chart, which I copied. R put fiberglass over bow hatch due to leakage.

August 27. Gathered another 16 coconuts. Charged batteries for another several hours. At this rate, we'll be here another week.

August 28. I husked coconuts. R fixed bow hatch and did some work on bilge pump. All the while the hum of the generator attests to the charging of batteries—from morning till night. Today's Wednesday. Winds willing, we shall be ready Saturday.

August 29. Husked rest of coconuts—we have 30 to take with us. Still charging batteries. Have decks cleared and ready for a swabbing—swabbed cockpit.

KAMUELA, HAWAII
SEPTEMBER 4, 1974

"KH61HG calling W7VXV, over."

In his secluded home on the mountainous northern slope of the Big Island, Shoemaker released the talk button and waited for a response. There was none.

"Come in W7VXV," he repeated. "This is KH61HG."

It was Wednesday night and Shoemaker had been calling Mac for the past twenty minutes. The expert ham operator had checked and rechecked his equipment. Everything was A-OK on his end, and he was tight on the same frequency he and Mac had always used for their radio communications these past months. The well-organized Mac would not forget their scheduled Wednesday-night talk. He was so precise. To Shoemaker, it seemed more plausible that his friend on the *Sea Wind* might be having trouble with his radio or antenna or even the generator. It was also possible that something had come up ashore and Mac couldn't get back to the boat in time for their weekly chat. Too bad, Shoemaker thought, because he had new letters for the Grahams, and he knew how much they liked hearing news from home.

"Mac, I don't know if you can hear me," Shoemaker finally said. "But I'll try you again next Wednesday night. Same time as always. Take care, pal."

The following Wednesday evening at exactly seven o'clock, an anxious Shoemaker, with Momi at his side, tried again.

But again, there was no response from the *Sea Wind*. For more than thirty minutes the only sound from the set was the muffled static of a radio channel not in use. There were no garbled transmissions or disrupted signals—nothing at all to indicate Mac was trying to contact him. Just maddeningly meaningless pops and hisses.

"There's just nothing," Shoemaker said resignedly to Momi. "I'm afraid something has happened."

When Shoemaker miserably flipped off his transmitter, his shirt was wet through with nervous perspiration. He was worried for his friends on Palmyra. Very worried.

Though it was still possible that equipment on the *Sea Wind* had failed, Mac had made no mention of having any problems during their last contact, August 28. And even if something had acted up, Curt knew that Mac could repair the damage from his complete store of spare parts, tubes, and wiring. Shoemaker just couldn't visualize the very capable Mac seated helplessly in front of a broken-down radio set or defeated by a malfunctioning generator.

So, where were Mac and Muff? Curt's thoughts went immediately to the hippie couple on the leaky boat who were almost completely out of food. Had they stolen the *Sea Wind* and left the Grahams stranded on the island?

First thing the next morning, Shoemaker called the U.S. Coast Guard and told the duty officer about his unsuccessful attempts to reach the *Sea Wind*.

"We can't do anything until we know a boat is missing," the officer replied.

"I tell you they *are* missing."

"Just because you couldn't reach them by radio doesn't mean they are in trouble," the officer explained patiently. "Boats sail to different ports all the time."

"But my friends wouldn't have left Palmyra without contacting me," Shoemaker insisted. "Something has happened to them."

"Sir, please try to understand. We need something more concrete than what you're giving me. We just don't have the manpower to track down every sailboat in the Pacific that hasn't been heard from for a week. I'm sorry."

"So am I," Shoemaker said before slamming the receiver down.

ON A BEAUTIFUL day with clear visibility, a twin-engine aircraft descended out of a pale-blue sky and dipped low over Palmyra Island, like an albatross circling for prey.

The pilot, Martin Vitousek, a University of Hawaii meteorological researcher, was a friend of Curt Shoemaker's. Vitousek was very familiar with the islands in this part of the Pacific. He'd first visited Palmyra some years earlier while conducting weather experiments in the area, and he'd returned to the island several times since.

Vitousek had taken off from Fanning, where he was involved in a research project. A week earlier, before he left Hawaii, Shoemaker had asked him to conduct an aerial search of Palmyra.

From above, the lagoon was its usual emerald-blue. He kicked one rudder pedal, banking the aircraft to the left, eight hundred feet above the tallest trees. This pilot knew better than to fly any lower because of the very real danger of running into a horde of Palmyra's birds, which could smash a plane's windshield or even cause its engines to stop running.

He swung over the wharf area and then out over the dolphins, where he knew visiting boats usually moored. Banking next to the right, he flew along the edge of the lagoon, over the area where Curt's friends reportedly had anchored their boat. He searched the clear water for a silhouette of a sunken boat. Then he made several sweeps over the interior of the island to give anyone down below a chance to come out to the sandy beach and signal for help. Finally, he flew above the farthermost shorelines along the outer rim of the island's compact archipelago.

After thirty minutes of intense and orderly searching, he leveled the wings and pushed the throttle forward. The plane strained to gain altitude.

Vitousek picked up his radio mike and called the University of Hawaii's powerful communications station, which was located on an Oahu mountaintop. He gave the operator a short message to be passed along to Shoemaker. Vitousek knew that Curt would be anxiously waiting for the results of the search. He was just sorry he didn't have good news at all.

For there were no boats in the lagoon and, other than the omnipresent birds, no signs of life anywhere.

Palmyra was deserted.

CHAPTER 15

MID-SEPTEMBER 1974

THE SAILBOAT'S RIGGING CREAKED with the undulating motion of the ocean. Her forward speed was erratic. A gust would cause a quick acceleration, but with no hand at the tiller to correct for the shifting winds, most of the breeze would spill from her sails and she would slow to a standstill.

A gurgling came from below, where the cabin was steadily filling with seawater pouring through several holes that had been opened in the hull.

A mile or so off Palmyra, and without a living soul aboard, the doomed *Iola* sailed on.

EARLY OCTOBER 1974

SUNNY JENKINS lived with her second husband, Tom Nichols, in a mobile home park hugging the Southern California coast just north of Los Angeles. She was taken aback late one afternoon when she received a telephone call from a man named Shoemaker who asked if she'd heard from her daughter.

"Well ... not for ... awhile," she stammered. Uneasy to be talking about her daughter with a man she didn't know, she asked, "Just who are you?"

"I live in Hawaii. Some friends of mine were on Palmyra Island. We were keeping in contact by radio, but it's been over a month since I've heard from them. My wife and I are worried about them. I know your daughter and her boyfriend were there at the same time."

"Where is this, now?"

"Palmyra."

"Where's that?"

"A thousand miles south of Hawaii."

"A thousand miles?" Sunny said incredulously. That sounded like the distance between New York and south Florida. Jennifer had sailed *that* far in that little boat?

"So have you heard from her?" Shoemaker asked impatiently.

"Yes, two letters. She never told me where she was. Just that she was . . . all right."

"When was her last letter?"

"A little over two months ago, I guess. Say, how'd you find me?"

"Jennifer gave the Leonards, who were on Palmyra with your daughter, a letter to mail to you. They took down your name and address off the envelope. I'd appreciate it if you'd call me if you hear from her."

Sunny took down Shoemaker's number, then asked him to spell the name of the island. "I'm glad to know where Jennifer is. I've been so worried."

For several seconds, there was silence on the line. "Well," Shoemaker finally said, "she's not there anymore."

"What? How do you know?"

"I had someone fly over the island. He didn't see any boats."

When they hung up, Sunny went to a bookshelf and found a world atlas. It hadn't been opened for years. In the index, she found small towns named Palmyra in Illinois, Missouri, New Jersey, Pennsylvania, Wisconsin, and upstate New York. But no island. Had she taken down the correct spelling? She flipped to the Pacific Ocean page, put her finger on Hawaii, and moved downward. There it was—Palmyra was a remote, tiny dot surrounded by blue. As isolated as the place looked, Sunny would have at least known for certain where Jennifer was, but evidently she had moved on.

Sunny remained still for a long time, staring at the map of the Pacific Ocean. It had been such a relief to get Jennifer's letters and to know she had safely reached her mysterious destination. But now, familiar fears and anxieties began gnawing again, more painfully than ever. Her baby could be in grave danger at this very moment. Where in the world had she gone in all that blue?

WHATEVER HAD happened to Mac and Muff, Shoemaker believed, had to have happened against their will. Any other explanation strained logic. They had planned to stay on Palmyra for a considerable time, perhaps a year, and if they had changed their minds, they would have alerted him by radio. The purpose of staying in touch was for him to know they were all right.

Just as certainly, Shoemaker knew that the Grahams' fate had somehow intertwined or collided with that of the hippies. That's why he had called the Leonards to see if they knew how to reach Jennifer's family. Shoemaker had been in contact with this couple several times since their return from Palmyra. When Shoemaker said that he'd lost radio contact with the *Sea Wind*, the Leonards reinforced his fears by explaining that they had sensed trouble brewing on Palmyra.

But Shoemaker still couldn't get the authorities to do a damned thing. Finally, he turned to his fellow ham operators for help. At the time, there existed the Mickey Mouse Network, an extensive chain of radio amateurs operating in the Pacific. Many of the members lived aboard small boats. The network was run by a gabby New Zealander named Robby. Shoemaker radioed Robby in New Caledonia and told him the story. Beginning the following night at six o'clock—when all the network's hams were supposed to be monitoring a specific frequency—Robby put out an urgent call for assistance in locating the *Sea Wind*. "We think there's a boat missing," the message began. "Be on the lookout for a white-and-blue ketch named the *Sea Wind*." Robby gave a complete description of the sailboat and her owners. Any possible sightings of the boat were to be radioed to him immediately. Finding the boat that the Coast Guard declined to search for became the top priority of the Mickey Mouse Network.

A BEAUTIFUL THIRTY-SEVEN-FOOT sailboat, its auxiliary engine purring evenly, slid quietly into Honolulu's Ala Wai yacht harbor on the afternoon of October 28, 1974.

The sparkling white ketch was trimmed in a fresh coat of lavender. It did not pull up to any of the many dozens of crowded boat docks, with hundreds of boats moored to them, but anchored instead out in the yacht basin.

Any boating enthusiast would have instantly noticed something peculiar. No name or home port was displayed on the boat's stern.

LATER THAT day, around five o'clock, FBI Special Agent Calvin Shishido, forty-one, a Hawaii-born Nisei, received a call at his Honolulu home from a clerk in the FBI office. The Coast Guard had called to report that a missing sailboat had just been spotted in the Ala Wai.

"Why call us?" groused Shishido, who had the day off. "So they found a missing boat. Big deal."

A few minutes later, the phone rang again.

This time it was Lieutenant Bruce Wallisch of U.S. Coast Guard Intelligence. "Cal, we've been carrying a sailboat reported missing for more than a month. It's a documented vessel, number 282330, registered to a Mr. and Mrs. Malcolm Graham. We think the boat is in the Ala Wai right now, but it looks like the owners aren't aboard."

"So maybe they went shopping."

"It looks like it's been repainted."

Shishido, a pleasant-faced man with a generally kindly disposition, was more interested in trying to keep his young son from knocking a cup of milk off the kitchen table. "Maybe someone got tired of the old color, Bruce. What am I supposed to do about it?"

Keeping track of the thousands of private boats in Hawaii was not an FBI responsibility. Missing boats were routinely a matter for the Coast Guard, but because Wallisch was so insistent that the owners might have been victims of foul play, Shishido reluctantly agreed to come down to the harbor.

After service in the U.S. Air Force, followed by college on the G.I. Bill, Shishido had gone to work for the Internal Revenue Service in 1962. A few years later he ended up in Washington, D.C., for the investigation into the Johnson administration's Bobby Baker scandal. Working closely with FBI agents in the Baker case, Shishido liked what he saw in these highly professional, well-trained investigators. He applied to the FBI and was hired in 1965 as a special agent. Since 1971, he had been assigned to the Honolulu field office.

At the Hawaii Yacht Club in the Ala Wai, Shishido met with Wallisch and a very excited Bernard Leonard, who had, two hours earlier, reported the arrival of the *Sea Wind*.

He and Evelyn had sailed over from Kauai for a few days. Long-time members of the Hawaii Yacht Club, they had docked the *Journeyer* at one of the club's boat slips in the Ala Wai and had spent the afternoon picnicking at a nearby seashore park. When they returned to the yacht club, Leonard had immediately recognized the unique and elegant silhouette of the *Sea Wind*.

As he had watched, a man had pulled away from the ketch in a dinghy. According to Leonard, the man was definitely not the owner, Mac Graham, but someone named Roy Allen.

The schoolteacher uncharacteristically stumbled over his words as the whole complex story came rushing out: his missing friends, mysterious Palmyra, the menacing Roy and desperate Jennifer, the striking differences between the *Sea Wind* and the *Iola*.

Shishido still wasn't convinced that a federal crime had been committed. In fact, he wasn't sure there was evidence of *any* crime having been committed. Despite Leonard's assumptions, the owners could be ashore on a shopping trip. Maybe they had given this fellow Roy a ride up from Palmyra. Shishido could think of all kinds of plausible scenarios short of boat theft and murder.

Still, he decided to take a closer look at the nameless boat. The three men climbed into a skiff and rowed out toward it. Since no one seemed to be aboard, they circled slowly, looking for clues.

Leonard immediately pointed out some spots of blue trim paint under the fresh coat of lavender.

Although he'd grown up in Hawaii, Shishido knew very little about boats or sailing, but he was impressed by the apparent significance of the details Leonard was discovering. A gilded figurehead was missing from the bowsprit. Many of the features still visible were Mac Graham's modifications. "I'm positive this is the *Sea Wind*," Leonard said firmly. "They stole the boat and repainted it."

He directed Shishido's attention to some netting that extended around the sides of the deck. "This used to be on the *Iola*, Roy and Jennifer's boat. They used it to keep their three dogs from falling overboard."

They headed back to the yacht club landing.

"The Grahams might have given them a ride back to Honolulu," Shishido said, still disinclined to leap to the worst possible conclusion.

"If the Grahams were in Hawaii," Leonard pressed on, "they would have called. There's a fellow on the Big Island they were talking to by radio every week. He was the first one to report them missing. They would have *called* him."

"How do you know they didn't?" Shishido asked, not even trying to play the tough interrogator. "You've been out of touch on your boat for a couple of days."

Leonard was doing a slow boil. "Don't be ridiculous! The Grahams would *never* have brought Roy and Jennifer back with them on their boat. I tell you, something terrible has happened to Mac and Muff! You have to arrest Roy and Jennifer and find out what they did to Mac and Muff."

"I don't have probable cause to arrest anybody," Shishido said softly.

"So what are you going to do?" Leonard demanded. "*Nothing?*"

Shishido looked knowingly at Wallisch.

The Coast Guard officer had agreed to Shishido's request to

post a lookout. "If he comes back," Wallisch said, "we'll go out and ask some questions."

"My God," Leonard groaned, "Mac and Muff are either stranded somewhere or . . . dead. Don't you understand?"

Wallisch told Shishido he would call him as soon as he heard of anyone boarding the *Sea Wind*.

Feeling there was nothing further he could do at this point, Shishido went home for a family barbecue.

Shishido was a veteran agent, not a hot dog. Playing by the rules protected him and the Bureau. He would take his time and let the Coast Guard carry out its investigation. With jurisdiction over any boat in U.S. waters, the Coast Guard could board a vessel, check its registration papers, and ask questions of crew members any time it pleased.

Although Shishido, at the time, had no inclination to reference the law, if he had he would have learned, of course, that Palmyra was a U.S. possession, and since the faraway island was located outside any state's jurisdiction, the FBI had jurisdiction over any crime committed on the island, be it boat theft or murder. But even if the worst *had* happened and the Grahams were victims of foul play, it still might not be a federal case. For instance, if the Grahams had come back to Hawaii on their boat and been killed *after* their arrival, it would be a matter for local authorities, not the FBI. One thing Shishido *did* know. His office would be overwhelmed if it took too seriously every citizen's anxious account of serious crime. Shishido had dealt with scores of Bernard Leonards, each one imagining himself to be Sherlock Holmes. He decided he had no reason to make a move yet.

THE NEXT morning, word spread among the early-bird crowd at the Hawaii Yacht Club that something big was coming down. No one knew exactly what, but the sudden swarm of armed Coast Guard personnel in the basin was good reason to guess that a gang of drug smugglers was about to get busted.

The harbor, as usual, was packed solid with private boats of all sizes, shapes, and colors, most tied up to the docks but a few dozen anchored on the water in neat rows. Ala Wai was the largest and busiest boat basin in all of Hawaii. Often, as was the case this morning, over five hundred vessels were moored there. Even from the picture window overlooking the marina, it was impossible for curious club members to pick out the most likely target in the jumble.

Bernard Leonard had stayed at the yacht club until late the previous evening after talking to the FBI agent, waiting for something to happen. Coast Guardsmen discreetly attempted to interview several people on boats adjacent to the *Sea Wind*. Leonard thought that was a mistake, because it might tip off Roy and Jennifer that they were being sought. When no one had boarded the *Sea Wind* by midnight, Leonard returned to his own boat. It had been a long, emotionally taxing day and night.

Promised that Coast Guard authorities would bring their cutter into the harbor the next morning in order to board the *Sea Wind*, Leonard was up at dawn and walked to Coast Guard headquarters at Pier 4 about a mile away. His self-appointed role was to help identify whoever was found aboard the boat.

A few minutes after he arrived at his office that morning at eight o'clock, the FBI's Cal Shishido received a hurried call from the Coast Guard. The lookout posted near the yacht club had just reported seeing a man and woman getting ready to leave the *Sea Wind* in a dinghy. Since the lookout had obviously missed their return to the sailboat during the night, the cutter's crew had been caught unprepared. It would take a few minutes to get ready, Shishido was told, and if he could get down to Pier 4 pronto, he could join in the pursuit.

Driven in a rush by another agent, Shishido arrived at the pier three minutes later. As usual, he wore a colorful aloha print shirt,*

---

*FBI agents in Hawaii would be unwise to wear dark suits favored by agents in other locales. Two years earlier, an FBI team—including Honolulu's special agent in charge—was staking out a dangerous felon in a crowded public place when two elderly women walked by and glanced at the conservative suits. One lady remarked to her companion: "Something bad must be happening for the FBI to be here." A revised dress-code policy was handed down by the SAC the next day. In the future, all agents in Hawaii were to wear aloha shirts so as to blend in anonymously with the bright-plumaged tourists and local residents.

which stood out on deck among all the blue dungarees of the Coast Guardsmen.

The Coast Guard cutter's engine was already rumbling when Shishido stepped aboard. He nodded to Wallisch and Leonard.

The Coast Guard officer started to say something, but a crackling radio report from a lookout interrupted: "The woman dropped the guy off at one of the docks in the harbor and headed back to the sailboat." Things were getting complicated. Now there were two separate quarries.

The deckhands cast off, and the forty-foot cutter was on its way, speeding toward the harbor entrance from its nearby base.

A second report from the lookout came in: the man on the dock, apparently trying to avoid Coast Guardsmen in the harbor, had shed his clothing and dived into the water.

It took only a few minutes for the swift cutter to arrive at the Ala Wai, where it immediately swung into the harbor. From its deck, Shishido and the others spotted the dinghy—with a woman aboard—now heading lickety-split for shore.

"That's her!" Leonard cried out. "That's Jennifer!"

When Jennifer spotted the cutter closing on her, she started rowing more rapidly. She had almost reached land already.

She made it to a pile of rocks, leaped from the dinghy, and scrambled over a low seawall like a spooked lizard. From the cutter, Leonard and Shishido saw her pause momentarily to allow a small dog to catch up. She scooped it up maternally in her arms and ran toward the nearby Ilikai Marina Hotel.

AFTER DIVING into the water, Buck Walker took several powerful strokes underwater, clearing the keel of a boat, then surfaced, gulped a deep breath, and began swimming under boats and docks alike, heading in the general direction of shore.

Lungs bursting, he finally surfaced between two boats. He heard some frantic yelling. "I lost him. Anybody see him?" Buck took another deep breath and went under again. When he came up next, he was in a narrow space under a dock. He heard footsteps pounding overhead and excited voices shouting.

He cursed to himself. *Goddamn dogs! She should have left them alone.* Not more than twenty minutes before, a man on a neighboring boat had yelled to Jennifer, on her way in the dinghy to the public rest room ashore, that the Coast Guard had been around the night before asking questions about them. She returned to the boat immediately, and told Buck. He had known then it was time to abandon the *Sea Wind*, and they had done so with dispatch. As they grimly rowed to shore, Buck's two dogs—left behind on deck—began barking loudly. Jennifer, apparently afraid they would disturb the neighbors, wanted to return and put them below deck. Buck had argued that the idea was crazy. When she insisted, he demanded she drop him off first at the nearest dock. They had intended to meet at the bathhouse on the beach. But as he was walking up the dock toward shore, he had spotted an armed Coast Guardsman off in the distance coming his way. Buck turned down a narrow offshoot of one dock, slowing his pace so as not to look suspicious. Pretending to be interested in the boats tied up on either side of him, he watched the serviceman out of the corner of his eye. While the detour had prevented a face-to-face encounter for the moment, it had also cut off Buck's access to shore. He was trapped. When, a minute or so later, the serviceman started getting closer, Buck didn't hesitate. He quickly stripped down to a bathing suit he had on and dove in.

Now, under a dock, Buck didn't move a muscle. He stayed where he was long after his teeth began chattering from the cold water.

IN HOT pursuit of Jennifer, Bernard Leonard and Lieutenant Wallisch had immediately gone ashore in a launch.

Shishido, still no more than an observer of a Coast Guard inquiry, elected to stay aboard the cutter.

Pulling up where Jennifer had abandoned the *Sea Wind*'s dinghy, Leonard and the officer ran toward the hotel. In the lobby, they rounded a pillar and spotted a woman crouching ludicrously behind a potted plant near the elevators. She was cradling a small dog.

Leonard, his heart pounding, nodded at the officer.

"Miss," the Coast Guardsman said, "you'll have to come with us."

Jennifer stood up, keeping a hold on Puffer. "Hi, Bernie," she said with a sheepish grin.

"Hello, Jennifer," he responded sternly.

"I want to tell you what happened. I really do. But can I go to the bathroom first?"

The officer replied that they had to return to the ship immediately. He put his hand under her elbow and led the way out of the hotel lobby.

Outside, he decided to tow the *Sea Wind*'s dinghy with the cutter's launch. He asked Leonard to stay with Jennifer in the dinghy for the short ride.

Once they pushed off from shore, Leonard looked solemnly at Jennifer and asked: "Are Mac and Muff alive?"

"You'll never believe what happened. They invited us over for dinner. They were going fishing and they knew they were going to be late. They told us to make ourselves at home. After dark, we turned on the masthead light and waited all night for them. They never showed up. The next morning, we went looking for them and found the Zodiac capsized. We searched for days and didn't find any sign of them. We left a few days later on the *Iola*, but she got hung up on the reef, and when we couldn't get her off, we went back and got the *Sea Wind*."

"You wouldn't have left on the *Iola*," Leonard said in a tone that suggested he wasn't buying one syllable of her story. "Not with the *Sea Wind* sitting there."

She looked at him, but didn't say anything.

They pulled alongside the cutter, which had come down the channel toward the hotel. They boarded and then climbed down a ladder to a compartment below deck. Cal Shishido was waiting with several Coast Guard investigators.

"Are you Jennifer Allen?" asked Wallisch.

"Yes—er, well, Jenkins," she stammered, sounding nervous. "Jennifer Jenkins is my name."

"What is the name of the boat you came here on?"

"The *Sea Wind*."

"Whose boat is it?"

"Mac and Muff Graham's."

"What happened to them?" the officer asked.

"They drowned on a fishing trip," Jennifer replied without hesitation. "It was an accident."

Shishido stepped in to advise Jennifer of her constitutional rights. The boat's owners were missing under suspicious circumstances, and this woman had ended up on their boat, which had been sailed to Hawaii. At the very least, he had reason to believe that the federal crime of interstate transportation of stolen property had been committed.* Of course, the agent was now far more concerned about the fate of the Grahams. If their deaths had truly been accidental, why hadn't Jenkins and Allen reported the incident to authorities immediately upon their return to Hawaii?

For the next hour, Jennifer recounted how she and her boyfriend had ended up on Palmyra, become friends with the Grahams, and been upset by their puzzling disappearance. This discourse was interrupted only twice—once when she finally was allowed to use the bathroom, and again when she was taken back to the *Sea Wind* to restrain Buck's dogs so that authorities could search the vessel. On the return trip to the cutter, Jennifer dropped off Puffer at a nearby boat whose owner agreed to look after the pet.

Developments in the search for Roy Allen were relayed to Shishido throughout the morning. Jennifer's boyfriend had not been seen since diving into the water. The pants and shirt he'd shucked at the end of the dock were brought to the cutter, and Shishido went through them.

Inside a wallet, he found a Hawaii driver's license and ID picture in the name of Roy Allen. There was also a separate small photo of the same man wearing a clerical collar.

Shishido held up the driver's license and asked Jennifer if this was her companion, whom she had previously identified by the name of Roy Allen.

*Under the U.S. Code, "interstate" transportation of stolen property occurs not only when the property is transported from one state to another, but from a U.S. possession, such as Palmyra, to a state.

"Yes," she said.

"Is he a minister?" the agent asked.

Jennifer smiled. "Universal Life Church. You know, that place in California that will ordain you through the mail for ten dollars."

"I see." He put the wallet down. "Tell me, if the Grahams were killed in an accident and you did nothing wrong, why were you attempting to flee?"

"We came here on a boat that doesn't belong to us." She looked as if she wanted to say something more.

"Is that all?"

She simply nodded.

Shishido later wrote up a summary of what Jennifer told him: His report read in part:

> Jennifer Jenkins furnished the following information: On the last Friday in August, 1974, she and Roy Allen were making preparations to leave Palmyra the next day. She was on the boat *Iola* while ALLEN was on shore. He returned and told her that they were invited to dinner at the GRAHAM'S boat the *Sea Wind*. ALLEN left the *Iola* and stated he was going to take a bath and went ashore. He returned shortly after and told her that the GRAHAMS told him that they were going fishing for the evening dinner and would be a little late but to make themselves at home. The dinner invitation was for 6:30 P.M. that evening. At about 6:30 P.M., she and ALLEN went aboard the *Sea Wind* to await the GRAHAMS' return. The GRAHAMS did not return that evening, and she and ALLEN spent the night aboard the *Sea Wind*.
>
> The next morning she and ALLEN conducted a search of the area and located a dinghy overturned in the lagoon at Cooper islet, part of Palmyra Island. The dinghy was the Zodiac dinghy which was used by the GRAHAMS the day before when they went fishing. The outboard motor on the dinghy was also overturned, and they found the gas tank floating in the lagoon nearby. They turned the dinghy upright, reattached the gas tank, and continued further searching in the Zodiac. They continued the search for the GRAHAMS until September 11, 1974,

and finally decided the GRAHAMS were gone. Since they did not know how to operate a radio, they were unable to call for assistance or to report the incident.

They rationalized the GRAHAMS last statement to them to make themselves at home to mean the GRAHAMS would like for her and ROY ALLEN to keep the boat if anything happened to them. They therefore tied a 50-foot tow rope to the *Iola* and attempted to tow it back to Honolulu with the *Sea Wind*. She was on the *Iola* steering and ROY ALLEN was on the *Sea Wind*. On September 11, the *Iola* ran into a reef while being towed out of Palmyra and when last seen was still stuck on the reef.

They arrived at Nawiliwili, Kauai, on the *Sea Wind* October 12, 1974. They stayed at Nawiliwili overnight and sailed to Pokai Bay, Oahu, arriving October 15, 1974. They stayed at Pokai Bay about one week, left and arrived at Keehi Lagoon on October 21, 1974. The next day, they docked at Kewalo Basin and dry docked the *Sea Wind* at the Tuna Packers. There, she and ALLEN repainted the boat another color. The boat was in dry dock for a week, and on October 28, it went back into the water, and they went to the Ala Wai Yacht Harbor, arriving there in the late afternoon.

She and ALLEN found $400 in currency on the *Sea Wind*, consisting of $20 bills—$300 in a book, and $100 in MALCOLM GRAHAM'S wallet located under the floor board of the *Sea Wind*.

She stated the *Sea Wind* did not belong to them but they loved it as much as the GRAHAMS and thought the GRAHAMS would like for them to have it. She also stated they did not report the incident at Palmyra to proper authorities upon arrival in Hawaii because they knew the boat would be taken from them.

Bernard Leonard, who had listened closely to Shishido's interview of Jennifer, was finding it almost impossible to remain silent. He believed Mac and Muff would never tell anyone to "make themselves at home" on the *Sea Wind* when they weren't there. And the idea that the Grahams would make such an offer to Roy and Jennifer, *of all people*, was preposterous.

Moreover, Leonard had quietly fumed when Jennifer now claimed that the *Iola* had gotten hung up on a reef at Palmyra while it was being *towed* by the *Sea Wind*—a direct contradiction of her story to him just minutes earlier that she and Roy had intended to leave Palmyra on the *Iola*, and while attempting to sail it, not tow it, out of the channel, it went aground, necessitating their returning to get the *Sea Wind*. Obviously, she had changed her story because he had scoffed at it. *She's a liar*, he thought. *And undoubtedly a murderer, too.*

Shishido handcuffed Jennifer and escorted her off the cutter.

By then, the news media had gotten wind of the action at the Ala Wai, and newspaper photographers and TV camera crews eagerly filmed Jennifer as she was led off the cutter on her way to FBI headquarters for further questioning. Her arrest—the opening volley in what promised to be a big story—made the lead of the evening news and the following morning's front pages.

Later that afternoon, Jennifer was booked into the Honolulu jail on charges of stealing the *Sea Wind* and four hundred dollars cash from Mac and Muff Grahamn. Bail was set at twenty thousand dollars.

AFTER HIDING under the dock an hour or so, Buck heard a group of more leisurely footsteps and quieter voices approach. As they passed overhead, a woman's voice asked, "What in the world has been going on around here?"

"Someone said they're looking for a murderer," a man answered.

But no one was there to see Buck Walker when, around noon-time, he finally emerged from the water—chilled to the bone, exhausted, desperate, frightened.

THE NEXT day, Cal Shishido headed for the Drug Enforcement Administration's office in Honolulu's federal building. He was following through on a hunch. Jenkins and Allen weren't your regular yachties. They were hippie dropouts, with all that that might imply. No large quantities of heavy-duty drugs had been found on the *Sea Wind*, just some marijuana seeds and stems in a small plastic bag. Even so, the couple had arrived in Hawaii on a boat that didn't belong to them—drug runners often used stolen boats to cover their trail when smuggling drugs in these waters—and Shishido suspected there might be a drug connection in the case. He needed any leads he could get on the mysterious Roy Allen.

At the DEA, Shishido showed the Roy Allen driver's license to the first agent he came across.

"Hey, that's Buck Walker," said the surprised DEA man. "Where did you get his picture?"

"You know him?"

"Yeah, we're after his ass."

Shishido couldn't believe his luck. For the very first DEA agent to know the fugitive's identity was more than he could have hoped for. Some aliases hold up for weeks, even months.

The agent walked over and handed the license to a colleague seated several desks away. "Tell Shishido who this turkey is," he said.

"Buck Walker," said the deskbound agent without a moment's hesitation. "He sold to an undercover agent, pled out, and skipped before sentencing."

"When?" Shishido asked.

"About six months ago. You got a lead on him?"

"He jumped off a dock at the Ala Wai two days ago and swam for it when he saw us coming," Shishido said.

"Whaddaya know. Buck Walker's back."

CHAPTER 16

SUNNY HAD BEEN SO conscientiously tending her roses that she nearly missed the phone. "Hello," she gasped, out of breath from hurrying into the house.

"Hi, Mom."

"Jennifer—thank God!" Sunny exclaimed. "Where are you?"

"Hawaii."

"Are you all right?"

"Yes and no. I'm not hurt or anything, but I'm in jail."

"*Jail?* Jennifer, what for?"

"For stealing a boat," she said. "Only we didn't really steal it. See, Mac and Muff, this nice couple on the island with us, died in a boating accident. We sailed their boat to Hawaii and the cops arrested me for boat theft. Will you bail me out?"

"Where's Buck?" Sunny asked warily.

"I don't know. He ran away."

Sunny thought quickly. If Jennifer got out on bail, she might well hook up with Walker and take off again.

"I'm not going to get you out, honey. Not now."

"Mom . . ."

"No," Sunny said firmly. "You're safe and sound. At least I know where you are. That's the way I want to keep it for now."

ON THE morning of October 30, San Diego–based FBI special agents Darwin Wisdom and Earl Harris drove out to see Muff's mother, Rose King, who lived in a modest bungalow on Meade Avenue in San Diego.

The visitors settled on the couch in the sensibly furnished living room. Mrs. King, frail and white-haired, sat with her hands clasped like a vise in her lap. She knew that her daughter and son-in-law had been out of touch, and their sailing friends in Hawaii were very concerned. Like any worried parent, she had tried to avoid thinking the worst. Surely, they would show up. They were so well prepared for anything.

Also present was Muff's sister, Peggy Faulkner, a demure woman in her mid-forties who was slimmer and taller then her sister.

Both women listened intently as the agents briefed them on the previous day's events in Hawaii. It sounded like the plot for a television show, not something that actually touched on the lives of one's own family.

For Mrs. King, the most frightening part was that the *Sea Wind* had been found in the hands of strangers, with her daughter and Mac nowhere around. They would *never* abandon their boat. "Where *are* they?" she asked forlornly.

"We don't know," Wisdom answered. "All we know is that your daughter and her husband are missing. With the Coast Guard's help, we'll be searching for them, of course. In the meantime, it would be helpful if you could provide us with some information."

After Mrs. King gave the agents a physical description of LaVerne, as she called Muff ("born on December 18, 1932, in Pueblo, Colorado, blond hair, blue eyes, 5-foot-3, 135 lbs., appendectomy scar," etc.), she gave them several letters Muff had sent from Palmyra. The agents also borrowed a recent photo of Mac and Muff, smiling and holding hands, aboard the *Sea Wind*.

"Just a few other matters," said Wisdom, sensitive to the worried mother's distress.

Mrs. King nodded.

"Do you know how much cash they had when they departed for Palmyra?"

"My impression is that they took four or five thousand dollars to Hawaii," Muff's sister answered for her mother. "I don't know if they intended to take that much with them to Palmyra. They had enough food and supplies on their boat to last them two years."

"Did either Mr. and Mrs. Graham drink?" Harris asked.

"Rarely." Peggy Faulkner seemed to have put up her guard. "Neither was a heavy drinker."

"There was that ticket, honey," Mrs. King said quietly, peering over the top of rose-hued bifocals at her daughter.

"My sister was arrested for drunk driving just before she and Mac left on their trip."

The agent was scribbling away in his pad.

"But it was very unlike her," Peggy added with conviction. "Really."

Muff had had a bad case of hepatitis when she was in her late twenties, Mrs. King explained, and the doctors had advised her to avoid alcohol.

"Do you know if anything was bothering her around the time of the drunk driving?" asked Wisdom, his curiosity roused.

Simultaneously, mother and daughter shook their heads no.

Muff had never told them of her fears.

AT 4:30 P.M. on November 1, some forty hours after Jennifer's arrest at the Ala Wai harbor, the *Tattarax*, an oceangoing tugboat skippered by Martin Vitousek, chugged into the Palmyra lagoon he had earlier flown over at Curt Shoemaker's request.

Aboard the dirty, rust-splotched hundred-foot tug was a ten-man search team that included the FBI's Shishido and Tom Bridges, Honolulu Assistant U.S. Attorney William Eggers, a representative of the U.S. Department of the Interior, several Coast Guard divers, and Jack Wheeler, who would be their island guide.

The trip from Honolulu had not been easy. Climbing aboard a Coast Guard C-130 at 7:00 A.M. on October 31, the expedition had flown from Oahu's Barbers Point Naval Air Station through an overcast that hung down the mountainsides like a dark, heavy blanket. Four and a half hours later, they landed at Fanning Island, where they boarded the tug for a twenty-two-hour trip to Palmyra, 175 miles to the northwest. Halfway there, a pump broke down and the toilets couldn't be flushed. A compartment below deck offered half a dozen bunks, but no one had slept much as the vibrating old tug plowed through choppy seas.

When they moored at the dolphins in the Palmyra lagoon, there were no other boats there, nor could prosecutor Bill Eggers, from where he stood on the deck of the tug, see any sign of people on the island. He had already noted, as they came through the channel, that there was no sailboat hung up on the reef where Jennifer Jenkins had claimed the *Iola* had gone aground and been abandoned. Almost certainly, she had lied, and he was pretty sure he knew why.

Taking charge of the mission, Eggers suggested they immediately begin a thorough search, even though some of the others wanted to rest from their journey. Once ashore, they paired up to fan out in different directions. Their objectives were obvious. First and foremost, to find the Grahams—alive, or dead. And second, to gather any physical evidence that a crime had been committed.

The jungle rose only a few yards away, yet there was a collective pause before anyone in the search party made the first move. No one looked forward to whatever awaited them inside the dense growth. And the raucous squawking of the birds was somehow strangely daunting.

Eggers himself, a square-shouldered veteran criminal prosecutor with a boyish grin during happier times, had a nasty intuition about this stifling-hot place. He hoped he was wrong, but he believed, as Shishido now did, that a monstrous crime had been committed here. People didn't give up a boat like the *Sea Wind* in a desolate place like Palmyra without a struggle. Whatever had happened to Mac and Muff Graham must have involved force and violence.

Eggers teamed up with Wheeler for the search. They walked around the West Lagoon's shoreline to the *Sea Wind*'s former anchorage. When they came across an old campfire site, Eggers found a stick and poked through the charred mess. At first, he uncovered only some empty, unmarked prescription bottles.

Mopping his face with a rolled-up sleeve already soaked with sweat, Wheeler watched the prosecutor jab at the refuse.

"My God . . ." Eggers muttered.

They were both shocked to see what looked like a mass of human hair among the ashes.

Eggers reached cautiously for the hair. It was coal-black.

When he separated the hair from the other debris, Eggers was relieved to see it was actually a wig—a type of "fright wig" worn by Halloween tricksters.

Probing deeper, Eggers retrieved several bits of cotton cloth— possibly from a shirt that had been burned—and two eyeglass lenses, one from nonprescription dark glasses and one clear prescription lens. He placed the recovered items in a gunnysack he'd brought along.

Wheeler led the way to the site of Roy Allen's camp, where the tent still stood. Inside, they found a bare cot, an armchair, and a bedside table upon which lay the beginnings of a homemade braided belt and a sketchbook with drawings of sailboat designs. In a corner of the tent a small bookcase held a variety of books and magazines.

Outside, on a bench, were quite a few tin cans and paper cups, all half-filled with dirt. Nearby, on the roof of the Refrigerator House, was a thriving garden of foot-high marijuana plants.

That afternoon, they all met back at the tugboat for ham and cheese sandwiches and chilled beer. Eggers asked the divers to gear up to check out the bottom of the lagoon near the dolphins. He didn't have to spell out what to look for. Two Coast Guardsmen, outfitted with scuba tank, face mask, and flippers, dived off the deck, while another stood guard with an automatic rifle. The sharks of Palmyra could be seen circling in the blue lagoon.

When nothing was found near the dolphins, the divers took a dinghy to the small cove where the *Sea Wind* had been anchored and searched the bottom carefully. Arousing the aggressive instincts of the sharks, the dive was soon suspended for safety reasons.

Eggers assigned each team new quadrants to search. He and Wheeler took a dinghy across the lagoon and beached it, then set out to wade across a stretch of knee-deep water—too shallow, they thought, for sharks.

Wheeler was the first to notice a sleek, gray shark at least six feet long circling lazily in the crystalline blue of the lagoon. "I don't think it'll attack," he said with a definite edge in his voice.

Suddenly, as if it had heard and was determined to disprove Wheeler's assessment, the shark moved soundlessly toward them, its curved fin breaking the surface like a submarine periscope. The wide snout left no doubt the creature had a mouth big enough to amputate a leg in one quick chomp.

They could not outrun it to shore!

Wheeler spotted a coral head nearby, and they ran awkwardly toward it, splashing and floundering about like a flight of wounded birds fighting to get airborne. Their tormentor brushed closely against their coral perch. Eggers saw a pair of eyes beneath the surface reflecting an eerie golden light. Now that they were out of the water, could the shark still see them?

Apparently not. And for this big fellow, out of sight was out of mind, as it swam on and was soon gone.

When they regained their composure, Wheeler and Eggers waded quickly back to where they'd left the dinghy. There would be no more dips in the lagoon this day.

By dusk, the searchers were back at the boat, thoroughly drained by the hot sun, the humidity, and the jungle. Wheeler and Eggers mesmerized the others with the story of their run-in with the "man-eater."

Gathered on the tug's deck as sunset shimmered over the water, they discussed what they had and had not found. There was not one shred of evidence that the Grahams were still on the island, dead or alive, nor had anyone found any physical evidence of any kind that even vaguely suggested foul play. Eggers and Wheeler had found and photographed a hatch cover on the beach near the dolphins, and Wheeler was sure it belonged to the *Iola*. But that didn't seem very helpful.

At dawn the next morning, the *Tattarax* left Palmyra. En route to Fanning, the tug sent a radio signal to a ham operator in Honolulu who had Mac Graham's sister standing by waiting to hear from the search party. Calvin Shishido identified himself.

"This is Mary Muncey," said a woman's unsteady voice over the radio. "Are my brother and sister-in-law alive . . . or dead?"

"I don't have an answer for you one way or the other, Mrs. Muncey," Shishido said, not telling Mac's sister, of course, that the searching party had expectantly brought along two body bags. "All I can tell you at this point is that we were unable to find any sign of either of them."

Mac and Muff Graham had vanished, not leaving so much as a footprint on Palmyra.

DARK-HAIRED, ATTRACTIVE Mary "Kit" Graham Muncey had flown to Honolulu the day after Jennifer's arrest. No one sitting next to her on the plane could have guessed that this self-contained woman was experiencing a family tragedy. Divorced (since 1969) and living in Seattle, she'd once been married to Bill Muncey, at the time the world's most famous boat racer. After years of watching her husband—the father of her three sons—hurtle across the water at two hundred miles an hour, Kit had learned to conceal her deepest fears beneath a placid exterior.

While waiting in Honolulu to hear word from the search party, Kit had surrendered to nostalgic reminiscences of her life with Mac. As a little brother, he'd been a terror. While growing up in Connecticut, they had been highly competitive and fought a lot. But everyone noticed that when Mac and Kit—shortened from Kitten, her father's pet name for her—weren't arguing, they were sharing toys and playing together like pals. They spent much of their time exploring the countryside around their home, using back roads and staying out of sight. When they'd come across a horse in a pasture, they'd climb aboard with no saddle or reins. "Oh, Mac, we had such great fun," she would have liked to remind him now. As adults, brother and sister had remained close. Kit was so pleased when Mac had found, in Muff, a loving woman to spend his life with. Mac had been just as supportive of her. Bill Muncey was a man's man—Mac's kind of guy—and her brother had been pained by her divorce from Bill, but he'd let her know that her happiness was paramount.

She had last seen her brother and sister-in-law six months earlier, in April. Knowing they were preparing to leave for a long voyage to the Pacific, she'd flown down to San Diego to spend a few days with them. Mac had been feverishly excited about this new adventure, but Muff, in a moment of girl-talk candor, had confided to Kit that she really didn't want to go. Alone with Mac, Kit gently chided him for not being more sensitive to Muff's feelings.

This trip was very important to him, he had replied, and he was confident that once they reached their island paradise, Muff would end up enjoying it, too.

For weeks now, Kit had been praying long and hard that Mac and Muff would be found on Palmyra—stranded, blazing mad over losing their boat, maybe a little hungry and parched, but alive. After hearing the distressing news from the search party, however, she realized she might never again see her brother or Muff.

Desperate for any information about what had happened on Palmyra, Kit agonized over whether she should contact Jennifer Jenkins in jail. She finally decided that she had no choice. She could not rest until she talked to the one person available who might know what happened to Mac and Muff.

Even if that person might have had a hand in whatever horrible fate had befallen them.

NOVEMBER 7, 1974

KIT WAS uneasy as she sat across from Jennifer in the Honolulu jail visiting room, looking directly into the wide-eyed gaze of someone who she felt probably knew everything but hadn't admitted to anything. If at all possible, she was determined to hide her suspicions.

"Has anyone told you about the sharks?" Jennifer asked.

Kit nodded. "Yes, Mac and Muff wrote about them."

"They're real bad in the lagoon. I think, you know, that's what might have happened. After they flipped their dinghy and fell into the water—well, the sharks—"

Kit tensed noticeably, clutching her purse.

Jennifer changed course. "As I said, we found the Zodiac turned over, upside down. I'm sorry." She lowered her head. "I'm really sorry. It was such a tragedy. Mac and Muff were wonderful people. They were good to us."

Kit could see that Jennifer had a bearing of unaffected friendliness. She obviously got along well with others—even the jail matron who brought her in seemed to like her. Kit could not easily picture Jennifer in the act of murder. Then again, she reminded herself, this could all be a very skillful act, the ploy of a manipulative little bitch who had always known how to use people. There was a slippery, evasive quality to Jennifer, or so Kit thought.

Mac's sister left the jail more puzzled than ever. Jennifer's story simply didn't add up. Kit well knew that the Zodiac, designed by the famed French oceanographer Jacques Cousteau, was reputed to be the most stable dinghy in the world. In fact, she had never heard of one flipping over, even in the hands of children or rank amateurs. Moreover, if Mac and Muff had actually disappeared in some sort of freak accident, why hadn't Jennifer and her boyfriend reported the incident as soon as they reached Hawaii?

Kit was firmly convinced that Jennifer was holding something back.

NOVEMBER 8, 1974
HAWI, HAWAII

AROUND NOONTIME, Buck Walker sat down at the picnic table beneath the shade of a banyan tree and spread out that day's *Honolulu Advertiser*. He was interested in only one story—and it was prominently featured on the front page, along with head shots of him and Jennifer. Even his two dogs had become media celebrities since being impounded by animal regulation officials. Dozens of people had called about adopting them.* Now that the FBI knew his real name, a detailed all-points bulletin had been issued for his arrest. The formal charge: boat theft. But the article focused on unexplained disappearances, rumors of conflict, and a possible double murder on an obscure, exotic island.

For ten days he'd been on the move. No one had noticed him come ashore after swimming the length of Ala Wai harbor. Luckily, he'd had some money in the swim trunks he'd been wearing under his trousers. He'd walked dripping wet into a clothing store

---

*After completing a six-month impoundment to ensure they were disease-free, Popolo and Sista were separately adopted in May 1975 by Oahu families.

and bought an aloha shirt, shorts, a straw hat, and wraparound sunglasses. Looking like a tourist, he'd lost himself in the large crowd of vacationers, occasionally glancing back to make sure no one had recognized him. He'd crashed at a friend's apartment that night.

The next day, he'd taken a bus to the airport, bought a plane ticket under the name of J. Evans, and, right under the nose of a Honolulu cop holding his picture, passed through the gate and boarded an Aloha Airlines jet for the short hop to Hilo. When he arrived, he'd walked from the sleepy airport to the nearest hotel, about a mile away—cab drivers, he knew, were among the first people the police contacted when looking for someone on the run. The next day, he popped in on Gina Allen at her little frame house in a run-down section of Hilo. She had broken up with her boyfriend and seemed pleased to see Buck. They spent the night together. The following morning she lent him some camping equipment and went shopping for a few other essentials for hiding out—food, matches, cigarettes, hunting knife, eating utensils, boots, jeans, shirts, and various toiletries. Later that day, she drove him thirty miles up Saddle Road into the island interior and dropped him off in the Kohala Mountains.

Buck camped out for a week in the desolate volcanic range, which has peaks almost fourteen thousand feet high, reading Carlos Castaneda and smoking marijuana. Once, stoned out of his mind, he stripped off his clothes and ran joyously through the Kohala forest during a light, warm rain, dancing to his own internal rhythms, feeling as wild and free as the occasional white-tailed deer he spotted. He could look down upon smooth black fields of pahoehoe lava or imagine that a pile of stones was a heiau, an abandoned Polynesian temple. But his physical comfort soon became a priority, as on Palmyra. He decided to chance going into town to get a hot meal and a good night's sleep on a real bed. He picked Hawi, the northernmost community on the Big Island, relatively isolated up near Upolu Point. Two roads led into the village—population 797—both unpaved and often impassable in bad weather. The sidewalks were wooden, suggesting a town right out of America's Old West. After hitching his way down Kohala Mountain Road, Buck checked into Room 19 at the St. Luke's Hotel, giving his name as Joe Evans. The unpretentious room cost $7.28 a night, and he paid for three nights in advance. It was Friday, November 8, as he perused the morning paper at the picnic table.

Though Buck hadn't noticed—because he was new in town himself—several strangers were eating lunch right then at the St. Luke's café. When they finished, they showed the waitress a photo of a man in a clerical collar.

"He's staying here," she said excitedly. "In fact, he bought a paper just before you came in." Pointing out the window, she added: "That's him right there across the street, sitting under the tree."

By the time Buck looked up to see them coming, it was too late.

"FBI! Don't move!"

Several revolvers pointed at his chest.

"Are you Bob Walker?" an agent asked.

"Buck," he corrected, closing the newspaper. "Yes, I'm Buck Walker."

"You're under arrest," said FBI Special Agent Henry Burns.

"No shit."

Buck was put in the backseat of a rented car, his wrists handcuffed under his legs.

Burns, thickset, about forty, climbed in beside Buck and read Buck his rights. That formality over, the agent sat back. "Mind answering a few questions?"

For Burns, the long moment that followed was tense with uncertainty. Stony silence is a suspect's strongest defense.

But Walker shrugged flippantly, with an air of arrogance. "Depends on the questions."

"Where've you been staying?"

"St. Luke's."

"Mind if we search your room?"

"I don't care."

Burns told two members of his team to search the hotel room.

"You forgot to tell me why I'm under arrest," Buck said sarcastically. "J. Edgar Hoover wouldn't approve."

"Boat theft. We've also got a fugitive warrant charging you with failure to appear."*

The old drug charge that had started it all.

"I'd like to ask you some questions about the Grahams," the agent said, taking out a small, creased notebook. "We're investigating their disappearance."

"Who said they disappeared?" Buck asked coyly.

"Jennifer Jenkins has made a statement."

"Ask away."

"To start with, when did you meet Jennifer?"

"In late '72, I guess." Buck looked off into the distance. "Been together ever since."

"You were living together?"

"Uh-huh."

"How did you get to Palmyra Island?"

"By boat," Buck said, smirking. "Know another way?"

"Your own boat?"

Buck nodded. "We bought her on Maui a couple years ago and fixed her up. Named her the *Iola*."

"When was the last time you saw the Grahams?"

"On August 30th."

"What happened that day?"

"I met Mac on shore and he invited us over to the *Sea Wind* for dinner that night. There was just the four of us on the island then. Jenny and I went over there about six o'clock that night. The Grahams weren't there. We waited about half an hour, then went aboard the *Sea Wind*. I remember Mac said they were going fishing for our dinner, so we just figured that they were late getting back."

"Did you see them leave to go fishing?"

"Yeah. They went in their Zodiac."

"What were they wearing?"

"Mac was wearing a T-shirt and shorts. Mrs. Graham was wearing a bathing suit and hat of some kind."

"You never saw them again?"

*"Jumping bail."

"No. We spent the night on the *Sea Wind*. In the morning, we went out and hunted for them. We found the Zodiac overturned about a hundred yards west of the *Sea Wind*."

"If it was only a hundred yards away, you must have been able to see the overturned dinghy without having to search for it," the agent said without missing a beat.

"It must have been farther away than that. Maybe half a mile."

"What did you do next?"

"Went over to the dinghy and turned it upright. Nothing seemed to be damaged. I took several pulls on the engine and it turned over. We spent the next three days looking for the Grahams. Never found a trace of them."

"Did you make any attempt to call for help?"

"We didn't have a two-way radio. There was a radio on the *Sea Wind*, but we didn't know how to use it."

"So, you left Palmyra on the *Sea Wind*?"

"We were going to tow the *Iola* to Fanning. We were using the *Sea Wind*'s inboard motor to get through the channel, with the *Iola* in tow, when the *Iola* got hung up on the reef. We couldn't get her off, so I cut our line and we kept going through the channel. We anchored the *Sea Wind* out past the reef, and I went back in the dinghy to try to free the *Iola*. I put up the sail and tried to get the wind to help her break free. But it didn't work. We took all our things off and put them on the *Sea Wind*."

"You just left the *Iola* on the reef?"

"Yes."

"And sailed off on the *Sea Wind*?"

"Right."

"So, you headed directly for Hawaii on the *Sea Wind*?"

Buck nodded. He obviously felt he had gotten past the hard part. "Kauai, actually. We spent the night there, then sailed the next day to Oahu."

The other agents returned to the car. They had found nothing of any value as evidence in the hotel room.

"Did you do anything to the *Sea Wind* after reaching Hawaii?" Burns asked as they pulled away from the curb.

"Yeah. We repainted her."

"Why?"

"Because she needed a paint job."

"Why did you take the name off the boat?"

Buck shrugged nonchalantly, as if he was beginning to lose interest in the conversation.

"You say the *Sea Wind* needed to be repainted," Burns continued.

"We'd been rammed by a swordfish on the way back to Hawaii. Its bill went through the hull. I had to go over the side to patch the hole so it wouldn't leak so much."

"That's why the whole boat needed to be repainted?" Burns asked disbelievingly.

"Yeah."

"When did you come to the Big Island?"

"About a week ago."

"Why?"

Buck looked at the agent as if he were a piece of dog meat.

"Because I didn't want to get caught, stupid."

The agent looked up from his notebook. "So, how'd you dispose of their bodies?" he asked abruptly.

"Fuck off."

So ended the FBI's first, and as it would turn out to be, last question-and-answer session with Buck Walker.

CHAPTER 17

SUNDAY, NOVEMBER 10, 1974

A DOZEN OR SO people, all deeply tanned and dressed in sports clothes, gathered quietly aboard the *Journeyer* for a short trip in choppy seas. Their collective mood was decidedly somber but not mournful. By common agreement this was not to be a funeral service, but rather an informal Hawaiian "service of aloha." On the other hand, though Mac and Muff were officially still only missing, not dead, like one coming out of anesthesia, everyone had slowly begun to face the sobering reality that it was time to bid a final farewell to Mac and Muff.

Bernard Leonard, wearing Bermudas and a bright-colored shirt, shut down the motor when they were a couple miles off world-famous Diamond Head. The boat bobbed up and down, and for a long moment the only noise was water slapping against the hull. Then a tall, graying man wearing sunglasses moved forward. An experienced yachtsman and coach of the University of Hawaii's sailing team, he was also a minister.

"On behalf of the families of Malcolm and Eleanor Graham," the minister began, "I should like to thank each of you for joining us in this service of aloha."

Kit, wearing a stylish sundress, was thankful that both mothers had decided against traveling to Hawaii. Elderly and frail, facing devastating loss as well as the strain of not knowing what had happened, they would surely have found the trip unbearable. *Yes, thank God they didn't come*, Kit thought.

"Mac and Muff and the *Sea Wind* sailed the oceans of the world together for many years," the minister went on. "Mac was a supremely capable seaman. A man for all seasons and all situations. A man content with life, yet not completely satisfied. There still were new horizons, and new landfalls beckoning him.

"Muff, I have learned, never felt quite so much at home upon the sea. She found power to overcome a fear of the great expanses of the oceans they traversed, in her confidence and trust in the man she loved. She would sail anywhere with Mac."

Kit could no longer hold back the tears.

"Their dream, their quest, was so wrongfully interrupted at Palmyra Island. But God has not forsaken Mac and Muff.

"We cannot fully understand the sad events that have led us to this service. We cannot know yet precisely what occurred at Palmyra, nor do we know for certain whether they are indeed dead, or—hope against hope—somehow still alive. But we can believe that wherever Mac and Muff are, God is watching over them."

The minister offered a prayer.

They all bowed their heads and held hands. Experienced sea

legs held them steady as the boat lurched in the waves.

"Oh God, we ask Thee to extend Thy loving arms to all those who have known and cared for Mac and Muff Graham. We pray that justice may be done, but ask that Thou would purge our hearts of the vindictiveness that would poison our souls and deny Thy concern and grace even for the incarcerated."

Leonard cringed at those last words. They were too close to Gandhi's admonition that one should hate the sin, but love the sinner. Leonard didn't feel capable of such a noble dichotomy right now. His friends Mac and Muff had obviously been murdered, and their beloved *Sea Wind* stolen. Leonard wanted justice, not mercy.

Kit was no less vindictive now. A few days earlier, a Honolulu newspaper photo had shown a handcuffed Jennifer being escorted to a court hearing by U.S. Marshals. Something about the scene disturbed Kit, but she couldn't immediately put her finger on it. With a horrified gasp, she suddenly realized it was the short-sleeved blouse the suspect wore. A peasant blouse with a distinctive embroidered yoke, it had been one of Muff's favorites. From that moment on, Kit despised Jennifer Jenkins.

"Particularly, we pray for Mac and Muff," the minister continued. "If, as seems to us inevitable, they indeed are gone from this life, then we commit their spirits into Thy sure hand. Lead them to their high island. Amen."

Leonard fired up the *Journeyer's* motor and the boat began a slow circle. Everyone stood silently at the railing and, one by one, dropped purple and white vanda orchids and red-and-white carnation leis over the side.

As Kit watched, the sprinkling of flowers began to drift away upon the wind-blown surface of the water, much as, she thought, her brother and Muff had been taken by currents and winds over the horizon to a far-off island named Palmyra on their final voyage.

SEATTLE, WASHINGTON

HER FIRST evening home, Kit went through a box of letters from Mac and Muff. Those from Palmyra were already held together in one pile by a single rubber band. She put them aside. The authorities in Hawaii had asked her to make photostatic copies of them so that they could read the Grahams' own account of their relationship with the couple on the *Iola*.

Also, Kit still had all the letters Mac and Muff had sent her from various other locales while they were on their honeymoon cruise. Nearly six years' worth. She took a stack of them and sat down on the couch in the downstairs den.

On the wall were a mask painted with vegetable dyes and a carved wooden spear, trophies brought by Mac from some distant corner of the world. Kit smiled. It was an endearing memory: Mac holding the mask to his face and hopping goofily around the room, performing what he swore was an authentic tribal dance.

She began reading. In one letter, dated July 16, 1962, Mac had written to her, "I love life and living so much that the constant realization of its passing hurts."

She picked up another letter, written in the fall of 1966, when Mac and Muff were heading up the west coast of Mexico on the final leg of their round-the-world trip. At the time, Mac had asked her not to tell their parents this story. It still took her breath away.

October 1966

Dear Kit,

The Gulf of Tehuantepec, feared by all ships for her 100-mph-plus winds, lay in our path. It is 200 miles across. We made 100 miles when the engine broke. Then, *chubascos*, the grand-daddy of all thunderstorms, hit us. Do we retreat 300 miles to the hardly adequate port of Acajutla, or try for the ports ahead on the other side of the gulf without a working engine? We turned back. I put the dinghy down and tried to tow with the outboard. We could make only one knot. We spotted a shrimp fishing fleet. They found someone to speak English with me over the radio and arranged for a tow from Camaroner #18. It was 200 miles to Salina Cruz. The skies darkened and the *chubascos* started moving in. We were pulled through huge seas and wind that made steering practically impossible. Hardly a moment in thirty hours did we not think of a chafed splice in our tow rope. If it broke, we would founder.

Muff is terrified, and every instant wanting to help. She is on my left, holding on, when an awful bolt of lightning splinters the world ahead with such an ear-breaking sound and ragged brilliance that with it comes the knowledge that this IS hell. The jagged shape of that bolt keeps violently twitching in our eyes, as the explosion of lightning turns our world an eerie blue-white. The mad steering goes on. I go forward to check the tow rope, leaving Muff at the helm.

Muff screams, "The breakers! We're in the breakers!"

The first roaring breaker seemed to tower over us. Our boat was at a fantastic angle. The wave came down. "This is it, Muff!" I yelled. I wanted to say I was sorry, but I didn't. I didn't want her to know I'd given up hope. The wave crashed down and hit our hull. Only the foaming top came over us, but the hatch was open and it poured inside. As the next roller broke, I saw the breaker engulf the shrimp boat. When it passed, #18 miraculously had held her position. I saw the tow rope chain come up hard. #18 was going at right angles to us. Something had to break. Our bow was virtually yanked toward her. She started climbing the swell. I screamed at Muff, "Hard left, damn it!" Then, "Follow him!" Muff was doing a wonderful job at the helm, and I felt horrible for yelling at her. With certain knowledge that no rope could hold that fantastic strain, I concentrated on readying the anchor for when we broke loose. But then, we climbed out over the last comber to safety, which must surely rate as the luckiest moment of our lives.

We are safe now in a Mexico port, getting our engine repaired. Will be home soon.

Love, Mac

Kit let the letter drop into her lap. They had made it that time, in part because they were a good team. She knew they had also survived a South Pacific typhoon, a perilous journey through the

Red Sea, and the close call with a pirate ship in the Mediterranean. How could they have disappeared now, not in a storm at sea, but on an idyllic island?

Kit found another letter, which Mac had written to himself. He titled it "Unconnected Fragments," and it was one of her favorites. It revealed a sensitivity in Mac that he did not show everyone. He had written it shortly after their father's death in 1973. A few "Fragments":

> The hours and days of working on the boat with the constant thought that I would be able to show Dad how well each piece fit—*someday*. The machinery all set for his inspection, with a rehearsed monologue. I wished to please him so. I would have liked to have shown him a happy family with grandchildren— and the painful list goes on. But I most horribly regret not being able to thank him for everything he gave me. There's one less kind, thoughtful, quiet man in this world. As for me, I am so afraid of the future that I can't enjoy the present. I want to live my life and be happy, but I don't know how. I think that "how" is not having to worry about the future.

Kit took solace in the fact that her brother, more than any person she knew, had lived life the way he wanted. She went to a nearby bookcase and returned with a worn photo album. She sat down and opened to a page that had a square black-and-white picture of her parents on their honeymoon, looking so young, so hopeful for the future. Daddy was an engineering student at MIT when they got married, and Mother was attending Miss Windsor's, an exclusive Boston finishing school. On the same page was a photo of the spacious family home where the bridegroom was born. Most of the money in the family had come from Grandfather (Malcolm) Graham, who at one time owned Remington Rand, only to quickly sell it for a profit. He became a Wall Street investor, and when the stock market crashed in 1929, Grandpa lost a fortune, though when he died in the mid-1940s, he left trusts for Mac and Kit (both then in their teens). At his direction, the trusts were not distributed to them until the mid-1960s. The inheritance tax laws in those days encouraged the skipping of a generation, so their father received nothing. (When she and Mac finally received their grandfather's trust assets—$120,000 each—they decided to buy their father a sailboat. "I'm too old for sailing," he protested. "Get me something with a motor." So they got him a new twenty-six-foot Chris-Craft cabin cruiser. By then, Mac had already bought the *Sea Wind* with his uncle's inheritance. And Kit, herself a sailing aficionado, had followed her brother's lead and, with her own inheritance from their uncle, bought a smaller, more modest vessel good for day sailing on Puget Sound.)

On the next page was a snapshot of Kit, age two, playing with a toy train set, on December 25, 1930. It had been her last Christmas as an only child. Mac was born on April 13, 1931, and there was a picture of him taken with Mother the following December 25. Kit read her own unevenly penned caption: "And then my brother joined us."

Pictures of Kit and Mac together filled the album's pages. Here was one she had always loved—the two of them, ages eleven and nine, at the beach in high summer. Dressed in old-fashioned tank-top swim suits, they were lying on their stomachs in the sand, flashing the camera identical pixie grins. Mac had made an enlargement of the picture and kept it in an album aboard the *Sea Wind*. Kit's original had faded, but she ran her fingers gently across the old print, as if reading Braille, as if touch could restore this lost moment in her life. "Oh, Mac, we had such great fun."

Kit looked up, and gazed unseeing at the African mask on the wall. "Mac, Mac," she whispered, shutting the album gently.

CHAPTER 18

TWO WEEKS BEFORE CHRISTMAS 1974, Buck Walker appeared in court to be sentenced on the MDA drug charge that had caused him to flee with Jennifer to Palmyra seven months earlier. U.S. District Court Judge Samuel P. King delayed sentencing, however, when court-appointed defense attorney Jon T. Miho made a surprise announcement.

"Mr. Walker is willing to take a polygraph test with respect to the disappearances of Mr. and Mrs. Malcolm Graham," the lawyer told the judge. "We believe the results will be of assistance in our discussions with the Government."

Assistant U.S. Attorney William Eggers agreed to the delay.

Soon after his client was escorted from the courtroom by armed marshals, Miho met in the hallway with reporters. "While a polygraph is not admissible in court," he explained, "results favorable to Mr. Walker could be used for plea-bargaining purposes."

It didn't take long for Jennifer's attorney, Mark Casden, to go public with her agreement to take a polygraph.

Jennifer had made bail on November 13 when her widowed aunt (Uncle Buddy had passed away two years earlier) posted a security bond listing her $120,000 Oahu home as collateral. Since then, Jennifer had been living with friends on the Big Island, but Buck had remained in custody in Halawa Jail since his arrest.

During Christmas week, prosecutors huddled with an FBI polygraph expert and came up with a list of proposed questions to ask both defendants. As previously agreed, the list was submitted to the defense attorneys for their review.

Within days, Buck Walker withdrew his offer to take a polygraph. It would later be hotly disputed whether Jennifer also backed off or the Government decided to administer the test only if both defendants cooperated.

While the legal skirmishing continued, the press trailed after the Palmyra case like ants scenting watermelon juice at a family picnic. Of course, the bare facts were intrinsically compelling—mysterious disappearances and a possible double murder set against the alluring backdrop of an uninhabited tropical island, an ocean voyage on a stolen yacht, the suspenseful capture of the two lovers who were the prime suspects.

Coverage of the story regularly made the top of the evening TV news in Hawaii, and was splashed across newspapers in bold, front-page headlines, often accompanied by pictures of the suspects and the victims, and provocative sidebar articles. "Woman Seized in Yacht Theft," headlined the October 30 edition of the *Honolulu Advertiser* in the first article on the case. "Is My Brother Dead? Mac Graham's Sister Asks FBI," read a headline in the November 4 *Advertiser*. "Palmyra Searchers Return but Won't Talk About Findings," announced the *Star-Bulletin* on the same day.

In San Diego, the case also made the front pages. "South Seas Dream Trip Tainted," reported the *San Diego Union* on October 30. "Yacht Wife's Premonition Recalled," revealed the *Tribune* on November 1. *People* magazine, in a November edition, featured "A Couple Who Loved the Sea Vanish in It," an illustrated multipage story that referred to Jennifer as a "scruffy social dropout" and Buck as a "tattooed drifter."

In Hawaii, at least, the names and faces of Mac and Muff Graham, Jennifer Jenkins, and Buck Walker were etched in the public mind. When Jennifer finally went to trial in mid-1975, every single member of her eight-woman, four-man jury admitted to having read, viewed, or heard about the case from radio, television, and newspaper accounts.

ON JANUARY 7, 1975, one week before Jennifer and Buck were scheduled to be tried together for the theft of the *Sea Wind*, Judge King granted a motion by Jennifer's defense attorney to sever their cases. They would be tried separately.

That day in court, both were present. Jennifer sat next to Buck, and they conversed intimately in the hushed tones of lovers who missed one another and were deeply worried about their future together.

At one point, Jennifer leaned over to her lawyer and said, "Buck has asked me to go first."

"What do you mean?" her lawyer asked.

"He wants me to be tried first. I said fine. Tell the judge."

It did not dawn on her that Buck might want her to be the try-out for his performance.

On January 13, Walker stood before Judge King on the old drug charge. He was given the maximum five-year sentence in federal prison.

SEATTLE
MARCH 1975

KIT NEVER expected to hear from Buck Walker, not ever. His letter arrived with the abruptness of a bolt of lightning. She sat now in her kitchen with his eight-page handwritten missive in her hands, utterly unprepared emotionally for what it had to say.

The envelope carried a March 11, 1975, Hawaii postmark. Jennifer had enclosed a short note, explaining, "Buck wrote to you some time back while we were in dry dock," but the letter had been "lost and forgotten in the shuffle."

In the upper-right-hand corner of the letter, Buck had penned, in his neat writing, "October—Hawaii."

Dear Kit,

It's difficult to write this, as the news we have to convey is very sad for us, and we know it will be so for you. I've made numerous attempts in this regard and each has always seemed inadequate. Even now I can find no words that seem appropriate to the circumstances. We are torn in many ways in this matter, yet we feel a deep obligation to communicate with you.

My name is Roy Allen and my wife is Jennifer. We've recently returned to Hawaii from Palmyra, where we met Mac and Muff, and although we were fellow inhabitants for only a couple of months on a remote atoll, we came to care very much for them.

Please prepare yourself for the worst.

Mac and Muff disappeared August 30th, and we haven't seen them since. We believe they died in a boating accident. They had gone fishing in the afternoon and never returned. The next day we found their overturned dinghy washed up on the beach.

All else that follows is an elaboration of circumstances, as well as our own thoughts and feelings. I hope you'll bear with my clumsiness in the telling.

The image of Mac that, for me, signifies his essence, is drawn from the day I first saw him. He was standing out on the bowsprit of the *Sea Wind*, directing Muff at the helm as they glided into the lagoon. He waved and smiled . . .

Kit felt bile rising. How was it possible for Mac's and Muff's murderer to have the incredible boldness to write her any kind of letter, much less this kind? she wondered. The very thought made her light-headed and caused her to perspire. She had to pause for a minute before continuing to read on.

. . . as I was rowing close by. I offered to help in getting the *Sea Wind* secured and he replied, "Nope, I can handle it." In this simple refusal, he seemed to imply much more; that as much as he appreciated the offer, he couldn't forgo the pleasure of doing it himself! There was an indescribable look about him when he smiled that I've felt always permitted him to say anything whatever with perfect graciousness.

Walker told of his admiration for Mac's "self-sufficiency," and Mac's "utter love and regard" for Muff. The two couples were "friendly and neighborly," Walker waxed on, sharing fish from their daily catches. He alluded to their having fun together at Jennifer's birthday party, "singing Happy Birthday and talking away a long evening."

Kit's eyes flitted back to the words "friendly" and "neighborly." Her hands trembled.

It may seen a little strange to you how we could derive so much enjoyment from simple pleasures. Of course, the setting is important. Palmyra is enchanting and mystical. There is a natural beauty that numbs the senses going hand in hand with hard realities: poisonous fish, sharks, scorpions, spiders, rats, mosquitoes, etc. There is the fear of serious injury because the nearest outside help is days away, and on the other hand, an eagerness for the challenge.

The humidity is usually uncomfortable, making a delight of a cold bath from stored rainwater. There is a sameness to the days, a silence composed of only sounds of nature, the pulse of the surf, the wind through the coconut trees, the nesting birds taking flight; an acute sense of being alone. Sharing a meal, a drink, a smoke, a conversation, playing chess, greetings as you pass going in opposite directions, all take on a pronounced flavor.

The chess games were a special treat, except that Muff didn't play. Mac and I were fairly evenly matched, while Jennifer beat us both on quite a few occasions.

Walker mentioned the planned trip to Fanning. He said Mac had invited him and Jennifer for a "bon voyage dinner" the night before their scheduled departure. He told of arriving at the *Sea Wind*'s anchorage around six o'clock, and not finding Mac and Muff. "Mac had mentioned earlier in the day that they were going fishing in the afternoon," Walker said, so he and Jennifer were not initially worried. But "the later it became, the more we worried."

Buck went on to tell of their searching for Mac and Muff in the morning and finding their overturned Zodiac not far away, "washed up on the beach." They searched for three days, he said, but found no other signs of Mac and Muff.

Kit tried desperately to concentrate on the details presented in

Buck's rendition, rather than give in to her growing urge to ball up the patronizing letter and chuck it into the garbage.

> Jennifer and I hardly spoke except for calling out for Mac and Muff, and we didn't get much sleep. In retrospect, I think we were in a mild state of shock at the loss. It was unbelievable. I can't say how much we miss them!

They stayed on the island another week or ten days, Walker went on, then decided to take the *Sea Wind* to Fanning, towing the *Iola*, and "report the matter there." But on the narrow passage out of the Palmyra lagoon, the *Iola* "crunched up on a coral head." When they couldn't free the damaged *Iola*, they set out on the *Sea Wind* for Hawaii.

> After a while we decided that going to Fanning wasn't a good plan because we'd be in a foreign jurisdiction and there was a question of whether the *Sea Wind* would be confiscated, leaving us homeless and stranded. We felt a great responsibility for the *Sea Wind*. She's a beautiful yacht and we've come to love her.
>
> One thing I might as well tell you is that Jennifer and I tend to be romantics, which often leads to rationalizations about life. I suppose this comes from being overanxious for something better, and we tend to color reality with our dreams. I mention this because I wish to be candid about everything, and I hope it'll aid in understanding something of us.
>
> Here in Hawaii, we've had to haul out the *Sea Wind* for repairs. (This is being written at the boatyard.) Last but not least, we wanted to get married . . .

Hadn't he said a few pages back that "my wife is Jennifer"? Just one small lie, Kit was sure, in comparison to the rest of the letter.

> . . . which we haven't felt the necessity to do before, but we've been talking of having children—the time for a wedding now seems completely right.

I realize this may be the wrong place to mention this, but we want to file a salvage claim on the *Sea Wind*. I hope I can make you understand all that we mean by this, as there are many factors involved. We've lost our own boat, market value about $10,000, although price tags have nothing to do with how a sailor values his vessel, whether she be a tub or a luxury yacht. We love the *Sea Wind* and we want, eventually, to continue with her in voyage around the world. Also, I've registered the *Sea Wind*, renaming her *Lokahi*, meaning "of one mind," which we think aptly sums up the spirit of our feelings. We haven't yet notified anyone about the true circumstances. We feel you should be the first to know.

There are many things we know you'll want to have whatever happens, and we'd like to ship them to you at the earliest opportunity. We would appreciate hearing your feelings about everything. We intend to write again soon. We want to keep you fully informed.

I know this letter must be a sensitive experience for you, and I know I've stated things badly. I seem to have great difficulty finding an end and a beginning, and in determining appropriate language for in between. I apologize for my lack, but we want and very much need an understanding.

Thank you for listening, and please let us know if there's anything we can do. We send all our deepest sympathies to you and others who will feel Mac and Muff's loss. We cared, we care.

Sincere regards,

Roy and Jennifer

P.S. We found about $400 aboard and used it on repairing and painting the *Sea Wind*. However, we'll return this amount to you if you feel it's the right thing to do.

Kit was convinced the letter was largely a pack of lies—and she didn't believe for a minute that Buck Walker had written it back in October 1974, from an Oahu boatyard. She could picture this glib, manipulative murderer hunched over a cot in his steamy Honolulu jail cell concocting these elaborate explanations in a desperate attempt to save his own skin.

Kit promptly called the FBI's Calvin Shishido, told him about the letter, and vented her outrage by reading him a few of the more unbelievable excerpts.

"It's just a bunch of nonsense written by a pathological liar," he said. "Don't let it get to you."

"I won't." She took a deep breath. "I just hope Walker and the girl get what they've got coming."

"Send me a copy of the letter. Maybe we can use it against them someday."

UNITED STATES v. *Jennifer Jenkins*, criminal action 74-160, began on June 19, 1975, in Judge King's courtroom in the Honolulu federal building on King Street. The street was not, as some Hawaii residents believed, named to honor the well-connected judge or his late father, who had been a territorial delegate to Congress from Hawaii between 1934 and 1942, but rather the Hawaiian royalty who formerly resided in the Iolani Palace, located across the street.

The unseasonably chilly morning did not deter the curious from crowding into those gallery seats remaining after the contingent of newspaper and television reporters pitched camp in the front rows.

At 9:05 A.M., prosecutor Bill Eggers approached the podium and began his opening statement to the jury by setting forth the nature of the three charges against the defendant: theft of the *Sea Wind*; illegal transportation in the interstate commerce of stolen goods, to wit, the *Sea Wind* and its contents; and theft from the *Sea Wind* of four hundred dollars belonging to the Grahams.

Murder had not been included, though the authorities were convinced that Mac and Muff Graham had been murdered, and that the killers were Buck Walker and Jennifer Jenkins.

Although it is commonly believed that the word "corpus" in *cor-*

pus delicti refers to the body of the victim in a homicide case, and that without a body there can be no prosecution, *corpus delicti* actually means "the body (that is, the elements) of the crime." Those elements have to be present, together with evidence that it was the defendant who perpetrated the crime, before there can be a successful prosecution. One of the elements in a murder prosecution is, of course, a dead body. (Other elements of the most common type of first-degree murder are malice aforethought, premeditation, and deliberation.) But the prosecution only has the burden of proving that an unlawful killing took place, not the burden of actually producing the body.

Nonetheless, it is self-evidently true that without finding the body in a homicide case, the prosecution's case is generally weakened. The automatic first defense for the accused is to claim that the supposed victim might still be alive. Also, if the defendant is prosecuted for the murder and found not guilty, he can never be prosecuted again for the murder—even if the body of the victim and other evidence, no matter how incriminating, is subsequently found—because of constitutional safeguards against double jeopardy. For this reason, prosecutors frequently wait a considerable period of time before filing murder charges, hoping that the body will turn up. There is no statute of limitation for the crime of murder.

Law enforcement officials connected with the Palmyra case agreed that sooner or later Buck Walker and Jennifer Jenkins would be prosecuted for murder, whether or not the bodies of the Grahams were ever found, and that the theft cases were only dry runs for the murder prosecutions—with the same witnesses and virtually the same circumstantial evidence.

The first Government witness was Kit Muncey, her face pale and wan from grief and worry. She was obviously ill at ease as she took the stand. But though she had never testified in court before and was as nervous as she looked, Kit *wanted* to be here. She wanted a hand in convicting Jennifer Jenkins. She only regretted that the charge was not murder.

Testifying that the *Sea Wind* and sailing were her brother's "whole life," she added that her brother and sister-in-law were experienced, competent blue-water sailors who had expertly prepared themselves for the trip to Palmyra.

Kit also attested to the characteristic stability of the Zodiac and Mac's skill in operating it safely.

In succeeding days of testimony, four Government witnesses—Larry Briggs, Jack Wheeler, Tom Wolfe, and Bernard Leonard—testified about events on Palmyra in the summer of 1974. Two themes were emphasized by them all: the *Iola* was in wretched shape, and Jennifer and Roy Allen were getting desperate for food. Leonard also testified about the details of Jennifer's flight from authorities on the morning of her arrest.

Lorraine Wollen, who lived with her husband on their sailboat at Pokai Bay, testified next that they had met Jennifer Jenkins and Roy Allen in October 1974, when they moored their boat in the adjacent berth.

"Did Miss Jenkins speak with you about how they obtained the boat they sailed into Pokai Bay on?" Eggers asked.

The morning the *Sea Wind* was to depart, Wollen answered, Jennifer invited her over for coffee. Afterward, as Wollen was about to leave, she noticed a photograph on the wall. "I asked Jennifer if it was a picture of the previous owners. She said it was, that the man had owned the boat for fourteen years and just got tired of all the maintenance that goes with a boat and decided to get rid of it. I got the impression Jennifer and Roy got a very good deal."

Later that day, according to her testimony, Wollen returned to her own boat after doing some errands and found a note from Jennifer explaining that she hadn't had time to pick up a roll of film at the Waianae Drugstore. She asked Lorraine to please pick up the prints and mail them to an address on Maui. Folded inside the note were a five-dollar bill and the stub off the film envelope.

Several days later, Wollen did pick up the prints, but before she got around to mailing them, she heard the news about Jennifer's arrest at Ala Wai. Thinking the pictures might be important evidence, she took them down to the Waianae police station.

"The policeman on duty spread the pictures out on the

counter, and told me he didn't think they were evidence, and gave them back to me. The next day, I mailed the pictures to Jennifer Allen at the address she had left."*

Eggers showed the witness five pictures, which she identified as the photos she had picked up for Jennifer.

The five photos entered into evidence by the Government showed the *Iola* under full sail next to the *Sea Wind*. Palmyra could be seen in the background.†

The pictures of the *Iola*, minus its front hatch cover, had been taken from the deck of the *Sea Wind*, the rigging of the *Sea Wind* being visible in the photo. Clearly, they contradicted Jennifer's statement to Shishido that the Iola got hung up, and was left, on a reef in Palmyra's channel. The little boat had obviously made it well clear of the channel and out to the open sea. The lack of a hatch cover suggested that Buck and Jennifer intended from the very start to scuttle her.

The Government attempted to discredit Jennifer's story about finding the Zodiac capsized by calling to the stand Kenneth White, an expert on small boats. White testified that he had examined the engine from the *Sea Wind*'s Zodiac and concluded that there was no evidence it had been submerged in salt water, as would have occurred if the dinghy capsized in the Palmyra lagoon. Furthermore, White characterized the Zodiac as "about the most stable water craft you can buy." He had personally tested the stability of Mac and Muff's Zodiac. "We put *four* men in it and took it out into the water and tried to capsize it. We could get just a little bit

---

*A friend of Jennifer's subsequently took them to the Honolulu jail and attempted to give them to her. An alert jail matron confiscated the prints and turned them over to the FBI.

†There were more pictures on the roll, but this jury would not see them. Cal Shishido had, of course, seen all of the photos, several of them being nude pictures of Jennifer and Buck in various poses aboard the *Sea Wind*. Shishido had to deal with a particularly sordid rumor going the rounds about the explicit nature of some of them. Agents and lawyers, time and again, had sidled up to him and begged to see the pictures of Jennifer having sex with a dog. There was no such picture. There were shots of a nude Jennifer lounging on the deck with the dogs, and petting Puffer.

of water into the boat by the four of us bouncing on one side. That's all."

When Eggers rested the Government's case, there had been a total of sixteen witnesses for the prosecution.

Jennifer was the only witness to testify for the defense. On the stand, she stuck mulishly to the story she'd told the FBI agent, including leaving the *Iola* behind on the channel reef after it got stuck there when she and Buck tried to tow it out of the channel behind the *Sea Wind*, etc.

On cross examination, Eggers showed her the photos of the *Iola* and *Sea Wind* sailing together in the waters off Palmyra. "Would you explain, please, at what point in time when you and Mr. Walker were on the island of Palmyra were the *Sea Wind* and the *Iola* together under full sail out in the ocean?"

"Never."

Shishido lowered his head so the jury could not see his smile. Unbelievably, Jennifer Jenkins had just denied something that had been conclusively proved before her very own eyes by the Government—that the *Iola* and *Sea Wind* were at sea together. Those five pictures shown to the jury did not lie.

In his closing argument, Eggers asked rhetorically: "What does this all mean? Well, all the evidence, I suggest, means Jennifer Jenkins was a desperate individual. She had a leaking boat, she was stranded on a remote island with no food, and a stone's throw away was the answer to both of these problems: transportation and food. She gave inconsistent stories after her return to Hawaii, and if the *Sea Wind* was properly taken possession of by her as a result of some unexplainable act of God or mishap that was caused to the Grahams, then would there be any need to tell inconsistent stories? She is guilty of stealing the *Sea Wind*, and she's guilty of stealing the four hundred dollars from the boat, and she's guilty of transporting these stolen goods in interstate commerce. I ask you to find her guilty as charged."

The jury swiftly returned a verdict. When it was read, Jennifer, waxen-faced, dropped back into her seat at the defense table. She had been found *guilty on all counts*.

On August 18, Judge King sentenced her to two years in federal prison for the theft of the *Sea Wind* and five years' probation on the other two counts.

Buck Walker, paying close attention to press accounts of Jennifer's trial from his jail cell, adjusted his story accordingly at his own trial in December. Testifying in his own defense, Walker did not make the same mistake of denying—in direct contradiction to photographic evidence—that the *Iola* and *Sea Wind* had sailed side by side off Palmyra. He told the jury that the *Iola* had indeed gone aground in the channel, but that he had been able to free her. Once on the ocean, Walker said, it was clear that the *Iola* had sustained significant damage and was leaking badly, so he and Jennifer abandoned their boat and sailed on in the *Sea Wind*.

Special Agent Henry Burns took the stand and testified that Walker's original version had been that he had failed to get the *Iola* free from the reef.

Inevitably, Walker was also found guilty on all counts and sentenced to a term of ten years, not to commence, however, until he had finished serving his five-year sentence on the MDA drug charge.

Walker's defense attorney suggested to the media that his client had been unfairly convicted of theft because of "public opinion, speculation and innuendo" that the Grahams had been murdered for their yacht and food.

In spite of the two convictions in the Palmyra boat theft case, the question of what had actually happened to Mac and Muff Graham was still unanswered.

The mystery of Palmyra Island was far from solved. There were those who believed it would never be.

CHAPTER 19

THE JUNGLE HAD RECLAIMED its own. The clearing Mac had hacked out next to the *Sea Wind*'s anchorage was again a tangle of vines and trees. Also hidden by returning foliage was the site of Buck's campfire, where Muff had confided in Jennifer one summer evening. The building Mac had used as a workshop still stood. Atop the workbench inside was a jar of rusted nuts and bolts, draped in the silken shroud of a spider's weaving.

Sharon Jordan and her husband Robert arrived on Palmyra the first week of November 1980. They had heard tales from other yachties throughout the Pacific about the disappearance of a sailing couple in the area. But they did not connect the incident with this island until they found, in a building in the jungle, some yellowed newspaper clippings about the case, apparently left by visitors who had stopped at the island *because* of the notoriety. The Jordans devoured every riveting word and offered each other various theories of what might have happened.

"The Grahams had sailed around the world and they ended up disappearing here," Sharon mused one evening as they sipped sherry aboard their boat.

"It certainly sounds like they were murdered."

"How horrible."

At that moment, Sharon was very glad that they were alone on the island. "You know, it could just as easily have happened to . . . us."

They vowed not to let the incident detract from the enjoyment of their planned stay of several months before moving on. They were circumnavigating the globe on their sailboat, the *Moya*, which Robert had built himself.

The following weeks passed quickly for the young, handsome

couple from Johannesburg. Sharon, a fitness buff with a slim, taut body to show for it, walked barefoot several miles each day along the lagoon's shoreline, often going entirely without clothes in the moist heat. Her tanned nimble figure, coal-black hair, and dark-brown eyes gave her the look of a Polynesian princess exploring her private tropical domain. Robert fished most mornings, did chores on the boat every day, and in the afternoon usually took a nap in a hammock secured in the shade between two sturdy trees.

On January 4, 1981, the sun rose in a cloudless sky. After a light breakfast of granola soaked in fresh coconut milk, Sharon and Robert climbed into their dinghy to go fishing. Actually, Sharon wasn't as interested in catching anything as she was in observing the schools of colorful reef fish—angels, butterflies, wrasses—that darted here and there in the lagoon.

As they passed by an old seaplane ramp on the south side of Cooper Island, Sharon watched a strikingly beautiful scarlet fish zigzag beneath them.

"Wait," she said. "I see something."

Robert stopped rowing and joined her in looking over the side. "What is it?" she asked.

"A boat."

Sharon wondered aloud if the wreck might have anything to do with the missing couple from California.

The next day, the Jordans began an ambitious salvage operation to raise the sunken boat. They collected a number of empty gasoline drums, filled them with lagoon water, and sank them next to the wreck. Wearing nothing but scuba masks, they dived the twenty feet to the bottom and began tying the drums to the boat, all the while keeping a wary eye out for sharks coming too close.

It took more than an hour to secure the drums. Without tanks, they had to surface often to take a breath. There were also a few interruptions when they had to get out of the water until curious sharks moved along. When the metal barrels were finally in place— each tied to the sunken boat by six to eight feet of heavy rope— Robert went down with a hand pump and Sharon took along a wrench. One by one, they uncapped each drum, ran a length of hose into its opening, and pumped in air, displacing the water.

When the tenth or eleventh drum became buoyant, the old boat rose a foot or two off the sandy bottom, as the Jordans watched excitedly, then stopped.

Sharon arrowed to the surface to catch her breath. When Robert joined her, they agreed they needed more barrels to achieve the necessary buoyancy. They sank four more and pumped air into them. Thirty minutes later, the boat broke the surface of the lagoon with a loud *whumph*.

Its metal hull was covered with yellowish barnacles, but the inscription "U.S.A.F." was clearly visible. The Jordans bailed the water out of the boat and pulled it to shore for closer inspection. Cigar-shaped with low sides, it obviously had not been designed for ocean travel. Robert thought it was probably a rescue boat. Near the stern, four rectangular storage compartments, about three feet deep, were built into the deck. Empty aluminum containers fit snugly inside two of the spaces.

The containers for the other two spaces were nowhere to be seen.

JANUARY 25, 1981

SHARON JORDAN set out for her daily constitutional along the westward shore of the lagoon. When she left, her husband was lying in their hammock, reading a book.

It was a beautiful afternoon, but hot, as usual.

She headed up the western shore of Cooper Island, following the high-water mark along the sand and coral. She always preferred the beach to walking inland, since she was curious to see what might have washed ashore during the night. She was rarely disappointed on Palmyra.

Spotting an especially pretty and unbroken shell, she kneeled down and brushed the sand away from it. Yes, she thought, a nice addition to her collection.

Striding on, she passed the old seaplane ramp, which reminded her of raising the rescue boat. Such a lark. This place brimmed with adventure. Maybe it really was paradise, she decided. They were alone, and happy, the weather was consistently balmy, and the surroundings were exotically beautiful . . . she'd told Robert she was in no hurry to leave, thank you very much.

About half a mile farther on along the shore of Strawn Island she noticed something glistening in the sunlight about ten yards away.

Her interest piqued, she walked closer, then recoiled and screamed. A human skull lay on the sand in front of her, a gold-capped tooth in its jaw sparkling in the sun. Other skeletal remains were scattered nearby.

Sharon dropped her shells and went down to her knees in the sand. *It's one of them. One of the missing couple.* But she knew the bones couldn't have been lying on the beach all these years.

There was an aluminum container nearby. Lying next to it were a lid and some wire that presumably once had held the lid and box together. From the position of the bones, she recognized immediately that they must have fallen out of the container. Inside the lid was a small bone, and a wristwatch, which she picked up. Despite the corrosion, she could see it was a woman's watch. The box could have been washed ashore by the latest storm, which had died down just the night before. Inside it, Sharon saw a small swatch of cloth. She also noticed charring on the box's interior surfaces.

Her gaze went back to the ivory skull. *This must be the woman.* One side of the skull was charred, too. She didn't want to touch the grinning *memento mori*, but knew she must. If left here, it might be washed away.

Gingerly, she picked it up and turned it over. In the left temple region there was a small round hole.

Her mind raced. The poor woman had obviously been shot, put in the box, and then—set on fire! "Dear *God*, oh dear God."

There was something about the aluminum box. She looked at it more closely and recognized it as identical to the two containers stowed in compartments on the sunken rescue boat. But there had been two empty compartments. *Two.* Here was one box; the other was still missing. *The man*, she realized with a chill. *The missing box must contain his body!*

Reluctantly, she looked down the shoreline ahead of her. Nothing. The second box, the one with . . . him inside . . . must still be underwater in the lagoon. She'd better get her husband right away so he could help her collect the rest of the bones before the next tide came and washed them away.

Fastidiously holding the skull out in front of her, Sharon Jordan ran back to the *Moya*, a raven-haired Godiva carrying a death's-head in paradise.

CHAPTER 20

LATE JANUARY 1981
FBI HEADQUARTERS, HONOLULU

CAL SHISHIDO WAS WORKING at his desk in the field office's "bull pen," the grungy squad room where agents worked at long tables, filling out reports, talking on the phones, and expelling enough cigarette smoke to produce the smoglike "vog" that lingers on the Hawaiian air after a volcanic eruption.

Shishido had been assigned to Honolulu for ten years now, longer than anyone else in the office. It was rather unusual for an agent to spend so long in one locale, but he had consistently spurned all offers of transfer—even ones promising promotion—because he loved Hawaii. His sons were going to his old high school, his elderly parents had retired nearby, and most of his other relatives and many of his closest friends still lived in the islands. And then there were the golf courses, some of the most neatly manicured and beautifully situated in the world. When Cal Shishido teed off at the majestic, coast-hugging thirteenth hole at Oahu's Klipper Marine Golf Course, with the surf crashing next to him and the fertile emerald hills of the Waiahole Forest Reserve in the background, he couldn't imagine moving to Cleveland or Pittsburgh or Washington, D.C. He was home.

It was an uncommonly slow afternoon at the office, and the bull pen was quiet. When all the agents were present, it was difficult to hear oneself think over the volume of chatter, let alone overhear a phone conversation. But now Shishido could clearly hear, from twenty feet away, the new guy manning the complaint desk, set up to handle calls from local authorities and the public.

"They found bones?" the agent was saying.

At that moment, Shishido's extension rang. A federal prosecutor was returning his call about a recent bank robbery case. When he hung up a minute or so later, Shishido noticed that the complaint-desk agent was still on the same call.

"Cannibals, maybe?" the young man chuckled.

Shishido made a note in the bank robbery file and put it back in a file cabinet.

"Give me the name of the place again. You'd better spell it," Shishido heard the agent say.

Cal looked at his watch. Maybe he'd head home early today. He had worked overtime on the weekend.

"P . . . A . . . L . . . M . . . Y . . ."

Shishido popped out of his chair and hurried to the complaint desk.

"Yeah, Y as in Yankee . . . R . . . A."

"Let me have that!" Cal unceremoniously grabbed the phone.

The new guy had only recently graduated from the academy in Quantico. He'd been in Hawaii barely six months. Christ, he'd been a college kid going to frat parties when the Grahams disappeared. He just wouldn't know.

"This is Special Agent Shishido."

The Coast Guard officer on the line reread the radio message that had been patched through from the yacht *Moya*. The officer, also new to the islands, knew nothing about the Palmyra case.

Shishido scribbled a few notes.

When he hung up, he pulled the Walker/Jenkins file.

One of the first people Shishido called next was Bill Eggers. Both men had always feared that the bodies of Malcolm and Eleanor Graham, even a trace of them, would never be found. When they had learned that Muff Graham wore prescription glasses, there was a fleeting hope that the partially burned lens Eggers had recovered from the old fire pit in the November 1974 search might be hers. But Muff's eye doctor had reported that it didn't match her prescription.

Eggers was elated at the reported discovery of bones and wished his old friend good luck on the next trip to Palmyra. Eggers would not be going along this time. He had left the U.S. Attorney's Office a year earlier and was now in private practice in Honolulu.

"My God, I can't believe it," he exclaimed. "The bones have *got* to be the Grahams'."

Shishido agreed. "I'd give my left nut to see the looks on the faces of Walker and Jenkins when they hear. They thought they had gotten away with murder."

NEWS OF the grisly discovery on Palmyra reverberated throughout the Hawaiian Islands. "Human Bones Found on Palmyra," "Murder on Palmyra," "Witness Describes Finding Bones on Palmyra," headlines across the islands screamed out.

On February 4, an FBI team headed by Cal Shishido left Hawaii for Palmyra. They were gone for six days. On the night they returned, television crews waited at the airport to film Shishido and another FBI agent as they stepped from the plane carrying the corroded metal box Sharon Jordan found on the beach. Up close, the rattling of bones could be heard inside the container.

That night's ten-o'clock news on KGMB-TV led with this story:

FBI agents returned tonight with a skull and bones found two weeks ago on Palmyra Island by a yachting couple from South Africa. The skeletal remains had been hidden inside a metallic container and apparently set afire and then weighted down and sunk in a lagoon. The container evidently broke free, and currents washed everything onto a coral-strewn beach, where they were discovered. The burning question now is, "Are those the remains of Malcolm and Eleanor Graham?" The San Diego couple disappeared mysteriously seven years ago on Palmyra, an idyllic island setting approximately one thousand miles south of Hawaii. Buck Walker and Jennifer Jenkins were subsequently convicted of stealing their yacht. Federal agents say it is incredible luck the bones and container were discovered at all.

Referring to the fact that the next tide might have returned the bones to the lagoon, where they could have sunk to the lagoon bottom or been washed out to sea through the channel, the report noted that the bones "may have been visible and reachable for only a few hours, and then would have been gone, probably forever. If connected to the Grahams, a few moments of luck may help clear up a seven-year-old mystery."

The speculation ended on February 17 when William C. Ervin, special agent in charge of the FBI's Honolulu office, announced that the remains found on Palmyra had been positively identified as those of Eleanor "Muff" Graham. A forensic odontologist had been able to make the identification by comparing dental charts and X-rays obtained from Muff's dentist in San Diego to the teeth and fillings in the skull.

On February 20, a federal grand jury in Honolulu returned an indictment against Buck Walker and Jennifer Jenkins for first-degree murder in the death of Muff Graham. (Walker and Jenkins were not charged with the murder of Mac Graham.) The grand jury charged "that sometime between, on, or about August 28, 1974, and on or about September 4, 1974, at Palmyra Island, in the District of Hawaii and within the special maritime and territorial jurisdiction of the United States, Buck Duane Walker, also known as Roy A. Allen, and Jennifer Lynn Jenkins, also known as Jennifer Allen, with malice aforethought did murder Mrs. Eleanor Graham during the perpetration of, or attempt to perpetrate, a robbery, thereby committing the offense of murder in the first degree."

Gruesome details began to be made public. "The aluminum box found next to the bones was too small to place a full corpse inside," a federal prosecutor in Honolulu told the press. "The body must have been cut up to fit into the box. There's a hole in the left temple of the skull and char marks on both the bones and the box. This body suffered intense heat."

Virtually every article or news story about the murder spotlighted Buck and Jennifer's suspicious conduct back in 1974—the theft of the *Sea Wind*, its repainting, Jennifer's flight from authorities in the harbor, Buck's escape, and so forth. Flat-out accusations in the news media were commonly reported: "Friends of the Grahams maintain that the two San Diegans were murdered by Walker and Jenkins." Even when there was no direct accusation, it was clear who the murderers were believed to be: "The Grahams had described the couple as ragtag nuisances they wished to be rid of"; "The Grahams radioed that they did not like the looks of Walker and Jenkins, *the only other people on the atoll*, whose yacht was in poor condition and without provisions"; "The Grahams' last transmission said Walker and Jenkins were out of food, cutting down coconut trees, and shooting fish with a handgun"; "The Grahams told Curt Shoemaker that Walker and Jenkins were desperate and out of food"; "The relationship wasn't a friendly one," etc. Even the headlines themselves went in the direction of presupposing guilt: "Walker and Jenkins Tied to Slaying of Pair on Cruise."

On March 5, Jennifer Jenkins, now thirty-four, turned herself in to U.S. Marshals in Los Angeles. The next day, she was freed on $100,000 bond, and she promised to appear in a Hawaiian federal courtroom on April 2 to enter a plea to the charge that she had taken part in the murder of Muff Graham.

Unlike his former girlfriend, Buck Walker had no intention of surrendering to the authorities.

When Cal Shishido attempted to get a line on Walker's whereabouts, he called the FBI office in Seattle. Last Shishido had heard, Walker was serving time at McNeil Island Federal Penitentiary in Washington State.

The agent called back in twenty minutes. "Walker escaped."

"*Escaped?* You're kidding. When?"

"Year and a half ago."

"Any leads?"

"Nope. No one knows where he is."

U.S. MARSHAL'S OFFICE
SEATTLE, WASHINGTON

WHEN DEPUTY U.S. Marshal Richard "Dick" Kringle, Jr., received word of the Hawaii murder indictments, he spun into action, teletyping information to headquarters in Washington, D.C., about Buck Walker and the discovery of human remains at a place called Palmyra Island.

Buck Duane Walker's case had been among eighty fugitive cases the U.S. Marshals Service Seattle office had received from the FBI in October 1979, when that agency relinquished its responsibility to hunt for federal prison escapees. Kringle, forty-four years old, had a streak of bulldog determination in his personality that suited his job.

Walker had escaped on July 10, 1979, from the minimum-security camp adjacent to the federal penitentiary on McNeil Island in Puget Sound, just southwest of Tacoma. He had either swum the two miles to shore or—according to one colorful rumor Kringle never entirely discounted—had been picked up in the water by a single-engine seaplane. Kringle learned that the U.S. Parole Commission had planned to parole Walker after he had served seven years. He escaped after logging close to five years.

When Kringle first received the case in late 1979, he wondered why Walker had been so desperate to escape, considering that the most difficult part of his sentence was already behind him. But in view of the murder indictment, the escape made perfect sense. The deputy could imagine Walker sweating each moment out in prison, fearful that the bodies of his victims might be found any day.

Kringle learned that before his escape at McNeil, Walker had obsessively stuck to a strenuous physical fitness regime, making his muscular build even more solid. Kringle also learned that Walker was very intelligent, with an IQ range of 130 to 140. A rabid reader as well, Walker had become something of a jailhouse lawyer, helping other convicts with their court motions and appeals in exchange for the most valuable prison currency: cartons of cigarettes. He also was a prolific correspondent, sometimes sending out a half-dozen letters a day. Reading copies of the surprisingly articulate and reasonably grammatical missives—routinely kept on file—Kringle noticed that Walker's tone never varied. The entire system was against him; he had been framed. From McNeil Island guards, Kringle learned that Walker had delved into the occult. "He thought himself capable of leaving his body," reported one guard.

According to Walker's file, he had been married twice,* and had fathered a daughter, Noel, born in 1967. Walker had married Noel's mother, Patricia McKay, in 1966, and they had divorced in 1972. McKay, who had been awarded custody of Noel, still lived in fear of her former husband. "I don't want him to know where I'm living," she told the feds. "You have to understand something about Buck. He's a classic psychopath. And he's never been questioned for even a fraction of the armed robberies he's committed."

Kringle noticed a pattern in Walker's buddies at McNeil Island and in the list of convicts he had written to in other institutions. They were the true incorrigibles—bank robbers, drug smugglers, extortionists, kidnappers, murderers. Kringle knew how this amoral brotherhood worked. When any member could call another as a witness in a trial, he did so, with the idea that it was easier for his friends to escape while traveling to and from court than while stuck behind prison walls. When someone like Walker hit the streets again, he was often set up in criminal enterprises by friends who had been out longer. Kringle knew that with such connections, Walker did not plan to go straight. That was fine with Kringle. Fugitives who stayed out of trouble were the most difficult to locate.

Kringle also knew about Jennifer Jenkins. Her name was

---

*On July 30, 1955, a week before he received three years' probation for burglary, Walker married his sixteen-year-old sweetheart, Tanya Logan, in Tijuana. Logan was granted an annulment in 1958, while Walker was serving his San Quentin stretch for armed robbery.

included on the McNeil Island list of Walker's correspondents. About eighteen months before his escape, Buck had written to her at a Santa Barbara address. There was no record of a reply.

January 18, 1978

Aloha Kekepania,

Hau'oli Makahiki Hou. I wish you new beginnings. How the fuck are you, baby? I'm writing because I've been thinking a lot about you lately and feeling the bitter wrench in my heart. I'm enclosing a present, which is about all I can come up with hereabout. They're a bunch of mad scribblings, which, in my egotistical state, I lump under the heading of quote poetry unquote.

We haven't communicated much over the last couple of years and you've become something of a stranger to me. Most of my thoughts about you nowadays are warm, some are bitter with disappointment, and there are times when I just can't help myself. I turn myself on remembering some vivid and vital things, beautiful things, that happened between us. Sometimes I can almost remember what you taste like.

The other evening I walked out on the back ramp to get a breath of fresh air, and stood there looking at the mountains, the waters of the Sound, across to other islands that abound in this area, and the setting sun was magnificent shining through a golden-reddish haze of the clouds. It's a terrible agony to experience anything beautiful in prison, because beauty here is always so tentative and there never seems to be any consummation. Some of the ugliest thoughts in the world must be thought by people in prisons, but I think some of the most beautiful thoughts come into our visions simply because we have such a need for them.

Ah well, Jen, my love (I hope you don't mind my calling you that for old time's sake) it's not such an enchanting world after all, is it? Too much manure for barefooted souls like us. If I had any juice with whatever gods there may be, I'd put in my strongest bid that they look after you and bless you with all you deserve, which would consist of an awful lot of love and consideration.

No more. I have to get back to work. Just wanted to say hello. Like hell! What I really want would take about a million words to express, and I'm not really feeling that creative. Take care and be good to yourself.

Aloha, baby.

Attached to the letter was Jennifer's "present," twenty-four pages of poems. Most were love lyrics, more than a few spiced with erotic images. Lines from one effort—entitled "Shall I Begin?"—caught Kringle's eye, and the deputy marshal smiled. Walker had written:

> No dungeon shall long contain me,
>   nor chains bind.
> Shall I begin
>   by walking on water
> or moving mountains?

Although a former sweetheart or accomplice could often be of assistance in locating a fugitive, it appeared to Kringle that Jennifer could not offer such help, having apparently ended all contact with Walker a long time before his escape. But, Kringle decided, locating the *new* woman in Walker's life could be the key to apprehending him.

Ruth Claire Thomas, thirty-nine, a short, bespectacled housewife, lived a humdrum existence with her stockbroker husband and two children in a tree-lined Olympia, Washington, housing tract. That is, until she joined the Aloha Club and went on one of its visits to McNeil Island to cheer up inmates from Hawaii. During regularly scheduled social hours in the prison's recreation hall, Ruth joined other club members in handing out fresh leis to the convicts as taped Hawaiian music played in the background. On her first visit, Ruth met Buck Walker. Soon she was returning just to see him. The day after he escaped, Mrs. Thomas left her family and vanished, but not before cleaning out the family savings account to the last penny.

JULY 31, 1981

A DUSTY PICKUP pulled off Interstate 8 in Yuma, Arizona, stopping at a gas station. Two men climbed out of the truck. They were wearing blue jeans and cowboy-style shirts with snaps and pointed pockets. Dressed pretty much like the locals, Deputy U.S. Marshals Dick Kringle and Don Baker hardly resembled law enforcement officers hot on the trail of a dangerous wanted fugitive.

Kringle had left Seattle a week before, first checking out a Lake Tahoe address that Ruth Thomas had recently used to acquire a new California driver's license. After he warned the residents of the penalties for aiding and abetting a fugitive, they confirmed that Buck Walker and Ruth Thomas had stayed there off and on that past summer and gave Kringle a Las Vegas address for Walker, which turned out to be a private postal drop. A few days later, Walker called the Las Vegas mailing center to request that his mail be forwarded to an address in Yuma, another private postal drop, located in an adult bookstore. Within the hour, Kringle was on his way to Arizona, where he rendezvoused with Baker.

At the local sheriff's office in Yuma, the duded-up lawmen discovered a federal narcotics task force working out of the office and Kringle showed the undercover officers Walker's mug shot.

"That's Sean O'Dougal," said Art Cash of the Drug Enforcement Agency. "We've seen him around but not for a few days. He's tight with a guy named Terry Conner. Conner owns a house in one of Yuma's nicer neighborhoods and drives a big Lincoln Continental. He likes people to think he sells enough greasy burgers at his hamburger stand to finance his life-style."

"This hamburger stand in town?"

"No, it's a truck-stop town called Wellton. About thirty miles east of here."

"Where does Walker hang out?" Kringle asked.

"We know where he hangs his hat when he's in town. I'll show you."

"By the way, what have you got on Conner?"

"Smuggling. Dealing. He's bringing in large quantities of Thai heroin. Your guy O'Dougal—or Walker—makes drug runs for him south of the border."

Kringle smiled narrowly. "That sounds like Bucky."

YUMA
AUGUST 4, 1981

BUCK WALKER still hadn't shown up.

Kringle decided against staking out the house on Elmwood Avenue where, according to the task force, Walker lived with a woman about forty named Luanne. "Walker is so con-wise, he might see our stakeout before we see him," he told Baker. "I want him to think it's safe to come home."

But Kringle and his partner did drive by the place several times every day. They were looking for a cocoa-brown 1976 Oldsmobile sedan bearing Arizona license ALF752, reputedly Buck's latest set of wheels.

As they drove for the nth time past the address at about nine in the morning on their fifth day in town, they saw a woman in a faded purple bathrobe taking the garbage out to the curb. She was in curlers, and she looked like bloody hell, but Kringle instantly recognized her.

"Ruth Thomas," he told Baker.

Now known as Luanne Simmons, Thomas, oldest of the molls among the Conner-Walker gang, had been dubbed the Den Mother by the task force. Pathetically enough, her main man, Walker, was known to be traveling with the youngest woman in the group—the fetching nineteen-year-old daughter of a McNeil Island ex-con. Willingly or not, Ruth Thomas apparently condoned the relationship, for everyone seemed to be one big happily villainous family.

"Still no brown Olds," Kringle said as they swung around the block. "Still no Bucky."

When his boss called a few days later, Kringle had to admit he couldn't anticipate when Walker would return to Yuma. "It could be tomorrow or it could be next month."

The next day, Kringle boarded a plane for Seattle, leaving Art Cash in charge.

AFTER MIDNIGHT,
AUGUST 12, 1981

A BROWN OLDS with Arizona plates rolled through the U.S. Customs checkpoint just south of Yuma. The tall, muscular male driver and a much younger female passenger were waved through after a glance in the trunk. The customs agent on duty failed to notice that this car was on the "Border Lookout" list.

At 2:00 A.M., a Yuma city policeman spotted the Olds in the parking lot of the Torch Light Motel on the outskirts of town. He radioed in an alert.

Art Cash and his men raced to the scene. All but Cash parked their cars down the street. He pulled his van into the lot next to the unoccupied Olds. He and the agent with him went into the back of the van to observe through the vehicle's one-way windows.

Ten minutes later, Conner and Walker walked out of Room 16. Both looked around edgily. Walker got into the driver's seat of the Olds and reached under the front seat for a paper bag. Conner opened the passenger's door and slid inside. He looked inside the bag, then pulled out an envelope from his pants pocket and handed it over to Walker.

Within seconds armed narcotics agents were descending on the two men. Walker and Conner were yanked out of the car, spread-eagled over the hood, patted down for weapons, and handcuffed.

Cash leaned into the Olds and pulled out the bag and envelope. The envelope was full of cash—at least several thousand dollars. The bag held hundreds of bright-colored capsules. Cash popped one open and tasted the powder. Barbiturates. Fresh from Mexico, Cash guessed.

He looked the big man in the face. "Buck Duane Walker," he said. "You're under arrest. So are you, Conner."

"There's some mistake," Walker said. "My name's Frank Wolf."

"Okay, Frank Wolf. You're under arrest."

Book Two

JUSTICE

NOTE: In Book Two, a number of in-depth legal discussions have been included in the hope that they will help explain the motivations behind the actions of the participants in this case, and how such actions are viewed in the context of existing law. I believe that these passages will enrich the reading of the book. However, because there are those who may be distracted by such legal asides, wherever possible I have put these legal observations—along with certain other material—in the appendix.

—VB

CHAPTER 21

LOS ANGELES
MARCH 8, 1982

"VINCE," MY SECRETARY ANNOUNCED over the intercom, "Miss Jenkins is here to see you."

I greeted my visitor in the reception room and was surprised to see her accompanied by a shaggy little dog with a graying snout.

"Mr. Bugliosi, I'd like you to meet Puffer," Jennifer said, leaning down to scratch the mutt behind an ear. "She's my baby." This was not the usual gambit of a murder suspect.

I ushered both visitors into my law library, and shut the door. Surrounded by wall-to-wall shelves of legal tomes, Jennifer and I sat across from each other at the long mahogany table that dominated the room. Puffer, with a quick wag of her tail, slipped under the table and curled up happily at Jennifer's feet.

"Puffer goes everywhere with me. She was at Palmyra."

"Maybe I should interview Puffer, too."

Jennifer laughed politely, crinkling the laugh lines at the corners of her large brown eyes. The alleged killer of the newspaper headlines had a disarming little girl quality about her.

I had first heard of Palmyra Island only a few weeks earlier. A friend had given me a copy of a three-part series, "Murder on Palmyra," that had appeared in the *Honolulu Star-Bulletin* the year before—an account of Mac and Muff's disappearance and presumed murder, the grisly discovery of Muff's skeletal remains and the first-degree murder charges against Buck Walker and Jennifer Jenkins. My friend knew Ted Jenkins—"he swears his sister is innocent"—and asked that I meet with Jennifer to consider representing her.

Though I suspect I'll always be thought of as a prosecutor, I have been a defense attorney since I left the Los Angeles County

District Attorney's Office in 1972. I must take a brief moment to add a degree of qualification concerning my defense work, which will help explain what I was looking for in my first meeting with Jennifer Jenkins.

During my career as a prosecutor, I learned that our criminal justice system has a tried-and-true way of filtering out people unjustly accused of breaking the law. Although most individuals arrested *have* indeed committed the offense for which they were arrested, a significant number have not. That mistake is often made on the spur of the moment and under pressure by uniformed officers (who are in my view, because of their daily risk of death, the poorest-paid members of our society). Most such mistakes are corrected at the next level, when plainclothes detectives investigate the case and interview the witnesses. Only when the detectives think the right person was arrested do they seek a criminal complaint from the district attorney's office. But the careful filtering continues. In Los Angeles County, for example, prosecutors reject about half of the cases brought to them. Most refusals to prosecute stem from a lack of sufficient evidence, but in some cases, the deputy DA may believe the wrong person has been arrested. Only when the charges against an individual seem both proper *and* strong enough to prove beyond a reasonable doubt in a court of law does the prosecutor file the criminal complaint. A preliminary hearing is then held before a municipal court judge, who decides whether the prosecutor has enough evidence to go to trial. As high a proportion as 15 percent of all criminal cases in Los Angeles County are dismissed at this hearing. Even when the judge sets the case for trial, the defense can file a motion requesting still another pretrial judicial review of the evidence, this time by a superior court judge, who determines whether or not there's sufficient evidence to warrant a trial. (Jennifer, by the way, had been indicted for murder in a federal court, where the filtering-out process is less thorough than in the state court system.)

Once a defendant has gone through all of these levels and the case has reached the trial court, it's probable that ninety-nine times out of a hundred, the true robber, rapist, or murderer is sitting at the defense table. In other words, most defense attorneys necessarily spend their careers defending guilty people.

"Everyone is entitled to be represented by an attorney" is the idealistic chant often recited by defense attorneys as justification for representing even the most vicious criminals in our society. The concept is unassailable, but idealism is rarely what motivates lawyers who represent guilty defendants. They take the work because trying cases is their livelihood, and they are ambitious to advance their careers. These motivations, while perfectly proper, are clearly not idealistic.

True idealism would be involved in a hypothetical situation such as the following. Suppose a family is brutally murdered in a small town, and none of the six lawyers in town is willing to represent the suspect because the enraged citizens are all convinced of the suspect's guilt and no lawyer wants to be ostracized in the community for attempting to get the suspect off. Finally, one attorney steps forward and says, "I don't care what my friends at the Rotary Club and the First Baptist Church say. This is America, and everyone is entitled under the Sixth Amendment to our Constitution to be represented by an attorney."

That would be idealism. I, too, would represent a defendant—even one I believed to be guilty of murder—if I were the only lawyer available, because the right to counsel is a sacred right in our society and much more important than any personal predilection I might have. But this type of situation simply does not exist in a city like Los Angeles, where 35,000 lawyers stumble over each other's feet for cases. So I am free to follow my inclination.

Since nothing in the canons of ethics of the American Bar Association says a lawyer has to represent everyone who comes to his door, I choose not to defend anyone charged with a violent crime unless I believe he is innocent or, if guilty, that there are substantially mitigating circumstances. (By the latter, I don't mean the question said to be asked about the victim by hard-bitten sheriffs in rural Texas at the start of any homicide investigation: "Did he *need* killing?") I investigate my own cases, and if I become satisfied in my own mind that the person is guilty, with no substantial mitigation, I routinely refer the case to other lawyers. I simply have no motivation whatsoever to knock myself out working a hundred hours a week, as I frequently do, trying to figure out a way to get some murderer off. Of course, theoretical purists might say I am prejudging the accused, and that a person cannot be considered guilty of a crime unless brought to trial and found so by a judge or jury. But under that argument, Adolf Hitler never committed any crimes, Jack the Ripper never committed any crimes, and the only crime Al Capone ever committed was income tax evasion.

Obviously, if a person, for instance, robs a bank, he is guilty of having robbed the bank, irrespective of whether or not the prosecution can prove this fact to the satisfaction of the jury. A legal verdict of "not guilty" doesn't change the reality of what he did.

My position is not a matter of high ethics. It's just that I would have a difficult time living with myself if I did otherwise. As a prosecutor, I handled some twenty-one first-degree murder cases before a jury. Every one of the defendants was convicted, and eight were on Death Row when, in 1972, the California state supreme court ruled that the death penalty, as then being implemented, was unconstitutional. How could I possibly start defending these same types of people in order to earn a living? If it came to that, I would rather stop practicing law and find another job. I am also not unmindful of the fact that were I to secure a not-guilty verdict for one of these defendants I represented, and he went out and did it again, I could rationalize all I wanted, but I would be partially responsible. If I had not deceived the jury, there would not have been a second murder.

In a nutshell, although I've never been a law-and-order fanatic, I do believe that those who have committed serious crimes should be severely punished, and I do not want to be in a position of actively seeking to thwart this natural justice.

One illustration of my dilemma in legal defense work is the case of Dr. Jeffrey MacDonald, the Princeton-educated former U.S. Army Green Beret who was accused of savagely stabbing to death his pregnant wife and two young daughters in their Fort Bragg, North Carolina, home one rainy night in March 1970. He was first charged with the murders that year, but the case against him was dropped. It was sometime in late 1973 or early 1974 that a woman friend of MacDonald's came to my office and told me that the doctor, who was then working as an emergency-room physician in nearby Long Beach, had learned that he was about to be reindicted. Would I be interested in representing him? We could talk about it, I said, if the doctor was innocent. "Tell him, though, that for starters I want him to take and pass a polygraph test." I was interested because the MacDonald case could provide the kind of high visibility I needed to start changing my public image from that of prosecutor to defense attorney. While waiting to hear from him, I telephoned the federal prosecutor handling the case in North Carolina and asked what he had against MacDonald. The prosecutor would not say very much, but did mention a few pieces of evidence to me, one of which was that fibers from MacDonald's blue pajamas were found embedded beneath the fingernails of his two-and-a-half-year-old daughter. That evoked in my mind the horrifying scene of a little girl crying out, "Daddy, Daddy, no," as she reached out and struggled against her father while he stabbed her to death. That was enough for me. I wanted nothing to do with the case. MacDonald's lady friend called a week later anyway to say that he did not think it was necessary to take a polygraph as a precondition to my representing him. Convicted of the triple murder in 1979, he was sentenced to three consecutive life terms in prison.*

Now, after reading the series about the Palmyra Island murder case, I was characteristically reluctant to defend Jennifer Jenkins. The way I saw it, if four people were alone on an uninhabited island and two were murdered, what was the likelihood that either of the other two people was innocent, particularly when both ended up in Hawaii with the victim's boat, acting very suspiciously? The Federal Bureau of Investigation, the U.S. Attorney in Hawaii, and a federal grand jury had examined the evidence and

---

*My disinclination to defend a murderer also resulted in my electing not to represent former San Francisco supervisor Dan White for the 1978 assassination murders of Mayor George Moscone and supervisor Harvey Milk when friends of White's from the San Francisco police department—White was a former officer—asked me to.

concurred that Buck Walker and Jennifer Jenkins had together committed the murders. And two juries had already found Walker and Jenkins guilty of stealing the boat together. Before I agreed to defend her, I had to be confident she was not a killer.

After the preliminary pleasantries, Jennifer told me her family had tried to contact me after the murder indictment in 1981. "My Uncle Harold called your office and left his name and number, but you were out of town."

I couldn't remember receiving any such message, but I had been in Chicago in the winter of 1980–81 for a three-month federal jury trial. In any event, Jennifer's family hired Barry Tarlow, a prominent Los Angeles criminal defense attorney. Soon he was replaced by defense attorneys Brian J. O'Neill and Leonard Weinglass. O'Neill had since withdrawn from the case, but Weinglass would remain as co-counsel if I agreed to represent Jennifer. Though I had never met him, I knew a little about Weinglass, who some feel is the most respected trial lawyer for the political left in America. His most famous case was the Chicago Seven trial, in which he defended the late Abbie Hoffman, Tom Hayden, and two other defendants. He had also been a defense attorney in the historic Pentagon Papers case.

In a major criminal trial, particularly a murder case, it is common for the defendant to be represented by two or even three lawyers. (Buck Walker had already lined up two court-appointed defense attorneys, Earle Partington and Ray Findlay, both from Honolulu.) On the other hand, as a longtime prosecutor, I'd never envisioned the day I would be on the same side of the aisle as the likes of Leonard Weinglass.

I told Jennifer I hoped she'd had nothing to do with the murders of Mac and Muff Graham.

She sighed. "I'm guilty of making some mistakes in my life, but I didn't kill Mac and Muff."

I watched her intently for a moment. "Then I assume you're willing to take a polygraph?"

"Yes," she answered with no hesitation. "I'll take whatever test you or the Government want to give me. Lie detector, sodium pentothal, you name it. And the jury can hear the results."

"Whatever they may be?"

"Yes."

What Jennifer had just said was extremely important to me. Most guilty people don't want to take any kind of a truth-discovering test. Even those who are willing have been told by their lawyers that the results cannot be introduced at their trial without their consent, which, if they fail the test, they obviously never give. Here, Jennifer had offered to not only take any test I or her accusers wanted to give her, but to let the jury hear the results, whatever they turned out to be. How could she possibly be willing to do this if she was guilty?

Jennifer had made a significant stride toward convincing me of her innocence.

"Anyway," she added, "Barry Tarlow had me take a polygraph test last year, right after the indictment. I passed."

I made a note to confirm that.

Now I wanted to get to the case. "Tell me everything that happened. Start at the beginning, when you met Buck, and take your time."

When I next looked at my watch, it was nearly 10:00 P.M., and Jennifer was far from finished with her story. I had, of course, slowed her down by asking for clarifications and interjecting questions.

"It's late," she said, trying to stifle a yawn.

"Let's call it a night. Jennifer, I repeat that I will not be able to represent you if it ever appears that you had anything *at all* to do with these two murders."

"Since I'm innocent," she said confidently, "that's fine with me."

I handed Jennifer a fresh yellow legal pad. "Whenever you think of anything favorable to your case, I want you to write it down. Make another list of everything you think is unfavorable, along with any explanations you may have. Next time we meet, we'll go over your notes."

She seemed reluctant to pick up the pad.

"What's wrong?"

"I have to concentrate all day at work."

"Do it when you get home."

"I like to relax then." It was that little girl I hadn't seen for several hours.

"Jennifer, the charge against you couldn't be more serious. You've already been convicted of the theft of the boat. If you're going to have any chance of getting a not-guilty verdict on the murder charge, you've got to work hard, very hard."

"I know," she said, but her tone suggested no real concern. She casually reached for the pad as she stood up.

A bit unnerved, I escorted her to the elevator. When I returned alone to the office, I went back into the library and sat down. Everyone had long since departed the suite I shared with two other attorneys. The only sound was the soft tap-tapping of my pencil eraser against the tabletop as I contemplated the exotic story Jennifer Jenkins had begun to tell.

Apart from the mystery of the case (and the fact it seemed almost fictional and was completely different from any of the other murder cases I had ever handled or knew of, most of which fall into routine categories and have familiar settings), I was immediately struck by the terrible irony of Mac Graham, reportedly (per the newspapers) wanting to get away from a big-city life that was becoming increasingly unsafe by going to a peaceful, idyllic South Sea isle, ending up brutally murdered and left at the bottom of a lagoon, a worse end than could have ever happened to him in San Diego.

What unimaginable hell exists right here on earth. Had the woman I just spoke to been responsible, along with her boyfriend, for the horrors that had befallen the Grahams in the summer of 1974?

Although I don't feel I'm particularly adept at judging people—especially early on—to me, Jennifer had not acted like a guilty person. I have interviewed and/or cross-examined many individuals who were guilty of serious crimes, and not one has ever been as matter-of-fact and detached as she. Guilty minds are normally beset with fears and suspicions that have a way of surfacing. I saw nothing but casualness and openness in Jennifer. On the other hand, neither did she act like an innocent person accused of committing the most heinous crime of all. Such defendants are usually angered by the cruel twist of circumstances that has them "standing in the dock" facing untrue charges, and they can't wait to prove their innocence to the world. Since Jennifer did not act entirely like either a guilty person or an innocent one, what it came down to on my first meeting with her was a simple visceral feeling that she was not involved in the murders. But obviously I still had my doubts. These would have to be addressed in many other meetings with her before I could make up my mind whether or not I should represent her. I also reminded myself of what an old-timer at the DA's office told me early in my career about a French adage: *Une femme ne révèle pas sa culpabilité aussi facilement qu'un homme.*—A woman does not reveal her guilt as easily as a man.

There was something in particular that bothered me. I did not realize what it was until the following morning, when I reviewed my notes over a cup of coffee in our sunny kitchen at home.

Although she had repeatedly expressed sadness at the deaths of Mac and Muff Graham, Jennifer did not talk as if *murder* had taken place on Palmyra, only two terrible accidental deaths for which *no one* was responsible. I confronted the issue head-on at our next session as soon as she, the loyal Puffer, and I were once again settled in the law library.

"Jennifer, it's clear that Muff was murdered. And undoubtedly Mac was, too."

She raised her dark-brown eyebrows in surprise, gazing at me as if I had offered a novel thesis. "As I said, they went fishing and never came back. We found their overturned dinghy. I've always thought they drowned or were attacked by sharks."

"The bones of drowning victims or people eaten by sharks don't show up seven years later in a metal box."

She shrugged. "Len Weinglass says they don't know *for sure* that Muff was ever in the box."

"Jennifer, please. Obviously, Mac and Muff were murdered, and no bluebird did it. We're not going to get anywhere shadowboxing with reality. Only four people were on the island. Either Buck and you did it together, or Buck did it alone. The circumstances simply don't permit any other reasonable conclusion. At this point, I'm willing to assume you weren't involved. Which makes Buck the lone killer."

"I just can't see Buck killing Mac and Muff. They were so nice to us—especially Mac. He was a prince of a man. He was always coming over and giving us fish he'd caught. He kept Buck in cigarettes. We played chess together." Her arguments seemed to summon up vivid memories. "They were *good people*, Vince."

"Yes, they sound like they were."

"Buck wouldn't have—" Her voice cracked. It was her first display of emotion.

She rose from her chair and nervously circled the table, running her finger along a row of law books as she passed in front of them.

"Last summer, at a hearing in Honolulu," she began, "I sat next to Buck in court. I hadn't seen him in years." (During our first session, Jennifer told me that she hadn't even heard from Buck since he'd written her from prison several years earlier. She said she did not answer his letter and assured me she no longer had any emotional attachment to him.) "Before court started, we had a chance to talk. I told him I had never believed anything different had happened to Mac and Muff other than they went fishing and had an accident. Buck said that's what he always thought had happened, too."

Finished with her brief tour of the room, she scratched Puffer behind the ear and sat back down. "I asked Buck how he could explain that Muff's body had *apparently* been put in a metal box. He said, 'Maybe Mac did it.'"

She looked up expectantly, perhaps waiting to see how that idea played with me. But I kept quiet.

After the slightest pause, she went on. "I told Buck that didn't make sense. If Mac wanted to kill Muff, he could have waited for us to leave the next day. They would have been alone on the island, and he could have done whatever he wanted. He could have reported to the authorities that Muff had fallen overboard in the ocean. He could have spent the rest of his life sailing the seven seas on the *Sea Wind*."

"What was Buck's response?"

She shook her head. "He didn't say anything. He just . . . shrugged, or something."

"Did you talk about anything else?" I asked.

"Well . . ." She looked a little embarrassed. "I asked him if he'd go first this time. See, he had asked me to go first during the theft trials, and I did. I was thinking he might want to return the favor this time."

"What did he say?"

"His exact words: 'I'm not sticking my neck in no chopping block.' The judge took the bench then, and we had to keep quiet. I haven't talked to Buck since."

"So, after you heard about Muff's remains being found along with the box, you *did* begin to suspect that Buck had murdered Mac and Muff?"

"No, not really. It just—confused me. I still don't believe Buck killed them. You have to understand, Vince. I loved Buck very, very much. More than any man in my life, before or since. And I knew the real Buck, the hidden Buck, better than anyone else did. Besides, I was with him every day on Palmyra. I just don't know how he could have done such a horrible thing right under my nose without my knowing it."

I leaned back in my hard wooden chair and watched her closely. Guilty suspects typically try, of course, to put the hat on someone else in order to lift suspicion from themselves. But Jennifer would not do that to Buck, even though I had given her the opportunity. She didn't even make any effort to distance herself from him. And somehow I didn't sense she was using clever reverse psychology on me.

"What have you written down on your note pad since we last met?" I asked.

"Nothing." She was back to being breezy.

Somewhat testily, I suggested that she keep the pad and make time to do the homework I had assigned her. I then asked her to continue her story where she had left off at our previous meeting.

In all, it would take three sessions for Jennifer to tell me her complete version of everything that had happened from the moment she had met Buck through all of the events on Palmyra, and on up to the present. In the meantime, I confirmed with Len Weinglass that Jennifer had indeed taken a polygraph examination. In fact, two. The first one had been judged by the examiner to be "inconclusive," but everyone agreed that one of the key questions had been ambiguously phrased. The second test, Len assured me, was a clear "pass."

By this time, although Jennifer had done everything possible to convince the world she was guilty, I was coming to believe she was innocent of murder. She was certainly guilty of having loved the wrong man, and she had shown bad judgment in a number of other ways. But I was moving in the direction of concluding that she was one of those rare criminal defendants who is not guilty as charged. Yet, because of one of the most unusual sets of circumstances I'd ever seen or heard of in a murder case, I knew that only a tremendous uphill legal battle would save her from being convicted.

MARCH 19, 1982

SINCE ALL of the case files were there, my first meeting with Leonard Weinglass was at his office in the Old Bradbury Building, an 1893 historical landmark located in a declining area near the L.A. County Courthouse. This five-story building, complete with an open courtyard, exposed elevator cages, and ornamental rails and banisters, was the kind of place you'd expect to see a gumshoe like Sam Spade hang up his shingle.

When I arrived, Weinglass was on the phone, so I took a seat in his waiting room. Close to hand lay the latest copy of *Mother Jones*, the self-proclaimed "magazine for the rest of us," a liberal, non-profit publication based in San Francisco. I smiled . . . of course.

In addition to the Chicago Seven and Pentagon Papers cases, Weinglass had defended Symbionese Liberation Army soldiers Bill and Emily Harris, and also been involved in the Wounded Knee defense, a Native American *cause célèbre*.

In a long article on him in the *Los Angeles Times* two years earlier in which he was referred to as one of the top trial lawyers in the country, "the Weinglass commitment" was summarized as a "brand of easy-riding radicalism that embraces both a concern for

the underdog and an absolute certainty that capitalism is dying."
The forty-eight-year-old barrister was described as anti-nuke,
anti-MX missile, anti-big oil, anti-macho interventionist foreign
policy, and anti-death penalty.

I couldn't imagine what Weinglass might think of my prosecutorial background—particularly, the notoriety I had received during some of my death-penalty cases. I suspected he was as
incredulous as I that we might end up on the same side in a court
of law.

When Weinglass appeared, he greeted me by my first name, suggesting I call him Len, and warmly grasped my outstretched hand.
Tieless and bearded, he had long gray-streaked brown hair, with a
neat round bald spot at the crown, a kindly smile, and a pleasant
voice.

As we settled into his sparsely furnished office, I noticed a large
framed sketch of Clarence Darrow on the wall behind him. (Weinglass had been selected as the first recipient of the Clarence Darrow Award in 1974.) To his right was a small bust of Ho Chi Minh.

Since our backgrounds were poles apart, I casually tried to
soften the image he might have of me. I explained that as a prosecutor I always abided by the old 5th Canon of Ethics of the American Bar Association that the primary duty of a public prosecutor
is to secure justice, not a conviction, and only if a conviction was
justice would I have anything to do with a case, and then, only by
prosecuting in a fair manner. I was proud, I said, of having been
called a "prosecutor with a heart" by one of the leading underground newspapers.

Hoping I wasn't sounding patronizing, I added that I was in
sympathy with the civil rights causes he'd been fighting for
throughout the years.

Len, with his smile in place, said he appreciated that. I was
amused that he made no effort to toughen any image I might have
had of him.

I remembered from the *Times* article that Len was content leading "a simple life," taking cases that did not violate his principles,
and getting by on ten to fifteen thousand dollars a year.

It is said that the principal element that distinguishes a profession from a business is that in a profession, one's primary obligation is to those he serves, not to himself. In this day and age, where the pursuit of dollars has become the top priority of so many lawyers, and where unconscionable fees as well as overbilling (for example, working one hour and billing for two or three, or billing at the lawyer's hourly rate for work which, unbeknownst to the client, the lawyer has the paralegal do) are commonplace, Len Weinglass is among the last of a dying breed.

"I imagine you've represented, along the way, quite a few people without a fee," I said.

His smile broadened. "That's true," he said, "but I've never gone without a meal." He had a lot of friends around the country, he explained, who happily provided him with room and board when his legal travels took him to their town.

"Allard Lowenstein lived the same way," I said.

I had come to know Lowenstein, the brainy, inexhaustible former Congressman and lawyer from New York, when he asked me to handle the legal proceedings in his group's attempt to reopen the investigation into the assassination of Senator Robert F. Kennedy. A close friend of the Kennedys, Lowenstein himself was later murdered. He'd become, I knew, kind of a cult figure. A movie was reportedly in the works on him, and it has been said that Lowenstein probably influenced more young people to become political activists in the 1960s than anyone else. Definitely a member of the "left," Lowenstein is believed by some to have actually triggered the downfall of Lyndon Johnson over the Vietnam War by giving a stirring call-to-action speech at a massive rally in New York City.

Weinglass's expression had darkened.

"I bring up Allard," I offered, "because he's the only other member of the activist left I've personally known."

"He was not trusted by the left," Weinglass said flatly. "I am *not* an admirer of his."

I smiled to myself, realizing just how far to the left Len Weinglass was coming from. (I would tell him, at a later time, that being as far to the left as he was, one would think he would have "both feet planted very firmly in the air," yet I found him to be a sensible, down-to-earth guy. He chuckled.)

With that, we turned our discussion to Jennifer Jenkins.

IN APRIL 1982, after further sessions with Jennifer, I made a decision to defend Jennifer Jenkins against the charge of first-degree murder. I made another decision: since Buck and Jennifer had been together throughout the Palmyra period, and both had seemingly been acting in concert thereafter, I would have to rewind the past and try to separate them. I instinctively knew that a key way would be to don my old DA's hat and prosecute Buck Walker at Jennifer's trial. Despite Jennifer's protestations, I was certain that Walker was responsible for the brutal murders of Mac and Muff Graham.

Weinglass, however, told me he was uncomfortable with this approach. "I'm afraid if Buck Walker goes down," he said, his voice filled with doom, "so will Jennifer."

From the moment I take a case right up to the time of a jury's verdict, I always have tremendous confidence I will win. For some inexplicable reason, the feeling comes over me that I can't lose. This trial would shake my confidence more than any case I had ever tried.

MAY 5, 1982

UNEARTHING A COPY of the transcript of Jennifer's boat-theft trial was not easy. But I had to have it. The transcript would undoubtedly be used by the prosecution to attack Jennifer's credibility at her murder trial whenever her testimony varied from it. However, Weinglass did not have a copy. He told me that one of Jennifer's former attorneys had the transcript, but when I spoke to the lawyer on the phone, he couldn't find it. Eventually, I learned it had been put in storage in a Los Angeles warehouse with other old unrelated files.

When I was finally able to lay my hands on the 749-page transcript, I discovered a number of substantive inconsistencies between what Jennifer had told me and what she had testified to in 1975. They were disturbing.

She had told me that she and Buck had found a 1961 signed will of Mac's on the *Sea Wind*. It provided that in the event of his death at sea, whoever he designated in another document (Jennifer never saw any other document) could take up to two years to return the boat to his sister, Mary "Kit" Muncey. Although she and Buck obviously hadn't been so designated in this other document, Jennifer argued strongly to me that the language of the will implied justification for their plan to sail the *Sea Wind* for two years before returning it to Muncey. But in her theft-trial testimony, other than mentioning that she and Buck had found Mac's will naming his sister, Mary Muncey, as the executrix of his estate, Jennifer had made absolutely *no mention* of this two-year grace period. On the contrary, she had testified that when she was arrested in Honolulu, she and Buck had been on their way to Seattle to immediately deliver the *Sea Wind* to Kit Muncey.

With respect to the all-important day in question—August 30, 1974, supposedly the day Mac and Muff disappeared—I found two major discrepancies. In one of our first sessions, Jennifer told me that Buck had the *Iola*'s dinghy *all day* on August 30; in other words, she couldn't have gone ashore unless he came and picked her up. It had occurred to me then that if Buck had possession of the dinghy that day, he would not have had to worry about Jennifer coming ashore while he was committing the murders. However, if *she* had the dinghy that day, then Buck would have had to worry about being caught, either in the act of killing Mac and Muff, or while disposing of their bodies. Buck's having the dinghy, then, would be one piece of circumstantial evidence going in the direction of supporting my argument to the jury that Buck had *alone* murdered Mac and Muff. But if Jennifer had the dinghy . . .

Now I learned that, contrary to what she had told me, she had testified that she, not Buck, had the dinghy on August 30.

The second discrepancy was also alarming. She had told me that on the morning of that same critically important day, she and Buck had gone back and forth between the *Iola* and his camp bringing things like a camping stove, lantern, and articles of clothing back to the boat in preparation for their departure. But she had not testified to this activity at her trial. Rather, the clear implication of her testimony was that she had stayed aboard the *Iola* all day.

Of course, I confronted Jennifer with these inconsistencies at our next meeting. She was not surprised and answered calmly. With respect to the will, she explained that her lawyers at the theft trial had advised her not to testify about the subject provision in the will or about her and Buck's plan to return the *Sea Wind* after two years. "They said it sounded unbelievable," she explained.

When I countered that even before she had any lawyers, she had failed to tell FBI agent Calvin Shishido about the will and its unusual provision, she replied that she had simply been too frightened and confused to tell him the whole story, and that she also knew that the provision, since it did not apply to them, gave them no legal right to take the *Sea Wind*.

But what she did tell Shishido was even worse, yet a third version of events. Testifying at her trial that she and Buck intended to bring the *Sea Wind* back to Mac's sister *immediately* but telling me they intended to wait for *two years* was bad enough. But when she told Shishido that the reason she and Buck never notified the authorities about what happened to Mac and Muff was that they knew if they did, the *Sea Wind* would be taken away from them, and they believed the Grahams would want them to have the boat, Jennifer was in effect telling Shishido that they *never* intended to return the boat. Why, I asked her with some heat, had she told Shishido this outrageous as well as very incriminating story? She answered that she couldn't admit the *real* reason why they never reported the Grahams' disappearance. Buck had insisted they couldn't have any kind of contact with the authorities because he was a fugitive. And when she spoke to Shishido, she was still protecting Buck's identity.

"What about your telling me that you were on and off the *Iola* during the morning?"

"I was."

"There's no reference to that in your trial testimony."

She shrugged. "I guess no one asked me."

"Jennifer, this is important. Very important. I'm going to ask you again—*who* had the dinghy that day? You or Buck?"

"As I remember, Buck had the dinghy that day," she answered, without hesitation.

I couldn't help but wonder whether Jennifer, in the years since her theft trial, had figured out the significance of who had the dinghy that day and had altered her story accordingly. It was a chilling thought with enormous ramifications.

"Then why did you testify in 1975 that *you* had the dinghy?"

She shook her head. "I honestly don't know. I've talked to so many people about the case over the years. Sometimes it's hard for me to remember what really happened that day. But I think Buck had the dinghy."*

I knew witnesses could become confused by all the questions and proposed scenarios suggested to them by the police, prosecutors, and defense attorneys, sometimes not remembering if something they are saying actually happened or was an image or thought implanted in their mind earlier by someone else. With the passage of time added—in this case, eight years—variations in anyone's story could be anticipated. But Jennifer's prosecutors would not look upon these discrepancies so charitably, and could use them to discredit her with the jury.

There was another, even more serious, problem I would have to deal with at Jennifer's murder trial. She admitted to me that she had committed perjury at her theft trial.

Not that her perjury surprised or shocked me. To people unfamiliar with court proceedings, the word "perjury" can set off lights and sirens. But in fact, perjury occurs at nearly every trial. A distinguished former member of the New York Bar once observed:

---

*I subsequently realized that under Jennifer's version of what happened, she *had* to have had the dinghy at least later in the day because she told me she went ashore by herself around 5:30 P.M. to take a bath and then meet Buck at the *Sea Wind* for their supposed dinner invitation with the Grahams. When I confronted Jennifer with this reality, she said she was more confused than ever as to who had the dinghy on August 30. Certainly the possibility exists that each of them had it during different parts of the day.

"Scarcely a trial is conducted in which perjury does not appear in a more or less flagrant form." Perjury is so common that attorneys are not only unsurprised by it, but even expect it.

Although Jennifer had told several lies on the witness stand, the main one concerned the final fate of the *Iola*.

She told me it was Buck's idea to leave Palmyra on the *Sea Wind* and that she had originally balked at the suggestion, finally relenting when he argued that the *Sea Wind*, left unattended in the Palmyra lagoon, would be vandalized. They would be respecting Mac's love for the *Sea Wind* by protecting her, Buck had said. That made sense to Jennifer and she had agreed. But I discovered that at her theft trial she had served up the story (the same one she told Shishido) about trying to leave on the *Iola* before it grounded on the reef, foolishly sticking to that lie even in the face of damning photographic evidence to the contrary. Jennifer told me that shortly after those pictures of the *Iola* and *Sea Wind* were taken, Buck had sunk the boat by opening up all of the *Iola*'s hull fittings.

"When I last saw our boat," Jennifer said, "she was sailing toward the horizon, slowly sinking. It made me very sad." She went on to explain that Buck, even before they left Palmyra, had concocted the story of the *Iola*'s grounding in order to justify taking the *Sea Wind*. He told her the authorities would never believe the true story—that they were acting out of concern for Mac's wishes.

There are two basic types of perjury in a criminal trial. In the first, a guilty defendant denies under oath that he committed the crime. The prosecutor merely blinks his eyes at this type of perjury and looks the other way, because he knows it is a form of self-defense that is inevitable. If the defendant were going to admit his guilt, he normally would have pled guilty and there wouldn't have been any trial. The second form of perjury is not self-defensive in nature. The most egregious example would be a witness knowingly accusing an innocent person of a crime. This type of perjury, if it can be proved, is not overlooked, resulting usually in a criminal prosecution.

Jennifer's lies were in the nature of self-defense; hence, relatively speaking, more understandable than the second type of perjury. But I still had reason for serious concern. Her lies under oath before the previous jury could very possibly destroy her credibility with the jury at her murder trial.

The inescapable reality I faced with Jennifer was the prosecutor arguing to the jury in his summation: "*Miss Jenkins admits she lied to another jury. She says she is telling the truth now. If we know she lied before under oath, why should we believe her now?*" If everything else she had done and said wasn't already enough, it could be a clinching argument to sway the jury against Jennifer.

"Well, what do you think?" Jennifer said. "Did I do a good job of making it tough for you?" She had a smile on her face, but she wasn't really smiling.

"I don't mind tough cases, Jennifer. What I resent about you," I said with a straight face, "is that even though you say you're innocent—and I believe you—you went around acting guilty. That's hypocrisy."

Jennifer chuckled, a real smile dissolving the rented one.

"Let me tell you, Jennifer, what the trial is going to be all about," I said. "The unique circumstances of this case come down to a matter of basic math. When four people are on a deserted island, two are murdered, and the remaining two take off in the victims' boat and otherwise act very suspiciously, as you and Buck did, most reasonable people would conclude that these two are guilty. So the prosecution's case is essentially going to be—almost has to be—that four minus two leaves two. And I'm just going to have to convince the jury that four minus two leaves one. And that the one killer is Buck."

Jennifer smiled once again. "Good luck," she said.

Her tone suggested that *I* was the one who had the problem and she was good-naturedly wishing me well in my effort to solve it. Jennifer was amazing, I said to myself.

I WAS TO have more problems preparing Jennifer for trial than with any other witness I could remember. Typically, when I interview a witness, I write down everything the witness says in narrative form, as if it were a straightforward factual account of events. Later, I convert the material into tentative questions and answers. In the nature of things, there will always be many modifications to my original Q and A, but with Jennifer, the changes were endless. Often, entire pages of questions became useless because she would add a different twist to an incident we had already covered in detail. I was also constantly having to expand my line of questioning because Jennifer would suddenly open up an entirely new area that needed to be explained or covered. The difficulty of preparing her for trial was reflected in the numbering of my pages of questions. It degenerated to the point where it was rare for one consecutively numbered page to follow another. For instance, between pages 43 and 44 there soon appeared pages 43 (a), 43 (b), 43 (c), and so forth. Then, later, for further additions between pages 43 (b) and 43 (c), I would have to resort to 43 (b) 1, 43 (b) 2, 43 (b) 3 . . .

Why was there always yet another layer of truth to be revealed? Another shadow in this hall of mirrors? After one particularly frustrating session with Jennifer, I admitted to my wife over a late-night snack that perhaps I was having so much trouble because I was "trying to fit a square peg into a round hole."

Gail's frank response was alarming. "I'm not sure I trust her."

"Why not?"

"When I met her, she didn't look me in the eye."*

"That doesn't make her a murderer, honey."

"I know. But it's more than that. I keep wondering how anyone could have been on that tiny island while Buck Walker was killing those people and not know anything about it. Where was she?"

"On the *Iola*."

"Doing what, Vince? Baking bread?"

"As a matter of fact"—I was almost too embarrassed to say it—"she was, among other things, baking bread on the day Mac and Muff disappeared."

*Len Weinglass, though he never said he did not believe in Jennifer's innocence, nonetheless remarked to me that she came across as "manipulative and untruthful," and in answering questions she frequently "shifts her eyes and hesitates, as if she's searching for the right answer." Len said he found these mannerisms "disturbing." But I did not see these things. One insight Len and I did agree on from the beginning: Jennifer was quite intelligent. Her capacity to grasp and understand virtually anything she was confronted with was impressive.

Gail said nothing more. She didn't have to. Her expression of utter disbelief said it all.

When my own wife, who is as level-headed as anyone I've ever known, suspected my client, I knew I had problems.

Gail was hardly alone in questioning Jennifer's innocence. A July 1981 public opinion survey in Hawaii commissioned by the Honolulu law firm of Hart and Wolff, which Leonard Weinglass hired to handle matters in the islands, showed how strongly the public there felt about the Palmyra case. In the survey, 205 adults were selected at random from lists of registered voters and questioned by telephone. Ninety-one percent of those surveyed said they had read or heard about the case of a sailing couple disappearing on Palmyra Island. Clearly, the Palmyra murder case had become Hawaii's most sensational crime story since the Massie murder case in 1931 (Clarence Darrow's last big case, and the basis for the novel and television film *Blood and Orchids*). To the key question, whether "the couple charged with the Palmyra murder" was guilty or innocent, the tally was a landslide. A staggering 95.8 percent believed *both* Buck and Jennifer were guilty of murder.

Not only did the unusual circumstances point irresistibly to the guilt of both Buck and Jennifer, but the media coverage only exacerbated the problem. Hitler didn't get much worse press in London than they got in Honolulu.

Obviously, there was an early defense motion for a change of venue to the mainland, where, away from the inundation of publicity, the chances of a fair trial would be increased. At a critical three-day July 1981 hearing in Honolulu before U.S. District Court Judge Ernest M. Heen, Dr. Jay Schulman of Columbia University, a recognized authority on public opinion, was called to the stand by Len Weinglass. Schulman founded the National Jury Project, an organization devoted to research and consultation on all facets of the American jury system, and for many years has been one of the nation's leading consultants to defense attorneys, prosecutors, the U.S. Justice Department, and Congressional subcommittees examining our judicial system.

Schulman testified that the 95.8 percent prejudgment of guilt was by far the highest he had ever heard of in a criminal case. It was "astronomically high," he said, even compared to other high-visibility cases. He cited the Patty Hearst case; polls preceding her trial had indicated only a 15 percent prejudgment of guilt. (And Patty Hearst, of course, was found *guilty*.) Schulman speculated that the reason for the low 15 percent in the Hearst case was the possibility of an alternative explanation for her conduct (i.e., that she had been brainwashed), which was lacking in this case. Schulman believed the unique facts of the case were such that the prosecution wouldn't have to prove guilt, as they are required by law to do.

"I think she [Jennifer] would have to prove her innocence before a jury could acquit her," Schulman told Judge Heen.

Testifying that he had examined hundreds of articles published in Hawaii's newspapers and reviewed transcripts of dozens of TV and radio news stories about the case, Schulman concluded: "My opinion is that the publicity in this case has reached almost every eligible juror in Hawaii. . . . It is a macabre story, a bizarre story. It has all the ingredients of a fantastically interesting soap opera."

Noting that people frequently don't read articles to the end, and often forget what they do read, Schulman said this case was different. "It so much captured people's imagination that they read it through and they assimilated a great deal of the total circumstances reported." The story "excites and courts the imagination. It offers the imagination the chance to wonder, to infer, to develop some closure of its own as to what happened." Coupled with "the paradisiacal romantic image of this remote island where all of this took place," Schulman said he could understand why his survey showed that people had "the highest recall of details of any case I have ever encountered."

On cross-examination, Assistant U.S. Attorney Elliot Enoki, opposing the change of venue for Jennifer's case, asked if it wasn't true that the "majority" of publicity had to do with Buck Walker—"his prior convictions for drugs and other things, his escape and being a fugitive?"

"No," Schulman answered. "Buck Walker and Jennifer Jenkins are always paired. *There is an inescapable conclusion that both of them were involved.* Because of this twinning phenomenon, in every piece of publicity on this case, Jenkins and Walker are twins: Jenkins is Walker's girlfriend; they had an association before they sailed to Palmyra; their association was obviously close on Palmyra; and they sailed the *Sea Wind* back to Honolulu together. The publicity has linked Jenkins and Walker constantly." Schulman's expert opinion was firm: it would be impossible for Jennifer to receive a fair trial in Hawaii.

Judge Heen disagreed. On August 12, 1981, Heen, a former U.S. Attorney for Honolulu, orally denied the change of venue motion.

On March 12, 1982, U.S. District Court Judge James M. Burns, Heen's successor, issued a written order again denying a change of venue for the Palmyra murder case.

But at the same March 12 session—four days after I first interviewed Jennifer and before I joined the defense as co-counsel—Judge Burns (as Judge King had done for the theft trials in 1975) granted Leonard Weinglass's motion to sever her case from Buck's. There would be separate trials for Buck and Jennifer.

'The July 1981 public opinion poll consistently contained responses such as these:
"It was a double murder of a couple who sailed down there to some island. A *murderer and murderess* stole a yacht."
"Jennifer Jenkins and her boyfriend were on Palmyra Island and I'm sure *they* murdered the Grahams."
"*They* left the bodies of a couple on the island and fled."
"*They* killed the people and took their yacht."
"*Jennifer Jenkins and Buck Walker* murdered the owners of a boat and stole the boat."
"A young couple ended up with another couple's yacht and the evidence would point to the fact that *they* murdered the couple who owned the boat."
"*Two hippie characters* murdered a couple on the island and took their yacht."
"I think it was very atrocious what *they* did. *Those people* deserve the maximum penalty. I don't know how *they* thought *they* could get away with it, especially since *they* brought the stolen boat back to Hawaii."

CHAPTER 22

A YEAR-LONG ROUND OF LEGAL delays began September 7, 1982, when Judge Burns denied Leonard Weinglass's double-jeopardy motion to dismiss, which was first presented to the court before I entered the case. I agreed the decision should be appealed, though I held little hope for success.

Len's major contention was that Jennifer had already been prosecuted in 1975 for the theft of the *Sea Wind*. He argued that since theft is a necessary element of the crime of robbery, prosecuting her now for a robbery-murder would constitute a *second* prosecution of the theft. Such a prosecution was barred, Len argued, by the double-jeopardy clause of the Fifth Amendment to the U.S. Constitution.

In opposition, prosecutor Elliot Enoki argued that an exception to double jeopardy exists where evidence of the main felony (murder) was not available at the time of the earlier prosecution. He noted that although authorities had long *suspected* that Jenkins and Walker were somehow responsible for the disappearance of the Grahams, the discovery of Muff's remains—powerful evidence that a murder had occurred—happened seven years *after* Jennifer's boat-theft prosecution. Therefore, Enoki claimed, the murder charge was in fact a new charge based upon that new evidence and did not constitute double jeopardy.

On May 31, 1983, the Ninth Circuit Court of Appeals denied Len's appeal, and six months later, the U.S. Supreme Court "denied certiorari" (refused to hear the matter), effectively putting to rest the double-jeopardy issue.

Several trial dates had been pushed forward while we awaited the outcome of the double-jeopardy appeal. On January 19, 1984, U.S. Magistrate Bert Tokairin convened a hearing in Honolulu to set new trial dates. I did not attend the session, but all three lawyers who did asked for continuances: prosecutor Enoki said he needed another six months to prepare for trial; Partington, Walker's attorney, had a five-month Army Reserve active-duty obligation beginning in May; and Len was involved in a criminal proceeding back East. (Kathy Boudin, a Weather Underground radical he represented, was charged with robbery and murder in the $1.6 million 1981 holdup of a Brinks armored truck in Rockland County, New York, that left two policemen and a Brinks guard dead.)*

After both defendants, through their attorneys, waived their right to a speedy trial, Tokairin set January 15, 1985, as the date for the Walker trial to begin, with Jennifer's trial to start immediately afterward. We were advised that the prosecution would seek sentences of life imprisonment for both defendants.

Meanwhile, Len continued his effort—parallel to that of Walker's attorneys—to win a change of venue. The people of Hawaii had already tried and convicted both defendants.

MOST PEOPLE on bail for the worst crime of all, murder, would have trouble getting a job shining shoes at a bus terminal. But Jennifer, despite the murder rap hanging over her head, had done remarkably well for herself. Recently promoted to branch manager of a Los Angeles telecommunications firm, she supervised six employees.

For her theft conviction, she had spent seven months (April to November 1977) at Terminal Island Correctional Institution off Long Beach, California, followed by ninety days in a Santa Barbara halfway house. At this low-security facility, she had been allowed to work outside as a sales clerk during the day. She also enrolled at the University of California at Santa Barbara, and in January 1978, as part of a work-study program, began a part-time job at the Center for the Study of Democratic Institutions, a well-known, left-leaning intellectual think tank. In February, when she was released from the halfway house, she quit school and took a full-time job

---

*Boudin eventually pleaded guilty and is currently serving a twenty-year prison term.

as a secretary at the center. That job ended in January of 1979, but she immediately began working as an executive recruiter for the firm of John Lawrence and Associates in Van Nuys. (An uncle was part owner.) In October 1980, Jennifer had purchased a comfortable two-story tract home for $100,000 in the scenic chaparral country of Simi Valley, a middle-class bedroom community northwest of Los Angeles with the highest per capita population of police officers in L.A. County. Interested in a job with greater opportunities for advancement, Jennifer joined the telecommunications firm in September 1982, selling expensive business telephone systems. She had a mortgage payment, a new car, and a good-paying job. I considered using the following argument to the jury: Would she have been as likely to devote the physical, mental, and emotional energy necessary to achieve such career success if she knew she was guilty of murder and would, in all likelihood, be convicted one day and spend perhaps the rest of her life behind bars? But I had no sooner contemplated using that argument than I realized that another interpretation was possible.

The prosecution could well argue in rebuttal that Jennifer might have been able to put the two murders behind her and go about making her way in the business world because she was extremely cold-blooded, perhaps even a sociopath who didn't think she'd done anything wrong and therefore had no feelings of guilt. (It is widely recognized that sociopaths guilty of crime are frequently able to pass polygraph examinations.) This entire point, I decided, might at best end up being a wash, and at worst suggest the possibility of some lethal quirkiness in Jennifer's personality rather than innocence.

During the double-jeopardy appeal and subsequent delays, I had continued working to prepare Jennifer for trial, developing a routine that varied little. Because she was now working quite a distance from my office, I would drive once or twice a month to her office after business hours—arriving after the worst of the rush-hour traffic and bringing with me a bag of the nut-and-raisin mix favored by many hikers. We nibbled on this trail mix—which we called "trial mix"—rather than take the time to go out to dinner. Further fortified by less healthful cups of coffee, we always worked well into the evening.

The dates we actually met, however, were never arrived at routinely. As often as not, she would call my office on the very afternoon of an agreed-upon evening session and cancel. One such call to my secretary, who came to expect them, inspired this note: "The princess slept on a pea last night. Has to cancel." Cancellation often led to conversations like the following: "What about Monday night then, Jenny?" "Sorry, Vince. *Monday Night Football* is on." Watching sports on TV, particularly her beloved Rams and Raiders, was a passion. "Tuesday night?" "I'm going over to my mother's for dinner." "Jennifer, the trial date is approaching, and we still have a lot of work to do. You act like you only have a drunk-driving case facing you in Honolulu." "Well, okay, what about the *next* Friday night?"

I sometimes got the feeling that Jennifer was agreeing to meet and prepare her defense more as a favor to me, even though it was she who faced the prospect of life imprisonment. Was the reality too terrible to confront directly on the conscious level? Or had she at some level, particularly in view of her previous conviction, actually given up hope?

Whatever continuances were being sought and granted, Jennifer was invariably in favor of them. "Vince," she explained once, "my career is going well and I'm enjoying life now. I can think of a lot better things to do than go to Honolulu to be tried for murder." How, I asked myself, was it possible for someone facing a charge of first-degree murder to "enjoy life" and put what she faced in the back of her mind? I had gained the distinct impression from Jennifer that with all the granting of trial delays, she felt the case might somehow die of old age.

"Jennifer, this is a *murder* case," I cautioned her. "It's not going to fade away. There's going to be a judgment day soon. That's when you take the witness stand. And we've got to be ready."

My stack of yellow legal pages with questions and answers for Jennifer kept growing. But she had yet to write a word on the pad I'd given her the night we met. Whenever I pointed this out, she would shrug, laugh, and say something like "Haven't had the time. I've been so busy," or "Other than when we meet, I try to put it out of my mind." Her casualness continued to amaze me.

An attorney benefits from his client's own helpful ideas and thoughtful insights. Jennifer had produced neither. Not once in nearly two years had she ever said, "Vince, I want you to check this out," or "I was thinking about what we were talking about last time, and I remembered something else I should tell you."

Yet despite the frustrations of preparing Jennifer for trial, on a personal level I still found her very likable, with an outgoing personality and ready sense of humor, and we invariably got along well together.

In fact, nothing in our encounters alerted me to the trouble I would have with her down the line.

ONE OF my main problems with Jennifer was her vague recollection of certain events, which caused her to vacillate and, more dangerously, introduced damaging inconsistencies that would certainly be exploited on cross-examination. Some inconsistencies were so subtle they only emerged clearly when I would discover that the lines of questioning I was preparing for her direct examination were taking me in conflicting directions.

There were several areas, however, in which Jennifer was consistent, and a few where she remained particularly resolute throughout the period of our trial preparation. For example, there was the question of Buck's influence after the Grahams disappeared.

"Buck gave me three options," she told me again and again. "I could sail away with him on the *Sea Wind*. I could go it alone on the *Iola*. Or I could stay on Palmyra by myself."

She felt Buck left her no option other than to leave with him on a sailboat they didn't own. "I didn't want to stay on that island alone," she explained, "and I was afraid to go by myself on the *Iola*."

From my first talk with Jennifer back in early 1982, I knew there was a central issue I'd have to thread my way through. It had been apparent to me that Buck was the dominant party in their relationship. Not only didn't this trouble me, I preferred* this cir-

---

*My argument that Buck Walker alone had murdered the Grahams would be more believable to the jury if Buck Walker was the dominant party in the relationship than if Jennifer were the boss (or even if they were equals).

cumstance, so long as she hadn't been completely under his thumb, which she assured me she was not.

If we couldn't make it convincing to the jury that Jennifer could and would stand up to Buck, the jury might readily conclude that she had been influenced to go along with the murders, even against her natural impulses not to. I stressed to her how absolutely critical it was that we show the jury she had drawn lines in the sand with Buck.

I asked for examples. "Anything," I said. "Even little things."

She thought for a moment. "Well, one time when we were living in the cabin on the Big Island," she said, "we got in an argument and he threw a plate of spaghetti at me and stormed out of the house. When he came back a few hours later, the spaghetti was still all over the wall and floor. I hadn't touched it. He ordered me to clean it up, but I told him he would have to clean up his own mess. He did. Buck knew his limits with me."

It wasn't much, but we were headed in the right direction.

IN EARLY February 1984, Len Weinglass and I met to discuss trial tactics.

There is no other profession with as many members who have managed to fashion for themselves out of thin air such a mighty and jumbo-sized image as that of the trial lawyer branch of the legal profession. Almost humorously, hundreds of trial lawyers in various sections of the country are known as "brilliant," "great," "high-powered," "silver-tongued," and so on. One reason why this high regard is so very easy to come by is the strong myth that *successful* trial lawyers are *supposed* to be these things, when in reality, so much less is required to achieve success.* (Many trial lawyers have these adjectives routinely applied to them who aren't even successful, merely having been associated, if even in a losing way, with one or more high-visibility cases.) In fact, if the average prominent trial lawyer met his reputation out on the street, they

---

*The media have been complicit in perpetuating the myth. For example, cross-examination as bland as pablum is routinely reported to be "rigorous," "grueling," or "withering." Why? Because cross-examination is *supposed* to be rigorous, grueling, and withering.

wouldn't recognize each other. Unfortunately, many clients have to learn about, and pay for this, the hard way.

When we finally got to trial, I was pleased to find that Len Weinglass approximated his reputation; I found him to be a very competent, professional, and experienced trial lawyer, and it was a real pleasure working with him.

But, pleasure aside, it immediately became clear at our first meeting on tactics that we had a major disagreement.

"I don't think we should concede there was a murder," Len said.

A chasm suddenly yawned between us.

"If we deny there was a murder, Len, we'll lose credibility with the jury. Credibility is essential when I give my final summation. The jurors will know, as everyone else does, that Muff was murdered."

Len's position was not outlandish. It went against every fiber of this veteran defense attorney to concede commission of the crime in a situation where at least an argument could be made, albeit weak, that the prosecution hadn't proved it beyond a reasonable doubt. In fact, standard defense attorney dogma is that you should always put the prosecution to the test on every major issue. From a tactical standpoint, however, I felt we should tell the world that a gruesome murder had unquestionably been committed on Palmyra, then go about proving that our client had nothing to do with it.

Although Len and I were co-counsel, with an equal say, it developed that whenever we had a divergence of opinion Len usually deferred to me. Not because he had to, but more likely because he's more agreeable than I. Out of the courtroom, I'm relatively easy to get along with. But when I'm on a case, the trial is open warfare to me. And in my battle to prevail I am frequently at odds not only with the opposing counsel (which is normal), but also with the judge, my co-counsel (if there is one), and sometimes even my own client. This may not be the prettiest of profiles, but it's an honest one.

HONOLULU

HAWAII'S LEGAL machinery turned full circle with the assignment of U.S. District Court Judge Samuel P. King to handle the two Palmyra Island murder cases. King had presided at the boat-theft trials of both defendants, and following their convictions, had meted out their prison sentences.

At Jennifer's sentencing, Judge King had commented: "I'm satisfied that quite a few of your explanations of what happened were, if not untruthful, certainly not the whole truth. Though you've not been charged with murder in this case, there is the underlying nagging question of just what happened to the Grahams."

With such a negative opinion of my client's earlier testimony (though an accurate one given her obvious perjury), I wondered how King would treat Jennifer at her new trial.

King, of Hawaiian ancestry, was born in Hankow, China, in 1917, and had ascended to the bench in part because of useful connections, both political and familial. In 1953, his father had been appointed governor of the Hawaiian Territories by President Eisenhower.

The King family was staunchly Republican, and the younger King, a graduate of Yale Law School, served as Hawaii's Republican Party central committee chairman from 1953 to 1955. During the 1954 elections, Sam King earned the sobriquet "Redbaiter" with this remarkable outcry: "No one is accusing *all* the Democrats of being Communists, but they are politically obligated to the Communists." In 1961, King was appointed judge of the First Circuit Court of Hawaii.

In 1970, showing how deep his political roots ran, he stepped down from the state bench to run for governor. He won the Republican primary, but was defeated in the general election by Democratic incumbent John Burns. King spent the next two years in the private practice of law, meanwhile serving on the Republican National Committee. In 1972, King received his reward for loyal service to the GOP when President Nixon named him to the federal bench.

As early as January 1982, Honolulu attorney Peter Wolff, then representing Jennifer as Len's co-counsel, had anticipated that King would be handling the Palmyra murder case. In a letter to Len at that time, Wolff wrote: "Both Earle [Partington] and I are concerned that Judge King has already made up his mind about the case. He has indicated pretty much that he has decided that both defendants are guilty of murder."

That possible predisposition aside, in King the defense finally found a judge who agreed that the Palmyra murder cases should be moved from Hawaii. The defense filed with the court yet another change-of-venue motion on June 8, 1984. This motion, virtually the same that two other federal judges had earlier denied, was granted by Judge King on August 8, 1984.

"The defendants previously were tried and convicted in the District of Hawaii on theft charges relating to the *same set of events* from which the present felony-murder charges arise," read Judge King's order. "That trial, as well as subsequent proceedings involving the defendants, received extensive media coverage. As a result, the local community is all too familiar with the Palmyra story. In sum, the likelihood of prejudice to the defendants and the attendant probability of an unfair trial in the District of Hawaii far outweigh any inconveniences that a change of venue would cause this court or the prosecution. Therefore, it is hereby ordered that the defendants' motion for a change in venue to the Northern District of California is granted." As is customary in federal court, Judge King would follow the case to its new locale.

From the bench, King's remarks to the attorneys were considerably less formal than his official order. "I'd like to be in San Francisco for the opera season," he said, smiling.

CHAPTER 23

SEATTLE
FEBRUARY 22, 1984

THE TYPICALLY WET, DREARY winter in the Pacific Northwest still dragged on. Deputy U.S. Marshal Dick Kringle was glad to have enough paperwork to keep him inside and out of the field for a few days.

Just past ten o'clock on this gray morning, the phone on his desk rang sharply. A deputy marshal was on the line from Los Angeles.

"Dick, we think Dougherty's in L.A.," the deputy marshal informed Kringle.

Joseph William Dougherty, forty-five, a hardened violent criminal, had once served time at McNeil Island, where he had become tight with Buck Walker and Terry Conner. Dougherty was now believed to be robbing banks in California.

"We staked out Dougherty's mail drop and found correspondence from Buck Walker at Marion," the L.A. deputy marshal went on. "Guess these guys are real tight."

"Yeah," Kringle snorted, "they're all members of the McNeil boys' club."

"The reason I'm calling is that I hear Walker is about to be paroled. What do you think of us following him to get to Dougherty? Would it work?"

"Whaddaya mean, *paroled*? Walker is waiting to be tried for murder and he's not about to be paroled. You must have heard wrong."

"Dick, Walker *does* have a parole date. I called Marion and they told me they'll be springing him on March 7th. Two weeks from now."

Kringle was suddenly alarmed. "There's a foul-up somewhere," he growled. Unbelievable as it might sound, he knew that such a nightmare was all too possible and he'd have to act fast.

Kringle had not thought much about Buck Walker in the past couple of years—there'd been no need to. Walker was safely tucked away at Marion Federal Penitentiary in Illinois, serving a series of sentences. Marion, the present-day equivalent of Alcatraz, is known among cons as "the End of the Line." It has the highest security level of any federal prison in the country. Only the "worst of the worst" federal offenders are sent to Marion, the most secure prison in the nation. Those inmates who have recently been convicted of violent offenses are locked up in single cells for twenty-three hours a day for the first four years of their sentence, and are even shackled to go to the shower.

Kringle had finally met his longtime prey a few months after Walker's arrest in Yuma. Walker had first been sent to Hawaii for arraignment on the murder charge, but was eventually brought to Seattle in handcuffs, leg irons, and waist chains to face the McNeil escape charge.*

Immediately after the call from the deputy in L.A., Kringle telephoned Marion and verified that Walker did indeed have a March 7 parole date. Kringle told an assistant warden about the murder indictment in Hawaii.

"There's nothing in his file about any murder indictment or detainer," the prison official replied.

It took Kringle several other calls to begin to put the pieces together. After Walker's Seattle conviction on the escape charge, he was sent to Lompoc Federal Correctional Institution near Santa Barbara, California. It didn't take long for someone in the prison system to decide that because of his escape Walker belonged at Marion, and he was transferred there in July 1982. Walker's prison record at Lompoc was kept in the prison's administrative offices, where inmates work in clerical jobs. When the file reached Marion, all reference to the murder charge had been purged from the file. Kringle had heard of such things happening before; all it took was a bribe, promise, or threat from one inmate to another, and Walker was capable of all three.

Kringle "called the world," as he later explained, to tell anyone and everyone that Buck Walker should not be paroled. Within forty-eight hours, Walker's parole date was canceled. He had come within fourteen days of being set free.

SOMEWHERE IN VIRGINIA
OCTOBER 5, 1984

NOEL ALLEN Ingman, a relocated witness under the Federal Witness Protection Program, sat across from Honolulu FBI Agent J. Harold "Hal" Marshall, the Palmyra case agent since Calvin Shishido retired from the bureau in 1982.

---

*Walker was subsequently convicted of the escape and sentenced to five years, the term to commence after his other sentences.

"Let me get this straight," said Marshall, whose thinning hair, broadening girth, pale complexion, and rounded shoulders made him look more like a bus driver than a G-man. "The first time you met Buck Walker was at McNeil Island?" His southern drawl was almost soothing.

"Right," said Al Ingman. "I'd already served three years in maximum security and had been transferred to the camp adjacent to the prison. I was working at the powerhouse when Buck was assigned there."

"When was that?"

"Late '77 or early '78."

"Who else was assigned to the powerhouse?"

"Terry Conner and J. W. Williams."

Ingman, a former schoolteacher who had graduated from the University of Alaska, looked older than his fifty-three years. It wasn't so much his graying hair or bottle-thick glasses as his deathly pallid, gaunt looks. A longtime heroin user, he had turned members of his own family into junkies.

Talking to the authorities had become another kind of habit for him. Under the Witness Protection Program since 1982, Ingman had already given testimony that helped convict a number of his former accomplices, including Terry Conner and Ruth Thomas. On the stand, he had admitted to complicity in Conner's drug-smuggling operation and described its inner workings. Conner helped finance the deals by committing bank heists, Walker transported the illicit drugs from Mexico into the United States, and Ingman himself acted as distributor for the ring.

In prison lingo, Ingman had turned snitch. In return, his whereabouts were kept a closely guarded secret, not even appearing on official reports or in-house documents. He was a marked man. The federal government had taken responsibility for keeping him alive.

Marshall had sought out Ingman because Ingman had passed the word that he had potentially damaging information about Buck Walker.

"What were your duties at the powerhouse?" Marshall asked, ready to take notes.

"The boilers were computer-operated, so we just sat in front of the computer and watched some dials. We took turns working eight-hour shifts. It was pretty laid-back. We smoked lots of dope."

"Marijuana?"

"Yeah, and Thai sticks. With the right connections, you could get about anything you wanted. We'd sit around all night, getting high and telling stories."

"True stories?"

"I didn't have the feeling that anyone was making stuff up. We all had been involved in a lot of—well, adventures over the years. Talking about them"—Ingman shrugged—"helped pass the time."

"What did Walker say about the Palmyra case?"

"Lots of things," Ingman said. "He told us how he dived into the water after his girlfriend was arrested in the harbor in Honolulu and how he swam under the pilings. After he was arrested, he said he managed to get a gun into jail, but that the gun was found before he could use it to escape."

"You're not telling me much, Ingman." Marshall, despite his easygoing manner and avuncular looks, could be tough and direct when necessary. He could stare like a basilisk.

Ingman got the point. "I remember Buck telling some story," he went on, "about being on Palmyra Island. There was this other boat with a couple on it. I guess they had gotten into some kind of hassle with them. Anyway, he made the couple walk the plank."

"Come again?"

"Yeah, you know, like they do in pirate movies. There was some comment about raw meat being thrown into the water by Walker to attract sharks."

"Did he *make* them go overboard?" Marshall asked.

Ingman took his time lighting a cigarette.

"The man went out on the plank, but I don't know if he jumped in with the sharks."

"Did Walker say whether his girlfriend, Jennifer Jenkins, was present during the murders?"

Ingman paused for a moment. "I don't remember," he finally said. "But I did ask him once whether he trusted her."

Marshall looked up from his notepad. "And?"

"He described Jennifer as a 'stand-up broad.' He said she would never talk."

HUNTSVILLE, TEXAS
OCTOBER 9, 1984

MARSHALL FOUND J. W. Williams in a Texas state prison. A four-time convicted bank robber who had twice escaped from federal prison, Williams had recently been convicted of raping a woman and leaving her for dead on a Gulf Coast beach. He was serving a minimum forty-year term for aggravated rape and attempted murder.

According to Al Ingman, Williams had been there the night Walker gave his version of the Palmyra murders, and was later involved in the Yuma-based drug-smuggling operation run by Conner and Walker.

Williams, a big man of about forty, had short-cropped brown hair and brooding dark eyes. Marshall guessed him to be of below-average intelligence.

Serving a long sentence and with other charges still facing him, Williams reportedly wanted to work out a deal. But Marshall insisted he wouldn't make any offer without knowing what Williams could tell him.

"You worked at the McNeil powerhouse in 1977?" Marshall began.

"Yeah."

"Who else was there?"

"Walker, Al Ingman and Terry Conner."

"Were there any guards in the powerhouse?"

"Naw. There were only two guards for three hundred and fifty inmates in the entire camp. It was pretty loose. We were pretty much on our own. We had a stereo, a television, even a sauna."

"Did you guys talk about your past activities?"

"Oh, yeah. We rapped all the time."

"Did you know what Walker was serving time for?"

"For selling MDA, I think."

"Did he ever talk about a Pacific island?"

Williams nodded. "He told us quite a bit about Palmyra."

"Did he talk about the missing couple?"

"One time he told us he put them on a rubber raft and set them out to sea with no water or food."

"Did you believe him?"

"I figured he probably took care of them, one way or the other, so there wouldn't be any witnesses when he stole their boat. Another time, he told us about making the couple walk the plank."

Marshall remained stone-faced. "Go on."

"Well, Buck said they tied the couple's hands behind their back and made them walk the plank."

"They?"

"Buck and his girlfriend. He said they were smoking dope and were dressed up like pirates. Buck said he had taken some chicken guts or something out of the refrigerator on the couple's boat and thrown it into the water to attract the sharks. I remember he said something about putting blindfolds on the couple at some point." Williams tended to add details hastily, as if he'd just remembered, or just thought them up, but the agent stolidly kept taking notes.

"Was Walker on drugs when he told you this?"

"Yeah, we were all loaded."

"What do you mean?"

"Smoking marijuana."

"Would you describe Walker as being lucid at that time? In control?"

"Oh, yes." He smirked.

"Were you still at McNeil when Walker escaped in July '79?"

"Yeah. I helped him."

"How so?"

"We built a raft using an inner tube from a tractor and a big sheet of canvas. We hid it in the forest near a cove."

"You could do all this without being seen by guards?"

"They figured because we were on an island we couldn't get off."

"Why didn't you escape with him?"

"I wanted to wait to be paroled. Not Buck. He was worried."

"About what?"

"He was always afraid they'd find something on Palmyra. He wanted to be long gone when they did."

"After you were paroled, you joined Walker and Conner down in Arizona?"

"Right. I was with Buck in Mexico when we heard about the bones being found on the island."

"What did he say?" The agent poised his pencil.

"Buck said the feds were falsifying evidence because that's not the way it went down."

"How so?"

"He said they never put the bodies in metal boxes."

FOR A HOST of reasons, including the avoidance of surprise at the trial, a criminal defendant has the right of "discovery," that is, the right to inspect or copy certain designated evidence of the prosecution. In most state courts, for example, the defendant can discover the pretrial statements of prosecution witnesses *before* the trial. In the federal courts, where Jennifer was being tried, the prosecution by statute doesn't have to release these pretrial statements to the defense until the prosecution witness has testified on direct examination *at the trial.* The defense is allowed only a short recess in which to examine the statement before cross-examination of the witness. In practice, however, only Assistant U.S. Attorneys who play unnecessary hardball avail themselves of this harsh rule. Fortunately for us, Enoki did not, and we received the FBI's interview reports—typed out on FBI Form #302 (and therefore called 302s)—long before Buck Walker's trial.

Enoki made an exception, however, for the statements of Ingman and Williams, which were kept from the defense until shortly before the Walker trial. Perusing them, I naturally recognized the possibility that Ingman and Williams were telling the truth. But prison informants are notoriously unreliable, not only because they are untrustworthy criminal types by definition, but also because they have a strong motive to fabricate—the expectation of a quid pro quo from the authorities. Moreover, the story Buck allegedly told Ingman and Williams at the McNeil Island powerhouse didn't make too much sense. I had heard of no "plank" on Palmyra (though any board, of course, could serve as a "plank"), there was no evidence that Buck and Jennifer had "pirates' clothing," and the chicken-guts twist sounded farfetched on its face. Furthermore, if Muff had been fed to the sharks, how had she ended up in the metal container? In addition, the impression I had increasingly formed about Jennifer precluded her from being involved in a brutal murder. And for her to compound the murder by joining in the torture of Mac and Muff and feeding them to the sharks was totally unbelievable to me. Besides, even if Walker had told Ingman and Williams what they said he did, that obviously didn't necessarily mean Walker had told them the truth. In fact, according to Williams, Walker had told him two completely different stories of how the Grahams met their death.

But even though I strongly believed in Jennifer's innocence, I of course could never be 100 percent certain. How could anyone who wasn't there be sure? And the possibility of her guilt, however remote in my mind, was something I had to deal with.

I don't think any lawyer in the country works any harder preparing his case than I do. More than once, the thought came to me that if Jennifer *was* guilty, there was something obscene about my making use of every ounce and fiber of my ability to get her off. Conceptually, the notion that I was not on the side of two decent people who had been brutally and nightmarishly murdered, but fighting with all my mental strength on the side of one of their cold-blooded murderers, was more than immoral to me. It was indescribably vile.

But I felt confident that this fleeting image was a false one. In discussing every detail of the case with Jennifer over so many hours, there simply was nothing, nothing at all in her demeanor or mannerisms, in her body language, that made me feel I was talking to a guilty person. There even seemed to be, always, a wholly valid or at least reasonably acceptable explanation for her inconsistent statements and failure to mention certain things to me.

My conviction wavered only on the few occasions when Jennifer's personality seemed to change almost freakishly before my eyes, from the normally passive, vulnerable, and reactive to the assertive, confident, almost mechanical. Suddenly, I was talking to a different person. At these alarming moments I could conjure up the image of Jennifer matter-of-factly telling Buck, before the murders, "You do _____, and I'll make sure that _____." These thoughts were naturally highly disturbing to me, but not frequent, and, I felt, normal under the circumstances.

I also had to consider that if a strong belief in someone's innocence, as I had with Jennifer, was not enough; if I had to be 100 percent sure of someone's innocence before I defended them, either I'd have to stop practicing criminal law or my wife would have to get a paper route.

In short, unless something came out of the blue, the die was cast. Jennifer and I would sink or swim together.

CHAPTER 24

SAN FRANCISCO
OCTOBER 26, 1984

JUDGE SAMUEL KING AND the various lawyers involved in the Palmyra case flew to the site of the upcoming murder trials for a hearing on pretrial matters.

I had not met the judge before, or the federal prosecutors, Elliot Enoki and Walter Schroeder.

In the informal setting of his chambers, Judge King looked and acted grandfatherly, complete with thinning gray hair, alert eyes magnified by glasses, and heavy jowls that shook like bowls of Jell-O when he chuckled. He always had a quip or two, even from the bench, and he appeared to enjoy making people laugh. I immediately like Sam King because he seemed to lack the silly pomposity found in so many judges. He was a regular guy.

Enoki, thirty-six, a straitlaced Japanese-American with a compact frame, had a perpetual wry smile that hinted he knew something no one else did. His straight black hair matted against his
forehead as if he'd just stepped from the shower. A native of
Hawaii, Enoki chose the mainland for his advanced schooling,
receiving his undergraduate degree in English literature from
Northwestern, and his law degree from the University of California at Davis. Four years with the state public defender's office in
Hawaii following law school convinced Enoki that he'd rather
prosecute the bad guys than defend them. Becoming an Assistant U.S. Attorney in 1978, in just six years the unmarried, hard-
working, and always gentlemanly prosecutor had risen to the
position of First Assistant U.S. Attorney, and had become the top
trial lawyer for the Honolulu U.S. Attorney's Office. Enoki alone,
backed by the investigative might of the FBI, would have been a
formidable courtroom opponent. But Walter Schroeder, a Department of Justice prosecutor in Washington, D.C., had recently been
assigned to assist.

Since it was unusual for a prosecutor from headquarters to be
sent to San Francisco to assist a Honolulu prosecutor (normally,
Enoki's co-prosecutor would be chosen either from his office or
the San Francisco office), when I spoke to Schroeder by phone the
first time, I asked if Steve Trott, a former fellow prosecutor of mine
at the Los Angeles District Attorney's Office, had personally had
anything to do with his assignment to the case. Trott was the third-
ranking official at Justice. Schroeder said Trott had, confirming my
hunch.* This move signified that the Government was taking special measures to win the Palmyra murder case. I knew nothing
about the unassuming, bespectacled Schroeder, but I suspected his
abilities would prove to be considerable. Unfortunately, this early
assessment was correct. Schroeder would unearth new and, if
believed by the jury, very damaging evidence against Jennifer.

At this brief session, King's first priority was setting firm dates for
the long-delayed murder trials. Both sides agreed that the date earlier

---

*Because Steve Trott had once made an uncommonly flattering remark about my
trial abilities, the thought had immediately entered my mind that my former colleague might have had a hand in the decision to dispatch Schroeder.

set for Walker's trial, January 15, 1985, was too soon. May 28, 1985, was agreed upon as the new date, with Jennifer's trial to follow.

We agreed there would be two alternate jurors in addition to the twelve regular jurors. At each trial, both the prosecution and defense would be able to "voir dire" (literally, "to speak the truth," but in law, refers to the questioning of prospective jurors to determine their impartiality and qualifications) prospective jurors. This is the exception rather than the rule in federal jury trials, where the jury panel is usually questioned only by the judge. However, each side would be limited to just one hour of voir dire.

After a discussion of several other housecleaning details—such as the hours of trial—King ended the session by saying he would hear all remaining pretrial motions on January 11.

That didn't leave much time for springing a few surprises I had in mind.

LOS ANGELES

FROM THE moment I decided to handle the case, I had literally scrounged around trying to come up with *some* evidence, *any* evidence, of Jennifer's innocence (other than her denial of guilt) to counteract all the evidence of guilt. And if the past was barren, I would have to look toward the future.

I wrote to Elliot Enoki in Honolulu, reminding him that a few years earlier Len Weinglass had made an offer that Jennifer take a polygraph examination—an offer Enoki had declined.

"I'm well aware that the reason you declined was that she really had nothing to lose," I wrote, "since if she failed the test, the results would not be admissible before the jury anyway."

I told Enoki I was prepared to take our earlier offer a very significant step forward—Jennifer Jenkins was willing not only to take a polygraph test, but to stipulate, in advance, that the results could be introduced at her trial, *regardless of what they were*.

I was not shooting from the hip. In fact, I had carefully researched the results of Jennifer's earlier polygraph tests. The first one, arranged by her then attorney, Barry Tarlow, was administered in Los Angeles on February 28, 1981, five days before she turned herself in to federal authorities. The polygraph operator was David Raskin, a noted polygrapher and professor of psychology at the University of Utah.*

Three key questions stood out in Jennifer's first polygraph test:

Question 5: Did you participate in any way in causing the disappearance of Muff or Mac Graham?

Question 7: Were you present when Muff Graham was killed?

Question 10: Did you participate in any type of plan to cause harm to Muff or Mac Graham?

To all three she answered firmly: "No."

On a scale where scores of +6 or higher indicate truthfulness (truthful goes up to +30), scores of –6 or lower indicate deception, and scores of less than 6 in either direction are considered inconclusive, Jennifer obtained a total score of +3, that is, "inconclusive." After Raskin gave Jennifer the results, she explained that she had a problem with Question 7. In his written report of the test, Raskin quoted her on this point: "Obviously, I was on Palmyra when Mac and Muff died. I don't know if they were killed or not, but they definitely died. I've always assumed their dinghy overturned and they were drowned and eaten by sharks. That question confused me. I said no but I was thinking yes. I'd like to take another test."

Raskin agreed but suggested they do so at his Salt Lake City laboratory, which had more sensitive equipment. The reexamination took place there on March 3, 1981. After Raskin reworded the key questions, Jennifer approved their content.

Question 5: Were you involved in planning the disappearance of Mac and Muff Graham?

Question 7: Did you take part in deliberately causing the disappearance of Mac or Muff Graham?

*Later, Raskin figured in the cocaine-dealing trial of automaker John DeLorean when the defense sought to introduce the passing results of a polygraph test he'd given DeLorean. The Government's polygraph expert had given DeLorean a separate test and concluded he was lying, and the trial judge declined to admit the results of either test.

Question 10: Did you have definite knowledge before this year that either of the Grahams had been deliberately killed?

Once again, she answered no to all three questions. This time, her score totaled +7. "According to the usual standard employed in the polygraph field," Raskin wrote to Len Weinglass, "a score of +7 is a definite truthful outcome."

My belief was that Enoki would refuse to agree to the offer I had made. Not only do prosecutors rarely agree to stipulate with the defense as to the admissibility of polygraph results, but I knew Enoki sensed an easy victory, and I therefore felt he would not want to open up any new side issue that could go the wrong way for him. But in the unlikely event he did agree, I had decided to let Jennifer take the test, as she continued to tell me she was willing to do. With a neutral polygraph operator, I felt her worst result would be "inconclusive." But a risk was involved (more, actually, for Enoki than for me, since having the stronger case, he had more to lose), one I was hoping to avoid. On December 6, Enoki surprised me by telephoning to accept my offer—on the condition, however, that an FBI polygraph expert administer the test.

I phoned David Raskin in Salt Lake City and told him what had happened.

"I don't have any confidence in FBI polygraph examiners," Raskin snapped. "The Secret Service has better examiners. I know, because I've trained a lot of them."

Raskin went on to warn me that Jennifer's previous polygraph results suggested she wouldn't ever receive any overwhelmingly "truthful" scores. "Don't get me wrong," he said. "I read the charts as indicating she's innocent. But at plus seven, where the truthful factor can go as high as plus thirty, she was only borderline truthful, not dramatically truthful."

Weinglass unhesitatingly opposed the Government's condition that the FBI administer the test to Jennifer. "I don't trust the FBI," he growled. "Never have and never will." I didn't share his feelings, but obviously I did not want to proceed without his concurrence.

Subsequently, I made a counteroffer that we use the Secret Service, but Enoki balked. The prosecutor wanted no one but the FBI to give the test. We were at an impasse, but it was an impasse I welcomed, feeling it would enable me to make an argument I had been contemplating all along.

BOOKS ON criminal evidence have sections called "consciousness of guilt," wherein all types of conduct and statements of an accused—flight, resistance to arrest, escape, destruction of evidence, silence in the face of an accusation, false or conflicting statements, etc.—have been held by courts to be admissible circumstantial evidence showing a consciousness of guilt. In addition to these conventional indications of guilt, as a prosecutor I had a passion for taking even unconventional and obscure specks of evidence and developing them into an argument showing consciousness of guilt on the part of the defendant.

Now, as a defense attorney, I find it very natural to argue the opposite side of the coin; consciousness of *innocence*, also illustrated by the conduct and statements of the accused. Strangely, however, the same books that have entire sections on consciousness of guilt never even mention consciousness of innocence. It's as if the pivotal mechanisms of the criminal justice system have been established to prove guilt, not innocence, perhaps the residual progeny of the notorious common-law rule (abolished by statute in England in 1701) that in cases of felony, the accused was not even allowed to introduce witnesses in his defense. It should be noted that the very term "circumstantial evidence" has come to mean circumstantial evidence *of guilt*. But there obviously can be circumstantial evidence of innocence, too.

If the jury were allowed to hear that Jennifer had offered to take a polygraph test and let them receive the results, I felt they would inevitably ask themselves why, if guilty, would she do this.

Absent a stipulation from both parties, courts routinely reject "polygraph evidence" on the ground that the test has not been proved to be scientifically reliable.* Judge King would, I believe, reflexively lump what I was seeking to do under that rule, even

---

*New Mexico is currently the only state which allows either party alone to introduce the results of a polygraph examination.

though the reliability of the polygraph was not involved here, only Jennifer's state of mind. To have a chance with Judge King, I'd have to arm myself with case law to support my position.

I spent a day and a half at the Los Angeles County law library reading virtually every case on polygraph evidence I could find anywhere in the country, only to discover that not a single one dealt specifically with the tactic I had created for Jennifer.

Though not precisely in point, I did finally find one, and only one, favorable case, *Commonwealth* v. *A Juvenile* (No. 1), 365 Mass. 421 (1974). Like Jennifer, the defendant offered to take a polygraph test and let the results come before the jury. The trial court denied the offer, but the appellate court reversed the defendant's subsequent conviction, noting that "in view of the possibly damaging consequences" of the defendant's offer to let the results of a "yet to be taken" test come in, there was sufficient ground for the judge to order the test and admit the results into evidence.

Of course, Jennifer's case was different in that I was not seeking, as in the Massachusetts case, to have any actual polygraph results received into evidence; I only wanted the jury to know she had *offered* to let the results come in. But the Massachusetts court had recognized that where the accused has something to lose this is justification for departing from the basic rule. Inferentially, at least, this ruling went in the direction of supporting my position.

I filed a motion with Judge King's court on December 19. In opposition to my motion, Enoki listed no authority to support his position (confirming my research that no court had yet dealt with the issue), simply arguing that the court "should not deviate from the well-accepted rule that offers to take polygraph examinations are as inadmissible as the results of unstipulated polygraph examinations."

I knew I was mounting an uphill battle.

HONOLULU

JANUARY 8, 1985

AT 4:00 P.M., a federal grand jury, on the basis of information provided earlier in the afternoon by Buck's two chums, Williams and Ingman, returned a superseding indictment against Jennifer Jenkins and Buck Walker. In addition to the felony-murder count already filed against them, both were now charged with a second count of premeditated murder.

The prosecution had welcomed the new information from the two inmates as a major break in the case. It was in their interest to believe that Buck Walker, like many a caged felon, had confessed under the pathetic illusion of prison camaraderie.

The prosecutors also wanted to believe their tale, particularly Williams's, that Walker had suggested Jennifer Jenkins participated in the killings. In fact, strong sentiment had developed among law enforcement officials that it was she, not Walker, who had been the brains behind the crime, while he had provided the brawn.

Would a trial jury believe unsavory types like Williams and Ingman when they took the stand?

The prosecutors were more than willing to take that chance.*

---

*Although testimony from the Government's two informants had, according to Enoki, been the basis for the addition of premeditated murder charges against *both* defendants, Len and I were not overly apprehensive about what the informants had told authorities. We knew neither Ingman nor Williams would be permitted to testify at Jennifer's trial about Buck's alleged statements implicating her in the murders. In the landmark 1968 U.S. Supreme Court case of *Bruton v. United States*, 391 U.S. 123, the court held that a defendant implicated in court by an *out-of-court* statement made by his codefendant is, in effect, being accused by his codefendant (i.e., Jennifer accused by Buck). Every person on trial has the constitutional right under the Confrontation Clause of the Sixth Amendment to confront and cross-examine his accuser in court. But the codefendant cannot be forced to take the stand, and if he does not voluntarily do so, the accused loses the right to cross-examine. Len and I were certain that no matter what happened to Buck at his trial, he would not take the stand at Jennifer's trial to testify against her. If he were found *not guilty* but testified at Jennifer's trial that he had, in fact, confessed to his prison buddies that he'd murdered the Grahams and that she was involved, this could form the basis for an indictment against him for the murder of *Mac* Graham. Even if found *guilty* of murdering Muff, he would automatically appeal his conviction, and if, down the road, the conviction was reversed, any admission at Jennifer's trial could be used against him at his retrial.

CHAPTER 25

WHEN HE TOOK THE bench to hear oral arguments on the final pretrial motions, Judge King asked which defendant wanted to be heard first. I yielded to Walker's lead lawyer, Earle Partington.

With black hair thinning on top and deep lines creasing his face, Partington seemed older than his forty-three years. A confirmed bachelor, teetotaler, and nonsmoker, he was a former assistant federal public defender in San Francisco and state prosecutor in South Rhodesia (now Zimbabwe) and Hawaii. His voice had a whiny edge that, combined with his feisty nature, would grate on judge and jury alike, but the wiry Partington savored his reputation as one of Hawaii's scrappiest attorneys.

Partington's first motion was an attempt to prevent the prosecution from introducing Walker's prior testimony in his theft trial at his murder trial, a clear signal that Walker might not testify at his trial. The motion was denied.

The Government, unable to locate its expert on small boats for the upcoming trial, sought to introduce his testimony from the theft trial. Partington's second motion, to exclude this testimony, was also denied. It was now my turn.

I started with my polygraph motion, admitting to the judge that this was a "novel issue" and adding that while I understood it would be challenging for the court to chart a new course, "any pioneer effort requires that kind of courage. Your only guide is common sense and the general principles of admissibility of relevant evidence." I carefully reviewed the points I had made in my written motion, including the Massachusetts juvenile case. "The Government hasn't come up with one single case to the contrary."

Judge King said he liked my argument; however, since the Government had accepted our original offer, but we had reneged and made the counteroffer that they then rejected, the situation had become too complicated and he didn't want the jury to get tied up on a collateral issue. He denied my motion. But I didn't give up all thought of getting King to change his mind.

So far, three defense motions had been presented, and three had been denied. I hoped this clean sweep wasn't a portent of the future course of the trial.

My next motion was the most important I would make in the entire case. It was the main reason for my having flown to San Francisco that morning. If the defense lost it, I feared the murder trial could very well be anticlimactic—rather like a tennis player stepping onto the court down one set and 0-5 in the second before the first serve of the match.

The Government lawyers, not satisfied with their strong case against Jennifer, were attempting to engineer a scenario that would, for all intents and purposes, convict her of murder before they called their first witness. I was resolved not to let them get away with it.

Let me back up and explain their scheme.

As indicated, felony-murder had been the first murder count filed following the discovery of Muff Graham's remains.

To put it in simplified language, under the felony-murder rule, if a killing takes place during the perpetration or attempted perpetration of an inherently dangerous felony, such as robbery (the felony alleged against Jennifer), burglary, rape, arson, etc., it is automatically first-degree murder, even if the killing was accidental.* The justification for a law that makes a killing first-degree murder in the absence of a premeditated intent to kill, or even *any* intent to kill, is to offer an additional deterrent to committing crimes that, by their very nature, create an increased probability of death.

---

*Theft, the crime Jennifer was previously convicted of, is not considered to be "an inherently dangerous felony." In shorthand terms, "theft" is simply the taking of another's personal property with intent to steal, as when a professional pickpocket lifts someone's wallet. But when the taking is accomplished by means of force or fear (for example, the victim handed over his wallet at gunpoint), "robbery" has been committed.

When the Government was fighting Len in one legal battle after another to prevent the felony-murder indictment from being dismissed on the ground of double jeopardy, it puzzled me very much that they didn't simply circumvent the whole problem by filing a premeditated murder count instead. I finally came to believe that their only reason for sticking with felony-murder was the hope they might somehow get before the jury that Jennifer had already been convicted of the theft of the *Sea Wind*. (There are many ways such things can surface at a trial, including the jury's learning it through the media.) And as lay people, the jury might very well get confused between the *theft* of the *Sea Wind* (what Jennifer had already been convicted of) and a *robbery* of the *Sea Wind* (what she was now on trial for). This confusion could only redound to her detriment, and make her conviction under the felony-murder theory even easier than it would be under that of premeditation.

On December 12, I had filed a written motion setting forth my concerns and asking Judge King to take the most unusual step of ordering the Government to amend its original indictment to allege premeditated murder rather than felony-murder. (Although there is no specific provision in the law allowing a judge to do this, I cited to the court some general legal authority for the trial judge's responsibility to ensure that the accused receive a fair trial.) I don't imagine too many defense attorneys have ever strenuously urged that their client be charged with premeditated murder, but I felt this strategy necessary in order to get the felony-murder count dropped from the indictment.

I contended that premeditated murder was the proper charge in this case because of the "irresistible conclusion that whoever murdered Mrs. Graham premeditated her murder. The felony-murder rule is an inappropriate and rather unconventional theory to proceed under given the facts of this case. It is traditionally invoked where the facts are for the most part not in dispute, as in the killing of a liquor store proprietor during the perpetration of a robbery. Only the identity of the perpetrator is in issue. In the instant case, absent a confession by the perpetrator of the murder of Mrs. Graham, it can be assumed that the facts will never be known."

Judge King had denied my motion, but in the Government's January 7 response to it, Enoki had finally revealed his true intention in charging felony-murder . . . and it was a lot worse than I'd suspected. Enoki's position was that the prosecution should be able to introduce Jennifer's theft conviction at her murder trial *"to establish an essential element of the felony-murder charge."* In other words, he wanted to introduce Jennifer's prior conviction for theft of the *Sea Wind* in his "case in chief" (the presentation of his evidence at the trial) as *conclusive and irrebuttable* proof of key elements of the *robbery* in the felony-murder charge!

Both my co-counsel, Len Weinglass, and Buck Walker's defense attorney, Earle Partington, thought the law allowed Enoki to do just that. I was equally convinced it did not.

The Government's strategy of trying to convict Jennifer of felony-murder by presenting proof of her theft conviction was momentous in scope. To be sure, several steps were necessary to achieve the Government's objective, but each step was simple, flowing quite credibly and naturally into the next. If the jury at Jennifer's murder trial believed someone committed a robbery of the *Sea Wind* (obviously, they would), and if they believed the robber also killed Muff Graham (again, they obviously would), *and if the judge instructed the jury that Jennifer's theft of the* Sea Wind *was an integral part of that robbery*, the jurors would surely reason thusly: since Jennifer committed *some* of the elements of the robbery—the theft elements of (1) taking the *Sea Wind* and (2) having the intent to steal—she must also be guilty along with Buck (who else was there?) of committing the remaining elements—i.e., (3) the taking of the *Sea Wind* by means of "force or fear" (of course), and (4) from the "immediate presence" of Muff Graham (liberally interpreted to include any place within sight or hearing). And since it's obvious the killing almost assuredly took place *during* the perpetration of the robbery, she'd be guilty of first-degree murder under the felony-murder rule.

Stated another way, if I had to concede that my client did commit *some* of the elements of the robbery that eventuated in Muff Graham's death, how could I argue she was innocent of the others? Any sensible juror would assume that either she alone committed the remaining elements, or aided and abetted Buck Walker in doing so. In my opinion, the prosecutors were not merely trying to deprive Jennifer of a fair trial, they were also determined to keep her from having any kind of *murder* trial, period. They wanted to have a trial only for *robbery*. If they could prove Jennifer committed that crime, her guilt in the murder would be assumed.

I told the judge how strongly I condemned the prosecution's scheme. "As a former prosecutor, I have to say I am very disappointed. I would never have attempted to do what they're trying to do here. Although I was a tough prosecutor, I was always fair.* You can't tell the jury going in [to a trial] that half the crime charged against the defendant has already been proved," I argued.

I turned to face the prosecutors. "That's what you're seeking to do, is that correct, Mr. Enoki?"

Enoki, evidently fascinated by a worn spot on the counsel table, didn't respond.

"By seeking," I said, "to have the theft conviction introduced to prove some of the elements of the robbery alleged in the present case—"

"Right," Judge King interjected. "Some of them. Not all."

"By definition," I went on, "that's telling the jury that the theft was a part of, and took place at the *same precise time* as, the robbery."

"If a person has been convicted of a criminal charge," the judge said unresponsively, "then if it's relevant, that *can* be used in a subsequent trial."

I sensed that Judge King didn't see what the Government was trying to do. Although you cannot commit a robbery without thereby also committing a theft, it's too obvious to even state that a theft committed at a different time than a given robbery would not be a part of *that* robbery.

Now that the judge appeared to be agreeing to go along with his plan, Enoki leaped in with both feet. The theory of his argument

*Under our system of justice, the defense attorney's only obligation is to his client, whereas the prosecutor has a dual obligation—not only to represent the state or federal government (as the case may be), but to do his part in insuring that the defendant receives a fair trial.

was the doctrine of "collateral estoppel," the prosecutor explained. "If a defendant was tried previously and legally convicted, any facts that were necessarily determined in that conviction the defense is barred [estopped] from relitigating in a subsequent trial." He added that to prove robbery, as required of him in the present felony-murder count, he had to prove four elements: (1) the taking of the *Sea Wind* (2) from the immediate presence of Mrs. Graham, (3) by means of force or fear, (4) and with intent to steal. The prosecutor said the first and fourth elements had already been established in Jennifer's theft trial.

"You can get those elements in by my instructions to the jury," the judge chimed in. *"You don't have to prove them."*

"That's correct," Enoki said. "Two of the elements of the theft conviction are necessary parts of my proof in *this* case."

Judge King looked squarely at me and asked incredulously, "You *still* say he can't do that?"

My answer was that the prosecution definitely could *not* do that because it would be "tantamount to telling the jury that the theft for which Miss Jenkins was convicted was a part of, and took place at the *same precise time* as, the robbery. We can't *tell* the jury that," I persisted, "because we do not *know* that. Even assuming Miss Jenkins is guilty of the theft of the boat, that theft could obviously have been completely unrelated to the robbery and the murder in this case. Let me give you two very reasonable possibilities, and there are more.

"If Buck Walker, without Miss Jenkins's knowledge or assistance, killed the Grahams during the perpetration of the robbery, and *thereafter*, Miss Jenkins, finding out about the robbery and the murder, steals the *Sea Wind*, she is guilty of the theft. But obviously, she had nothing to do with the robbery or the murder. The theft she committed was a different theft. Or in another scenario, if Mr. Walker killed the Grahams without Miss Jenkins's knowledge or assistance, and Miss Jenkins believed that the Grahams had died an accidental death, and thereafter she steals the *Sea Wind*, she again is guilty of the theft, but not guilty of the robbery or murder. Because these possibilities exist, your honor, the jury cannot be told that as a matter of law they do *not* exist.

"The prosecution is seeking to take elements of one crime, the theft, and transpose them over to another crime, the robbery. You can't do this. And I don't know why they would even want to because I think it's automatic reversible error.

"I have to question whether they're acting in good faith. The problem is that I can't give them credit for good faith without thereby convicting them of a lack of knowledge of fundamental criminal law."

Enoki took this thrust impassively.

Judge King was listening to every word. "The Government argues collateral estoppel," I continued, intent on keeping my one-man audience. "The requirements for collateral estoppel are simple enough. The issue to be decided must be the same as that involved in the prior action. In the prior action, the issue must have been raised, litigated, and actually adjudicated. In the case before you, the indictment alleges robbery. In the prior action, the 1975 theft case, the jury did not have the robbery issue before it. The robbery issue was not raised, nor was it litigated, nor was there any adjudication of it. So the jury that convicted Miss Jenkins of theft did not, by their theft conviction, say that the theft took place as a part of the robbery of the *Sea Wind*. How can we now say that it was?"

I pressed on, telling the court that to tell the jury the theft was a part of the very robbery for which Jennifer was on trial was to take away from the jury's consideration "virtually the sole issue at this trial."

The judge replied that even if the theory of collateral estoppel were not applicable, Jennifer's prior conviction could still come in during the prosecution's case in chief.

If collateral estoppel did not apply, I asked Judge King, then under what theory *could* Jennifer's prior conviction come in. The "willy-nilly" theory? "Please give me a theory I can address myself to," I said.

Judge King, showing signs of beginning to lose his patience, asked if I actually intended to argue at the murder trial that my client *didn't even steal* the *Sea Wind*.

"Of course we're going to argue that."

Court: "She did *not* steal it?"

"Yes, of course."

Court: "What do you mean?"

"Judge, why would I get up and tell the jury that what this other jury did is automatically right, that juries are never wrong?"

Court: "That's what we are arguing about right now. That you can't relitigate something that has already been decided."

"So in other words, I am precluded from asking her on the witness stand what her state of mind was when she departed with Mr. Walker from Palmyra on the *Sea Wind*. She is literally prohibited from saying, 'I didn't intend to steal the *Sea Wind*,' because as a matter of law, she *did* steal the *Sea Wind*."

Court: "I suppose she can say anything she wants to."

"How can she if the court is going to tell the jury that as a matter of law she *did* steal the *Sea Wind*, and therefore to disregard her testimony in that respect?"

Court: "Right."

"And that she is committing perjury when she testifies that she never intended to steal the *Sea Wind*."

Court: "I don't know about perjury. Defendants have elastic memories."

"I am not going to stipulate that she is a thief in front of the jury. And if the court wants to tell the jury that she is—"

Court: "I don't want to do a damn thing! I am sitting here with the Government telling me they want me to say that, and I am listening to you as to why I shouldn't."

We had slipped off the road to a related issue, and I returned to the central issue: whether or not Jennifer's theft conviction could be introduced by the Government as a part of the robbery being charged.

"If the court can give me a theory that allows them to do this, then I can respond to it. The *only* theory that's been propounded by the prosecution is collateral estoppel, but it simply does not apply here."

Court: "I understand your argument." He hadn't said he agreed. Merely that he had finally understood.

At that point, Judge King called a short recess.

As I walked out into the hallway in search of a drinking fountain, I wasn't confident that the judge—even if he actually had understood my argument—would go along with my motion and prevent the prosecution from pulling off one of the smoothest, sneakiest tricks I'd ever seen attempted in a court of law. In light of the judge's vacillating comments, I was deeply worried.

When we went back into session, Judge King addressed Enoki. "Mr. Bugliosi has a point, you know. You *are* trying to argue that the two elements of the precise robbery for which she is on trial have already been proved by the prior theft conviction when, as a matter of fact, it could be that you are talking about a *different* theft. I will grant Mr. Bugliosi's motion with respect to the inadmissibility of the theft conviction in the Government's case in chief."

Judge King *had* understood.

At the defense table, Len leaned over and whispered, "Congratulations. You turned the judge around."

Partington was shaking his head in bewilderment as we all left the courtroom. "Good work, Vince, but I still think that under the law the Government unfortunately has the right to do it," he said.

There was one more battle to be fought concerning Jennifer's theft conviction. On cross-examination of her at the murder trial, could the Government ask her whether she had been convicted of stealing the *Sea Wind* (along with money found aboard)? Typically, they could. In this case, I felt they could not, and had filed a ten-page motion setting forth my arguments.

Judge King said he would decide this second issue at the trial. If we lost, bad as that would be, it wouldn't come close in its consequences to losing the ruling we had just won.

It had been a trying morning, and I was glad to accompany the other attorneys to a restaurant across the street and unwind over lunch.

"Buck looks like an accountant," Len offered midway through the meal when the discussion got around to how Buck and Jennifer had changed in appearance since 1974.

Partington smiled, obviously pleased with Len's assessment.

"But then again," my co-counsel added with a wink and devilish grin, "would anyone here want to take a sailboat ride with him?"

Los Angeles

My pretrial interviews with Jennifer continued, as did my frustration with her refusal to believe that Buck Walker had murdered Mac and Muff Graham. She maintained her skepticism in the face of my efforts to lay out evidence which pointed toward his guilt.

Take, for example, the *Sea Wind*'s masthead light, a single, beacon-type light mounted at the very top of the front mast. In reading Jennifer's theft-trial transcript, I noted that Tom Wolfe had testified about accompanying the Grahams on a Palmyra exploring expedition from which they expected to return after dark. In anticipation of this, Wolfe explained, Mac had turned on the masthead light before leaving the *Sea Wind* so that they wouldn't have to locate her and climb back aboard in total darkness. Remembering to flip on the light in the middle of the afternoon was the act of a careful and prepared boatman, a description everyone agreed fit Mac Graham.

But Jennifer had testified that on August 30, when she and Buck went to the *Sea Wind* around 6:30 P.M. for their bon voyage dinner, Mac and Muff were not there, the masthead light was not on, and she and Buck thereafter turned it on to help Mac and Muff find their way back in the dark.

Pointing out Wolfe's testimony to her, I asked Jennifer, "Didn't it strike you as odd that Mac hadn't switched the masthead light on before he and Muff left, inasmuch as he supposedly told Buck they might be late?"

"Not at the time," she answered.

"What about now?"

"I guess so," she said. Her expression, as impassive as a cigarstore Indian's, remained unchanged.

And then there was the apricot brandy. I asked Jennifer to repeat in detail what she and Buck had done aboard the *Sea Wind* that night as they waited for the Grahams. She said that when they went below they had found "certain things" set out on the table.

"What things?" I asked. "Be specific."

"Apricot brandy and vodka. Dry-roasted peanuts. Olives. Oh, and a box of cookies. Buck said Mac told him they'd lay food out for us in case they weren't there when we arrived."

"And what did you do then?"

"I poured myself a glass of apricot brandy, Buck poured some vodka for himself. Buck took the box of cookies and we went up on deck."

After our session that night, I sat in a chair in my den until almost two in the morning, with my ever-present yellow legal pad in my lap. Comparing my interview notes with Jennifer's theft-trial testimony, I reran over and over the scene of Jennifer and Buck aboard the *Sea Wind* on the all-important evening of August 30. If Buck had been aboard earlier in the day, as I suspected, either while killing the Grahams or afterward, it was conceivable that there was something visible on the boat that could have given this away. Even the brightest, most cautious crook can make a mistake. Among my scrawled notes before finally going off to bed was this one: "Ask Jenny what her favorite drink is."

At our next meeting, she answered without hesitation: "Apricot brandy."

"Did Mac and Muff know that?"

She paused to consider. "No," she said. Although she'd had cocktails aboard the *Sea Wind* once or twice before, the Grahams had never served apricot brandy. "So it never came up."

"Buck knew apricot brandy was your favorite drink?"

"Sure," she said, shrugging, apparently not aware where I was headed.

"Doesn't it appear to you that Buck had to be the one who put out the bottle of apricot brandy?"

She looked at me searchingly, but said nothing for several moments. I let her work it out for herself.

"I see your point," she finally said almost inaudibly. Her face fell.

The masthead light and apricot brandy were two pieces of evidence I presented to her which, for the first time, seemed to shake Jennifer's conviction that Buck Walker was innocent. But she wavered only briefly. Right up to her trial, the bottom line for her remained unchanged. Jennifer simply couldn't accept that Buck had killed the Grahams.

CHAPTER 26

PIRACY IN PARADISE: '74 VOYAGE ENDING IN MURDER TRIAL
—San Francisco *Chronicle*

S.F. TESTIMONY BEGINS IN PIRACY-MURDER TRIAL
—San Jose *Mercury News*

SAN FRANCISCO
MAY 28, 1985

IT WAS A BRIGHT, WINDY morning in this picturesque city by the bay. The air was naturally fresh, electric. Cable cars chugged up and down steep hills past quietly elegant hotels and world-class restaurants. Tens of thousands of commuter cars roared over the spiderwork bridges that feed into elevated highways curving around and into the towering business district. Glimpsed through the tall buildings in a myriad of shapes and designs, the sky was a vast cyclorama of blue, a backdrop dwarfing the melodrama promised by the press.

At the Civic Center, Old Glory snapped in the breeze atop the flagpole outside the twenty-story federal courthouse on Golden Gate Avenue.

A two-block stroll from the courthouse is the dome-topped San Francisco City Hall, where on the morning of November 27,

1978, the youthful-looking Dan White murdered Mayor George Moscone and Supervisor Harvey Milk, adding his bloody page to a city's history.

AFTER AN early jailhouse breakfast, Buck Walker was loaded into an unmarked U.S. Marshal's van with barred windows and accompanied by armed guards on the drive across town from his temporary lockup at the county jail to the courthouse's basement parking lot, which was guarded by shotgun-toting marshals. It was the kind of scene that in a Sam Peckinpah film would jump-cut to a massacre.

At 9:30 A.M., Judge Samuel King entered the courtroom. At a long counsel table perpendicular to the bench and to the judge's right were Elliot Enoki and Walter Schroeder, both looking somber in their dark-blue three-piece suits. At an identical table opposite the prosecutors were lead defense counsel Earle Partington, nattily dressed in a gray wool suit with a rose-colored shirt and maroon tie, and co-counsel Ray Findlay, a younger man with a full head of salt-and-pepper hair, his eyes hidden behind tinted glasses. It was Findlay's courtroom style to blend into the woodwork, not grab for the limelight—rather the opposite tack from his co-counsel's. Between the two defense lawyers sat the big, quiet, inscrutable-looking man accused of murdering Muff Graham.

Walker, now forty-seven, had aged considerably in the eleven years since Palmyra. His neatly combed hair was receding, and with the thirty extra pounds and a double chin he looked as soft as Pillsbury dough. It would be difficult for the jury to picture him as the swaggering, powerful, ruggedly handsome man of the photos taken in 1974. His eyes stared coldly out of black horn-rimmed bifocals that he frequently pushed up the bridge of his nose with his right index finger. He was wearing a flower-splotched Hawaiian shirt, a Western-cut corduroy coat with elbow patches, and cola-brown polyester slacks—what he would wear to court every day of his trial. There was a chalkiness to his complexion that was to be expected, considering he had spent the last three years and nine months since his arrest in Yuma behind bars. Whenever he spoke to his attorneys, he whispered behind a cupped hand, never making the slightest disturbance in court. But lurking beneath his stolid CPA demeanor was an unmistakable malevolence that most people who came near him sensed in their very bones.

Judge King introduced himself to the pool of sixty prospective jurors at the commencement of jury selection. ("I'm sixty-nine and I've been married forty years to the same woman," he said with a smile. "I have four and three-quarters grandchildren.") He asked each juror a few preliminary questions, then turned the questioning over to Enoki and Partington.

Shortly before noon, the prosecution and defense agreed to accept the jury, along with two alternates, and the jury was sworn.

That afternoon, Enoki delivered the Government's opening statement. "I don't think you will have any problem giving this case your undivided attention because it is truly a case involving a very unique setting," he began, then summarized the charges against the defendant, told the jurors about Mac and Muff Graham and their *Sea Wind*, described Palmyra, and explained how the Grahams had ended up alone on the island with Buck Walker and Jennifer Jenkins eleven summers earlier. The Government lawyer went on to give the jury a preview of the evidence the prosecution intended to present at the trial. As the motive for the murder, he suggested that Walker and his girlfriend were stranded on the island and virtually without food.

Sitting in the front row of public seats, a fragile but intense-looking woman in her fifties clutched a wadded tissue in one hand while keeping her blank gaze leveled on the prosecutor. In the preceding ten years, Kit Graham McIntosh had undergone several major surgeries, including one for a benign brain tumor. Next to her, holding her hand, sat her second husband,* Wally McIntosh, a

---

*On October 18, 1981, Kit's ex-husband, Bill Muncey, fifty-two, was at the controls of his unlimited hydroplane, *The Atlas Van Lines*, in a race off the coast of Mexico when rapid acceleration caused to bow to lift out of the water, flipping the boat over backward (called a "blowover" by boat racers). Muncey, who during his three-decade racing career drove with a verve and wizardry that became his trademark, was struck in the neck by a propeller blade and expired before reaching the hospital. His funeral in San Diego was attended by several thousand mourners.

tall, sweet-mannered retired engineer. Married since 1977, they had flown down from their home in Seattle, and neither would miss a moment of the trial. "I like being able to see what's going on," Kit said, smiling pleasantly to a reporter in the hallway during a recess. "Mac was my only brother and I loved him dearly." Her smile disappeared and her eyes clouded. "I want everyone to know that Mac and Muff were real. I'm going to sit here and remind them."

As she took her seat next to her husband, Kit recalled how grateful she'd been that her mother, who died a year earlier, did not have to endure this public presentation of the evidence. Muff's mother had not even lived to hear of the hideous discovery on Palmyra. She had gone downhill fast after Muff's disappearance, passing away not quite two years later. The cause of death, according to one family friend: a "broken heart."

After Enoki sat down, Ray Findlay stood to deliver the defense's opening statement. He buttoned his drab, rumpled suit and looked almost apologetically at the jury.

In a singsong voice, he went over the geographic layout of the island, emphasizing the abundance of coconut palms and edible fish and crabs. "No one was going to be starving to death on this island," he said. "No one was going to be desperate from hunger. They had food, and they were bartering for food."

At this point, Judge King interrupted testily. "You get to argue the case later," he barked. His jowls had turned beet-red with startling speed, and his words had a bite that, by the end of the trial, would be all too familiar to the defense.

"Yes, your honor," Findlay said respectfully.

Throughout the trial, Judge King, in the presence of the jury, would make his lack of respect for defense counsel clear not only in what he said but also in his tone of voice and theatrical gestures. Fist-pounding would accent his words when he was upset with them, as would tapping his pencil on the base of the microphone mounted in front of him. This tic would cause an amplified *tap-tap-tap* to echo throughout the courtroom, signaling to all and sundry that the defense was once again pushing him toward an explosion.

Findlay continued his opening statement. Twice more he would be interrupted by the judge's harsh admonitions. "There is no fight or argument that Mr. Walker is a boat thief," the defense attorney said, rocking nervously on the balls of his feet. "He stole the *Sea Wind*, yes." But, Findlay claimed, this theft occurred only after the Grahams had disappeared.

Findlay ended his remarks on the theme that would prove to be Walker's principal line of defense—that murder did not occur on Palmyra, only accidental death. "The Grahams went out fishing in their small inflatable dinghy. We don't know if that Zodiac hit something in the water, or flipped because of a gale.

"I believe the evidence will show one thing: nobody knows how or when Muff Graham died, and nobody can point to any evidence which proves beyond a reasonable doubt that the defendant, Buck Walker, committed *the murder*."

In loose language that no one would hold him to, the defense attorney had just contradicted himself unwittingly, conceding the fact there *had* been a murder—perhaps the main point at issue in the Walker trial.

LEN WEINGLASS and I attended Walker's trial, as did Ted Jenkins. We all listened carefully to the testimony of each witness, knowing that most would be giving almost the same testimony against Jennifer. When someone left the stand, Len would remain seated in order to monitor the start of the next witness's testimony while I rushed out to the hallway to intercept and interview the witness who had just stepped down.

The Government's first witness, Larry Briggs, took the stand shortly after court convened on the morning of May 29. Under questioning by Walt Schroeder, the charter boat captain for the *Caroline* told how he had helped tow the *Iola* into the lagoon on June 27. "By my standards," he testified, "the *Iola* did not appear to be a seaworthy boat. It was very run-down." He averred that Hawaii to Palmyra is "what's known as an easy sail." What about the reverse? "It would be much more difficult because you would be going against the wind and the sea. You would have a rough trip in *any* boat."

Would you have attempted such a trip in a boat like the *Iola*? Schroeder asked.

"No, I wouldn't. Unless I had no choice."

The message was clear: the *Iola* couldn't make it back to Hawaii, but Buck and Jennifer had a choice. The *Sea Wind*.

On cross-examination by Findlay, Briggs confirmed that sharks were plentiful in the lagoon. Then, in an effort to show that not everyone on the island feared Buck Walker, Findlay attempted to ask the witness if it was true that one of the amateur radio operators aboard the *Caroline* had gotten along well with the defendant.

Court: "I will sustain the objection."

But no objection had been made.

Taking his cue from the judge, Schroeder shot out of his seat and objected to the question.

"Objection is sustained," ruled Judge King.

Findlay seemed stunned. "But, your honor, the relationship—"

"*Sustained,*" the judge bellowed.

"The witness can observe—"

"Overruled! Overruled!" Judge King yelled. "The question is objectionable!"

The defense attorney, trying to recover from the sting of the judge's outburst, took a moment to collect himself. Finally, he asked the witness whether he had ever seen the ham radio operator in question in the company of the defendant.

"If I did," Briggs answered, "I have no recollection of it at this time."

"Do you recall making a statement to the Federal Bureau of Investigation—"

King half rose from the bench, his face flushed. "You are going to get into real trouble *soon*," he roared, "if you try to get around my ruling."

"Judge . . ." Findlay offered weakly.

The judge directed the jury to leave the courtroom. By then, of course, the damage had already been done. The jurors had seen the judge demean the defense counsel, surely diminishing in their eyes the attorney's stature and credibility. What the jurors didn't know—and had no way of knowing—was that the judge had been wrong on the law to boot. Findlay properly wanted to ask Briggs about what social intercourse he had observed between the defendant and others on Palmyra. He technically had not laid an adequate foundation for his question (this was not the basis for King's ruling), but he was properly attempting to use an earlier statement Briggs had made to the FBI to jog the witness's memory.

Outside the presence of the jury, the judge continued ranting about Findlay's effort to circumvent his ruling. Sitting there, I began to get a sinking feeling in the pit of my stomach. Was this a preview of Jennifer's trial? If standard courtroom practice pushed this judge to the verge of meltdown, what would happen when I attempted an unconventional defense, as I was planning, and in my aggressive style?

IN ALL, the prosecution would call six eyewitnesses to the midsummer 1974 events at Palmyra Island: Briggs, Jack Wheeler, Bernard and Evelyn Leonard, Donald Stevens, and Thomas Wolfe. A common thread ran through their testimony: Buck and Jennifer were running out of food; their boat was unseaworthy; and, since none had ever seen Buck and Jennifer on the *Sea Wind*—although they themselves had visited there—or otherwise associating with Mac and Muff in any way, hostility between the two couples was assumed.

Following up on an FBI 302 report that referred to letters the Grahams sent to Mac's sister, I had requested copies of the letters and had recently received them from Enoki. The correspondence, although inadmissible hearsay, made clear to me that the two couples *had* associated on Palmyra and were, in fact, at least outwardly civil to each other, even though each had hoped to find themselves alone there.

Concluding an innocuous cross-examination of Wheeler, Findlay said, "Your honor, I have no further questions."

Unbelievably, Judge King scolded Findlay before the jury: "Before you *ever* say 'no further questions,' you always consult Mr. Partington."

"I don't think . . ." Findlay stammered in amazement.

The judge continued the stern lecture. "Always just say to me, 'Could I have a second?' and then turn around and look at Mr. Partington."

What King was instructing Findlay on like a child was a matter of courtroom coordination to be determined only by the attorneys, not the judge. King's conduct was outrageous.

Two of the prosecution witnesses I feared most followed Wheeler to the stand. Bernard and Evelyn Leonard were charter members of a club I had facetiously dubbed "the Hawaiian Connection." This group, which included Curt Shoemaker, agreed with those law enforcement officials who believed that Jennifer had been the real brains behind the Palmyra murders.

The judge's behavior during the defense's cross-examination of Bernard Leonard was a repeat of what had happened to Findlay during his cross of Briggs, though this time Partington was the target, again right before the eyes of the jury. Findlay had been handling the cross of Leonard, asking for details about the geography of Palmyra, when Partington stood and made a reasonable request.

"May I have a moment with Mr. Findlay, your honor?" Partington asked. "He hasn't been to Palmyra. I have."

"He seems to be doing all right. If he wants any help, he will turn around and ask you," Judge King said sharply.

Partington looked hurt. "I wanted to explain something—"

"Make it fast! Let's not spend five minutes."

The two attorneys for the defense had every right to consult with each other at this point—as they finally did—but not before the judge had once again signaled to the jury that the defense team did not deserve even a modicum of respect. (Outside the presence of the jury, King continued his choleric abuse of defense counsel. Among his demeaning remarks were: "Get off that!" "Finish your objection!" "Have you tried any criminal cases before?" "I've *heard* your arguments.")

After only a few days of this treatment, Partington had a full-fledged case of shingles. The painful skin ailment inspired the courthouse crowd to produce a wave of pointed jokes about his succumbing to a nervous disorder during the biggest trial of his career. "Isn't shingles what lawyers are supposed to hang out once they pass the bar?" teased his own investigator.

When I approached Bernard Leonard in the hallway after his testimony, he acted coolly toward me, as I had anticipated he would. To be frank, he braced as if I had slithered out from under a rock.

It's been said that former CBS anchorman Walter Cronkite could influence millions of Americans just by raising an eyebrow while delivering the news. I feared that Leonard could have the same type of influence on the jury. It was now close to twelve years after the events that occurred on Palmyra, and we were in San Francisco, far from the uninhabited atoll. Many things can change in a dozen years, including one's appearance and demeanor (Buck Walker was a perfect example). I knew the jury would necessarily place considerable weight on the testimony of people who had been on Palmyra that summer of 1974. These people had seen Jennifer as she was *then*, and had observed, firsthand, what took place between Buck and Jennifer and the Grahams. On the stand at Jennifer's trial, Leonard and his wife, by body language and tone of voice, could shrewdly reveal to a jury drinking in their every word and gesture how strongly they believed her to be guilty, thereby influencing the jurors against Jennifer. I knew I probably could not shake Leonard's personal belief in Jennifer's guilt, but I hoped I might be able to soften him to the extent that he would testify without undue bias in his every word and gesture.

From a March 12, 1982, telephone interview Len Weinglass had with the man, I knew this task was going to be difficult, if not impossible. Leonard had characterized Jennifer as "capable of doing whatever she puts her mind to," including passing polygraph tests. Buck was clearly "a crook," he had told Len, but Jennifer was "clever, aggressive, and cunning." She was the "instigator," the schoolteacher claimed, and "she got Buck to do it. He did it. Jennifer planned it." Leonard also told Weinglass that he had no desire to talk at greater length with the defense because "anything I tell you is going to help you and I don't want to help Jennifer."

On January 3, 1984, I had made my own attempt to open communications with Bernard Leonard, writing him a letter.

I told him up front that the tone of my letter could perhaps be characterized by him as bold, but because of the position he had taken, and in view of the fact that Jennifer's liberty was at stake, I hoped he'd countenance the language I used. I tried to appeal to his reasoning. Since he was a teacher, I thought he himself would find the inflexible position he had taken in this case—the seemingly irrevocable prejudgment he had made without having access to all the facts—to be incompatible with his training and orientation. I went so far as to remind him of the profound lament of Socrates, one of history's greatest teachers, that the only thing he knew for sure was that he did not know anything.

I next sought to appeal to his sense of fair play, asking him if he thought he was being fair-minded when he personally judged Jennifer guilty even though he had not examined any of the evidence.

I told Leonard that after spending countless hours studying and examining all of the documents, transcripts, and available evidence in the case, as well as interviewing Miss Jenkins in depth, "I am personally convinced she is completely innocent of the murder charge pending against her."

I closed with this appeal: "If you would be kind enough to afford me the opportunity of meeting with you at any time and place designated by you, I am confident I will be able to furnish you with compelling justification for the conclusion I have reached. If I fail to do so, you certainly will not have surrendered anything other than an hour or so of your time. I believe you will find we both want justice in the death of your friends, Malcolm and Eleanor Graham. It has been said that truth, oftentimes admittedly an elusive fugitive, is the mother of justice. Only if we are open-minded in our inquiry, Mr. Leonard, can we help insure it does not suffer a miscarriage in this case."

I told Leonard that I eagerly awaited his reply to my letter.

But Leonard sent no reply.

After introducing myself to him now, I quickly reminded him that I wouldn't be representing Jennifer if I thought she was guilty of murder. He stood with slightly stooped shoulders, his long, grim visage radiating all the warmth of a clerk in the Department of Motor Vehicles.

"Lawyers don't care whether their clients are guilty or innocent," he all but sniffed.

"I assure you I do."

For the briefest of moments, he seemed to consider that possibility. "I've had eleven years to think about this thing," he said. "Believe me when I say Jennifer is an expert at convincing people of her innocence. She has the ability to convince anyone of anything. She's a pathological liar."

We were walking as he talked, and I led the way to the entrance of an unoccupied room nearby that I was using to interview the witnesses.

"There is no way in the world Mac and Muff would have invited Buck and Jennifer to dinner on the *Sea Wind*, or told them they could make themselves at home until they returned," Leonard concluded.

I immediately agreed that both the dinner invitation and the "make yourself at home" remark were complete fabrications.

Leonard seriously pondered my admission. Obviously surprised and intrigued, he followed me into the room.

"The dinner invitation is Buck's story," I explained as we sat down, "not Jennifer's. Buck told her that they had been invited to the *Sea Wind* for dinner. Jennifer has never said she heard it directly from Mac of Muff. In fact, she says she never saw the Grahams at all on August 30th."

"The day of her arrest at Ala Wai," Leonard said defiantly, "Jennifer told me, and I quote, 'Mac and Muff invited *us* over for dinner.'"

"As a teacher, Mr. Leonard, I'm sure you're more than familiar with colloquial English. 'Us' was just shorthand. It doesn't mean that Mac of Muff told her this personally. As she understood it from Buck, *they* had been invited over for dinner."

"Yes. Okay." Meaning: point taken, get on with it.

We went on to discuss how the *Sea Wind* was not locked when Jennifer and Buck boarded her on the evening of August 30. "Mac always locked his boat," Leonard insisted, "even when he left it for a short time."

"Do you think Jennifer had any way of knowing that?"

Leonard paused. "Probably not."

As we parted, I felt that possibly I had tempered Bernard Leonard's harsh judgment of Jennifer or at least reawakened his sense of fair play. Not until his appearance at her trial would I find out what effect, if any, my letter and my conversation with him would have.

Back in the courtroom, Evelyn Leonard, a woman in her late fifties with high cheekbones, a slim build, and feather-cut auburn hair, had followed her husband to the witness stand.

Describing the last time she saw Muff, she said, "Muff was crying very hard and she said she would never leave the island alive."

TOM WOLFE, who visited Palmyra aboard the *Toloa*, testified next to his being attacked and bitten by Walker's dog, Buck's ineptitude in catching game fish, the dwindling food supply aboard the *Iola*, and the building tension between the couples on the *Sea Wind* and the *Iola*.

Concluding Wolfe's testimony, the prosecutor brought up the missing rat poison. The witness, eager to reply, recalled that he had noticed the boxes of poison missing the day before his departure and warned Mac.

The next witness was Curt Shoemaker, whose ruddy complexion, sun-bleached hair, and rolling gait lent credence to his boast that he had logged ninety thousand miles of blue-water sailing in his lifetime.

Walt Schroeder, who continued handling the Government's witnesses, elicited testimony from Shoemaker about his schedule of radio communications with the Grahams. Then came a specific recollection of their last contact that hit the courtroom like a bombshell, particularly in view of the rat-poison testimony the jury had just heard.

"Do you recall if the subject of your last conversation with Mac Graham on August 28th ever turned to something that was then taking place?" Schroeder asked.

"Well, toward the end of this contact, I could hear a voice in the distance. Then Mac said, 'Wait a minute. Something is going on.'

So he went up topside and he came back and said, 'There is a dinghy coming over to the boat.' And his comment was, 'I guess they've made a truce,' or something like that. Then he told me to hang on while he went topside again."

"Did he return to the radio?"

"Yes, he did," Shoemaker said. "He came back in maybe ten or fifteen seconds and *said something about their bringing a cake over.* And he said, 'I better find out what's happening.' Mac signed off at that point."

"Did you hear anything in the background while Mac was telling you about these events?"

"Yes. I heard a woman's voice, and there was laughter, and I believe Muff was talking, too. It sounded like two females' voices."

From my review of the transcripts of the two theft trials, I knew that Shoemaker, with every opportunity to do so, had never mentioned anything about a cake or a truce in his earlier testimony. Incredibly, Findlay, in his brief cross-examination, did not bring out this critical contradiction. Had Walker's defense lawyers not *read* the theft-trial transcripts? Our copy had ended up in a warehouse; perhaps theirs had, too.

When the court recessed for the day shortly after Shoemaker's testimony, I stepped into the hallway and overheard a group of spectators discussing the sailor's story. "So now we know *how* they did it," one said. "Yeah," agreed another, "they laced the cake with rat poison. Man, what a way to go!"

The flippant analysis was devastating to Jennifer. What was the likelihood that Buck alone would have baked a cake and used his culinary skill to lace it with rat poison? It was Jennifer who kept the oven hot with her various concoctions. If the gallery assumed the Grahams were poisoned to death, why wouldn't the jurors, also? I knew little about the effects of rat poison on humans, but if it could actually cause death, I suspected the end would not come quickly. The Grahams would undoubtedly take sick, but have plenty of time to radio Shoemaker or someone else for help. The fact they didn't seemed to negate death by poisoning. (Tom Wolfe had also told me that one explanation he had considered for the rat poison's disappearance was that Mac had taken it with the intention "of wasting Buck's pit bull.") But, of course, I couldn't be confident the jury would feel the same as I.

I went immediately to the U.S. Attorney's Office on the sixteenth floor and confronted Schroeder.

"The rat-poison testimony couldn't possibly be more prejudicial, and it has no probative value," I argued. "What you're trying to do, Walt, is impregnate the jury's mind with the possibility that Buck and Jennifer poisoned the Grahams, even though you have no evidence of any kind to support such a thesis." My main concern, of course, was that the prosecution would attempt to use Shoemaker's rat-poison testimony at Jennifer's trial.

Schroeder dismissed my inference. "Vince, we just wanted to show that the Grahams knew about the missing poison, and because of it, this increased the suspicious feelings the Grahams had about Buck and Jennifer, making it all the more unlikely they would invite them to dinner."

Despite Schroeder's protestations, I was unconvinced.*

I knew I would have to come down hard on Shoemaker during my cross at Jennifer's trial when he repeated, as I obviously knew he would, his testimony about Buck and Jennifer's allegedly bringing cake to the Grahams on the evening of August 28.

As for the testimony by Tom Wolfe concerning the rat poison itself, I was determined to keep it from ever being heard at Jennifer's trial. Whatever the effects of the poison, the mere mention of it would be toxic.

ONE MESMERIZED spectator seated in the gallery was Patricia McKay, a large-boned, hefty woman in her mid-fifties with long graying hair. Buck's ex-wife had sculptured features, and the set of her jaw, though softened by years and a few extra pounds, suggested she'd been a real looker in her day.

Her presence had caught Buck by surprise, because they hadn't

*Sure enough, Elliot Enoki in his closing argument at the Walker trial, did not argue that the missing rat poison decreased the probability that the Grahams would invite Jennifer and Buck for dinner.

been in contact for years. Although they exchanged greetings by notes passed to Partington, Patricia was careful not to let people know who she was. She was here not to lend Buck support, but rather, as she would later explain, "to see for myself the case against him. I needed to know." She intended to fill in details of the evidence for Noel—her and Buck's nineteen-year-old daughter, who was sure her father was being framed.

Patricia had never had such feelings. Buck had been a crook when they met and fell in love in 1961, she insisted, and she was convinced he'd stayed a crook after their 1972 divorce. Of course, there had been a time, at the beginning, when Patricia believed in Buck, too. And when things were good, there was a lot of passion and love between them. When things were bad, it was horrible. Patricia had often feared for her safety, even after the divorce. "I always felt that if Buck killed anybody, it would be me. Our relationship was that volatile."

Sailing around the world on his own beautiful yacht had long been Buck's dream, Patricia recalled, and during their early years, he'd sit hunched over the kitchen table for hours drawing elaborate yacht designs. Once he sent away for a kit of sailboat plans, thinking he'd build one himself.

When she first saw a picture in the newspaper of the *Sea Wind*, a chill had gone through her. The Grahams' ketch looked very much like Buck's dream boat.

TRIALS NEVER proceed swiftly, except in novels or the movies, and during the ensuing days, a long line of additional prosecution witnesses dutifully took the stand.

The defense's cross-examination of these witnesses was consistently uninspiring, failing, for the most part, to make any dent in the witnesses' version of events. The mediocre performance of the defense attorneys was hardly enhanced by King's continuing assault upon their competence in open court. Remarks like "You are wasting a lot of time," "Stop this nonsense and go on to another question," and "Now, move on" found their way into his splenetic repertoire.

During a recess, one of the newspaper reporters covering the trial approached Findlay in the hallway.

"He's a peppery judge," the reporter said.

"The judge is so bad, it's unbelievable," snapped a disgusted Findlay, making no effort to keep his comments off the record. "It's more than his demeanor. His prejudice against our side goes to substantive issues."

I knew that King's conduct would likely influence the jury against Walker, since it would be a small step for a lay person to reason that a judge who treated the prosecutors with collegial respect and the defense with such disdain must not like *the cause the defense attorneys were representing*. But Partington and Findlay stuck with their submissive stance, not unlike steers being led to the slaughterhouse.*

It was obvious that King was like a loose cannon on the bench, unmindful of the prejudicial effect to the defendant his outbursts in court would have on the jury.

I hadn't decided how yet, but I already knew I would have to come up with some way to help insure that King acted much differently during Jennifer's trial. If I had anything to say about it, I wouldn't even countenance one such outburst, much less the steady stream of them Walker's attorneys endured.

FRANK MEHAFFY, a Sacramento, California, college teacher, bland of demeanor and expression, testified he was aboard his boat at Kauai's Nawiliwili harbor on October 12, 1974, when a ketch he identified as the *Sea Wind* pulled up to the pier. The next day, he met the couple on the unfamiliar craft—Roy Allen and Jennifer Jenkins.

Mehaffy was the first prosecution witness to mention a mysterious hole in the hull of the *Sea Wind*. According to him, Roy Allen explained that a swordfish had speared his boat just below the waterline on the trip from Palmyra.

---

*In a March 21, 1991, letter to me, Partington said that the way he and Ray Findlay acted "in regard to Judge King's conduct toward us" was a "tactical decision based on consultation with, and instructions from, our client." These tactics, he said, were imposed on them by their "ethical obligation" to their client.

Kit, who shook her head in disbelief once or twice during Mehaffy's story, was convinced that the hole was made by a stray bullet during the brutal murder of her brother and sister-in-law. The prosecutors obviously had the same suspicions and introduced the evidence in order to suggest this scenario to the jurors.

During a recess, a rangy fellow sitting in front of me turned around to strike up a conversation. An outdoors type in his mid-thirties with a neatly trimmed Vandyke, he said he was a building contractor from Los Angeles.

"What brings you up for the trial?" I inquired.

"I'm going to testify."

When I explained who I was, he told me he was Joel Peters, "Not *the* Joel from Ala Wai harbor?" I said quickly.

"Yeah," he shrugged.

"I've been looking for you for a long time, Joel. In fact, four years."

"You're kidding."

I was not. I asked him to step out into the hallway, where I found Len huddled with Ted Jenkins, mulling over some aspect of the trial. I introduced Peters.

"This guy right here, Joel—I never knew his last name before now—is one of the key witnesses for Jennifer's defense," I said spiritedly, holding on to the surprised contractor's arm. "I've been looking for him ever since Jennifer told me about him. I asked Enoki about someone named Joel, and he said he'd never heard of him. I called all over looking for him."

"The FBI called me about a month ago and asked me to testify," Peters explained. "I guess they'd been looking for me, too. I left Hawaii years ago. Moved to Los Angeles."

Len and Ted looked bewildered.

"Don't you remember who Joel is?" I asked. "He's the guy Jennifer delivered the *laundry* to on the morning of her arrest even though the Coast Guard and FBI were pursuing her. That's great evidence."

Len and Ted both nodded vacantly, obviously not sharing my elation.

"Wait until the trial," I promised them. "You'll see what Joel is going to do for us."

Len and Ted both gave me amused if-you-say-so-Vince smiles and resumed their conversation.

On the stand for the prosecution, Peters testified that he first met Jennifer and Buck on the Big Island in the fall of 1973, then ran into them on Maui early the following year when they were preparing the *Iola* for launching. In Ala Wai harbor in October 1974, he saw Buck rowing by and hailed him. "Buck pointed out a boat he said was his," Peters testified, adding that it didn't look at all like the same boat he had seen Jennifer and Buck refitting in Maalaea Bay. Shown a photo of the *Sea Wind*, he identified it as the boat.

The next witness, Katherine Ono, clerked at the Hawaii State Harbors Division. Using Harbors Division documents to refresh her memory, Ono testified that on October 18, 1974, a man named Roy Allen, "a very grubby individual wearing shorts," filed boat registration forms with her for a "homemade sailboat named the *Lokahi*," claiming he had completed it that year. The craft was "an Angleman wooden ketch, thirty-seven and a half feet long by 11.9 feet wide, by 5.7 feet draft from bridge to port, powered by sail and inboard" (the exact description of the *Sea Wind*), colors "white and violet," according to Allen's answers on the form. Ono assigned the boat Hawaii state hull number HA25946C0672.

Taking the stand dressed in a tight-fitting black skirt and scarlet raw-silk blouse, Sharon Jordan, with her Polynesian looks, deep tan, and straight black waist-length hair, was right out of *Mutiny on the Bounty*. In her clipped upper-class accent, she testified with poise to finding skeletal remains beside a metal container on the northern shore of the Palmyra lagoon in January 1981.

Up to now, the horror of what had happened on Palmyra had been deflected by testimony that was relevant to the issue of guilt, but unrelated to the actual acts of atrocity that had taken place. Like a sudden cold sweat, the atmosphere of the trial was changed in an instant by the slow, creaking arrival of a silvery metal box* being wheeled into the courtroom by an FBI agent. There was a

---

*The aluminum box measured thirty-three inches long by twenty-three inches wide, and was eighteen inches deep.

sudden silence in the courtroom. The rust-stained container was riddled with holes, some caused by corrosion from the lagoon waters, others by experts conducting evidentiary examinations. The box and lid, Government exhibits 28 and 29, sat squarely before the jury for the first time.

Everyone's attention was riveted to the box that, in all likelihood, had for seven years been Muff Graham's coffin at the bottom of the Palmyra lagoon.

During cross-examination, Partington worked a line of questioning designed to open the possibility that the bones and box could have washed ashore separately—implying that Muff Graham's remains had never been *inside* the container. But Jordan steadfastly and articulately resisted all his attempts to separate the bones from the container, a separation which was vital to Partington if he was to have at least a hint of credibility when he argued to the jury at the conclusion of the case that Muff Graham had not been murdered.

Partington had considered Jordan so important a witness he had traveled to Johannesburg to interview her. But even with this type of preparation for cross-examining her, he was not able to diminish the impact of several key observations. Jordan's word picture of Muff Graham's remains spilling out of the upended container onto the beach was too memorably vivid.

Jordan: "I found a wristwatch* and small bone inside the lid of the box. The rest of the bones looked like they had fallen out of the box, and were in a crescent shape in the immediate vicinity of the box. I also found a piece of wire near the box, twisted in the shape of the box, that had obviously been around the box at one time, as if to keep the lid on."

Partington got into a disagreement with Jordan about what she had told him in South Africa. "Do you recall saying to me that the vegetation was growing in the box in such a way that the box was

---

*An April 7, 1981, FBI report described the watch found by Sharon Jordan as a seventeen-jewel Westclox brand, and stated that the last time displayed by the watch was around 12:15. It could not be determined, naturally, whether that was a.m. or p.m. Also undeterminable, of course: whether or not the watch had stopped ticking at or near the time of Muff's death.

wedged in and you actually had to hack the vegetation away to get it out?"

Jordan: "I don't recall saying that."

Partington glowered at the witness. "Do you recall my saying to you that if there was vegetation already growing in the box and wedging the box in, how could the bones have just recently spilled out, as the Government contends? To which you replied you hadn't thought of that, and the bones couldn't have just recently spilled out of the box?"

Jordan: "I don't recall saying that."

After Harry Conklin, a former Coast Guardsman, next testified to having observed Buck dive into the water at Ala Wai harbor on the morning of October 29, 1974, and escape, FBI agent Henry Burns, the bull-necked twenty-two-year veteran of the Bureau who had arrested Walker on the Big Island in November 1974, gave details of his interview with the prisoner on the drive to Hilo.

Burns testified to Buck's telling him about the dinner invitation from the Grahams on August 30, 1974; his and Jennifer's going to the *Sea Wind* that night and the Grahams' absence; the discovery of the overturned dinghy on the beach the following morning; his belief they had died an accidental death, etc.

Ken White, the missing boat expert whom the prosecution had finally located in Texas, took the stand to tell the jury he'd found no salt water in the Zodiac engine. This was now the third jury to hear that there was no indication at all that Mac and Muff's dinghy had overturned in the lagoon, thereby knocking another pillar or two out from under the Walker defense team's accidental-death argument.

Witness Frank Ballintine, who had sold and serviced Zodiacs for eighteen years, described it as "probably the most stable boat you can find." He'd heard of only one Zodiac capsizing in the whole of his career, and that had happened in thirty-foot waves forty miles out at sea.

Next, Calvin Shishido, now retired, testified about his 1974 and 1981 trips to Palmyra.

Enoki asked the former chief investigator to identify the contents of a large cardboard carton. The jury was now to see the incomplete remains of Muff Graham for the first time. Six plastic bags contained various bones. Out of the carton last came the skull. Shishido identified the lot as the remains he had recovered from the Jordans and subsequently sent to the FBI laboratory in Washington, D.C., for identification and analysis.

Shishido was next shown a wristwatch. "Do you recognize exhibit 27?" Enoki asked.

"Yes. Sharon Jordan gave it to me. It was later identified as a lady's Westclox watch."

"That watch has never been positively connected to anybody, has it?" Judge King asked.

Enoki confirmed that it had not.

Shishido also identified Buck's .22-caliber Ruger Bearcat pistol, which he had found aboard the *Sea Wind.**

The Government next called Joseph Stuart, who testified to meeting Buck Walker (introduced to him then as Roy Allen) at a party at his Honolulu home in October 1974.

Stuart: "He told me he was playing chess with this couple that owned a boat on Palmyra Island . . . this couple ran out of money and they put up the boat. Whoever won the game would get each other's boat."

Enoki: "According to him, what happened?"

"He said he won the game and got their nice boat. They got his old boat."

"What was the context of this conversation? Was it a joke or what?"

"He told it as a true story, sir."

BESPECTACLED AL Ingman, the next prosecution witness, looked as nervous and ill at ease as a Baptist in a bordello, never once even glancing at his old cellmate, Buck Walker.†

---

*This .22 had been purchased by Buck Walker's brother, Don, in 1963, and was still registered to him.

†J.W. Williams was brought to San Francisco for the Walker trial but was not called to the witness stand. To date, Elliot Enoki will say only that he decided against calling Williams after speaking to him there. "I can't go into why I didn't call him," explains the prosecutor, "because it isn't a matter of public record."

On direct by Schroeder, Ingman elaborated on the details of Walker's alleged prison confession at McNeil Island in the spring of 1979: "He mentioned forcing the man to walk the plank."

"Did he say what he meant by 'walk the plank'?"

"Yes, walk off the edge of the boat."

"Did he ever tell you whose boat he used when they made this man walk the plank?"

"It was my understanding it was the man's boat, because I believe that Buck and his girlfriend were invited by this couple to dinner."

"Did Mr. Walker tell you that this man said anything as he was being made to walk the plank?"

"He mentioned that the man was crapping all over himself and sniveling when he was being made to walk the plank."

"When Mr. Walker told you about this man sniveling and defecating, what was his demeanor?"

"He was laughing."

"Did Mr. Walker ever say that he did, in fact, murder this couple?"

"There was a statement made about—I don't recall the term— offing, or knocking them out of the box, or blowing them away, some jailhouse term like that."

"Did he mention this term with respect to just the man or with respect to both of them?"

"I think to both of them, but I'm not sure."

If the jury believed Ingman's testimony, this, of course, was the fall of the blade for Buck.

Ingman testified that in a motor home in Tijuana, Mexico, at a later date, he asked Walker if he was worried about rumors that his girlfriend might cooperate with the authorities in turning state's evidence against him, and that Walker "seemed concerned about it, but he didn't think she would."

Ingman went on to testify that shortly after the press reported discovery of "bones in a box on Palmyra," he'd gone to Mexico to give Walker ten thousand dollars to complete a transaction in their drug-smuggling operation. Walker, Ingman said, had a house in Puerto Escondido, a small fishing village near the southernmost tip of Mexico, and was living with a "younger girl." He said he told Walker about the accounts of a "box floating up with a woman's remains in it. I said something about how strange or fantastic it was that a box could come floating up after that much time."

"And what did Mr. Walker say?" asked Schroeder.

"He said that it was bullshit, that he didn't put her in a box."

"Did he say what he did with her body?"

"No, he didn't."

On cross-examination, Partington got Ingman to admit that he was stoned on grass when Walker told the bloody tale in the McNeil prison powerhouse, as well as to share a fact of prison life: "There is a lot of storytelling that goes on in prison, things that aren't true."

Ingman also admitted that he once supported a four-hundred-dollar-a-day habit by dealing drugs, and had supplied heroin to his two sons, one of whom subsequently died of an overdose.

Partington established Ingman as a "professional witness" by pinning down the amount of Government money he had received over the years for testifying against various individuals—$7,800 before he even entered the federally funded Witness Protection Program, $28,000 afterward. The money, Ingman said, was only to help defray his subsistence, housing, and medical costs.

"If the Government did not believe you were cooperating with them, you would not have received this money, isn't that correct?" Partington asked.

"I suppose so."

Richard Taylor, who with his brother Carlos had planned to sail to Palmyra in the fall of 1974 to resupply Buck and Jennifer, came to the stand as a prosecution witness, but the sullen scowl frozen on his long, pinched face left little doubt that he was only reluctantly testifying against his old pal.

He confirmed that he had received the letter Buck and Jennifer had written on Palmyra. "Buck asked me to bring epoxy," Taylor said. Asked what it was used for, he replied: "For patching fiberglass." He recalled that the couple also needed food supplies, "mostly flour and sugar."

Why had he and his brother never arrived to rescue their friends? According to Taylor, they had lost their storm jib during a severe blow on a cruise off the Hawaiian Islands.

He said he next heard from Buck and Jennifer when they reappeared in Oahu. In fact, he visited them on their new boat in Ala Wai harbor on October 27—just two days before the federal dragnet pulled tight on the repainted *Sea Wind* and her passengers.

"What did Buck tell you about their new boat?" Schroeder wanted to know.

Taylor looked as if he'd just swallowed vinegar. "Buck said they were down on Palmyra," he began uneasily, "and there wasn't much to do. He had played a lot of chess with a man on the other boat. After a while, the man owed him so much money that they—traded boats."

"During this conversation, did he ever mention anyone on Palmyra drowning or capsizing or disappearing?"

"No, sir, he did not."

On cross, Findlay elicited that Taylor had spent three weeks on Palmyra in 1977. When he said he had a "foreboding feeling about the island," Findlay asked why.

"It was more than just the fact that it was a ghost-type island," Taylor said. "It was more than that. It seemed to be an unfriendly place to be. I've been on a number of atolls, but Palmyra was different. I can't put my finger on specifically why. But it was not an island I enjoyed being on. I think other people have had difficulties on that island." Intended translation: maybe the island itself, not Buck Walker, had mysteriously done Mac and Muff in.

After establishing that Taylor had owned and operated Zodiac dinghies, Findlay next asked: "From your experience in operating a Zodiac, can you tell us whether it is possible for someone to be thrown from a Zodiac; for example, in a situation where a sharp turn is made?"

"Absolutely." Taylor brightened, as if this was just the kind of question he had been waiting to hear. "In fact, we had to rig our own Zodiac with safety lines, because there is really nothing to hold on to."

Buck Walker still had some friends in the world.

CHAPTER 27

THE JURY WOULD NOW hear testimony on the key issue at the Walker trial. To prove that Muff Graham had been murdered, thus refuting the defense's main argument that she had died accidentally when the Zodiac overturned in the lagoon, the Government called to the stand a platoon of medical and scientific expert witnesses. Their often complex and abstruse testimony would consume hundreds of pages of transcript.

Dr. Oliver Harris, a forensic odontologist (a specialist in the study of teeth and their surrounding tissue) with a sparse, balding crown and reading glasses that he kept putting on and taking off, testified to his examination of the skull and its mandible, or lower jawbone, which was detached ("fractured out by blunt trauma") from the skull when found on Palmyra. He cited other evidence of blunt trauma: fractures to an upper left molar in Muff's skull and a lower right molar in the jawbone, as well as to the crown of tooth number 13 at the gumline and the apices (tips) of the roots of tooth number 30. There were also "fracture lines" in the lower jaw. He asserted that these fractures most probably occurred either pari mortem (at or near the time of death) or postmortem (after death).

"Could the fractures have occurred antemortem—prior to death?" asked Enoki. In other words, could the trauma have been sustained in a nonhomicidal context, like a fall or some other accident?

"In my opinion, they could not. The pain of the fractured tips of the roots of the molars would be so severe, so intolerable, that the subject would immediately want to seek the services of a dentist. And the fracture to the jawbone was of such a nature as eventually to cause death unless the person sought out a physician for treatment."

The jury knew that Mac could always call for medical or den-

tal help on his radio or sail the *Sea Wind* to Fanning or some other
island for assistance.

Enoki asked the dental expert what degree of force would have
been necessary to cause these fractures. To split the jawbone from
the skull, the expert said, and fracture the roots of teeth, which are
"deeply embedded in bone," would require "extreme force. It's not
characteristic of an automobile accident. It would be more characteristic of a sledgehammer, a ballpeen hammer, or some other
heavy round object." Multiple blows were involved, Dr. Harris
added.

One juror bowed her head . . . another stared directly at Buck
Walker. The others seemed to retain their focus on the expert, who
had assumed the affectless monotone of a dispassionate observer
inured to testifying about such matters.

On cross-examination, Partington asked if anything in the
marine environment or any other natural phenomenon could have
caused the "blunt trauma" to the teeth and jawbone.

"I know of nothing in the marine environment that could cause
fractures like that."

The curator of anthropology at the Smithsonian Institution in
Washington, D.C., was called to the stand next. Douglas Uberlaker
was the FBI's sole consultant in forensic anthropology since 1977.

The tall, professorial Uberlaker, dressed like a Princeton faculty
member in tweed jacket, wool slacks, and Weejuns, stated that he
had examined the skull, jawbone, and other skeletal remains at the
request of the Government. "The skeleton was not complete, as
there were a few missing parts," he explained. "So, it was not possible to put it all completely back together." But the find was sufficient, he asserted, to conclude with confidence that the skeletal
remains derived from one individual, "a Caucasian woman approximately five feet four inches tall."

Enoki read into the record a stipulation that the remains were
those of Eleanor Graham.

"There appears to be a whitish area on the top portion of the
skull. Do you see that?" the prosecutor asked.

Uberlaker owlishly regarded the skull he held in his hands. "Yes.
There is a white area, what we call calcination, on the upper left

part of the skull that extends more or less from the eye area back over the left top of the skull, and then back down to about the center [of the rear] of the skull."

"Did you reach a conclusion as to what caused that area to be white?"

"Yes. Given the extreme whiteness of that area, the best causal factor I would attach to that is extreme heat applied to that very localized area over a period of time."

"Could this intense heat be caused by direct sunlight?"

"I don't think so. You might get that extent of bleaching from the sun with years of exposure, but you would also get a type of erosion that we don't see here. That suggests to me that the heat source was something more intense than the sun."

"Greater than a fire?" Enoki asked.

"It would not be a bonfire or a wood-burning fire, but some sort of heat source that could generate extreme temperatures."

"Would an acetylene torch have that kind of heat capacity?"

"Yes."

Another horror.

Partington objected that Enoki was leading the witness. With a shrug, the judge gave the prosecutor a perfunctory warning. But the image was indelible: *an acetylene torch.* There was now scientific testimony which indicated that Muff's beloved husband's own implements had probably been used on her by her murderer. The horror was cruelly refined.

Their thinking clearly legible in their unguarded expressions, jurors could not resist studying Buck Walker, stoically unmoved at the defense table. Was this rather ordinary-looking fellow capable of such savagery toward Muff? And had he done the same to Mac?

Enoki's direct examination of the anthropologist proceeded implacably with the cadence of a slow march. The witness briskly ignored the sensational nature of his testimony, as if giving the basics to undergraduates in an anatomy class rather than revealing dramatic evidence at a major murder trial.

"Were you able to determine when this heat was applied to the skull in relation to death or decomposition?"

Uberlaker sat back in the hard wooden witness chair and

crossed his long legs, as if dying to retrieve a meerschaum pipe from his pocket, clamp it between his teeth, and strike a match while pondering further. This man clearly enjoyed supplying the missing pieces of a forensic puzzle, but stingily, one at a time.

"Well, it's difficult to say exactly," Uberlaker answered cautiously. "The borders of the calcination area suggest that something had to have been present to protect the nonaffected bone from also getting that extreme heat. In other cases that I have seen like this, that has *always* been flesh."

Could the whitening have been caused by fossilization, Enoki asked, seeking to eliminate all possible natural causes. The answer was no. Fossilization, Uberlaker explained, is a "very long-term process."

"Did you note any wear or erosion by some other source on the skull?"

"Yes. On the front left side of the skull, across the face, are five very flat abraded areas that we term "coffin wear." There also appear to be several smaller areas on the right side of the face. If a skeleton has been in a coffin for many years, the slow movements caused by gyrations of the earth could cause abrasion of the bone against the flat surface that it's lying against."

The jury didn't have to be told that the "coffin wear" was from the container.

Still seeking to negate a defense argument in support of accidental death, Enoki asked: "And did you see any evidence of a shark attack or bite on the skeletal remains that you examined?"

"No."

"Would you have expected to see such evidence if a shark had attacked this individual?"

"Yes. Sharks will attack with a tremendous amount of force. They will rip and remove large sections of flesh and even bone, leaving behind very chiseled-like imprints of their teeth."

To conclude, Enoki asked the anthropologist if he had reached a conclusion as to what caused the hole in Muff's left temple.

"No. It's in a part of the skull that's very thin and is one of the most easily damaged areas."

During cross-examination by Partington, Uberlaker admitted

he hadn't been at all surprised to find a hole in the skull, or fractures to some of the other bones—the *long* bones of the skeleton.
"There are natural phenomena, such as abrasion, that can produce
a hole in the skull and . . . I can think of a lot of natural circumstances that would produce breakage of bone that don't involve
foul play or criminal activity."

A new mystery surfaced without warning on cross-examination.
Uberlaker testified that he had observed "several blackish deposits
on the top of the skull" which appeared to be "remnants of burn
material."

Partington eagerly asked, "Didn't you express the opinion to me
when I spoke to you at the Smithsonian that the burning which
caused the black deposits, as opposed to the whitening, had taken
place *years after death*?"

"Yes," the anthropologist answered casually just before stepping
down.

But the implications were not casual. Was it possible that someone had set fire to Muff's remains years after she was murdered? If
so, who? And why?

A pasty-skinned man with thick glasses and unruly hair sticking
up like bulrushes hurried forward to the stand. He was the man
who in every homicide case is supposed to tell the jury with scientific precision how the victim died. But Dr. Boyd Stephens, chief
medical examiner and coroner for the City and County of San
Francisco, testified that on examining the skeletal remains at the
request of the Government on April 16, 1985, he found "no recognizable cause of death."

Enoki asked the witness if he had made any "findings" in regard
to the damage to the skeletal remains.

"Yes. The radius and ulna—the forearm bones—on the left
forearm have transverse fractures, meaning they are broken across.
Both the right and left tibia—the lower leg bones—have a twisting fracture."

"What amount of force is required for a twisting type of
fracture?"

"A considerable amount of force in a living individual. It's usually a rotational force, frequently seen in skiing accidents. It usually

implies that some part of the extremity is fixed or restrained while the body is rotated around it, or the body is fixed while the extremity is rotated."

As this latest expert continued on, I realized that all of us—the jurors, the attorneys, the judge, and the spectators—were anxiously hanging on every word of what, for the most part, amounted to nothing more than sophisticated, argot-ladened speculation. I gazed hard at Buck Walker. Through it all, there he sat, taciturn and still, the only person on the face of the planet, in my view, who knew *exactly* what had happened. Yet he sat there like the rest of us, giving the impression he was being educated or tantalized along with everyone else. I wondered whether he could be thinking, *What stupid jerks all of them are. That's not how I did it.* Or was he thinking how very lucky he was to be living in the United States of America, where authorities who *knew* he had committed the murder had to spend hundreds of thousands of dollars and sink years of investigation into the effort to prove his guilt to a jury? (Of course, the same authorities were equally certain that my client was involved in the murder.)

In addition to the various fractures, Dr. Stephens testified that the five flat areas on the skull near the left eye and left cheek were flattened to the extent "that a ruler can be placed" across them.

Asked by Enoki if, in his expert opinion, the abrading surface could have been the container, Stephens replied that indeed the inside walls of the container were "consistent" with the abraded areas on the skull.

Dr. Stephens confirmed that there was evidence the skull had been exposed to heat. "This is not the type of heat we see from sun exposure," he said, obviously getting into it with relish. "We are talking about an accelerant or a gas that is burning. To burn something like that, you would need about eleven hundred degrees Fahrenheit or higher." Stephens was more categorical on the next important point than Uberlaker had been: *"This burning took place while there was tissue on the skull. The tissue and moisture protection are the explanation for the irregular margins. The burning, I believe, happened at or near the time of death."*

Enoki: "Is there enough gas given off by a human body's decomposition to float a container the size of Government exhibit 28?"

"Yes," Stephens answered. He explained that the most common gases given off by decomposing human remains are methane, hydrogen sulfide, and carbon dioxide. As they displaced the water inside the box, they would "literally make the body a lifting force. We have had cases here in San Francisco Bay where a human body floated to the surface with as much as two hundred pounds of weight attached to the body."

"Those weren't in concrete boots, were they?" Judge King asked.

Soft chuckling filled the courtroom.

"Various types of weights were added to the body," Dr. Stephens responded with a smile, "for reasons other than good health. The average body in San Francisco Bay will float in about ten days. Obviously, if the weight is added, it takes a longer time."

Enoki, tenacious as a terrier, returned to the possibility that the hole in the skull *might* have been caused by a bullet. Again, Dr. Stephens was more accommodating than the previous witness.

"Did you reach any conclusion as to the hole in the left side of the skull?" the prosecutor asked.

"No. But I don't believe it is an abrasion."

"Have you ruled out the possibility that this hole was caused by a gunshot?"

"No, I have not."

Primed for damage control, on cross-examination Partington elicited the medical examiner's admission that he had tried to determine the presence of "foreign material" around the hole by taking X-rays and films. "With lead bullets, when they penetrate a bone, lead is deposited, isn't that true?" he asked.

"That is correct."

"You found no evidence of lead [around the hole], did you?"

"No, counsel." The reply was straightforward, but the tone was acrid.

The defense attorney then asked if Dr. Stephens, given the Government's theory that the bones were once inside the container, expected to see the areas of abrasion on the skull he'd testified to. The witness said he could visualize the abrasions to the skull, which would be held "somewhat in position" by the ligaments on the vertebrae, but would have expected to find areas of abrasion "on many of the other bones" as well.

"Which you did *not* find?"

"I did not find."

The witness said there had to be "another element in the box that fixed the skull" more firmly, or it would not have worn only on those five specific surfaces. The most likely element "to fix the skull," Dr. Stephens concluded, was sand.*

It was an opening Partington hadn't expected. "You cannot preclude the possibility that this abrading took place while the skull was embedded in sand amidst coral *outside* the box?" he now asked.

"I cannot preclude that. It only requires that there be movement, a flat surface, and that the skull be against that flat surface, and change its position five times." With that answer, Partington had created the theoretical possibility that Muff's body had never been in the container—again, the *key* issue, since Walker's defense was accidental death.

Obviously, if Muff *had* been placed in the container, accidental death could not be persuasively argued. The mood at the defense table lightened.

The next four witnesses were FBI technicians assigned to the Bureau's laboratory in Washington, D.C. On the stand, they spoke in carefully phrased, precisely articulated sentences, having long ago polished their skills as scientific witnesses. Their purpose was to put Muff's body securely back in the container.

A metallurgist, William Tobin, testified that he'd conducted a series of examinations on the container and concluded that there had been intense heat *inside*, evidently produced with the aid of a hydrocarbon accelerant—"something like gasoline, kerosene, or fuel oils." The factors upon which he based his opinion, he explained, were traces of sulfur and carbon found inside the container. "They are by-products of hydrocarbon-based fires."

*Sharon Jordan had testified that when she found the container, there were several inches of sand at its bottom.

In addition, the expert said that when he cut out a section of the container and examined it under a high-powered microscope, he observed "a very abnormal variation in grain size" between the metal on the inside and outside surfaces of the container. The larger grains on the inside showed that the surface "was subjected to elevated temperatures," while the outside surface "was not simultaneously exposed to the atmosphere, but rather, to a very severe quenching medium." That medium, in his best judgment, was water.

Enoki wanted to know if the several corroded holes on the lid and bottom of the container would have prevented it from floating to the surface. No, the witness replied, he had seen "much heavier containers that had human bodies in them, even with chains and weights, and with large triangular holes cut out, rise from the deep ocean and float to the surface."

Next, chemist Roger Martz recounted a series of tests—solubility studies, infrared analysis, X-rays, gas chromatography and thermotography—he had conducted on the container. On the inside surface, he'd discovered a "waxlike material, which contained fatty acids, and the calcium salts of those fatty acids. The substance, called adipocere, is the product of the natural fats in the body being changed chemically under decomposition. Martz said adipocere forms after death when "the body is taken away from air, such as would occur underwater."*

He went on to explain that calcium salts or fatty acids are not unique to human beings. They could also be formed by animals. If so, he said, cholesterol is detectable. But he found no trace of cholesterol.

During cross-examination, Partington sought to raise the possibility that the calcium salts and fatty acids were residues of plant decay. The chemist doubted that plants have enough fatty tissue to form the kind of deposit he'd found, but admitted that he was no plant expert.

Agent Chester Blythe, the microscopy expert, testified that he'd

---

*Dr. Stephens had previously narrowed it down further. "Adipocere is most commonly associated with water that is still, such as a lake or lagoon. It would not form well in a stream," he said.

conducted a microscopic examination of a small piece of "faded, greenish-color, cotton cloth" found stuck to the bottom of the aluminum container. "The fibers exhibited characteristics which are associated with burning," he concluded.

Agent Roy Tubergen, the serologist, or expert in the study of blood, testified to performing a phenolphthalein screening test on residue from the bottom of the container. The test, he explained, was so sensitive it could detect even a single drop of blood in ten thousand parts of water. "I got a positive result on the box," he said.

The serologist performed the same test on a swatch of a dark red portion of the cloth found in the container. Result? Again, positive for the presence of blood. But the phenolphthalein test only determines the presence of blood, not whether it's human or animal. The next test *did* make that determination. Tubergen performed an Ouchterlony test—taking the swatch of the blood-stained cloth and extracting the blood from it using a saline solution, then placing the extracted blood in a gel on a microscopic slide and subjecting it to various reacting agents—and found the unmistakable presence of *human* protein in the blood extracted from the fibers of the cloth.

So much for Partington's *plant*-in-the-box theory.

The Government team had done their homework. Step by step, the cumulative scientific evidence had made it clear that a human body—obviously that of Muff Graham—had at one time been inside the container. Partington's accidental-death theory, though dying a slower death than had poor Muff, was well on the way to rigor mortis, it seemed.

But the defense had yet to present its case.

The jury had heard two days' worth of complex medical and scientific testimony, often delivered in numbing jargon and sewing-machine rhythms. It was a relief for everyone when Enoki returned to calling witnesses who didn't have a ten-page *vita*.

By the end of the day on June 5, the Government had called its last witness. Enoki was expected to rest his case the following morning.

Before Judge King sent the jurors home, he reminded them, as was his daily custom, not to discuss the case, read newspaper articles about it, or watch the TV news coverage.

After the jurors departed, Partington made a motion for a judgment of acquittal as to Count One of the indictment. This was the felony-murder count I had previously asked the court to remove from the indictment, which Judge King had declined to do.

But now, Judge King, no doubt to Enoki's surprise, looked at the Government table and asked: "How do you *connect* her death with the robbery?" The judge's question implied that the Government had not presented evidence that the killing took place "*during* the perpetration" of the robbery, a circumstance that had to be proved before the felony-murder rule would apply.

Enoki: "Well, if in a bank robbery the defendant takes the bank teller along with him and kills her later—I don't mean three weeks later, I mean in the process of taking her away from the scene— that's connected to the robbery."*

Judge King was unmoved by the prosecutor's argument, and granted the defense motion. Of course, if felony-murder had been the only count in the indictment, as it had been originally, and hence dismissing that count would have set Buck Walker free, Partington would have had about as much chance of winning his motion as of persuading Kit Muncey to step up as a character witness for his client.

Before the marshals escorted him from the courtroom, Walker grinned smugly at his attorneys and gave Partington a good-old-boy pat on the back.

Walker might have considered the felony-murder dismissal a major legal triumph, but I thought it more a matter of the Government's being prevented from pursuing an inappropriate charge.

With the defense set to present its case, the charges against Buck

---

*I was amazed that Enoki didn't buttress his argument by specifically citing to the court the whole line of prosecution cases holding that the requirement that the death be *connected* to the robbery should be liberally construed, with no strict causal relationship needing to be shown. Moreover, the precedents allow the connection to be shown by circumstantial evidence, i.e., by inference.

Walker had been whittled down to a single count of premeditated murder.

JUNE 6, 1985

THE FIRST defense witness was Charles Morton, a criminalist who was the director of the private Institute of Forensic Sciences in Oakland. Morton testified that his examination of the metal container revealed no "direct evidence" indicating there had ever been a body inside. On the other hand, he added, he had found nothing to "exclude that possibility."

In his never-say-die effort to keep the bones out of the box, Partington wanted to know if the expert had found any evidence suggesting that the abrasion to the bones had taken place inside. The answer: "I looked for areas in the box that would show that. I found only relatively light abrasion to the interior of the container in a couple of areas."

Obviously, Partington would have preferred the complete absence of discernible abrasions.

On cross, Enoki asked: "If the container were partially filled with sand, wouldn't the sand provide another surface for possible abrasion of a human bone?"

"Certainly," the criminalist replied without hesitation.

Enoki next used the defense witness to elicit a critical piece of testimony to bolster the argument that the reason Muff's remains were found right alongside the container was that they had once been inside. After all, how else could they have gotten there?

"By the way," the prosecutor now asked, "bones don't float, is that correct?"

"That's correct," the defense criminologist replied.

Next, a serologist from the same institute testified that he had cut out a section of the piece of green cloth found in the container for examination. His tests had not shown evidence of human protein in the blood (ostensibly contradicting the findings of the FBI serologist), meaning that the blood could be either human or animal.

Now, it seemed, Partington wanted to suggest the novel scenario that a bleeding animal—not a human being—might have been inside the container.

Enoki swiftly dealt with this ploy on cross. "There is really no way for you to contradict the finding [of the Government's serologist] that there was in fact human protein on the cloth in a different section of it, is there?" (The Government's serologist had already testified that because of the saline solution used in his testing, that sample of the cloth had been "consumed in the examination.")

"In a different section? In other words, that he could have tested that I didn't test?"

"Yes."

The defense expert pursed his lips. "I cannot contradict that possibility," he conceded.

The expert dental witness for the defense was an intense, studious-looking odontologist experienced in treating burn victims. Dr. Duane Spencer testified that his examination of Muff's teeth revealed no evidence of burning. He also said that the conclusion of the Government's odontologist that the fractures to Muff's teeth had to have been caused by "blunt trauma" erroneously presupposed that the trauma occurred at or near the time of death. "Teeth are the hardest object in the body, harder than bone," but after death, "teeth dry out and become brittle, and it doesn't take much force to break them."

Going beyond his area of expertise, Dr. Spencer offered a possible cause for the abrading on the skull. "When a body is floating in the water, it will usually float on its stomach, arms down, in what is called the 'dead man's float.' If the body ends up that way on the sand or beach or rocks, that face could just rub into the sand or whatever the abrasive material might be. I believe that could be an explanation for the abrading on the face."

Enoki brought out on cross that Dr. Spencer had never before testified in a court of law as to the cause of injuries to a human body.

Undaunted, Dr. Spencer challenged the prosecution expert's opinion that if the fracture to the gum line had occurred prior to death, the pain would have been so great that the person would immediately seek dental care. People have different thresholds of pain, he pointed out. Whereupon Enoki countered: "Wouldn't you say that the overwhelming majority of humans would seek dental treatment if the crown of their tooth was fractured off at the gum line?"

"It would seem so, but there are people walking the streets of San Francisco right now, if you look in their mouths," Dr. Spencer sniffed, "you would be *appalled* by what you'd see there."

The defense, further pursuing the accidental-death theory, and in an effort to show that the Grahams' dinghy might have capsized in the lagoon, next called a U.S. Air Force meteorologist to the stand. The witness spotlighted the extraordinary remoteness of tiny Palmyra when he testified that even though his job was to provide aviation forecast mission support "throughout the entire Pacific region, I had never heard of Palmyra until the events of this case came up."

Thumbing through satellite weather pictures of the Palmyra area, the weather forecaster said that on August 27, 1974, they showed "very intense" thunderstorm activity that subsided by the 28th. On the 29th and the key day of the 30th, the heavy weather had moved about one hundred miles north of the island. Defining a squall as a "burst of wind," Major Rodney West of the 20th Weather Squadron stationed at Hawaii's Hickam Air Force Base said that the thunderstorms north of Palmyra on August 30 could "possibly" have created squalls with a velocity of up to thirty-five miles per hour for several minutes on Palmyra that day.

(The Government's meteorologist, the chairman of the Department of Meteorology at the University of Hawaii, had earlier testified that August 30 appeared to be a "fine weather" day on Palmyra. He had noted a "heavy shower zone" north of the atoll in late August and early September, but said the likelihood was that it had only generated, if anything, a southeast trade wind "probably somewhere between seven to ten or eleven miles an hour" over Palmyra. He found it "extremely difficult to imagine" any sudden storms or squalls there during this period. Everyone knows how weathermen disagree on future weather. We had now learned they also disagree on the past.)

Findlay next called an expert in the operation of Zodiac dinghies and asked whether or not a strong wind could flip or overturn a motorized Zodiac. The witness said it was possible if winds exceeded twenty knots (twenty-three miles an hour).

The defense theory that the Grahams drowned when their boat capsized required that the jury accept quite a string of *ifs*: *if* there were squalls on Palmyra on August 30; *if* the lagoon, normally placid even during tempestuous seas outside, was uncharacteristically turbulent; *if* Mac and Muff just happened to be in the lagoon during the several minutes of a squall; *if* the Zodiac was not, as Government witnesses had testified, almost impossible to capsize; and *if* Mac and Muff, thrown in the water, had been unable to get back to their dinghy or to shore.

But Partington and Findlay were doing their best to convince the jury that these ifs added up to a reasonable doubt of Buck Walker's guilt.

University of Hawaii marine biologist Richard Grigg, still lithe and rangy like the big-time competitive surfer he had once been, next testified about a trip he made to Palmyra in August 1984 on behalf of the Walker defense.*

The biologist explained that one objective of the excursion had been to search for the missing second container from the rescue boat. They did not find it after numerous scuba and snorkel dives that totaled sixteen hours underwater. The divers had seen plenty of blacktip sharks, though. Were they afraid? "Not really," Grigg

---

*Several other defense-oriented people went along, including Partington, Chris Cannon (a San Francisco–based federal public defender then assigned to the Walker case), Len Weinglass, and Norman Sanders, who would eventually appear as a Walker defense witness. Also on the trip: two divers and a pair of crewmen for the party's chartered sailboat. Partington and Weinglass had visited Palmyra previously, in January 1982, shortly after they both came on the case. On that earlier trip, the two defense lawyers, along with Stuart Hilt, a Honolulu private investigator, and Roger Coryell, a Honolulu photographer, were flown to the island by Martin Vitousek aboard his twin-engine aircraft.

shrugged. "With sharks, you are safer staying right against the bottom than swimming on the surface. Most accidents with sharks occur at the surface, the sharks being attracted by splashing or some sort of agitation in the water." The jury was also told that sharks have "very, very poor vision" and compound it by closing their eyes when they attack. A gray reef shark, however, with one bite "could take a pound of flesh with no problem." Grigg said he saw many gray reef sharks ("They are only about six feet long, but they are perhaps the most aggressive shark in the Pacific") outside the lagoon, but only one inside. He said that although the lagoon's blacktip sharks were also aggressive, they "wouldn't take a very large bite" of a human, since most were smaller. Grigg's laconic testimony had not been overly helpful to Partington, who peppered him with questions suggesting the Grahams could have been killed by sharks.

To rebut the Government's position that the metal container had surfaced after Buck dumped it in the lagoon, Partington next inquired about the stability at the bottom of the lagoon. Grigg described the bottom sediments as "very fine," and metallic pieces of debris scattered around the lagoon bed as "coated," as if they had been undisturbed for years. "The bottom [he found the deepest point to be around 150 feet] is very stable. There is no indication that a box, such as the metal container, could be moved on its own. There is just not enough wave or current energy along the bottom to move *anything* once it was lodged on the bottom."

Grigg and his associates conducted a survey along the entire length of the beach connecting Strawn and Cooper islands in which they counted the number of items of flotsam—floating material that had washed up on the beach—every fifty feet.

"What was the purpose of that survey?"

"To determine to what extent the site where the box and bones were found was a cul-de-sac."

"Did you find any area that collected more debris than any other?" Partington asked.

"Yes, the box and bones site."

"Do you know why that is?"

"It is a place of confluence, meaning concentrated current where more objects than normal collect."

In other words, the defense was suggesting, the finding of the bones near the container didn't necessarily mean they had once been inside.

Partington had done a good job with Grigg, a credible witness. Enoki, obviously sensing that the man would only strengthen under fire, merely asked a few benign questions and sat down.

Although his *Toloa* shipmate, Thomas Wolfe, had appeared as a prosecution witness, Norman Sanders came to the stand on the other side. In 1981, he had read Australian press accounts of the discovery of Muff Graham's body in "a steel box on Palmyra Island" and had written to the authorities in Honolulu offering to be of assistance to the prosecution, but the U.S. Attorney's Office eventually decided not to use him. Partington put on his traveling shoes in late 1983 for a trip to Australia to recruit the former college geology instructor as a defense witness. Sanders, now an Australian citizen and the first American-born politician ever to be elected to the senate of the Australian Federal Parliament, had subsequently been hired by the defense, all expenses paid, to conduct geological experiments on Palmyra during the August 1984 trip. The bearded Sanders, his head lifted high, had a puffed-up demeanor on the witness stand that sometimes made him seem fatuously self-confident.

Sanders shared with the jury his melodramatic impressions of the island during his short stay there in 1974. "Palmyra is one of the last uninhabited islands in the Pacific. The island is a very threatening place. It is a hostile place. I wrote in my log: 'Palmyra, a world removed from time, the place where even vinyl rots.' I have never seen vinyl rot anywhere else. I said, 'Palmyra will always belong to itself, never to man.' It is a very forbidding place."

Because the presence of blood in the water enhances the probability of a shark attack, Partington elicited testimony from Sanders that he observed Mac slash at small sharks in shallow water with his machete. Sanders identified two photos he had taken of Mac: in one, his left calf bandaged, he posed with a machete; in the other, he stood in ankle-deep water holding the machete up in the air as a small shark approached his feet.

Partington, pursuing the defense's boat-accident theory, next asked if there were any obstructions in the lagoon that would be hazardous to small boats.

"It's full of steel spikes that stick up and concrete blocks in various places. There are a lot of underpinnings that you couldn't see well at high tide and which are a hazard to a small boat. At low tide, you can see them and avoid them."

To cast doubt on the credibility of all the prosecution witnesses, Partington suddenly changed course, asking about a conference telephone conversation Sanders had with the Government attorneys following the 1984 trip to Palmyra.

"A voice sounding like Mr. Schroeder's said, 'Well, these defendants are nasty people. They are killers. Why are you working for the defense?' Another voice then came on saying, 'We are just joking around here, Dr. Sanders,' as if that person felt this was not a proper thing to be saying," Sanders recalled for the jury. He then flashed a smug smile in the direction of the prosecutors, as if to say, *That'll teach you.*

If this was the heavy-handed way the prosecutors dealt with one witness, had other witnesses been cowed by the prosecution's tactics? That was the question Partington wanted the jury to consider.

At the defense's behest, the court then accepted Sanders as an expert witness in coastal geomorphology. Sanders explained that he had spent a number of hours at the site where the bones were found, studying beach erosion on the lagoon shore. The defense attorney asked his witness for any conclusions he arrived at as a result of his experiments.

Sanders seemed to relish the moment. "There was evidence of a *great* deal of coastal erosion, as well as accretion, which is the opposite of erosion. Accretion occurs where the sand builds up on the lagoon shores. Both these movements are very rapid on Palmyra. This is a sign of extremely rapid beach fluctuations."

Partington asked if Sanders's analysis of the sand samples showed them to be abrasive. The witness said yes.

Judge King interjected with a smile: "They use sand for sand-paper, don't they?"

"Yes, they do," Sanders said.

Court: "So it would, indeed, be an abrasive?"

"It would, indeed, be an abrasive."

Partington, ignoring this needling, pressed on. "In view of the sand movement you have testified to, what might happen to a skeleton on that beach over a period of time?"

"It would be buried in the sand," the witness said. "The sand buildup could cover a skeleton or anything else that was there. It would lie there until some action dug it out."

A one-man band for the defense, Sanders rendered his judgment that Buck and Jennifer's boat was seaworthy. In fact, his overzealous attempts to do well for the defense provoked Judge King numerous times: "Just wait for the question." "Keep it short. We don't want all your mental processes." "Could we get to it as fast as possible?" "Briefly, briefly!"

On cross, Schroeder, after a struggle, got Sanders to admit that he had sensed a "great deal of tension between Mac and Muff and Roy and Jennifer" and that, to his knowledge, the two couples did not associate with each other.

All eyes riveted upon the next witness, a stunning brunette in her late twenties who approached the witness stand with the casual poise of a woman unaccustomed to being ignored. With her bright floral prints, stylish sandals, and flashing smile, Galatea Eatinger glided through the courtroom with the freshness of a tropical breeze.

Under questioning by Findlay, Eatinger testified she had lived in Hawaii for ten years and in June 1980, aboard a small fishing boat called the *Aquaholics*, visited Palmyra. Friends on three other boats—the *Kiave*, the *Luty* and the *Hawaiian Moon*—also made the journey.

"On this occasion in the summer of 1980, did there come a time when you discovered a bone?" Findlay asked.

"Yes."

A bone? Found on the island seven months *before* Sharon Jordan's discovery? I had to shake my head at the Erle Stanley

Gardner theatrics. Was the beautiful mysterious witness actually going to produce amazing evidence that would turn the trial around?

The courtroom was suddenly so still that I was aware of the soft tapping of the court reporter's fingers on the keys of her stenographic machine.

Findlay had the witness mark on the chart of Palmyra the exact location where she had found the bone. She put a circle on the lagoon shore about midway between Strawn and Cooper islands— a couple of hundred yards east of Jordan's find.

She found the bone "washed up, close to the bushes," as she was "looking on the ground for crabs." When she picked it up, it was "very clean, with a little bit of green algae growing on it." She immediately thought of the "case of the missing couple."

She showed the bone to her friends and kept it for about three weeks before throwing it overboard where the *Aquaholics* was moored at the dolphins.

Findlay entered into evidence a diagram of the bone Eatinger had drawn for the defense several months earlier. Placing several pages from a book of human anatomy in front of the witness, Findlay asked if she could find anything that looked like the bone she had found.

"It was this bone," she said, pointing to a picture of an adult humerus, the long bone of the upper arm that extends from the shoulder to the elbow.

On cross, Schroeder threw into question the witness's credibility by getting Eatinger to admit she had at first thought she'd found a thighbone.

He then asked what had caused her to dispose of the bone if she had really thought, as she testified on direct examination, that it might pertain to the Palmyra murder case.

"It was rather grisly and uncomfortable for me to keep, and it kept getting in the way," she explained lamely. "Every time I reached for something, the bone would be there." She gave a fetching shudder.

Eatinger went on to say that although she had never told the authorities about her find, she had told a sailing friend, defense witness Richard Grigg, and he had immediately recruited her for the defense team.

NEXT, SEVERAL witnesses were called in an effort to discredit the testimony of prison snitch Al Ingman that Buck Walker told him he had killed the Grahams. Two half sisters of his each claimed Ingman introduced them to heroin at a young age, and labeled him "untruthful."

The testimony began to sound like a broken record, perhaps diluting the defense effort by repetition. Ingman's twenty-two-year-old niece, Tamee Cyphers, called him a "very untruthful, manipulative person." When she was sixteen, she said, her uncle had taken her to an Arizona motel room and instructed her to have sex with his friend Terry Conner. She did, and remained with Conner for a year—until his 1981 arrest at the Torch Light Motel—and had his baby. A pathetic story, but not particularly germane.

Ingman's stepmother was contemptuous. "Al has never been truthful. He has more or less lived in a fantasy world. He seemed to fantasize about what things would be, and lied about what they really were."

Ruth Thomas, now in her forties, appeared next. Life on the run with lawbreakers followed by a prison stretch had taken a severe toll on the former social worker. Buck Walker's ex-lover looked drawn, even gaunt. As she passed the defense table, she and Walker exchanged weak smiles. After being sworn in by the clerk, she looked again at the man who had upended her life, this time with sad eyes and no expression.

"Where do you reside, Ms. Thomas?" Partington asked.

"The federal correctional institution at Pleasanton [California]," she answered quietly.

Thomas explained that she had been arrested in 1983 for conspiracy to distribute heroin. She had been convicted the following year after Al Ingman testified against her. "He's a liar," she said softly.

Thomas reviewed her live-in relationship with Walker, which had lasted from July 1979 until mid-1981. Several times the judge had to ask her to speak up. The demure Thomas clearly took no pleasure in being the center of attention. She denied that Walker had ever been involved in smuggling drugs or guns.

Partington brought out that the FBI's Hal Marshall had visited her in prison in early 1985 to recruit her to testify against Walker. "He said he could help me. I took that to mean that if I would testify to what he wanted me to, he'd help me get out of prison."

"Did you understand him to be asking you to lie?" Partington asked.

"No. He didn't ask me to lie. But I think if I had, I would be out of prison."

Later that same afternoon, the defense called Terry Conner.

Over six feet tall, Conner, forty-one, had a shiny forehead framed by receding lank hair. Quick to present a boyish smile, he projected an astonishingly sunny disposition, considering that he was currently serving sentences totaling seventy years for separate bank-robbery convictions in Arizona, Utah, and Oklahoma, as well as a 1984 conviction for conspiracy to distribute heroin.

Conner had traveled under armed escort from his cell at Leavenworth Federal Penitentiary in Kansas to San Francisco in order to testify on behalf of his old friend Buck Walker. With a studied cool that seemed sadly juvenile, the two men gave each other half-waves as he passed the defense table.

Under Partington's direction, Conner recalled serving time with Walker and Ingman at McNeil Island from 1978 to 1979. Walker did not trust Ingman, he said, and had never told any incriminating stories about events at Palmyra Island. "To the contrary," Conner testified, Buck had denied killing the Grahams. "Buck told me he admired and respected those people on Palmyra. I have known Buck for a long time. I feel he has always been a man of his word, of high principles. To me, he has a lot of personal integrity," Conner said unabashedly about the man with a five-page rap sheet.

When Partington concluded, Enoki moved slowly to the podium, a prowling jungle cat tensed to spring. After he brought out on cross that Buck Walker's character witness had used six aliases in the past, he asked: "Did each of the bank robberies you were convicted of involve taking hostages?"

"It involved taking the bank manager to the bank, and emptying the vault out."

"Involuntarily, I gather."

"Yes. No one was ever hurt, though."

"You used a weapon in each of those cases, didn't you?"

"Yes." Conner's voice had dropped a notch. His boyish grin faded.

Things did not improve when the prosecutor expanded on Conner's checkered criminal history by noting that he and Walker had been arrested together in 1981 on the drug charge in Arizona. For the clincher, Enoki got Conner to admit that in April 1985 a hacksaw blade had been found in his Leavenworth cell.

"Mr. Conner, isn't it true that you asked the defendant, Mr. Walker, to get you out of Leavenworth to testify here today?"

"Yes."

"Isn't it true that you wanted to use this opportunity to escape from prison?"

As if on cue, Conner looked at the jury, showed his upraised palms, and smiled that mischievous but endearing smile of his. "If I got the opportunity," he said, shrugging.

The spectators laughed, as did the jury.

To almost no one's surprise, the defense rested its case without calling Buck Walker to the stand.

JUNE 11, 1985

CLOSING ARGUMENTS in the Walker case began fourteen days after the jury had been selected. In the interim, fifty-two witnesses had been called to the stand—thirty-four by the prosecution, eighteen by the defense.

Enoki, in his familiar monotone, stressed two major prosecution themes: the *Iola* was unseaworthy, and Buck and Jennifer were out of food.

"Did they want to continue to eat fish, coconuts, crabs, and Runway Salad, when, just two hundred yards away, were the Grahams and the *Sea Wind* with 'every provision known to man'?"

Enoki contended that Walker had the motive, the means ("He had a pistol, and he was not reluctant to use this weapon on the island"), and the opportunity to commit murder. In fact, he said, Walker was "one of only two people on earth who could have committed the murder."

The prosecutor summarized the testimony of Sharon Jordan and several of the Government's expert witnesses, saying that the evidence and scientific findings refuted the claim that Muff Graham might have died by drowning or in any other accidental way.

He cited the evidence of murder: the body had been in the container (the bones being found right next to the box; the abrasions on the skull from "coffin wear"; the human protein in the blood on the cloth; the waxlike substance containing fatty acids and calcium salts of those acids, consistent with the decomposition product of human fat underwater); the skull had been burned, apparently while the flesh was still on it; sledgehammer-type blows causing several fractures to the bones, etc.

And, Enoki pointed out, there was considerable evidence that no drowning had occurred: the vaunted stability of the Zodiac; the placidity of the lagoon ("Even in storms, the lagoon only had waves of one foot by some estimations, two feet by the highest estimation"); the fact that the obstructions were located in shallow water, etc.

Enoki reminded the jury of Buck Walker's long letter to Kit Muncey (which he had introduced earlier over defense objections) and contended that Walker had obviously written the letter well *after* his November 8, 1974, arrest (the envelope bore a Honolulu postmark of March 11, 1975), but backdated the letter to October 1974.

In the letter, "Mr. Walker has the audacity to explain to Mac's sister that he was going to write all along," Enoki fumed, "and that he had some salvage claim that he thought he might be filing on the vessel."

Refuting the defense contention that the bones and container had washed ashore separately, Enoki noted that even the defense criminalist had conceded that "bones don't float." Also, the fact that the bones were found grouped together on the beach proved "they must have been held together, as a container or box would hold something together." As further evidence that Muff had not washed ashore as a drowning victim, Enoki cited testimony Dr. Stephens had given that when flesh is on the body, rats or other rodents gnaw first of all around the orbital areas of the eyes and the nose. "Rats, of course, are not like humans. They don't wipe away fingerprints, they don't wipe away evidence. The evidence of gnawing marks around the eyes and nose area should have been there if Muff's body had washed ashore from a drowning." Instead, the rat gnawing was limited to the tibias, the larger bones of the lower legs.

Enoki bore down. "Innocent people don't have to falsify evidence like disguising a boat, reregistering a boat, and fleeing from authorities by diving in the water and getting away. These are circumstances, the court will instruct you, which can be considered by you as consciousness of guilt.

"I ask you to return a verdict that reflects the true circumstances of this case, and that is that the defendant, Buck Walker, murdered Eleanor Graham."

After a fifteen-minute recess, the jury returned to hear Partington's final remarks.

The defense attorney started off defensively: "Jurors believe we lawyers talk too long, so I will endeavor to be brief, but I am sure you will find I have talked too long anyway and I apologize in advance." And on dubious ground: "This is where we present the evidence most favorable to our side. I am not going to pretend to you that I am here to be objective. I am not. I am here to be a partisan for my client, to raise doubts."

Sensibly, he conceded that Buck Walker was a boat thief. "Please understand that merely because he is a boat thief doesn't mean he is a murderer. It's a giant step from stealing a boat to killing someone."

Partington predictably argued that the *Iola* was seaworthy and that Buck and Jennifer, though very low on food, could have survived on fish, crabs, and coconuts. He likened the alleged motive in this case to a poor person waiting for a rich aunt to die. "If the Government's argument is carried to the extreme, when your Aunt Minnie dies unexpectedly and leaves you her millions, that's evidence that you murdered her." This analogy did not evoke nods of agreement from the jury. One lantern-jawed juror in the second row gave Partington a look that could freeze fire. The defense attorney went on to caution that motive alone should not be used to convict anyone.

His client left Hawaii and was fleeing from a drug charge, Partington continued, which accounted for many of Walker's actions after the Grahams disappeared.

Partington valiantly tackled some of the most damaging scientific evidence. He suggested that the bones washed ashore separately from the container and had been buried in the sand for a long period of time. The sand and rocks caused the abrasions, he said, while the sun and perhaps also a campfire on the beach scorched the skull. It was in this setting that the fractures and gnawing of rodents occurred. If the abrading to the skull had taken place inside the container as the Government argued, he asked, why were there virtually no signs of abrasion to the inside walls of the box? As to the bone fractures: "There is nothing unusual about bones exposed over a period of years having some fractures." Partington also noted that the waxlike substance in the box was also consistent with plant-life decomposition.

As to the burning on the skull that may have taken place years after death, "That means that somebody had to have tampered with these bones, and if that's true, all of the Government's scientific conclusions are suspect."

Concerning Galatea Eatinger's testimony: "We know from the remains recovered [by Sharon Jordan] that the bone found by Miss Eatinger could not have come from Mrs. Graham, because that would make three humeri. And we all know we only have two arms each. Therefore, that bone would have to come from Mac Graham. What does that tell you? Mac Graham is not in the second missing box at the bottom of the lagoon. Mac Graham is scattered about the lagoon, consistent with a drowning, or shark attack.

"The Government is suggesting that the defense is relying on a Zodiac accident to explain what happened to the Grahams. No, we are not. What we are saying is how can it be said beyond a reasonable doubt that the Grahams did *not* fall victim to a boating accident or shark attack?"

After arguing that no murder at all had been committed, Partington switched gears and proposed that *if* one had, Jennifer Jenkins alone could have been the killer.

"She was the navigator on the trip to Palmyra. Obviously, she is not empty-headed, as celestial navigation requires skill. When the arrest was made at the Ala Wai, Jenkins ran like crazy. We know that Walker had at least two other reasons to run. He had stolen the boat, and he was a fugitive from a federal drug charge. But Jenkins wasn't a fugitive from anything. Yet, she fled. Why?

"Mr. Shoemaker testified he heard female *voices* over the radio. So, apparently, Jenkins was permitted on the boat. If you ask me, that is rather strong evidence that if there was an opportunity to commit a murder on the *Sea Wind*, only defendant Jenkins had the opportunity, because, according to the Government, Walker would never have been permitted aboard."

Describing Al Ingman as a "paid Judas, the ultimate con artist," considered by his own family to be a liar and manipulator, Partington told the jurors, "If you doubt that Al Ingman is telling the truth, the Government's case comes apart like a house of cards.

"If the Government wants to prove a murder, they are going to have to do a lot better than they have done during this trial. Thank you."

It had not been a very stirring summation.

After a lunch recess, Enoki had his last chance to speak to the jury and give each nail a final tap. In a brief and confident rebuttal, the prosecutor reminded the jury that the Government did not have to solve all elements of the mystery. "We are not required to prove such things as what precise means were used to kill Mrs. Graham, what was done with her remains after she was killed, or any number of other things Mr. Partington has rattled off. All the prosecution is required to do is prove that Mr. Walker killed her with malice aforethought and premeditation."

Responding to Partington's contention that no murder had been committed, the prosecutor said: "Sharon Jordan's unrefuted and unforgettable testimony alone is worth at least ten experts. She was there, and she told you what she saw. It looked exactly like the bones had come out of the box.

"Look at the wristwatch she found on the lid of the container," Enoki said, holding up the rusty watch for the jury to see. "There is not much remaining of it and no one has identified it as being Muff Graham's. But you can see that the part not completely encrusted with rust is a silver-colored metallic watchband. If you will look at exhibit 8A, the picture of the Grahams on the *Sea Wind* at Palmyra, you will see that on her left wrist there appears to be a silver-colored band remarkably like this silver watchband."

In any event, Enoki argued, proving Muff was murdered "did not hinge on the Government's proving the bones were in the box." For instance, he said, was not Muff set afire while flesh was still on her body? "Wouldn't that be enough for you to conclude, in conjunction with the other evidence in this case, that Muff had been murdered?"

WITH THE testimony and arguments concluded, Judge King read aloud pages of instructions the law required him to recite to the jury before it began deliberating. He droned on for almost half an hour. At one point, like a fatigued grad student working in his carrel, Buck Walker took his glasses off, rubbed his eyes, then went back to following along on his copy of the instructions.

At 2:57 P.M., the judge told the jury, "You have the case." He informed the relieved jurors they would not be sequestered at night. He suggested they proceed to the jury room and work for a few hours, then come back for an hour or two after the Government treated them to dinner. He also advised them to make no commitments for the next couple of days and to plan to report to court each morning and deliberate throughout the day and into the early evening until they reached a verdict.

The first business at hand for any jury is the selection of a foreman or forewoman. The Walker jury chose gray-haired Charles Simmonds, a veteran of two previous juries.

Eleven jurors had already decided how they would vote. When Simmonds sent a note to the court clerk asking to see some of the evidence, it was basically to satisfy the jury's collective curiosity. They passed around some of the pictures that had been introduced at the trial, and each took time for close-up looks at the container, the bones, and the skull. When they read the postdated letter Buck had sent Kit, the jurors were both amazed and angry . . . amazed that Buck had written so articulately and with such obvious intelligence, and angry that he had had the colossal nerve to say the things he did to Kit.

None of the jurors believed Al Ingman, the convict who claimed Buck had admitted murdering the Grahams. Nor did they believe the other two convicts, smiling Terry Conner and pitiable Ruth Thomas. "And Norman Sanders just wanted to get his name in the paper," said one disgusted juror. While agreeing that they liked the judge, they also picked up on his bias in the case. "I think he's looking to get Buck convicted," said a juror. "So was the defense," another quipped. Everyone laughed.

After they exhausted their fascination with the various pieces of evidence and pondered to themselves over a cup of coffee, Simmonds asked if they should take a vote. The affirmative replies came in chorus. A woman juror passed out slips of paper for the secret-ballot vote. The foreman collected the slips and tabulated them: eleven for conviction, one undecided.

It didn't take long for the jurors to identify the lone holdout. The big, heavyset guy who had sat quietly in the back row was pleasant enough, but, some of them thought, a little slow upstairs. When they politely asked him why he was undecided, he replied that he just didn't know exactly *how* Buck Walker had killed Muff Graham.

"Wait a minute," said Robyn Schaffer, at twenty-two the youngest member of the jury. "You *do* think Walker killed her?"

"Sure," said the holdout. "I just don't know how."

Several people started talking at once, but the foreman took over. They did not have to solve all of the mysteries of the crime, he explained patiently. This was one murder case probably no one ever would. All they had to do was determine whether the defendant was guilty or not guilty. When the holdout juror smiled and nodded in agreement, Simmonds said, "Let's take another vote."

AT 4:40 P.M., the jury buzzed the judge's clerk to report they had reached a verdict. It took thirty minutes to collect all of the lawyers and bring Buck Walker back up to the courtroom.

The jury, having suspended work for twenty minutes so that one juror could move his car from a lot that closed early, had deliberated for the incredibly short time of one hour and twenty-three minutes. The jury hadn't even waited to have one meal together on the Government. Buck Walker hadn't even left the courthouse yet! He had been sent down to the basement for return to county jail, so sure had everyone been that the jury would not return a verdict in its first few hours of deliberation.

When the guilty verdict was read by the court clerk, all four attorneys who had lived with the case for so long remained curiously expressionless, as did Mac's sister, Kit.

Not so the defendant.

He grimaced, tight-jawed, and stared down at the carpeted floor, as if steeling himself. Then he slowly lifted his gaze to the jury box and locked eyes with young Robyn Schaffer, who swore that if she lived to be a hundred she would never forget the stone-cold anger aimed at her by the convicted murderer.

EIGHT DAYS later, the incorrigible Terry Conner and his prison pal, Joseph Dougherty, escaped while the two were being transported by a pair of rookie Deputy U.S. Marshals to an Oklahoma City courthouse.

Dougherty had flipped out a sharp object and pressed it against the throat of one of the marshals, while Conner disarmed them. Charming Conner, who had entertained the jury and spectators at Walker's trial, wanted to kill the two marshals, but a nervous Dougherty talked him out of it, and the marshals were left handcuffed to a tree. The escapees sped away in the U.S. Marshals Service vehicle.

Conner was apprehended by FBI agents in a motel near Chicago on December 10, 1986. He was charged with committing several bank robberies while he was on the lam, including more than one in which the bank president's family was held hostage at home while the bank vault was cleaned out. In one robbery, the take exceeded $700,000

SAN FRANCISCO
JUNE 28, 1985

A PALE, HAGGARD-LOOKING Buck Walker remained mute when Judge King asked if the defendant had anything to say before he was sentenced.

Calling the killing of Muff Graham a "particularly heinous crime," Judge King sentenced Walker to life imprisonment. He pointed out, however, that anyone sentenced in federal court to life is automatically eligible to apply for parole after serving ten years. For that reason, the judge ordered the life sentence to run consecutive to (that is, to follow) Walker's earlier sentences.

As a stoical Walker stood before the court that afternoon, he still had eleven years to serve on his various convictions for drug possession, escape, and interstate transportation of stolen property.

CHAPTER 28

LOS ANGELES

ONE OF THE FIRST calls I received after the Walker verdict was from a *Los Angeles Times* reporter who had covered the Walker trial. "The swift verdict doesn't bode well for Jennifer," he said.

It is extremely unusual for a jury in a murder trial to return a verdict so quickly. Even more so when there is such a dearth of hard, factual evidence, and when there is complicated scientific and medical testimony. CBS Radio went overboard and called the swiftness of the verdict "unprecedented." Everyone connected with the case, including the judge and the prosecutors, had expected the jury to be out for a day or two at the very minimum. Though anticipating the guilty verdict, I too was surprised by the speed with which it was determined. It was now obvious that the typical rules requiring substantial evidence to convict didn't apply here. *The unique circumstances of the case were a substitute for evidence.* In a normal case, if the defendant denies committing the crime, at least theoretically any one of millions of other people could have. But in the Palmyra case, if Buck and Jennifer didn't do it, there was no one else. The prosecution *didn't need evidence* in a case like this.

Jennifer was jolted by Buck's conviction.

"I still find it difficult to believe that someone I loved so much could have been so dishonest with me," she said sadly. "I guess I always felt I could keep him out of trouble. I figured once we left Hawaii, there would be less temptation. I mean, how much trouble could he get into on a deserted island?"

Len, too, was shaken because he had approved of the Walker defense team's effort to raise doubts, through scientific testimony, that a murder had occurred. Now Len reconsidered his position and decided that as of the moment, he was starting to come around to my position for Jennifer's trial.

In a telephone conversation, I told Enoki that I would concede the murder of Muff Graham in my summation, but only if he presented evidence of it in his case in chief. "You don't have to do it in quite the same depth as you did at the Walker trial," I said, "but before I concede it, I do expect you to put on scientific and medical evidence that a murder was committed." Actually, Enoki had little choice. As the prosecutor, he *had* to prove the crime of murder.

It soon became apparent that Jennifer's trial would be delayed because of conflicts on Judge King's judicial calendar. My dreamy client continued to be pleased with any and all such delays.

But they worried me. Up to now, as I tried to make Jennifer understand, the prosecution had been concentrating mostly on

Buck. Now that he had been convicted, all their time and resources would be directed toward fortifying their case against her. "There's nothing to gain and much to lose by continuing to delay the trial," I counseled. "We already have our defense, and it's not going to get any stronger. Right now, the prosecutors and FBI agents are sitting around a table in Honolulu, wondering how they can make their case against you even stronger than it already is."

My principal fear was that federal agents would rush out to interview all of Jennifer's former cellmates—as they did Buck's— and come up with a witness willing to testify against her. I asked her if there was anyone she had talked to about the case at Terminal Island who, she felt, might be the type to lie that she had made an incriminating statement. She couldn't think of anyone. How about outside of prison? Again, she drew a blank. She trusted the world.

In late August 1985, the trial was set for February 3, 1986, giving us, and the Government, six additional months to prepare.

As the trial was approaching, Jennifer received a letter from a man named Joe Buffalo, whom she described as a friend she knew in Hawaii in 1975. According to Buffalo (per Jennifer, a "part Indian with long thick hair and a big beard"), FBI agents had recently contacted him and tried to unearth something they could use against Jennifer. A rudely awakened Jennifer telephoned me anxiously with the news. "You were right," she said solemnly.

AS MATTERS now stood, there would actually be more incriminating evidence against Jennifer at her murder trial than there had been against Buck Walker (informant Al Ingman would not appear, but we now knew the jury hadn't believed his testimony against Buck anyway), and *he* had been convicted in almost record time.* With only a few exceptions, all of the circumstantial evidence that convinced him would be used against Jennifer. But in

---

*Moreover, Jennifer would be telling her jury the very same story (dinner invitation, Grahams not present on *Sea Wind*, discovering the overturned dinghy on the beach the next day, belief the Grahams had died an accidental death, etc.) that Buck's jury had heard, and his jury had not bought it.

addition, there were the preposterous lies she had told to the FBI's Calvin Shishido, the conflicting story she had told to Bernard Leonard, the lies she had told Lorraine Wollen, and the provable perjury she had committed at her earlier trial in Honolulu—all of which, the prosecution would argue, showed a definite consciousness of guilt on her part. Additionally, although Walker's boat-theft conviction had been overturned on appeal because of a technicality involving an erroneous instruction by the judge to the jury, Jennifer's conviction in the theft of the *Sea Wind* had been affirmed. This, too, might find its way into the trial.

At Jennifer's murder trial, the prosecution would essentially use the same witnesses and evidence that they had relied on at her theft trial. The only real difference would be that there was now a dead body. But a dead body was not evidence against Jennifer. It only changed the charge from theft to murder. In effect, then, since the earlier jury that convicted Jennifer of theft had been presented with basically the same case that would be presented against her at her upcoming trial, they had implicitly convicted her of murder. This was so because the conclusion that Muff's death was somehow tied in to the theft of the *Sea Wind* was irresistible. I just hoped that nothing new against Jennifer would surface, no matter how small.

It's hard to get too much smaller than the outer shell of an ant, but, unbelievably, this subject suddenly took on considerable importance.

In a second reading of the cororner's report on the postmortem examination conducted on Muff Graham's remains in April of 1985, I noted something potentially explosive that the prosecution had not brought out at the Walker trial. "In the marrow of the long bones there is deposited coral and sandy-like material which is layered in a fashion indicative of water exposure," the coroner wrote. *"From this, recognizable portions of insect exoskeletons [outer shells] are removed. These are portions of ants.* The ants show anatomic features of a small, dark-colored ant approximately 4-5 millimeters in length." Exactly when, I wondered, had the ants crept into the bone marrow?

Within a few months after I got on the case in 1982, Len and I had agreed that he would handle all of the medical and scientific witnesses, since he wanted to contest the issue of whether Muff had been murdered and these witnesses would be establishing that fact for the Government. Because the coroner, Dr. Boyd Stephens, was therefore one of Len's witnesses, I telephoned Len and asked him about the ant exoskeletons. Len said Dr. Stephens had told him that the ants would have crawled into the marrow only while the body still had flesh on it and was freshly deceased, *not* if the bones were dry of oil, which, I assumed, they would have been when they were washed ashore in the container in 1981. I realized that the ant exoskeletons could go directly to the issue that concerned me the most: whether or not Jennifer had been involved in the murders.

My argument to the jury had to be that Buck murdered Mac and Muff without Jennifer's knowing about it. Therefore, *immediately* after murdering them, he would have had to put their bodies in the containers to hide them from her. But if what the coroner told Len was correct, it would go in the direction of Jennifer's having been involved, because it would indicated that the bodies were left out on the ground long enough for the ants to get into the bone marrow. If Buck had not been rushed, then he was not hiding the bodies from Jennifer—powerful circumstantial evidence, the prosecutor could argue, of her involvement in the killings.

Since the ant exoskeleton evidence would go only to the issue of Jennifer's guilt, not Buck's, it was understandable that the prosecution had not introduced it at the Walker trial. But if they had done their homework, they would undoubtedly use it at Jennifer's trial. This type of hard-to-controvert physical evidence could illuminate a critical part of the darkness cloaking the Palmyra murders.

Though the case was a mystery, were we actually being reduced to studying ants and their habits in our efforts to learn what happened?

After thinking about it further, I called Len back and asked him if he would mind if I handled the ant exoskeleton issue. He didn't.

Cursory research revealed that ants are strictly terrestrial creatures—they never go into water. Therefore, the ants had entered the marrow of Muff's bones either before her body was put inside the container and sunk in the lagoon or after the remains were washed ashore. But the latter was not possible, according to Dr. Stephens, because the bones had no flesh on them by the time they washed ashore in 1981. But was the coroner right? Would ants enter the powdery marrow of dry bones? I had to find out, even if the answer was not something I wanted to hear.

I soon learned that the study of ants was called myrmecology, a branch of entomology. Several phone calls eventually led me to Roy Snelling, an entomologist with the Los Angeles Natural History Museum for twenty-five years whose specialty happened to be myrmecology. Snelling and a professor at Harvard were considered the top two ant experts in the country.

The next day, I drove to the L.A. Natural History Museum, located in a mammoth stone building across the street from the University of Southern California. The museum, Snelling had proudly informed me, contains the largest collection of ants (presumably dead ones) in North America.

I finally found Snelling's office, cluttered with books, professional journals, and stacks of papers. About fifty, Snelling was lanky and easygoing, though his face was deeply lined. He was dressed in faded blue jeans and a plaid shirt in earth tones. His long, braided hair was parted in the middle and kept in place by a headband, betokening his Cherokee Indian ancestry. He had taught entomology courses at USC and written many articles on ants.

To my relief, Snelling told me that ants very definitely *would* go into the marrow of bones bare of all flesh. "Even when there's no flesh on a bone, oil from the bone would still be present, and that's what would attract the ants."

"So when the bones washed ashore in 1981, seven years after the murders, there would have still been sufficient oil in them to attract ants?"

"Oh, yes. Oil from the bone, which is really liquefied fat, is very slow to volatilize [evaporate]. Even a bone twenty to thirty years old and apparently completely dry would still have enough oil to attract ants."

What about the fact that the bones in this case had been exposed to water? Wouldn't water hasten the evaporation process?

"Yes. Water does leach the oil out more rapidly than if the bones were in a dry environment. But it still would be a very long process, taking many years, particularly since the bones were in a container, which would cut off the rush of water against the bones."

"When you say many years, you mean what?"

"At least ten or more years," Snelling said.

The description of the ants in the coroner's report, the ento-mologist continued, fit the genus *Solenopsis*, found in many parts of the world, including the Pacific. "They are also known as grease ants," Snelling said, "because they are particularly attracted to oils and fats of any kind, human or otherwise."

Snelling went on to explain that bone marrow would be more prized by the ants than muscle tissue, since it is a "fatty" substance.

All of what Snelling had said so far applied only if the ants got into the marrow in 1981. What if it happened in 1974, when there would have been far more oil in the bones to attract ants? I asked the key question: how long would it have taken for ants to get into the marrow of Muff's bones if her body had been left exposed on the ground after her murder in 1974?

"Well, to start out with," he said, unconsciously tugging at the end of one of his braids, "ants can't penetrate through bone, so there would have had to be a fracture of the bone for them to get into the marrow."

"The bones with ant exoskeletons in their marrow *were* fractured."

"Even with the fracture, it would have taken the ants *days* to penetrate the skin and get into the marrow."

I tensed. The probability that Muff's body had lain out on Palmyra for *days* was extremely damaging. Buck would not have been hiding the body from Jennifer. And therefore . . .

Snelling blinked at my palpable discomfort.

"Is there any way, any way at *all*, that the ants could have got-ten into the marrow quickly?" I asked urgently.

"When I said 'days,' that assumed that the fractures were internalized. But if the fractured bones had penetrated the surface of the skin, as in a compound fracture, then the ants would have had *immediate* access into the marrow."

I relaxed quite visibly. Muff's horribly fractured leg and arm bones could very well have punctured the outer layer of her skin and thereby exposed the marrow. The ants could have gotten inside the marrow even in the short time it would have taken Buck to get the container and hide Muff's body from Jennifer.

On my way home, I reviewed what I had just learned. The ants could have gotten into the marrow in three types of situations, two of which would *not* point in the direction of Jennifer's guilt: (1) at the time of the murder, if the fractured bones had punctured the skin, or (2) in 1981, when the dry bones, still with enough oil in them to attract ants, were washed ashore.

I couldn't prove what had actually happened, but I now knew the prosecution couldn't either. Before I left his office, Snelling had agreed to testify as an expert for the defense. With his testimony, the jury could not conclude that the presence of ant exoskeletons in the marrow of Muff's bones necessarily pointed in the direction of Jennifer's guilt. I still hoped the subject wouldn't come up at all, but if it did, we were prepared.

The ant exoskeleton issue had spotlighted the as yet futile search to learn what had really happened on the remote island of Palmyra in the late summer of 1974. Only two people had survived. Of the two, I did not believe that Jennifer knew what had taken place, and Buck Walker, who surely did know, wasn't talking. What other living creatures knew? If the dogs could only talk, I thought.

A WEEK BEFORE THANKSGIVING, 1985

WITHOUT CONSULTING me, Len had advised Jennifer that because of the strength of the Government's case, it would perhaps be wise to "negotiate the best deal possible" with the Government. When Jennifer told her brother about this, he asked for a meeting at my home in Los Angeles. Jennifer and Len drove over, and Ted Jenkins flew down from the Bay Area.

Len took the plunge. "I think we should give serious consideration to approaching Elliot Enoki about a plea bargain," he said. "I don't know if he'd go along with it, but if he does, maybe we can get second-degree murder or even manslaughter. Enoki will probably insist on a minimum prison sentence of two years."

Ted and Jennifer exchanged glances, but neither said anything.

"The Government has a very strong case," Len continued, as if rushing to forestall disagreement. "In a sense, stronger than against Buck, and we have virtually no defense but Jennifer's denial. I remind everyone how swiftly the jury convicted Buck."

Ted raised his eyebrows. "Vince?"

"I'm against any effort to plea-bargain," I answered. "There's no question they've got a strong case, but I still think we can win." I spelled out the strengths of our case, stressing that Jennifer's testimony would be "very important," and also noting that we would present a strong "character defense" to show Jennifer's revulsion toward violence. I added that I had finally found a witness, Bill Larson (Don Steven's shipmate on the *Shearwater*), who would testify that relations between the Grahams and Jennifer and Buck were friendly, thereby making it much more plausible that Jennifer would believe Buck's story about the invitation to dinner. "And in all candor, I'm going to make a powerful summation." I added, directing my words at Jennifer: "But obviously, it's up to you, Jenny."

At last, my client spoke, and per usual, there was ambiguity. Yes, she was opposed to a plea bargain, but if we *could* work out a deal with the Government, she wouldn't agree to spend more than six months in prison.

"Enoki will never agree to that," Len said.

I didn't like Jennifer's qualified response. "Jennifer, if you are innocent," I said, "as I believe you are—as all of us in this room believe you to be—how can you plead guilty to *anything*? I mean, how can you possibly stand up in front of the judge and say you were involved in killing Muff if you weren't?" I added that this wasn't like cutting a deal in a drunk-driving case. "For the rest of your life, you'll be branded a convicted murderer. That's something you have to think about."

She agreed she did want to think about it.

"I only ask one thing of you, Jennifer," I said. "Whatever you decide to do, make up your mind soon, not just before the trial. I don't want to waste one more day preparing for trial." Was I shouting down a well?

She said she'd let us know her decision in a few days. The team, at least for now, was more like queen bee and entourage.

I suspended all work on the case until her decision. Yes, this was precious time that was needed to prepare for trial, but I wasn't going to spend one second more than the hundreds of hours I'd already put into the case if she chose to cop a plea.

A long week later, Jennifer called and said she was not going to plead guilty to anything.

"That's great! We're going to do it, Jen."

She laughed nervously. "I guess my life's in your hands now, Vince."

DECEMBER 24, 1985

PROSECUTOR ENOKI ADVISED US by phone that FBI agents had recently gone to see Buck Walker in prison. There could be only one reason for such a visit.

"I'll bet they've made Buck some kind of offer for a reduced sentence if he testifies against Jennifer," I told Len.

He wondered aloud what Buck could have told them.

When we received the final list of Government witnesses, however, Buck Walker was not listed.

Apparently, he had said no to incriminating his former lover.

CHAPTER 29

PERHAPS NO OTHER ISSUE in the case tested my resolve not to represent a murder defendant I believed to be guilty as much as that of the tidal activity on Palmyra on August 30 and 31, 1974. And frankly, I wasn't overly impressed with myself.

At her theft trial, Jennifer had testified that "between 4:00 and 5:00" on the afternoon of August 30, she heard the motor of the Zodiac dinghy going "out and away" from where she was on the *Iola*. When I interviewed her she put the time "somewhere around 4:30 P.M." I planned to argue at the trial, of course, that what Jennifer had heard was Buck operating the dinghy with Mac and Muff's bodies inside, and that after dumping the bodies in the lagoon, he overturned the dinghy on the beach to lead Jennifer to believe it had capsized in the lagoon and the Grahams had died an accidental death. Assuming it took Buck about ten minutes to deposit the bodies in the lagoon and overturn the dinghy once reaching shore, that put the time around 4:40 P.M.

Both at her theft trial and to me, Jennifer said that they commenced searching for Mac and Muff the following morning at dawn and found the overturned dinghy on the beach "just after dawn." The dinghy was "about a foot and a half or two above the waterline." (Jennifer told me that the Zodiac was perpendicular to the shore, with the stern—where the motor is located—being closest to the water.) She recalled that the water was *not* at high tide. Therefore, if there was a high tide between approximately 4:40 P.M. on August 30 and dawn on August 31, chances are the water would easily have washed up the beach more than two feet and soaked the Zodiac's motor with salt water. But the prosecution had established that the motor was absolutely clean, showing no trace of salt water.

With this background, I should have immediately tried to ascertain whether there had, in fact, been a high tide between these two times. But my knowledge of anything having to do with the sea was so deficient that initially it never even occurred to me there might be a record somewhere of tidal activity on Palmyra.

Long after I had come to the conclusion that Jennifer was innocent, this whole issue finally crystallized in my mind. Like every other issue that enters my mind when I try a case, I promptly wrote it down on my yellow pad: "Check to see if there's any record of whether there was a high tide on Palmyra between 4:40 P.M. on 8/30 and dawn on 8/31." Although I felt there probably wouldn't be any such record, once I write a reminder down on my pad, it of course never goes away until I cross it off. My note serves as a nagging reminder of work undone.

I originally made a few calls locally seeking to find out if anyone, anywhere, would have the answer to my question, but no one I spoke to seemed to know. Not getting the answer to my specific question, I simply went on to the long list of other things I had to do.

I knew, of course, that if a tidal record existed somewhere, and if it showed there *was* a high tide between 4:40 P.M. on August 30 and dawn on August 31, 1974, that would probably mean Jennifer had made up the whole story about finding the Zodiac overturned on the beach. And if she had invented this story, she was probably guilty, with Buck, of murdering Mac and Muff. Since I had already concluded that Jennifer was innocent, I obviously did not want there to exist any evidence of her guilt. *Not wanting* the evidence to exist was one thing. But not making every effort to find out whether it *did* exist was something else altogether, and that's what I found myself doing. I simply was not pursuing the high-tide issue the way I have a habit of doing things, feeling almost relieved each time I failed to get the necessary information.

This procrastination went on for almost a year. Finally, I decided to stay on the phone until I found the answer, good or bad. I was eventually referred to someone in Seattle, who in turn directed me to the Tidal Datum Quality Assurance Section of the National Ocean Service (NOS) in Rockville, Maryland. No matter what one is seeking in life, it seems there's always someone, somewhere, who makes it his business to be knowledgeable about it.

The first person I spoke to in Maryland said that the tidal information I wanted was available, that on their charts Palmyra was Tidal Station 2721; and that as part of the instrumentation for recording tides, there was a camera on Palmyra. A camera? Unbelievable. The thought immediately entered my mind—*was it possible* (a one-in-ten-million chance) that the camera had witnessed the murders? If so, where was the film now? I was aware of the surreal notion that one can't go anywhere in the world, even the most remote corner, without someone watching. Later, however, I learned from others at NOS that there was no camera on Palmyra. What they did have there was a tide gauge (with a pressure sensor) mounted underwater on a piling in the lagoon on Sand Island. Also, the tides had been actually measured at Palmyra only during three periods: from May 30, 1947, to December 31, 1948; January 1 to November 12, 1949; and February 19 to March 26, 1967. These measurements, which were made simultaneously with those in Honolulu, enable the NOS to determine at any other time what the tides are on Palmyra. From the observed tides in Hawaii, which are taken daily, the NOS knows what mathematical correction to make to determine the tides on Palmyra. These determinations, though officially classified as "predictions," are amazingly accurate.

When I asked the NOS people the key question—was there a high tide on Palmyra between around 4:40 P.M. on August 30 and dawn on August 31, 1974?—they said they didn't know when dawn was at Palmyra on August 31, that I'd have to call the Naval Observatory in Washington, D.C., to find this out. Also, of the two high tides approximately every twenty-four hours and fifty minutes (the average daily tide cycle throughout the world), one was a "high high" and the other was a "low high," when the water, of course, wouldn't go quite as far up the beach. Similarly, there was a "low low" and a "high low" tide during the same period. It would be best if they sent me all the tables, they suggested, and if I couldn't figure them out, I could call back.

Meanwhile, I called the Naval Observatory to learn when dawn had occurred on Palmyra on August 31, 1974.

"Well, actually," I was told by an astronomer, "there are three phases of twilight."

"I'm sorry," I said. "I'm only interested in dawn, not twilight."

It turns out that "dawn" is not a term used by the Naval Observatory. It's more poetic than scientific, I was told, a subjective term to describe daylight or natural illumination in the morning, rather than a quantitative term. And "twilight" is used by the observatory not just to describe the period from sunset to nightfall, but that period in the morning between daybreak and sunrise—what most of us call dawn. And there are three types of twilight: civil, nautical, and astronomical.

I was already confused and wondering whether I'd be able to get what I needed. Obviously, the first step was to get a definition of all these types of morning twilight. I was told that "civil twilight" in the morning starts when the center of the sun is six degrees below the horizon, and ends at sunrise (sunrise being when the top rim of the sun's disk first appears in view). "Nautical twilight" starts earlier, when the sun is twelve degrees below the horizon, and "astronomical twilight" is when it is eighteen degrees below.

I explained to the astronomer that what he was telling me was very educational but, I pardoned the play on words, "really not that illuminating" to a lay person such as myself. I had virtually no framework of reference. "Could you define these three morning twilights," I asked, "in terms more understandable to me?"

So often in life people who are experts do not know how to communicate their specialized knowledge to others. In fact, it's probably the rule rather than the exception. Fortunately, I was talking to an exception. He patiently explained that generally speaking, astronomical twilight begins around one and a half hours before sunrise and is the time in the morning at which the upper atmosphere, receiving sunlight from the sun below the horizon, reflects part of it back to earth. Because of this increased lightness in the sky, the stars and planets can no longer be photographed. Nautical twilight begins around one hour before sunrise and is that period when the fifty-three stars used for navigation at sea are no longer visible to the naked eye. Civil twilight is about half an hour before sunrise, the time at which one no longer needs artificial illumination (such as car headlights) to see during outdoor activities.

Now we were getting somewhere. When lay people use the word "dawn," he explained further, they are usually describing a time somewhere between nautical and civil twilight, when "it first begins to get light in the morning."

Looking at his tables, I was informed that on the morning of August 31, 1974, in the Palmyra region of the Pacific, astronomical twilight was at 4:32 A.M., nautical twilight at 4:56 A.M., and civil twilight at 5:21 A.M.

Fair enough, I thought. I now had something concrete to work with. I next had to find out what Jennifer meant by "dawn."

When I asked her, she replied, "You know, when it first starts to get light in the morning."

"You *don't* mean that time of morning when it's light enough to see everything without artificial light?"

No, she said, *before* that.

So, as the astronomer had suggested, by "dawn" we were talking about halfway between nautical and civil twilight. Or approximately 5:08 A.M. on Palmyra on August 31, 1974.

Jennifer elaborated that by "just after" dawn (when they found the dinghy), she meant around five minutes later. That brought it to 5:13 A.M. She also said that by the time they called out and searched the immediate vicinity for Mac and Muff, set the dinghy upright, reattached the engine, and motored off, it was around ten or so minutes later. That brought it to around 5:23 A.M.

Of course, all these times were just estimates. The actual times could have been, and almost undoubtedly were, at least slightly different. But since the estimates were all I had to work with, they assumed virtually the same importance as the actual times.

Naturally, I eagerly awaited the tidal activity tables from NOS, which I received as a certified copy a week or so later. The tide tables covered the "Central and Western Pacific Ocean and Indian Ocean" for the year 1974.

Was there a high tide at Palmyra *between* 4:40 P.M. on August 30 (the approximate time I was assuming Buck overturned the Zodiac) and 5:23 A.M. on August 31, 1974 (the approximate time I was assuming that Buck and Jennifer motored off in the Zodiac that morning)? Adding one hour for Daylight Saving Time to the standard times always used in the tables, the first entry looked good. There was a high high tide in Honolulu at 15:07 (3:07 P.M.) on August 30, 1974; i.e., almost an hour and a half *before* Jennifer heard the Zodiac engine. But this was Honolulu, and there was a one-hour-and-nineteen-minute addition to correct for Palmyra, bringing the high high tide on Palmyra to 16:26 (4:26 P.M.), just fourteen minutes *before* 4:40 P.M.

Factually, this was okay, but trialwise, a problem. It would look pretty "convenient" to the jury that the high high tide was just fourteen minutes before the critical time of 4:40 P.M. (and just four minutes before Jennifer heard the Zodiac in the lagoon).

In any event, that took care of the high high tide. What about the next high tide, the "low high"? Was it, as I hoped, after 5:23 A.M. the following morning? And sufficiently after to offset the earlier "convenient" time problem? Maddeningly, the low high tide was at 5:35 A.M.; after 5:23 A.M., fortunately, but again, only twelve minutes after the approximate time Jennifer said she and Buck motored off in the Zodiac. The whole scenario would just look too pat to the jury. There's a high high tide fourteen minutes before the dinghy is overturned, and no high tide (either high high or low high) between then and when Jennifer and Buck motor off in the dinghy, the next one being twelve minutes later. In other words, Jennifer was saved by around fourteen minutes on one end and around twelve minutes on the other. If the jury received the tidal evidence, they might very well conclude, I thought, that Jennifer's testimony was contrived. I knew, of course, that it wasn't. Jennifer had *already* testified at her theft trial to her times and had *already* given me essentially the same times, all *before* I received a copy of the tidal report. But how could the jury know for sure that she had not somehow picked up this information earlier? After all, what were the mathematical probabilities against Jennifer's being protected in her testimony by only a matter of minutes, *twice* within a twenty-four-hour period?

Because I felt the jury might feel that Jennifer and perhaps even I were involved in a fabricated defense, I decided against introducing the report into evidence, despite Jennifer's and Len's urging that I do. My reasoning was that if the jury concluded that Jennifer's testimony was fabricated, the ball game would be over for us. But if there was no evidence one way or the other on the issue, I could at least fashion an argument that would render the whole matter inconclusive in the jury's eyes.

However, I wasn't about to give up yet. If the defense could disassociate itself from the NOS report, the problem of contrivance would most likely vanish. I decided that just maybe I could get the best of both worlds by showing the report to Enoki and getting him to introduce it at the trial.

"What the heck is this?" he said when I laid out the tidal tables before him.

I passed along some of my newly acquired education about tidal activity, admitting to him my problem, and suggesting the evidence could hurt either the Government or the defense as much as help us. But in the interest of justice, I went on, to reach a fair verdict the jury should have all available information on this issue. I wasn't being completely candid. As stated, I had concluded there was a possibility (if the jury smelled a fabrication) that the defense could be hurt by the report *more* than the report could help us.

Enoki thought it over, but declined. Later, I made a motion to Judge King for him to take "judicial notice"* of the entries made in the certified NOS report (which again would dissociate the defense from the report), but King denied my motion.

As a result, Jennifer's jury would not receive any evidence about

---

*To save time, courts will recognize, when relevant, the existence and truth of certain facts that are universally regarded as common knowledge, such as historical events, dates, geographical features, and so forth, and furnish these facts to the jury as a substitute for formal proof. Hence, neither side has to introduce evidence to prove these facts. However, facts that are not of common knowledge but are capable of determination by resort to sources of "reasonably indisputable accuracy" can also be the subject of judicial notice. It was this latter type of notice I asked the court to take.

the times of the high tides on Palmyra on the days of August 30 and August 31, 1974.

For emotional and personal reasons, however, I was pleased I'd taken the time to get to the bottom of the tides issue. I was also confident that at the trial I would be able to make use of the information I had learned about the two types of high tide. In the end, I felt more confident than ever that I was representing a truthful client caught up in a most unusual set of incriminating circumstances, and one who was innocent of murder.

CHAPTER 30

LOS ANGELES
JANUARY 29, 1986

LEN PHONED THE WEEK before the trial was scheduled to start. He had checked into a San Francisco hotel a few blocks from the federal courthouse and was going over his files in preparation for trial. My wife and I planned to head north the following morning and stay at the same hotel.

"Vince, after reviewing all the evidence," Len said ominously, "I'm convinced the only chance we have is to keep Jennifer off the witness stand. I think she's the weakest part of our case."

I was greatly surprised. "Len, not only isn't Jennifer the weakest part of our case," I responded sharply, "she's our *entire* case. We have nothing else. This isn't the type of case where other witnesses can give testimony pointing to her innocence. All we have is Jennifer. Without her, I'd have to throw eighty percent of my final argument out the window."

"But she doesn't have to testify for you to argue reasonable doubt."

"Obviously, I'm going to argue reasonable doubt. But I need to argue her *innocence*, too."

"Other than her word, there's no evidence of innocence even if we do put her on the stand," he countered. "If you argue innocence to the jury, you'll lose points with them. Stick with reasonable doubt. We won't be saying she's guilty, of course. You'll be arguing there's a reasonable doubt here and a reasonable doubt there."

Len wasn't just playing devil's advocate the way co-counsel sometimes do with each other to identify soft spots in a case. He sincerely felt she would look so bad on cross-examination she would do much more harm than good. But I had spent a great number of hours preparing Jennifer, and I was confident she'd hold up well on cross. Len was not so convinced.

"The reason she has to testify," I told Len, "is that her conduct and lies, without any explanation from her, make her look very guilty. But Jennifer has an explanation for everything she did, and obviously, only she can give these explanations. They have to come from her lips."

Len suggested that crucial explanations of her actions could be "inferred" from the evidence.

"Len, I don't have to tell you that final argument has to be based on evidence that comes from that witness stand. Without Jennifer's testimony, there is no evidence as to precisely why she said or did any of these very incriminating things. I could only *speculate* about her motivations. I respect your judgment and I know this is a professional call on your part, but either she testifies or you're going to have to try this case alone."

"Maybe you're right," he said tentatively. By the end of our conversation, Len sounded agreeable to—though none too enthusiastic about—Jennifer's taking the stand.

As I began preparing for the trip to San Francisco, I considered the matter of Jennifer's testifying to be settled once and for all. As it turned out, I was wrong, twice over.

SAN FRANCISCO
FRIDAY, JANUARY 31, 1986

I HAD JUST finished shaving when the phone rang in my hotel room around nine in the morning. It was Jennifer, calling from her brother Ted's place in Lafayette, a suburb across the bay. During the trial, she and Sunny would be staying with him and his family at their sprawling custom-built house. Sunny and Ted, supportive as ever, planned to attend the trial every single day. (Jennifer's father had died the year before.)

I had arrived in the Bay Area late the previous afternoon and spent the evening at the hotel poring over last-minute details with Len. Neither of us had mentioned our telephone conversation of two days earlier.

"How was your trip?" Jennifer asked cheerily.

"Good."

"You play your tapes?"

"Yeah, most of the way."

(Other than tennis, my main hobby for years has been to record on my own tapes the best records of recording artists throughout the world when they were at their peak. The tape I mostly played on the way to San Francisco was my favorite, the best recordings, from the early 1940s to the present, I could find of the most beautiful Latin American standards, such as—"Perfidia," "La Paloma," "Yours," "Siboney," "You Are Always in My Heart," "Cien Años," etc. Artists like Mario Lanza, Placido Domingo, Julio Iglesias, and, to me, the finest Latin American singer ever, the great Chilean, Lucho Gatica, are on the tape.)

"Did Len talk to you about my not testifying?"

"Yes," I said. "I assume you told him it would take a team of wild horses to keep you from the witness stand?"

There was a disturbing pause on the line.

"Jennifer, I don't like your silence."

"Well . . . I think it's something we should at least talk about."

As surprised as I had been at Len's recommendation, I was utterly dumbfounded now. My mind reeled. I had explained to Jennifer, more than once, why her testimony was so vital. "All the jurors sitting in the box know that if they were in your shoes, and if they were being charged with a murder they did not commit, no one could keep them from shouting that fact from the highest mountain." I had told her that there's no sound in any courtroom as loud as the defendant's silence when witness after witness has given testimony pointing to the defendant's guilt and the defendant doesn't take those few steps to the witness stand to proclaim his innocence.

"There's nothing to talk about, Jennifer," I now fumed. "It's a closed issue. Either you take the witness stand or I'm going back to L.A." Images of all too many frustrating interviews with her came crowding in.

She paused again, this time not nearly as long.

"Okay, okay. I'll testify," she said, once again as if doing me a favor.

But I was too angry to let it drop. "I have to say I'm very disappointed, Jennifer. I'm much more upset with you than I am with Len. He's thinking about your not testifying purely from a professional standpoint. But what's your explanation? You should be dying to testify and proclaim your innocence. You know that nearly everything you said and did in this case reeks with guilt. You appear as guilty as sin to everyone."

"Not to my friends," she interjected, driving me further up the wall.

"I'm not talking about your friends, dammit. I'm talking about the kind of people who are going to be on the jury." Once again, as I hung up, we seemed back on course.

Before heading for court for some pretrial matters that afternoon, the four of us, at Ted Jenkins's suggestion, met at a coffeehouse across the street from the courthouse. With its freshly squeezed orange juice, rich dark coffee, and homemade pastry, this unpretentious and cozy refuge would become a frequent stop for all of us throughout the trial, particularly on those mornings when we hadn't had time for a regular breakfast where we were staying.

Jennifer was wearing one of the new outfits she'd purchased during a shopping trip with Len. He'd wisely counseled her to keep her attire simple and tasteful, "nothing outlandish," and to choose lighter hues than she usually wore. Len's theory was that lighter colors give one a softer look. This day, she wore a tan jacket and skirt with a white silk blouse. It would have been difficult for anyone to guess that this well-dressed businesswoman was about to be tried for murder.

We were still passing the cream and sugar when Ted threw an unexpected curve. "I want to hear Len's views on whether or not Jennifer should testify. Then I'd like to hear from Vince." Jennifer's brother had a rapid staccato manner of speaking that bordered on brusqueness. Clearly, he was used to being listened to.

"I can't believe this," I bristled. "You mean this issue *still* hasn't been resolved?

"Vince, I'd like to hear both sides," Ted said.

Len reiterated the same points he had pursued with me on the phone two days earlier, though with much less vigor. For the third time, I outlined my position, concluding that this case offered no options.

"Jennifer *has* to testify."

My last words were spoken directly to Jennifer. I had noticed that she hardly glanced at either Len or me as we took turns speaking. She kept busy folding and refolding her paper napkin into new and apparently engrossing shapes. She acted like an uninterested bystander to something that had nothing to do with her.

"Vince has made a persuasive case," Len admitted.

Ted nodded.

I wondered if his sister had been tempted not to testify out of sheer laziness. That would fit her m.o. Facing the jury and the prosecution would be a difficult, draining ordeal, and Jennifer had yet to show any willingness to work hard on her case. The notebook I had given her at our first meeting so long ago was still as empty as a bird's nest in winter. At times, I felt like grabbing her by the shoulders and shaking some sense into her. *"Jennifer, for Christ's sake, wake the hell up! You're on trial for murder!"*

In fact, despite the many hours I had spent with her during more than three years of preparing the case, Jennifer Jenkins remained an enigma to me.

All feeling the strain from this tense encounter, we walked across the street and up the flight of steps to the courthouse. After passing through the security checkpoint, where our briefcases were X-rayed as we stepped through a metal detector, we took an elevator to the nineteenth floor. Visiting Judge Samuel P. King had been assigned a courtroom at the far end of the long hallway.

As I thought about what I was about to say to Judge King, I remembered my last chat with Earle Partington after the Walker trial. "It was the worst experience I've ever had in a courtroom with a trial judge," he said. "It was terrible. He browbeat us in front of the jury and showed his bias for the prosecution. The tension and pressure were so great that after the trial, I took a week off and went to Cabo San Lucas in Baja, just to recover."

Unfortunately, behavior as outrageous as Judge King's is not uncommon in courtrooms throughout the land.

A WORD ABOUT judges.

The American people have an understandably negative view of politicians, public opinion polls show, and an equally negative view of lawyers. Conventional logic would seem to dictate that since a judge is normally both a politician and a lawyer,* people would have a markedly low opinion of them. But on the contrary, the mere investiture of a twenty-five-dollar black cotton robe elevates the denigrated lawyer-politician to a position of considerable honor and respect in our society, as if the garment itself miraculously imbues the person with qualities not previously possessed. As an example, judges have, for the most part, remained off-limits to the creators of popular entertainment, being depicted on screens large and small as learned men and women of stature and solemnity who are as impartial as sunlight. This depiction ignores reality.

As to the political aspect of judges, the appointment† of judgeships by governors (or the President in federal courts) has always been part and parcel of the political spoils or patronage system. For example, 97 percent of President Reagan's appointees to the federal bench were Republicans. Thus, in the overwhelming majority of cases there is an umbilical cord between the appointment and

---

*Judges, with the ironic exception of Justices of the U.S. Supreme Court, must be lawyers. No non-lawyer has ever sat on the U.S. Supreme Court, although Lyndon Johnson did try to get non-lawyer Dean Rusk, his Secretary of State, to accept a nomination.

†If not appointed (the usual situation), to become a judge one has to run, like any other politician, for the office.

politics. Either the appointee has personally labored long and hard in the political vineyards (as we have seen was the case with Judge King), or he is a favored friend of one who has, oftentimes a generous financial supporter of the party in power. As Roy Mersky, professor at the University of Texas Law School, says, "To be appointed a judge, *to a great extent* is a result of one's political activity." Consequently, lawyers entering courtrooms are frequently confronted with the specter of a new judge they've never heard of and know absolutely nothing about. The judge may never have distinguished himself in the legal profession, but a cursory investigation almost invariably reveals a political connection. (Of course, just because there is a political connection does not mean that the judge is not otherwise competent and qualified to sit on the bench. Many times he is.) Incredibly, and unfortunately, the political connection holds true all the way up to the U.S. Supreme Court, where, for instance, the last three Chief Justices—Earl Warren, Warren E. Burger, and, to a lesser extent, William Rehnquist—like so many of their predecessors in history, have all been creatures of politics.

Although there are many exceptions, by and large the bench boasts undistinguished lawyers whose principal qualification for the most important position in our legal system is the all-important political connection. Rarely, for instance, will a governor seek out a renowned but apolitical legal scholar, such as a highly regarded law school professor, and proffer a judgeship.

It has been my experience and, I daresay, the experience of most veteran trial lawyers that the typical judge either has no or very scant trial experience as a lawyer, or is pompous* and dictatorial on the bench, or worst of all, is clearly partial to one side or the other in the lawsuit. Sometimes the judge displays all three infirmities.

It's always a great relief and pleasure to walk into court and find

---

*Federal judges, who are appointed for life, are even more insufferably pompous than their state counterparts. When one is not, he prompts this type of remark: when U.S. District Court Judge Anthony M. Kennedy was nominated for the U.S. Supreme Court in 1987, Ronald Zumbrum, the director of the Pacific Legal Foundation in California, said: "If you picture a federal judge, he does not fit it. He has a low ego threshold and he has no airs about him. *He is a normal person.*"

a judge who has had trial experience, knows the law, is completely impartial, and hasn't let his judgeship swell his head. There are, of course, many such admirable judges in this country, but regrettably they are in the decided minority.

For whatever reasons (undoubtedly the threat of being held in contempt of court ranks high), the great run of lawyers are intimidated by judges and continue to be outwardly respectful even when publicly humiliated by them. The lawyers' complaints are made in private to each other and to their families. Commonly heard at any watering hole for the courthouse crowd is one lawyer crying to another over his first drink of the evening. "The judge is *killing* me in court."

The judge's obligation in a jury trial is to be totally impartial, the decision on guilt being the exclusive province of the jury. For instance, federal judges take a swearing-in oath to "impartially discharge and perform their duties." But time and time again a judge makes it very clear to the jury which side he prefers. This is a corruption and bastardization of our system of justice by the very people whom the law entrusts with the responsibility of insuring that it works properly and equitably.

Unfortunately, jurors usually assume that whatever the judge says or does in court is correct and justified. As we've seen, Judge King demeaned and humiliated the defense attorneys in the Walker case without justification, and they were very mild-mannered in response. Yet unbelievably, a juror was overheard in the elevator saying, "The defense attorneys have been giving poor Judge King a lot of trouble." Because Judge King, in contrast, treated the prosecutors with respect, the jurors drew another inference (correct or otherwise), the most serious one to the defense that could possibly be made: that the judge sided with the prosecution. During the trial, Jennifer's brother remarked to a stranger in the elevator that Judge King seemed to be very biased toward the prosecution. "Well," the man responded, "he must have done a lot of research into the case and knows what happened." Ted later noticed, to his shock, that this man was actually a Walker juror! After the trial, a more discerning juror was even more direct. "It was obvious the judge was out to convict Walker," said Robyn Schaffer.

The problem that confronted me now was obvious but knotty, and potentially perilous. Thus far, Judge King had been very friendly toward me, even abnormally deferential. For example, while the lawyers in the Walker trial were discussing proposed jury instructions with the judge in his chambers, I sat off to the side as an observer. During a lapse in the discussion, Elliot Enoki turned to me and asked if I had ever had one of my murder convictions as a prosecutor reversed on appeal. (The answer is no.) Before I could respond, Judge King interjected, "They [the appellate courts] wouldn't dare." Obviously, King was just joking, but his quip nonetheless showed a certain measure of respect for my work.

Yet it was abundantly clear that although Judge King was neither pompous nor, believe it or not, as tyrannical as many other judges in action, he still had a short fuse and was capable of an angry outburst in open court at any lawyer whose conduct displeased him. Whenever this type of thing happens in court, the lawyer nearly always comes out the loser, and his credibility with the jury inevitably suffers.

My demeanor in court is somewhat freewheeling. Add my confrontational manner of cross-examination, and I knew I would have no difficulty irritating King. If so, and if he were to react against me as he had against the defense in the Walker trial, how would I respond? No mystery there. If he waxed intemperate and demeaning in front of the jury, I would be several degrees tougher in my response, right in front of the jury. Maybe I'd be held in contempt, but at least I would retain my stature with the jurors. I'd rather be held in contempt and pay a fine than allow the judge, in the presence of the jury, to demean me and threaten my credibility with the jury. My personal style before a jury is to try to gain their respect. Although I obviously want them to like me also, I not only feel uncomfortable making an effort in this regard, but am too absorbed in the trial anyway. What I try to convey to the jury is sincerity, honesty, substance, and stature. They all add up to credibility, which I want to have with the jury above all else.

Clearly, if I could completely avoid a verbal confrontation with Judge King in open court, I (and my client) would be much better off. My best hope, I had decided, was forthrightly to place the judge on notice, before the trial, that I wasn't going to accept any maltreatment before the jury, and that if he chose to disregard my admonition, he'd have to pay a price himself before the same audience. I aimed for checkmate before the game began.

AFTER WE had discussed the usual mundane legal matters in open court, Judge King seemed a little perplexed when I said there were some other items for discussion that did not lend themselves to the formality of the courtroom. "They're of a personal nature, your honor," I explained. Since I was planning to speak bluntly, I wanted to do so in private and not risk embarrassing him in front of any members of the press, who were closely covering these early skirmishes in the Palmyra murder case.

Except for the panoramic view of the bay out the window, the judge's chambers were unremarkable. We were surrounded on three sides by the traditional dusty law tomes. The judge took off his black robe and hung it on a hook, then sat casually at one end of a small conference table. He wore a white shirt, rolled up at the sleeves, and no necktie. Len and I sat to his right, and the two prosecutors opposite us.

Even on the bench, Sam King was more informal than most of his colleagues, and in his chambers, he was understandably more so. In such a setting, King was even given to cracking his share of jokes. It was on this note that I began.

"Judge, you're a paradox," I said. "Your personal demeanor is less formal than most judges, but your courtroom rules are more restrictive. I'm going to raise a few issues with you because you have already demonstrated a certain flexibility. Too many judges, particularly federal judges, have well-deserved reputations of being pompous asses who can't be talked to."

The judge started to smile, but quickly thought better of it. His dry expression said, *Thanks a lot for your backhanded compliment.*

"Fortunately for us," I raced on, knowing the ice could be very thin, "you don't fall in that category. My first point—do we always have to stand up in court when we address you?"

"No." He had not hesitated.

"Good," I said.

"Secondly, I would appreciate it, judge, if we wouldn't be restricted to the microphone at the podium. A great number of courts in this country don't have microphones and people get along very well. On cross-examination, I find it more effective to move around."

"I'll let you leave the microphone," King said more amiably, "but don't get close to the witness."

"That's my third point. I know you do not want us to approach the witnesses, and only if we request and are granted permission can we do so. But we're officers of the court. I don't think that witnesses should be elevated in importance over the lawyers. This definitely goes in the direction of the lawyers' losing stature in the jury's eyes, because from the jury's own experience in life, it's completely unnatural to get consent before approaching someone."

Judge King declined. "Allow me my idiosyncrasies," he said. This wasn't pleasing, but it wasn't a major problem.

"My next point is that both lawyers for each side should be able to object to a question. Permitting this does not impose any new burden or inconvenience on the court, but not permitting it (as was King's rule) can result in serious detriment to both sides." Under King's edict, if a witness of mine was asked an improper question on cross-examination but I didn't catch it, Len could not make an objection on behalf of the defense. And by the time he could whisper the nature of the impropriety to me so that I could object, the answer would already be on the record. It made no sense to hobble the defense or the prosecution in this way.

"Declined," King said. "Next point?"

Now I was getting the distinct impression that King was not listening to logic, but was sticking to his rules because they were his rules, period. He was not displaying the flexibility for which I had just praised him.

But I went on.

"Next point. If we have to discuss any matter with you, why can't we approach the bench?"—something King did not permit. "I had a federal jury trial in Los Angeles a few months ago, and we approached the bench five to ten times a day. To call a recess inconveniences the jury, consumes a lot more time, and sometimes makes the lawyer requesting the recess look bad in front of the jury."

"Declined."

Okay. Now it was going to get interesting.

"Judge, on these other matters *you* had all the say. I had no say. I was just offering suggestions. On this next point, I *will* have a say. This goes to the stature and credibility a lawyer has to have in front of the jury. I can't speak for the other lawyers, but if I do anything that displeases you in the slightest, I expect you to register your displeasure outside the presence of the jury." Pointing a finger at him, I said, "What I'm saying is that you are *not* to demean me, in any way whatsoever, before the jury." I had given my voice a rough edge, and Judge King's face was darkening noticeably, but he said nothing. "If you have anything derogatory to say to me, call a recess."

"I'm *not* going to take the bench worried about you being overly sensitive, Mr. Bugliosi," the judge finally shot back. "Just because you're sensitive doesn't mean I'm going to be afraid to act as I've always acted."

"I'm not sensitive at all, judge. You can call me a horse's ass outside the presence of the jury. But before the jury, I will not be demeaned in any way whatsoever," I said forcefully.

Elliot Enoki, Walt Schroeder, and Len Weinglass had sat quietly, figuratively looking the other way, evidently not wanting to have any part in this discussion. That was fine with me.

"If this were a court trial, no problem," I said. "But in a jury trial, when the judge does this it unquestionably hurts the client. The court has enormous stature with the jury, and the slightest negative comment carries with it considerable damage. My credibility before that jury is what we're talking about."

The judge made no immediate response. He just looked at me, as if studying a creature he could not readily classify. The breezy friendliness that had existed between us had vanished like a breath upon a mirror.

"The thing I'm most concerned about going into this trial, Judge," I continued, lightening up a bit, "is that Jennifer's right to a fair trial might be, excuse the phrase, *shipwrecked* by some type of prosecutorial misconduct or by the court's indicating to the jury a bias in favor of the prosecution. If either of these two things occurs, I'm going to take it to the mat *right in front of the jury*. I have to. I have no choice."

I rose to my feet. "Judge, I hope you're not offended. I only say these things because of my grave concern for my client's right to a fair trial."

The judge smiled, actually *smiled*, as easily as Eisenhower.

He's shell-shocked, I thought. I had a feeling what I had just told him wouldn't completely sink in for a while.

"I understand," Judge King said quietly.

He extended his right hand and we shook hands.

After we left the judge's chambers, Len looked at me with a tight smile. "In all my years of practicing law, Vince, I've never heard a lawyer talk to a judge like you just did."

"What do you think? Did I go too far?"

"It's hard to say. But you made your point, and I have a feeling it will probably be for the better."

I was relieved to hear that from my co-counsel. If he was wrong, we'd have hell to pay.

FEBRUARY 1–2, 1986

THE LAST weekend before trial blurred into long hours of non-stop work, for there was still much to do. I was staying just two floors above Len, so we both went up and down the stairs or the elevator numerous times to consult with each other. Not taking time even to go out to a nice restaurant for a real meal, we lived on the less than adequate bill of fare of a coffee shop adjoining the hotel. Few cities anywhere can cast a spell like San Francisco. But I knew that the upcoming trial could just as well have been in Helena, Montana. I would not have the time nor the inclination for the special charms of the city by the bay.

On Sunday afternoon, a mystery of sorts was solved. But, as was very much in keeping with this case, an even greater mystery was created.

Many months earlier, I had noticed on the Government's inventory list that the authorities had found a wallet on the *Sea Wind* with a California driver's license and various credit cards in the name of Dannell Donald Petersen, a dentist who practiced just north of San Diego in suburban Carlsbad. I had asked Jennifer who Petersen was and why his wallet was aboard the Graham's sailboat, but she said she didn't know anyone by that name or anything about the wallet.

Earle Partington had left all of his files behind in San Francisco with Len, who had discovered an FBI report of an interview on the Petersen matter that for some reason neither Len nor I had received from the prosecutors along with the other FBI 302s.

On October 31, 1974, at his home in Encinitas, ten miles down the coast highway from his office, Petersen told the agents he had lost a wallet containing two hundred dollars in cash and various credit cards at Maalaea, Maui, in December of 1973. He recalled that he had dined on a little, run-down sailboat with a young couple who had invited him aboard. They had met that evening at a nearby beachfront bar. After he left the boat, he discovered his wallet missing and returned to search for it. He told agents that the couple had refused to allow him to come back aboard, but agreed to check around themselves. They returned topside after a few minutes, claiming it could not be found. Understandably unhappy with this sequence of events, Petersen had gone to the Maui police. Officers went down to the marina and questioned the couple, but the dentist's wallet was never recovered—that is, not until the *Sea Wind* was impounded and thoroughly searched almost a year later, in October 1974.

In the FBI 302, Petersen described the people he suspected of stealing his wallet. The man was "possibly nicknamed 'Butch,' about 35 years old, over 6 feet, 200 pounds, brown collar-length hair, possibly a front tooth missing or broken off." The woman was "about 30 years old, around 5 foot 3 or 4, brown curly hair, a former cocktail waitress at a sailors' bar in Wailuku, Maui, and she had a foul mouth." According to the doctor, the couple had three dogs: a small, furry mutt, and two big, surly hounds that had remained tied up while he was on board.

The agents showed up at Petersen's Carlsbad office on November 14, 1974, to show him mug shots that might identify the couple. He unhesitatingly picked Jennifer Jenkins from among five women and Buck Walker out of five men.

Len told me he had already spoken to Jennifer about the Petersen incident but she had been unable to recall it. I immediately phoned her from Len's hotel room, and she still drew a blank.

"Jennifer, the police came down to the *Iola* and questioned you and Buck about the wallet. How is it possible you can't remember this?"

"What can I say? I just don't," she insisted.

After this conversation, Len and I pondered what could have happened.

"Maybe Buck stole the wallet," Len offered, "and she didn't know anything about it."

"But even if that were the case, wouldn't she have at least remembered the police coming down to the boat and questioning them about a missing wallet?" I said.

We also thought that perhaps Jennifer had drunk too much that night and simply couldn't recall any of the events. She rarely, in those days, hit the pillow without significant amounts of some mood alterer in her system.

With the rush of other last-minute matters we had to attend to, Len and I put the wallet incident in the back of our minds. Neither of us could imagine any legal theory the prosecution could devise to introduce the matter before the jury.

We both were troubled, however, by the disturbing possibility that Jennifer, at some time prior to Palmyra, had engaged with Buck Walker in any kind of unlawful activity. But, of course, that did not make her a murderer.

WITH THE trial scheduled to start in the morning, my yellow-pad sheets of paper, covering every aspect of the trial (even case law authority to overcome anticipated objections, and optional lines of follow-up questions dependent on how a witness on cross-examination answered a particular question), rose to a height of almost a foot. Although the clear trend in the legal profession is toward fewer and fewer notes on direct examination, cross-examination, and final summation (so recommend instructors at many law schools and trial lawyer seminars), I do the opposite, almost to an obsessive, perhaps even unnecessary extreme. But I believe in the adage that the war is won before the first battle is fought, and thus far in my career I've been able to orchestrate most of the trial *on paper* before ever entering the courtroom. Arguments, counterarguments, questions, objections—the whole gamut takes place on my yellow pad before the trial even starts. My objective, of course, is for the trial to be merely the acting out of the scenario or script I've already written. Granted, unusual things happen at a trial, but if I've done my homework, even many of these occurrences can be anticipated and prepared for. In my unremitting quest to be completely ready for trial, I find that in effect *I try the case against myself.*

Reducing what's in one's mind to writing is very tedious and time-consuming, of course. In fact, working on my yellow pad is the hardest part of trying a case for me. But in my opinion, it is the only way to try a *complex* lawsuit, and the only way to make a superior presentation of my case, as opposed to a good or merely adequate one.

For instance, in preparing my cross-examination, I might know, in my mind, what point I want to make, but it might take me a half hour of sweat on my yellow pad to work out the very best way of establishing this one point on cross. Before I ask my key question, I might decide I have to ask ten preliminary questions, and in a particular sequence. Some of these preliminary questions I may rewrite three or four times because when I examine them closely I may see that the witness might be able to discern the direction in which I am taking him.

Likewise, in preparing my final summation, I might know what point I want to make, but when I try to articulate it on my yellow pad, oftentimes my pencil comes to a stop. It's at this moment that I realize I didn't quite understand my point as well as I thought I did, or even if I did, I certainly realize I was unable to extemporaneously articulate the point with the clarity and power I want.

The standard explanation of lawyers who religiously avoid the pain and agony of the yellow pad is that if a lawyer does all that preparation and has everything written down, he can't be flexible, and can't think on his feet when something not covered by his notes occurs. If that's not a classic *non sequitur*, I don't know what is. Is instant improvisation and flexibility the domain only of those who are unprepared?

As with all my trials, I was ready for this one. There was only one difference. As opposed to every other jury murder case I had ever tried, I didn't feel I had a "handle" on this one. There were too many things I didn't know. It wasn't enough to jar my confidence, but there was a certain sense, albeit slight, of a lack of equilibrium.

CHAPTER 31

FEBRUARY 3, 1986

AT 9:30 A.M. SHARP, court clerk Kathy Harrell, who was a graduate of the University of San Francisco law school and a member of the state bar, cleared her throat and announced, "Calling criminal action 84-0546-02, *The United States of America* versus *Jennifer Jenkins*."

"Mr. Enoki, are you ready?" Judge King asked.

"Yes, your honor. Elliot Enoki and Walter Schroeder for the United States."*

"Mr. Bugliosi?" the judge queried.

"Ready, your honor," I said. "Vincent Bugliosi and Leonard Weinglass for the defendant Jennifer Jenkins."

More than eleven years had passed since the disappearance of

---

*Since both Enoki and Schroeder came from out of town, they were being assisted in the selection of a local jury by Ben Burch, an assistant from the San Francisco U.S. Attorney's Office.

Mac and Muff Graham . . . eleven long years of extensive official investigations, court proceedings, legal delays, rumor and innuendo, sensationalistic press coverage, and exhaustive prosecution and defense preparation. But finally, the murder case against Jennifer Jenkins was going to be tried.

From the defense table, I scanned the faces among the panel of sixty prospective jurors. Some looked sleepy, others mildly curious, a few resentful at being summoned from their homes or jobs for this inconvenient civic duty. Among them were the dozen men and women who would decide Jennifer's fate.

All were seated in the gallery on polished benches lined in rows like church pews. A wide aisle dividing the rows of benches ran from the two sets of double doors at the courtroom entrance to a low wooden barrier and swinging saloon-style gate. Beyond the gate were the long tables for the prosecution, on the left, and the defense, on the right, where Jennifer sat between Leonard Weinglass and myself. Above it all rose the judge's tall mahogany bench, beneath which the court clerk's table squatted.

The judge read from a prepared statement. "Jennifer Jenkins has been charged with murder in the first degree in an indictment returned by a grand jury in the United States District Court for the District of Hawaii." He read the felony-murder count first, followed by Count Two, which alleged "that at some time during the period from about August 28, 1974, to about September 4, 1974, at Palmyra Island, Buck Walker and Jennifer Jenkins, with a premeditation and malice aforethought did willfully, deliberately and maliciously murder Mrs. Eleanor Graham, in violation of Title 18, United States Code, Section 1111(a)."

Voir dire, the questioning of the prospective jurors, was about to begin.

In my opinion, the greatly restricted scope of permissible questions on voir dire reduces jury selection to at best one-third art and skill and two-thirds guesswork. Many experienced trial lawyers concede that after a lengthy and vigorous voir dire, the twelve jurors they end up with are frequently no better than the twelve originally seated in the box by lot. Why? Because the juror one side wants is nearly always one the other side does not. As each side excuses jurors who look good for the opposition, very little progress is normally made.

Nonetheless, a surprising number of lawyers consider voir dire the most important part of a trial. Obviously, it would be if a lawyer had the uncanny insight and ability to select jurors who would end up voting for his cause, regardless of the evidence. But since no lawyer has ever been found who can do this, or even come close, the reality, in my opinion, is that voir dire is far from being the most important part of the trial. Lawyers have a significant amount of control over every other area of the trial, and assiduous preparation pays enormous dividends. During voir dire, a lawyer operates mostly by fallible instinct. If even after years and years of marriage many husbands and wives don't really know each other, how can there be any reliable way of evaluating prospective jurors by means of a few rounds of questions and answers? Because of this, voir dire has always been the one part of a trial I've never felt confident about.

Trial lawyers joke that prosecutors typically look for conservative, crew-cut Nordic types during voir dire, while defense attorneys look for long-haired fellows in well-worn cords and tweeds.

More specifically, it's generally supposed that artists, sculptors, writers, musicians, and others in the arts, including the liberal arts, tend to be more sympathetic toward defendants in criminal trials. The same assumption is applied to people in the "helping professions," like nurses and social workers, as well as to Italians, Hispanics, Jews, and blacks. Single people who are not deeply rooted in the community, clerks, factory workers, and anyone who prefers reading a book to watching television are all considered defense-oriented personalities. On the other hand, defense attorneys obviously challenge anyone who works in law enforcement, and are similarly wary of secretaries, who, according to a national jury survey, are the most prosecution-oriented of all occupational groups. The only inference I've been able to draw from this statistic is that secretaries have to go along with the boss, and in the courtroom, symbolically, the boss is the government. Engineers, scientists, accountants, and bookkeepers are generally considered pro-prosecution jurors as well, perhaps because they are trained to be objective and reach conclusions based solely on facts, not emotions.

But all of this vague conjecture ignores the reality that, not uncommonly, the juror in the characteristically defense-oriented profession turns out to be a staunch member of the John Birch Society, and the juror in the prosecution-oriented profession belongs to the ACLU.

In our discussions, Len and I agreed that someone from a so-called pro-prosecution discipline like engineering might actually be good for us in this particular case, where the prosecution did not have hard, demonstrable proof. Len also felt (and not having a strong feeling one way or the other, I went along) that women jurors close to Jennifer's age might be unfavorable. Though he felt they might have some instinctive partiality toward her going in, on balance, he feared they'd be against her, thinking, "I never would have gotten involved with someone like Buck Walker and done the things she did."

With the help of friends in the San Francisco Federal Public Defender's Office, Len found a local researcher who, for a nominal fee, ran background checks on the entire jury panel—getting details that could not come out on voir dire, such as political party affiliation. It was nice having someone of Len Weinglass's savvy and contacts in the legal profession as co-counsel.

As names were called at random by the court clerk, the first twelve jurors came forward, passed through the swinging doors, and took seats in the jury box.

The judge informed the jurors they'd be "hearing a lot about an island in the Pacific, near the equator." He asked how many were "yacht people," and four people raised their hands.

From the judge's preliminary questioning, we soon had thumbnail profiles of everyone in the box.

"I'm sixty-one years old," began juror Clarence Lessa when the judge's focus of attention reached him. "My wife works with me in my business in Fremont. It's Orange Julius. It's okay if I get a plug in, your honor?"

"Sure," said a genial Judge King.

Soon it was the prosecution's turn to ask the questions. Although it is not the sanctioned purpose of voir dire, lawyers use it to begin the process of educating and indoctrinating the jury to their side.

"Ladies and gentlemen," Enoki began, "if the judge instructs you that circumstantial evidence is as valid as direct evidence, would any of you have any beliefs that would make it difficult for you to accept that premise of law?"

No juror spoke up or raised his or her hand.

"Would any of you require the Government, in order to prove a point, to actually have a person come into court and say, 'I saw this happen,' as opposed to establishing through some other means that a certain fact or event occurred?"

Again, no response.

"Is there anyone here who cannot accept the law of accomplice liability? Meaning that somebody can be guilty for something someone else did?"

Again, the answer was a silent, unanimous no.

With this last question, Enoki confirmed what Len and I already suspected. The prosecution's theory was that Buck Walker actually committed the murders, but with Jennifer's knowledge and assistance.

When our turn came, Len led off.

"As you sit here now," he said to the jurors, "you have to have the state of mind, under our law, that requires you to presume that Jennifer Jenkins is innocent. Does anyone have trouble with that?"

No juror did.

To a specific juror, Len asked: "In your experience, do you find sometimes that experts can be wrong?"

"Oh, of course," the juror answered.

Len asked if anyone had ever had a woman friend in her twenties who became involved with a man whose activities put her in jeopardy.

"Yes," one of the jurors said. "I have a friend who had a boyfriend who abused her, and she wouldn't let him go." (All other things being equal, we wanted a juror with this background, and the prosecution did not. They eventually excused her.)

Alluding to the jury that Buck Walker had been convicted of murdering Muff Graham, Len asked: "Can you all accept the proposition that under our system of justice each person is to be judged separately, apart from anyone else, on the merits of the case that's involved in their particular situation?"

No negative replies.

Len proceeded to turn the questioning over to me. My opening goal was to indoctrinate.

"Judge King has already told you that the indictment in this case is no evidence of guilt against Miss Jenkins. To elaborate further, an indictment can be analogized to a theater ticket," I said to the jury. "It only enables the prosecution to get into this courtroom with their case, and once they're here, like a ticket to the theater, it has no value or significance whatsoever." I asked if anyone had any quarrel with this reality, and the answer was no.

Pursuing the grand jury indictment further, I said, "Normally, only the prosecution presents its case at the grand jury. And that's what happened in this case. No defense was presented, and Ms. Jenkins did not testify, nor was she invited to testify."

Before I could ask the jury if they understood that what happened in this case was typical, Enoki was on his feet, predictably objecting to my line of questioning, and Judge King sustained the objection.

Although this wasn't conventional voir dire on my part, I didn't want the jury to start the trial thinking that another group of jurors ("grand" jurors, no less) had already evaluated *both* sides of the case and concluded that Jennifer was guilty.

I continued to indoctrinate the jurors under the thin guise of a question: "In this case, ladies and gentlemen of the jury, we intend to prove, and we are confident we will prove, that Miss Jenkins is completely innocent of the charges against her. However, do you all realize that we have absolutely no legal burden to do so? That under the law, the prosecution *always* has the burden of proof?" The jurors indicated they understood this.

So far, for the most part, the questions from all of us only required the jury to answer yes or no. This type of voir dire is just fine with the jurors. Since the courtroom is an unfamiliar and somewhat intimidating setting for them, they are very reticent about speaking up. But to get any insight into their minds, I needed to hear their voices, their intonations, their choices of words. And this can only be done if the question is framed in such a way that they are forced to give more than a yes-or-no answer. This is what I now did.

"As Judge King told you, the prosecution must prove guilt beyond a reasonable doubt. That's a very high burden of proof. I want to ask each of you at this time how you personally feel about this rule. For instance, do you feel it's fair? That it should be as high and difficult a burden as it is because a person's life and liberty are at stake? Or do you perhaps feel it's unfair, unrealistically high, and therefore the burden should be lower? Or perhaps you may feel that our judicial system should reexamine this entire rule, to determine whether we should keep it or modify it in some other way. Whatever your state of mind might be, I want to hear from you, and I want you to try to be as expressive as possible."

Some of the responses: Juror Clay Gillette: "I feel it's a *very fair* rule. I don't think anything should be changed."

Carol M. Steagall: "If someone accused someone of something, then they should have the burden of proof. You can't just arbitrarily go out and say somebody did something without saying, 'This is why,' or support it."

Joseph F. Lockary: "I don't have an alternative. I'm sure that sometimes people who do commit crimes go free. But there are also people who have been proven guilty, who are innocent. It's not foolproof. I . . . basically agree with it."

The jurors were now talking. A lot.

Clarence Lessa: "I feel a lot of people get away with a lot of things in our society. I really feel that we're a little too easy, and we forget our victims. That's the part that bothers me." He certainly sounded like a prosecution juror.

"Well," I inquired further, "the situation being what it is today in America—we're losing the war on crime and drugs—do you therefore think the burden of proof should be lowered to make it easier for the prosecution to secure a conviction?"

Lessa: "Well, I think that the problem is something deeper than that. I think it's something beyond what we can do maybe. I think our court system is as good as it's going to be. I think that it's fair. And I think that there's other areas that need to be attacked."

After his first response, I was inclined to excuse Clarence Lessa. But his answer to my follow-up question revealed that he was not unthinkingly law-and-order, that his objections were sensible. Also, he fit Clarence Darrow's main criterion for a defense-minded juror; he smiled a lot. We decided to take a chance on Lessa.

I felt quite the opposite about Joanne M. Murphy, a forty-five-year-old Catholic schoolteacher. Her stern response: "It's here, so I'll follow it."

"Well, if you were empowered with the authority to change it," I pressed, "what would you do? Would you lower the burden to make it easier for the prosecution?"

The invisible shades behind her eyes slammed down.

"I don't know what I would do really."

Moving on, the jury had been told by Judge King that there could only be, of course, two possible verdicts in the case. Guilty and not guilty. Speaking to two Scottish-born jurors, I said: "You're aware that in your homeland there are three verdicts?"

Irene Angeles and James McGowan answered no.

"I believe it's guilty, not guilty, and *not proven*," I said.* "Have you heard of that in Scotland?"

Neither had.

As I do in every case, I proceeded to ask each prospective juror his or her hobby. Prospective jurors are always asked their occupa-

---

*In Scottish criminal procedure, where conviction or acquittal is decided by the majority vote of a jury of fifteen, the jury can return a verdict of "not proven," a finding designed to cover the situation where there is a suspicion of guilt but one not sufficient to remove all reasonable doubt. Scottish wags refer to the verdict as "not guilty, but don't do it again." The principal criticism of the Scottish system has been that a lingering stigma attaches to one whose trial culminates in a "not proven" verdict. I was concerned that if Mrs. Angeles and Mr. McGowan, whom I otherwise wanted on the jury, had deeply ingrained within them the unique Scottish rule and ended up having a suspicion of Jennifer's guilt but weren't able to express this suspicion formally (as they would in their homeland) with a "not proven" verdict, they might feel constrained to opt for a guilty verdict. Their complete unfamiliarity with the rule eliminated that problem.

tions, but a person's hobby is far more revealing. Many people don't particularly enjoy their jobs, but no one dislikes his hobby. Employment as an accountant or salesman doesn't tell me nearly as much about a person as does a penchant for deer hunting or community volunteer work. The answers of the jurors varied all the way from sailing and fishing to needlepoint and woodwork.

"No one has mentioned watching TV yet," I said with a smile. "I thought that was popular. I guess it's not."

"We don't admit it," said a voice from the panel.

Everyone laughed.

Back to business, each side handed the judge a sheet listing its peremptory challenges ("peremptory" because no reason at all has to be given), and prospective jurors were excused. "Please remember," the judge said kindly, "this is not a reflection on your intelligence, good looks, or patriotism."

The jury we finally ended up with consisted of seven women and five men ranging in age from thirty-six to seventy-four. Two alternates were also chosen.

Almost immediately, I began worrying about a juror perched right in the middle of the front row.

Frank Everett, who was dressed very conservatively, had a rock-solid jaw and florid complexion, as if the good American red blood coursed close to the surface. This Kansas-born, deep-dyed Republican was a retired engineer, and Len and I were gambling that he and Michael Nevins, an electrical engineer, would be professionally unimpressed by the Government's lack of hard evidence in the case. Everett had previously served on a criminal jury that had found the defendant guilty, but the case involved child molestation, and Len and I had been inclined to discount it. But now, watching sourpuss Everett as he scowled constantly at the world from front and center, I began to feel we had made a grave mistake. We had decided to excuse him when we first prepared our list, but when we got down to our tenth and last peremptory, we decided instead to challenge someone we disliked more.

As the judge was telling the jurors to return to court promptly the next morning and advising them against discussing the case with anyone, I leaned over to Len, pointed to Everett's name on the jury list, and whispered, "This guy is just the kind of juror always wanted as a prosecutor."

Len grimaced.

I shrugged, shaking my head.

It was too late now.

CHAPTER 32

THE TRIAL BEGINS

FEBRUARY 4 DAWNED CRISP and sunny. Hurrying the few blocks from my hotel to the courthouse, laden with my stuffed briefcase and an extra armful of papers, I fleetingly acknowledged it was going to be one of those bright, zestfully invigorating winter days, a patented San Francisco specialty. Too bad I would miss it.

"One thing, your honor, before you bring in the jury," I said, rising. "There's going to be reference at this trial to the transcript of Jennifer's theft trial. The question is, how should we refer to it?"

My co-counsel interjected that he understood that "witnesses would be instructed by both sides to say they testified at an 'earlier proceeding,' without indicating it was a theft trial."

"Yes," agreed Judge King. "That's what I thought we had agreed to."

We had, but I was suddenly having serious doubts about it. I spelled out my worries. "It's conceivable, particularly since the jury knows that Buck Walker has been prosecuted and convicted of murder, that they may think the 'earlier proceeding' against Jennifer was also a prosecution for murder, the same murder charge she is now facing. That would be very harmful to Miss Jenkins."

Since she wouldn't be standing trial again had she been acquitted, I reasoned the jury might conclude that Jennifer had been previously convicted of murder and, as they'd read about so often in the news, the conviction had been reversed on a technicality and sent back for retrial.

"I would rather have them know it was a theft trial," I said, "as opposed to speculating that it was a murder trial."

It was finally agreed we would say that the prior transcript came from Jennifer's theft trial, with no reference, of course, to her conviction.*

One familiar spectator in the crowded courtroom was Wally McIntosh, who sat in a front-row seat, just as he and his wife had during the Walker trial. Kit, recovering from another cancer operation, had to remain home this time. But her interest in the Palmyra case had not slacked. Mac's sister had obtained Wally's solemn promise to call her each evening and brief her on the day's events, which he chronicled in a spiral notebook. Several weeks earlier, she had mailed out nearly a hundred copies of a one-page letter addressed to the "Friends and Complement of the Sailing Yacht SEA WIND." In it, she wrote: "Jennifer Jenkins' murder trial is scheduled to start on February 4th in San Francisco. It is still our hope to be able to be there, inasmuch as my husband and I still feel strongly about her involvement. Thank you all for your continuing support. This has been a difficult period for everyone involved. We can only hope that justice will finally be served."

When the jurors entered the courtroom at 9:50 A.M., Judge King read them several brief instructions, and advised them that Buck Walker would *not* be "available"† to testify for either side in the case, and not to concern themselves with the reason why.

"Mr. Enoki, you have the opening statement for the prosecution?"

"Yes, your honor."

In the opening statement, a lawyer gives the jury an overview of his case and tells the jury, before the commencement of the evidence, what he intends to prove by that evidence.

---

*The day before, during a recess, Judge King had finally granted my motion that when Jennifer testified, the prosecution could not ask her, on cross-examination, about her theft conviction.

†Both the prosecution and the defense had been notified by Walker's lawyer, Earle Partington, that Walker would not testify.

Placing a legal pad filled with neat handwritten notes atop the podium, the usually sober-countenanced Enoki allowed the corners of his mouth to curl in a slight smile, said good morning to the jurors, and began the prosecution of Jennifer Jenkins for the murder of Muff Graham.

After giving a brief history of Palmyra, he rolled a portable television in front of the jury and showed a videotape from a flight over the island. Next, he began homing in on the events of 1974, pointing out that it took Jennifer and Buck almost twenty days in their "weathered vessel" to reach Palmyra—twice as long as the trip normally took.

"The *Iola* was battered during this trip, and arrived at Palmyra leaking and without a working engine."

He went on to assert that the unseaworthiness of the *Iola* effectively marooned Miss Jenkins and Mr. Walker on Palmyra, absent other transportation."

He continued, "In addition, the *Iola* was not stocked with enough supplies, and Miss Jenkins began bartering for food, and asking others on Palmyra for supplies. By the end of August 1974, food supplies aboard the *Iola* had dwindled to the point that they were even out of staples like flour."

In contrast, Enoki described the Grahams' "unique and immaculate" *Sea Wind* and her well-stocked stores.

"The relationship between the two couples had deteriorated by August to the point where they barely associated. Miss Jenkins and Mr. Walker were not seen by others aboard the *Sea Wind* at Palmyra, although other visitors arriving after them were invited aboard the Grahams' vessel. Muff Graham even said that she did not trust Miss Jenkins or Mr. Walker. In addition, there was a fear of Mr. Walker *and Miss Jenkins*. In fact, Muff Graham—"

I sprang to my feet. "Your honor, before we proceed any further, I think there should be an offer of proof [outside the presence of the jury]. He seems to be getting into hearsay that he'll be unable to prove." I knew Muff Graham had been afraid of Buck Walker, but no one had ever reported that Mac or Muff had also been afraid of Jennifer.

Enoki withdrew his remark before the judge even ruled on my objection.

In his low-key delivery, Enoki told the jury they would hear from Curt Shoemaker about his last radio contact with his friends on Palmyra.

As soon as the *Sea Wind* reached Hawaii in October, Enoki continued, it was promptly repainted. "Mr. Walker removed the name *Sea Wind* and reregistered it as the *Lokahi*. Miss Jenkins made no mention of the Grahams or their disappearance to anyone they met. Instead, they told some people the *Sea Wind* had been won in a gambling game."

In recalling Jennifer's arrest, Enoki brought out her flight from the authorities in the Ala Wai harbor, and the many inconsistencies in her story.

Enoki concluded by saying that after all the evidence was in he was confident the jury would "find Jennifer Jenkins guilty of murdering Eleanor Graham."

With that, he took his seat.

Len Weinglass next delivered a solid forty-five-minute opening statement for the defense. His courtroom demeanor was friendly and pleasant; he was rather like a favorite uncle sharing an engrossing tale with family members at the Sunday dinner table. He spent some time talking about why Jennifer had every reason to believe that the Grahams had died in a boating accident. "Based on what she saw—the Zodiac overturned on the beach—she believed there had been some kind of mishap in the lagoon: that the Grahams either fell out of their dinghy, had an episode with the sharks, or the boat rammed an object and turned over." Weinglass told the jury that on Palmyra, Jennifer "had no reason to suspect Buck Walker of doing anything wrong, *if in fact Buck Walker did*." My co-counsel was not completely abandoning the theory that Muff Graham might have died an accidental death.

In discussing the discovery of the bones by Sharon Jordan, Len said, "No one can tell any of us how the container precisely got to where it was found or how long it had been there. Inside the container there is evidence of charring. But I don't believe anyone can tell us *when* that fire occurred. That container had been on the

The *Sea Wind* under sail, San Diego.
From the collection of Kit Graham McIntosh.

Muff Graham in
Tahiti, 1962.
*From the collection
of Kit Graham
McIntosh.*

Mac and Muff Graham aboard the *Sea Wind* in Aden, 1964.
From the collection of Kit Graham McIntosh.

Buck Walker making repairs to the *Iola*.

The faces of Buck Walker.
Credit: David Shapiro

Birds over the airstrip at Palmyra.

Aerial view of the lagoon at Palmyra Island, showing airstrip, top right, and channel, bottom left.

The coastline
of Palmyra.

Mooring site of the
Sea Wind at
Palmyra, looking
southeast.

Hermit crabs on
a dead fish.

The "dolphins" (in the distance) in the lagoon where the *Iola* was moored.

The *Sea Wind* at Palmyra, with Muff on deck and Mac in the Zodiac.

Jennifer Jenkins with Puffer, aboard the *Iola*.
Defense exhibit.

Buck's tent.

Strawn Island, where the bones were found.

An investigator testing the stability of the Zodiac in the lagoon.

Sharon Jordan, at the bone site.

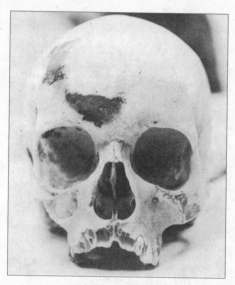

The skull.

The coffin.

island for seventeen years prior to 1981. And the experts will say: 'I can tell you there was a fire, I can't tell you when.'

"The skull is white," Weinglass continued, "indicating intense heat. But it could have occurred while there was flesh on the skull, or years later when the flesh was off, and the skull was in sand, and someone applied heat to that part which might have been sticking out of the sand. Is it conceivable that the skull was burned years later by someone else? This is the mystery within a mystery in this case."

Len promised that the defense would produce a witness who had boarded the *Iola* at Palmyra and considered it to be seaworthy. "Other people will tell you they didn't think the *Iola* was seaworthy. But they weren't on it. The man who was on it, Don Stevens, will tell you the boat was seaworthy."

I waited for the prosecution to object, but both Enoki and Walt Schroeder remained silent. Although a lawyer is forbidden from arguing the evidence during opening statement, my co-counsel, like the seasoned trial lawyer he is, had done just that ("But they weren't on it") and gotten away with it.

"I think the believable evidence in this case will show that there was no threat of starvation on Palmyra. That Buck and Jennifer had a boat they could have gotten to Fanning on, and they were planning such a trip to get food. And that there was no open hostility between Buck and Jennifer and the Grahams."

Len concluded by saying that after the jury heard all the evidence, he was "convinced" they would conclude she was not guilty.

AFTER THE noon recess, Palmyra Island caretaker Jack Wheeler was called to the stand by Walt Schroeder as the Government's first witness.

As at the Walker trial, it soon became apparent that Schroeder, for the most part, would get the Government's case into the record, while Enoki would handle the bulk of the cross-examination and argue the case to the jury. At all times, both lawyers showed conventional prosecutorial deportment; somber and brimming with righteous indignation.

"Based on your experience as a sailor and your observations of the *Iola*, what condition was the boat in?" Schroeder asked.

"I would have to say it was run-down," answered Wheeler, adding irritably that he'd heard a pump on the *Iola* pumping water out of the bilge every single day he was on the island, indicating that even in the protected waters of the lagoon, the *Iola* was constantly leaking.

"Mr. Wheeler, did you ever talk to the defendant in this case, Jennifer Jenkins, about her going to Fanning Island, one hundred and seventy-five miles southeast of Palmyra, to obtain food?"

"I did."

"Do you recall what you said to her?"

"I told her that sailing against the two-knot current which prevails there, and since it's also against the wind, would make it impossible."

"Do you recall what else you told her?"

"Then I suggested, as an alternative, Samoa, which would have been fairly simple, although much further—about fifteen hundred miles away."

"I believe you had a Drake transceiver on your boat similar to the one aboard the *Sea Wind*?"

"That's correct."

"Now, did the defendant, Jennifer Jenkins, ever come aboard your boat and *use* your two-way radio?"

"One time."

"And did you show Miss Jenkins how to use that radio when she came aboard?"

"No."

"Did you show her how to operate the push-to-talk switch?"

"No."

Jennifer had told the FBI's Calvin Shishido that she did not contact the authorities when the Grahams first disappeared because neither she nor Buck knew how to work the *Sea Wind*'s radio. (The *Iola*, of course, had no ship-to-shore radio.) But the testimony Schroeder had just elicited suggested that Jennifer *did* know how to use the type of two-way radio aboard the Grahams' boat.

I leaned over to ask Jennifer if she'd ever gone aboard Wheeler's boat to use his radio.

Quite casually, she replied she hadn't.

"Didn't you hear what he just testified to?" I whispered more urgently.

She shrugged. "He's obviously wrong."

"How's the jury going to know that, Jennifer?" I said curtly.

"No further questions," Schroeder soon announced.

Court adjourned for the day, and I pursued Wheeler into the hallway, where I told him in front of a gathering group of spectators that Jennifer unequivocally said she'd never used his ship-to-shore radio.

"I never said she did," he answered gruffly.

I was taken aback. "Well, you certainly strongly implied that in your testimony just now, Mr. Wheeler."

Wheeler shrugged. "I called *for* her."

At that moment, the prosecutors stepped into the hallway. I called to Schroeder, who frowned and came over.

"Walt, this witness is saying that Jennifer did *not* 'use' his radio. She 'used' it only in the sense that Wheeler operated it for her benefit. You elicited testimony that indicated to the jury that she personally operated it."

"I told you she never operated the radio," an annoyed Wheeler said to Schroeder.

Schroeder nodded in agreement.

The Government lawyer, knowing all along that Jennifer had never operated Wheeler's radio, had posed his questions in such a way as to create the impression that she did.

"Is there any question in your mind now, Walt, as to what the true facts are?" I asked Schroeder.

"No," the prosecutor said.

"When Mr. Wheeler testifies on redirect tomorrow, I want you to bring this out immediately in front of the jury," I said with obvious irritation in my voice. The jury had been deliberately misled on a not too insignificant matter.*

---

*Before the judge took the bench the following morning, Schroeder came over to me at the defense table to apologize for creating the wrong impression. I readily accepted his apology. Subsequently, Schroeder played everything straight by the book.

The first night of the trial was a typical one for me. I worked well into the early-morning hours polishing and modifying the lists of questions I'd be asking on direct and cross-examination.

I also waited up each night for that day's transcript to be delivered to my hotel by the court reporter as soon as his assistants finished typing up and copying the two-to-three-hundred page document. Sometimes it was as late as two or three in the morning when the front desk clerk would call and say a package had arrived for me. Reading the "dailies" is very helpful in preparing for the next day's examination of witnesses. Important words that somehow elude you when uttered in court are seen for the first time.

I also worked every night fine-tuning my final argument, and would do so right up until the moment I stood for summation.

Trials require considerable physical stamina on the part of all involved.

With a life in the balance, there was little time now for rest.

CHAPTER 33

WHEN JACK WHEELER WENT back on the stand the next morning, Len Weinglass began his cross-examination by establishing that the oldster had always found Jennifer to be pleasant.

Asked if it was true that Jennifer had baked several cakes for the Wheelers during the ten days before their departure from Palmyra, the witness said he thought she had baked only one for them. When Len pointed out that at Jennifer's theft trial Wheeler had testified she had baked "several very good cakes" for his family, the witness allowed that his memory of such culinary events was probably better in 1975.

The old military rescue boat was still sitting in a warehouse when he accompanied the search party to Palmyra in November 1974, Wheeler said.

"Did you check to see if all four containers were still in the holes in the rescue boat?"

"I did not." Weinglass was planting another seed that maybe, just maybe, the murders had not taken place while Buck and Jennifer were on Palmyra a few months earlier.

Regarding his assessment of the *Iola*'s "run-down" condition, Wheeler admitted he'd never actually set foot on the vessel. As for the daily pumping, he offered that, given the length of the voyage down from Hawaii and the age of the boat, water in the *Iola*'s bilges wouldn't have been unusual. "It was no big deal," he shrugged.

It was obvious that Wheeler was not the most credible of witnesses. For instance, he had testified in 1975 that the prevailing winds at Palmyra around the time of the year in question are "easterly," while under direct examination by Schroeder he described them as "northeasterly" winds. When asked to explain by Weinglass, Wheeler blithely responded, "A knowledgeable person would know that in the northern hemisphere, if I said easterly, we're talking about northeast." (Actually, per the Government's meteorologist, Dr. Ramage, who testified at the Walker trial and would testify at Jennifer's trial, the prevailing winds around Palmyra in August and September are *southeast* trade winds. Since Fanning lay southeast of Palmyra, sailing from Palmyra to Fanning would therefore be directly against the wind.)*

When it came to Len's challenging Wheeler's opinion that a Palmyra-Fanning trip would be "impossible," however, the experienced sailor hung tough.

"When Jennifer mentioned her plans about going to Fanning for supplies, it's true, is it not, Mr. Wheeler, you told her the trip would be difficult?"

"*Very* difficult."

---

*Winds are described by the direction from which they are coming. Ocean currents, on the other hand, are described by the direction in which they are going. Hence, an easterly wind is coming from the east and going toward the west, whereas an easterly current is coming from the west and going toward the east.

"But you didn't tell her it would be 'impossible'?"

"I don't know the exact words," Wheeler said.

"You can't tell the court or the jury that you told Jennifer that it would be 'impossible' to go to Fanning."

"I couldn't say. I think I was trying to tell her that *she couldn't make it.*"

Len and I had elected not to wait for Walt Schroeder's correction of Wheeler's testimony about Jennifer's presumed operation of his radio.

"Do you recall having a discussion with Mr. Bugliosi after court yesterday?"

"I know I talked to him."

"Did he ask you if Jennifer Jenkins ever used the radio on your boat?"

"I think I did the talking for her. She just told me what to say, I believe."

"To your knowledge," my co-counsel said, "she didn't even know how to use your radio."

"That's correct."

As Len took his seat, Jennifer was smiling. My own gratification would be short-lived.

On redirect, Schroeder asked Wheeler the subject of the message he'd sent over the radio for Jennifer.

"It was in regard to another boat coming down with food. I don't know who we were talking to."

"Do you recall where you were sending the message to?"

"It was to Honolulu."

Unbelievable. Overnight, the Government had developed testimony that was even *more* incriminating than what had just been retracted. If Wheeler was right, within just days of the *Iola's* arrival at Palmyra in late June the food shortage aboard the *Iola* was already so urgent that Jennifer needed to radio for more supplies immediately.

Jennifer scrawled a note and put it in front of me. "Did not send radio message in June. Jack confused."

Based on our knowledge of the case, Len and I agreed with Jennifer, but after huddling, we decided not to challenge—on re-cross—Wheeler's latest testimony. With Wheeler, things could get worse for us before they got better. Instead, we hoped the jury would accept our chronology of events and clarification of the matter through later testimony.

WHEELER WAS dismissed, and outside the presence of the jury, Judge King asked both sides where we stood on the latest polygraph issue.

There had been an earlier discussion as to whether the defense could bring out Jennifer's acceptance of a Government offer made way back in 1974 for her to take a polygraph examination.

Jennifer told me that though both Buck and she had initially agreed to take the test, Buck had later decided against it. She said she had been willing to go ahead, however, but the Government said the offer applied only if both went along.

Enoki had earlier asked the judge for time to research the Government's position on this issue and had made several phone calls to Hawaii. "From what I gather," he now reported, "the prosecutor in the theft case agreed to give a polygraph" to both Jenkins and Walker. Indeed, the Government flew in an FBI polygraph operator and, following standard procedure, furnished a list of questions to the couple. "After reviewing the questions, Mr. Walker decided he didn't want to take the polygraph and refused to do so," Enoki said. "And after Mr. Walker's refusal, Miss Jenkins also refused to submit to the test."

Jennifer was tugging at my coat sleeve. "That's *not* what happened!" she hissed. This was the first time I had ever seen Jennifer express any emotion about the case. She could sit, apparently blasé, through the erroneous testimony of Jack Wheeler, and in fact remain indifferent throughout the several years of trial preparation, but this polygraph issue had touched some nerve.

"I *wanted* to take it"—she was still yanking my sleeve—"but after Buck said no, they wouldn't let me!"

Judge King advised that if he allowed us to tell the jury about Jennifer's willingness to take the 1974 polygraph, the Government would be permitted to present its own version of why the polygraph agreement imploded.

"I'm not going to pursue it, Jennifer," I said quietly.

"Why?" She looked stricken.

"There's too much to lose by getting into a dogfight with the prosecution on this issue. They've already told us what they're going to say. They're going to have a couple of witnesses from the FBI and U.S. Attorney's Office take the stand and say you refused to take the test."

"But that isn't the way it happened. I want you to fight this."

"I'm not going to take on the Government on this issue, Jennifer," I said. "The jury will have just as much or more reason to believe several federal officials than they will to believe you. And if they believe the Government witnesses, this means they'll believe you are lying, at *this* trial, when you testify that you never refused to take the test. There's no way I'm going to create an enormous risk like that, Jennifer. We've got enough problems. When you're already being mauled by a bunch of bears in the forest, you don't shout out, 'Bring on more bears.'"

Jennifer looked as if she still wanted to try to convince me otherwise when I told the court that the defense did not wish to present evidence on the polygraph issue.

THE GOVERNMENT next called Bernard Leonard to the stand. It was very clear that Leonard and his wife, together with Shoemaker and Shishido, would be by far the most damaging witnesses against Jennifer. The Leonards had made it their personal crusade to see Buck Walker and Jennifer Jenkins convicted of murder. I had no doubt that they honestly believed that both Buck and Jennifer had committed murder, but I also considered their bias so great that they might not hesitate to do whatever was necessary to ensure the second conviction in the case. Had my pretrial contact with Leonard had any positive effect? I'd soon find out.

"Is the individual who identified herself to you on Palmyra as Jennifer Jenkins in the courtroom today?" Schroeder asked.

"Yes."

"Could you point her out, please?"

"She's right there," Leonard answered quickly, pointing a long finger at Jennifer. Somehow, he made the simple words sound like an identification not just of the person, but of the murderer of Mac and Muff Graham. Obviously, all my pretrial efforts aimed toward keeping Leonard from using this type of accusatory tone had failed.

Leonard testified that the *Iola* was in "very poor shape and very unseaworthy. It was a carvel-planked boat [a wooden boat built upon ribs] and the planks were fastened to the ribs. As the boat gets old and tired, the planks start to wobble and warp, letting water in." He then volunteered, as would be his wont throughout: "So this boat had all those problems, and was also fiberglassed. When you fiberglass a carvel-planked boat it's a last-ditch effort."

"While on Palmyra, did Jennifer Jenkins say anything to you about their trip on the *Iola* from Hawaii?" Schroeder asked.

"She said that at times during the trip she was knee-deep in water down below."

"Did you have occasion to talk to Jennifer Jenkins about how they would manage to leave Palmyra?"

"She said that she wasn't going to leave the island on that boat."

This was explosive testimony I had never heard before. At a minimum, Leonard's last statement flatly contradicted what Jennifer was going to testify to: that after Mac and Muff disappeared, she wanted to leave Palmyra on the *Iola* and had to be *talked into* taking the *Sea Wind* by Buck.

Leonard went on to testify that Jennifer had told him she and her boyfriend were low on food and interested in bartering various boat-equipment items in exchange for supplies. "We did not barter with *them*," he said emphatically.

Although Leonard said he personally visited the *Sea Wind* "close to twenty times" and he and his wife were "quite often" dinner guests of the Grahams, he said he never once saw Jennifer or Buck aboard the *Sea Wind*, or either of the Grahams on the *Iola*. In fact, Leonard said, he had never once seen the Grahams even "associating" with Jennifer and Buck.

Leonard testified that Mac Graham always locked the door to the *Sea Wind*'s cabin whenever he and Muff left their boat.

Asked if the Grahams had ever invited him aboard the *Sea Wind* at a time they were not going to be present, Leonard said with conviction, "No. I don't think the Grahams would ever have done that." Schroeder was like a balloonist watching his craft steadily inflate, just adjusting the lines every now and then.

When asked if he and his wife had decided to leave Palmyra early, Leonard answered that they had, then volunteered, "There was an uncomfortable feeling. The *Iola* people were not the usual type people that we were used to meeting on cruises."

Asked about the last visit the Grahams had made to the *Journeyer*, Leonard didn't answer directly but started to launch into another narrative, and I objected, adding for the jury's edification, "He obviously likes to volunteer information."

The judge sustained the objection, cautioning Leonard to answer only yes or no to questions that called for such responses.

Schroeder: "Who was present during this last meeting?"

"Mac, Muff, Evelyn, and myself," Leonard said through tightly compressed lips.

"Did you notice if Mrs. Graham was showing any emotion while she was talking to your wife?"

"Yes."

"And what was she doing?"

"She was crying."

"After you sailed away from Palmyra, did you learn from your wife why Mrs. Graham had been crying?"

The question called for hearsay, and I objected, at which point Leonard blurted out over my objection, "All these yeses don't tell the story."

"*You* are not on trial for anything," Judge King snapped at him. "Just answer the questions that are asked."

Everything Leonard volunteered was prejudicial to Jennifer— and I was glad to have the jury see that the judge had heard enough, too.

As a matter of strategy, I try to make as few objections as possible in a jury trial. Constant interruptions irritate the jurors, who must sit there in weary forbearance. Moreover, if the jury concludes from the lawyer's objections that he is trying, by technicalities, to keep them from hearing relevant evidence, his credibility in their eyes is hurt. But Leonard was supposed to answer questions, not try the case himself.

Leonard next testified that as he and Jennifer were being towed out in her dinghy to the waiting Coast Guard cutter on the day of her arrest, she told him that she and Buck had found the Zodiac capsized "over at" Paradise Island. Also, that she and Buck had attempted to sail away from Palmyra on the *Iola*, but got stuck on the reef in the channel. Minutes later aboard the Coast Guard cutter, Leonard said he was appalled when Jennifer changed her story and told the authorities that she and Buck had first attempted to *tow* the *Iola* out of the lagoon with the *Sea Wind*, taking the Grahams' boat only after theirs got hopelessly hung up on the reef.

The prosecutor's final line of questioning concerned Jennifer's request that she be allowed to go to the bathroom after the Coast Guard cutter had tied up at the Ala Wai's Hawaii Yacht Club. Leonard explained that because he was a club member, he had a key to the rest room, which he unlocked for Jennifer.

"Do you recall if she took her purse in with her?"

"Yes."

"How long was she in the rest room?"

"It seemed like a long time. *Longer than was necessary*," Leonard again volunteered, continuing his unpaid summation for the Government.

"Did you hear or observe anything while Jennifer was in the rest room?"

"The toilet flushing. It was one of those valve-type toilets that you can repeatedly flush, and it was just constantly flushing."

Leonard explained that his wife, Evelyn, arrived about then, and he asked her to go in to check on Jennifer.

"And what happened then?" asked the prosecutor.

"She came out with Jennifer."

"No more questions, your honor."

The prosecutor's obvious intent was to suggest strongly that Jennifer had disposed of incriminating evidence of some kind while alone in the rest room.

As I've mentioned, my style on cross-examination is more confrontational than the norm. One reason may simply be my assertive personality, but another is the principal technique of cross-examination I employ to destroy credibility: the "why" question. When I feel a witness is lying, I just about know that he would not have acted—in a given circumstance—as a truthful person would have. Frequently, I already have evidence in hand that he did not. To expose his untruthfulness, I first elicit answers on preliminary matters (blocking off escape hatches), answers that, when totaled up, show he would be expected to take a certain course of action. The witness having committed himself, I then ask him what course he in fact took (unnecessary if what the witness did is already in the record), and follow this up with the "why" question, an inherently confrontational and argumentative approach. If time after time a witness is unable to satisfactorily justify conduct of his which is incompatible with what would be expected of a reasonable person, the jury will usually conclude that his testimony is suspect. Among other techniques, I used this type of cross-examination with Bernard Leonard.*

---

*Virtually all human beings, from childhood on, regularly cross-examine those with whom they interact. And the main technique they employ is to ask "why," or "how come." Wife to husband: "If your meeting ended at eight o'clock, why did you get home at ten-thirty?" Girl to boy: "You say you like me so much. *How come* you didn't ask me to the dance?" Yet ironically, this most natural, instinctive, and practiced of all cross-examination techniques is frowned upon by the very people who need it most: trial lawyers. Books on the art of cross-examination, from Francis L. Wellman's 1903 classic *The Art of Cross-Examination* on down, all advocate *never* asking an adverse witness "why" he did or did not do something the lawyer feels is implausible. Louis Nizer, in his book *My Life in Court*, says: "One can quickly spot a bad cross-examiner if he asks 'why.' " The reason given is that the "why" question gives the witness free rein to explain away his conduct, and in so doing, he also frequently incorporates within his explanation to the open-ended question a statement extremely damaging to the questioner's case.

Admittedly, real witnesses, unlike their fictional counterparts in novels and on the screen who crumple under the pressure of the first or second good question, are as elusive as all hell. When cornered on the stand, for some strange reason they seem to secrete a type of mental adrenaline that gets their minds working as fast as silicon microchips. But if the lawyer has blocked off all avenues of escape, a witness can't go somewhere when he has nowhere to go.

Sometimes, several possible escape routes have to be blocked off. Because of the nature of the testimony of the Government's witnesses in this case, however, that wasn't necessary.

I began my cross on the topic of the suspicious toilet flushing. "Can we assume, Mr. Leonard, that you felt that Jennifer may have been flushing something down the toilet she should not have been?"

"That entered my mind."

"That what she was flushing down the toilet may have had some connection with what happened on Palmyra?"

Leonard: "It would naturally follow."

"There's been a stipulation from the prosecution that later that same day, Mr. Leonard, the FBI interviewed you and your wife. Can you tell this jury *why* you never saw fit to tell the FBI agents about the toilet-flushing incident?"

Leonard hesitated. "The agents were there outside the rest room," he said.

"So, it's your testimony then that they *knew* what happened, and therefore you didn't have to tell them. Is that correct?"

"I suppose."

"*Why*, then, did you tell these same agents that Jennifer was seen rowing in a dinghy in the harbor, and was subsequently caught by the Coast Guard? *Why* would you have had to tell the FBI *that* information?"

Leonard hesitated again, shifting in his seat. "I don't remember that I told them that. They were there. Did I tell them that?"

At this point, I strode to the prosecution's table and placed Leonard's FBI 302 in front of Schroeder. Pointing to the relevant page, I quietly asked Schroeder if he would stipulate that Leonard, as the 302 showed, *had* told the agents this information. Probably thinking that he shouldn't do anything to rattle his own witness, the prosecutor refused. But I was very confident the jury had got the message from what had transpired before their eyes.

Returning to the podium, I asked: "Mr. Leonard, on June 15, 1975, you were interviewed about this case by William Eggers, an Assistant U.S. Attorney, is that correct?"

"I talked to Mr. Eggers many times."

"Are you prepared to testify now, *under oath*, that you told Mr. Eggers about this toilet-flushing incident? Are you prepared to testify *under oath* on that point?" I repeated, facing the jury, and not even looking at the witness.

Leonard paused, as if beginning to realize his misstep. "I don't remember having told anybody about it," he finally said.

"In fact," I bore down, "the first time you've told anyone about this toilet-flushing incident is today in court, almost twelve years after it happened. Isn't that true?"

"If it wasn't asked, I have a hard time getting out anything of the story," Leonard responded, without blushing.

I would return to Leonard's alleged difficulty in getting his point across.

"Mr. Leonard, you testified that Jennifer told you she'd never leave Palmyra on the *Iola*. Is that correct?"

"That's correct."

"I'm interested in your state of mind with respect to this statement she allegedly made to you. You've certainly always felt, have you not, that this statement was relevant to the question of what happened to the Grahams on Palmyra, and why Buck and Jennifer ended up with the *Sea Wind*. Is that correct?"

"That's right."

"Again, Mr. Leonard, can you tell the judge and this jury, *why* then, when you were interviewed by the FBI on October 29, 1974, you never told them about this statement that she reportedly made to you?"

"All I can say is we answered the questions that we were asked. They probably didn't ask that *particular* question."

"Mr. Leonard, how *could* they have asked you that question? How would they have known if you didn't tell them?"

"We told the story and they asked particulars that they wanted to know about. If we left that detail out, then I don't know. I don't remember."

"So even though your state of mind was that Jennifer Jenkins's statement that she's never going to leave Palmyra on the *Iola* was relevant to what may have happened to the Grahams, *by golly, if they didn't ask you the magic question, you weren't about to tell them. Is that correct?*" I said, my voice rising in pitch.

"I don't . . . know." Leonard sounded like one of his worst students, quite a transformation.

Even though I knew I would hear from the prosecution or

judge with my next question, I wanted the jury to know exactly what I thought of Bernard Leonard's selective memory. "You've come up with a lot of these things just out of whole cloth, haven't you, Mr. Leonard?"

"Mr. Bugliosi, please," the judge said patiently. "You'll get a chance to argue the case later."

So far, I'd been impressed with the latitude I'd received from Judge King in cross-examining Leonard. Some inexperienced judges don't realize how aggressive and even antagonistic cross-examination can properly be, and regularly sustain objections that the attorney is being "argumentative."

I pressed further, slinging verbal darts in the direction of the witness stand. Leonard agreed with me that a witness on the stand *in court* is only supposed to answer questions.

"But on direct examination today, didn't you volunteer a lot of information for this jury, Mr. Leonard, without being asked?"

"I tried."

I paused a moment. I wanted the jury to let his bold admission sink in.

"But *out of court*, where you *can* volunteer information," I went on, "you have to be asked the magic question before you give information, is that correct?'

"Well, that's pretty argumentative," Judge King said mildly.

I withdrew the question. Again, the message to the jury was clear.

The two most damaging pieces of his testimony out of the way, I essayed other matters.*

Since final summation has to be based on testimony and evidence at the trial, I proceeded to elicit a series of answers from Leonard that would serve as bases for argument during summation.

---

*One matter concerned Leonard's testimony on direct examination that Jennifer told him she and Buck found the overturned Zodiac "over at" Paradise Island, which is on the opposite side of the lagoon from where she subsequently said she and Buck found the Zodiac. I asked Leonard if it was possible she had told him that the dinghy had *capsized* near Paradise and that he misunderstood this to mean they had *found* it there.

"She said they found it capsized on the beach at Paradise Island," he answered firmly.

Yes, Leonard replied to my seemingly random question, in daylight on Palmyra, if one was on shore, or on one of the boats tied to the dolphins, one could see and identify the operator of a dinghy in the middle of the lagoon; yes, a dinghy is not the type of boat one would operate at sea because it would "swamp" (sink or be filled with water); yes, he and his wife had been served meat by the Grahams on the *Sea Wind*, etc.

As we moved quickly through a number of topics, Leonard admitted that he'd never had a conversation with Buck Walker involving more than "three or four words," but he and his wife had had many "friendly conversations" with Jennifer.

"Your wife discussed recipes with Jennifer, is that correct?"

"That's correct."

"And on the day you left Palmyra, your wife took a picture of Jennifer with her dog, Puffer, is that correct?"

"That's correct."

"So at least at the time you left Palmyra, you and your wife were not on unfriendly terms with Jennifer. Is that correct?"

Leonard paused so long before answering that even the court reporter made note of it in the transcript.

His answer, when it finally came, was delivered most begrudgingly. "I think that would be correct."

I wanted the jury to understand that the Leonards' very negative feelings toward Jennifer started *after* they learned of the disappearance and probable murder of Mac and Muff.

Since Jennifer intended to testify that she and Buck got along reasonably well with the Grahams, the defense had to start countering the prosecution position that they did not. I asked:

"And do you remember telling the FBI on October 29, 1974, Mr. Leonard, that the Grahams were also friendly with Buck and Jennifer; however, not extremely friendly because of their different life-styles?"

"I imagine I would have said something like that."

"And is that your present testimony?" I asked.

"That's my feeling."

"You were aware on Palmyra, were you not, that on several

occasions the Grahams went fishing and gave part of their catch to Jennifer and Buck?"

"That's correct."

I next got Leonard to concede that he had seen Jennifer and Buck gathering such food as land crabs, coconuts, and palm hearts, and that edible mullet and papio were available in the lagoon.

I asked Jennifer to stand up. "The last time you saw Jennifer on Palmyra, did she appear to be about the same weight as she is right now, Mr. Leonard?"

"That's correct."

As she stood now before the jury, Jennifer, although not at all heavy, did not look as if she'd missed too many meals. How deprived of food could she have been back then?

I moved on to Leonard's description of Buck to the FBI. "You described him as being around six feet two inches tall, muscular, medium to long-length hair, wearing dark glasses, having tattoos and some front teeth missing."

"That sounds like my description."

"Not the type of person you would like to meet in an alley, much less on a deserted island like Palmyra. Isn't that correct?"

"I had no fear of Buck Walker. I had no feelings that way," Leonard said without hesitation.

This was a shrewd answer. Leonard sensed that I was trying to separate Jennifer from Buck and didn't want me to get away with it. But I had brought out before the jury a physical description that made Buck sound like a very coarse, rough-hewn individual, precisely the image I wanted as I unofficially prosecuted him at Jennifer's trial.

I asked Leonard if he considered himself a law-abiding citizen who believed in certain principles upon which this country and its Constitution were based.

"Yes."

"Among those principles is the presumption of innocence. Is that correct?"

"*Without having knowledge of the facts*, yes," Leonard said alertly.

"*Concerning knowledge of the facts*," I responded, "at the time of the disappearance of Mr. and Mrs. Graham on Palmyra on or about August the 30th, 1974, you were about a thousand miles away. Is that correct, Mr. Leonard?"

"That's correct."

I had no further questions.

HAD THE toilet-flushing incident and Jennifer's conversation with the Leonards about not leaving Palmyra on the *Iola*, two important, counted-upon pieces of evidence against Jennifer, really taken place? On re-direct, a worried Schroeder made a shaky effort to rehabilitate Leonard's credibility on these issues.

"Mr. Leonard, on October 29th, the day that Jennifer was apprehended, would it be safe to say that things were pretty hectic around the Ala Wai that day?" Schroeder asked, his voice steeped with concern.

"That's true."

"A lot of people were running and scurrying around?"

"That's true."

I didn't feel the need to belabor before the jury on re-cross a point they had already heard: even if the hectic situation somehow caused Leonard not to mention these two incidents on October 29, he had had numerous other opportunities during the following years to do so, and hadn't.

After four hours on the stand, Bernard Leonard was dismissed, ending his nearly twelve-year campaign to do what he could to see Buck Walker and Jennifer Jenkins tried and convicted of murder on Palmyra.

We were at the end of the day. Judge King had handled the cross-examination like a real pro, and after the jury left the box, I told him so.

The judge gave me a smile, but it was forced.

We were no longer friends, that much was clear.

CHAPTER 34

BEFORE EVELYN LEONARD TOOK the stand the following morning, there was a lively discussion regarding the Government's intention to ask about her last conversation with Muff Graham in which Muff allegedly told her that she was in fear of her life and knew she would not leave Palmyra alive. This dramatic testimony was inadmissible hearsay unless, as the prosecution was arguing, the state-of-mind exception applied.

Walt Schroeder recalled Mrs. Leonard's account of her friend's fears and her desperate weeping. "We would argue to the jury that obviously a woman in the state of mind Muff Graham was in would never have extended a dinner invitation to Walker and Jenkins on August 30, 1974."

(The reason the Government would continue to make, throughout the trial, a concentrated effort to prove that no dinner invitation was ever made—and that if Buck told Jennifer it had, she would have had no reason to believe him, as she claimed she did—is that when Jennifer testified about the dinner invitation, they could argue she made the whole story up. And if she was lying about the dinner invitation, she undoubtedly was involved in the murders.)

"We will not offer evidence that there *was* a dinner invitation," I responded, "only that Buck *told* Jennifer there was." Since both sides agreed there was no invitation, I argued, Mrs. Leonard's inflammatory testimony should not be allowed. "This exception to the hearsay rule requires that Muff Graham's state of mind be *in issue,* but there is no such issue here because we agree there was no invitation."

The judge went against me, and ruled that the jury could hear about the dramatic conversation.

My last hope was to somehow restrain Mrs. Leonard from volunteering her biased opinions throughout her testimony. I remarked to the judge that I thought she was even more biased than her husband, "if that's possible."

Judge King well remembered Evelyn Leonard's demeanor during her testimony in the three previous trials. "She was emotionally involved as long as she was on the stand," he said.

When Evelyn Leonard took the stand, it didn't take long for me to see she was a different woman from the Walker trial. Her words were the same, but her delivery was not nearly so emotional and animated. She spoke with a flat intonation that suggested she'd taken something to calm her nerves. Len whispered to me that her husband's undoubted report to her of what he had been put through on cross-examination had probably had an effect.

Not that she wasn't still biased. When Schroeder asked if she'd ever gone aboard the *Iola*, instead of simply answering no, she said quietly, *"Never."*

Although more precise and organized than Enoki, like his fellow prosecutor, Schroeder lacked flair, even more so. He was obviously content to be a competent legal technocrat. Well-prepared for his witness, as usual, he methodically elicited from Mrs. Leonard everything he and Enoki felt the prosecution needed in their effort to convict Jennifer, deftly placing each piece in the mosaic of evidence against her. Some testimony overlapped with what the jury had already heard. Obviously, the Government wished the repetitions to have a cumulative effect by trial's end.

Once again, the jury heard the very damaging (if believed) testimony that Jennifer had vowed never to leave Palmyra on her leaky craft—"She said, 'There's no way I'll leave on the *Iola*,'" Mrs. Leonard recited softly. "She was very definite about that."

To her, Buck was an eerily frightening figure. "I would be scrubbing the decks or doing something topside and he would row past our boat. I would speak to him but he would never acknowledge me. Never speak back. He'd just watch what I was doing, making me uncomfortable." (In my "prosecution" of Buck, this was testimony I intended to elicit on cross-examination. Why the prosecution elicited it, or felt it was helpful to their case, was never made clear.)

"How many times did this happen?"

"Many times," she said, with an involuntary shiver. "At least ten times."

"Was it your original intention to stay on Palmyra for two weeks?"

"No. We had planned on spending the summer there."

"For some reason you decided to leave early?"

Mrs. Leonard paused pensively, her fingers playing with the string of faux pearls around her neck. "I felt uncomfortable. I felt threatened. I suggested to my husband that we leave."

Even during the worst weather she had ever observed while at Palmyra, the waters of the lagoon were calm, Mrs. Leonard explained, never more than a one-foot chop.

Now Schroeder wanted to know about her last conversation with Muff.

"I was . . . I was quite . . . This is so hard." Mrs. Leonard swallowed with effort, evidently fighting a strong surge of emotion. "I was fairly anxious about the situation. And I knew Muff was very anxious. I asked her if she couldn't try to leave . . . try to persuade Mac to leave Palmyra."

"Did you tell her why she should leave?"

"Yes. I said this was not a safe place to be. It would be wise if they would leave." ·

"Do you recall how she responded when you told her this?"

"She . . . she was crying. She would have liked to have left, she said. But Mac was not interested in leaving."

"And did she say anything else?"

"She was afraid for her life. She said she knew she would not leave the island alive."

Schroeder let this answer reverberate.

Expressions in the jury box varied, from the usual stony face of Frank Everett, whom I had named the "Kansas Rock," to an elderly woman juror sadly shaking her head. A younger woman juror looked on the verge of tears. A couple of the jurors looked squarely at Jennifer—probing, analyzing.

The prosecutor's final line of questioning concerned Jennifer's famously lengthy visit to the rest room. Mrs. Leonard had little to add, testifying that she went in to check on Jennifer, who emerged from a stall, purse in hand.

Although on direct examination of my own witness I normally ask questions in a reasonably predictable chronology, on cross-examination I purposefully skip about from issue to issue, trying to keep the other side's witness off-balance and distracted from what's coming next.

I began my cross of Mrs. Leonard by making a guess. If wrong, I had nothing to lose.

"Mrs. Leonard, at the time you left Palmyra, you were running low on provisions, were you not?"

"We had enough provisions for our return to Hawaii."

"And that was about it?"

"That was about it." (I had guessed right.)

"Now, if you had stayed the entire summer, since you still had to get back home, how were you going to get by on such low provisions?" I asked.

"All right. We fish. We eat what is available, as we had suggested to Jennifer—coconuts, crabs, and so on."

"So you had originally intended to live off the land on Palmyra, is that correct?"

"We would supplement our stores with food that we found, yes. Which we did."

Some yardage had been made. However, unlike Buck and Jennifer on the *Iola*, the Leonards could have easily motored at any time to Fanning, or Christmas, or some other island for provisions.

Since I suspected that, like her husband, she had developed and nurtured her negative feelings about Jennifer in the twelve years since Palmyra, and *after* the fate of the Grahams became known, I asked her about the letter Jennifer had given her and her husband to mail to Sunny Jenkins. She acknowledged this.

"And you did in fact mail that letter for her, did you not?"

"I did not."

Mrs. Leonard explained that for some reason she would "never know," she had decided to keep the letter "in a drawer in the cabin of our boat."

Score a point for the prosecution. I had fallen into that one.

(A legal maxim which I reject out of hand is this: "Never ask a witness a question unless you know what the answer is going to be." While this legal caveat is valid for direct examination of one's own witness, it clearly is not always valid for cross-examination. Although the ideal situation would be to know, in advance, what the adverse witness's answers to all of your questions are going to be, the reality is that inasmuch as you frequently have not had an opportunity to interview the witness [as was the case with Mrs. Leonard, whose husband, at Buck Walker's trial, had requested that I not interview her when she left the stand], of necessity, cross-examination often is a trek through new terrain, and experience, caution, and instinct are one's only guide. With Mrs. Leonard, my instincts proved faulty. I would accept this antiquated commandment only if it were amended to read: "Never ask a question concerning a matter *critical* to your case without being *reasonably sure* what the answer is going to be.")

On more than one occasion I had asked Jennifer to give me all of the letters she'd sent to her mother from Palmyra. She hadn't done so, and I'd neglected to keep after her. It turned out that the only letter her mother had not received was the one Jennifer had given the Leonards to mail.

Mrs. Leonard's surprise answer tended to show that way back in 1974 she had already had uneasy feelings about Jennifer and Buck, and that her ill feelings about the *Iola* couple were not completely of recent, and hence contrived, origin.

Nonetheless, I was able to elicit from Mrs. Leonard that the Leonards had given Jennifer some oil and flour on Palmyra, and that they and Jennifer had exchanged books. She also confirmed her husband's testimony that she had had a number of friendly chats with Jennifer. All of this suggested normal, casual, even amiable relations—particularly with Jennifer—in the summer of 1974, not rampant, pervasive ill will.

I was now ready to handle Jennifer's alleged comment that she would never leave Palmyra on the *Iola*. "If I sound a little harsh in my questioning of you, Mrs. Leonard, please know that I feel nothing but tremendous sorrow for what happened to the Grahams," I began. "You realize, Mrs. Leonard, that although Buck Walker and

Jennifer Jenkins were together on Palmyra, he and she are two separate and distinct people in the eyes of the law? You realize that, do you not?"

"Yes."

I asked if she had considered Jennifer's comment "a potentially threatening statement or in any way foreboding to the other boat owners on the island."

"I felt she meant what she said."

"I repeat. Did you think it was potentially threatening to the other people on the island?"

"Well, it threatened me. It was a threatening remark. I discussed it with Mac and Muff."

"So, at the very moment Jennifer said it, it sounded a little foreboding to you, frightening. And you felt a potential danger to the other people on the island?"

"Yes, I felt threatened myself."

"Mrs. Leonard, you were interviewed several times by the FBI agents in this case, were you not?"

"Yes."

"When you spoke to the FBI, you certainly wanted to help them, did you not?"

"Of course," she answered somewhat indignantly.

"You wanted to give them information that would aid them in their investigation into the disappearance of the Grahams. Isn't that correct?"

"We helped them in any way possible."

"Now, inasmuch as you felt that Jennifer's statement about never leaving Palmyra on the *Iola* was a threatening one, can you tell the judge and the jury *why* you never, at any time, told the FBI about what Jennifer allegedly told you?"

"We answered questions we were asked."

If she could replay her husband's testimony, I could repeat my previous line of cross-examination.

"So, if they didn't ask you the specific question 'Mrs. Leonard, did Jennifer ever tell you that she would never leave Palmyra on the *Iola*?' you would not have told them. You would never have volunteered this information on your own to them, is that correct?"

She was digging in. "I would have answered what they asked me."

"But, Mrs. Leonard, how could the FBI possibly ask you about this alleged statement that Jennifer made to you? How would they know if you didn't *tell* them?"

"I didn't tell them . . . I wasn't asked. If . . . I don't understand what you're trying to get at."

"Well, how could the FBI ever find out about this threatening remark that Jennifer allegedly made if you didn't tell them?"

Mrs. Leonard, her face watermelon-red, became flustered. "I had told . . . Okay. What . . . what I had told . . . You don't understand what I'm trying to say to you. If you're asked something, you respond, just like I'm trying to do with you. If you feel things, it's very difficult to put that across unless you're asked. Okay? At the time we left Palmyra, and I was with Muff, this was a very difficult time. Because we were leaving that place, and we . . . we shouldn't have left, so . . . ."

Her rambling incoherence was evident to everyone, and having achieved my aim, I helped her out of her tangled syntax by asking another question. "Do you know a lawyer by the name of William Eggers, formerly an Assistant U.S. Attorney?"

"Yes. I met him in the first trial."

I asked her *why* she had not mentioned Jennifer's statement when he interviewed her before calling her as a witness in that trial.

"He didn't ask," she responded, eyes narrowing.

"But Mrs. Leonard, again, how *could* he ask you? He wasn't there on Palmyra, you were."

"I just didn't tell him."

I stuck to the same theme in questioning her about the toilet-flushing incident, bringing out that the first time she had told *anyone* about this incident was a year earlier, when Walt Schroeder and the FBI's Hal Marshall had visited her home in Kauai.

"That would have been ten years after all this supposedly happened. Is that correct?"

"Yes," she said coldly.

When she finally stepped down from the stand, Evelyn Leonard gave the Government lawyers a friendly if wan smile as she passed by. There would be only two other prosecution witnesses whose credibility I'd try to impeach in the same way I had the Leonards', but it would be days before I would face Curt Shoemaker and Calvin Shishido.

In the meantime, there were other Government witnesses called to the stand, such as Joseph Stuart, the appliance-store owner who again testified that Buck told him the new sailboat was won in a chess game. The white-haired Stuart said Jennifer was within earshot of this conversation.

"During the afternoon, did Miss Jenkins say anything to you that was contradictory to Mr. Allen's statement about how they acquired the boat?" Elliot Enoki asked.

"No, sir," Stuart answered. "There were no contradictions made."

Since I viewed Stuart's testimony as being actually helpful to Jennifer's defense, I asked no questions on cross-examination. It was Buck who had told the lie, not Jennifer, and she could hardly be expected to contradict him in front of Stuart and the other guests.

The next witness was Joel Peters, whom I'd been so delighted to find in attendance at the Walker trial.

Peters repeated his tale of having met Jennifer and Buck on the Big Island in 1973 and then seeing them again in early 1974 on Maui, where they were preparing their thirty-foot sailboat for a Pacific cruise. When he ran into the couple at the Ala Wai in October 1974, Peters said, "they" pointed out their boat, a different boat, at anchor in the harbor.

When Peters asked how their cruise had gone, they had talked some about Palmyra Island.

"Was there any discussion of any accident or disappearances or mishaps on that island?" asked Enoki.

"No."

I had talked to Peters at considerable length in the past few months, and I was now prepared to try to turn him into a witness far more valuable to the defense than he'd proved to be for the Government.

I first got him to clarify that only Buck, not Jennifer, pointed to the *Sea Wind*, and that Buck had said, "That's *my* boat."

"Mr. Peters, you were still moored in the Ala Wai yacht harbor on the morning of October 29, 1974. Is that correct?"

"That's correct."

"On the previous evening—October 28th—did Buck and Jennifer come by your boat to pick up a bundle of dirty clothing of yours to take to shore with them and wash along with their clothing?"

"Yes."

Peters stated that he was asleep aboard his boat on October 29 when he was awakened about 2:00 A.M. by Coast Guard personnel asking questions about Jennifer and Buck.

"You're aware that around nine or ten o'clock in the morning on that same day, October 29th, Jennifer was placed under arrest?"

"Correct."

"*Before* she was arrested that morning, you saw Jennifer alone in her dinghy near her boat and told her that the authorities had been by earlier looking for her and Buck. Is that correct?"

"That's correct."

"*Shortly after* you had told her that the authorities were looking for her, do you recall Jennifer coming to your boat to bring back your laundry?"

"I don't clearly recall at this time," Peters said, backing down on a very critical point.

"I've spoken to you several times in Los Angeles. Is that correct?"

"Correct."

"Do you recall telling me, every time I have spoken to you, that *after* you told Jennifer that the authorities were looking for her and Buck, she came by your boat alone—not with Buck Walker—to return your clothing to you? Do you remember telling me that?"

"Yes."

"And is that correct?"

"I believe it's correct."

"In any event, she *did* return your laundry. You got that laundry back that morning?"

"I believe so, yes."

"And to the best of your recollection now, this happened *after* you informed her that the authorities were looking for her and Buck?"

"To the best of my recollection, yes."

"Is it a fact that shortly after she returned your laundry to you, you became aware of Jennifer being placed under arrest in the harbor?"

"That's correct."

On re-direct, Enoki wanted to know if the laundry Jennifer had returned to Peters was dirty or clean.

"At this point," Peters said, "I don't remember whether it was dirty or clean."

"Do you recall telling me previously that you thought it was dirty?"

"No, not clearly."

The prosecutor apparently wanted to indict Jennifer for not having done Joel's laundry as promised. The point was that Jennifer had taken the time to return the clothing even though she knew that the authorities were in hot pursuit. I would have a lot to say about this in my summation.

As Peters stepped down from the stand and passed in front of the defense table, Jennifer smiled at him and whispered, "It was clean, Joel."

He nodded and grinned.

The Government next called Donald Stevens. The square-jawed Stevens, wearing a navy-blue sweater, looked like the quintessential man of the sea. In a husky voice, the naval architecture graduate from the University of Michigan said he designed ships for a living in Portland, Oregon. He'd logged some twenty thousand miles of ocean sailing, including a visit to Palmyra in July 1974 aboard his sailboat, the *Shearwater*, with his friend Bill Larson.

Asked by Schroeder to describe the condition of the *Iola*, Stevens responded that she was an "older-looking boat, slightly run-down." He also noticed cracks in the fiberglass "between the wood planks," indicating water leakage.

Stevens said he and Larson spent most of their time working on the *Shearwater* and exploring Palmyra. In between, they visited with the other folks on the island. Jennifer told him the *Iola* had leaked during the trip down from Hawaii, necessitating constant pumping. He also learned that her provisions were low. "We gave them a bag of corn flour and several tins of corned beef," he said.

Schroeder brought out that the Grahams had on one occasion come aboard the *Shearwater* and that Stevens had visited the *Sea Wind* three times. But not once had he seen Jennifer Jenkins or Roy Allen aboard the Grahams' boat.

Stevens said he went out on the Zodiac with Mac more than once. "He handled the dinghy very aptly. He was a competent and experienced sailor."

The witness recalled the time he and Larson were invited by the Grahams to explore on the opposite side of the lagoon, and he and his friend had invited Jennifer. When Muff found out Jennifer had been invited, she was displeased, telling Stevens and his friend they shouldn't have invited her.

Although the naval architect's testimony on direct was not help-ful to the defense, it was refreshing after that of the Leonards. Clearly, he was not out to "get" Jennifer. Stevens replied in a care-ful, thoughtful way, never offering more than he was asked. At the start of cross-examination, Len underscored this not-so-subtle difference.

"You don't feel like you belong to either side in this case," Weinglass said. "You're just here to tell the truth."

"That's right."

Len wanted to know if in the nine days that Stevens was on Palmyra, he had come to know Jennifer well.

"Yes."

"Did you find her to be friendly?"

"Yes."

Stevens, who testified he had actually boarded the *Iola*, repeated his testimony at Buck's trial that although he would never have purchased the *Iola*, he felt the boat was "seaworthy."

Next, Stevens refuted Jack Wheeler's testimony that sailing from Palmyra to Fanning would have been impossible because of the pre-vailing winds and current. When the *Shearwater* departed Palmyra under sail, Stevens explained, they headed east to a point just north of Fanning, at which point they turned north toward Hawaii.

"You could have just dropped down into Fanning while under sail?"

"Yes, we could have."

"So, in your opinion it would be possible to sail from Palmyra to Fanning?"

"Yes."

If the Government had not called Stevens to the stand, we certainly would have had reason to do so.

In pursuance of the accidental-death possibility, Len next brought out that Stevens had been in the Zodiac when Mac was racing so fast that the nose of the craft "planed" out of the water as high as twenty-five degrees before settling down to a fifteen-degree angle. And yes, Stevens agreed, there were plenty of aggressive sharks at Palmyra.

On re-direct, Schroeder wanted to know if returning to Hawaii from Palmyra would be a more difficult sail than coming down.

"Yes, because it's against the wind *and* current."

"Would it not be a somewhat frightening experience to be sailing a thousand miles against the wind and current on a boat that was leaking?"

Stevens didn't answer directly, only saying that "if it was leaking, it would tend to leak more going against the wind."

Tom Wolfe, now sporting a full beard, but wearing a conservative dark-blue suit befitting his occupation as a consulting engineer, next came to the stand.

Wolfe, who had logged "pushing forty or fifty thousand miles" at sea under sail, testified he "would not have taken a long voyage in the *Iola*," that the boat "did not appear to be seaworthy to me."

Wolfe was a critically important witness, since he and his crew mate had been the last persons to observe the relationship between the Grahams and Buck and Jennifer, just two weeks before the murders.

"Did you ever have occasion to talk to Miss Jenkins about how she and Roy got along with the Grahams?" Schroeder asked.

"Yes, she indicated to me, well, the best way to express it," Wolfe said, "would be that both couples had come down to Palmyra expecting to live on a deserted island as the only couple, and there were other people there, and it had been an irritation to both of them. Both couples felt that the other had invaded their privacy." Wolfe said it was his impression from talking to Jennifer that the two couples were no longer speaking to each other.

Thus far, this was the strongest* and most damaging testimony at either Jennifer's or Buck's trial that there was friction between the two couples, since this allegedly came from Jennifer's own lips.

"Did Jennifer ever talk to you about the state of their food provisions?" Schroeder asked.

"Yes, she did."

"And what did she say about that?"

"She said they were out of nearly everything. No sugar. No flour. No meat."

"Did she mention what they had been eating?"

"Coconuts and fish."

"And did she say anything about that?"

"She said she was sick and tired of eating coconuts and fish."

Wolfe went on to say that Jennifer characterized her efforts to grow a vegetable garden as unsuccessful.† He said he gave Jennifer

---

*Muff's letters, being inadmissible hearsay, were never introduced at the trial. Moreover, even they did not reflect any ill feelings about Buck and Jennifer on Mac's part, only Muff's. Likewise with Mrs. Leonard's testimony, which only dealt with Muff's, not Mac's, fears. And there had not previously been any testimony or indication at all that Buck and Jennifer harbored any resentment toward the Grahams.
†The Government had already marked as an exhibit (for the jury's eventual scrutiny once it was received into evidence) the log of the *Iola*, found by the authorities on the *Sea Wind* on October 30, 1974. We had requested that any passages relating to drug use be excised, along with coarse sexual excerpts (for example, Jennifer's July 16, 1974, entry, "R and I smoked some hash and had an exquisite fuck," and an August 4 entry where she said that she had challenged Buck in a chess match "for a body rub and bj—which much to his chagrin I won. Finest rub of the year and an excellent bj and fuck thrown in"), fearing such references would unjustifiably prejudice some jurors against Jennifer. The Government had consented, on the condition that any mention in the log of Jennifer's considerable efforts to plant a vegetable garden be similarly expunged. (However, the agreement did not preclude either side, independent of the log, from inquiring of any witness about Jennifer's efforts to grow vegetables.) The prosecutors feared that even the potential existence of a vegetable garden went counter to their position that Jennifer and Buck faced starvation. We felt we'd easily come out ahead. Since the putative vegetable garden hadn't produced any vegetables, as Wolfe, the prosecution's own witness, had just testified, there was no way its existence could hurt the prosecution, whereas Jennifer's and Buck's affinity for drugs and Jennifer's latrine language could only have a negative impact on the jury.

flour and sugar out of pity, and that she subsequently baked and delivered a loaf of bread to the *Toloa*.

Like Stevens and the Leonards, Wolfe said he'd visited the *Sea Wind* a number of times and had had the Grahams over to his boat, but not once had he observed such reciprocal visits between the Grahams and Jennifer and her boyfriend.

"What did you observe regarding the *Sea Wind*'s food supplies?" Schroeder asked.

"The *Sea Wind*'s food supplies made my mouth water. They had canned hams and big, whole frozen turkeys and chickens. All sorts of fancy foods, canned and otherwise. Large bags of flour and rice."

Court now recessed, and the jury filed from the room. A few minutes earlier, during a lull in the questioning, I had gone over to Schroeder and reminded him that before he attempted to introduce Wolfe's testimony concerning the missing rat poison, he should ask for the recess.

It was now time for the judge to resolve an issue I had raised in a written motion on the eve of trial as to whether the Government should be allowed to introduce testimony that was so prejudicial at Buck Walker's murder trial.

"What are you going to ask the witness, Mr. Schroeder?" Judge King asked once the door to his right closed behind the last juror.

"Your honor, Mr. Wolfe had observed a fairly good supply of rat poison in a shed on the island. On the day before he left the island, he observed that the rat poison was gone. He got very concerned and he told the Grahams about this."

Schroeder said it was important in establishing the state of mind of the Grahams. The jury might infer, he continued, that if the Grahams were aware that this rat poison had been taken from the shed, they would have been far less apt to invite Jennifer and Buck aboard the *Sea Wind* for dinner on August 30.

Obviously, that was not the real reason the prosecution wanted to slip in the rat-poison testimony.

"Let me hear from Mr. Bugliosi."

"Your honor," I said, "there's a very cogent reason why the rat-poison testimony should not come in." I referred to Rule 403 of the Federal Rules of Evidence, which provides that evidence should be excluded if its probative value is substantially out-weighed by the danger of unfair prejudice.

"The Government realizes that the danger of unfair prejudice is great if the rat poison comes in," I continued, "and that's why, in their brief, they never even attempted to respond to my Rule 403 objection, even though it was the centerpiece of my brief. There is only one reason why the Government is offering the rat-poison testimony: to imply to the jury that the Grahams were poisoned to death. They want to do this by way of a free ride without produc-ing one speck of evidence that Muff Graham was poisoned to death, and they don't have the candor to admit that to this court.

"They want the jury to believe that the cake that Buck and Jen-nifer allegedly brought to Mac and Muff was laced with rat poi-son. At Buck Walker's trial, they even called Shoemaker for the cake testimony *immediately after* Wolfe testified to the rat poison. Not a coincidental coupling of witnesses, I am sure. The court has my declaration under penalty of perjury about the enormous prej-udice that most likely occurred at Buck Walker's trial when that testimony came in—spectators in the corridor speculating that the cake was laced with rat poison.

"Their contention that they're offering the rat-poison testi-mony to show that the Grahams wouldn't have invited Buck and Jennifer aboard the *Sea Wind* is just pure buncombe. They don't need it to prove that point. They have all types of other evidence, including Muff's apparent deathly fear of Buck, the cultural differ-ences between the two couples, and testimony that the Grahams would never invite someone aboard their boat if they weren't pres-ent. So it should also be excluded as cumulative."

Telling the court that with respect to the Government's moti-vation, "I don't smell rat poison here. I smell a rat," I said the defense was "extremely concerned about this issue. I can't tell you how serious this—"

"You don't have to," Judge King said. "Otherwise you wouldn't argue."

"But this particular issue is more—"

"Have you finished your argument?" the judge interrupted.

"Yes."

Looking to the Government lawyers, Judge King asked dead-pan: "Any rebuttal?"

Schroeder acknowledged that the defense would be entitled to a cautionary instruction from the court that the rat-poison evidence be considered by the jury only as it related to the state of mind of the Grahams. "But Mr. Enoki is familiar with the forensic evidence on whether or not poison was found in the skeletal remains of Mrs. Graham."

"Well, there wasn't any found, was there?" asked the judge.

Enoki now stood next to his co-counsel. "We have no evidence of poison in the bones," he admitted.

Judge King was ready to make a ruling. "I'm satisfied that the rat-poison testimony should be excluded in this case for the reasons Mr. Bugliosi gave. You already have all the state of mind you need, and also, this particular piece of evidence is more prejudicial than probative on that issue. I will sustain the objection to the evidence about the rat poison. Let's call the jury back." It was a crucial victory for the defense.

From my several telephone interviews with Wolfe, on cross-examination I put him in the same "fair and factual" category of Government witness as I did Don Stevens and several others. I knew he would allow me to extract a number of points favorable to Jennifer.

First, I elicited Wolfe's testimony that he became aware while he was on Palmyra that on occasion Mac Graham would bring some of the fish he caught over to Buck and Jennifer. Next, I established that Wolfe had been in the Graham's Zodiac dinghy many times. Asking Wolfe to stand up and take a look at the aluminum box found next to Muff's remains, I asked if the container would fit inside Mac's Zodiac.

"It would be bulky, but you could get it in."

Moving along, I asked a series of questions the answers to which would help me make the argument in summation that Buck Walker not only murdered Muff Graham, but he did it alone and without Jennifer's knowledge:

Was it the witness's impression, I asked, that Buck slept alone in his tent on the island at night and Jennifer slept aboard the *Iola*?

(Jennifer, of course, would herself testify that Buck lived on shore, but independent corroboration was important.)

Wolfe retreated a tad from the positive statement he had made to me during my interviews of him. "That was my impression," he said, "but I never saw any conclusive evidence of that."

I next showed the witness Buck Walker's .22 revolver, which had been found on the *Sea Wind* when it was searched by authorities in the Ala Wai harbor. "This was the revolver you saw Buck Walker remove from his tent before you went fishing?"

"That's correct."

In the argument I had already crafted, I needed to show that the revolver Buck had on Palmyra was taken by him aboard the *Sea Wind* back to Honolulu.

I asked Wolfe about the time he and the Grahams had gone exploring and Mac, anticipating a return after dark, had turned on the *Sea Wind*'s masthead light. Wolfe confirmed the incident, noting that it was particularly important at Palmyra to leave lights on in the event of a planned return after sunset because the island was close to the equator. "Once the sun started to go down," he added, "darkness fell very quickly."

"It's true, is it not, that from where your boat and the *Iola* were situated, looking toward shore, you could not see anything at all, except heavy foliage and vegetation?" I asked.

"Well, as I recall, that's correct, yeah."

I next elicited that it was no exaggeration to say that "millions of birds" lived on Palmyra and were very noisy.

I now moved on to other matters:

"Where was Mac's workshop located in relation to the *Sea Wind*?" I asked.

"The workshop was very close to the *Sea Wind*, fifty feet maybe. But you had to walk into the trees to reach it."

"You saw Mac in the workshop many times without Muff being present?"

"I saw him at the workshop at times when Mrs. Graham was on their boat."

"You testified yesterday about this conversation you had with Jennifer with respect to the relationship between the Grahams and

Buck and Jennifer," I said. "During this conversation, *Jennifer told you, did she not, that she and Buck were going to Fanning?*"

"That's correct."

If there was one piece of unequivocal testimony I wanted out of Wolfe more than anything else, this was it. I had asked the question with fingers figuratively crossed, since Wolfe, though impartial, could be unexpectedly and disconcertingly indefinite in some of his answers.

I next elicited the fact that when Buck Walker's dog bit Wolfe, Buck never even apologized.

"Mr. Wolfe, would you describe for the jury, who never met the man, your impression of Buck Walker? What type of person was he?"

Schroeder came to his feet. "Your honor," he said, "we would think that that would be irrelevant."

If Buck Walker was a nonperson at this trial, that was just fine with the prosecution. But it wasn't for the defense.

Court: "Overruled."

"He didn't talk a lot," Wolfe finally answered. "It was very, very hard to get any conversation out of him. He was difficult for me to relate to, personally."

"Did you tell me, in describing him, that 'he was a scary guy'?"

"Yeah, I remember. And that's true."

"You also told me you became afraid of Buck Walker. Is that correct?"

"No, I wasn't afraid of Buck Walker. I was *wary* of him."

"What about Jennifer?" I asked. "Were you afraid or wary of her at all?"

"My relations with Jennifer were always friendly, cordial."

"Did you tell me that you liked Jennifer?"

"I said I sort of liked her."

Finally, I wanted Wolfe's help on suggesting to the jury why Buck would have put the bodies in the aluminum boxes and dumped them in the lagoon.

"There's just a few inches of soil above the coral rock on Palmyra?" I asked. "Is that correct?"

"That is correct."

"So, one could not dig a deep hole on the island?"

"Not with any conventional tools, no."

On re-direct, Schroeder asked Wolfe if it would be difficult for a man to climb into the Zodiac after loading aboard *two* boxes the size of the one in the courtroom.

"I think he'd have trouble getting himself into the Zodiac with two boxes aboard."

"After you were bitten by the dog, did Jennifer apologize or say anything to you?"

"No, she didn't."

Jennifer had told me she had.

Schroeder wanted to know what Wolfe thought about a trip to Fanning on a sailboat with no motor.

"It would have been very tough," Wolfe replied. "Fanning is directly upwind from Palmyra. And there's big waves and lots of wind and that's a very rough trip in a small boat."

"Would you have been willing to go to Fanning Island in the *Iola*?"

"No. No way."

On re-cross, I came back to the aluminum boxes. "Mr. Wolfe, if one wanted to, one certainly could get on the Zodiac with two of these containers aboard. Is that correct?"

"Probably one could get the two boxes in there and sit on one of them."

As Tom Wolfe stepped down and walked from the courtroom, I knew he must have been relieved that the Palmyra chapter of his life had just ended. A short visit to an isolated Pacific atoll twelve years earlier had come to require his testimony at *four* criminal trials in Hawaii and California. Curiously, appearing at Jennifer's murder trial may have been the most difficult, because of an incident only a month earlier at his rented Puget Sound beach home in the Seattle suburb of Magnolia.

One night, a fierce storm with howling winds and driving rain had hit from the south. By morning it had cleared, and Wolfe went out at first light for a walk along the shore. Just forty feet from his house, washed up on some rocks, lay a long tube of what looked to be a rolled-up navigational chart. Wolfe flicked some seaweed away and unrolled his finding. Unbelievably, it was a chart of *Palmyra Island*!

In telling me this strange tale, Wolfe wondered what forces in the universe could have caused the Palmyra chart to wash up literally at his doorstep on the eve of Jennifer's trial. "Finding that damn chart was eerie, Vince. I'm not the superstitious type, but I'll admit, it *really* shook me. It was as if Palmyra—the island itself—had reached out and touched me from three thousand miles away."

CHAPTER 35

THE GOVERNMENT'S NEXT TWO witnesses, Dr. Douglas Uberlaker, the anthropologist, and San Francisco chief medical examiner Dr. Boyd Stephens, would provide, with slight variation, the same scientific and medical evidence they had at the Walker trial. This time, though, their testimony would be helpful to the defense as well.

We needed this evidence because I planned to use much of it to prosecute Buck and exonerate Jennifer. For instance, I had already prepared arguments on why a sledgehammer-type instrument rather than a gun was probably used on Muff, why there were only *localized* burn marks on Muff's skull, and so forth. In fact, if the Government never presented this evidence, the defense would have had to do so. But this would have involved spending a considerable amount of time and effort working with the various experts, and the cost of their witness fees, plus their transportation, hotel, and meals, would have been exorbitant, if not actually prohibitive. The defense budget for such expenses was not substantial,* and Len and I did everything possible to pare costs without com-

---

*Jennifer's brother paid for all the legal fees and bills in this case. Not every sister is lucky enough to have a brother like Ted Jenkins.

promising the quality of our defense. So, unwittingly, Enoki was underwriting an important part of our case.

It was now time for Jennifer's jury to see what was left of Muff Graham—the woman she was accused of murdering—in death.

Asked by Enoki to identify the contents of the cardboard box before him, Uberlaker peered inside, but removed nothing.

"Do those appear to be the same skeletal remains of an adult Caucasian female that you examined in 1981?" asked Enoki.

"Yes, they do."

"Would you examine the contents of the box and see if the skull you examined is in there?"

Uberlaker reached into the box with his long, thin hands, rustling the collection of plastic bags. He lifted out Muff's skull, holding it in the casual way a shopper might balance a cantaloupe at the produce stand before deciding to buy it. To the anthropologist, this was nothing more than a scientific specimen to be examined and analyzed. Uberlaker smiled, actually smiled, and said nonchalantly: "This appears to be it."

"Is there an exhibit number on the side of it?" Enoki asked clinically.

"Government exhibit 24,"* Uberlaker said, reading the tag.

Everyone in the courtroom understood this had once been Muff Graham, and we were all faced with the stark reality that a human being now lay in tagged pieces piled in a supermarket carton. The two openings where Muff's eyes had been had an uncanny way of catching a shadow from the overhead lights. Whenever Uberlaker moved the skull, the shadows narrowed or widened, rather like shifting eyes watching over the proceedings. Only a few of her top teeth, so white and gleaming in life, remained. They were now badly yellowed and broken. The gold cap on the upper left was perfectly intact, however, as it had been when its bright gleam caught Sharon Jordan's attention. Muff's bottom row of teeth, the jury would soon learn, was set in the

---

*Despite the many court and jury murder trials I've handled, I've never become inured to violence, or its handiwork. Even the reference to any part of the victim as an "exhibit," while proper and unavoidable, has always seemed somehow sacrilegious to me.

detached jawbone, which carried another exhibit tag and was still inside the box in a plastic bag.

A pallor had settled over the faces in the jury box. Every juror in a murder case awaits that moment of connecting with the victim for the first time. Almost invariably, it is evoked by a gruesome photograph of the murdered victim. Seldom do grisly remains like a skull and bones come before a jury. The jurors had seen photos of a smiling Muff standing next to her husband aboard the *Sea Wind*. They knew that the disassembled skeleton in the carton was not an anthropologist's research material, but belonged to the same Eleanor "Muff" Graham, loving wife, devoted daughter, attentive friend. Now: murder victim. For the jurors, their responsibilities had suddenly transcended civic duty. There was now a visceral bond to *their* victim that would not dissipate during the trial. Such a bond, though not necessarily detrimental to the accused, can never be helpful.

After Uberlaker ruled out sunlight and fossilization as the reason for the whitened area on the left side of the skull, Enoki asked if the simple process of decomposition and decay could have caused the whitened area. Uberlaker responded that in examining in excess of ten thousand skulls in his twenty-year career, some of them tens of thousands of years old, he had never seen "natural processes that had an effect like this one."

The inference was inescapable. Muff had been *burned by human hands*.

After Enoki read a two-sentence stipulation that the remains were those of Mrs. Eleanor Graham, Weinglass began his cross-examination. It was soon clear that Len had receded even further to his original position of challenging the murder. He asked, "You can't tell the court and jury, based on your examination of the skeletal remains, what the cause of death was?"

"No, I can't."

Len then asked, "In your examination of the skeletal remains, you found no signs of foul play?"

"No."

Judge King registered unhappy surprise. "You found *no* signs of foul play?"

"There's nothing on the skeleton," the anthropologist answered evenly, "that I can positively say is an indication of foul play."

Uberlaker was demonstrating what trial lawyers all know. "Experts" don't always testify like experts. He had testified on direct examination that "extreme heat" was applied to Muff's skull "at about the time of death" by nonnatural means. This was certainly an indication of foul play.

Still doggedly pursuing the non-murder theory, Len asked: "Now, you've previously stated under oath [at the Walker trial] that you found some black residue areas on the skull indicating a second burning *years after* the flesh was off the skull, isn't that correct?"

"Yes."

"When the prosecutors visited you in 1984, did they tell you that Gilbertese natives had visited the island five years after the disappearance of Muff Graham and had left just seven months before the bones were found?"

"No." Still outwardly dispassionate, the witness nonetheless perked up with scientific curiosity.

"If you had this information, and given your opinion about a second burn on the skull that occurred years after death, would you have inquired as to the ritual practices of the Gilbertese natives?"*

"Well, perhaps I would have. Or I might have recommended to the investigative officials that they look into it."

"But that wasn't done."

"It wasn't done."

Tinged with exoticism, the "second burning" possibility deepened the mystery of the case.

Weinglass now asked about the hole in the skull. "In your written report did you write, 'The hole in the left temporal area appears to have been made by erosion, not by trauma or projectile'?"

"That sounds correct."

Enoki lowered his head. In his opening statement, he had suggested that the hole in the skull was from a gunshot.

---

*Weinglass said his purpose in interjecting the reference to the Gilbertese was "to create a kind of smoke screen." He said he had heard or read that the Gilbertese have a ritual of putting human corpses into containers and setting the remains on fire. But Len forgot to mention this ritual in his question to Uberlaker.

Weinglass asked next about the fractures to Muff's bones. "You can't tell if those fractures occurred prior to death or during the process of death or years after death, can you?"

"I think I can say, fairly confidently, they did not occur a long period before death because there's no evidence of a healing process that took place. But," continued the doctor whose specialty was the detritus of death, "I cannot determine whether or not those fractures occurred at about the time of death or long after death."

"So, those fractures which you found could have occurred in the bones years later?"

"Theoretically, yes."

With Len contesting the murder, while I had already announced to Enoki that provisionally I would concede it, I couldn't help but wonder if the prosecutors were thinking, *What type of fractured defense is this?* But it was a disagreement in tactics that fortunately was not injurious to our cause.

Although Len was handling all the medical and scientific witnesses, I worked closely with him and suggested a question here and there to elicit testimony I needed for my summation. On one occasion, if the jury was listening closely, Len sounded as if he was trying to proceed in two opposite directions at the same time. I had Len (after he had just asked questions designed to show the possibility of *no* foul play in Muff's death, and that the whitening to the skull could have occurred as a result of a fire on the beach long after Muff's death) ask Uberlaker two other questions. First, could an acetylene torch (which the jury knew Mac had on Palmyra, and hence was available to Buck) have caused the whitening? Yes, Uberlaker answered. Second, could the whitening have been caused by the application of the torch for as short a time as five minutes? Again, yes.

It was one thing for Uberlaker, the expert witness, to have given clearly inconsistent testimony previously ("extreme heat" being applied to Muff's skull "at about the time of death" was no sign of foul play), but with Len's last two questions the jury probably thought the good doctor's confusion had become contagious and infected my co-counsel.

Uberlaker had no sooner stepped down from the witness stand than portly Dr. Boyd Stephens was already ambling across the courtroom in a sport coat that looked as if it had shrunk. His coat clashed with his slacks, too short by several inches, and his bow tie was crooked. Dr. Stephens evidently had weightier matters on his mind than stylish wardrobe.

Dr. Stephens supported his description of himself as an expert in the "morbid sciences" by estimating he'd examined "many thousands" of dead bodies, including persons who had died by fire, drowning, gunshot, and other assorted calamities. However, the pathologist once again admitted that after examining the remains of Muff Graham, he was unable to determine the cause of death.

Enoki asked Dr. Stephens if he found any evidence of stabbing on the skeletal remains.

"No," Dr. Stephens replied.

"Any evidence of poisoning?"

"No."

With the rat-poison testimony excluded, this interchange did not harm the prosecution. But what benefit did Enoki hope to achieve?

"Did you specifically test for poison?"

Why was Enoki continuing to pursue this matter when there was no evidence of poison?

"No, but if a person had been exposed, for instance, to arsenic over a long period of time and it was actually in the bone substance, then I should have picked up on it. *A short exposure I wouldn't have seen.*"

It seemed Enoki was trying to drop a seed in the jury's mind that there may have been poison in the cake that Jennifer and Buck had allegedly brought to the Grahams on August 28. But how could I respond without making the possibility even more prominent in the jury's mind than it might already be in its unstated but implied form?

Enoki next explored the possibility that Muff had been shot to death, and in more depth than he had at the Walker trial. Under his questioning, Dr. Stephens said the hole above the left ear in Muff Graham's skull had a "very roughened margin" associated with "coning," which he defined using the example of a BB shot hitting a plate-glass window. The force causes a concentric (circles with a common center) expansion of the hole in the direction of travel; that is, the hole gets larger as the force pushes *inward*. But since the hole in the skull in this case was larger on the outermost surface of the skull, the prosecutor asked for an explanation.

In a "contact gunshot" wound, in which the muzzle of the gun is touching or very close to the body, the gas pressure generated by the burning of gunpowder in the closed confines of the skull would cause *reverse* coning, said Dr. Stephens. "In other words, the coning would be in the opposite direction of travel"—the hole would be largest at the force's initial point of entry and would get smaller as it proceeded inward.

"If this hole is a gunshot wound, it's a contact gunshot wound," Dr. Stephens concluded.

If Muff had been shot, then, it had been at point-blank range, execution-style.

The absence of an exit wound did *not* rule out a gunshot wound, Dr. Stephens said. "We've had many examples of contact gunshot wounds where the bullet does not make it to the other side of the skull."

Enoki asked for permission to approach the witness with Buck's revolver in his hand.

"I'll let you take it up there," Judge King said. In an aside directed to me, the judge said dryly, "There are some exceptions, Mr. Bugliosi. Skulls and guns."

During a recess several witnesses back, I'd asked the court clerk to ask the judge whether I could approach the witness during my cross. The clerk had returned from Judge King's chambers with his answer: *No.* Then, five minutes later, she had come back and said the judge had changed his mind. I could approach the witness, but only if I asked for permission to do so *before the jury*. I told the clerk, "Tell the judge I reject his counteroffer." *Credibility* with the jury. Enoki had approached witnesses with the skull and now the gun, but each time he had been required to ask permission in front of the jury like a schoolchild asking to go to the bathroom.

Dr. Stephens held the gun with the aplomb expected of someone with a working knowledge of the various means of death. "I've examined this before," he said. "It's a .22-caliber Ruger Bearclaw."

"Is there anything about this pistol or the caliber of this pistol that would preclude it from being the source of that hole in exhibit 24, the skull?"

"No, there is not. A .22-caliber pistol has all the capabilities necessary to make such a wound, both in penetrating the skull and even producing the reverse coning."

After a short recess, Weinglass approached the podium with his characteristic smile and friendly greeting. His kindly courtroom style never faltered.

He asked if Dr. Stephens knew that Uberlaker, the Government's anthropologist, had thought the hole in the skull was caused by erosion.

"Yes, I have heard that. And I disagree."

"If it is a gunshot wound, and if that gun were held up against the head that way, and fired, the fact it was held right up against the head would reduce the sound?"

"That's true. It would reduce the sound."

"And I believe you told me that if this had happened, that someone standing two hundred yards away, if there were trees rustling and other background noise, they wouldn't hear the gunshot."

"They might not. Two hundred yards is two football-field lengths, just to put it into perspective."

Weinglass shuffled some papers, then asked, as he had with Uberlaker, if the whitening on the skull might have occurred to the bare bone while other areas were protected by, for example, sand on the beach.

"I cannot rule that out."

"And you also said that for every hypothesis here, there's a significant amount of argument against the hypothesis."

"Yes. It almost sounds like Newton's theory of forensic medicine. For each hypothesis, there's an equal and opposite."

After Enoki's brief re-direct, Judge King asked the witness if he thought the burn marks were from one or two burnings. One, said the medical examiner.

On re-cross, Weinglass emphasized this latest conflict between the Government's two expert witnesses. "Are you aware that Dr. Uberlaker believes the burn marks indicate two burnings?"

"No, I wasn't."

If two distinguished experts in the fields of pathology and anthropology couldn't agree, one could hardly expect the jury, or anyone else for that matter, to resolve all of the mysteries of the Palmyra Island murder case.

AS DR. BOYD Stephens was concluding his testimony, two women jurors from the Walker murder trial appeared in court. They had come separately, and their arrival within minutes of each other was purely coincidental. They smiled and gave each other half-waves from opposite sides of the gallery. They were there for the same reason.

"We heard so much about Jennifer," said Dorothy Nelson. "I was . . . well, curious."

"I wanted to see her for myself," explained Robyn Schaffer, who had been so unnerved by Buck Walker's wrathful stare. "I don't know if Jennifer did it or not, but I *do* know she had terrible taste in men."

ALL FOUR of the FBI crime lab experts who had taken the stand at the Walker trial came forward to repeat their findings. The microscopy expert testified to his discovering the piece of cotton fabric stuck to the bottom of the container and determining it had been exposed to "extreme heat or burning"; the chemist to the series of complex tests he'd conducted which allowed him to identify a "waxlike" substance found inside the box as indicative of fatty acids given off from a human body in a state of decomposition in an anaerobic (airless) environment, such as underwater; the serologist to his performing the screening tests for human protein on the piece of fabric and receiving positive results; and the metallurgist to the aluminum alloy inside of the container having been subjected to an intense fire fueled by an accelerant.

On cross, Weinglass asked the metallurgist: "This container had been on the island of Palmyra, if we accept Mr. Wheeler's word, for at least seventeen years prior to 1974. Could you tell the court and jury when, during that seventeen-year period, the fire that you claim you detected occurred in this box?"

"Not specifically."

"The fire might have been anytime from 1957 to 1974 before it was put under water?"

"Yes."

"And you told me out in the hall before you testified, did you not, that you thought the fire might have been fifteen or twenty minutes in duration?"

"You asked me what kind of time frame I would offer as to requiring the type of effects I saw on the interior of the container [enlargement of the grains of the metal], and I indicated *I wouldn't expect all the characteristics to exist below fifteen or twenty minutes*, but they could have occurred from a fire that lasted *hours*."

When Len finished with his cross-examination and returned to the counsel table, I asked him what reason he had had for eliciting this latter testimony. Len had wanted to show the brevity of the fire (the longer the fire, the less likely Jennifer's story that she saw no smoke on Palmyra on August 30) but had been given a *minimum* of fifteen or twenty minutes—a dangerously long time for our purposes. As they used to say in the courts of southern Louisiana, the prosecution had been given a lagniappe (gratuity).

The Government's last expert witness was Dr. Oliver Harris, the odontologist from Walker's trial, who once again testified to his finding the evidence of blunt trauma to an upper left molar in Muff's skull and a lower right molar in the jawbone. Asked by Enoki for examples of blunt-force trauma, the odontologist answered, "A large round rock, a sledgehammer, but not a fist. A fist could not deliver that much force."

On cross, Weinglass asked if the expert knew whether the fractures had occurred at the time of death.

"No, I do not know that."

As expected, the expert testimony had been gruesome as well as technical. Sledgehammer-type blows to the head, leg bones wrenched back and broken, an acetylene torch searing Muff's head, and her body being set on fire—scarcely conceivable as actions of the pleasant-looking woman seated beside me. But to convict her of murder, the jury would *not* have to picture her swinging the sledgehammer or wielding the torch. It would be sufficient to conclude that she'd been *involved in the decision* to kill the Grahams.

I sat at the counsel table, studying the two rows of jurors, trying to sense somehow their feelings about the case, but their faces were as unrevealing as those at a black-tie poker game. Had they already convicted Jennifer in their minds, and were just going through the motions, as for all intents and purposes another jury had at Buck's trial?

The answer was days away, but rapidly approaching.

CHAPTER 36

THE ASSISTANT U.S. ATTORNEY who had successfully prosecuted the boat-theft cases—only to lose Walker's conviction on appeal—was now in private practice in Honolulu. William Eggers, immaculately dressed in a steel-gray pinstripe suit, came to the stand to testify about the November 1974 search of Palmyra.

Eggers, understandably, had the appearance and mannerisms of someone more comfortable asking questions in a court of law than answering them. The suntanned former prosecutor went on for several minutes—with few interruptions from Enoki—describing in detail the atoll's terrain, his group's search, and their failure to find any sign of the Grahams or any indications of foul play.

On cross, Weinglass began, "The beach at Strawn Island—there are parts of it where the land comes close to the water's edge and other places where the land is set back, creating small bays?"

"Yes."

"There are parts of that beach that are six and eight feet above the high-water mark?"

"There are parts that are dry, yes."

Len next had Eggers relate his and Jack Wheeler's frightful experience with a shark in the Palmyra lagoon.

"Aside from the sharks, did you find the atmosphere on Palmyra to be hostile?" Len now asked.

"I did."

"In what way?"

"I've thought about that," Eggers said contemplatively. "I've been in distant places during my life, and I still haven't determined whether it was the nature of the case I was helping to investigate, or the island itself. I'm uncertain to this day."

What was it about this remote, uninhabited island that so many rational people unexplainably found eerie and foreboding?

Eggers stepped down at 3:50 P.M. on Friday, February 7. The jury was excused until Monday morning.

Throughout the trial, I was increasingly concerned about Jennifer's continuing lack of proper interest in the case. Except for a very few instances, she sat passively at the counsel table, showing little of the interest or anxiety typical of a defendant charged with murder. It was strange to watch.*

Nonetheless, at the end of each day, I still reminded Jennifer to do her homework, much as I had reminded my two children, Wendy and Vince Jr., when they were younger. She was supposed to be going over her copy of my tentative Q and A, now a mound of 143 yellow legal-pad pages. She invariably complained of

*Jennifer *did* exhibit a keen interest in one of the trial participants. For some time, I'd known that unattached Jennifer was attracted to Len, who was also single. In fact, her dreamy looks at him had been so obvious that I finally warned her to cool it whenever the jury was present. "If you can be so visibly caught up with one of your lawyers even in a courtroom when you're on trial for murder," I cautioned, "the jurors may wonder what you might have been capable of doing on a deserted island with the man you loved. They may draw the inference you would have done *anything* for Buck." Jennifer had duly toned down her Len-gazing. Though they usually lunched together during the trial, I'd detected no reciprocal romantic interest on Len's part. He conducted himself toward Jennifer in a professional manner throughout.

fatigue or headache, so I knew I couldn't rely on her own initiative. I urged Ted to keep the pressure on her. More serious-minded and reality-grounded than his sister, he would always assure me he would do what he could. "She can go home with you and have a nice relaxed dinner," I would say, "and maybe rest for an hour or so, but then you've got to get her to work on the Q and A. She's going to be on the stand soon. She has to work." I also lobbied her mother to pressure Jennifer.

This weekend—when we were well into the prosecution's case—was a turning point for Jennifer. For the first time in our entire association, I began getting anxious calls at my hotel from her: "Vince, what about this?" or "I know I said this last time, but after some further thought it's not quite accurate." Never before had she taken such an active role in her defense. Finally, I guess, it had hit home that she was about to testify at her own murder trial. On Saturday, she took a room at the hotel and we worked late together the next two nights. So little time remained.

"There's one juror I don't like," Len confided as the three of us took a late-night breather in the twenty-four-hour coffee shop next to the hotel.

I flashed immediately upon the Kansas Rock, whose presence worried me well nigh incessantly. I'd noticed he took notes whenever one of the prosecutors was asking questions, but sat with his arms folded across his chest, a grim Buddha, whenever Len or I stepped to the podium. I had the sinking feeling he had already judged Jennifer guilty and was gathering tidbits from the Government's case for persuading other jurors during deliberations.

"The Kansas Rock?" I asked.

"No. It's one of the guys in the back row. He's always looking at us with such a dour expression. Like he's disgusted."

Great, I thought. *Before they've even heard the defense's case we've already got two jurors against us.*

More than once that weekend, Len fretted about the "dour" juror. Aside from the Kansas Rock, I'd not noticed any unusually hostile juror, but then I generally don't spend much time eyeing the panel. As soon as the jury entered the courtroom Monday morning, I asked Len to point out the worrisome juror. When he indicated juror number fourteen, I cracked up. Number fourteen was an alternate juror, the second alternate at that, and wouldn't participate in deliberations unless *two* regular jurors fell by the wayside. Short of an outbreak of Legionnaires' disease on the jury, Joseph Winston, a thirty-four-year-old hospital administrator, would never have a hand in deciding Jennifer's fate.

"Why are you so concerned about an alternate?" I asked, laughing with relief.

Len, ever the worrywart, said somberly, "Let's hope no one gets sick."

TRUE TO form, the Kansas Rock had his pen and notebook ready when Curt Shoemaker settled in the witness chair to testify for the Government.

The nautical-looking Shoemaker wore an old blue blazer festooned with gold buttons, over a flamboyantly patterned aloha shirt unbuttoned to mid-chest, wrinkled tan chinos, and scuffed white deck shoes. Now retired from the Hawaiian Bell phone company, he lived only part of the year on the Big Island with his younger wife, Momi, who still worked for the company. The rest of the time he sailed to faraway ports like Fiji and Tahiti on his fifty-seven-foot-yacht, the *Sivada*, which he'd designed and had built to his own specifications.

The Government entered into evidence Shoemaker's radio log for April through December 1974. In his own handwriting, the notations showed he had reached the Grahams from Hawaii on eight dates in July, and (eventually settling on a regular once-per-week contact) on August 7, 14, 21, and, finally, 28.

I knew Schroeder would elicit basically the same testimony Shoemaker had given at the Walker trial: the conversation between himself and Mac on the 28th, including the suggestive stories of the cake and the truce. Technically, his line of questions would be calling for hearsay.

Even so, I planned to waive all hearsay objections, knowing, as I've mentioned, how jurors tend to resent an attorney who wants to suppress relevant information. After all, what Mac allegedly said to Shoemaker on the last occasion he and Muff were heard from *was* extremely relevant, and the jurors would unquestionably want to hear it. I wouldn't attempt to keep them from doing so.

Shoemaker proceeded to repeat his testimony at the Walker trial, concluding by noting that after signing off with Mac on the evening of August 28, 1974, he had unsuccessfully tried to contact the Grahams three more times between September 4 (the next scheduled call) and September 18.

At least in this trial, the "cake" wouldn't be improperly coupled with testimony about missing rat poison. Nevertheless, Shoemaker's testimony caused very serious problems for us. For starters, although the *Iola's* amateurish log contained references to far less substantive matters, such as "Some rain in a.m." and "in P.M. back to Zane Grey," it made no mention of any visit to the *Sea Wind* on August 28. The prosecutors and FBI agents in the case believed that Jennifer had omitted the visit from her log for the very good reason that she and Buck had murdered Mac and Muff at that time. If the jury believed Shoemaker's testimony about the cake and truce, the damage to our side would be immense.

I headed toward the podium to commence my cross-examination of Shoemaker. After explaining to him that for convenience's sake I intended to refer collectively to his testimony about the cake and truce as the "cake-truce incident," I asked: "This last contact with Mr. Graham on the evening of August 28th, 1974, you say commenced at 7:10 P.M. and you signed off at 7:50 P.M. Is that correct?"

"Yes."

"And this incident took place right near the end of your radio contact?"

"That's right."

"Apart from this cake-truce incident, was the rest of your conversation with Mr. Graham on the evening of August 28th basically just routine conversation?"

"Prior to that, yes."

"Nothing that stands out in your mind?"

"No," he said.

"Okay. So, the cake-truce incident is what you remember most about this conversation you had with Mr. Graham on the evening of August 28th, 1974?"

"Yes."

"It sticks out in your mind above all else, is that correct?"

"Yes."

"Is the cake-truce incident the type of thing that if you live to be a hundred years old—and I hope you do, sir—and someone asks you to relate what took place during this very last contact that you ever had with Mac Graham, it would be the very first thing that entered your mind?"

Shoemaker emphatically agreed. It was something he'd never forget.

"Mr. Shoemaker, about two months after your last contact with Mac Graham, specifically on October 30th, 1974, do you remember being interviewed by FBI Special Agent Tom Kilgore at the police station in Hilo, Hawaii?"

"Yes, I do."

"And the express purpose of this interview was to find out what you knew about the Grahams and their disappearance? Is that correct?"

"Yes."

"And you certainly wanted to be helpful to the FBI agent and tell him whatever information you had which you felt was relevant?"

"Yes."

"And you told the FBI agent—I'm holding in my hand a report of your interview with Mr. Kilgore—about your radio contacts with the Grahams, did you not?"

"Yes."

"And you told him your last contact with Mac Graham was on August 28th, 1974, did you not?"

"Yes."

After next eliciting from Shoemaker that he *had* told Kilgore several insignificant, mundane things Mac had told him during this last contact, I asked:

"Mr. Shoemaker, is there any reason *why*, during this entire interview with Mr. Kilgore, you failed to mention the cake-truce incident that you've testified to here today? Any reason at all, sir?"

"No. If I did fail to—I don't remember. I'm sure I did, though."

"You're testifying now *under oath* that you are positive you told Mr. Kilgore about this cake-truce incident? You're positive about this?"

"Well, I'm not positive, but I'm . . . I feel that I did at that time. Because I was relating everything I knew to him."

I nodded, as if agreeing completely.

"Certainly you would want to tell him about that because that's the thing that sticks out in your mind above everything else. Isn't that right?" I asked.

"Well, yes. Yes."

(To impeach—challenge the credibility of—Shoemaker, I could not at this point introduce Agent Kilgore's report, even though it contained no reference to the cake-truce incident. You can use a witness's prior written statement to impeach his testimony, but here the prior statement was written by Kilgore, not Shoemaker. And Enoki had refused to stipulate that Shoemaker never told Kilgore this information. Since the jurors saw me holding Kilgore's report in my hand, however, they might draw the correct conclusion that Shoemaker had not told Kilgore. But if there was any doubt in the jury's mind about Shoemaker's not mentioning the cake-truce incident to Kilgore, I felt my next series of questions would remove that doubt.)

"Mr. Shoemaker, on June 25th, 1975, you testified at a theft trial in Honolulu. The clerk will hand you a photostatic copy of your testimony at that proceeding."

Shoemaker, still seemingly oblivious to what was happening, looked casually at the pages of transcript from Jennifer's boat-theft trial.

I directed him to read to himself certain numbered lines in the transcript. I then asked: "At that trial, to these questions did you give the following answers?" I proceeded to read aloud the prosecutor's questions and Shoemaker's answers.

Question: "What was the nature of that *last radio contact* with Mac Graham on August 28th?" Answer: "Like all the other contacts. He [Mac] related his experiences on the island. What he was doing, what he found. We talked about everything from rain to birds, sharks in the lagoon, and everything. How to fish, and what fish were poisonous. I was trying to help him out as much as I could. Also, there had been other boats on the island, and I was relaying messages from some of these other boats to their parents, and I was handling, in other words, third-party traffic."

Since Shoemaker seemed to be drifting off into matters that obviously could have taken place during conversations before the one on the date in question, the prosecutor brought him back once again to the last contact. I continued reading to the jury.

Question: "What was the nature of your *last conversation* with Mac Graham? What was the nature of *that* communication with you?" Answer: "Well, he had spoken about this prior to this. I think one of the dogs of the other two people on the island had almost attacked his wife. So there seemed to be a problem. It was a boat that had gone down there that was—according to him he said it was unseaworthy and leaking badly, and the people on the boat were having a hard time, apparently, running out of food, and these were the ones with the dogs. There were several dogs, but I think there was only one that was causing the trouble." Question: "That conversation was on the *28th of August*?" Answer: "That was on the *28th*, the *last time* I heard from them." Question: "Did you have another contact with him after that?" Answer: "No. That was the last time I heard from him and he said that the other boat was leaving the next day."

I now looked up from the transcript. "Did I read the questions and answers correctly, sir?"

"It sounds . . . yes."

"Mr. Shoemaker, I've counted seven, seven references in the transcript I just read to the fact that this was the last contact you ever had with Mac Graham. So there was no confusion as to which conversation this was. You've testified earlier how this cake-truce incident stood out in your mind above everything else. Something you would never forget as long as you live. If it actually happened, as you claim it did, can you tell this jury and Judge King *why*, when you were specifically asked to relate what was said and what took place during this very last contact that you ever had with Mac Graham, that you never felt the cake-truce incident was memorable enough or important enough to mention?"

"Mention to who?"

The whole room felt a gear disengage, I thought.

"To the lawyer who asked you to relate what took place during that conversation."

"What lawyer?"

"The person that was asking you the questions, sir, that I just read to you."

Shoemaker paled. "Well," he stammered, his lips visibly quivering. "I was only . . . answering the questions that were asked."

I had no further questions.

On re-direct, Schroeder tried his best to repair the obvious damage. "Do you recall whether you mentioned the cake-truce incident to FBI Agent Hal Marshall?"

"Yes, at my home," Shoemaker said quickly, grabbing for the life preserver. "That was last year. I discussed it with him then."

"And you specifically mentioned that incident at that time?"

"Yes."

But this was some eleven years *after* it supposedly occurred. Shoemaker's involvement in the notorious Palmyra Island murder case had undoubtedly been a dramatic peak in his life. He could be likened, I thought, to the fisherman who lets a big one get away, and the fish keeps getting bigger and bigger with each retelling. Nonetheless, although Shoemaker had fared badly on cross-examination, he didn't come across at all like the devious, lying type; he looked more like the sort of guy who goes on stage when the magician asks for volunteers. In terms of believability with the jury, that was a plus for him.

ROBERT MEHAFFY, the Sacramento college teacher, testified to the *Sea Wind*'s entering Kauai's Nawiliwili Harbor on the evening of October 12, 1974, and setting anchor next to his boat. The next day, "it was just after dinner when we heard a knock on our hull. We opened the hatch, and this couple was next to us in a dinghy.

They had a bottle of wine. They introduced themselves as Roy Allen and Jennifer Jenkins. We invited them aboard, and they stayed about three hours."

Jennifer did most of the talking, though her boyfriend did talk some, Mehaffy said. The couple mentioned a recent trip to Palmyra, but gave no details. The woman told a story about being shadowed by a large swordfish while they were becalmed at one point during their return to Hawaii. "She said this fish kept circling the boat. They heard a thump, but didn't think anything about it until later, when they went below and found the boat taking on water. They pumped out the water, and she said they found the bill of the swordfish sticking through the hull into the bilge area. They said they put an outside patch on the hole."

"Now, from your experience as a sailboat skipper," Schroeder asked, almost purring, "did you find the story to be plausible or credible?"

"Well, I told Roy at the time that it seemed to me kind of unlikely that a swordfish would have a bill strong enough to go through the oak hull of their boat."

"Did you ever ask Jennifer or Roy to show you the evidence of this swordfish attack?"

"When we were talking about it, I just simply said, 'I would like to see that. I'd like to see a hole a fish could put through a boat.'"

"Did Jennifer or Roy ever offer to show you this . . . swordfish hole?"

"No. They mentioned they had to leave the next day because the boat was still taking water, and they wanted to go someplace where they could haul it out to effect more permanent repairs."

Prior to trial, I had asked Enoki to stipulate to the following entry in an *Encyclopedia Americana* article: "The excellence of the swordfish's bill as a weapon and the power of its attack is attested by their frequent piercing of boats and even of large wooden ships, through which the sword has been deeply thrust before breaking off." Enoki had refused, telling me I'd have to call my own expert witness on this point. I surmised that the Government intended to argue that the hole was probably caused by a bullet. Why else would they be resisting the swordfish-hole theory?

Mehaffy testified that two weeks after meeting the couple, his boat was moored at the Hawaii Yacht Club in the Ala Wai harbor when their ketch entered the harbor and anchored a hundred feet or so away. The date was October 28. "As they dropped anchor," he continued, "there was a man helping me tie up another boat and he looked across the channel and said, 'That's the Grahams' boat.' I said, 'No, that's Roy and Jennifer.' He said, 'Oh, my God,' and hurriedly left."

"Do you know who that man was?" asked Schroeder.

"Bernard Leonard," said the witness.

Based upon my pretrial interviews with Mehaffy, I had intended to bring out some things I felt would be very helpful to Jennifer. But Schroeder did my job when he asked if Mehaffy had observed Jennifer and Roy at any time the following morning.

"Yes, when they left the *Sea Wind* in their dinghy to row ashore."

"Do you recall which one of them was rowing?"

"As I remember, it was Jennifer."

"Did you see either of them later?"

"Well, just a few minutes later, Jennifer rowed *back* to the boat. She was there for just a very few minutes. She was rowing back toward shore the next time I noticed. It was then that the Coast Guard patrol boat came into the harbor and speedily headed toward her."

The prosecutor had just unwittingly provided corroboration for Jennifer's story about returning Joel's laundry.

Cross-examination is limited to those matters covered by the direct examination, but I asked Judge King to permit me to take Mehaffy as my own witness on direct, which he allowed me to do.

I began by establishing Mehaffy as an expert sailor who had taught sailing classes and written articles about the sport. "Mr. Mehaffy, if a boat doesn't have an engine, can it sail—by way of what is called tacking—against the wind?"

"You can never sail *directly* into the wind. But by attacking first one side of the wind source and then the other—what we call tacking—it can go towards the direction that the wind is coming from."

Tacking was never discussed at Buck Walker's trial, although the Government urged the proposition that a sailboat without an engine could *not* sail against the wind from Palmyra to Fanning. Knowing nothing about boats and the sea, I had never heard of tacking before, but it made no sense to me that sailboats, plying the Mediterranean in ancient days long before any thought of combustion engines, could proceed at sea only with the wind at their back, or against it with oarsmen. Knowing that Fanning was against the wind, I had asked Jennifer about this and she was the one who first told me about tacking, explaining this was the way Buck and she had intended to sail to the island.

"Can you explain to the jury in a little more detail what's involved in this technique called tacking?" I asked Mehaffy.

"What you have to do is to get the sail to curve, and then as the wind comes by the sail, instead of pushing the boat, it sucks the boat ahead. When the wind comes around the side of the sail, it creates turbulence in the back that draws the boat ahead."

"Is this aerodynamic principle roughly analogous to the wind on top of an airplane wing forming a suction which holds the airplane up?"

"Yes, sir."

"So by tacking, then, even though the wind is against you, you can actually advance and proceed forward."

"That's correct."

"Does the bow of the boat, when you're tacking, have to be slanted in excess of any angle from the wind line?" I asked.

"Yes, about forty-five degrees from the wind source."

"If the angle is less than forty-five degrees, you can't tack forward."

"Yes, you're not going to go forward."

"Let's assume that not only the wind is against you, but also the current. If the wind velocity is greater than that of the current, can one tack forward against the wind *and* the current?"

"Yes."

When Schroeder took my place at the podium, he was obviously concerned over the testimony just elicited. "Mr. Mehaffy, would it be safe to say that you cannot tack everywhere? That there are conditions when you would, for example, be proceeding directly into the wind and the current where it would be extremely difficult to tack?"

"Well, in really light winds, say less than five miles an hour, and you're trying to tack into that with the current against you, you're not going to go very far, very fast."

Incredibly, up to a point, the greater the winds against you, the easier to make forward progress in a sailboat. In hoping to make the trip sound impossible, the Government had already stressed how strong the winds would have been between Fanning and Palmyra.

"Would it be safe to say," Schroeder went on, "that there are certain directions and points on the globe where it's commonly known to sailors that sailing from one point to another is extremely difficult or almost impossible?"

"Yes," Mehaffy answered. "An example being from Honolulu to San Francisco. It's very difficult without going due north out of Honolulu for eight hundred miles before you turn east."

"And would not another variable involved in sailing a difficult course, and trying to tack, be the condition of your boat?"

"Yes. Definitely."

"If your boat was unseaworthy, it would be extremely difficult, would it not?"

"Not so much difficult as dangerous. Because when you're tacking, that puts more strain on your boat. So if your boat were not seaworthy, it could tear apart."

Schroeder had done a good job in bringing up the seaworthiness of the *Iola* as a factor. But on defense, we'd strongly made our point that Jennifer had reason to believe that she and Buck *could* have made it to Fanning by tacking.

THE NEXT two prosecution witnesses, James Wollen and his wife, Lorraine, had testified at Jennifer's theft trial. Originally from Tacoma, Washington, they'd spent 1974 through 1976 living aboard their twenty-seven-foot sailboat, the *Juno*, at Pokai Bay in the town of Waianae on Oahu's western shore.

James Wollen testified to meeting Jennifer and Roy Allen in

mid-October 1974 and visiting them aboard a blue-and-white ketch they claimed was theirs. He had noticed the name *Iola* painted on the back of the boat.* Wollen was certain of this point for a good reason: he'd been born and raised in a small Kansas town named Iola.

Wollen identified a photograph of the *Sea Wind* as "the *Iola* from Pokai Bay."

Mrs. Wollen once again testified to her picking up the snapshots for Jennifer—the pictures that showed the *Iola* and *Sea Wind* sailing alongside each other in the open sea.

She had visited "the Allens" once aboard their boat, Mrs. Wollen explained. "It was very, very nice. I remember seeing things like china and crystal. It was quite plush." She repeated Jennifer's telling her how she and her boyfriend had come into possession of the beautiful yacht—they'd purchased the boat from a man who had had it some fourteen years and had become tired of the maintenance.

"Did she ever mention the names Mac or Muff or the Grahams?" Enoki asked.

"No."

"Did she ever mention anyone disappearing or having any accidents on an island named Palmyra?"

"No."

There was but one point I wanted to bring out on cross-examination—that there was a picture of the previous owners on the cabin wall of the boat.

"I don't remember that, no," Mrs. Wollen said.

I flipped to a page of Jennifer's theft-trial transcript and read a

---

*Jennifer told me that at some point in time before Pokai Bay (she couldn't remember when—it could even have been while they were still on Palmyra) Buck removed the name *Sea Wind* from the stern of the boat and painted the name *Iola* on. Upon leaving Pokai Bay, Jennifer and Buck had sailed the *Sea Wind* to Honolulu, where Buck registered the Grahams' boat under the name *Lokahi* on October 18, 1974. Under its new name (but with *Iola* still on its stern) the *Sea Wind* was in dry dock at the Hawaii Tuna Packers boatyard in Honolulu from October 22 to 28, 1974. There it was hauled out, the patched swordfish hole repaired, and the entire boat repainted, covering up the name *Iola*.

brief portion of her testimony in which she recalled noticing a picture on the cabin wall and asking Jennifer if those were the previous owners and being told yes.

"Do you recall testifying to that on a previous occasion?" I now asked.

"Yes, I do. I guess I don't remember the picture now, and that's throwing me."

KEN WHITE, the Government's boat expert, testified to his detailed examination of the nine-and-a-half-horsepower Evinrude engine from the *Sea Wind*'s Zodiac not revealing any evidence of salt water inside the motor. White had found no evidence of corrosion, either. "Corrosion from salt water is immense," he explained.

With his testimony, the Government proved beyond a shadow of a doubt that the Zodiac had *not* capsized in the Palmyra lagoon.

White went on to describe the complicated procedure for starting an engine after it has been immersed in salt water—taking the spark plugs out, drying them off, using the primer bulb to force gas through the carburetor system while extracting all the water, and finally, using a flywheel puller to clean out the magneto. (Jennifer was going to testify that Buck did none of the above, and yet the engine roared to life after he pulled the cord several times.)

White added that there was no sign that a flywheel puller had been used. "You find some scarring tissue on the side of an engine when a flywheel puller has been used. I didn't find such scarring on the Evinrude. . . . It was a very clean engine."

"Did you find any markings on the cowling [the housing] of the Evinrude that could have been left by coral?" asked Enoki.

"No, I didn't."

The prosecutor knew Jennifer would testify that the dinghy lay on the lagoon beach, described by several witnesses as mostly coral.

On cross-examination, Weinglass tried to soften White's last finding. "You weren't asked to look at the cowling at the time of your examination. You were looking to see if there was salt inside the engine. Isn't that right?"

"No. We also were asked to see if there was any abrasive areas on the Zodiac. And we did check out the engine cowling also."

At such times, it's best to move on. Rapidly.

But I was not greatly worried. Buck could have turned over the Zodiac and left it on the beach in such a manner that the cowling would not scrape against coral. After all, the Zodiac was going to be all his in the near future.

I HAD LONG believed that the next witness, retired FBI Special Agent Calvin Shishido (who was now working for a Honolulu law firm as a private eye), was among the most critically important witnesses against Jennifer. In light of Ken White's testimony, if the jury believed that Jennifer had told Shishido, as he claimed, that she and Buck found the Zodiac overturned *in* the water of the lagoon, this could devastate her credibility with the jury and very strongly indicate her guilt.

Shishido unbuttoned his beige suit jacket and made himself comfortable on the witness stand as he waited patiently for the first question. Obviously, he had been here many times before.

Enoki had Shishido relate what Jennifer had told him when he first interviewed her on the Coast Guard cutter.

". . . she said they found the Zodiac dinghy with the outboard motor *overturned in the water* the following morning. The gas tank was detached and floating nearby. . . . They continued their search for the Grahams until about September 11th, I think she said, at which time they made sail for Honolulu aboard the *Sea Wind*."

"Do you specifically remember her mentioning that the Zodiac was found overturned *in* the water?" Enoki asked, wanting to nail the point down.

"Yes."

Enoki asked Shishido what Jennifer had told him nearly twelve years earlier about the fate of the *Iola*. "She said she boarded the *Iola* and Roy Allen boarded the *Sea Wind* and they used a tow rope of approximately fifty feet in length to tow the *Iola* with the *Sea Wind*. But the *Iola* got hung up on some rocks, and they were unable to dislodge it. So, they left the boat there, and sailed away on the *Sea Wind*."

"Did she say anything further about why they were using the *Sea Wind*?"

"She stated that since the Grahams had invited them to dinner and said to 'make yourselves at home,' she rationalized that to mean that if anything should happen to the Grahams, she and Roy could take possession of the *Sea Wind*." Shishido smiled slightly.

"That's what Miss Jenkins said?" Enoki asked, just this side of open sarcasm.

"Yes."

Enoki wanted to know if Jennifer had mentioned why she and Roy Allen had not reported the disappearance of the Grahams to the authorities when they reached Hawaii.

"She said she did not want to report the disappearance of the Grahams because she was afraid the authorities would take the boat away from her."

Shishido testified to his inspecting the *Sea Wind* after Jennifer's arrest to look for evidence. He noticed that on the stern of the boat, "underneath the new paint you could see the name *Iola*," which had been painted over. Among other things he found Buck's .22-caliber Ruger Bearcat pistol and the *Iola*'s log, but no log pertaining to the *Sea Wind*, nor any diary written by Mac or Muff Graham.

Shishido told about the November 1974 search of Palmyra and its lack of results. When he returned to Palmyra in February 1981 to recover the bones found by Sharon Jordan, he also recovered the aluminum container, its lid, and a length of wire found next to the bones. "I slipped the wire around the container and lid to see if it would fit," the ex-agent said. "It did. It fit snugly."

Enoki handed Shishido several photos, which the former case agent identified as showing Sharon Jordan pointing to the general area where the bones were found, "right in front of a line of bushes on shore." At the prosecutor's direction, Shishido stood and went to a map on a tripod beside the witness stand and marked the spot.

He described it as a "coral shelf that extends from the land into the lagoon," occasionally submerged completely. "When it gets to the deep-water area, it makes a sheer drop. The shore is made up of rocks, coral, and little bits of sand."

Enoki showed the jury an aerial videotape of the area, then sat down.

The judge looked my way. "Are you ready for cross, Mr. Bugliosi?"

My awareness of the importance of this witness must have been obvious to the jury by the reams of documents and transcripts I lugged to the podium with me.

"Yes, your honor."

I had no doubt in my mind that the witness I was about to cross-examine was a completely honest one. I also felt, however, that he was not the most reliable one, at least insofar as this case was concerned. I first established for the jury's edification that *all* FBI agents are called "special agents" (hence the witness before them was not part of an elite group of "special" agents within the FBI) and that he, Shishido, was the *only* witness who had testified before the grand jury that indicted Jennifer.

"On the morning of Miss Jenkins's arrest," I continued on with Shishido, "you received word, by way of a radio communication from the Coast Guard personnel surveilling the *Sea Wind*, that Jennifer and Roy Allen were observed leaving the *Sea Wind* and boarding a dinghy. Is that correct?"

"Yes, that's correct."

"Sometime thereafter," I now asked in my prosecution of Walker (since Harry Conklin, the Coast Guardsman who had testified at Buck Walker's trial to having observed Walker dive into the water, did not testify at Jennifer's trial), "you learned that the man whom you believed to be Roy Allen had gone ashore, stripped his clothing off, dived into the water, and disappeared. Is that correct?"

"That's correct."

"With respect, Mr. Shishido, to your interview of Jennifer on the Coast Guard cutter on October 29, 1974, she was very, very eager, was she not, to tell you what happened on Palmyra?"

"Yes, sir, she was."

"In fact, she was so eager that while you were advising her of her constitutional rights, she kept interrupting you because she wanted to tell you what happened?"

"Yes, that's true."

"And you had to actually stop her so you could read to her all of her rights. Isn't that correct?"

"That's right."

"Did you tell her that she had a right to consult with an attorney before you spoke to her?"

"Yes."

"And she told you she didn't want a lawyer?"

"That's true."

"In fact, right off the top, she said, 'The boat doesn't belong to me. It belongs to the Grahams.' Isn't that correct?"

"Yes."

To increase the likelihood that Shishido's recollection of his interview with Jennifer was unreliable (most important, her alleged statement that she and Buck found the dinghy overturned *in* the water), I first sought to weaken his credibility as a witness.

"Did you tape-record your interview of Jennifer?" I asked.

"No, sir, I did not."

"Is there a reason for that?"

"Well, we've found that when we do that, we rely too heavily on the tape recorder and don't pay attention to what's being said. And later, when we go to make the transcription, oftentimes we can't transcribe the recording itself because the words get slurred or there is some other outside noise."

"So you feel that now, almost twelve years later, it's better for the jury to rely on your recollection of what Jennifer told you as opposed to listening to a tape-recorded conversation?" I asked incredulously.

His answer was fairly stunning. "I would answer yes," he said evenly. "On some tape recordings, you can't make out parts of the question. You can misconstrue an answer if you don't fully understand the question."

"But if someone wanted to verify whether your recollection of what she told you is accurate, there would be no way in the world to do so, isn't that true, Mr. Shishido?"

"Well, I guess scientifically, no."

"Her words are lost forever, is that correct?"

"Well, they're in the memorandum that I prepared shortly after the interview."

I asked if he had taken written notes for preparing that memorandum, and he answered that he had.

"Do you have those notes with you?"

"No, sir, I don't."

"Do you know what happened to them?"

"They were destroyed after I prepared my memorandum of the interview. That was the practice back then."

"It's not the practice now?"

"No, sir, it's not."

"You've been cross-examined many times in court by defense attorneys, have you not?"

"Yes."

"And almost invariably, the defense attorney wants to see your notes of any interview you've had with their client, isn't that correct?"

"No, sir."

"They don't ask you for your notes?"

"Well, on some occasions, yes, they have."

"Knowing that they sometimes ask for your notes, is there any reason why you would destroy the notes?"

"It was just . . . actually, if they ask me for my notes, I can say they're in typewritten form because I dictate *from* my notes."

"I imagine there would have been an FBI case file on Jennifer?"

"Yes."

"And rather than put your original notes in that case file, you just tore them up and threw them in the wastepaper basket?" I stopped and looked scoldingly at Shishido, treating the jury to a disbelieving glare.

When he answered, Shishido's voice was barely audible: "At that time, yes."

I paused for several beats.

"Approximately how long did you interview Jennifer on the cutter?" I continued.

"I think it took a total of about an hour, maybe forty-five minutes, somewhere in that area. At the FBI office, where we took her later, I believe it ran about an hour and a half."

"So, we're talking about, what? Two and a half hours total?"

"Roughly, yes."

"Would you characterize your memory, Mr. Shishido, as being average, below average, or what?"

"I would say it's average. On occasion, it's above average."

He conceded that Jennifer did most of the talking during the two interviews that day and concurred with my description of her words as "gushing out," particularly at the beginning.

"And you condensed what she told you during this two-and-a-half-hour period into a brief two-and-a-half-page report?"

"Well, that's true."

"I take it that of necessity, the great bulk of the words in the report are *your* words, not hers. By that, I mean you couldn't put everything she told you in two and a half pages, so you had to summarize, in *your* words, what you recall she told you. Is that correct?"

"That's true."

"If a disinterested party were to look at your report, would there be any way for them to know what words are yours and what words are hers?"

"Well, I guess they would have to listen to my side. They would have to listen to hers."

That was not possible, of course, without a tape recording of the conversation. We were being asked to take Shishido's word for exactly what Jennifer said in the interview.

"But your report doesn't indicate which words are your words and which are her words."

"Well, I said she furnished the following information. When I do that, this is what she's telling me."

"But she would tell you something and then you would put down what she told you in *your* words?"

"Yes, unless I used a quotation."

"Do you find any quotation marks there in that two-and-a-half-page report?"

Shishido slowly perused the copy of his report he had taken to the stand. "No. No. I don't see any, not in *this* one," he finally answered.

"Do you think it's important, in serious matters like this, to indicate in your report which words are yours and which words are those of the person to whom you are talking?"

"Yes, I think it is," he said tonelessly.

I was deriving no pleasure out of embarrassing Calvin Shishido in open court. There's probably no finer, cleaner, more competent investigative agency in the world than the FBI, and Shishido was a salt-of-the-earth agent who had just done his job pretty much by the book. To be honest, I felt a little sorry for the witness. On the other hand, his testimony was threatening my client's life and liberty.

"Did you prepare your report in this case the day after you interviewed Jennifer, or later on the same day?"

"The very next day," he said.

"Did you formulate that report from your memory of what she told you or from the notes you had taken?"

"From both memory and the notes."

I quickly flipped to the appropriate page in my portable library. "In 1975, at a hearing in this matter, you testified: 'I made a note of as much as I could *remember* in the memorandum I wrote.' It sounds like the following day, you based your report not on notes you took the previous day, but on what you could remember."

"Well, that's not what I meant," he answered weakly.

Having laid a foundation that Shishido's credibility as a witness in this case was suspect, I proceeded to the key issue of whether or not Jennifer, during the interview, had told Shishido that she and Buck found the Zodiac overturned in the water of the lagoon. First, I elicited that although Shishido testified on direct examination that Jennifer told him the Zodiac was found *three-quarters of a mile* west of the *Sea Wind*, his report gave no indication where (other than in the water) Jennifer said she found the dinghy.

Then I brought out the inconsistency that at a hearing on November 8, 1974, he had testified that Jennifer had told him the Zodiac had been found a *half mile away* from the *Sea Wind*.

"I would say that if the earlier testimony said half a mile, that was more correct than what I said today," Shishido conceded.

A small point, to be sure. But every fleck of evidence that undermined Shishido's reliability as a witness was valuable.

"With respect to your testimony today that Jennifer told you they found the Zodiac overturned in the water of the lagoon, at the hearing in this case on November 8, 1974, at page thirteen of the transcript, you testified as follows: 'She told me they searched the next morning for the Grahams. During the search they found the Zodiac dinghy that was used by the Grahams the night before. The dinghy was overturned. It had an outboard motor which was also overturned. They also found a gas tank that belonged to the dinghy floating nearby in the lagoon.' "

I put the transcript down and locked gaze with the witness. "Mr. Shishido, when you say 'they found the dinghy overturned' and then say they found the gas tank 'floating nearby in the lagoon,' doesn't it sound from the context as if you recalled her telling you they found the dinghy *on shore*, and the gas can floating *in the water* nearby?"

"No, sir, it does not. When you're on the stand testifying, you just go into the general details oftentimes. And I may have done that in that instance. But at the time of the investigation, my recollection is that she said the dinghy was found overturned in the lagoon. But if the motor had overturned *in* the lagoon, how could they have turned it upright, attached a gas can, started the motor, and continued the search? Because the motor I doubt would have run."

"That would have been a good question. Did you ask her it at the time?" I wanted to know, getting the ball back over the net.

"I may have."

"What did she say?"

"I don't remember the answer."

"And there's no tape—"

"*My guess* is she said, 'Well, I don't know, we did it, you know.'"

"We just have your memory of this, is that correct?"

"Yes."

I walked as close to Shishido as I thought I could without ask-ing Judge King for permission to approach the witness. Looking deeply into his eyes, I summed up his testimony. "Actually, Calvin," I said, lowering my voice and speaking almost conversationally, "you really don't have the best recollection *of what she told you* at all. Isn't that true?"

The former FBI agent, his confidence and composure on the stand having gradually faded, said quietly, "I don't have perfect rec-ollection. That's right."

It was a dramatic courtroom admission, but Shishido's credibil-ity had been so damaged in the last half-hour that he had little choice. His principal testimony—that Jennifer had told him they found the Zodiac overturned in the water, as opposed to on the beach—was now at least open to question.

It was still an issue, however, and I knew I had to travel some additional miles with other witnesses to convince the jury that Jennifer had told Shishido the dinghy was found on shore, and that his critical entry to the contrary in his report was in error.

As we moved on, Shishido acknowledged that Jennifer had gone to the rest room at the yacht club after she had boarded the Coast Guard cutter. The next critical question was whether he had required her to empty out her purse in his presence on the cutter beforehand, or later at the FBI office. But before posing it, I wanted to get him to commit himself to a position that would paint him in a corner. In other words, if Shishido had considered Jennifer a suspect while on the cutter, the great likelihood was that he would have had her empty out her purse *before* going to the rest room, as Jennifer claimed. I needed this testimony to knock out the Leonards' implication that Jennifer had flushed incriminating evidence down the toilet. I expected Shishido would readily con-cede that Jennifer was considered a suspect while on the cutter. But I was wrong. It was about as easy as getting the Pope to say he wasn't Catholic.

"At the very moment that you brought her on the Coast Guard cutter, she was a suspect, is that correct?" I began.

"Well, I wouldn't say immediately when she was brought to the cutter she was a suspect. I didn't think of her so much as a suspect, but as a witness."

I was going to have to dig. "You had instructed the Coast Guard to keep the *Sea Wind* under surveillance, had you not?"

"Yes."

And Shishido conceded, of course, that he had joined in pursuing Jennifer in the harbor.

"And yet, in your mind, she was just some *witness* you wanted to talk to?"

"Well, that's true, because at this point, I felt that we had no real jurisdiction but to assist the Coast Guard in trying to determine to whom that boat belonged. Now, when it came to the point where the Grahams were not there, that the Allens were in possession of the boat, then, of course, my concern came for the safety of the Grahams, and that possibly there could have been some foul play."

"So you did suspect foul play *before* you even spoke to her."

"Well, not really, because at that point, I really didn't know if the Grahams were just left stranded on Palmyra. But foul play in the sense of illegal possession of the boat, yes." Shishido had become as elusive as mercury.

"So, you were very suspicious."

"Not really. Just because we didn't see the Grahams on the boat at the time, didn't mean that . . . maybe they had gone shopping and their guests, the Allens, were still on the boat. Those were questions I had. At the time, you know, there were a lot of possibilities."

I pressed on, feeling almost like someone enticing a wary bird with crumbs. "Mr. Shishido, you've already testified that at the very beginning of your interrogation of Jennifer you advised her of her constitutional rights. Is that correct?"

"Yes."

"If you only viewed her as a witness when she first came aboard the cutter, why at the very beginning did you advise her of her constitutional rights?"

"Because, like I told you, there were several options open in my mind. There could possibly not have been a crime, but then there also was the possibility that there was a crime. Say of murder."

"But you do not advise a simple witness of their constitutional rights, do you?"

"Well, sometimes I do. It depends on whether I feel that the witness may have some complicity in a particular crime."

Shishido was trying to justify the unjustifiable. Like any witness, he was not eager to admit that his actions didn't make sense. Since I had started bearing down, Shishido appeared increasingly less comfortable on the stand. He no longer rested his hands on the railing, but nervously folded and unfolded them in his lap. At times, he seemed bewildered by my questions. Occasionally, he looked toward the prosecution's table like a Little League pitcher, with bases loaded, seeking cues from his dad in the bleachers.

"If Jennifer had given you a good explanation for what happened to the Grahams, and why she was on the boat, you would not have considered her a suspect, is that correct?" I sensed that we were finally near the crux.

"That's true."

"But in point of fact, in your mind she did not give you a good explanation."

"That's right."

"So, *right near the beginning of your interrogation* of her, she *did* become a suspect in your mind. Is that correct?"

The veteran agent frowned. "That's correct," he at last said.

"In fact, at that point, if she had said to you, hypothetically, that she had an appointment at the beauty parlor and she didn't want to stay on the cutter any longer and she wanted to leave, you would not have let her go."

"I would have detained her at that point."

Finally: "Now, isn't it standard routine procedure in the FBI, Mr. Shishido, to have a suspect at that point empty their purse, or bag, or what-have-you, to protect the agent from any hidden weapons?"

Shishido looked distinctly troubled. "That's true."

"Another reason why this is done is that many times incriminating evidence is found in the purse or bag, is that correct?"

"That's true," he acknowledged again.

"And in this case here, you *did* have Miss Jenkins empty the contents of her purse in your presence aboard the Coast Guard cutter. Isn't that true?" He had to agree, I thought.

"That's true . . . well . . . on the Coast Guard cutter, I don't remember that I asked her to empty the contents of her purse. I thought it was later, at the FBI office, that I did that."

"So, you're telling this jury, then, that even though she was a suspect in a case possibly involving murder, you let her leave your presence on the cutter and go into a rest room with a purse that you hadn't looked into? Is that what you're telling us?"

"That's right. Now, *you* may say she's a suspect—"

"We're talking about what *you* considered her situation to be, not what *I'm* saying. You've already testified you thought she was a suspect."

"Right. But a suspect in the theft of a boat."

"We're also talking about *murder*, Mr. Shishido," I said loudly.

"Well, it's just . . . well, I really don't know about the murder yet, at this point."

I shook my head solemnly for the jury and laid the issue to rest at that point, going on to a series of miscellaneous matters characteristic of my method of establishing bases for summation:

I had Shishido confirm that he had seen and heard the Grahams' Zodiac being operated and the motor "made a very loud noise"; that at the time he interviewed Jennifer, he thought the man she was with was named Roy Allen, and Jennifer had never informed him that Roy Allen was Buck Walker; that when Lieutenant Wallisch of the Coast Guard tried to take Puffer away from Jennifer so an animal regulation official could impound her, Jennifer had refused (although Shishido could not remember Jennifer's having cried) and eventually she had been permitted to turn the dog over to Joel Peters, etc.

I next handed the witness Government exhibit 16, the inventory of items from the *Sea Wind* that had been turned over to FBI custody.

"Item number 26 reads: 'Navigational logs contained in a five-by-eight plastic folder.' Could that have been the log of the *Sea Wind*?"

"Well, I really don't know."

"You testified on direct examination that there was no log of the *Sea Wind* found aboard the boat. Are you willing to amend your testimony now to state that the navigational logs, inventory item number 26, may have been the log of the *Sea Wind*?"

"Well, no, I wouldn't change my testimony because I still don't remember seeing any logbook for the *Sea Wind*."

"Yet these 'navigational logs' certainly were not the log of the *Iola*. You agree on that?"

"Yes. Because we have the log of the *Iola*."

"So, item number 26 is some other log, and you don't know what it is."

"That's right," Shishido said. "I really don't know what that is."

"And you don't know where item number 26 is at the present time?"

"No, sir, I don't."

I switched topics.

"Jennifer told you in 1974, to the best of your memory now, that they found the overturned dinghy about three-quarters of a mile west of where the *Sea Wind* was moored. Is that correct?"

"Yes."

"And, as it turns out, the skeletal remains of Muff Graham were found in 1981 in the same general area in which Jennifer said the dinghy was found overturned."

"That's true."

Shishido had testified that during the November 1974 search, the Coast Guard's frogmen had dived only in and around the areas where the *Sea Wind* and the *Iola* were known to have been moored.

"The reason for the limited search was that the lagoon was lousy with sharks, is that correct?"

"Yes," he answered. "And the sharks were coming in, getting too close to them. And we feared for their safety."

"So the entire lagoon was never dredged at the bottom to try to find Mr. Graham's body or the second container?"

"That is correct."

Finished with the witness, I returned to the defense table, interested now in seeing where Enoki would try to plug the holes. Sur-

prisingly, he started off in a direction I thought would prove helpful to the defense.

"Now, Mr. Bugliosi asked you about Miss Jenkins's eagerness
to answer your questions," Enoki began. "Did she also refuse to
answer some of your questions?"

Shishido regained some of his self-contained, confident manner.
"She did. She refused to answer some questions."

"Do you know the subject area of the questions that she refused
to answer?"

"Well, my recollection is—I believe it was based around the
identity of Roy Allen."

I had no questions on re-cross.

During Shishido's testimony on the witness stand, the defense
had clocked some serious mileage.

AS THE Government's case wound down, Sharon Jordan was
summoned. Her light summer dress and white sandals suggested an
afternoon of croquet upon the lawn of a country manor. She still
wore her long raven hair straight down her back and was still a
naturally pretty woman who, without a smidgen of makeup or
trendy fashion accent, could cause men's heads to swivel. She
smiled at the judge before taking her seat. Judge King beamed back
like a raffish uncle.

She had traveled twelve thousand miles from her native South
Africa to tell yet another jury about her macabre discovery of
Muff's skeletal remains in 1981. What had first caught her attention as she was walking on the beach of the lagoon, she told a rapt
jury, was something "glittering in the sunlight." She approached
the object. It turned out to be a "gold tooth in a skull."

"A wristwatch and *what* was found in the lid?" an elderly lady
whispered to another spectator as Jordan continued her story.

"A bone."

"A boat?"

"A bone."

"Oh, my God."

Schroeder asked if a high tide would come up past the spot

where the remains were found. Yes, Jordan said, high tides would reach all the way up to the naupaka bushes, some feet farther in. (In fact, it was almost preternaturally fortuitous that the skeletal remains were not only washed ashore when someone was on the island, but that this someone, Sharon Jordon, just happened to be walking along that precise part of the beach when she was. The very next high tide would probably have pushed the bones into the undergrowth out of sight or dragged them back into the lagoon where they would have sunk and most likely been lost for eternity. The box alone would have meant nothing.)

After describing how she and her husband had raised the old Air Force rescue boat from the bottom of the lagoon, Jordon said there were four storage-hole compartments on the boat "but only two of the compartments had containers in them." The other two had been missing, she said. The jury knew that one of them was sitting before them right in the courtroom and the other was most likely Mac's coffin in the lagoon or sea.

There wasn't much for the defense to ask the young woman, but Len brought out her well-founded opinion that no one could starve on Palmyra. "The food situation was super," she offered in her pleasantly accented English. "There were coconuts, lots of different types of crabs, the fishing was good, there were eggs, palm hearts. We ate pretty well in the five months we were there."

THE ONLY white person now living on Christmas Island, John Bryden was a rugged outdoorsman who spoke with a Scots brogue as chewy as haggis. Weary of contemporary life in Scotland, he had moved in 1969 to Christmas Island, part of the Gilbert Islands (which included Fanning, Washington, and numerous other islands), seeking a blend of adventure and peace of mind in a less complicated society. He'd found both in his island kingdom. In 1979, he had been hired to start a coconut plantation on Palmyra, which was three hundred miles to the northwest of Christmas. As general manager, Bryden brought with him sixteen young Gilbertese men as laborers. Along with his men, whose Micronesian dialect he spoke fluently, he spent fourteen months on the atoll before determining that conditions militated strongly against a profitable commercial venture.

Bryden testified that in May 1979, after deciding that the old rescue boat, which they had found in a cluttered shed located a few feet from the water's edge, was beyond repair, he had his crew drag it down the seaplane ramp into a fairly deep part of the lagoon, where it sank.

From a photo produced by Enoki, Bryden identified the rescue boat found by the Jordans as the same craft his men had unceremoniously scuttled. He could not remember whether any of the containers inside the boat's four storage-hole compartments were missing at that time.

Bryden confirmed that he was familiar with the lagoon shoreline in the area where Jennifer claimed she and Buck had found the overturned Zodiac (and where Jordan had found Muff's remains).

"How big is the beach in that area?" Enoki asked, trying to shore up the probability that lagoon waters would have reached the allegedly overturned dinghy, and therefore gotten salt into its motor.

"There really isn't much beach. At low tide, it's dry. At high tide, it's covered by about eighteen inches of water at the most. The sandy area is just a little strip along the water's edge at high tide. It would be about a foot wide there."

"After that foot or so, you would hit the brush line?"

"Well, you would hit the jungle even before that in some spots. The bushes grow out into the water in some places there."

During one of Len's two trips to Palmyra he had stopped off at Christmas Island and interviewed Bryden in his rustic beachfront cottage home as his young, native wife served coconut milk laced with gin. But there was little to cross-examine Bryden on.

Weinglass: "It's true, is it not, that you found, in your living on the island of Palmyra for fourteen months, the island to be a foreboding place?"

"There were times when it felt like that," said Bryden, who didn't look at all like the kind of person who scared easily. "It sometimes felt a little bit spooky."

A discussion of the food supply on Palmyra resulted in this exchange.

"Did you bring pigs with you to Palmyra?" Len asked.

"Yes. We had two pigs, but we never got to eat them because we . . . they were . . . we lost them."

Judge King, incredulously: "You *lost* them?"

"Yes," the Scotsman answered soberly. "They fell in a hole, sir, and they . . . they drowned."

IN AN obvious attempt to retrieve the damaged credibility of Curt Shoemaker, the Government had flown in FBI Special Agent Tom Kilgore from Honolulu. Involved in the initial stages of the investigation, Kilgore had interviewed Shoemaker on October 30, 1974.

"Agent Kilgore, did Mr. Shoemaker tell you about his last radio contact with the Grahams?" Schroeder asked.

"Yes."

"Did he tell you about an incident with respect to a cake coming from the other boat?"

"Yes. He mentioned to me that the people from the other boat, who I was led to believe were the Allens, were either there [aboard the *Sea Wind*] or they were to be with them at a later time."

"And what did he say that they had with them, or were bringing with them?"

"A cake," the witness answered.

"Now, did you include that cake incident in your 302 report?"

"No. No I did not." The agent explained that he didn't imagine, at the time, that the cake had anything to do with the disappearance of the Grahams.

"Was the case classified as a homicide investigation at that time?"

"No, it was not. It was classified as a crime on the high seas."

"Mr. Kilgore," I began on cross, "when is the *very first time* anyone ever asked you if you recalled Mr. Shoemaker telling you about a cake?"

"A couple days ago."

"No one, prior to a couple of days ago, asked you if you recalled Mr. Shoemaker telling you about a cake?"

"That's correct."

"Your interview with Mr. Shoemaker took place on October 30, 1974. This is mid-February, 1986, almost twelve years later. Right?"

"Yes."

"And you've investigated hundreds of cases since then, have you not?"

"Yes."

"At the time Mr. Shoemaker supposedly told you about this cake incident, in your mind, this was just two people bringing a cake to two other people. Right?"

"Yes."

"It was totally insignificant to you at the time you heard it. Is that correct?"

"Yes."

"The obvious question: How can you possibly remember, twelve years later, something which, at the time you heard it, you admit was totally insignificant?"

"I recall that particular instance of a cake, simply because . . . that it was quite difficult for someone to bake a cake on a boat."

I smiled at Agent Kilgore. "You mean you haven't heard before about people making cakes on boats?"

"I have never had someone serve me cake on a boat."

Kilgore had gone from the untenable statement that it is difficult to make a cake on a boat to the irrelevant observation that he had never been served cake on a boat.

"With respect to this last radio contact with Mac Graham, Mr. Shoemaker didn't tell you anything about a *truce* being mentioned by Mr. Graham, did he?"

"No."

The last Government witnesses were close friends of the Grahams.

Harry Steward, a very formal man in his seventies, was at one time U.S. Attorney for the Southern District of California in San Diego. A yachtsman himself, Steward explained that he and Mac had hit it off when they first met by chance at a marina. "Mac was the most knowledgeable man about sailing I have ever met." Steward estimated he'd been aboard the *Sea Wind* a hundred times or more.

"And during that hundred or so occasions," Schroeder asked, "did the Grahams ever invite you to go aboard at a time when they were *not* going to be personally present?"

"No."

"Now, in your opinion, would Mac and Muff ever have invited someone they did not know well or did not care for to come aboard the *Sea Wind* at a time when they were not going to be personally present?"

"No, no," the witness said emphatically.

Karl Kneisel, an Ichabod Crane type with dry, tousled hair and a flaming sunburned long nose, rated Mac "the best sailor I ever ran across" and concurred that the Grahams were fastidious in choosing guests to board their beloved boat. "They were old-fashioned about yachting etiquette."

"Did Mac have an acetylene torch aboard?" Schroeder asked.

"Yes, he did. He considered it a piece of his cruising gear which was indispensable to do metalwork with."

After a parade of twenty-seven Government witnesses, the prosecution closed with this final horrific image, one the Walker jury also had: Muff Graham's corpse searing in the roar of her beloved husband Mac's own acetylene torch. It was enough to curdle anyone's stomach.

CHAPTER 37

FEBRUARY 12, 1986

IT WAS A COLD AND drizzly morning in San Francisco, as a late-winter storm approached from far out in the Pacific, where all the bad weather on this coast originates.

Soon to unfold inside the monolithic federal courthouse on

Golden Gate Avenue, in the heated comfort of a nineteenth-floor courtroom, was the final act of a long-running murder mystery that had also begun far out on the world's most turbulent ocean.

The lineup of defense witnesses was considerably shorter than the Government's. Our star witness would appear last. We had not publicly announced that Jennifer would testify in her defense, but everyone knew she *had* to explain in her own words why, if she was innocent, everything pointed to her guilt.

Before summoning the jurors, the court heard two defense motions. The first was my motion for a judgment of acquittal on the felony-murder count under Rule 29(a) of the Federal Rules of Criminal Procedure. For the same reasons he had dropped the felony-murder count in the Walker trial, Judge King granted my motion forthwith. Next, Len made a lengthy motion under the same rule to dismiss the premeditated murder count. Since this was the only count remaining against Jennifer, he was asking that the entire case be dismissed. This motion, contending that the evidence presented by the prosecution "is insufficient to sustain a conviction," is made by defense attorneys in virtually every case and almost as invariably denied. Nevertheless, Len made a good argument, and it was apparent that he held Judge King's full attention.

Weinglass asserted, "There's no evidence as to how the death occurred. No proof to show what happened on Palmyra. There's no evidence of any connection of Jennifer Jenkins to a killing. There's no bloodstain, there's no murder weapon, there's no fingerprint, there's no footprint. There is nothing that would tie her to the act of murder."

He argued that "participating in the theft of the *Sea Wind* does not automatically mean" that Jennifer had participated in a murder, but that there was a danger here of one crime overlapping the other in the collective mind of the jury. If the case went forward, Len argued persuasively, then when Jennifer testified, "what will come out is the fact that she had made untruthful statements about the *Sea Wind* and about the *Iola*. The Government will seize on those untruthful statements and argue to the jury that she can't be believed. And the focus of the jury will shift from the failure of the

Government to prove their case, to: 'Can you believe Jennifer Jenkins, who previously made untruthful statements about the *Sea Wind*?' So the Government will have the benefit of a bootstrapping," Weinglass said in conclusion.

After hearing from Elliot Enoki, Judge King predictably denied Len's motion. Obviously, the case *had* to go to the jury. Among other things, as Enoki pointed out, the theft of the *Sea Wind* could not be separated from the murder, since the motive for the murder had been to steal the boat.

I now told the judge I was concerned about how he was going to tell the jury that the felony-murder count had been dropped.

"Well," Judge King said whimsically, "let me try something on you and see how you like it."

"Okay."

"'Ladies and gentlemen, *I* have removed Count One from your consideration. It's no longer before you.'" Judge King smiled benignly, no doubt confident that he'd forestalled all objections.

"There's a little problem with that," I offered.

"What?" His eyes widened.

"The jury could conceivably draw the inference from your language that you feel there was no merit for the felony-murder count to proceed, but the fact you did *not* dismiss Count Two indicates you feel there *is* some substance and merit to that count. May we help you in the formation of what you tell the jury?"

"Suggest something, and we'll talk about it. I have no pride of authorship."

AFTER THE midmorning recess, the judge read the jury a statement dashed out by the defense and prosecution working together. It was an improvement over what he had been planning to say. Rather than "I have removed Count One from your consideration," he explained:

"Count One has been removed from your consideration. It is no longer of concern to you and you should not speculate as to the reason for its removal. The fact that it was removed from your consideration should not influence your verdict with reference to the remaining count, which verdict you must base solely on the evidence."

With that, the defense case began.

Our first witness was Bill Larson, who had been with Don Stevens on the sailboat *Shearwater* at Palmyra in July 1974. The tall, sandy-haired Larson was now an engineer for the Syndyne Corporation in Vancouver, Washington.

Stevens had been a prosecution witness at both theft trials, as well as at Buck's murder trial. While poring over Walker's 1975 theft trial transcript when I first got on the case in 1982, I saw where Stevens had mentioned that his (unnamed) friend aboard the *Shearwater* attended a potluck dinner party at Buck's tent. Mac and Muff had been present, too. Stevens had remained aboard his boat because of an ear infection. We *had* to have at least one independent witness to help counter the overall impression that there was bad blood between the Grahams and Buck and Jennifer. Otherwise, the jury would likely disbelieve Jennifer's story that she had found nothing unusual about the Grahams' supposed dinner invitation. Although I had more than once asked Jennifer if there was *anyone at all* who could be such a witness, she had been unable to think of a soul. Grasping at straws, I telephoned Stevens at his home in Portland, Oregon, for the name and phone number of his former shipmate. When I called Larson at his home in Vancouver and he confirmed being present at the dinner and said that the relationship between the Grahams and Buck and Jennifer at the get-together seemed very cordial, I felt like Moses spotting Aaron in a roomful of Egyptians. With so precious little affirmative evidence for the defense, otherwise routine information becomes exhilarating. When I reported back to Jennifer about Larson, she did not remember him by name. When I explained he was the fellow from the *Shearwater* who had attended the potluck dinner, she said, "Oh, yeah, that guy. Yeah, he could tell about Mac and Muff having a nice evening with us." Irked, I asked why in hell she hadn't mentioned Larson before. As usual, I hadn't really gotten through. She simply laughed her hearty laugh. "I just forgot."

With Larson, as with almost any witness, there was some scuff on the shine. In the FBI's 302 report of a telephone interview with him, he characterized Jennifer as "the leader of the two." *Leader enough to mastermind murder?* I had delved into this issue in my pretrial interviews with Larson. Urged to clarify, he said he hadn't felt very strongly about Jennifer's leadership role, basing it mostly on the fact that she was the "talker" of the couple, and had once yelled at Buck, who had said nothing in return. Also, Larson had been impressed that she had acted as navigator on the *Iola*, even though she lacked ocean sailing experience. On balance, I felt it was worth calling Larson for the defense.

Although I had prepared Larson for trial, Len asked me if he could handle Larson on the stand, and I had no objection. Len first brought out that even before the dinner, Larson had accompanied the Grahams and Jennifer on a boating and exploration trip. As testimony arrowed toward the dinner party, seven or eight jurors—but *not* the Kansas Rock—began taking notes.

As to that night, Weinglass asked, "In your view, did it appear to be a friendly relationship between Buck and Mac?"

"Yes, it did."

"You watched Buck and Mac playing chess?"

"Yes."

"And when you saw Muff and Jennifer talking, did it appear, from where you were, to be a friendly conversation?"

"Yes, it did."

"Based on your observations of Jennifer with the Grahams, how would you describe their relationship?"

"It was friendly."

"Did you detect any animosity or hostility?" Len asked.

"No, I didn't."

The next line of questioning was adroitly designed by Len to show that even if Mac and Muff hadn't liked Buck and Jennifer, Jennifer could not have known it from their behavior.

"Now, did you see or hear any comments or behavior by Muff Graham, *in Jennifer's presence*, that would lead you to believe that Muff and Jennifer were unfriendly or hostile to each other?"

"No, I did not."

"Did you see or hear any behavior or comment of Muff Graham, *in Jennifer's presence*, that would lead you to believe that Muff was unfriendly or hostile toward Buck Walker?"

"No."

Finally, Larson recalled visiting the *Sea Wind* one afternoon when Muff happened to be alone. She served him ice-cold Kool-Aid, a sybaritic luxury on a deserted island in the tropics. "It was refrigerated. It was something we hadn't had in almost fourteen months."

"Did you comment to Muff on your appreciation of the Kool-Aid?" Len asked.

"I thought it was very good and said that we ought to share it with everybody on the island."

"Did Muff respond to that suggestion?"

"Yes. *She said that she didn't want the other two to actually be on her boat.*" I tried not to show my inner reaction.

In his brief cross-examination, Enoki asked whether Jennifer or Buck had ever asked the men aboard the *Shearwater* for supplies of any kind.

"Yes," Larson answered. "Jennifer did a couple of times."

"What did she ask for?"

"Sugar or flour, I believe. I'm not positive."

Enoki sat down. The Government had apparently overlooked what Larson had said about Jennifer's apparent domination of Buck. We were prepared with a response, of course, but not being put on the defensive was a plus for the defense.

I now called FBI Special Agent Tom Kilgore to the witness stand, and first asked, poker-faced, whether he'd ever testified for the defense before.

"Yes, sir."

We both smiled.

"Not too often, though?"

"No, sir."

The jury had, of course, already heard his account of an interview with Curt Shoemaker on October 30, 1974. I wanted to cover an interview conducted the *previous* day with the Leonards.

"Did it come to your attention that the Leonards had called the FBI requesting an interview?" I asked.

"Yes."

Both had denied, during my cross-examinations of them, ever calling the Bureau to solicit an interview.

"In fact, they had called the FBI office several times. Is that correct?"

"That's my understanding," the agent said.

"And your purpose in interviewing the Leonards was to secure from them whatever information they had to help you in your investigation of the disappearance of the Grahams?"

"Yes."

"During your interview of them, did either one of them tell you that while they were on Palmyra, Jennifer Jenkins told them that she would never leave Palmyra on the *Iola*?"

"Not that I can recall."

"If either one of them had told you this, would it have been the type of information you would have put in your report of the interview?"

"Yes."

On cross-examination, Schroeder asked Kilgore if it had been "pretty hectic" that day at the Ala Wai when he interviewed the schoolteacher and his wife.

"Yes."

"How long did you spend interviewing the Leonards?"

"I would say close to thirty minutes, maybe a little more than that."

"Would you agree that thirty minutes could not be called an in-depth interview?" Schroeder asked.

"Oh, by no means."

On re-direct, I elicited that Kilgore's interview notes came to nearly five typewritten pages, including such trivia as the Leonards' telling him that the Grahams had a dinghy with an outboard motor and Buck cut down coconut trees with a chain saw.

"So you put in quite a few little details in the report, isn't that true?"

"Yes."

"Thank you," I said. "Nothing further."

THAT AFTERNOON, a disheveled middle-aged man who looked like Willie Nelson's clone sauntered to the witness stand. Larry Seibert wore his sun-bleached hair long, like an aging hippie, and appeared quite comfortable in faded blue jeans and a military-style jacket. I had spent some time and effort finding Seibert, whose occupation seemed to be "beachcomber."

Seibert lived on a boat in Oahu's Keehi Lagoon and used the P.O. box of a Honolulu garment factory as his business address, though he didn't work regularly there or anywhere else. I had started looking for him in early 1982 but was unsuccessful until February 1983, when I caught him by phone at the Honolulu home of a friend of his. Seibert not only confirmed, as Jennifer had told me, that he had seen a broken-off swordfish bill stuck in the hull of the *Sea Wind*, but also that she had told him privately that Buck had lied about how they came into possession of the boat.

Under Len's questioning, Seibert now testified that he had first met Jennifer and Buck in the fall of 1973 when they were fixing up the *Iola* at Maalaea Bay boat harbor.

He next saw Jennifer and Buck in October 1974, when Buck called to invite him over to Pokai Bay to visit the couple on their newly acquired ketch. He had learned about the swordfish attack during that social visit.

"Did you see the patch on the outside of the hull?" asked Weinglass.

"Yes, yes. But I also saw a part of the fish sticking through the hull from the inside."

"And could you describe for us what that part of the fish looked like?"

"It looked like the mangled-up bill of a swordfish."

"About how long was it?"

"It was about six or eight inches long. What was left of it."

Now on to the second pertinent topic.

"In the course of your being on the *Sea Wind* that day, did you have an occasion to ask Buck how he got the boat?" Weinglass asked.

"Yes, I did. He told me he had won the boat playing chess with the previous owner in a series of games," Seibert answered.

"Now, was Jennifer there when he told you that?"

"Well, she wasn't sitting at the table with us, but she was somewhere around."

"Did you sometime after that ask Jennifer if the story that Buck had related to you was true?"

"Yes. She said that it had not been true. That he hadn't gambled with the guy."

On cross-examination, Schroeder tried to show that Seibert, being a friend of Jennifer's, might lie for her.

"You were good friends, were you not?"

"Well, we were fairly good friends."

Schroeder showed Seibert a photograph of him on board the *Iola* when the vessel was finally launched successfully.

"You have a bottle of champagne or wine in your hand. Is that correct?"

"Yes."

There was a slight pause as Schroeder changed key.

"The swordfish bill is not something that you simply stumbled across. They said, 'Larry, we've got something we want to show you.' Would that be correct?"

"Something like that, yes."

"And they took you and showed you this bill."

"Right."

Now the Government lawyer turned his attention to the second important part of Seibert's testimony.

"Isn't it a fact, Mr. Seibert, that Buck and Jennifer *both* told you that they won the boat?"

"Only Buck told me."

"Do you remember being interviewed by FBI agents Richard Bramley and Roy George Hamilton on October 31, 1974?"

"Yes."

"And during this interview, you signed a statement, did you not?"

"Yes."

"And did you not, during that statement, say, '*They* said that after *they* had won the boat, they departed the island on the boat they won, and the previous owners of the boat departed in the *Iola* for Fanning Island'? Did you say that to the FBI?"

"I might have used the word 'they' at that time, but—"

"Would you like to see your statement?" Schroeder asked pointedly.

"I saw the statement. I know what it says. But I'm not very good at always making sure that I'm using the proper pronoun or whatever you call it. And the word 'they' should have been 'Buck.'"

"So, in October 1974, you said 'they.'"

"Yes, I said 'they.'"

"And today, you're saying 'Buck.'"

"I have always said 'Buck' except for that one time that I used the improper pronoun."

(Schroeder should have known that the jury might think he had intentionally misled them if it was brought out on re-direct, as it was, that later in this very same interview Seibert had clearly said, "*Roy Allen* related the following story to me—that *he* won the boat gambling, playing chess with the previous owner who *he* referred to as being a wealthy millionaire who did not worry about losing the boat or approximately a thousand dollars in cash that *Roy also* won gambling.")

Schroeder elicited from Seibert that it was only after Jennifer's arrest that she had told him, in Halawa Jail, that Buck had lied about how they acquired the *Sea Wind*.

Schroeder had one more line of questions to challenge Seibert's credibility. "You went to the Unites States passport office with Buck Walker, did you not, and you signed an affidavit that he was Roy A. Allen?"

"Yes, I did."

"Nothing further, your honor."

BY THAT Friday, February 14, the advancing storm had finally arrived in full force, dumping four inches of rain on the San Francisco Bay Area on Valentine's Day. (Non-Californians may forget that much of the state is susceptible to severe damage from rains that, elsewhere, would cause little but traffic jams and bad jokes.)

"Mother Nature has interfered with us," Judge King explained that morning as we gathered in his courtroom at 9:30 A.M. "Juror Nelson is doing fine, but he can't get here. Highway 101 is wiped out at Petaluma, and so is another road below it. He's being evacuated from his home and he's moving to a friend's house. Mrs. Rico can't get here either. She got as far as Petaluma, and then had to go back home. There are two other jurors we haven't even heard from."

Before adjourning for the three-day President's Day weekend, Judge King issued a novel order. "The paper says several days more of rain, so I hereby order that it cease raining by Tuesday morning. Let's see how that works." He smiled roguishly and left the bench.

Heading out of the courtroom, Len, Jennifer, and the prosecutors reached the door at the same moment. "Since we're short jurors, maybe the judge should change his ruling on Rule 29 and dismiss the last remaining count," Weinglass joked.

Enoki, smiling narrowly, didn't miss a beat. "She can always plead."

"I'll plead guilty to jaywalking," Jennifer chirped, adopting dry humor like one of the courthouse crowd. "Really, Elliot, you find something I'm guilty of and I'll plead."

The prosecutor stiffened as he spoke in a resonant baritone. "I know lots of things you're guilty of, Jennifer."

Unfazed, Len was still holding the door open, keeping his kind but crooked smile in place, as the tableau froze.

Enoki headed for the eighteenth floor, where he had set up shop in an office borrowed from the U.S. Attorney. He would, no doubt, spend most of the weekend there, preparing for the prosecution's most important cross-examination of the trial. Walt Schroeder and Hal Marshall trailed like worker ants. Schroeder gripped a briefcase in one hand, and the bulky FBI agent carried, as he did at the end of each day, the carton containing Muff's bones. The judge's clerk, frankly squeamish about them, had asked him to be in charge of the grisly evidence. "No problem," Hal had said. "A few bones don't bother me." As the friendly agent was prone to do, he told the clerk a story to illustrate the point. "My daddy was a sheriff in Texas," he said in his deep drawl. "Down around the Gulf. One time he had to fish out a big old swelled-up drowning victim. He wrapped the body in a blanket he always kept in the backseat of the car. That Sunday, we used that very same blanket for a little family picnic. No problem." When the young clerk looked stricken—no doubt the desired effect—her tormentor grinned broadly and added innocently, "Mind you, the body wasn't still in the blanket."

LEN AND I spent Saturday working at the hotel. We ventured out on Sunday, driving across the Bay bridge and continuing east for another thirty miles to Lafayette, the leafy suburb where Ted and his family lived.

Jennifer, attired in sweat clothes, invited us into the spacious family room. The three of us discussed some of our upcoming witnesses and the points we needed to make with each. Jennifer's testimony was very much on my mind, of course, and I took the opportunity to run her through several portions of newly designed Q and A. As always, when we zeroed in on areas vital to her defense, my summation was not far from my thoughts. As it turned out, Jennifer was also thinking about my final argument.

"Vince, are you going to argue my innocence?" she asked out of the blue. There was an edge to her voice.

"You've got to be kidding, Jenny. Of course I am."

"I don't know. Len doesn't think you should. That you should only argue reasonable doubt." She looked directly at Len, apparently to take over the argument. Evidently, he'd been working on Jennifer. His hope, undoubtedly, was that with her support, I would reconsider, even though I thought I'd made it very clear to him why I needed to argue *both*.

After Len outlined—once again—his legalistic reasons for my arguing only reasonable doubt, I smiled derisively at my client. "Jennifer, you *do* want me to argue that you're innocent, don't you?" I said sarcastically.

"Well, I'd like to see what you're going to say," she countered.

"Ordinarily, Jennifer, I would show my argument to you. But not now. You're only going to hear it, not see it," I said sharply. "I never thought I'd see the day," I added, raising my voice, "when I'd have to get the goddamn approval of my client to argue that she is innocent."

Jennifer, blinking wildly, said nothing.

"Let's go, Len," I said as I stalked to the door, not wanting to spend any more time in the presence of our client.

In the car heading back to the city, Len and I discussed the issue more rationally. By the time we got back to the hotel, we had buried once and for all the innocence vs. reasonable doubt matter. But working on the case into the early-morning hours, I bristled whenever I thought of Jennifer's conduct. I probably should have been more understanding. She was simply a lay person totally unschooled in the law who was consistently influenced in her thoughts by one of her lawyers, a fine lawyer at that.

The next morning, my bedside phone rang early.

It was an apologetic Jennifer. "Obviously, I have total confidence in how you're going to argue the case, Vince. I was out of line last night. I'm sorry."

BY EARLY Tuesday morning, the judge's order had worked. The storm had ended, and the day was bright and clear.

We were set to put our character witnesses on the stand. At the low-rent hotel near the courthouse where we had put up all of these witnesses, and with Jennifer present, I conducted my final interview with Deborah Noland, an old friend of hers who had moved to Hawaii in 1972. We sat down together a few minutes after seven in the morning.

A petite woman in her thirties, Noland, her long, dark hair gathered in a bun, wore granny glasses and sandals. A mother of two, she worked on the Big Island for a counseling program that helped abused women.

In 1973—then "a kid of nineteen and pregnant"—Debbie and her boyfriend, unabashed hippies in search of an alternate lifestyle, had arrived on the Big Island. Mutual friends had written Buck and Jennifer's names on a matchbook, and the couples ended up living together for a time on the two-acre parcel of rugged forest-land where Buck had helped his father build his cabin.

Although most of this background information would not come out in her testimony, I had accumulated pages of notes from my several telephone interviews with Noland. "I *liked* Jenny right away," she told me. "She's real easygoing—a loving person. She took good care of me, like a big sister or even a mother. She was a vegetarian at the time and she made sure I was eating right for my baby's sake. She always kept busy around the place. Buck, I remember, spent a lot of time in bed, reading. One title sticks out in my mind: *The Master Game*. It was about getting your mind together. He read it over and over. He liked self-help and Zen books, too. And murder novels." Eventually, she warmed up to the quieter Buck, too, despite some disturbing tendencies. "When he got mad, he would go out and shoot his gun. He never beat Jennifer, but later, after I worked with abused women, I realized that Buck had psychologically abused Jennifer and taken advantage of her kindness."

In my final interview with Debbie that morning, I asked a question Judge King would probably sustain an objection to, but I needed to know the answer in case I decided to try to elicit it.

"Debbie, you witnessed the relationship between Jennifer and Buck. Do you think Buck had enough control over Jennifer to get her to go along with murder?"

Noland didn't answer right away. In fact, her silence gradually became alarming.

I interrupted the long hiatus with a nervous chuckle. "God, that pause could bury us, Debbie. Don't worry. I won't be asking you that question."

But Noland had completed her ruminations. "Jennifer is not that kind of person," she said firmly. "She couldn't kill anyone."

Later, Jennifer explained that people in Hawaii speak and react slowly because they are "laid-back. They just aren't as quick in their conversations as most of us are," she said.

Native son Sam King, with his whiplash tongue, would have loved that gloss.

Before the jurors took their seats that morning, I advised Judge King that I wanted to introduce Buck Walker's 1975 theft trial testimony about his activities on the all-important day of August 30, 1974. Because of Walker's unavailability at this trial, I believed his testimony to be admissible under the "former testimony" exception to the hearsay rule. "The only hurdle that has to be negotiated, as I see it, is whether the testimony is relevant," I told the court.

It *was* relevant, I went on, because it supported Jennifer's testimony "that she was told by Buck Walker about the dinner invitation; i.e., she's not saying that the dinner invitation was made by the Grahams, only that Buck *told her* it was. This previous testimony of Walker's contravenes the prosecution's position that the dinner invitation is a story that was concocted by both Miss Jenkins and Buck Walker."

Enoki, determined to keep out Walker's testimony, countered that the prosecutor in the boat-theft case did not cross-examine Walker about the issue of his activities on August 30, 1974; therefore, it did not meet the cross-examination requirement of the former testimony exception rule.

I quickly pointed out that the very language of the legal rule involved says that former testimony is introducible if the opposing side had an *opportunity* to cross-examine, as the prosecution did. Their failure to seize the opportunity was irrelevant.

Enoki wouldn't let go. The "former testimony" exception also required a similar motive to cross-examine, he said. Since Walker's testimony had been given in a *theft* trial, the aim of cross-examination would be different from that at this murder trial.

The prosecutor and I stood only a few feet apart, as tense and almost as physically close as boxers before the bell, as we staked out and defended our positions in front of the judge. Neither of us wanted to lose this one.

"The Advisory Notes to 804(b)(1) say that only a 'substantial' identity of issues is required to satisfy the requirement of a similar motive in cross-examination," I said. "The issues *don't* have to be identical. But actually, they are identical in this instance."

"Yes," the judge concurred thoughtfully, rubbing his chin. "Everybody was *talking* about theft at the theft trial, but everybody was *thinking* about murder. I think Mr. Bugliosi is right."

The Jenkins jury would hear from Buck Walker in absentia.

After a short recess, the jury was called in and Debbie Noland drifted to the stand.

SINCE NEARLY everything Jennifer had said or done after the Grahams' disappearance pointed toward her guilt, I had been on a constant, intensive search for evidence, *any* evidence, that might help prove her innocence. Early on, I had decided to put on character evidence to that effect; namely, that her caring and physically passive nature would be unlikely to produce the violent act of murder. (In a related vein, although I found a federal case that would allow such evidence, United States v. Staggs, several phone calls to forensic psychiatrists confirmed that there is no test yet devised by the psychiatric community to determine whether or not someone is capable of a violent act, or likely or not to have committed such an act.)

Character evidence is the most *indirect* type of evidence that can be offered at a criminal trial, since none of it relates to the actual circumstances of the crime charged. The defense of "good character" in a criminal case dates back to the time of Charles II in the seventeenth century, but it is not a frequent defense at a criminal trial, and if handled clumsily, can be perceived by the jury as indicative of a weak case.

Jennifer had given me the names, addresses, and phone numbers of friends who could testify to her nonviolent character, and I was eventually able to reach and interview them all.

Len agreed that a character defense was a good idea in the abstract, but feared that the Government, in rebuttal, might be able to introduce all of Jennifer's actions that showed *bad* character, including her theft conviction of the *Sea Wind*. I remembered from my days in the DA's office, however, that the prosecution would be restricted under the law to presenting evidence bearing only on that particular character trait about which the defense witness testified. In this case, therefore, the Government could only present evidence that Jennifer *was* a violent person. As it turned out, Judge King gave the impression that he shared Len's interpretation. But after I cited my supporting cases (*Mitchelson* v. *United States*; *United States* v. *Curtis*), Enoki himself acknowledged that my position was consistent with the law.

The main caveat I had with a character defense was the lurking danger that the Government might be able to find some evidence in Jennifer's past indicating a violent nature. Such a revelation would not merely cancel out the testimony of our entire platoon of character witnesses. If someone, for instance, had seen Jennifer throw a broken bottle at someone's head, this would be specific, affirmative evidence that would, understandably, weigh more heavily than all of our generalized character testimony. I warned Jennifer of the risks involved in a character defense and asked her repeatedly if she was absolutely sure there was no violent behavior the Government would be able to dredge up from her past. Anything at all, even slapping someone hard on the face, even a *threat* to be violent. Jennifer placidly assured me there was nothing.

On the phone, in writing, and finally in person, I reminded each of our character witnesses to confine their testimony to the issue of Jennifer's being a nonviolent person. If they inadvertently strayed from this narrow path and testified, for instance, that Jennifer was a "nice" or "good" or "honest" person, or one with "high morals," since these are general terms, virtually anything negative about Jennifer would be allowed in rebuttal. Thus, the door would swing wide open for the two petty-theft convictions, the conviction for the theft of the *Sea Wind*, and perhaps even the marijuana conviction. Fully aware, then, of the dangers inherent in a character defense, I nonetheless felt, in view of all of the other factors, that taking the risk was advisable.

With Debbie Noland, I began not with precise character-defense questions but by eliciting testimony from her that corroborated some very important points Jennifer would soon testify to. Noland alluded to certain "problems" she saw in the relationship between Jennifer and Buck, and I asked for illustrations.

"For one thing," she said, "Buck had a thing for weapons. Guns, mostly. Jennifer just didn't want the guns in the house. She didn't want any part of that."

"Would they argue about it?"

"Yes. They argued often about the same thing, the guns."

"Was she able to get him to remove the guns from the house?"

"Yes, the guns were taken out of the house."

I prodded her to go on.

"They were . . . totally different people."

"In what ways?"

"Jennifer was peaceful, easygoing. She loved nature. She went to the beach a lot. She loved animals. Buck stayed in the house most of the time. And he had a firecracker personality. He was nice for one minute, and then he would explode on the spot."

When I asked for examples, continuing with my "prosecution" of Buck, she said that if Buck and Jennifer were having a disagreement, Buck might get so angry that "he would just run outside and throw rocks at her van."

"Was Buck kind of domineering over Jennifer?"

Debbie paused, as she had earlier that morning at the hotel, but, to my relief, soon answered clearly, "Yes."

"Would you say you had a close relationship with Jennifer during this period of time?" I asked.

"Yes. I . . . I became very close to her," she said demurely.

"Based on your knowledge of Jennifer and your association with her, do you have an opinion as to whether she's a violent or nonviolent person?"

"Definitely a nonviolent person. Loving to animals, to people, mothering everybody. She's so giving."

Because of the likelihood of surprise and consumption of time, most courts permit character testimony relating to specific acts only on cross-examination, not direct. However, this was a gray area of the law ("not *generally permissible*" per Advisory Notes to

Rule 405), and I intended to make an effort to slip in such specific testimony from Noland on my direct.

"What caused you to believe that she was nonviolent?"

"Are we getting into specific acts now?" an alert Judge King asked. "I thought you weren't supposed to get into that."

I didn't respond, but swiftly took another tack with the witness. "Did she *speak* about nonviolence?"

"Yes, she—"

Enoki cut her off. "I'm not sure what the answer is going to be, but it could call for a statement about specific acts."

Court: "Yes. I thought that what you were getting into was not permissible under the rule."

"Well," I said, "I think the bald declaration of the nonviolence certainly is helpful, but what caused the witness to form that opinion I think is important."

When I stubbornly tried, yet a third time, to get into specific acts, Judge King said, with studied calm: "Mr. Bugliosi, we're going to have a little problem with this. Because you and I both know the rule. It's almost a formula. 'Do you know the defendant?' 'Yes.' 'Do you have an opinion?' 'Yes.' 'What is that opinion?' I'll sustain the objection."

A remarkably restrained Judge King was continuing to keep his tongue in check before the jury. I knew he would have roared at Buck Walker's attorneys—and perhaps at me, if I hadn't confronted him earlier in chambers—for blatantly trying to dance around a ruling of his two consecutive times.

Not once throughout the trial had Judge King indulged in a tantrum or in any other way belittled me or Len in open court. He had shown irritation with me a few times outside the presence of the jury, though he never seemed upset with Len. In and out of court, my co-counsel had a personality that seldom rubbed people the wrong way. It was sometimes difficult to recall that this nice-guy Weinglass had battled it out in court with crusty old Judge Julius Hoffman in the historic Chicago Seven conspiracy trial while a nation watched in fascination or partisan anger.

In any event, with or without specific acts, Noland's testimony was decidedly helpful. The judge just wouldn't let me put the icing on the cake.

On cross-examination, Enoki asked rhetorically, playing more to the twelve jurors than to the witness, "It's your opinion then that in spite of her association with Mr. Walker and knowing the kind of person he was, Jennifer was still capable of being a nonviolent person?"

"Definitely." Debbie Noland's tone was pleasingly decisive.

"I gather she also demonstrated," Enoki went on, "as part of that character, a capacity to tolerate violence in other people."

The judge sustained my objection, deeming Enoki's question "a little philosophical."

Our next witness, Rick Schulze, was a lawyer from the mainland who, within a year after moving to Honolulu in 1963, had made partner in the firm of Bill Quinn, a popular ex-governor. Schulze had left in 1970 to put up his shingle in tiny Kamuela—population 2,500—on the Big Island.

Schulze entered the courtroom attired in the colorful casual dress I'd come to expect of Hawaii residents—a lightweight summer sport coat, white open-weave shirt with playful orange tie, navy-blue slacks, and scuffed high-top desert shoes.

I first brought out that Schulze had served four years as a district judge in Honolulu and had been elected to the state's 1968 constitutional convention, chairing the committee charged with reapportioning political districts.

He recalled meeting Jennifer in 1970, when she was staying at a mutual friend's house.

"After we met, I saw Jennifer weekly throughout 1970. In December of that year, I married my second wife, and Jennifer was among a few friends who came and stayed at our house for the week before the wedding to help us with all the preparations. After that, Jennifer would visit us once a month or so, and my wife and I would visit her at the cabin in Mountain View."

"When you were with Jennifer, did you have conversations with her, philosophical conversations?" I asked.

"Yes, we talked in deep ways, conversations about very profound things. About how we feel about life. Jennifer and I had a very close relationship."

"How would you describe Jennifer to the jury?"

At this point, as if on cue, Schulze turned his head toward the jury and made eye contact with several of the people who would decide her fate. "Jennifer is a very unusual person," he said earnestly. "She is a very giving person. She was always concerned with helping other people. She didn't pay a lot of attention to her own problems. She is a very sound, reasonable person."

"Did you ever have an argument with Jennifer?" I asked, for a reason that would become clear. I was successfully skirting Judge King's "formula."

"Well, I don't know if it . . . was an argument. But there was an occasion when Jennifer and I certainly had a meeting of wills."

"Would you describe that to the jury?"

"Jennifer lived on the other side of the island, maybe sixty or seventy miles from us. I had just built a new house—it would have been in 1973—and she came to visit, bringing her little dog, Puffer. Jennifer is very, very close to her dog. Puffer went everywhere with Jennifer. We had a long discussion over whether Puffer could come into our house to sleep with Jennifer that night. It seems silly now. But I never allowed my dog to come in the house, and I thought he would feel really bad if her dog came into the house. So, I wouldn't let her bring Puffer in. Jennifer felt that she couldn't possibly leave Puffer outside overnight."

"What eventually happened?" I asked.

"What happened was that Jennifer finally cried, and went out and slept in the car with her dog."

"Overnight?"

"Overnight."

I felt that Jennifer's handling of the situation was surely revealing.

I next asked Schulze if he was aware of any of the men in Jennifer's life, and he said he'd met two of her boyfriends.

"Did these two men fall into a pattern?"

"Yes, they did."

"In what way?"

"Contrary to Jennifer's nature, her boyfriends tended to be scruffy, coarse men. Crude—crude men."

"Did you find this to be incompatible with her nature?"

"On the surface, you would think so. But underneath, Jennifer is a helper of people. She thought she could save these fellows."

"Give them some type of spiritual guidance, in other words?"

"She was very much a spiritual counselor, yes."

"What type of person was Buck Walker?" I asked, continuing my prosecution of him.

"Buck Walker was a burly kind of guy, coarse, crude, I thought. He was also very paranoid. His idea of other people was that they were all out to get him. He was always talking in terms of defending himself against others who were going to come and get him. And he had a lot of fascination with weapons. He talked about them a lot. And he had them around."

"Do you recall telling me he was the type of person who, if he joined a group, would join one like the Minutemen?"

"Yes," Schulze said. "That would be his kind of group."

"Did Jennifer indicate to you how she felt about Buck?"

"Yes."

"What did she say?"

"Like other friends of Jennifer's, I kept insisting that she get rid of this guy. But she saw some spark of goodness in him, something in there that she thought with the proper love and acceptance could be nurtured in him and brought out."

"Mr. Schulze, based on your association with Jennifer, do you have an opinion as to whether she's a violent or a nonviolent person?"

"Yes, I do."

"And what is that opinion?"

"In my judgment, Jennifer is very clearly a nonviolent person. I have never seen her exhibit violence in any form. And my conversations with her have been in great depth, and I have found that deep down she has a very marked respect and love for humanity in general, and for individuals in particular. I cannot imagine Jennifer involved in violence in any way."

I paused. This was the heart of our character defense. *I cannot imagine Jennifer involved in violence in any way.*

"Thank you, Mr. Schulze. No further questions."

Schroeder began his cross-examination in textbook fashion. "Mr. Schulze, I gather you base your opinion as to Jennifer's character for nonviolence on the fact you never witnessed any acts of violence on her part, is that correct?"

"In part, that's correct."

"And obviously you never observed Jennifer under circumstances of deprivation or desperation. Would that be correct?"

"Your honor," I interrupted, "the question assumes a fact not in evidence. It's an overcharacterization of the evidence."

"Yes," the judge said, then amplified to Schroeder: "You used words which are really your conclusion. I'll sustain the objection, and the jury should ignore the question."

Schroeder studied his notepad for a moment, reloading.

"Now, Mr. Schulze, during the times that you associated with Buck and Jennifer, did you ever have occasion to find any aspect of Buck's demeanor and personality objectionable?"

"Oh, yes."

"He talked of violence to the extent that you became weary of it?"

"Yes."

I sensed that Schroeder, smooth and businesslike as always, was setting Schulze up for something, but I couldn't figure out what.

"Among the people who knew Buck, was anyone afraid of him?" the prosecutor asked blandly.

"Yes. Jennifer's friends began to shun her—or not to shun her so much as just not wanting her around if Buck was with her. And my wife and I—we became that way too, a little."

At that moment, Schroeder strode over to the defense table, handed me a document with a flourish, and asked that it be marked as a Government exhibit. It was a January 7, 1975, letter from Schulze to, of all people, Judge King. I had never seen it before, nor did I know of its existence. I read it quickly. It spoke glowingly of Buck, saying, among other things, that Schulze did not consider him a violent person. My witness had written this testimonial on the eve of Judge King's sentencing of Walker for the boat theft. I asked for a recess.

With the jurors out of the room, I pointed out that under the law of discovery the Government should have furnished the defense with a copy of the letter before trial. (In that case, I would have brought it out myself on direct examination to reduce its impact.) The Government's attempt to introduce the letter thoroughly confused the judge.

"I've read the letter, Mr. Schroeder," Judge King began, "and I can't understand why you want to use it. As a matter of fact, I can't understand why the defense would possibly object to you using it."

"For the reason Mr. Bugliosi objects to it," Schroeder said quite reasonably, "we want it in."

"It's incredible," the judge said. "Do you really want to prove that everything bad that's come out about Walker was untrue?"

Schroeder: "Well, your honor, the witness diametrically contradicted himself."

Court: "I understand that. But now you want to prove that Buck is *not* a violent person? Is that what you're trying to prove?"

Schroeder: "We want to demonstrate the standards of this witness's ability to assess violence. This letter was a glowing tribute to Mr. Walker, and how Mr. Walker was nonviolent."

Court: "I understand that. And that's why I can't understand, for the life of me, why you possibly want it in. And I can't understand, for the life of me, why the defense objects to it. Maybe I'm operating in a never-never land where rational thought is irrelevant."

Judge King closed his eyes and pinched the bridge of his nose like a man who has just seen double. Actually, he had everything in reverse when he assumed the Government would want to prove that Buck was violent, and we would want to prove he was nonviolent. Obviously, the Government would benefit by showing that Walker was nonviolent (although, as would soon become clear, this was not the reason they wanted to introduce the letter), for this would increase the likelihood of his not having committed the murders by himself—that is, increase the likelihood of Jennifer's involvement. Conversely, I wanted to show that Buck was violent, that he had it within himself to murder Mac and Muff alone. But the judge and the Government would have to wait until my summation to learn this reasoning of mine. For now, I made a merely perfunctory objection, which the judge overruled.

When the jury returned, Schroeder sped to his point. "Mr. Schulze, did you write a letter to this court on January 7, 1975?" he asked, spoiling for a clash with the witness he felt he couldn't lose.

"Yes," said the witness.

As Schroeder savored the words of the letter he read aloud, Schulze verified having written all of them, including the lines "I have never had occasion to find any aspect of Buck's demeanor or personality objectionable. . . . Whenever I have seen him in the company of others, he has always been courteous and respectful of their desires."

"In your letter, did you write that you had never seen any indication that Buck was violent or even that he was particularly aggressive?"

"I did say that."

"Did you also say, 'Among this group [people the witness knew who also knew Buck], Buck had no reputation for violence that I am aware of'?"

"Counselor, I said in the letter, and I repeat here, that I have no knowledge of violent acts by Buck," Schulze said, clearly having lost some altitude. "He was always courteous with me and always respectful. And whenever I saw him, he was that way. I never actually saw him engage in a violent act or even a very aggressive act."

"But you were apprehensive of him?"

"No, counselor, I was weary of him. I tired of his paranoia, his attitude that other people had existence only, really, to hurt him in some way. But I never felt any personal apprehensions about his presence."

When Schulze added that many things had happened since he wrote the letter to cause him "to look back on the letter with a small amount of embarrassment," Schroeder interjected, "The event you are referring to would be his murder conviction?"

I was heartened by the nature of the question, certain that Schulze could reap advantage from it.

"Yes, and I believe he escaped from custody at some time," the witness responded. "And I had begun to hear lots of stories that there may have been some aspects of his character I wasn't aware of or, at least, weren't manifest at that time."

Inadvertently, the Government was aiding my effort to shock the jury with Buck Walker's loathsome background. Now they knew that he'd escaped from custody, a fact I had intended to try to elicit from Jennifer over a predictable objection from the prosecution.

Schroeder now tried to turn the screw on my witness. "And just as you once vouched for Buck's character for nonviolence, you are now appearing here today to vouch for Jennifer's character for nonviolence."

Schulze folded his arms across his chest. "Well, it's not exactly the same because I'm here in San Francisco in person under oath in this courtroom testifying for Jennifer Jenkins. And this letter I wrote I did so at someone's request. Maybe Jennifer's or maybe Buck's lawyer's—I don't remember. There is a difference in the magnitude between the two, it seems to me."

"So, you would say that Jennifer is more nonviolent than Buck was nonviolent?" Sarcasm, in small doses, can be effective.

"There are *no* traits in Jennifer that indicate violence."

"But you were confident, yet, that Buck was nonviolent as well?"

"Somewhat."

Judge King was getting testy. "Haven't we exhausted this subject, Mr. Schroeder, *please*?"

Schroeder instantly realized that he had nothing further.

During this byplay, I discovered by careful rereading that Schulze's letter was not entirely a glowing tribute to Buck; in fact, the lawyer had set down some observations that were more in keeping with his testimony this day.

Thus, on redirect, I could ask, "Did you say on page two of your letter to the judge that 'Buck is big and occasionally looks mean and people speak about this'?"

"Oh, yes, I did."

Our next witness looked as if she'd been born in the same 1960s time capsule with Debbie Noland. Leilah Burns, like her husband, Donald, still favored floppy sandals, peace symbols, and ponchos. The Burnses were a pleasant couple, soft-spoken, sensitive, and peaceful. Both were completely convinced that their good friend and soulmate Jennifer had had nothing to do with the disappearance and murder of the Grahams. I had originally planned to call them both, but Len cautioned that if we called too many character witnesses, the jury might suspect we were relying too heavily on this line of defense. Len's observation made sense, so we called only Leilah as a witness.

On the stand, Leilah told Weinglass that she and her husband had lived in Hawaii for fourteen years on a sailboat moored permanently at Oahu's Keehi Lagoon. She had known Jennifer ever since the day in early 1974 when the *Iola* sailed into Keehi. Jennifer and Buck had stayed there for five days, Burns said, and the two women, hitting it off from the start, visited daily. The next time they had seen each other was when Leilah visited Jennifer in jail after her arrest. After Jennifer made bail, she came to live with the Burnses and their two young children (then ages four and seven) on their boat for eight months. It was quite long enough for Leilah Burns to form a strong opinion about Jennifer's character. "In my view," Leilah told the court and jury, "Jennifer is a very gentle, loving, caring, and considerate person. She's not capable of being violent."*

---

*Something that would not come out in court this day: Leilah Burns had told me that Jennifer habitually talked in her sleep. Leilah admitted to listening carefully to Jennifer's nocturnal comments in the close quarters of the boat, where their bunks were only a few feet apart, wondering whether or not she would talk about Palmyra or the Grahams. She had assumed that a guilty person would, like Lady Macbeth, cry out guilty phrases in the night. Jennifer had *not once* talked in her sleep about Palmyra or the Grahams, Leilah assured me, and furthermore, Jennifer always seemed restful and at peace in her sleep. At first, I told Mrs. Burns we would ask her about this on direct examination, but in the end, I decided we shouldn't because there was an opposite side to the coin. The prosecution could argue that if Jennifer's story about two people (whom she supposedly liked) losing their lives just a short while back by drowning or shark attack was actually the truth, then being the gentle, compassionate person the defense claimed she was, why hadn't she tossed and turned in her sleep even over that fact?

Way back in 1974, when Jennifer was first arrested and Leilah Burns was interviewed by the FBI, she had remarked that she could vouch for Jennifer's good character. In answer to Len's open-ended question about how she could have had such a strong feeling about Jennifer after knowing her for only five days, she responded, "I got very close to her. *I really felt she was a good person.*"

I winced inwardly. Conceivably, the very broad term "good person" could give the Government license to bring out all of Jennifer's previous misdeeds.

Enoki came forward for cross-examination. "Mrs. Burns, I gather you would agree with the proposition that Jennifer is an intelligent person?"

"Yes."

"Did you, in fact, tell the FBI that Buck appeared to be the muscle in the relationship and Jennifer was the brains?"

"No, I did not."

"Did you say words to that effect?"

"I can't even imagine it being interpreted to that effect. I did not know Buck."

"You'd never met Buck?"

"I had met Buck one day. He came on our boat and spent a couple of hours and really, I talked to Jennifer the whole time."

"You don't dispute that Jennifer was the more intelligent, or appeared to you to be the more intelligent of the two, do you?"

"No, I don't dispute that," Leilah said. "But I honestly could not say that because I don't know Buck."

"You've never seen Jennifer in a situation where she was in a remote area in need of food, have you?"

"No."

"You will admit, Mrs. Burns, that some people who are non-violent in some situations can react with violence under other situations?"

"I imagine so."

"Now, in response to one of Mr. Weinglass's questions, did you describe Jennifer as being a *good person*?"

Enoki had spotted the opening.

"Yes."

"Okay. Did you mean to imply by this that she was an *honest* person also, in your opinion?"

Although Judge King had not relaxed his inane rule that only the lawyer who called a witness could object to questions on cross, I wasn't about to abide by it. In the time it would take me to advise Len to object, even if it was only a split second, the witness could have already answered. Enoki knew the answer would logically be that Mrs. Burns felt her friend *was* honest. He was maneuvering, obviously, to bring up Jennifer's three prior theft convictions on the rationale that honest people don't steal.

"Objection," I immediately blurted out. "Beyond the scope of direct examination."

The judge scowled at me. "You have Mr. Weinglass right next to you to make the objection," he said.

"I'll join in the objection," Len quickly said.

Court: "Mr. Enoki, I'm going to sustain the objection to that. She was called for a very limited purpose."

"Then I would request that her testimony relating to Jennifer Jenkins as being a 'good person' be stricken," Enoki said, "because I am not allowed to cross-examine on what that term means to the witness."

Judge King reminded the prosecutor, a shade curtly, that he had already sustained my objection.

But Enoki was undeterred. An experienced trial lawyer, he knew there is almost always another way to skin a cat. Wheeling back to the witness, he asked, "Have you become aware of any information that you know personally, or that you have been told of from other people, that would be inconsistent with Jennifer being a good person?"

I knew exactly where Enoki was going. It was an old prosecution ploy. If the witness had answered no, which was predictable, Enoki's next question would have been automatic: "If you *had* heard or been told *that Jennifer had three times been convicted of theft*, would you still feel she was a good person?" All of Jennifer's damaging past would lie before the jury.

Pressing my luck, perhaps, I immediately objected again. "It's too broad, your honor. Also, it's beyond the scope of direct."

The court again sustained my objection. "She wasn't called to testify that Jennifer was a good person," Judge King admonished Enoki.

"*I* can't help what *she* said," Enoki retorted. "I didn't ask that question, your honor. It came out in her answer to Mr. Weinglass's question."

"Let me help you *out*," the judge exploded in a burst of impatience new and no doubt startling to this jury. Turning to Leilah Burns, the judge asked more genially: "What do you mean by 'good person'?"

"I love her."

"You love her? Fine."

"I think she's a good person," added Burns, who was struggling to keep from being intimidated by prosecutor or judge.

"Any other questions?" the judge asked Enoki.

The distinct implication was that there had better not be. "No, your honor," said a newly compliant Enoki.

I took a deep breath. That had been a close call for the defense. We'd felt the bullet breeze past, but it hadn't touched a whisker.

When Leilah Burns reached the safety of the corridor, she literally fell into the arms of her husband. "I hope I did all right," she whispered. She was crying, but softly, like someone in mourning.

Our final character witness was Lawrence Seltzer, who had known Jennifer ever since she had baby-sat for his family in Toronto twenty-five years before. Beginning in 1979, she had worked for nearly four years as a recruiter for his executive search firm in North Hollywood. The portly, graying businessman said he felt Jennifer was "incapable of violence. And I would say she's incapable of assisting anyone in the course of violent behavior."

"Would it be safe to say that you never observed Jennifer in a situation where her survival would have been threatened?" Schroeder asked on cross examination.

"No, I did not. . . . But we had seventeen people working for me at one time with a variety of personalities, and I found that Jennifer got along with them. As a matter of fact, frequently she would try to act as a peacemaker when we had stressful situations."

When Seltzer stepped down, we had one last witness (before Jennifer) waiting in the hallway. Dr. John McCosker, director of San Francisco's Steinhart Aquarium, was considered the Bay Area's leading ichthyologist, or fish expert. When Elliot Enoki had refused to stipulate to the *Encyclopedia Americana* article that stated a swordfish's bill was capable of penetrating the hull of a boat, I had gone looking for an expert who could so testify. I viewed Dr. McCosker as a very important witness, but others on the defense team were less convinced.

Right off the top of his head, McCosker had given me a couple of examples of swordfish damage to boats and assured me that the bill was quite capable of penetrating the *Sea Wind*'s inch-and-a-quarter-thick hull. (Most wooden sailboats, I learned, had only inch-thick hulls.) I had asked him to conduct some research and prepare himself for trial. Now the marine biologist waited in the corridor with an actual swordfish bill in hand.

McCosker was prepared to tell the jury about several documented incidents. In two museums, he would testify, are portions of the hulls of large whalers penetrated by swordfish; in one case, a bill actually pierced through thirteen inches of wood, and in the other, the fish rammed through twenty-two inches of wood. There was also the documented case of a swordfish punching an inch-deep hole in a copper-sheathed vessel named the *Dreadnaught*. At the moment, though, Dr. McCosker was on hold, since Len vehemently disagreed with my calling him to the stand. We took a short recess to discuss the issue in the hallway.

"I know McCosker is going to say that a swordfish bill can penetrate the hull of a boat, but," Weinglass argued, "on cross it'll come out this is extremely rare. That's a very weak position."

Of course, I didn't plan to wait for the Government to bring this out on cross. "I'll bring out on direct that it's rare, but we need McCosker because without him the jury could think it's *impossible* for a swordfish to put a hole in a boat. Impossibility is infinitely worse than extreme rarity." But Len held his ground.

As I saw it, the whole swordfish issue reflected on Jennifer's credibility. If the jury disbelieved this story, they would be likely to deduce what the Government wanted them to: that the hole was a bullet hole, and Jennifer's lie was an attempt to cover up her complicity in murder.

My already prepared Q and A of the respected ichthyologist aimed to bolster Jennifer's account with learned expertise:

Q: "I take it you're familiar with swordfish?"

A: "Yes."

Q: "Could you describe this fish for us?"

A: "It is a mackerel-like fish of the *xiphias gladius* species."

Q: "How large is the fish?"

A: "Very large. Its body can equal the size of the largest sharks in the ocean."

Q: "And is it an extremely strong fish?"

A: "Astonishingly strong."

Q: "What about its speed?"

A: "Its powerful forked tail and a sail-like dorsal fin give it a power and speed in swimming equaled by few other oceanic animals."

Q: "What about its bill?"

A: "The bill is a prolongation of the forepart of the skull. It turns into a horizontally flattened sword composed of vomer, ethmoid, and premaxillary bones."

And so on . . . until we got into McCosker's specific examples, from which the inference could be drawn that a swordfish could definitely have penetrated the inch-and-a-quarter-thick wooden hull of the *Sea Wind*. Granted, the incidents McCosker would cite weren't as common as bad debt, but they *did* happen, an undeniable fact tending to corroborate Jennifer's story.

But for some reason, Len was more determined on this point than on any other since we had become co-counsel.

Jennifer had originally agreed with me, but Len had gotten to her. "I agree with Len," she said. "It could be dangerous."

"*Not* calling him could be dangerous," I shot back.

As our discussion grew increasingly animated, several members of Jennifer's family descended upon us. All had been lobbied by my co-counsel. Nonetheless, I was holding firm until Jennifer's fifteen-year-old nephew chimed in, urgently beseeching me not to call the fish expert. When it reached that extreme, I could only smile in resignation. Len had gracefully given in to me on several other matters during the trial. Against my better judgment, I now decided to lay down my ichthyological arms. At least, I thought, we had Larry Seibert's swordfish-hole testimony, however arguably biased.

WE WERE down to our last witness, the puzzling young woman sitting at the defense table. Before she took the stand, however, I had to deal, by way of stipulation, with the repercussions of an explosive jailhouse interview Jennifer had given to *Honolulu Advertiser* reporter Bruce Benson two days after her arrest. I had learned about it only three weeks before the trial, when Enoki sent me a copy of the article.

In his October 31, 1974, front-page byline scoop, Benson quoted Jennifer making some damaging, even outrageous statements. After telling Benson "Mac's last words to us were, 'Make yourselves at home until we get back.' I'm sure he didn't expect to go out and die. But that's what we did: We made the boat our home," she gave this explanation for not reporting the disappearance of the Grahams to the authorities when she and Buck reached Hawaii: "They would have confiscated it—they would have taken the boat. We didn't have anything to prove that it was ours. He didn't really give us the boat. He just said make yourselves at home. I realize that's a rationalization on my part, *to keep something that I love.*"

Jennifer's statement that she made the rationalization "to *keep* something that I love" ran completely counter to what she was now saying—that she always intended to eventually return the boat to Kit Muncey. Although Shishido had already testified that Jennifer had told him she didn't report the Grahams' disappearance for fear the authorities would take the boat away from her, her use of the word "keep" with Benson was even stronger, and not as open to interpretation.

Moreover, prior to reading this jewel, I had worked up a cross-examination of Shishido on the issue of whether Jennifer had actually told him, as he claimed, that she "rationalized" Mac's alleged last words, "Make yourselves at home," to mean that she and Buck could take possession of the *Sea Wind* if the Grahams didn't return. Such a deduction by Jennifer was, on its face, ridiculous, and Jennifer wasn't sure she had given Shishido precisely this explanation. (Jennifer's purported use of the word "rationalized" was particularly worrisome. If she was capable of making such a preposterously self-serving "rationalization," would the jury assume she was capable of rationalizing away murder as well?) The Benson article virtually proved that Shishido had quoted Jennifer correctly, at least on this point.

Jennifer also repeated to Benson the lie she'd told Shishido about the *Iola*'s running aground on the reef and so forth. The article concluded with Jennifer's disturbingly flip quote: "The *Sea Wind* wanted to go around the world again, and I wanted to go with it."

Characteristically, Jennifer had never mentioned anything to me about this article, but she did calmly confirm, when I asked, that Benson had quoted her accurately.

"Jennifer, how in the living hell could you tell this guy Benson something so outrageous as 'the *Sea Wind* wanted to go around the world again,' and you wanted to go with it?" I bellowed.

"I don't know. I don't know. It was a crazy thing to say." For once, she didn't try to grin herself off the hook.

"Thanks, Jen. We really need crazy things like this in our case," I retorted.

The prosecutor had waited until the last minute to signal his intention to call Benson as a witness to repeat the highlights of his exclusive interview.* Riffling back through a newspaper clipping file so incomplete it did not include the October 31st interview, I found another article by the reporter, published the day before. In it, Benson wrote about Curt Shoemaker's last radio contact with

---

*I do not mean to imply that Enoki's waiting so long was calculated misconduct. Enoki is a highly ethical prosecutor, and my guess is that the Benson matter was just an oversight on his part.

the Grahams and extensively quoted Bernard Leonard. I underlined one paragraph in red: *Leonard said Shoemaker was told during the last radio transmission from the Grahams that they had invited Allen and Jenkins to dinner, presumably as a going-away party, since the man and woman were to depart from Palmyra aboard the Iola the next day.* I was confident this was wrong, and something had been lost or garbled in the transmission between Shoemaker, Leonard and Benson. I didn't believe for a moment that there had been such an invitation (even if there had, this in no way would have militated against Buck still having murdered the Grahams), but I knew that Enoki, at all costs, would try to prevent the jury from hearing that there may have been, for it directly contradicted his position that no invitation ever existed. He would have to shoot down this article while defending the accuracy of the same author's jailhouse interview. I was soon on the phone negotiating long-distance with my courtroom opponent. We ended up agreeing that neither of us would call Benson and worked out a stipulation that I now read to the jury.

"It is stipulated that if Bruce Benson, a former reporter with the *Honolulu Advertiser*, were called as a witness, he would testify as follows: That he interviewed Jennifer Jenkins on October 31, 1974, and among other things, Miss Jenkins told him that the day after the Grahams did not return to their boat, the *Sea Wind*, she and Roy Allen found the Grahams' dinghy about a half mile down the beach in a westerly direction from where the *Sea Wind* was anchored, and that it was overturned as if it had flipped over. Also, that since the wind was from the southeast, she and Roy Allen figured the dinghy flipped over around Paradise Island. Furthermore, that as she and Roy Allen were taking their boat and the *Sea Wind* out of the channel on Palmyra, their boat got hung up on the reef and they unloaded things from their boat onto the *Sea Wind*."

Enoki had accepted a quid pro quo with me that markedly favored the defense. In exchange for keeping the dinner invitation out (which was of no use to the defense anyway, since I intended to tell the jury I did not believe there had been one), and including the story about the *Iola's* going around (a lie we already had to explain away anyway, because Jennifer had repeated it to Shishido),

I not only kept out the damaging and outrageous statements Jennifer had made to Benson, but I got into the stipulation the very key fact that she had told Benson she and Buck found the Zodiac on the *beach*. Also, I managed to get in that Jennifer told Benson she and "Roy" had assumed the Zodiac had flipped over *near* Paradise Island, and because of the wind from the southeast, their inferential belief that the dinghy had floated *to* where they found it on Strawn Island, thereby rebutting Bernard Leonard's testimony on this point.

During a short recess before I called Jennifer to the stand, I told Judge King that Jennifer would be giving a lot of testimony relating to her state of mind. Although such testimony is normally admissible, it often engenders objections, and I told the judge that rather than having legal skirmishes before the jury or asking for a recess to argue each objection, I wanted to resolve, at least in general terms, the admissibility question before Jennifer took the stand.

Judge King declined. "I usually have the experience of ruling on objections at the time they are made. That's about all I get paid for, actually."

"I told you I'm giving you good grades on your handling of objections," I said, deadpan.

"Thank you. A-plus would not be enough," he replied.

The jury was summoned.

"Call your next witness, Mr. Bugliosi," Judge King said.

"The defense calls Miss Jennifer Jenkins."

CHAPTER 38

WHEN I CALLED JENNIFER'S NAME, I looked back at her and nodded encouragingly. *You'll do fine,* I said with my smile.

She stood and walked purposefully to the witness stand. The

heels of her pumps clicked softly on the waxed floor, the only sound audible in the hushed courtroom. Every eye bored into her, but she did not wilt. When she faced the clerk, she raised her right hand with determination and confidently voiced the oath to tell the truth, the whole truth, and nothing but the truth.

There wasn't an empty seat in the courtroom.

I scanned the faces of the transfixed jurors. Were they thinking that here was the one person in the courtroom who could solve the mystery surrounding the events on Palmyra Island? Did they wonder if she would tell everything she knew? Or did they suspect she'd turn out to be evasive and untruthful and keep what she *really* knew locked inside forever? One thing was for sure. It was obvious the jurors couldn't wait to hear from Jennifer. It was written all over their collective countenance.

For her big day in court, Jennifer was wearing one of her smart new suits—a baby-blue ensemble with a white silk blouse—and little makeup. At Len's suggestion, she wore no lipstick at all. "Your upper lip is very thin," he had told her, "and lipstick accentuates this. Thin lips are cold-looking."

When the clerk asked the witness to state her name for the record, the response came in a clear, steady voice: "My name is Jennifer Jenkins."

Once she sat down in the witness chair, however, Jennifer suddenly looked vulnerable, and smaller. The microphone in front of her rose up nearly to her forehead. Of course, she *was* very vulnerable.

My direct examination of Jennifer would differ from most. Feelings are generally not a major part of a criminal trial. Testimony, in the main, concerns whether the defendant did or did not do certain things. But here, we had to get into Jennifer's feelings in just about everything she said and did. It was the only way I had any hope of convincing the jury that behind Jennifer's seemingly guilty conduct was an innocent state of mind.

After some preliminary background questions—she would be forty in July, she was unmarried, and so forth—I asked what I had long known I would first ask her of substance when she took the stand. "Jennifer, you're probably going to be on the stand for two or three days," I began, "but right at the top of your testimony, I want to ask you these questions. Did you kill, or participate in any fashion whatsoever, in the killing of Mac or Muff Graham?"

"No." She looked away from me and toward the jury. "I swear"—her voice remained firm—"by all that I hold dear, that I've never harmed any human being in my whole life." Her eyes began to fill with tears.

"Do you have any personal knowledge of who may have killed them?"

"No. I do not."

Now we could get on with the rest of my direct examination.*

"When you were indicted for the murder of Muff Graham in February of 1981, did you turn yourself in?"

"Yes."

"Were you released on bail shortly thereafter?"

"Yes, that same day."

I brought out that she had continued to be free on bail, and "gainfully employed," since that time.

Jennifer went on to say she was currently the branch office manager of a telecommunications company in Los Angeles. She told about meeting Buck Walker at the Hilo apartment complex in April 1972. "We were both there to visit friends. We caught each other's eye." She graced the bittersweet memory with the faintest of nostalgic smiles.

I asked her to briefly describe her relationship with Buck before the trip to Palmyra.

She sighed deeply. "I was twenty-five and he was about thirty-five when we met. He was a very strong, dominating person. He

---

*As is typical for me, for the most part on my direct examination of Jennifer, I stayed at the podium with my yellow pad of several hundred questions, doggedly trying to get into the record—literally *force* into the record—the facts and evidence upon which my case was based. I wanted the jury to focus their attention almost exclusively on Jennifer and her testimony, relegating my role to mere facilitator. (On cross-examination, however, I am apt to roam every inch of the courtroom floor, and my style is much more forceful and demonstrative, becoming, along with the adverse witness, a part of the drama on center stage.)

liked to have his own way, liked to be in charge. And I guess I'm the type of person who doesn't make unnecessary waves."

"Are you suggesting to this jury and this judge that you would do whatever he told you to do?"

"No, absolutely not."

I proceeded to have Jennifer cite examples where she drew the line:

"Without going into all the things that two people living together might disagree about, Jennifer, did the two of you have any differences with respect to guns?"

"Yes."

"What were those differences?" I asked.

"Buck liked guns, and I've always had an extreme aversion to them. On two occasions, he brought firearms into the house, and we had a number of arguments about it. Ultimately, he took them out."

"Jennifer, you've heard testimony at this trial that Buck did, in fact, have a gun on Palmyra?"

"Yes."

"Why did you go along with this?"

"Buck insisted that anyone who was going to sail in the open seas had to have some means of protection, and so I went along with that."

I returned to examples of Jennifer's standing up to Buck. "Did you tell me once about an incident involving spaghetti?"

She told how Buck had slung the pot of spaghetti against the cabin wall at Mountain View, splattering pasta and tomato sauce everywhere. "I just left it there. The next day, he asked when I was going to clean it up. I told him I didn't do it. 'You did. You clean it up.'"

"Did he, in fact, clean it up?"

"Uh-huh."

There would be more examples of Jennifer's standing up to Buck later in her testimony.

Getting before the jury Walker's hard-core criminal history was an essential part of my continuing strategy to prosecute him. I anticipated an objection from Enoki whichever way I attempted to do it, but particularly if he first had the opportunity to argue the matter, orally or in a brief, to the judge. I decided that questions to Jennifer would be the best way, forcing Enoki to show the jury, if he objected, that he did not want them to hear this very relevant information. There was no ethical problem, since there was no question in my mind that the information, being part of the basis for Jennifer's state of mind with respect to Buck (a key issue in the case), was legally admissible. However, because of improper rulings by courts, not all legally admissible evidence gets into the trial record.

I asked Jennifer when she had become aware of Buck's "background." Enoki did not object. She replied that he informed her soon after they started living together that he had been convicted of armed robbery, but explained that he was only nineteen at the time and that the gun had not been loaded.

The cat was out of the bag. For the first time in the trial, the jury now knew that apart from Buck Walker's having been convicted of Muff Graham's murder, Jennifer's lover was a convicted felon.*

"Did you learn when you were living with him in Mountain View that he'd been convicted of a *second* armed robbery here in California, and that he'd also been convicted of a burglary in the past?" I continued on.

Again, Enoki did not object.

"Not at that point. I found out about that since."

"Did you learn at that time that in 1966 and 1967 he was committed to a state mental hospital for the criminally insane in California?"

Again, there was no objection.

"He told me about that," Jennifer answered. "He said he was just feigning insanity so he wouldn't have to go back to San Quentin."

"Even though you only knew at the beginning about the one robbery conviction, were you disturbed about the fact you were living with someone who had that type of a background?"

"Yes, but I had found out about this after we had started living

---

*The jury had previously heard from defense witness Rick Schulze that Walker had once "escaped from custody." However, custody can result from not only a felony, but a misdemeanor, and of course, one can be in custody without having been convicted of a crime.

together . . . and we were already in love." I hoped the jury might begin to see that this four-letter word meant more to Jennifer than to more practical-minded people.

"Would you tell the jury and the judge what it was about Buck Walker that attracted you to him?"

"Well, Buck was bright and articulate and personable," she answered. "I knew he had a bad background, but I felt he had a lot of potential and—"

She stopped abruptly. "I—I thought I could help him." She took several deep breaths, trying to calm herself.

In the stilted decorum of a courtroom it would have been difficult for Jennifer to testify to her erotic attraction for Buck, but she would admit privately that in his arms, she'd experienced the most gratifying sex of her life. I planned to allude to this physical attraction whenever possible.

"Was there anything else about Buck that attracted you to him?" I asked, hoping that at least the women on the jury might empathize with Jennifer's powerful feelings for a man others found so frightening and repugnant.

"I found Buck attractive. He was a big, strong man. He made me feel—safe and protected."

I next had Jennifer summarize what led up to Buck's arrest on the Big Island for illegal drug sales. She said it all started when "a friend from the mainland brought some pills" to Hawaii and asked Buck if he knew a buyer. Buck put him in touch with someone, and that person, who turned out to be an undercover agent, later came back twice to Buck promising him a lot of money "if Buck could get some more pills." When Buck did, he was arrested.

"What was your state of mind with respect to what happened to Buck?" I asked.

"He was entrapped," she said boldly. "He wasn't selling drugs before the undercover officer started enticing him. I thought it was unfair." She recalled Buck's concern that the drug bust would send him back to San Quentin. "He was terrified of that place. He told me terrible stories about San Quentin."

"Did he make any vow with respect to not going back to San Quentin?" I asked.

"He said he would *never* go back to San Quentin."

"How did you feel about Buck's decision to jump bail because of his fear of San Quentin?"

"Well, at first I didn't think running was the right thing to do. But—I loved Buck too much to see him return to San Quentin."

Jennifer related her family's unsuccessful efforts to dissuade her from running away with Buck. "It was very hard to go against their wishes, but I felt Buck needed me."

During this testimony, Sunny and Ted, though after all these years still plagued by their failure to keep her from sailing off into harm's way, remained expressionless in their front-row seats.

Moving on, I elicited from Jennifer that Buck had acquired a passport under the alias Roy Allen before they left for Palmyra, but that she had used her real name on hers.

Jennifer next explained, in response to my question, that she soon realized that flour, sugar, oil, and other supplies were dwindling more rapidly than she had estimated, fully one-third having been consumed on the trip down.

Eliciting Jennifer's admission about these food problems was consistent with the pattern I would pursue throughout my examination. With two calculated exceptions, I intended to raise every negative circumstance, every inconsistency, discrepancy, and incriminating thing she had said or done. I wanted to cross-examine Jennifer myself, on my terms, leaving nothing more than a plate of leftovers for the prosecutor; *in other words, I wanted to conduct Enoki's cross-examination for him.* If he reprised the points I covered, he'd be going over old ground with the jury, with the impact almost surely being diminished.*

---

*This preemptive tactic frequently converts an opponent's left hook into a left jab. If it does not do that, it will usually shave at least a few decibels off his trumpets. It indicates to the jury that the evidence cannot be all that bad if the preempting lawyer matter-of-factly and almost cavalierly brings it out himself on direct examination of his own witness. (In some situations, I have refined this tactic by actually calling an opposition witness as my own.) In this case, having Jennifer admit, on direct examination, to her lies and all the other negative evidence against her was far better than having these things come out for the first time on cross by Enoki asking, "Isn't it true, Miss Jenkins, that . . ."

"As you know, Jennifer, there has been testimony at this trial that you and Buck were in relatively poor shape as far as food was concerned during your stay on Palmyra. Did you consider the situation desperate?"

"No. It wasn't great, but it *definitely* wasn't desperate."

"Was it your state of mind, when you arrived on Palmyra, to live solely off the provisions you had brought with you?"

"No. We planned to supplement our provisions by living off the land, off foods available on Palmyra."

"On a given day, if your diet, as indicated by your diary, consisted of fish from the lagoon and coconuts from the island, would this mean that your food provisions on board the *Iola* had been completely depleted?"

"Absolutely not," Jennifer said. "It just meant exactly what I said. We were supplementing and using those foods available to us on Palmyra in conjunction with our stores."

"You were trying to stretch out the stores you had as much as possible?"

"Right."

She went on to explain that they quickly learned which fish from the lagoon could be safely eaten. She noted the many uses she'd discovered for the wealth of coconuts on the island. "We made milk shakes, ice cream, cookies, sour cream, butter. Coconuts are a very nutritious food."

After establishing that Jennifer would frequently need her "diary" to refresh her memory about events that occurred on Palmyra, I handed her a photostatic copy of the *Iola*'s log. It had, she explained, become more of a daily journal or diary during her sojourn on the island.

"What other foods did you find on Palmyra?"

"There were lots of crabs."

"Would you read your July 17th diary entry to the jury?"

"'I never saw so many land crabs in my life,'" she recited, "'and they tasted delicious.'"

"Did you attempt to grow a vegetable garden?"

"Yes. I had brought all kinds of seeds down, vegetables and fruit seeds, and we attempted to grow a vegetable garden."

"Were you successful at all in growing vegetables in the garden?" (A far better question than a prosecutor's "Isn't it true, Miss Jenkins, that your effort to grow food on Palmyra to help sustain you was completely unsuccessful?")

"No," Jennifer answered. "The hermit crabs used to climb up everywhere and raid them."

"I take it, Jennifer, you would have preferred, during this period of time that you were on Palmyra, to have had a more diverse diet—more meat, fruit, and vegetables. Is that correct?"

She smiled at the understatement.

"Yes."

By late August 1974, their food supplies had fallen to about *seven days'* worth of food, Jennifer said. Pointing out the apparent discrepancy that an earlier, August 15 diary entry estimated only about "ten meals" left, I asked Jennifer how they could still have had seven full *days* of provisions remaining by *late* August.

"Well, more and more at the end, we relied heavily on those foods that were available to us on the island. I was conserving our stores because I never wanted to fall below a week's supply."

Did a period of a week have any particular significance? I asked.

"Yes. We were planning to go to Fanning Island to get supplies. I wasn't sure exactly how long it would take, but I knew that a week was the absolute outside. So, I didn't want to go below a week's supply."

Although her two previous answers satisfied my next question, the subject was so critical I couldn't leave the matter open for the jury to interpret. I had her turn to her August 23 entry, just seven days before the key day of August 30, and said: "It reads: 'No dinner save a coconut milk shake.' I asked: "Did that entry mean that you did not have any food left whatsoever at that point other than the coconut milk shake?"

"No, it didn't mean that at all," Jennifer insisted. "It just meant that all I had to eat that day was a coconut milk shake. By choice."

I asked Jennifer if she considered herself a big eater.

"No, I'm not a big eater."

"How many meals do you usually eat a day?"

"I usually eat one meal a day."

"Do you sometimes go a day without eating?"

"Yes."

"Jennifer, in late August of that year, did you have any sense of malnutrition at all?"

"No, not at all."

"To your knowledge, how was Buck doing?"

"He looked fine."

"Had either of you lost any weight on Palmyra?"

"No."

I next asked her to describe briefly the couple's relationships with the various visitors to Palmyra that summer. She told how Jack Wheeler and his son had helped free the *Iola* from the reef and how, in succeeding days, Jack had given them advice about how to live and eat on Palmyra.

Jennifer said Bernard and Evelyn Leonard "seemed cordial enough." She described her efforts to barter with them for food. "Evelyn said she'd trade for some things, but when I went over to her boat to do so one day, she said she wasn't feeling well. She said she had a tooth inlay problem," and Jennifer didn't go aboard.

"So you didn't get the impression that she didn't want you on the boat. She simply didn't feel good that day."

"Yes. She was always very friendly to me."

"Would you look at your July 13th entry and see if there is any reference to this tooth inlay problem and your not going on the boat?"

"Yes. It says, 'Evelyn wasn't feeling well. A reoccurrence of tooth inlay.' "

Jennifer recalled the Leonards' bringing books and rice pudding over to the *Iola* the day they left, her birthday, and Evelyn's snapping her picture with Puffer. She described how Bernard shouted farewell from the bow of his boat. "He waved and yelled, 'Goodbye, Jennifer. Have a happy birthday and a wonderful year.' "

Jennifer explained that she had baked for Don Stevens and Bill Larson, using flour and sugar they supplied, and exchanged books and magazines with them.

And though Tom Wolfe and Norman Sanders "weren't on the island very long," Jennifer said she got along well with both of them.

I asked her to relate the incident of Wolfe's being bitten by one of Buck's dogs.

"Tom came over to the Refrigerator House, and I guess he somehow startled Popolo, and Popolo lunged at Tom and nipped him."

"What type of dog is Popolo?"

"He's a pit bull."

In response to my question, Jennifer went on to say that even before Palmyra, she and Buck had trouble with Popolo, who would chase cars down the street, barking ferociously.

I wanted to show that the attack did not indicate, as the Government wanted to suggest, that Buck's dogs were starving. This particular dog, like many others of its breed, had been flat-out mean.

"You heard Mr. Wolfe testify that you didn't apologize when he was bitten?"

"Right. And I can't believe that I didn't apologize to him. Buck was yelling and screaming at Popolo and hitting him, and I wanted him to get Popolo out of there. Tom went running off. I'm sure I apologized to him but perhaps he didn't hear me in all the confusion."

When I asked Jennifer about little Puffer, my witness grinned for the first time on the stand. She eagerly told the jury how much Puffer weighed (twenty-five pounds), how intelligent and sensitive she was, and how the two of them liked sleeping in the same bed. "On my last two jobs," Jennifer added, "she came to work with me and she slept on a little pillow under my desk."

I was presenting this evidence for the jurors to draw their own conclusions, presumably favorable. I was not about to argue in my summation, however, that someone who loved animals was unlikely to commit murder. Enoki could respond that Hitler also loved animals, once saying that the more he got to know humans, the more he loved animals. While millions were dying in his gas chambers, the Führer showered affection on Blondie, his purebred German shepherd. Charles Manson also said he loved animals more than human beings and would rather kill a person than a bird or even a rattlesnake.

I had saved the Grahams for last. "With respect to Mac and Muff, during your stay on Palmyra, how often would you see them or talk to them?"

"Just about every day we would see one or both of them."

"And did you feel you got to know them fairly well?"

"Yes."

"How would you describe Mac Graham?"

"Mac was a wonderful man," she answered warmly. "He was full of life and very outgoing. He would come by the boat frequently and bring us fish he caught. I think he fished more frequently because he knew we could use it."

And Muff?

"She was always very nice to me. Muff was much more reserved, kept much more to herself than did Mac. And she wasn't happy. She wasn't happy to be on Palmyra."

"Did you have any animosity whatsoever toward either Mac or Muff?"

"No, absolutely not."

"To your knowledge, were you aware of any animosity or ill feeling that either one of them had toward you?" I asked.

"No."

"So, if they harbored any bad feelings toward you, you were not aware of them?"

"Right. They were both always friendly."

I asked if she or Buck ever had any kind of an argument with either Mac or Muff on Palmyra. Other than the problems with the two big dogs (which she set forth), she said, no.

"How would you describe the relationship that existed between the Grahams and you and Buck on Palmyra that summer of 1974?"

"It was friendly. Not especially close, I suppose, but definitely friendly."

"Jennifer, you heard Tom Wolfe's testimony at this trial that you told him *neither* you and Buck, nor the Grahams, wanted the others on the island. Do you recall telling him that?"

"I told Tom that both Mac and Muff, and Buck and I, had specifically chosen Palmyra because it was an uninhabited coral atoll. We had all come down there specifically to be alone, and I believed that this desire continued with—with Mac and Muff. But as it turned out, having Mac and Muff there was very good for us. Mac helped us in a number of ways. He brought us fish, and he tried to repair our outboard motor. Once our generator went out and he repaired that. So, having them there was good."

"Did you ever try to barter with the Grahams for food?"

"No."

"Inasmuch as you apparently did do this with the people on the other boats, why not with the Grahams?"

"Mac and Muff were down there for a prolonged period of time, so I knew they needed all their stores. I just offered, you know . . . wanted to barter with those people who were on their way to places where there were stores they could purchase."

It was getting late. Jennifer had been on the stand for more than two hours, and she looked fatigued. I turned to the judge and suggested this might be a convenient time to recess for the day.

"All right," said Judge King, taking my cue. "We'll recess until 9:30 A.M., and it won't rain hard tomorrow."

Outside the whole day, cold drizzle had given jewel-like San Francisco the mournful aspect of an Iron Curtain capital in the 1950s.

WEDNESDAY MORNING, FEBRUARY 19, 1986

WE ALL arrived in the courtroom with dripping raincoats and folded umbrellas generating small puddles. During the night, the skies had loosed another torrent of rain that showed no sign of easing. Mother Nature was most definitely in contempt of court.

For her second day on the stand, Jennifer wore a high-neck blouse and beige suit with buttons that were large, round, and brown, like her eyes. She had slept little the night before, Sunny informed me in a mother's worried tone.

As usual, the courtroom's gallery was packed.

At the podium, I said good morning to Jennifer, then commenced day two of my direct examination, continuing to take her through the events on Palmyra in essentially a chronological fashion.

I asked her if the entries in the diary concerning the Grahams constituted the total number of contacts she and Buck had had with Mac and Muff that summer. No, she said, the diary referred only to "some of the times we saw one another," nor did it even refer to every time she and Buck together visited the Grahams on the *Sea Wind*, a total she estimated as "maybe three or four times." She said it was hard to remember the exact number because it was "a long time ago."

I asked if there were times when either she or Buck would visit the *Sea Wind* without the other one along.

Yes, Jennifer said, "especially Buck. He used to go over to play chess with Mac more frequently." And she would occasionally go over by herself with coconut butter and coconut milk she'd made.

I had Jennifer read aloud a diary entry that involved a social evening Buck and Jennifer had spent aboard the *Sea Wind* on July 9: "'On our way to bathe took some coconut butter to Mac and Muff. Never got to bathe but had a very enjoyable evening with them, drinking wine, which tasted fine. And then some rum which was a bit too much for me on an empty stomach. Got pretty drunk—smoked two cigarettes. Mac had given R some Bull Durham earlier in the day. Then gave him a pack of some other cigarettes. He has a friend for life now.'"

"Jennifer, you've heard testimony from prosecution witnesses that they never saw you and Buck on the *Sea Wind*?"

"Yes."

"From where your boat and the other boats were moored at the dolphins, could one see the *Sea Wind*?"

"No."

"And why is that?"

"The *Sea Wind*—Mac had backed it into this little cove [as I had her indicate on the chart of the island]. And it was totally horse-shoed by land. And there was a little jut of land that came out helping to form the cove. So, there was no line-of-sight vision."

"Did this portion of Cooper Island jutting out into the lagoon have heavy vegetation and tall trees on it?" I asked.

"Yes."

She estimated the distance between the *Iola* and *Sea Wind* as two hundred yards.

Between July 6 and August 26, there were a total of twenty-three entries concerning Jennifer's and Buck's contacts with the Grahams. I had Jennifer read each one to the jury.

"The contact, then, between and among the four of you was of a considerable nature? Is that correct?"

"Yes."

The Walker jury had never heard this fact.

With regard to the August 22 entry that the Taylors wouldn't be arriving until the end of October, Jennifer said she and Buck had decided, upon hearing this news from their friends via Mac's radio link with Shoemaker, that they would have to make a trip to Fanning to pick up food supplies.

"You heard Mr. Wolfe's testimony that you told him that you and Buck were planning to go to Fanning?" I asked, reminding the jury of this corroboration of Jennifer's present testimony.

"That's right."

I asked Jennifer how she and Buck had intended to pay for the food they were going to purchase on Fanning. She answered that they had sold their generator to Mac for fifty dollars. Also, she said, they figured they could get temporary work at Fanning to pick up some extra money. "All we really needed was staples. I wanted to get dog food, rice, flour, sugar, beans, things like that." She also said they planned to trade some of their belongings on Fanning.

"After going to Fanning, was it your intention then to return to Palmyra?"

"Yes."

I moved on to a new area, a highly critical one for which I'd laid much groundwork earlier.

"Jennifer, were you aware that Fanning was against the wind— if you were to sail from Palmyra to Fanning?"

"Yes."

"Was that of concern to you?"

The nonchalance with which she answered was almost as telling as her words themselves. "When you're sailing into the wind, all you have to do is tack." She shrugged as if to say even nincompoops know that. "It's a harder sail, but we'd tacked before."

"Where did you have an opportunity to tack before?"

"We'd tacked intra-island among the Hawaiian Islands. And we'd tacked when we were approaching the channel to come into Palmyra."

"Jennifer, looking at the June 21st entry in your diary, is there any reference to tacking on that date?"

"Yes. 'Though winds were light last night and are brisk southeast today, we're having trouble relocating our island. *Tacking* from east to southwest.'"

"Did you know one way or the other whether the *current* would be in your favor or against you en route to Fanning?"

"I did not know."

"Even if you had thought the current as well as the wind were against you from Palmyra to Fanning, would that have affected your decision to go to Fanning?"

"No, it wouldn't have. In talking to Mac about it, he said he didn't think we would have a problem getting to Fanning. He said we might make it in as little as two or three days."

Jennifer went on to say she had tacked against both the wind and current before.

"You *did* think the trip to Fanning would be difficult. Is that correct?" I asked.

"I knew it was, yes, going to be difficult."

"Jennifer, does your diary reflect your intent to go to Fanning, and your preparations for the trip?"

"Yes."

I had Jennifer read portions of her entries for August 25— "Husked some coconuts for the trip"—August 26—"Mac brought by Fanning chart, which I copied"—and August 28— "Winds willing we shall be ready Saturday."

"Jennifer, going back to your August 23rd entry, does it say: 'Mac gave us fifty dollars for the generator'?"

"Yes."

"However, if you look at your August 26th, 27th, 28th, and 29th entries, there's a reference to your *still* having the generator, and it was being used to charge the batteries for the trip to Fanning. Is there any explanation for this?"

Looking down at her diary, Jennifer brushed an independent lock of hair from her face. "Well, Mac had given us the money on the 23rd. But he knew we needed to use the generator to charge the batteries. And he didn't have any objection to that. We were just going to give him the generator before we left." She spoke easily about Mac, as if recalling a friend.

"Continuing on, Jennifer, with the issue of your ability to get to Fanning with the *Iola*, you've heard testimony at this trial questioning the seaworthiness of the *Iola*, have you not?"

"Yes." Her eyes flared briefly.

"In your opinion was the *Iola* seaworthy?"

"Uh-huh. We—we wouldn't have left Hawaii on her if she wasn't seaworthy."

"What does the word 'seaworthy' mean to you?" I asked.

"Well, I see 'seaworthy' as a relative term. I think that some boats are more seaworthy than others. Some are newer boats, they have better rigging and better sails, and they pick up less water. But 'unseaworthy' is an absolute. 'Unseaworthy' means the boat will sink. The *Iola* was definitely seaworthy."

"Jennifer, you heard Mr. and Mrs. Leonard testify that you told them you would never leave Palmyra on the *Iola*. Did you say this?"

"No. Absolutely not. I—I don't know where they got that. I always assumed I would leave Palmyra on the *Iola*. That was our boat."

"At any time while you and Buck were on Palmyra, did you ask any of the people there—like the Wheelers, the Leonards, Tom Wolfe or the others—if you and Buck could hitch a ride with them? That is, leave Palmyra with them on their boat?"

"No, never."

"Did that thought ever enter your mind?"

"No."

"Either en route to Palmyra or when the *Iola* got hung up on the coral heads coming into the lagoon, did the *Iola* sustain any major damage?"

"She did not."

"Did the *Iola* leak en route to Palmyra?" I asked. "Did it take on water?"

"Yeah, just about all wooden boats leak. And she did leak."

"You heard Mr. Wheeler testify that even on Palmyra you were bilging the *Iola* every day while he was there?"

"Yes."

"Is that true?"

"When we first came in, it probably is true. We had just completed a long sea voyage. And Buck wanted to get the bilge totally dry to see if we had sustained any damage when we had bonked ourselves on the coral heads. So, for the first several days, we probably were bilging."

After that, they pumped out the bilge only a couple times a week, she said, "not because there was so much water, but any water that stood in the bilge threw off a musty odor."

I elicited from Jennifer that when they bought the *Iola*, they were told it had eighty gallons of fiberglassing on it. "Many, many, layers," she said.

"What's the significance of many, many layers?"

"Well, the more layers you have it means that you could have a crack on the outside—without it necessarily going all the way through. Tom Wolfe testified that he saw a crack. He could have seen a crack on the outside. It may or may not have caused a leak."

Out of the corner of my eye, I noticed that Enoki was taking fewer notes than usual. Was this a good omen or dire augury? Had he discerned that I was covering all the bases, leaving him nothing meaningful for cross? Or was he so fully prepped to rake Jennifer over the coals that he didn't need any more notes?

Jennifer, by the way, was handling herself extremely well. She'd not yet surprised me with a single unexpected answer—a testimonial to our wrackingly thorough preparation.*

"While on Palmyra, Jennifer, did Buck move off the *Iola* and into a tent on shore?"

"Yes."

"Why did he do this?" I asked.

"Well, the *Iola* didn't have adequate headroom for Buck. Buck was—over six feet tall. And we had about five feet five inches of headroom, which was perfect for me, but he had to slouch all the time in the boat's cabin. He wanted a camp on shore, where he would have walking-around room."

"Did Buck want you to move off the *Iola* and move into the tent with him?"

"Yes, he did."

"Did you go along with that?"

"No. I decided to stay on the *Iola*. I was looking forward to having some privacy after those close quarters."

"Were you still in love with Buck at that point, though?"

"Oh, yes. Very much so."

We began to grapple with the thorny cake-truce issue.

"Going to the day of August 28th in your diary, Jennifer, you heard Mr. Shoemaker's testimony that on the evening of the 28th Mac told him, during a radio communication they had that night, that you and Buck brought a cake to Mac and Muff, and Mac felt that it was to bring about a truce between the Grahams and you and Buck. You heard that testimony?"

"Yes."

---

*A week before Jennifer testified, Len rented a videotape camera and suggested I put Jennifer through her direct-testimony paces, followed by our critique of her "performance." I was opposed to such a dress rehearsal, and the camera went back unused. This type of thing is becoming fashionable in big cases, and I feared that Enoki, aware of the practice, might ask Jennifer on cross if Len and I had put her through such a filmed rehearsal. Since directing a witness to sit, act, and gesture in a certain way (frankly, I wouldn't have known what to tell Jennifer anyway—my only advice to her was to be natural) smacks of contrivance and insincerity, I felt that that one question, if asked by Enoki, would do far, far more harm to Jennifer's credibility in the jury's eyes than any possible benefit derived from a rehearsal.

"Your August 28th entry makes no mention of bringing a cake to Mac and Muff. Does that mean that you disagree with Mr. Shoemaker's testimony on this point?"

"I can't remember exactly what happened on the 28th, eleven or twelve years ago. That's a long time. But I can say that Mac had just brought us by the Fanning chart a day or so before. And certainly baking a cake as a thank-you for him doing that is consistent with the type of thing that I would do."

I asked Jennifer at what time of day she normally wrote her diary entries. She answered it was usually late in the afternoon, but before dark. "After dark, it was very difficult to write with the lighting we had on the *Iola*."

If the jury believed this visit had taken place, since it was in the evening, this testimony might help explain why there was no diary mention of it. But I wanted additional reinforcement. "Did your daily entries comprise everything that you did on each particular day?" I asked.

"No, it wasn't a total recap of everything. I just more or less wanted to mark the day in some way to separate one day from the next."

"So, it's your testimony that this visit *could* have happened?"

"Yes. It could have happened."

"You just don't know one way or the other."

"Right. I can't remember."

"What about Mr. Shoemaker's testimony that Mac told him that he felt the purpose of this cake, assuming you brought a cake, was to bring about a truce between you and Buck and the Grahams? How do you feel about that?"

"Well—there couldn't be a truce," she answered. "There wasn't any quarrel. We didn't have any feud going on. Mac was helping us all along. There wasn't a problem."

"So that part of his testimony—"

"That part is absolutely incorrect."

"Going now to the crucial date, August 30, 1974, was Buck still living by himself in a tent on shore then?"

"Yes."

"And you were living alone on the *Iola*?"

"Yes, with Puffer."

Some jurors smiled.

"Okay. You've reviewed that August 30th entry prior to your testimony today?"

"Yes."

"Does the entry include everything that took place on August 30th?"

"No. Like most all of the other entries, it's . . . just an overview of the events of that day."

"Would you please read to the jury *that part* of your August 30th entry, that part which you wrote on August 30th."

Jennifer cleared her throat and began reading.

"'All-out effort day. R was up bright and early, scavenging butts at Mac's workshop. R wangled a couple of games of chess, a stash of coffee and tobacco. to go, plus an invitation to dinner. Not bad for before 9:00 A.M. Next was coffee. Cleaning, swabbing, stowing—removed canopy, baking bread, all around cleanup effort both on boat and ashore. Was going to bake bread in outdoor oven to conserve fuel, but time and energy would not allow it. Undoubtedly, upon return, I'll have no alternative—only hope the fuel lasts till then.'"

I asked when exactly that day she had written the entry. She said she thought it was sometime in the afternoon. "While I was baking bread, probably. Before going over to Mac and Muff's boat for dinner. As I've said, I usually wrote the entries during the daylight hours. And I knew we would be getting back late from Mac and Muff's."

"Now, when you say in your August 30th entry, 'R *was up* bright and early, scavenging butts at Mac's workshop,' do you mean Buck slept on the *Iola* the previous night, and was up bright and early?"

I was trying to anticipate and answer every question any juror might conceivably have about the entry for this all-important date.

"No," Jennifer answered. "He slept at his tent. And he came by the *Iola* about 9:00 A.M., and told me that he'd been over to Mac's."

"Was approximately 9:00 A.M. the first time you saw Buck that day?"

"Yes, that was the first time."

"You've testified that your diary entries do not contain every-thing that happened on a particular day, Jennifer. Do you remem-ber everything that took place on August 30th, 1974?"

It was critical that I elicit testimony from Jennifer about what happened—beyond her diary's account—on that key day; particu-larly Buck's whereabouts, how many times she saw him, and at what times and locations. But how could she look back, so many years afterward, and remember such details? When I first raised the issue with her, she had assumed she remembered as much as she did because Mac and Muff had disappeared that day. But I feared an argument could be made that what took place *prior to her learn-ing of their disappearance that day* (i.e., prior to 6:30 P.M.), wouldn't have had much relevance to her. Therefore, *unless she had been involved in the murders*, I could see the jury thinking, she had no rea-son to remember these otherwise insignificant pre-6:30 P.M. details. The one exception would be if she immediately suspected Buck had done away with the Grahams. Then she would have had a reason to go over in her mind, that very evening and the days thereafter, everything that had taken place. But she said she hadn't suspected Buck at the time. How could she now, almost twelve years later, summon up the details of her interaction with Buck prior to 6:30 P.M. on August 30, 1974? In answer to that question, Jennifer eventually came to the conclusion that it must have been all the preparation for the Fanning trip that enabled her to remem-ber most of what took place that day, particularly between Buck and her. I was reasonably comfortable with this answer, which she would give at the trial.

Sensibly, Jennifer admitted that she didn't remember everything about that day. "But it is more clear in my mind, I guess, than a number of other days because we were getting ready to go to Fan-ning the next day. That was a reason for all the activity, all the things to get ready to go."

"However, because it was almost twelve years ago, your mem-ory is not perfectly clear. Is that correct?"

"That's correct."

"You've already read your August 30th entry up to a certain point. Could you expand, if you can, on what Buck told you when he came over to the *Iola* at approximately 9:00 A.M."

"Well, he said Mac had said that he and Muff were going to go fishing, and they'd catch all the fish they could. Anything that we didn't eat that night for dinner, he wanted to give us to take on our trip."

"Was this going to be somewhat of a bon voyage dinner for you and Buck?"

"Yes."

I asked if she felt that the dinner invitation was unusual at all.

Jennifer shook her head. "No. Not at all. Mac and Muff had had bon voyage dinners for others."

"Did Mac and Muff frequently fish for their dinner?"

"Yes, they did. Fresh fish is much more of a tasty meal than things that come out of cans."

"Getting back to the chronology of events, after Buck came by around 9:00 A.M. and told you about the dinner invitation, what's the next thing that happened, as far as you can recall?"

"Well, then I went over to Buck's camp and . . . he made some coffee, we had a cup of coffee. And I . . . we made a couple of trips back and forth together carrying things from his camp area to the *Iola*. And then I stayed on the *Iola* getting those things stored."

"These trips that you and Buck took between the *Iola* and the tent—approximately how long did that take?"

"Well, the tent was quite close to the *Iola*. So, I would say probably . . . an hour, maybe an hour and a half, altogether. All the trips back and forth."

"So that would take us to approximately ten-thirty or eleven o'clock?"

"Someplace in there, yes," she agreed.

"What were your plans for the remainder of the day at that point?"

"Well, I was going to stay on board the *Iola* and do all the things required to make her shipshape, getting everything stowed away, and swabbing and cleaning. And I wanted to do a lot of baking for the trip. And Buck was going to get his camp in order. He had all of this furniture that didn't belong to us, that we'd accumulated from various buildings on the island. Beds, and tables, and chairs, and things like that. And he was going to move all of that furniture to the Refrigerator House, and bring the tent, which was ours, back to the *Iola*."

"To your knowledge, did Buck actually bring the furniture to the Refrigerator House that day?"

"I don't know."

"From August 30th to September 11th, when you left Palmyra, did you ever go to Buck's tent area, or to the Refrigerator House?"

"No, I don't remember going there at all during that period."

"Did Buck bring the tent back to the *Iola* that day?"

"No, he didn't."

"Did you ask him why he did not?"

"Yes. He said it was dilapidated and falling apart, and just wasn't worth bothering with."

"Did you agree with Buck's assessment of the tent?"

"Well, he knew it better than I did. He was living in it. It didn't appear to leak, but I guess it could have been mildewed."

Jennifer said that after seeing Buck between 10:30 and eleven A.M. that morning, she next saw him "two or three hours" later. "It was sometime in the early afternoon. I remember him coming by the *Iola* and saying something."

"I take it you can't recall every time you saw Buck that day."

"No."

"When Buck would come by, would he always come aboard the *Iola*?"

"No. Not always. Sometimes he just talked to me from the shore."

"When is the next time that you recall seeing Buck that day?"

"It was several hours later, around four."

"And what happened at that time?"

"He came by, and he said that he'd been on his way to bathe, and he had run into Mac, and that Mac had said that he and Muff were still doing all kinds of things around the camp—and they hadn't gotten a chance to go fishing yet. But he said they were still going to do that. And so we should come over around six-thirty.

And that if they weren't back by then, we should just go on board and make ourselves at home, and they would be along presently."

"Would there be anything left out for you?"

"They said they would leave out some nibbles or something."

Jennifer went on to testify to her hearing, a half hour or so after Buck left, Mac's dinghy being operated in the lagoon.

"Would you please go to the chart, Jennifer, and with the pointer, indicate to the jury the direction in which you sensed, from the sound, that the Zodiac was traveling?"

"Well . . . here's where the *Iola* was, and here's the *Sea Wind*. It sounded like it was going further away from the *Sea Wind* and the *Iola*."

She indicated a path starting from the area of the *Sea Wind* and proceeding in a westerly direction away from both the *Sea Wind* and the *Iola*.

"You heard the sound of the Zodiac going away from you. Did you hear it coming back that day?"

"No."

"From the cabin of the *Iola*, could you see outside?"

"Yes. There were windows. And also I could see out the opened hatch."

"So, you would not have to go on deck to see what was happening in the lagoon?"

"Yes, that's correct."

"However, if the Zodiac dinghy were being operated or driven in the direction that you have indicated, could you have seen it from the cabin of the *Iola*?"

"No," she answered.

"Why not?"

"Because of that same jut of land that separated the *Sea Wind* from the *Iola* and with all the dense foliage."

"If someone were operating a dinghy, let's say in the middle of the lagoon during daylight, would you have been able to see and identify the operator from the *Iola*?"

"Yes."

Asked if there was any way she might have confused Buck with Mac, Jennifer said no, because they "didn't look anything alike."

"From the *Iola*, could you see any boat leaving or entering the channel?"

"Yes."

The courtroom was perfectly still, so I knew everyone was following Jennifer's testimony closely. Everyone, that is, with the possible exception of Judge King's wife, Ann, who had accompanied her husband to San Francisco. Other than those days when she enjoyed shopping in the city's countless boutiques, she sat quietly in the back row of the courtroom, busily knitting colorful sweaters for her grandchildren, only occasionally looking up from her work.

"After you heard the dinghy, when is the next time you recall seeing Buck?" I asked.

"Buck came by . . . maybe an hour later, an hour and a half, something like that. And he said that he was going to go bathe, and did I want to go with him."

"And did you?"

"No. I was still baking."

"You testified earlier that around 4:00 P.M., or thereabouts, Buck came by and told you that he had been on his way to take a bath, when he claimed he bumped into Mac. Were you surprised that an hour and a half later, he still hadn't bathed?"

"No, I didn't think anything of it."

"You never gave it a thought at that point?"

"No."

"Did you agree to meet each other later?"

"Yes. I told him that when I was through baking, I would go take a bath. And he said he would meet me over at Mac and Muff's."

"When is the next time that you saw Buck as far as you recall?"

"On my way to bathe, Buck was coming back from bathing."

"Did you talk to him at that point?"

"I said I would see him at Mac's."

At ten-thirty, the judge asked if it was a good time for a fifteen-minute recess, and I said it was. I sped down to the law library on the sixteenth floor of the courthouse to research a point of law.

In the hallway, I saw Jennifer, who was being cooled down like an overheated racehorse. Her brother and mother were at her side, walking her slowly. As I passed her, I patted her gently on the back and told her she was doing just fine:

When Judge King took the bench shortly after ten forty-five, I was, unfortunately, nowhere to be seen and was unaccounted for. I had simply stayed a minute too long in the library.

"He'll be back in a moment," Len bluffed gamely.

"I hope so," Judge King sniffed. He had not called in the jury, and wouldn't do so in my absence.

Lawyers are required to await every whim or impulse of judges as a matter of course. But seconds have a way of stretching swiftly into intolerable eons when a judge is waiting for a lawyer. It's the universe upended.

"I tell you what," the judge barked, his cheeks flaming. "You call me when Mr. Bugliosi's ready. I don't wait for the lawyers. They wait for me."

Judge King left the bench with powerful strides.

Just as I barreled through the double doors into the courtroom, the door to his chambers closed with thumping finality.

CHAPTER 39

AFTER A WAIT OF SEVERAL MINUTES—possibly he was evening the score—the judge materialized, mounted the bench, and signaled the bailiff to summon the jury.

I apologized for my tardiness.

Judge King nodded curtly. "You may resume."

"Jennifer, on August 30, 1974, did you see either Mac or Muff at *any* time that day?"

"No, I didn't."

"Did you hear any screaming or gunshots?"

"No."

"Or any other sound that aroused your attention?"

"No."

"During the period of time that you were on Palmyra, other than when Buck fired at fish in the lagoon, were you aware of any guns being fired on the island?"

"Well, once—I don't remember whether it was someone from the *Shearwater* or the *Toloa*—they told me that they were with Mac and Muff when they had been target practicing."

"Did you hear any gunshots that time?" I asked.

"No, I didn't."

"Was it difficult or easy to hear things on the island?"

"It was difficult."

"Would you relate for the jury the various sounds that inhibited one's ability to hear things on the island?"

"The birds made a terrific racket with their squawking. And there were the sounds of the ocean breaking on the outside shore, and the water in the lagoon lapping against the boat. There were also the winds, and the winds rustling through the trees would make quite a bit of noise. The dense foliage muted sounds, too."

"Did you see any fire or smoke on the island on August 30, 1974?"

"No."

In answer to my question, Jennifer said one "couldn't see anything on shore from the *Iola*."

"So, you couldn't see the *Sea Wind* or Buck's tent or the Refrigerator House or anything else on the island?"

"That's correct."

"From the *Iola* you just saw a wall of green foliage. Is that correct?"

"Yes."

Jennifer explained that when she arrived at the *Sea Wind*'s anchorage at six-thirty that night, Buck had already been there, waiting for her.

"Was it getting dark around that time?"

"It was approaching sunset."

Was the masthead light of the *Sea Wind* on?"

"No."

"Were the Grahams on the boat?"

"No. I hailed them and there was no answer. And their Zodiac wasn't tied to the side of the boat, which was usually an indication that nobody was aboard."

"Everything appeared to be still?"

"Yes," she said.

"What happened next?"

"Well, Buck and I just sat there at the lanai area for maybe ten or fifteen minutes or so, talking. And then Buck said that we should go aboard because they had said that if they weren't back by six-thirty, to go aboard and make ourselves at home. So we did."

"What did you observe once you went aboard the *Sea Wind*?"

"There were some things left out on the table in the kitchen area. There was some alcohol and some nibble things."

"Did it appear to you or did you believe that what had been left out had been left for you by Muff?"

"Yes."

I purposefully didn't bring up the apricot brandy. It was evidence favorable to my prosecution of Buck, but I feared the jury might think it sounded contrived so that Jennifer could point the finger of guilt at her former lover. It was one of those two-edged swords peculiar to the trial of a lawsuit. If it somehow came out on cross-examination, of course, the suspicion of contrivance would be substantially reduced, and this is what I was hoping for.

"What did you and Buck do at that point?"

"Well, we poured ourselves a drink, and I think Buck grabbed a box of cookies. We both went topside and sat and waited for Mac and Muff."

"Was it getting darker then?"

"Yes."

Jennifer said that by around seven o'clock, it was completely dark.

"So you're on deck with Buck and it's around seven o'clock and the Grahams are not there. What's your state of mind at that point?"

"I started getting very worried. They knew that we were coming over and I knew that it was dangerous to be out on the lagoon after dark."

"Why is that?"

"Well, you couldn't see where you were going. You wouldn't know whether you were in the middle of the lagoon or if you were getting toward the shore. And there were metal poles sticking up in the water. I . . . got worried . . . about Mac and Muff."

Since the recess, Jennifer had been answering my questions rather dispassionately. She had been responsive and detailed, but not clearly engaged emotionally. But now her composure began to crack at the seams.

"Did Buck appear to be worried?"

"I . . . I don't know."

I gave her a moment to recover. She sipped from a cup of water and took a deep breath. She patted her nose with a tissue she had balled up in her hand.

"Would you tell the jury and Judge King what happened next—the sequence of events?"

"I went looking for the switch for the masthead light," Jennifer said haltingly. "I put it on so that if Mac and Muff were coming in the dark, they would be able to see the boat. And then . . . I was just mostly up on deck, watching and listening for them."

"What happened next?"

"Buck said that he was hungry and he was going to open something to eat. I told him that I didn't think he should, because if . . . when they came back, they would see that we had eaten something of their stores, and that wouldn't be right. It would be embarrassing."

"What's the next thing that happened?"

Jennifer testified that she stayed on deck most of the night, listening and looking out across the lagoon, trying to see if she could see any type of light or anything Mac and Muff might have been using trying to signal. She finally dozed off and awakened around dawn. She immediately woke Buck up, he got the Grahams' other dinghy (wooden), and they started to search for Mac and Muff.

"From your starting point in the cove, you could have proceeded, I guess, in one of three directions. Across the lagoon or to the left or to the right. Is that correct?"

"Yes."

"Who was operating the Grahams' wooden dinghy?"

"Buck was."

"In which direction did he go?" I asked.

"He went off to the right, going along the shore."

"What's the next thing that happened?"

"I spotted the Zodiac dinghy a ways up the coast from where the *Sea Wind* was."

"Approximately how far from the *Sea Wind*?"

"Maybe a quarter mile or half mile—something like that. I'm not sure."

"Was it on the beach?"

"Yes, it was on the beach."

"The dinghy was not in the water?"

"No. The dinghy was on the beach."

"Was any portion of the dinghy in the water?"

"No. It was about a foot and a half, two feet above the waterline."

I had Jennifer go again to the large chart of Palmyra to her right and mark the approximate location of the beached Zodiac.*

"What did you and Buck do at that point?"

"Well, the dinghy was upside down on the beach. And I thought maybe they had turned the dinghy over themselves as protection from the night. And I knocked on the dinghy and called their names. And then I peeked under it and they weren't there."

"Didn't you think Mac and Muff would have simply walked back to the *Sea Wind* instead of staying underneath the dinghy all night?"

"Well, it would have been hard in the dark, and with all the vegetation, to make it back."

"What's the next thing that happened?" I asked.

---

*It is not clear from the chart of Palmyra where Cooper Island ends and Strawn Island begins. Although Jennifer told Shishido she and Buck found the overturned dinghy on Cooper Island, the X she placed on the chart to designate the dinghy's location is closer to the words "Strawn Island" on the chart than to the words "Cooper Island." Also, a half mile (the distance she told Shishido, me, and *Honolulu Advertiser* reporter Bruce Benson the dinghy was from where the *Sea Wind* was anchored) appears closer to Strawn Island than to Cooper.

"I remember I started to call their names. Then Buck and I went up this rise that was there and I continued to call out their names and look around."

She had controlled herself almost too well in these last answers, but my next questions restored the human element.

"What was your state of mind at this particular point?"

"I was just about *frantic*."

"How did Buck appear to be taking it?"

"I was so upset, I didn't notice."

"What's the next thing that happened?"

"We came back down the hill, and down the beach a little ways I saw the gas tank from the dinghy. Buck went down and got the gas tank. The two of us turned the dinghy right side up and moved it into the water."

"So, the gas tank was also on the beach?"

"Yes."

This had to be burned in.

"It was not in the water?"

"No."

"Jennifer, based on your previous testimony, am I correct in assuming that from where the *Iola* was moored, you would also be *unable* to see the location where you and Buck found the dinghy because the portion of Cooper Island protruding out into the lagoon obstructed your line of sight?"

"That's correct."

"Jennifer, did you tell FBI agent Calvin Shishido that you found the dinghy *in* the lagoon?"

"I don't remember exactly what I told Mr. Shishido, but I found the dinghy on the beach. If I said in the lagoon, it could have been to differentiate between finding the dinghy *on the beach in the lagoon* as opposed to *on the beach on the ocean side*."

"Did you tell Agent Shishido that you saw the gas tank of the dinghy floating in the lagoon near the dinghy?"

"No, he got that wrong. I told him that I thought the gas tank had floated to shore."

"After you found the gas tank, did Buck reattach it to the dinghy?"

"Yes."

"What happened next?"

Jennifer thought a moment. "Buck tried starting up the Zodiac dinghy, and he pulled the cord a bunch of times, and finally, the motor started. And we took the wooden dinghy back to the *Sea Wind* and started searching for Mac and Muff in the Zodiac."

"Where did you and Buck search for Mac and Muff?"

"We searched all over the lagoon. We just started going around the whole lagoon, as close to the land as we could get, looking on the shore to see if there was some sign of them."

I gestured toward the map. "There are three lagoons on Palmyra: the West, Center, and East lagoons. Is that correct?"

"Yes."

"Did you search all three lagoons?"

"The first day, we searched the Center Lagoon and the West Lagoon. Access to the East Lagoon was difficult. We didn't go over there because it wouldn't have been feasible [because of the causeway] for the dinghy to have floated from the East Lagoon to where we found it."

"And you found nothing in your search?"

"Right."

"How long did you search that first day?"

"We searched all day," she answered. "At some point during the day, after we completed going around the lagoon twice, Buck said that they were nowhere. He wanted to give up. And I said *no*, that we couldn't give up."

Jennifer stopped abruptly and breathed deeply.

"But Buck said he was hungry," she continued, "and we went back to the *Sea Wind* and got something to eat."

"What happened next?"

"We went back out and searched. We went across to Paradise and Home islands because from the way the ripples were in the lagoon, it looked like that would have been where the dinghy could have floated from. We searched all of those two islands on foot."

"And you found no trace of Mac or Muff on Paradise or Home islands?"

"That's correct."

"What did you and Buck do that night, August 31, 1974?"

"We stayed on the *Sea Wind*. I don't really remember what we did. I was physically and emotionally exhausted. I'm sure I slept."

"What did you and Buck do the next day—that would be September 1st?"

"We searched."

"Where did you search?"

"The same area. That was all there was to search."

"Where did you and Buck spend this second night?"

"On the *Sea Wind*."

They searched the East Lagoon the following morning, she explained, describing it as a "last-ditch" effort.

"So, when you went into the East Lagoon, you were kind of grasping at straws."

"Yes."

"What about the following day? Did you search that day?"

"Buck said it was ridiculous, that they were gone. But I went out for a little while by myself. He was right."

"So, you finally discontinued your search at this point?"

"Yes." She looked down. Despite Len's stylish dress code, she had taken us all back to the simpler, confused young woman entangled in a tragedy hundreds of miles from civilization.

"And you did not find the slightest trace of them? Footprints in the sand, or a signal fire, or anything at all?"

"Nothing."

"At the end of your search, was it your belief, at that point, that Mac and Muff were dead?"

"Yes." Jennifer's voice lowered to a barely audible whisper.

I asked what she thought had happened to them, and she said she believed they had had a boating accident and either drowned or were attacked by sharks.

"Jennifer, we have since learned, of course, about the skeletal remains of Muff Graham being found next to the aluminum container—the strong implication being that she was murdered. But I want to ask you what your state of mind was way back then at the time of Mac and Muff's disappearance. You didn't find it improbable that the Zodiac had flipped over in the lagoon?"

"No, I found it upside down. It was obvious it had flipped over."

"What about the fact that, according to several witnesses who testified at this trial, the Zodiac was a very stable craft?"

"I didn't know any of that then, but I don't know that it would have made any difference."

"Why is that?" I asked.

"I had seen Mac taking the Zodiac across the lagoon and the nose would kind of be in the air. And I knew there were obstructions in the lagoon, and I had been with Don Stevens and Bill Larson when the dinghy propeller hit the coral head or something. It made a terrible noise, and had to be repaired."

"And I take it you didn't find the possibility of a shark attack improbable?"

"No. There were sharks all over that lagoon and they were everywhere, and aggressive."

"Did you ever swim in the lagoon?"

"*Never.* I wouldn't even wade in that lagoon."

"Did you ever see anyone else swim in the lagoon?"

"No, I didn't."

"Jennifer, going back to the end of your search for Mac and Muff when you concluded that they were dead, did you believe everything that Buck had told you up to that point?"

"Yes, Buck didn't do or say anything to make me think anything other than Mac and Muff had gone fishing and not come back."

"Would you characterize yourself as a suspicious person?"

"No. My mother has always told me that I'm too trusting."

Sunny smiled weakly, but Ted's eyes were riveted on the jury. Seated next to him, his teenage son nervously gnawed at a fingernail.

I knew the jury, during deliberations, would certainly examine and analyze most probingly the entries for August 30 and 31 and September 1, 2, 3, and 4. After pointing out that Jennifer had already read to the jury that portion of her August 30 diary entry which she wrote before going over to the *Sea Wind* that day, I now asked her to read aloud the remainder of that entry.

She read: "'And then tragedy. And overnight, a whole new set of alternatives beset us.'"

"When did you write that part of the entry?"

"It was several days later. In looking at the diary, it looks like it was probably written on September 4th."

"Would you please read to the jury your August 31st, September 1st, 2nd, and 3rd entries?"

"August 31st says: 'No sleep all night. Searched all day. Found upturned dinghy. No other signs.' September 1st: 'R says he feels no hope of finding anything, but still we search.' September 2nd says: 'And search.' September 3rd says: 'And then? What to do.'"

"When were these entries of August 31st, September 1st, 2nd, and 3rd made?"

"I think they were all probably made at the same time on September 4th."

"Why was the last part of the August 30th entry, and the August 31st, September 1st, 2nd, and 3rd entries made on September 4th?"

"Well, I didn't have my diary. And I was more involved with searching for Mac and Muff than with writing in a book."

"You say you didn't have your diary. Was it back at the *Iola*?"

"Yes."

"And you and Buck were staying on the *Sea Wind* during that period."

"Yes."

"Why were you staying on the *Sea Wind* instead of the *Iola* during that period?"

"If Mac and Muff could make their way back to the *Sea Wind*, I wanted to be there."

"Jennifer, your September 1st entry says, 'R'—referring to Buck—'says he feels no hope of finding anything.' The word 'says' is in the present tense. Yet, you say you believe you wrote the entry three days later, on September 4th. Is there a reason for that?"

"I don't know. I guess Buck said it on September 1st, and I was writing it as the September 1st entry, so I put it in the present tense."

"So, each diary entry then was written from the perspective of what happened that day?"

"I guess so. I guess that's the reason."

"Why are your entries for August 31st, September 1st, 2nd, and 3rd so brief, Jennifer?"

Anyone would wonder why she would write fifty-word entries on routine days and spare only a few words for a catastrophe.

"Mac and Muff's deaths just affected me too deeply," she said, clutching her handkerchief. "I couldn't write about them."

"Jennifer, your September 4th entry reads: 'And the decision to depart followed by a great deal of preparation while we all grow fatter and fatter on ham and cheese and pancakes and turkey and chili and all the things we hadn't had for so long. And the dogs feed on corn beef hash.' Can you explain this entry to the jury?"

"I really don't know what I was thinking back then. The words sound very calloused. We had been eating a lot of coconut and fish. I guess after I knew that Mac and Muff were gone, I just didn't think it was so terrible to eat their food anymore."

I asked Jennifer what she and Buck decided to do when it appeared clear that Mac and Muff were dead.

"Well, Buck said to me, 'What do you think we should do?' I told him we should notify the authorities, but he said we couldn't do that because he was on the run and he didn't want to have any contact with any authorities."

"How did you respond to this?"

"I argued with him. I felt very strongly that we had to report what had happened to Mac and Muff. And he got really mad and yelled that didn't I see if we contacted the authorities, there would be questions and he'd be held?"

"What further discussion did you and Buck have on what to do?"

"Buck told me that he wanted to sail off in the *Sea Wind*."

"How did you respond to this?"

"I told him that we couldn't. That she wasn't our boat."

"Did Buck offer or attempt to offer any justification at all for taking the *Sea Wind*?"

"Buck said he didn't think that Mac would want us to leave the *Sea Wind* on the island unattended to be vandalized."

Some listeners snickered, but, like all good pretexts, Buck's had some basis in fact, as I next brought out.

"Did you agree that there was a vandalism problem on Palmyra?"

"Yes, it was obvious. Trucks were riddled with bullet holes and tires were slashed and buildings were ransacked."

"Did this fact—the possible vandalism and pillaging of the *Sea Wind*—persuade you that the *Sea Wind* should not be left unattended on Palmyra?"

"I agreed that Mac would not want the *Sea Wind* abandoned to looters."

"So did you have any suggestion to Buck at that point?"

"I told Buck I wanted to take the *Sea Wind* and the *Iola* over to Fanning. And then we could get our supplies and come back to Palmyra on the *Iola*."

"Leaving the *Sea Wind* at Fanning?"

"Yes."

"What did Buck say to this suggestion?"

"He got really upset and said I could do anything I wanted. But he was taking off on the *Sea Wind*, and I could do one of three things—come with him, stay on Palmyra, or sail off on the *Iola* by myself."

"Did you feel that you were capable of sailing the *Iola* by yourself?"

"No."

"You didn't want to try. Is that correct?"

"That's correct."

"So Buck gave you three options, is that correct?"

"Yes, but I didn't really think there was a choice."

"You decided that you had better go with Buck?"

"Yes."

"Was the fact that you really had no other option the only reason that you went with him?"

"No. I loved Buck. I wanted to be with him."

"Did Buck say what he intended to do upon leaving Palmyra?"

"He said he was just going to continue fleeing on the *Sea Wind*."

"Did he say how he intended to travel on a boat that was not registered to him?"

"He said he wanted to take the *Sea Wind* back to Hawaii and reregister her."

"What did Buck say, if anything, about the danger of going back to the very place where he was wanted by the law?"

"He said Hawaii was the only place he knew of where he could just go in and reregister the *Sea Wind* on his word alone."

"Did Buck say what would happen if you and he sailed outside the United States without reregistering the *Sea Wind*?"

"He said that since the *Sea Wind* papers were in the Grahams' name and our passports identified him as Roy Allen and me as Jennifer Jenkins, there would be questions and that he would be held."

I took a sip of water. As I did, I eyed my least-favorite juror.

The Kansas Rock sat impassively as ever, arms tightly folded against his chest and a slight hint of repugnance on his face, as if beholding a mockery. We apparently hadn't budged him one single inch.

When I looked back at my legal pad, it was like peering into the face of an old, trusted friend. The questions and answers I felt I needed to help secure a *not guilty* verdict were scribbled before me in pencil. But this could only be so if the jurors listened and were open-minded. *Damn* the Rock!

"Did anything happen thereafter, Jennifer, while you were still on Palmyra, which eased your mind somewhat about the entire problem?"

"Yes. I had been reading various papers I had found that Mac had written, and I found a will."

"Was the will signed or unsigned?"

"It was signed by Mac."

"Do you recall the date of the will?"

"It was 1960 or 1961, I think."

"And what did the will say, to the best of your recollection?"

"There was a part in it that said if anything happened to Mac, that he wanted some person, who would be designated in another document, to complete a circumnavigation of the globe and return the *Sea Wind* back to the mainland of the United States within a period of two years."

I had the clerk hand Jennifer a copy of the will. After she quickly scanned and identified the document as a copy of the will about which she had just testified, I read the following stipulation to the jury: "That this seven-page document is a true and accurate copy of a last will and testament signed by Malcolm Graham, Jr., on April 26, 1961, and found on the *Sea Wind* by law enforcement authorities when the *Sea Wind* was inventoried on October 30, 1974, at the Ala Wai yacht harbor in Honolulu. So stipulated?"

Enoki stood. "Yes," he said. "I agree to that."

I asked Jennifer to read aloud the section in question.

"'In contemplation of a lengthy trip in my ship the *Sea Wind*,'" she read, "'and in the event that I am not married at the time of my death, I direct that a person whom I shall so designate by separate document shall have charge and custody of the ship *Sea Wind* on its round-the-world anticipated cruise to whatsoever port and via whatsoever route the so designated person may wish, with the direction that this so designated person shall dock the *Sea Wind* in a port within the limits of the United States, excluding the states of Hawaii and Alaska, within a two-year period following my death.'"

"Jennifer, did you think that the trip which brought Mac and Muff to Palmyra was the round-the-world trip referred to in the paragraph of the will you just read to the jury?"

"No. I knew that was a different trip. An earlier trip."

"At that particular time you found the will, were you searching for something to make you feel better about what you and Buck were doing?"

Enoki came to his feet objecting to my question as leading the witness.

"Well, it's a little bit leading," the judge conceded, "but I'll let her answer."

"Yes," Jennifer answered.

"With respect to this other document Mac referred to, you knew that whomever Mac would have designated, it would not have been you and Buck?"

"Yes, of course."

"So how did this clause or language in Mac's 1961 will give you any solace or comfort?"

"It gave me a glimpse into Mac's mind," Jennifer explained, "and made me think that maybe what Buck wanted to do wouldn't be that terrible to Mac as long as we were able to get the *Sea Wind* back to the mainland within that two-year period. It showed me that, at some point in time, Mac had envisioned the possibility of somebody other than himself sailing the *Sea Wind*."

"But you knew that you and Buck would not be the people Mac would designate to do this."

"But we were the *only* people there. There was nobody else on the island to get the boat anyplace except us."

"After you got it back to the mainland, I take it the boat should have been returned to—"

"Kit—Mary Muncey. Mac's sister and heir. Yes."

"Did you think Buck had any intention of returning the boat to Mary Muncey?"

"Well, initially, when Buck said he wanted to take the boat, I hadn't found the will yet. After I found the will, I showed it to Buck and he read it. And I told him that the only way I would feel comfortable doing what he wanted to do was if he promised that we would get the boat back to Mary Muncey within two years."

"So, you extracted this promise from him?"

"Yes." The jurors were rapt, studying her expression without revealing their own thoughts at all.

"Prior to your extracting this promise from him, was it your state of mind that he may have intended to keep the *Sea Wind* for a very long period of time?"

"Yes."

"And perhaps not return it at all?"

"Yes."

"So are you telling this jury and Judge King then that you intended to go along with Buck in keeping the *Sea Wind* for up to two years?"

"For *up* to two years. I wanted to get the boat back sooner. I told Buck that he didn't need the boat, that we could just take the boat back to the mainland. But he didn't want to do that right away."

"So two years was the outer limit you would go along with it?"
"Yes."

"Did he indicate to you that he would separate himself from the *Sea Wind* just before it was turned in?"

"Yes. And then I would contact Mary Muncey and the authorities and he would be safe."

"Let me ask you this, Jennifer. Did you think the language of that will gave you any legal right whatsoever to take possession of that boat?"

"No," she said, lowering her voice. "I knew it gave us no legal right."

"You also knew, did you not, that what you were doing was wrong?"

"Yes, I knew the right thing to do was to contact the authorities to tell them what happened to Mac and Muff, and if we were going to take the boat at all, to take it directly back to the mainland of the United States and get in touch with Mary Muncey."

"In leaving Palmyra on the *Sea Wind*, which is a boat that did not belong to you and Buck, did you think that you were stealing the *Sea Wind*?"

"No. I never planned to steal the *Sea Wind* and I never intended to keep her."

"You can't speak for Buck, but as far as you were concerned, you had no intent to steal that boat?"

"That's correct."

Now we moved on to the topic of the other sailboat at Palmyra, the *Iola*, about whose fate Jennifer had lied over the years:

"Buck had told me it was impossible to tow the *Iola*, so I thought we would just leave her tied up at the dolphins. But he said we couldn't do that because she would continue to take on water and ultimately she would sink and become a navigational hazard in the lagoon."

"So what did you and Buck do with respect to the *Iola*?"

"Buck towed the *Iola* out of the lagoon with the *Sea Wind*. Puffer and I were on her. Then Buck came over and got Puffer and me and took us over to the *Sea Wind*. And he went back to the *Iola* and opened up all her through-hull fittings and just headed her off into the ocean."

"In what direction was the *Iola* headed at that point?"

"South by southeast."

"And you assume that the *Iola* sank in the ocean?"

"Yes."

"Did you observe it sink in the ocean?"

"No."

"Jennifer, at a previous proceeding in 1975 for the theft of the *Sea Wind*, you testified that in towing the *Iola* out of the channel, the *Iola* went aground in the channel and that you could not get it free. So you and Buck left it in the channel. You are aware you so testified?"

"Yes."

"That testimony, I take it, was not the truth. Is that correct?"

"That's correct."

"How did you come up with this story?"

"Buck told me that if anybody ever asked what happened to the *Iola*, I shouldn't say that we sunk her because that would sound very bad. It would sound as though we had stolen the *Sea Wind*."

"Did you think there was any merit in what Buck was telling you?"

"I didn't feel we were stealing the *Sea Wind*. I guess it did sound like it had merit because I did it."

"When you were interrogated by FBI Agent Shishido on October 29, 1974, did you tell him this same untruthful story?"

"Yes, I did."

"At this earlier proceeding, Jennifer, back in 1975, you took an oath to tell the truth, did you not?"

"Yes, I did."

"And with respect to your not testifying truthfully on this point, you violated your oath. Is that correct?"

"Yes."

"Why did you do this?"

"I was advised that if I didn't testify consistently during that proceeding, that it would go badly for me."

"You say 'testify consistently.' Consistent with what you had told FBI Agent Shishido?"

"Yes."

I had debated whether Jennifer should testify *who* it was who had so advised her. She had told me it was one of her two lawyers (the other had "gone along" with the idea). I realized that most probably the prosecutors would contact him. If he denied so counseling her, they might very well call him as a witness and it would become a big, contested issue we could lose. Even a victory wouldn't be much comfort, since Jennifer *had* committed perjury. I finally decided that Jennifer should testify on direct merely to what she was advised. If, of course, she was asked on cross-examination by whom she was advised, she'd have to identify the lawyer.

"Going back for a moment, you testified that Buck, on the *Sea Wind*, towed you and Puffer on the *Iola* out of the channel. Once out of the channel, were any photographs taken by either you or Buck?"

"Yes, I took some photographs of Buck on the *Iola*."

These were the very photographs, of course, about which Jennifer had lied at her theft trial.

"You testified earlier that you discontinued your search for Mac and Muff on September 3, 1974. Yet, you never left Palmyra until September 11th. What did you and Buck do during this period?"

"We loaded all the things from the *Iola* onto the *Sea Wind* and we gathered all the things that were on shore from Mac's workshop and brought them back on the *Sea Wind*, and we just generally made her shipshape, stowed everything away, and made her ready to go."

Jennifer's diary suddenly, and strangely, terminated on September 10. I asked her why.

"The next day, the *Iola* was sunk. And the diary was the log of the *Iola*."

I asked Jennifer if anything unusual had happened to her and Buck on their way back to Hawaii. She began her longest answer since taking the stand. I leaned slightly against the podium, listening to her narrate in detail the swordfish incident. I knew it in my sleep.

"Jennifer, where was the name *Sea Wind* located on the sailboat?"

"It was on the stern," she answered, "and I think it was in another place on the side somewhere."

"Did either you or Buck remove the name *Sea Wind* from the boat at Palmyra?"

"Yes, Buck did."

While they were at Pokai Bay, she said, Buck invited Larry Seibert to visit.

"When Seibert visited you, he asked you and Buck how you had come into possession of the boat, is that correct?"

"Yes."

"Did Buck respond to this question in your presence?"

"Yes."

"And he said that he, Buck, had won the boat in a chess game with a multimillionaire?"

"Yes."

"What, if anything, did you say or do at this point?"

"I just cringed."

"And Seibert at some time thereafter asked you if what Buck told him was the truth?"

"Yes."

"What did you tell Seibert?"

"I told him no, it wasn't the truth."

"Any time, Mr. Bugliosi," the judge interrupted.

I glanced at the wall clock above the jury box, surprised to see it was almost noon. The morning had flown by for me, and I could easily have forged on. But Jennifer definitely looked as if she needed time out.

"This would be a good time, your honor."

"We'll break for lunch, then."

As people in the gallery stood, stretched, and began filing out of the courtroom, Jennifer went over to her brother to say something.

While talking to Len, I noticed Sunny Jenkins standing alone, a worried frown on her vulnerable, friendly face. I could imagine what kind of hell she was enduring. I went over to try to soften her ordeal.

"She's doing fine," I said.

"You think so, Vince?" Her voice cracked.

"Yes. Len agrees. He just said she's doing great. Go have lunch and relax a little, Mrs. Jenkins."

I didn't take my own advice. In the empty courtroom, I remained at the defense table, going over the pages of questions I would be asking Jennifer that afternoon. (Throughout the trial, I made use of the noon recess, bringing my lunch so I could work in the courtroom or the law library of the U.S. Attorney's Office, or eating and working in the cafeteria downstairs.)

The bailiff, after making sure I was aware of my fate, locked the courtroom doors and himself went to lunch.

Jennifer was holding up emotionally and covering the details I wanted her to—of that much I was certain. But there was no way to know whether or not the jury was believing a single word she was saying.

THAT AFTERNOON, 1:45 P.M.

"JENNIFER, DID you have any conversation with anyone at Pokai Bay concerning repairing the damage to the hull of the *Sea Wind* caused by the swordfish?" I asked.

"Yes. With Lorraine Wollen, one of the witnesses at this trial."

"And what did she tell you?"

"She recommended Tuna Packers in Honolulu as the best place—the least expensive place to haul out and repair the damage."

"You heard Mrs. Wollen testify that when you invited her aboard the *Sea Wind* for coffee at Pokai Bay you told her that the previous owners of the *Sea Wind* got tired of maintaining it, so they sold it to you and Buck?"

"Yes."

"Did you in fact tell her this?"

"Yes."

"Do you recall the circumstances surrounding your telling her this?"

Jennifer responded eagerly. "Yes. She had wanted to come on board and see the boat, because it's such a unique-looking boat. And so I invited her on board. While she was there, she saw the pictures of Mac and Muff on the wall, and she asked: 'Who are these people?' I told her that they were the previous owners. She wanted to know why they had gotten rid of the boat. I told her that . . . they had just gotten tired of maintaining it."

"Was there a reason that you didn't tell her the truth?"

"I couldn't tell her the truth. If I told her the whole story . . . she would have asked me if I had reported it. I mean, Buck was sitting right there. And I just . . . I couldn't tell her the truth."

"Is Mrs. Wollen the only person you ever told this story to?"

"Yes."

"Was there any reason why you kept Mac's and Muff's pictures on the wall of the *Sea Wind*?"

"Yes. I never wanted to change anything about the boat. I wanted to keep it just the way they had it."

Jennifer testified that after repairing the hole in the hull, they scraped the barnacles off the bottom, sanded the hull and covered it with bottom paint (a special type of protective paint), and then repainted the rest of the boat's exterior above the waterline.

I now wrestled with this ostensibly incriminating act of repainting the *Sea Wind*. I asked if repainting the boat was normal boat maintenance. Jennifer answered yes, that whenever you "haul out a boat," as they had done, one normally repaints the boat, since "one does not haul a boat out frequently."

"Were you in favor of repainting the boat?"

"Well, as long as we were hauled out, I didn't see anything wrong with painting the topside of the boat. But Buck wanted to change the color of the boat, and I was against this."

"Why were you against changing the color?"

"I didn't want to change it from the way Mac and Muff had it."

Topside, the *Sea Wind* had been white with blue stripes. Jennifer said they repainted the white areas white, but painted lavender over the blue.

"Was it your intent when you repainted the *Sea Wind* to disguise its identity?"

"No. I didn't feel that any color that boat was painted would alter it, or disguise it. It was a very unique boat. Mac had customized the cabin, and it had an old-style rigging on it called 'dead-eye' rigging. It was just a totally unique boat."

"Did you feel that anyone who saw that boat, who had seen it previously, would recognize it immediately?"

"Yes."

"Irrespective of what color you painted it?"

"That's correct."

"Did Buck, while you were in Hawaii, in fact reregister the *Sea Wind*?"

"Yes, he did."

"Did he have any discussion with you about whose name should be listed on the registration as the owners of the boat?"

"Yes."

"What did he say?"

"He was filling out the papers, and indicated that there was a place there for—I don't know whether it was Mr. and Mrs., or whatever. He wanted to fill in my name on it. And I told him absolutely not."

"Why did you say that?"

"I felt it was wrong. I certainly didn't want my name on it."

"And you, in fact, did not put your name on that registration document. Is that correct?"

"That's correct."

"Jennifer, you testified earlier that on Palmyra you realized that the right thing to do would have been for *you and Buck* to notify the authorities of what had happened, but that Buck wouldn't allow this because of his fugitive status. But now that you were back in Hawaii from Palmyra, is there any reason why you didn't notify the authorities *on your own* about what happened on Palmyra?"

"I couldn't do that without placing Buck in danger of being apprehended."

"In other words, you felt that if you did this without Buck's knowledge, when the authorities came to the *Sea Wind* the questions that would inevitably follow would lead to his identity?"

"Yes."

"Did you and Buck have any specific plans as to where you were going to go once you left Hawaii?"

"We ... we didn't have ... really long-range plans. We knew we had to leave Oahu as soon as possible, because that's where his arrest warrant would have been issued from. And we thought perhaps we would go over to the Big Island just to figure out where we were going to go from there."

Jennifer testified that although she couldn't contact the authorities, it was her intent to contact Mary Muncey just before she and Buck left Hawaii, and inform her of Mac and Muff's disappearance.

"Did you know where to get in touch with her?" I asked.

Jennifer cleared her throat. "Yes. There were papers on board that gave her address."

"At the previously referred-to theft proceeding in 1975, did you testify that it was your intention upon leaving Hawaii to take the *Sea Wind* back to Mary Muncey?"

"Yes."

"I take it that was not the complete truth?"

"No, it wasn't the complete truth. I planned to *ultimately* get the boat back to her. But we weren't going to be taking it directly from Oahu to her."

Asked why she and Buck had pulled into Honolulu's Ala Wai harbor, where someone might recognize the boat, Jennifer said they needed diesel fuel, which was not available at Tuna Packers.

She testified that around eight o'clock on the morning of October 29, 1974, she climbed into the *Sea Wind*'s wooden dinghy and began rowing toward shore to use the rest-room facilities, explaining that one is "not supposed to use a bathroom in a boat when you're in harbor."

"You may continue," I said when she hesitated.

"So, I was rowing over to the public bathrooms, which took me in pretty close proximity to Joel Peters's boat. The previous day I had offered to do Joel's laundry with ours, and he'd given it to me. Anyway, he was on deck and he told me that the authorities had been there the night before and were looking for the two of us."

"What did you do at that point?"

"I went back and woke Buck up and told him what Joel had said."

"At this point, you did not know whether they were looking for Buck Walker on the MDA matter, and you for assisting him in his escape, or for Roy Allen and you for being on a boat that did not belong to you?"

"That's correct."

"What was the thing that was uppermost in your mind, if you recall?"

"Buck's fugitive status on the MDA matter was uppermost in my mind."

"After you told Buck what Joel had told you, what's the next thing that happened?"

"Buck said that we had to get off the boat right away. So we went and got into the dinghy, and were on our way to shore. And Buck's dogs were on top, topside, and they were both barking. I told Buck that I wanted to go back to the boat and put them below. And I just then remembered Joel's laundry. I told him I wanted to get Joel's laundry back to him."

"What did Buck say to that suggestion?"

"He said that I was crazy. He said he was going to get off at the dock first."

After dropping Buck off, Jennifer said she went back to the boat, put the two dogs down in the cabin, grabbed Joel Peter's laundry, and took it back to him. As she was rowing toward the bathroom, where she and Buck had agreed to meet, she saw "this big Coast Guard cutter pull into the channel" and come at her "really fast."

"What was your state of mind at the point where they were barreling down at high speed directly toward your boat?"

"I was scared. I rowed really fast."

"Was it also your state of mind to get away from them because you felt you had done something wrong?"

"Yes."

"And what did you feel you had done wrong?"

"Well . . . I was with Buck, and Buck was on the run. And as far as I knew, me being with Buck made me a criminal, too."

Then she added these crucially important words: "What you have to understand is that Buck's state of mind became my state of mind. Buck was a fugitive on the run, and I was running with him."

"So his reality became your reality?"

"Right."

(It must have been on the fourth or fifth time that Jennifer and I were going over why she had said and done so many incriminating things that she uttered these words for the first time: "What you have to realize is that *Buck's reality became my reality*. He was a fugitive on the run and I was running with him. That was the state of my consciousness." Sometimes, a spontaneous remark perfectly distills the essence of a situation. This one went to the very heart of Jennifer's incriminating actions, and I felt it would help the jury to see how an innocent person who is traveling with, and emotionally bound to, a guilty person may talk and act toward others the same way the guilty person does. I wrote the words down verbatim and told Jennifer I wanted her to use them on the witness stand. Alongside the remark, on her copy of our tentative Q and A, I had jotted a reminder: "Extremely important. Remember verbatim." She had come close enough.)

"Is there anything else that you thought you had done wrong that caused you to try to get away from the Coast Guard cutter?" I asked.

"Yes. I . . . I knew that . . . we should have reported what had happened to Mac and Muff to the authorities. And also we were on a boat that wasn't ours."

Jennifer gave details of being found by the Coast Guard officer and Bernard Leonard in the lobby of the Ilikai Marina Hotel.

"Mr. Leonard testified that while you and he were on the dinghy going back to the Coast Guard cutter you told him you had found the Graham's dinghy on the beach on Paradise Island. Did you tell him that?"

"No. He misunderstood if he thought I said I found the dinghy on Paradise Island. That was just where I thought it had flipped over, by Paradise Island."

"Jennifer, did you tell Mr. Shishido the same thing you've testified to here in court about the circumstances surrounding the disappearance of Mac and Muff?"

"Yes. I told him the truth about what I thought happened to Mac and Muff."

"Did you tell Mr. Shishido that the reason you never notified the authorities about the Grahams' disappearance was that you were afraid they would take the boat away from you?"

"I probably said something like that."

"Was this the truth?"

"No."

"Why did you tell him this then?"

"Well, he asked me why I was on the boat, and why I hadn't turned the boat in. And I couldn't tell him the truth. I couldn't tell him that it was because of Buck's fugitive status. So I guess . . . that was just what popped out of my mouth."

I moved quickly to emphasize this important point.

"You didn't feel you could tell him the real reason, is that correct?"

"Right."

"That you were trying to protect Buck?"

"Yes."

In answer to my question, Jennifer testified that during the FBI interrogation, she found out for the first time whom they were looking for. They kept talking about Roy Allen.

"And you never told them that Roy Allen was Buck Walker?"

"No."

Since Jennifer's effort to protect Buck was so central to my summation, I presented further evidence of her effort.

"Jennifer, Mr. Shishido testified that you told him you first joined Roy Allen on the *Iola* in late April of 1974 while the *Iola* was moored in the Keehi Lagoon on the island of Oahu. You testified earlier, however, that you and Buck moved to the island of Maui in October of 1973, and Buck bought the *Iola* there that same month. And the boat, which you and Buck lived on, was moored in the Maalaea Harbor in Maui. Do you recall that?"

"Yes."

"Why did you change the date and location to Mr. Shishido?"

"I was afraid that otherwise they would find out that Roy Allen was really Buck Walker."

"You felt the authorities would be able to check and ascertain that you were really with a Buck Walker at the correct time and place?" I prompted.

"Yes," she said.

"Did you tell Mr. Shishido that you and Buck rationalized Mac's statement—Mac's *alleged* statement—to Buck to 'make yourselves at home' to mean that the Grahams would have wanted you and Buck to take possession of the boat if anything happened to them? Did you tell Mr. Shishido that?"

"I'm sure I said something to that effect."

"Was this a truthful statement on your part?"

"No."

"Why did you tell him this?"

"Again, he was questioning me as to why we hadn't turned the boat in. And I couldn't tell him the real reason, so . . . I don't know why I chose those words, except that was . . . as I knew it, the last words that Mac had told to Buck. And they just came out."

"The last words that Buck *told you* that Mac had said?"

"Yes."

With respect to the toilet-flushing incident at the yacht club, Jennifer said she didn't flush anything out of her purse. "I was in the rest room for a long time, longer than usual. My stomach was really upset," she told the jury.

"How long after you had originally set out to go to the bathroom were you permitted to do so?" I asked.

"It seemed like forever. Probably at least a couple of hours."

Actually, there was *another* toilet-flushing incident, the details of which I decided to have Jennifer volunteer to the jury. "While you were at the FBI office in Honolulu, did you flush anything down the toilet from your purse that you did not want the authorities to see?"

"Yes."

"And what was this?"

"When I was taking the things out of my purse—I think they were cataloguing everything—I found a piece of paper that had the name Buck Walker on it. So, I crunched it up, and when I went to the bathroom, I flushed it down the toilet."

"Had you emptied out the contents of your purse earlier that day?" I asked.

Jennifer had told me that at the beginning of her interview on the Coast Guard cutter they had inspected the contents of her purse. (Later, at the FBI office, they had catalogued everything.) But after listening to me and Shishido go around and around on this issue, she now retreated, but just a bit. "It seems to me that when I went on board the Coast Guard cutter someone took my purse, but I really don't remember what happened."

Jennifer testified that when she visited Buck in jail after she was released on bail he gave her a letter to mail to Mac's sister, Kit Muncey, and she did so.

"Did he ask you to write a cover letter for him to her?"

"Yes. He said he wanted me to say that the letter he wrote was written while we had the boat in dry dock. When it wasn't."

"And that something had happened to the letter to delay its mailing?"

"Yes, he told me to tell her that the letter had gotten misplaced, and that I had come upon it and I knew that Buck would want her to have it."

"Actually, to your knowledge, his letter to her was written later while he was in jail. Is that correct?"

"Yes."

"And did you in fact write the cover letter that Buck requested of you?"

"Yes, I did."

I asked her why she had been willing to misrepresent to Kit when and where the letter was written.

"I did it for Buck. And I thought it was a beautifully written letter, and all the events that were in it about what happened to Mac and Muff were true. There were some other things in it that weren't true. But I thought that the main thing was that it talked about our relationship with Mac and Muff, and the accident, and what had happened on Palmyra."

"So, the contents of the letter referring to Mac and Muff's disappearance, the heart of the letter, you felt that that was true."

"Yes."

"And that was the main thing you were concerned about?"

"Yes."

I next explored further Jennifer's relationship with Buck, by far the longest intimate relationship she'd had in her entire life. Yes, they had discussed getting married and had even gone so far as to take a blood test, she told the jury. She considered herself Buck's common-law wife.

"So in your mind your relationship with Buck was something akin to marriage?"

"Yes."

"Do you have any further emotional attachment to Buck?"

"No."

I paused a few moments.

"Jennifer, as this jury here, and this judge, are your witnesses, as God above is your witness, did you have anything at all to do with the deaths of Mac and Muff Graham?"

"No, I didn't." She looked to the ceiling for a moment, composing herself. "I never doubted that Mac and Muff had died in a boating accident."

"You may take the witness," I told Enoki.

CHAPTER 40

ON THE WITNESS STAND, Jennifer waited, unsmiling, but evidently quite comfortable. All the work getting her ready for this moment had given her—and me—confidence that she was prepared for the pitfalls of cross-examination.

Elliot Enoki approached the podium with no apparent enthusiasm. After putting his papers down, he made sure his coat was buttoned, then lingered, head down, looking as lifeless as a rag doll.

Professionally, I could almost feel sorry for my counterpart. He was like someone about to give a speech identical to the one just delivered by the previous speaker.

With two calculated exceptions, I felt assured I had conducted the major points of Enoki's cross-examination for him. I had raised every negative, incriminating thing Jennifer had ever said or done in connection with the case, and had given her ample opportunity to give plausible reasons for each and every action.

My two calculated exceptions covered pieces of evidence that, if the two prosecutors were to overlook anything, seemed the most likely candidates to me.

The first was Jennifer's filing of a salvage claim on the *Sea Wind* on May 22, 1975, just two months before her theft trial. She told me this had been her lawyer's idea. If she didn't, he said, everyone would believe she and Buck had stolen the vessel. He reasoned that a thief wouldn't have the audacity to file a salvage claim. Jennifer said she argued that it made no sense to do so because the *Sea Wind* belonged to Mac's heirs, but he persisted in his urging and she acquiesced. She told me that the salvage claim never came to court, and she didn't know what had happened to it.

I viewed the salvage claim as particularly damaging to Jennifer, because if the jury did not believe that her lawyer was the instigator, it was completely inconsistent with her testimony that she intended to return the *Sea Wind* to Kit Muncey after two years. Even if the jury *did* believe that her lawyer had influenced her, it was just one more example of someone getting Jennifer to do something she didn't want to do. His getting her to commit perjury was bad enough. I thought this salvage claim might slip by both Enoki and Schroeder, since they weren't on the case at the time of the theft trials, and the only reference to it I'd found was one short article amid the sea of newspaper clippings.

The second item I'd skirted was Jennifer's testimony at a motion-to-suppress hearing in Honolulu on January 24, 1975, that the only alternative open to Buck and her on Palmyra was to take the *Sea Wind* because they "were stranded" on Palmyra. When I asked Jennifer about this devastating testimony, she said this did not, as it appeared, refer to a belief in the unseaworthiness of the *Iola*. Rather, it was a lie to go along with the other lie that the *Iola* had run aground in the channel.

I had first seen a reference to the motion-to-suppress hearing in one of the documents furnished to the defense by the Government, but there was no copy of the transcript in our files. I asked Enoki for a copy and found the "stranded" remark in it. This appeared to be a highly damaging piece of evidence that confirmed exactly what the prosecution was saying, and I was greatly relieved when Jennifer had a satisfactory explanation. I didn't, however, want her to have to give it before the jury. Since Enoki had up to then furnished the defense with every transcript of a court proceeding in the case, it crossed my mind that the prosecutor might not have had this transcript in his own files, had ordered a copy for me, and, in the rush of things, not taken the time to read it himself.

"MISS JENKINS," Enoki finally began, straightening up and tucking one hand in his coat pocket, JFK-style, "as I understand it, you deny stealing the *Sea Wind* after the disappearance of the Grahams?"

"I never planned to steal the boat," she answered evenly, "and I had no intention of keeping her."

"Okay. At the prior theft proceedings that Mr. Bugliosi asked you about, you steadfastly denied to that jury stealing the *Sea Wind*. Is that correct?"

"Yes."

Enoki was already struggling with a subject I had covered matter-of-factly during my questioning.

"Yesterday, you admitted, did you not, that you had no legal right to the boat?"

"Yes."

"You knew that you were doing wrong. You admitted that yesterday, didn't you?"

"Yes."

"Concerning the letter Mr. Walker wrote to Mary Muncey, you did review it before you sent it off?"

"I read it, yes."

"I think you testified that not everything in there was true. Isn't that right?"

"Yes."

"In fact, that letter contains the statement that the *Iola* wound up on the reef as you were leaving Palmyra. Correct?"

"Yes."

"So, you knew Mr. Walker was lying to Mrs. Muncey about that?"

"Yes."

At the podium, Enoki paused.

"You indicated in your testimony that you were not trying to disguise the *Sea Wind* at all by repainting it. Is that right?" he asked.

"I did not believe that changing the color of that boat would in any way disguise her."

"And did you tell Mr. Walker that?"

"I did."

"And what was his response?"

"He just said he wanted to change the color. He said we were either going to paint her yellow or I could pick a color I liked better. Yellow is one of my least favorite colors, so I chose lavender."

"Didn't Mr. Walker's comments cause you some concern that he might be repainting the boat to disguise it because he was never going to return it?"

"He had made a promise to me when I showed him Mac's will. Buck promised me that we would get the boat back to the mainland of the United States within that two-year period specified in the will."

With respect to the swordfish incident, all the maneuvers Enoki had made to question the hole in the boat turned into smoke. Although he examined Jennifer in depth about the incident, none of his questions could in any way be considered challenging. They were more in the nature of simply finding out what had happened. Such as: "Now, did I hear you correctly that you discovered you were struck by the swordfish sometime later that evening? Is that correct?"

Enoki asked if the gold figurehead of a woman was in place on the bowsprit of the *Sea Wind* when Jennifer and Buck took possession of the boat at Palmyra.

"Yes," Jennifer said. "At some point, the figurehead ceased to be on the boat, but . . . I don't know when that was."

"I gather by your answer that you did not remove the figurehead yourself?"

"That's correct. I don't remember seeing it after we left Palmyra."

"Do you recall whether the name *Sea Wind* was on the running boards of the vessel when you took possession of it on Palmyra?"

"I don't remember, but it probably was."

"Do you remember if it was there when you got to Hawaii?"

"I don't remember. It probably wasn't. I think Buck had removed all the names. Mr. Wollen testified that the name *Iola* was on the boat. So . . . at some point in time, Buck must have removed all the *Sea Wind* names, and put the name *Iola* on. But I don't remember where and when that happened exactly."

Enoki was making good headway in one important area: Jennifer was beginning to say she didn't remember or recall certain things. Her memory, the prosecutor could later argue, had conveniently been much sharper on direct than on cross-examination. I hoped the jury would see that most of the things she couldn't remember were more trivial than the matters we had covered on direct.

Enoki touched on the subject of whether or not there had been a diary or log written by the Grahams aboard the *Sea Wind*. Jennifer said she "didn't specifically recall" finding anything that resembled a diary or log book.

"How about Mrs. Graham's clothing? Did you look through what she had?"

"I saw that she had clothing there. I didn't go through it, per se." There was a peevish tone in her reply I would have preferred she didn't have.

"Did you wear any of her clothing?"

"I don't recall wearing any of her clothing. I'm not sure."

"Do you recall the outfit in which you were arrested?"

"No."

Enoki asked the clerk to hand the witness two mug shots taken on the day of her arrest.

"Does that refresh your recollection in any way as to what you were wearing at the time you were arrested?"

"Yes. But I don't know whether that was . . . Muff's blouse I was wearing. I mean, I've . . . I had a blouse just like that, too."

"You took four hundred dollars in cash that you found on

board the vessel?" Enoki asked, repeating a point I had already elicited on direct examination. "Is that correct?"

"Yes," she said.

"You told Agent Shishido that you thought the Grahams would have wanted you to have the *Sea Wind*, is that correct?"

"The problem with that conversation was he was asking me questions that I could not answer honestly without placing Buck in jeopardy, so I came out with certain responses. Did I think that Mac wanted me to have that boat? No, I knew Mac wanted his sister to have the boat."

"I understand that. But at some point in that conversation, you do admit telling Agent Shishido that you rationalized the Grahams would have wanted you to have that boat. Whether that statement was true or not, you did make that statement to Agent Shishido."

Jennifer grimaced slightly.

"Yes."

"And you didn't mention to Agent Shishido the will that you had discovered on the boat. Isn't that right?"

"I probably didn't. I don't recall mentioning it."

"Telling Agent Shishido about your discovery of the will would not have impaired Mr. Walker's ability to escape, would it?" the prosecutor asked, leaning forward.

It was a good question, but Jennifer was prepared.

"No," she said. "But I knew that the will didn't give me any legal right to that boat. So why would I tell him about it?"

"On direct examination, I believe you indicated that it made your mind feel a little bit easier that you had found the will,* and seen in the will that Mac at one time wanted someone to have his boat in certain circumstances."

"But I didn't feel that the will was any justification for us keeping the boat, not legally. Not morally."

"You testified on direct examination that you weren't sure where you were going after you left the Ala Wai yacht harbor."

---

*Enoki had earlier entered into evidence a copy of a later will, the probated will of Mac Graham (San Diego Superior Court) signed by Mac on June 26, 1973.

"Yes."

"Do you recall Mrs. Wollen saying that she had asked you where you were going, and you told her the South Seas?"

"I could have easily told her that," Jennifer answered. "I don't recall."

"When you testified in your theft trial, you indicated to that jury that you were going from the Ala Wai to the mainland to return the boat to Mrs. Muncey."

"Yes."

"And that was a lie. Correct?"

"Ultimately, I did want to get the boat to Mary Muncey," she said firmly.

"Was it because it would possibly have been a defense to the theft charge that you told that jury that you were returning the boat to Mrs. Muncey?"

Enoki was zinging Jennifer now. My having brought out the matter on direct examination could take out only some of the sting, not all.

"No. It was because that's what I knew should be done. And that's what I would have done if it was my choice to make."

"Okay. So you deny that you were setting up the defense of 'return of property' by saying to that jury that you were returning the boat to Mrs. Muncey."

"I deny that, yes."

The prosecutor asked Jennifer if she had ever considered the possibility before leaving Palmyra that by some remote chance the Grahams had got lost and were perhaps injured and alive somewhere on the atoll.

"I would never have left Palmyra if I thought there was any chance that Mac and Muff were there."

"So you were—as of the time you left Palmyra Island—you were absolutely positive in your own mind that they had both died."

"Yes."

With that, court adjourned for the day. Jennifer had tasted only forty-five minutes of a cross-examination that would resume first thing in the morning.

Adjournment at this point in the proceedings was a break for the Government. Enoki had the rest of that afternoon and all night to prepare for his final assault on Jennifer's credibility.

9:37 A.M., THURSDAY,
FEBRUARY 20, 1986

ENOKI ADVISED the court outside the presence of the jury that the Government intended to call a rebuttal witness at the end of the defense's case and wanted to be able to cross-examine Jennifer now on the witness. He added that he assumed the defense would object to the testimony of the witness.

Indeed, we *did* object. When Enoki handed over an FBI 302 report just the previous afternoon—while I was still questioning Jennifer—Len and I had seen immediately what the Government was up to, and we both knew that the law did not permit it. But since we didn't have the legal citations to the cases on this point, Len went to the library that night for supporting authority prohibiting the prosecution from pulling this witness out of the hat at the eleventh hour.

Enoki told Judge King he wanted to call to the stand one George Gordon, a resident of Hawaii who claimed he met Jennifer Jenkins in a bar on the Big Island in 1975, shortly after her boat-theft conviction. In his interview with FBI Agent Hal Marshall, Gordon claimed that he and Jennifer had been drinking together, and during the course of the evening she had made several remarks about the Palmyra case.

Enoki said the witness would rebut Jennifer's testimony on several points.

Weinglass broke in. "Your honor, yesterday the prosecution handed us a statement that they have a witness who they found back in December 1985."

"Oh," Judge King said, raising his eyebrows, "they didn't tell you about him?"

"They purposefully withheld the existence of this witness from the defense," Len charged, "although they took his statement on

January 6, 1986, one month before this trial began." Len pointed out that under all the cases, including *People* v. *Carter*, a California supreme court case, witnesses like Gordon are precluded from testifying in rebuttal so as to avoid, as the *Carter* court ruled, "any unfair surprise that may result when a party who thinks he has met his opponent's case is suddenly confronted at the end of the trial with an additional piece of crucial evidence."

Judge King looked at Enoki. It was his turn.

Enoki simply said he didn't think he was required, under the law, to inform us of the existence of the witness, and went on to set forth the six points Gordon would testify to. "First, that Jennifer was scared, insecure, and not comfortable on Palmyra. Second, that she wanted to leave the island. Third, that she was afraid the *Iola* wouldn't make it away from Palmyra and that the craft would sink. Fourth, she had wanted to obtain some passage with the Grahams, but that was either denied or refused for the reason that the Grahams didn't want to take her or weren't leaving or some other reason he's not sure of. Fifth, that the two couples didn't get along very well."

Enoki's next and final point was the one I feared most. He said Jennifer had told Gordon that "if Buck Walker told his story, she would be in some trouble." (The FBI report quoted George Gordon as saying: "Jennifer told me if Buck Walker spilled his guts, she would be in a lot of trouble.")

When I now asked Jennifer about George Gordon, she said he was a "beach guy" who worked on cars. She said she had never been intimate with Gordon, but had had drinks with him once or twice, and said she could not recall having any such conversation with him. Gordon's statement, especially the "spilling the guts" part, *did* sound unrealistic to me. Even if Jennifer were guilty, it seems highly unlikely she would make such a clearly incriminating remark, particularly to a casual acquaintance. But on the other hand, why would Gordon lie?

Obviously, the purported "spill the guts" statement was a hundred times more serious than any of the others. If true, and if believed by the jury, the statement came close to being an outright confession to the murders. As Enoki pointed out to the court, "would be in a lot of trouble" couldn't refer to the theft, since at the time of this alleged statement she had "*already* been convicted of the theft charge." However, Jennifer told me she thought it was *before* her theft trial that she had drinks with Gordon.

Len told the court that Enoki told him that "the witness was drinking at the time he allegedly heard this statement."

"Who *is* George Gordon?" Judge King asked, bemused.

"Mr. Gordon is a former, well, he was an auto mechanic at the time these statements were made at a bar in the Puako area of the Big Island," Enoki said. "And he is now a charter fishing boat captain in Maui. I want to correct something Mr. Weinglass said. I told him Mr. Gordon would testify that Jennifer Jenkins, not Mr. Gordon, was intoxicated at the time the statements were made. I would assume that he had something to drink. But he will deny he was in any way intoxicated or under the influence of alcohol."

The judge predictably sustained the defense objection to George Gordon's testimony; the jury would never hear from the former auto mechanic. But the Gordon statement was quoted in the following morning's *San Francisco Chronicle*, where any member of the jury could read it.

The FBI had become aware of Gordon while looking for witnesses with knowledge of Jennifer's relationship with another man after her return from Palmyra. This lover had, like Buck Walker, spent time behind bars and had a history of violent activity. *That* relationship the jury *would* hear about later, and the implications were almost as serious as those of the Gordon matter.

Resuming his cross-examination when the jury was back in place, Enoki asked if Jennifer knew that by helping Walker flee, she herself was breaking the law.

"I wasn't sure whether my going with Buck was wrong legally or not. But I thought that it might be. I didn't know."

"And you knew if you turned him in," Enoki continued, "it was your understanding that he faced a lengthy prison term. Isn't that right?"

"Yes."

I scribbled on my pad, "How is this helpful to prosecution?" A few seconds later, I added: "It can't be."

Enoki changed the subject to the condition of the *Iola*, asking Jennifer specifically about the frequency of pumping out the bilge while the boat had been moored at Palmyra.

"Twice a week, probably."

"How deep was the water in the bilge when you pumped it out?"

"Oh, maybe a couple of inches."

"Did you ever state to Mr. or Mrs. Leonard that you never wanted to leave Palmyra on the *Iola*?" he asked.

"Absolutely not."

"While you were on Palmyra, did you ever think that the *Iola* would not get you off the island safely?"

"My major concern with getting off of Palmyra was in our ability to navigate, without a motor, out the narrow channel, because of the problem we had coming in. I spoke to Mac about that, and he said that I shouldn't worry about it, that if the winds were bad, that he could push us out with the Zodiac dinghy."

"Other than that, did you ever have any doubts about the *Iola* getting you off of Palmyra to somewhere else, wherever that may be, with safety?"

"No, I didn't. No."

The prosecutor's cross-examination was typical—not really very cross. This is the style one sees day in and day out throughout the nation's courts, not the aggressive demeanor portrayed in fiction. Perhaps in this one area lawyers could learn from dramatists. When one is trying to destroy credibility, the primary purpose of cross-examination,* although the questioner does not necessarily have to be continuously aggressive, and although some of his questions may be velvety in nature and tone, it's my belief that most of his questions should have a cutting edge to them. Either Enoki didn't agree with this, or such an approach simply wasn't in his nature. In

---

*Another purpose is to elicit additional facts that will favor the questioner's side of the case. Cross-examination is a valuable but dangerous art that is mastered by few, and this is why more cases are lost on cross-examination than won. Nonetheless, it remains, as one legal scholar observed, "the greatest legal engine ever invented for the discovery of the truth," taking the place in our system of justice which torture occupied in medieval times.

fact, as is the conventional practice, Enoki never once asked Jennifer a "why" question during his entire cross-examination of her.

Enoki next asked if Jennifer recalled having asked the Taylor brothers to bring seagoing epoxy, which is used to repair leaks below the waterline, down to Palmyra. She answered that this was Buck's realm, and she did not "know anything about that."

A crucial area of examination for the Government involved Jennifer's insistence that she and Buck had planned to travel to Fanning for new supplies.

She denied that Jack Wheeler had used the word "impossible" to describe a trip from Palmyra to Fanning. "He indicated it would be difficult."

"You did know that the trip would have been against the wind?"

"Yes."

"Mr. Wheeler told you there would also be an approximately two-knot current that was against you on the trip to Fanning. Correct?"

Jennifer considered that a moment.

"I don't recall him saying that, but he may well have . . . I knew it was going to be a difficult sail."

Enoki persisted on the issue of the current between Palmyra and Fanning, wanting to know if it would be necessary to know its speed in order to navigate.

"The way I navigated was I took sights. I saw where I was, and knew where I was going, and I took a compass heading that would take me in that direction."

"So, you're saying it didn't matter to your method of navigation . . . the speed of the current?"

"That's correct."

"Doesn't there ever come a point," Enoki probed, "where the current might become so strong that you are simply unable to make progress tacking?"

"I never experienced that," Jennifer said.

"Would the speed of the current have been relevant to determining how long it would take you to get from Palmyra to Fanning?"

"Yes."

"And the state of your provisions would be affected by how long it would take you to get from Palmyra to Fanning, would it not?"

"Yes, but it was, I mean, Fanning should be like a two-day trip. So, by me planning for the possibility of it taking five, six, seven days—I was saving a seven-day supply—that would cover, as far as I was concerned, any situation of being becalmed and having it take longer than it should."

Asked how she and Buck were planning to get back into the Palmyra lagoon upon their return from Fanning, Jennifer said they had discussed two possible ways. "One would be to wait for an advantageous wind that would be coming from behind us to sail up into the lagoon, and the other way would be if we were having trouble doing it, I'm sure Mac would have come out and helped us."

"You were expecting the Grahams to be there upon your return?" Enoki asked.

"Yes. They were going to be staying for a long time."

Enoki veered to yet another subject I had covered on direct. Couldn't she and Buck have left the *Sea Wind* at Palmyra, sailed elsewhere, and alerted the authorities *anonymously*? Though I had asked Jennifer this precise question during our trial preparation, I had elected to omit the "anonymous" part of it on my direct examination of her.

"That's what I wanted to do."

"And you say that Buck convinced you not to do that?"

"Right. Buck was absolutely adamant."

"If you had left the *Sea Wind* on Palmyra, and you had gone to another port in the *Iola*, did you feel that Mr. Walker would have physically prevented you from making a phone call or any other kind of report to the authorities?"

Jennifer paused. "I don't know the answer to that question."

"You were aware, prior to leaving Palmyra, that Mac Graham had regularly scheduled radio communications with Curt Shoemaker. Is that right?"

"Yes."

"And you were aware that, obviously, those radio communications would no longer be met by the Grahams?"

"Yes."

"Neither you nor Mr. Walker used the *Sea Wind*'s radio at all. Is that correct?"

"That's correct."

"Did either of you *try* to use the radio?"

"No." (Jennifer had testified on direct that she didn't know how to operate the *Sea Wind*'s radio, and didn't believe Buck did either. The radio on the *Iola*, she explained, "was different. It was just a receiver, not one you talked out from.")

Gaining speed, Enoki now asked Jennifer, "You will agree that contained in your diary are many details about what you did on Palmyra?"

"Uh-huh."

"You wrote down things like going fishing?"

"Yes."

"You wrote down where you went on certain days?"

"Yes."

"You wrote down who you saw and what you did?"

"Yes."

"You even wrote down arguments you had with Mr. Walker. Is that right?"

"Yes."

"But there is nothing in this diary about you and Mr. Walker arguing about whether you were going to leave Palmyra on the *Sea Wind*. Is there?"

"That's correct."

Enoki's intended implication was clear. *No argument had ever taken place.*

"I believe you stated on direct examination that the latter part of your diary entry on August 30th where it says 'And then tragedy' was not written August 30th?"

"Yes, that's correct."

"There are other entries in that diary where you did write about the day's events after the completion of the day, are there not?"

"There are a number of them, yes."

"But you didn't do this on this particular day, August 30th, correct?"

"That's correct."

Next was the inevitable attack I had tried to soften: Jennifer's prior perjury.

"Now, you do admit—you testified about telling a previous jury, at your . . . at a theft trial where you were the defendant—that the *Iola* ran aground in the channel. Is that correct?"

"Yes."

"And you said it while you were on the witness stand like you are today, correct?"

"Yes."

"And that means you took the oath before you testified?"

"Yes."

"So, when you told the jury that while towing the *Iola* out of the channel it had hung up on the rocks, you knew you were lying and committing perjury?"

"Yes."

"Now, as I understand your testimony, the reason you did this was because Mr. Walker told you on Palmyra not to tell the truth. Is that correct?"

"Yes, he said I should say the *Iola* had gone aground, and that that's why we had to go back and get the *Sea Wind*."

"Yet, when you got to Hawaii, Mr. Walker told people that he had won the *Sea Wind* in a chess game. Isn't that right?"

"Yes."

"Isn't that totally inconsistent with even the rehearsed version of what happened?" Enoki asked, illustrating the maxim that false-hoods not only disagree with truths, but usually quarrel among themselves.

"No," Jennifer said coolly. "He was only talking about if the authorities asked us."

With respect to Jennifer's testimony on direct that she was cau-tioned about the inadvisability of changing her story at her theft trial, Enoki asked: "You're not suggesting that one of your attor-neys in that case told you that, are you?"

"I wouldn't want to say that they told me to lie, but I was advised by one of my attorneys that if I testified inconsistently with statements that I made to the FBI, the trial would probably go poorly against me."

"Just so the record is clear, neither Mr. Bugliosi nor Mr. Weinglass were involved in that case?"

Jennifer raised her voice.

"Absolutely not."

"Did your attorneys at the theft trial know that the true fact was that the *Iola* had not run aground and you had not left it there?"

"Yes."

Enoki next elicited from Jennifer that at her theft trial she denied taking the photographs of the *Iola* and the *Sea Wind* in the open sea off Palmyra.

"That was a lie, too?" he asked.

"Yes, it was."

"Do you recall Bernard Leonard testifying that you also told him that you attempted to *sail* out of the lagoon on the *Iola*, and it wound up on the reef and that's when you went back to get the *Sea Wind*?"

"I think I do, yes."

"I gather you deny saying that to Mr. Leonard?"

"No. With all that was happening that day, I could have easily told Mr. Leonard that story, but then when I was speaking to Mr. Shishido, it got to where I spoke more close to the truth."

"Isn't it true the reason that your story changed between Leonard and Shishido was because Mr. Leonard told you that you would have never left on the *Iola* if the *Sea Wind* was sitting there?"

"No, it didn't change for that reason."

Noon recess.

BEFORE THE afternoon session resumed, Judge King asked each side, since we were nearing the conclusion of the trial, to submit instructions to the jury we wanted him to add to his standard instructions. There was one instruction I wanted him *not* to give, and because my request was so unusual, I had alerted Judge King before the trial began so that he would have time to mull it over at length. I handed him an article I wrote in 1981 titled "Not Guilty and Innocent—the Problem Children of Reasonable Doubt."*

"For your reading pleasure," I told the judge with tongue in cheek, referring to the very dry subject matter.

"I'm sure," he muttered.

The article dealt with the critical distinction between the terms "not guilty" and "innocent." (It is nothing short of incredible that with legal treatises having been written on virtually every point of law imaginable, apparently none had ever been previously published on the subject in America. At least, none is listed in the Index to Legal Periodicals, or the Criminal Justice Periodical Index.) The genesis of the distinction is in the requirement that guilt must be proved "beyond a reasonable doubt." But what does that hallowed phrase actually mean?

The doctrine of reasonable doubt is, as Sir Winston Churchill once said of Soviet Russia, "a riddle wrapped in a mystery inside an enigma." "This elusive and *undefinable* state of mind," said J. Wigmore, the foremost authority on the law of evidence. "It is coming to be recognized that all attempts to define reasonable doubt tend to obfuscate rather than clarify the concept," said E. Morgan, another authority. However, one all-important principle is implicit in the term—namely, that a jury does not have to believe in a defendant's innocence in order to return a verdict of not guilty. Even their belief in his guilt, if only a moderately held one, should result in a not-guilty verdict. To convict, their belief in guilt must be *beyond a reasonable doubt*.

In federal courts throughout the country, the judge properly instructs the jury that to convict, guilt must be proved beyond a reasonable doubt. Inconsistently, however, in the very same instruction (#11.06 of *Federal Criminal Jury Instructions* by Devitt and Blackmar), the judge tells the jury: "You are here *to determine the guilt or innocence of the accused*." Under existing law, this added instruction should not be given since it is not the central purpose of a criminal trial to decide the factual question of the defendant's

*Published in *Mississippi College Law Review* in Jackson, Mississippi, and *Criminal Justice Journal*, Western State University School of Law in San Diego.

guilt or innocence." Yet even the U.S. Supreme Court in case after case* continues to define loosely and erroneously the jury's function in a criminal trial. Needless to say, far less insightful state,† county, and municipal courts throughout the land, as well as authorities on the criminal law,‡ make the same mistake.

To a lay juror—in fact, to anyone—"guilt" means that a person *did* whatever he is charged with doing, "innocence" that he did *not* do it. The completely reasonable assumption I wanted to erase from the jury's mind was that their *ultimate* duty was to determine whether Jennifer did or did not participate in the Palmyra murders.

While a defendant's guilt or innocence obviously is the most important *moral* issue at every criminal trial, the *ultimate legal* issue for the jury to determine is whether or not the prosecution has met its legal burden of proving guilt beyond a reasonable doubt. If the jury does not fully understand this critical distinction, its ability to fulfill its function as the trier of fact will almost necessarily be impaired.

In American criminal jurisprudence, a not-guilty verdict can result from one of two states of mind on the part of the jury: that they believe the defendant is innocent and did not commit the crime; or, although they do not believe he is innocent and *tend* to believe that he did commit the crime, the prosecution's case was not sufficiently strong to convince them of his guilt beyond a reasonable doubt.

Instead of the correct term "guilty or not guilty," the incorrect "guilt or innocence" has insidiously crept into the American language and consciousness. Although the precise date and locus of its misconceived birth are not known, it has led a very robust life,

---

*E.g., Chief Justice William H. Rehnquist, in *Arizona v. Fulminante*, 111 S. Ct. 1246 (1991): "The central purpose of the criminal trial is to decide the factual question of the defendant's *guilt or innocence.*" *Jackson v. Denno*, 378 U.S. 368 (1964): . . . "there must be a new trial on *guilt or innocence.*"

†E.g., Texas Criminal Pattern Jury Charges, section 0.05, "Your sole duty is to *determine the guilt or innocence* of the defendant."

‡See *Perkins on Criminal Law*. "Criminal Procedure is the formal machinery established to enforce the criminal law. It includes 1.) accusation of crime, 2.) *determination of guilt or innocence* and 3.) disposition of those convicted."

shows no signs of aging, and, as we have seen, has been invested with the imprimatur of the highest court in the land.

When jurors are deliberating, the media report that they are deciding the "guilt or innocence" of the accused. And a defendant found "not guilty" is usually reported by the press to have been found "innocent." So, too, in novels, theater, movies and television. With this constant inundation, jurors naturally believe that their purpose at a criminal trial is to determine whether or not the defendant committed the crime. Even in the absence of such a deluge, they would almost automatically make this assumption. After all, though the prosecutor and defense attorney get caught up in the adversary process—with its attendant unblushing effort to maximize advantages and minimize disadvantages—jurors have a much more pristine view of justice. To them, justice is finding out the truth and then giving a person his due. And the question "Did the defendant commit the crime or not?" is much more compatible with their concept of justice than what they view as the gamelike "Did the prosecution prove it beyond a reasonable doubt or not?"*

Instead of clearly and unequivocally disabusing jurors of their misconception, courts throughout the land repeat the incorrect notion. Along with judges, the great bulk of prosecutors use the term "guilt or innocence." (In the Walker trial, Enoki told the jury: "We are determining Buck Walker's, not Jennifer Jenkins's, guilt or innocence in this particular case.") And defense lawyers everywhere can be heard arguing to juries that the prosecution has not proved guilt beyond a reasonable doubt, and in the next breath stating, "Now, in determining the guilt or innocence of my client, take into consideration . . ." In fact, the textbook of the Association of Trial Lawyers of America states that "the determination of guilt or innocence is the sole province of the jury, and is the essence of our system."

---

*This is not the forum to debate whether guilt or innocence should be the issue at a criminal trial. Many philosophical and societal considerations are involved. But since it is *not* the issue, as long as juries are told (along with the correct instruction) that it is, thousands of defendants throughout the nation will continue to be tried before juries who are misinstructed on the most fundamental issue at a criminal trial.

What it all comes down to in an actual courtroom situation is this: if the question that is *uppermost* in the jurors' mind when they retire to deliberate is "Did he do it or did he not do it?" as opposed to "Did the prosecution meet its burden of proof or did it not?" then even though the evidence against the defendant is only moderately strong (as opposed to the requisite very strong) the jury will probably be psychologically attuned to a conviction.

For this reason, I asked Judge King to delete all of the many references to "guilt or innocence" from his instructions, particularly the charge to the jury that it was *its duty* to determine the guilt or innocence of the accused. The judge said he had read my article, and although he had never thought of the matter before, had to agree with my conclusions. But he hastened to add, "Look, I've been giving the guilt or innocence instructions for years. How do you expect me not to give basic instructions that are in Devitt and Blackmar, that are a part of the standard instructions of the federal courts given everywhere? In all my years, I've never been asked not to give these instructions."

I had saved my ace in the hole. "What if I furnished you with evidence that the coauthor of your book of instructions doesn't use the term 'guilt or innocence' in his own court?"

"What do you have?" the judge said.

I showed him a long piece about my article in *The National Law Journal* of March 1, 1982. A staffer had contacted Judge Edward J. Devitt (Chief Judge, United States District Court for the District of Minnesota), the horse's mouth, for his comment on my article. After reading it, Devitt remarkably told the *Journal* he didn't use the phrase "guilt or innocence" in his own courtroom. (The judge uses the phrase in no fewer than ten instructions in his own book, which is cheerfully parroted by federal judges throughout the country.)

"Okay," Judge King said, after reading the article. He agreed to delete all uses of the phrase "guilt or innocence" in instructions to Jennifer's jury.

While not a pivotal victory, it perhaps could, in company with others, help me persuade the jury to return a verdict of not guilty. Of course, I still intended to argue Jennifer's innocence to the jury, *but not in the context that her "guilt or innocence" was the ultimate issue for them to decide.*

WHEN COURT went back into session, Enoki resumed his cross-examination. "*When you found the Zodiac,* Miss Jenkins, do you recall whether the tide at that time was high or low?"

It wasn't the first time he'd phrased a question in a way that indicated—grammatically, at least—that he was accepting Jennifer's version of events. Of course, Enoki did *not* believe her and was trying his best to destroy her credibility on the witness stand. It was simple carelessness on his part not to qualify his questions with "allegedly" or "you claim" or some other terminology to signal to the jurors his disbelief.

"I don't have a specific recollection, but I know that it wasn't high tide, I mean, I don't know where in between low and high it was."

"Okay. Would it be fair to assume that at high tide, the Zodiac, from where you found it, would have been partially in the water?"

"I . . . I don't know that."

"Okay. It was one and a half feet from the water when you found it. Correct?"

"Yes, it was about one and a half to two feet from the water when I found it."

"And the gas tank was approximately the same distance from the water?"

"Yes."

"You remember Agent Shishido testifying that you told him you *found* the Zodiac overturned in the lagoon and the gas tank was floating nearby?"

"Yes."

"And you deny telling him this?"

"I told him that I thought the dinghy had overturned in the lagoon, and that both the gas tank and dinghy had floated ashore."

Enoki asked Jennifer about her testimony regarding the various obstructions in the lagoon. Wasn't it true, he asked, that the lagoon was shallow enough in the area where the steel poles stuck up out of the water for the Grahams to walk to shore if their Zodiac had struck one and tipped over? Jennifer agreed it was shallow enough, but went on to describe again the occasion when she and Buck were rowing their own dinghy across a shallow stretch of the lagoon.

"He got out of the dinghy, and the sharks came after him immediately. So, I felt that even if Mac and Muff had their boating accident in shallow water and had been thrown out, that—you know, that was the image that was in my mind of what might have happened."

"Then you were not thinking of a drowning?"

"I just . . . all I knew was that I found the dinghy upside down. And in searching for Mac and Muff, I found them nowhere. It was evident to me that *something* terrible had happened."

When Enoki asked if Jennifer was—by August 30, 1974—tired of living on Palmyra, there was a long pause.

"I don't know how to answer that question," she finally stated. "If I had my choice of someplace to go, I would not choose Palmyra. I felt that way then. Palmyra was not my favorite place to be."

"Did you want to leave Palmyra for reasons other than going to Fanning and getting resupplied?"

"No, my preference would have been to wait for Richard Taylor and his brother to come down."

"You do admit that you were eating virtually nothing but coconuts in the last week in August?"

"Well, and fish. And we did have stores. But I was touching the stores as infrequently as possible."

Enoki read the August 25 entry from Jennifer's diary: "'For the first time in three days we'll have something other than coconuts for dinner—beans.' So that would mean that on at least August 22nd, 23rd, and 24th, you didn't have anything except coconuts for dinner."

"Yes, sir."

"Do you recall telling Tom Wolfe that you were sick and tired of eating coconuts and fish?"

"I could have easily said that."

"I gather you were eating the food on the *Sea Wind* from the time of August 30th onward?" Enoki asked.

"Yes."

The next subject on Enoki's list was the cake-truce incident the jury had heard so much about. "The 28th of August is the date on which the cake-truce incident, as Mr. Bugliosi refers to it, supposedly occurred," the prosecutor said. "Now, as I understand your testimony, you don't remember whether you took a cake over to the *Sea Wind* on the 28th?"

"That's correct."

"Now, you were running out of food supplies at that time, were you not?"

"Yes."

"Wouldn't a gift of food from you have been an important event for you at that time?"

The scenario being advanced by Enoki was obvious: the murders occurred on August 28 after Jennifer and Buck had gone to the *Sea Wind* with a cake, and she did not mention the visit in her diary because the Grahams were murdered that night.

"I brought things over to Mac and Muff periodically, things that I had made for them," Jennifer said. "Without having it in the diary to refresh my memory, I would not remember it at this point."

"Well, you did put in the diary for the 28th that you husked coconuts, and charged batteries, and a few other things that you did that day. Correct?"

"Yes."

"But there is no entry for going to the *Sea Wind*, or taking a cake to anyone that day."

"Yes. That's correct."

"Now, I believe your testimony also was that Mr. Shoemaker relating that Mac Graham had said something about a truce on that day must be incorrect?"

"Yes."

"Because there was no need for a truce in your view of what was going on?"

"Yes."

Enoki stared at Jennifer for a few moments. "If you were getting along at that time, was there any reason for you to tell Mr. Wolfe that you weren't getting along with the Grahams?" he finally asked.

"I don't believe that I ever indicated to Mr. Wolfe that we weren't getting along."

Enoki now began to take Jennifer over the events of August 30. "You said that Mr. Walker first mentioned this dinner invitation at approximately 9:00 A.M. Is that correct?"

"Yes."

"Between eleven o'clock and very late in the afternoon—when you were on the *Iola*—you had the *Iola*'s dinghy. Isn't that correct?"

"I believe that's correct."

"Because otherwise you would be on the *Iola* with no way of getting ashore. Correct?"

"Yes." When Jennifer hedged by adding that it was "possible" that Buck had the dinghy since she "didn't need it" during the day, Enoki quickly firmed up her original position.

"A few days earlier you had gotten into an argument with Mr. Walker about him taking the dinghy and leaving you stranded on the *Iola*. Correct?" Enoki asked.

"Is that in my diary?"

"If you want to look at it . . . I believe it's August 19th."

"Yes, I see it."

"It says there: 'R came by to bake cakes and cookies which once again infuriated me . . . then sunshine. But I was stranded as he took the dinghy to shore. Slight confrontation, and to our separate corners for the night.' Correct?"

"Yes."

"Now . . . do you recall testifying in your theft trial that *you* had the dinghy on August 30th?"

"I don't specifically recall, but I generally had the dinghy on the boat. So I could have easily testified to that, yes."

"So, you *did always* have the dinghy that day, as far as you can remember?"

"As far as I can remember, yes."

This, of course, was a critical issue I had discussed in detail with Jennifer long before the trial, and she had told me that Buck had the dinghy that day. Her current version, the same as her theft-trial testimony, could be taken to imply that Buck had not worried that she might come ashore without warning. *Enoki could now argue that Buck's lack of concern showed that she had been involved in the murders.*

Enoki next queried her about hearing the sound of the Zodiac's engine at some point that afternoon. "I believe you indicated on the chart that the motor sounded to you like it was going away from you, along the shore of Cooper and Strawn islands. Is that correct?"

"Yes, the sound was getting further away."

"By 'further away,' you mean further away from where you were on the *Iola*?"

"Yes."

"So, the sound could equally have been going in a direction from the *Sea Wind* into the middle of the lagoon as well. Is that correct?"

"Yes."

"Now, after you heard the Zodiac motor, did you actually hear it shut off, or did it just sort of disappear into the background?"

Again, a question worded in a way that, if taken literally, actually accepted Jennifer's version of events.

"I just . . . I know that at some point I either ceased to hear it, or ceased to listen to it. One or the other."

"I gather during all these times that you saw Mr. Walker during that day, you didn't see any bloodstains on him?"

"No."

"You didn't see any scratches, or any indications that he was injured?"

"No."

"What was he wearing that day? Do you remember?"

"He was wearing a pair of shorts."

"That was his customary attire?"

"Yes."

"Was he wet at all during any time of the day?"

"He perspired a lot, so he was always kind of—"

"Well, I mean, wet to the point where it was obvious he had been in the water. Were his shorts wet, or was his hair wet?"

"I don't . . . I don't remember anything like that."

"Do you recall any peculiar smells about him, such as smoke or gasoline or kerosene?"

"No."

"You found no bloodstains or signs of a struggle when you went on board the *Sea Wind* that night?"

"No, nothing like that."

"Nothing unusual?"

"Nothing unusual," she repeated.

"Was the door to the cabin of the *Sea Wind* already open, or was it not open?"

"It was open, as I recall."

"Do you remember if there was any sign of someone having broken into that area?"

"No, I didn't notice anything like that."

"After awhile on the *Sea Wind*, you went below deck, correct?"

"Yes."

"And is that where you saw what you thought they had left out for you?"

"Yes."

"Are you able to recall specifically what was left out for you?"

"There was *a bottle of apricot brandy* and a bottle of vodka, and some cookies . . . and a couple of other things."

I had made the right decision about the apricot brandy. I'd now be able to explore the matter on re-direct.

Enoki asked a series of questions about Walker's "explosive personality" and criminal past. By the fourth or fifth query, Jennifer was teary-eyed and looked downcast.

"You knew that he had a prior conviction for armed robbery?"

"Yes," she whispered.

Enoki was now ready to spring his big surprise.

If someone had suggested there probably was something important in Jennifer's personal background that I didn't know about and could be used against her at this trial, I would have scoffed at the suggestion. But I was wrong.

The prosecutor placed a hand on each edge of the podium, bracing himself for his final fusillade. "You've heard testimony from witnesses that you were a nonviolent person?" he said with an intonation that portended danger.

"Yes."

"Is it also your testimony that you wouldn't associate with violent people?"

"I would not associate with anybody that was doing any violent acts."

"Do you consider shooting people to be violent?"

"Yes. Shooting people is violent."

It was obvious that Enoki had something, and I listened uneasily, fearing the worst.

"Now, in 1975, or 1976, you were residing in the Puako area of the Big Island. Is that correct?"

"Yes."

"During the time that you lived in Puako in 1975 or 1976, did you come to have a boyfriend named Joe Buffalo?"

"Yes."

Joe Buffalo? I thought a moment. Yes, that was the "friend" of Jennifer's who'd told her the FBI had contacted him about her. When she received the letter from Buffalo, Jennifer told me Buffalo had told her he had nothing to tell the authorities about her. Because of this, coupled with the fact that he wasn't on the list of prosecution witnesses Enoki had furnished us before the trial, I therefore assumed he was no one to worry about. I was correct in assuming Buffalo had nothing incriminating to say about Jennifer, and hence would not be a witness against her. It was what the authorities had to say about Buffalo that was the problem. For some inexcusable reason on my part, I neglected to explore with Jennifer just who Buffalo was (not that my knowing this would have changed anything, but at least I would have been better prepared to handle the issue). And during my first interviews with Jennifer, when I had her account, in chronological order, for all of her movements and activities during her several-year Hawaii period, somehow Jennifer's brief affair with a man named Joe Buffalo had slipped through the cracks.

Enoki now asked: *"And you became aware while you were going with Mr. Buffalo that he had shot and killed a man in California. Isn't that correct?"*

"Yes."

I didn't quite freeze like a deer in headlights, but I remained expressionless, not wanting the jury to sense my surprise and alarm.

"You also knew that he was wanted by authorities in connection with that shooting incident?"

"No, I didn't know that then. When . . . when the authorities came and arrested him, that was the first time I found out that he was . . . still wanted."

"You did know that he was trying to keep a low profile in that area?"

"Right. I . . . I . . . he had been officially released from prison. And a low profile was something that in retrospect . . . I know he was keeping. But I didn't know that he was being looked for, or wanted, or anything like that."

"You thought that the reason he was trying to keep a low profile was because he was trying to conceal his prison background, is that it?" asked Enoki.

"No. He was just wanting to keep a low profile, just generally. I don't know."

"You testified that you were aware that Mr. Buffalo had been released from prison before he came to Puako. Correct?"

"Yes."

"You were aware that his release was inadvertent, correct? That he was mistakenly released?"

"Not at that point, not until after he was rearrested."

I knew the prosecution would now argue that the Buffalo affair showed that Jennifer's relationship with the homicidal Buck Walker was *not* just situational but a way of life with her. One could reasonably conclude that she willingly associated with these birds because of her own feathers. Being involved with not just one but two murderers within a period of only two years seemed far too much for coincidence. *It was a pattern.*

Enoki was gathering his notes, like a news anchor after sign-off. Only he'd ended, not begun, with the day's top story.

"Thank you," he said. "Nothing further, your honor." Enoki proceeded to request, and was granted, a fifteen-minute recess. Because of Joe Buffalo, I needed it more than he did.*

After grilling Jennifer about Buffalo during the break, I began my re-direct examination of Jennifer where Enoki had left off.

"With respect to this fellow, Joe Buffalo, when did you live with him in Hawaii?"

"1975, the latter part."

"Did he tell you that he had killed someone in *self-defense*?"

"Yes."

"And you believed him?"

"Yes."

"Did he ever do anything violent while you were with him?"

"No, never."

"To your knowledge, was he leading a law-abiding life throughout the period of time that you were with him?"

"Yes, he was."

"What was your attitude about Joe Buffalo's past?"

"I knew he had a rough background and I thought I could help him. He was generally . . . he seemed generally interested in putting his past behind him and living within the rules of society."

"At the time you had this relationship with Mr. Buffalo, you had not yet suspected that the Grahams may have been murdered?"

"Correct."

Because of the importance of the issue, I wanted to underline this fact in the jury's mind by repetition: "So, when you were living with Mr. Buffalo, it was your state of mind that Mr. and Mrs. Graham had died an accidental death?"

"Yes."

"The Buffalo association, then, was long before you began to suspect that maybe the Grahams were murdered."

"Yes."

I hoped this had reduced the pattern down to a coincidence in

*But on re-direct I would not have to put out brushfires like Jennifer's salvage claim of the *Sea Wind* or her "stranded" remark, because Enoki had missed both points in his cross-examination. My gamble in not bringing them up on direct had paid off.

the jury's eyes, lessening, at least somewhat, their speculation that she had *knowingly* lived with *two killers*. Knowingly, she had been involved with only one person who had taken the life of a fellow human being (in self-defense at that, she believed). And that person was Joe Buffalo, not Buck Walker.

SINCE ENOKI had tried to impeach Jennifer's testimony that she and Buck had found both the Zodiac and the gas tank on the beach (using an allegedly *inconsistent* statement she had made to FBI Agent Shishido), I was now entitled, under the rules of evidence, to introduce any statement she'd made *consistent* with her present testimony, but only if made *before* the alleged inconsistent statement. Although her theft-trial testimony was given *after* her statement to Shishido, I nonetheless now asked Jennifer (without provoking the objection Enoki should have made): "At your theft trial, did you testify that you found the Zodiac dinghy overturned *on the beach* about a half mile or so to the west of the *Sea Wind*?"

"Yes."

"Did you also testify you found the gas tank of the Zodiac *on the beach*?"

"Yes."

"Jennifer, are you familiar with the fact that there are two high tides and two low tides approximately every twenty-four hours?"

"Yes."

The crucial significance of my next question wouldn't be apparent until my summation: "Are you also aware that of the two high tides, one is a high high tide where the water goes the farthest up on the beach, and one is a low high tide where the water does not go quite as far up?"

"Yes."

And now, finally, I could ask Jennifer about the apricot brandy.

"You testified that when you and Buck arrived at the *Sea Wind* on the evening of August 30, 1974, among other things, apricot brandy and vodka were set out. Is that correct?"

"Yes."

"Was vodka one of Buck's favorite drinks?"

"Yes."

"Was apricot brandy one of your favorite drinks?"

"Yes."

"You had had drinks on the *Sea Wind* prior to the 30th of August with Mac and Muff?"

"Yes."

"Had you ever had apricot brandy with them?"

"No."

"Had you ever communicated to them, as far as you can recall, that apricot brandy was one of your favorite drinks?"

"No," she said, "I don't recall ever mentioning that to them."

"When you found apricot brandy set out there in the cabin, and also vodka, did it occur to you at that time that it may have been Buck as opposed to the Grahams who set those alcoholic beverages out there for you?"

"No."

"Has it occurred to you since?"

Enoki jumped to his feet. "I will object to that as irrelevant, your honor."

Court: "Overruled."

"Yes," Jennifer answered sadly.

"When did it occur to you?" I asked.

Enoki objected again and was again overruled.

"When you were interviewing me and brought it to my attention," Jennifer answered.

Court: "How long ago?"

"Oh, God," Jennifer shrugged. "I don't know."

Court: "A year ago?"

"A few years ago."

Court: "Two years ago?"

"Two or three years ago," she said.

Court: "When Mr. Bugliosi was first interviewing you?"

"Yes."

"You did not volunteer to me when I was interviewing you that apricot brandy happened to be one of your favorite drinks?" I asked.

"No."

"I asked you whether it was. Is that correct?"

"Yes."

"Jennifer, going on, there has been some testimony about your attorneys, during the 1975 theft trial, giving you certain advice. Has either Mr. Weinglass or I told you or implied to you in any way that you should not tell the truth at *this* trial?"

"No, not at all. Both you and Mr. Weinglass have always indicated that you wanted me to tell the whole truth."

"Absent our telling you this, Jennifer, what was your state of mind with respect to testifying truthfully at this trial?"

"I was always determined to tell the truth at this trial."

"No further questions," I said.

Judge King cleared his throat noisily. "I have a few," he said.

I wasn't happy at that prospect. When a judge starts asking questions of a defendant, the jury might infer that he doesn't believe the defendant.

"You didn't find any log on the *Sea Wind?*" the judge asked.

"I don't remember at this point either finding one or not finding one," Jennifer said. "I could have come across a log of the *Sea Wind*, and it probably wouldn't have meant much to me."

Court: "You don't recall?"

"Right."

Court: "Somebody said you came over to the *Sea Wind* with a cake on August 28th. Did that happen or didn't it happen?"

"It could have easily happened and I didn't put it in my diary. Mac had loaned me the Fanning chart and I could have easily baked him a cake as a thank-you for that and taken it over. It's not in my diary and I don't remember."

Court: "Your diary mentions the Fanning chart?"

"It does mention the Fanning chart."

Court: "What day does it mention it?"

"I think it was the 26th. It says [reading], 'Mac brought by the Fanning chart' on August 26th."

Disturbingly, Judge King returned once again to August 28: "You have no clear memory of going over there on the 28th?"

I didn't like the obvious hint of disbelief in the judge's voice.

Jennifer shook her head. "I really tried to remember."

Judge King had no further questions. Finally, Jennifer's ordeal was over. Altogether, she had been on the witness stand for just short of three days.

Judge King waited until virtually the end of the evidence in the case to finally rule in my favor on my motion to introduce into the record Buck Walker prior testimony (at his theft trial) concerning August 30, 1974. This ruling would enable me to draw a telling inference in my summation. After I read to the jury that part of Buck's testimony (set forth infra), the Government called one familiar face in rebuttal. When FBI Agent Shishido took the stand, Walt Schroeder asked him to describe the defendant's demeanor during his interview of her on October 29, 1974.

"I would say she was very confident and somewhat matter-of-fact in relating the story as to what happened at Palmyra Island."

"And during that interview did she, at any time, cry when talking about the Grahams' disappearance?"

"No, sir."

"Did she cry during any other part of the interview?"

"No, sir."

"Did she, at any time, demonstrate any sorrow, sadness, or any similar emotion when talking about the Grahams?"

"No, sir."

"Did she show any emotion whatsoever during any part of the interview?"

"No, sir."

"Nothing further," said Schroeder.

"Mr. Shishido," I asked on cross-examination, "do you think the observations you have just made on the witness stand are in any way relevant?"

"Do I think they are relevant? Yes."

"Did you therefore put any of these observations you say you had about Jennifer Jenkins into your report, your 302 report?"

Cal Shishido set his mouth in a tight line.

"No, sir."

When Shishido was dismissed, Enoki asked for a moment. He and Schroeder had a quick whispered conference.

"The prosecution rests," Enoki said.
"The defense rests," I echoed.

CHAPTER 41

THE JURORS DEPARTED FOR the weekend, and the lawyers gathered in chambers for the final round in a battle I'd begun with Judge King early on.

Judges customarily put a time limit on lawyers in summation, often as short as one or two hours. They give no valid reason for this limitation. None exists. When pressed, they'll generally contend that whatever has to be said can be said in the time allotted and add that a long-winded lawyer bores the jury and ends up hurting his case. Too many lawyers routinely accept these limitations. But since I consider summation decisively important and invest a great amount of time and effort in its preparation, I normally need considerably more time than most judges initially offer.

Just before Jennifer's trial began, Judge King had agreed to allow me as much time as I wanted in summation, although he had previously indicated that two hours for each side seemed appropriate. But a few days before summation was to begin, he told me in chambers that my limit would be five hours. When I reminded him of his previous commitment, he ignored me, saying crisply, "Five hours." I told him I needed at least six, maybe seven hours, adding that I thought the case was going to be won or lost on final summation and that I didn't want to shortchange my client. I pointed out that since there were so very few known facts in the case, it would all finally come down to argument, to drawing subtle inferences. "It's going to be very difficult to persuade the jury to let Jennifer walk out of court," I argued. "There are just too many things against her. A considerable number of arguments and inferences are going to have to be made, and to make all of them, and in the right way, I need extra time. We already know what one weak argument got her. She was convicted of the theft." But Judge King didn't budge.

"Judge," I persisted, "if I determine, as Jennifer's lawyer, that I need extra time to make some important arguments and you refuse to give me that time, that's denying Jennifer her right to a fair trial."

"So take it up on appeal," he snapped.

"I'm not interested in having the courts upstairs reverse a conviction. I'm only interested in a verdict of not guilty."

"And I'm only interested in moving this trial along. Five hours is more than enough time," the judge said firmly.

I was thoroughly disgusted. All we were talking about was an extra hour or so in a very important murder case that had already been around for eleven years. Moreover, if I decided that the extra time was necessary to adequately represent my client's cause, what right did the judge have to question my judgment? I responded testily, "If I make the assumption that your appointment as a judge was merited, why don't you make the assumption that if I decide I need extra time, I know what I'm talking about?"

"Mr. Bugliosi . . ." Judge King said, bristling, but he did not continue his thought.

I had more to say, of course. I quoted cases from around the turn of the century, when long summations were common (short time limitations are so accepted today I couldn't find any modern appellate cases dealing with the issue in a substantive way). A 1905 case: "How can the court know, in hours and minutes, how long the argument ought to be? As argument progresses, he may interdict idle repetition, but while counsel speaks to the point, how can the court forbear to be patient, and hear what is said?"*

But Judge King again repeated the five-hour limitation. I had only one card left, one I felt forced to use, though it was embar-

*And an 1893 case: "It is very difficult for a judge to determine, in advance, what limitation should be imposed upon counsel, what period may be necessary to enable counsel to present, in the aspect deemed by *them* important, the case of their client."

rassing to me. In an effort to convince Judge King that my long arguments weren't two hours of substance and the rest just adornment, I handed him an issue of *Courtwatchers' Newsletter*, a paper for Chicago trial buffs. The editor, commenting upon an eight-hour summation of mine to the jury (the judge had originally set a two-hour limit), said, "Mr. Bugliosi's performance today was the finest I have ever seen, and I have been a court watcher in Chicago for twenty-one years."

"I don't give a damn what someone says about you in Chicago or some judge in 1893 or 1905 has to say," Judge King barked. "You'll have five hours. Not a minute more."

I informed Judge King that although I had had disputes with judges on the issue in the past, in the end, no judge had ever restricted my time in summation.

"Baloney!" he bellowed.

"Are you calling me a liar, judge?"

"Mr. Bugliosi," he said, visibly controlling himself, "I've already ruled."

I had no doubt that Judge King was finally getting even, in his way, for what he perceived as my disrespectful confrontation with him at the beginning of the trial. He had come a long way from the day he had jested that the appellate courts wouldn't dare reverse a conviction of mine, but he had held his tongue before the jury, and up until now, that was all that mattered.

I now wondered if I would end up paying a higher price in the long run for my challenge to Judge King's authority.

MONDAY MORNING, FEBRUARY 23, 1986

THE GOVERNMENT would open this morning with its summation, and I would follow after lunch. If by the end of the day I was not at the midway point, my plan was to have Jennifer personally intervene with the judge. On the trial record, she would state that she wanted me to make every single argument on her behalf that I felt was needed. Most judges would probably not deny such a request from a defendant, but I was not convinced King would yield to Jennifer's plea. Over the weekend I had reluctantly excised about an hour's worth of summation. While doing so, I uttered more than one profanity (although I had to concede that other than the time limitation on summation, King had handled the trial well).

What if, despite my cuts, I ran past five hours and Judge King strictly held me to the five-hour limitation? Should I continue to talk, forcing the judge to look like a fool in front of the jury for insisting that I cease talking when it was obvious that I was building logically to my peroration?

When the jurors entered the box shortly after 9:30 A.M., Elliot Enoki, his left hand in his suit coat pocket and a pencil in his right hand, was already at the podium, primed to make his opening argument for the Government.

"May I proceed?" Enoki asked.

"You may," said the judge.

Speaking in a low-pitched voice with little emphasis, Enoki explained that first-degree murder required not only malice aforethought but premeditation. "It is for you to determine whether in the circumstances of this case, the killing took place with premeditation."

Enoki stayed with his focus—obvious as early as voir dire—that Buck Walker murdered Muff Graham and Jennifer helped him, or perhaps even instigated the murder.

"The law imposes responsibility in a murder case on more than just the person who does the actual killing. You don't escape the grasp of the law by merely letting someone else perform the crime of which you are a part. In fact, *an accomplice does not have to even be present at the scene of the crime or even know all the details of how the crime is to be committed.* In this case, you can find Jennifer Jenkins guilty if she aided and abetted Mr. Walker in any way in murdering Mrs. Graham." That would include, Enoki pointed out, her "inducing" or even merely "counseling" Walker.

"Now, the judge will instruct you that the law does not view circumstantial evidence as having any less weight or value than direct evidence."

He was approaching the legal heart of the Government's case. "The concept of circumstantial evidence is an important one for the prosecution, since quite obviously we have no eyewitnesses to any killing. However, it is our position that the circumstantial evidence in this case leads to the conclusion that Jennifer Jenkins is criminally responsible for the murder of Eleanor Graham on Palmyra Island."

Because of the "most unique circumstances of the case," Enoki asked who else but Buck Walker and Jennifer Jenkins could possibly have committed the murder. "*There was no one else there,*" he said pointedly.

Enoki quoted me as saying that Walker was "the kind of guy you wouldn't want to meet in a dark alley," but reminded the jury that Jennifer never saw her lover in that light. "She lived with him for more than a year prior to the trip to Palmyra. She knew he was on parole. She knew he had been arrested on drug charges. She knew he carried guns. She agreed to help him escape from those drug charges, even though it meant breaking the law herself. So, we are talking about a woman who not only had no hesitancy about associating with an ex-convict, and a person on the run from a pending prison sentence, but she actually *assisted* him in doing this.

"She devoted her money, her time, and even her labor in preparing the craft they used to escape, the *Iola*. She was willing to sail off with him into one thousand miles of ocean without even knowing how to navigate. So, we're talking about an adventurous woman, one who was clearly willing to take a lot of chances with Mr. Walker. And she appeared to be attracted to those same qualities that caused others to be alarmed about him.

"The converse is likewise true. Mr. Walker thought a lot about Miss Jenkins. He knew she could turn him in at any given time, yet he was willing to take the same voyage off into parts unknown with only her as his companion."

Reminding the jury what kind of people Mac and Muff Graham were, Enoki said, "If you were to pick two couples that would be the least likely to get along on a deserted island, you couldn't get much further apart than these two couples. The one major identical characteristic is they both wanted to be on Palmyra alone. And that served to make them even further apart. Because they resented each other's presence."

Enoki conceded that some evidence proved interaction between the two couples, but added: "No one ever saw Miss Jenkins or Mr. Walker *aboard* the *Sea Wind*. For all of Miss Jenkin's claims of interaction with the Grahams, after July you will find in her diary that there is no reference to her or Mr. Walker being aboard the *Sea Wind*."

After reminding the jury of Muff's being upset when Don Stevens and Bill Larson invited Jennifer to go on an island outing with the Grahams, Enoki moved on to Jennifer and Buck's food situation. They were low on supplies "from the outset," he said; "the evidence is clear they were facing a severe food shortage. There is no doubt she told Tom Wolfe when he was there—and he left the island on August 17th—that she was sick and tired of eating coconuts and fish. Certainly it was not by choice that she was reduced to this diet."

Enoki suggested that it would have been harder for Buck and Jennifer to live off the land than for someone like the Grahams, whose motorized dinghy enabled them to troll for fish.

The prosecutor struck at the issue of the *Iola*'s unseaworthiness. He summarized the testimony of various visitors to Palmyra who had noticed cracks in the fiberglassed hull of the *Iola* and heard regular pumping of the boat's bilge.

"There's a big difference between *thinking* that your boat might make it to another island, and *knowing* that your boat is going to make it. The difference really is that your life hangs in the balance. We're talking about one hundred and seventy-five miles of ocean between Palmyra and Fanning, and two people who had all kinds of problems sailing *with* the wind and *with* the current down from Hawaii. In fact, they took on so much water during their trip to Palmyra, they had to pump every day after they got there.

"And so you have to put yourself in the position of Miss Jenkins and Mr. Walker, looking at that trip, looking at the wide expanse of water, listening to people warn them—Mr. Wheeler told them it was an impossible trip—a trip that was *against* the wind and *against* the current. Miss Jenkins knew quite well how dangerous it would be to try to sail to Fanning. She even told the Leonards that she'd never leave Palmyra on the *Iola*. That's the degree of confidence she had in the *Iola*.

"I would like you to keep in mind what is really the bottom line of this never wanting to leave Palmyra on the *Iola* question. She never *did* leave Palmyra on the *Iola*. And that is, after all, what really brings us here in this trial. Jenkins and Walker not wanting to leave Palmyra on the *Iola*, and having left it on another boat."

Enoki reminded the jurors of Jennifer's "curious diary entry" of August 5, 1974, just weeks before the Grahams' disappearance, that she and Mr. Walker spent the night "drooling and dreaming" about their next boat.

Enoki next discussed the all-important cake-truce testimony, reminding the jury what Curt Shoemaker had said about his last communication with the *Sea Wind* on August 28. "Not only was the visit unexpected by the Grahams, but it's in the nighttime on top of it. There was a reference from Mac of a 'truce.' Now, this contradicts all of Miss Jenkins's claims that there was nothing but a normal relationship going on between these two couples. The word 'truce' implies not the rosy picture that was painted by Jennifer Jenkins.

"You recall Tom Wolfe saying that Miss Jenkins said the two couples were not really getting along—or his impression was that they were not really getting along and not talking. The Leonards testified they left the island due to the situation they saw there. And recall, finally, Muff Graham saying she feared she wouldn't be leaving Palmyra alive when she talked to Evelyn Leonard on their departure. Muff was crying at the time. It's not the picture of the cordial relationship that Miss Jenkins told you about." *Enoki pointed out that after this unexpected nighttime visit to the* Sea Wind, *the Grahams were never heard from or seen again.*

Enoki, in effect, had just told the jury he believed that Mac and Muff Graham had been murdered *on* August 28, 1974. If this was true, then inferentially my client was a murderer.

He turned to Jennifer's diary entry for that date. "There is absolutely no reference to a visit to the *Sea Wind*," he said. "In fact, there is not even a reference to the Grahams, or to her baking on August 28th. Nothing. I would submit to you that it's a pretty significant event to be taking not only this cake over to the Grahams, but both of them are going over to the *Sea Wind*. So, it's not like it's an idle visit, where she happens to wander over by herself.

"Here she is baking a cake for the Grahams, when she has been begging for flour most of the summer. And the week prior to this she is eating nothing but coconuts for at least three days. And she's also giving this food, this cake, to people who didn't even need it, when about two weeks prior to this, she was down to ten meals plus rice. And she is now about to go on a voyage to Fanning, for which she needs all the supplies she can keep. *This is not at all consistent with merely repaying the Grahams for the mere borrowing of the Fanning chart.* You'll recall that's the only thing she could think of as a conceivable reason.

"But baking a cake is one hundred percent consistent with getting on board the *Sea Wind* when you've been having problems with the occupants. It's kind of like bringing a peace offering, in appearance. When in reality, this turned out to be, I would submit, more like a Trojan Horse to get aboard the *Sea Wind*.

"If she had visited the Grahams that day after having had difficulties with them, or even if she just baked a cake for them, the event would have been more significant to her than writing down that Mr. Walker was husking coconuts, or the other insignificant events she *has* written down for August 28th."

Enoki flat out did not believe any of Jennifer's diary entries for August 30, "the day Miss Jenkins says the Grahams disappeared. *There's nothing to establish that date as the date of the Grahams' disappearance, except her testimony and her diary!* And I submit to you that both of those things are false. There is nothing that would have prevented her from writing the entries in the diary *after* August 28th—*after* killing the Grahams. How much better a way to avoid detection than to falsify succeeding entries?

"There's an absence of information in these succeeding entries about critical points that she says occurred or in fact did occur. There's nothing about the *Sea Wind* or about taking the *Sea Wind*. Remember, she says she disagreed vehemently with Mr. Walker, and argued with him about it. Yet, there's nothing about that in the diary.

"There's also nothing in her diary about the *Iola*, and what happened to her. There's nothing in it about not notifying the authorities. Recall that she said Mr. Walker told her not to do that. Remember, she called the diary a kind of journal of events, yet there's not a word about *any* of these things. And most absurd of all, she claims that the reason she stopped keeping this diary was because it really was the log of the *Iola*, and the *Iola* sank on September 11th. The last entry is September 10th. And yet, there's not a single word about what happened to the *Iola*."

Enoki now reached his conclusion on this issue. "This diary was written to cover up a crime. But it isn't just the crime of theft that's being covered. It's also the crime of murder."

He next started summarizing the scientific and medical evidence in the case, arguing that it proved Muff did not die as a result of a drowning or shark attack, as Jennifer said she had assumed, but was murdered. Much of this recapitulated the prosecutor's summation at the Buck Walker trial.

"In order to reconcile," Enoki then went on, "this scientific evidence, and the other evidence in the case, with Miss Jenkins's diary and with her testimony, let's look at what Mr. Walker has to do all by himself, without any assistance, without being observed, and without any sound that Miss Jenkins can hear, except for the sound of the Zodiac going away from the *Sea Wind*.

"First of all," the sincere but unemotional prosecutor continued, with no attempt at drama in his voice or gestures, "he has to find both Grahams. Then he has to kill them both. Then he has to try and burn Eleanor Graham's head with an acetylene torch that he would have to get from Mac's workshop. He has to get at least one, and undoubtedly two, aluminum containers out of the old rescue boat that, in 1974, was still in the warehouse.

"Then he would have to take at least one of these containers from the warehouse to wherever he's killed Eleanor Graham. And I would submit he has to do that with Mac Graham as well. He would then have to find some wires to wrap around the containers so the lid wouldn't just pop off when he dropped them into the water. Then he'd have to weight each container down so it would sink.

"Following that, he has to burn Muff Graham's body in the container for, we were told by an expert, at least fifteen to twenty minutes.

"He then has to get both containers down to the lagoon and load them into the Zodiac by himself with the bodies inside. We're talking about carrying that container with a one-hundred-and-forty-pound woman in it, another with a one-hundred-and-eighty-pound man inside it. They don't call that dead weight for lack of any reason. It's just dead weight in that container. And loading it into a soft-sided rubber Zodiac is not like loading it into a van or bus or something that's parked there. We're talking about a boat."

Never pausing for effect, Enoki went on to say that Walker would then have had to take the dinghy out into the lagoon, dump the bodies overboard, return to shore—without Miss Jenkins hearing the Zodiac motor—beach the dinghy upside down, detach the gas tank, and walk half a mile back to the bath area, where Jennifer said she saw him that afternoon.

"In addition, if either of the killings were done on the *Sea Wind*, he would have to, of course, clean up whatever evidence was left behind, because there was nothing unusual aboard the boat, according to Miss Jenkins, when she arrived."

Enoki argued that if Walker had caught up with the Grahams and murdered them on shore, then he would have had to break into the *Sea Wind* to set up the drinks Jennifer said were there when she arrived.

"And," the prosecutor added, "he's also, according to Miss Jenkins, making appearances periodically throughout the day at the *Iola*. During this time, he would have to have done all of this not only without Miss Jenkins seeing him do anything, but without her seeing any smoke or without noticing any evidence about him, such as blood, injuries of any kind, gasoline. She didn't notice anything.

"And he supposedly decides to kill two people and hide it from his girlfriend, when she could take the *Iola* dinghy ashore at any time and catch him in the act. This person, who supposedly thought enough in advance to go and set up the drinks on the *Sea Wind*, didn't think about taking the dinghy away from her." Her story just didn't add up, the prosecutor said.

"But worst of all about her version of what happened, she claims she never even had any suspicions of foul play. Yet, she knew Mr. Walker was convicted of armed robbery. She knew he loved to carry guns. He had a 'firecracker personality' that could explode on the spot. She knew he was arrested with a loaded gun in the drug deal. She knew he kept booby traps when they lived on the Big Island. Yet her testimony is she did not suspect any foul play."

The prosecutor looked directly at Jennifer, not a flicker of feeling on his face. "No one has described her as naive. She was twenty-eight at the time, not sixteen or eighteen or twenty. She has been described as intelligent, and she appeared to be intelligent on the witness stand. How could any intelligent person *not* suspect foul play with a man of Mr. Walker's background? And yet that's what she would have you believe. She suspected *nothing*.

"I submit to you that her story about what happened in the Grahams' disappearance, and what happened on Palmyra, was just the beginning of a continuous stream of lies about the events on Palmyra that she told, and has told, ever since she left that island."

Enoki's tone of voice and whole demeanor seemed to be: "We all know that she's guilty of the murders, and has told one lie after another in the hope that you won't see the obvious." He condensed the stream of lies: "Miss Jenkins tells Lorraine Wollen she got the boat from a man who was tired of doing maintenance on it after fourteen years. It got even worse when she gave her statements," Enoki charged. "She told Bernard Leonard they found the Zodiac near Paradise Island. Her defense is that Mr. Leonard is mistaken about that. But there is no misunderstanding about the other lie she told Bernard Leonard: that she and Walker tried to *sail* the *Iola* off Palmyra, but it ran aground in the channel, so they went back and they got the *Sea Wind*. Leonard tells her it's not believable they would have left on the *Iola* with the *Sea Wind* sitting there, so she changes her story, and instead tries to make it more believable. When she spoke to Agent Shishido a few minutes later, instead of sailing the *Iola* out and running up on the reef, now it's that they were *towing* it out, and it got hung up on the reef. When she told Agent Shishido about the *Iola* winding up on the reef, she had forgotten she took these photos of the *Iola* on the open sea. When she gets to her theft trial, she still says the *Iola* wound up on the reef, and she denied taking the photographs. Another lie."

These photos proved at her theft trial that her story was a lie, the prosecutor said. "So she knows that story wouldn't fly here. So she tells you that the *Iola* really didn't hang up on the reef after all. And that Walker and her attorney told her that these were the lies that she should tell to the theft jury."

Enoki's next point could alone, *if believed*, convince the jury Jennifer was probably involved in the murders. "Here's another example of the same changing of the story," he said. "She told Shishido the Zodiac was found overturned *in* the water, and the gas tank was floating nearby. Now, she disputes meaning that the Zodiac was in the water. But it's clearly what Agent Shishido remembers from that interview, and what he understood her statement to mean. And there's certainly no misunderstanding about something floating. You can't float if you're on the beach. Agent Shishido had no misunderstanding about where she said the Zodiac was, because what did he do? He took the Zodiac motor to Ken White to see if that motor had ever been underwater. He would never have done that unless his understanding was that she meant it was in the water. Then when she hears Mr. White's testimony at her theft trial that the motor couldn't possibly have been underwater, her testimony became, after that, that it was not found overturned in the water, but on the beach.

"She testified that when they found the Zodiac it was one to two feet from the water. And that it was not high tide at the time they found it.

"Well, you'll recall Mr. Bryden testifying that there were two highs and two lows in tides every day at Palmyra. And supposedly Mr. Walker, according to Miss Jenkins's version of what happened, left the Zodiac out there sometime between 4:00 and 5:00 P.M. because that's when she heard the motor going away.

"And it's there overnight, supposedly, and into the next morning when they find it. *Now, it would have to have gone through at least one high tide at that point.* And I would submit to you that being one or two feet from the water, and *not* being high tide, would mean that at high tide that motor must have been *in* the water for some period of time. But there's no evidence of this in Mr. White's examination."

Enoki went on. "I would also like to point out to you that she wrote a letter to Mac Graham's sister, but only after she was arrested. She did not inform the sister, or any relative, or anyone else, about the disappearance until *after* her arrest.

"Even in her letter to Mrs. Muncey, she lies about Mr. Walker's letter that's enclosed, saying it was written much earlier when, in fact, it was written in jail.

"You can see the pattern that Miss Jenkins has illustrated, in that she doesn't admit something until either she's caught in a lie on it, or she knows that it's not going to benefit her to keep up this particular story.

"But she can't escape the one thing that is really obvious about this situation. If someone winds up dead, and the only motive for the murder is stealing their property, then when you show up with their property, you are it.

"The motive of the killing is a theft of the *Sea Wind* and its supplies. There's no other motive. *And Miss Jenkins has the same motive as Mr. Walker.* She even thought nothing of using the clothing of Muff Graham and taking the four hundred dollars that was on board."

Enoki reminded the jury that at her theft trial, Jennifer testified that she intended to return the *Sea Wind* to Mac's sister and, therefore, wasn't really stealing. "But she denied at this trial that this was in defense to the theft charge. What do you think the defense was, if it wasn't that? I mean, she was on trial for *theft*, and she was found sitting on the boat, so she told the jury: 'I was going to return the boat.' Of course it was for the purpose of defending against that charge."

"This isn't a theft trial, so now she can admit to you that she lied about planning to return the *Sea Wind* to Mrs. Muncey directly from the Ala Wai. So, she does admit it. But that doesn't make her testimony truthful in this trial either. It's kind of like, if you would, peeling off layers of a story—it's like taking one mask off and finding another one underneath. And you can take that one off and there's another one there.

"Remember that she sat in the very same place—the witness chair—took the same oath eleven years ago, and told people just like yourselves all those lies that she is now admitting. And she certainly didn't tell them that those were lies. And all she's doing in this trial, ladies and gentlemen, is covering up a murder instead of a theft. She can now admit the lies that went to the theft because she's not on trial for that here. I would ask you not to fall for this series of lies that she's been making since 1974."

Characterizing Jennifer's version of what happened on August 30, 1974, and her diary entry for that date as unworthy of belief, Enoki concluded: "What remains is the August 28th arrival of Miss Jenkins and Mr. Walker, in the darkness, at the Grahams' boat with both of the Grahams there, bearing a most unlikely gift of food. An event that is not mentioned at all in that diary. The fact remains that Muff Graham was murdered, and the last persons that were there were both Miss Jenkins and Mr. Walker. They both had the means, the motive, and the opportunity to commit murder. And Miss Jenkins, the only one that's on trial here, certainly has not provided a believable explanation of the evidence and events that occurred there.

"One can only conclude that the cake she made in the depth of their food shortage was for the purpose of setting up the boarding of the *Sea Wind*, and the eventual murder of Eleanor Graham.

"We're talking not about the nonviolent woman that she claims she was, but one who showed no hesitation to assist Mr. Walker in whatever he did. And she immediately went on to another man who shot and killed someone else in California.

"The evidence shows in this case that Mr. Walker and Miss Jenkins found themselves in a position where killing was necessary to get off that island with the security they wanted. *There is no evidence to suggest that Miss Jenkins would hesitate to help Mr. Walker in that endeavor.*"

During Enoki's summation, Jennifer alternated from locking her eyes on him to staring grimly at the tabletop, as she was doing at this moment. Not once during his argument had she looked into the faces of the men and women who would decide her fate.

"It is time, after eleven and a half years," Enoki now concluded with unmistakable conviction, "that you find Jennifer Jenkins guilty of murder.

"Thank you."

Enoki had given a good opening argument, and his obvious sincerity and belief in his case were definite pluses. If there was a weakness in the prosecutor's argument, it was that he failed to draw any new or otherwise arresting inferences from the evidence. Though he effectively reminded the jury of all the points which made his case strong, I doubted he had further strengthened the prosecution's case against Jennifer by causing the jury to reflect, "That's a very good point. I never thought of that!"

I could only hope the jury wasn't thinking that there was no need for any "new thoughts" about Jennifer's guilt—that, like the Walker jury, they already had more than enough.

CHAPTER 42

IT WAS NOW TIME for the defense's summation. To me, summation is the most important part of the trial for the lawyer, the climax of the case. As the Roman historian, Tacitus, said: "The breastplate and the sword are not a stronger defense on the battlefield than eloquence is to a man amid the perils of prosecution."

Usually, the very first thing I think about when I get on a case and begin to learn the facts is: *what* am I going to argue, and *how* can I best make the argument to obtain a favorable verdict? In other words, I work backward from my summation. Virtually all of my questions at the trial, and most of my tactics and techniques, are aimed at enabling me to make arguments I've already determined I want to make.

In fact, before the first witness at a trial has even been called, I've usually prepared most of my summation to the jury. As soon as I learn the strengths and weaknesses of my case, I begin to work on how I'm going to argue these strengths, and what I'm going to say in response to the opposition's attacks on the weaknesses. Getting an early start on my summation, and continuing to expand and modify it during the trial, gives me ample time to develop arguments and articulations.

A great number of trial lawyers do not feel that final summation is the most important part of the trial. And I have never really understood why.

In life, if one wants someone else to come over to his viewpoint, isn't it all-important *what* one says and *how* one says it? Is a trial any different? Isn't the lawyer trying to convince someone, in this case, the jury, of the rightness of his cause? Therefore, shouldn't most of his preparation and efforts be directed toward this final appeal to the jury?

Not so, say many experts. As Louis Heller, a former justice of the New York supreme court and before that a prominent trial lawyer, writes in his book *Do You Solemnly Swear*, "An address to the jury should be *extemporaneous* and reflect spontaneity."

In my opinion, a summation must either be written out or set down in a comprehensive outline. The problem with even an outline is that although all the points the lawyer wants to make are there, he does *not* have the all-important articulations; that is, he does not have his points expressed in the most effective way. It's simply not possible to powerfully articulate a great number of points, one immediately following another, extemporaneously. There *is* a best way to make a point, and to find it takes time and sweat on the yellow pad. But whether one should write out one's summation or put it into an outline, it has been my experience that the majority of trial lawyers—even many high-priced ones in major, nationally publicized criminal trials—do neither, addressing the jury after scandalously little preparation. Far too often this results in their delivering arguments which are disjointed and sterile in articulation, and which, most injurious of all to their clients, omit a number of salient facts and inferences.*

In a complex trial involving many witnesses and thousands of pages of transcript, to discuss the highlights and nuances of the case, draw the necessary inferences, and in the most telling sequence, always seeking simplicity and clarity of expression, requires an enormous amount of written preparation.

The one advantage in arguing extemporaneously is to be able to talk with the jury eye to eye, with the candor of spontaneity. But if a trial lawyer is willing to put in the hours, he can have such a grasp of his written or outlined argument that, like an actor on stage whose lines flow naturally, he can deliver it to the jury giving the appearance of spontaneity. (Mark Twain knew whereof he spoke when he said that "it takes three weeks to prepare a good ad lib argument.") If I've had adequate time to prepare, I only have to glance at my notes sparingly. I can look at one word on a page, and the whole page is vivid in my mind.

Final argument is nothing more than a speech, and I know of no generally accepted great speech in history that was not carefully prepared before it was delivered. Lincoln's Gettysburg Address consisted of only ten sentences. Of his 271 words, 202 of them were

*What I have just said may be difficult for the reader to believe, but unfortunately it happens to be true. (There is all the documentary evidence one would need to support this; namely, the trial transcripts.) One could give a great number of examples, but here are a few relatively recent ones. Three different authors comment on three separate summations for the defense. All three cases were sensational, nationally publicized criminal trials, and all three lawyers have not just regional but national reputations.

1. "He rose from the defense table, grabbing an unruly stack of notes. He spoke for less than forty-five minutes, but as I cringed in my seat, trying to follow his disjointed discourse, it seemed like a lifetime."

2. It was "two hours of rambling, sometimes incoherent, and consistently repetitive harangue. He had not begun to cover most of the specific points he had intended to include in his argument."

3. "It was generally agreed that his closing argument was remarkable; most remarkable was the fact that no two people who heard it agreed on what was said. The jurors' faces showed not the slightest indication whether or not they were following his sequence of events."

just one syllable. But these historic words went through five drafts and were the result of two weeks' thought and preparation, handwritten on two pages that were in front of him as he spoke.

The conventional wisdom is that a summation should be succinct, focusing only on the main points in the case. Not only can't a lawyer keep a jury's attention for more than an hour or so, it is said, but discussing the smaller points only clutters and dilutes the thrust of the main arguments. I may be wrong, but my personal opinion is that this couldn't possibly be a more serious mistake—in many cases, perhaps a fatal one. Juries, unaccountably, often base their verdict on (or are heavily influenced by) the most tangential, seemingly insignificant points. Just as in surveying the ocean bed "no rock or prominence can be left unnoted with safety to the mariner," a lawyer should want to be heard on virtually every point in the case. Likewise with inferences. Though I don't exactly put a bib on the jury and spoon-feed them, I also don't assume they're going to see everything I want them to see without my help. So often in life, things are only obvious once they are pointed out.

Moreover, I do not agree that it is difficult to hold a jury's attention for more than an hour or so. In fact, it is not difficult to keep their attention for an entire day or two if the lawyer can deliver a powerful, exciting summation that is sprinkled with example, metaphor, and humor; and particularly when he makes it obvious to them that he has a lot of important observations to make about the case, and they can only fulfill the oath they took to reach a proper verdict if they listen to him closely—that is, *if he convinces them that they need him.*

I had put in a considerable number of hours writing, polishing, and going over the summation I was about to give. Curiously, I had formulated the broad conceptual structure of my argument while strolling through Boston Common one sunny Sunday afternoon shortly after I got on the case.

I was ready, and feeling, as usual, very confident. My confidence would manifest itself most clearly to the jury in the words I used, and the way I uttered them. No matter how weak my case is, *if I believe in it,* as I did here, my selection of words and intonation will suggest that it is the strongest case imaginable. And I mean every word I say. When delivering a summation, a trial lawyer has to be confident before a jury, or at least appear so. It is one of the most essential ingredients of a successful trial lawyer. If he is not confident, the jury will pick it up immediately—from the way he talks, the way he walks, the expression on his face; most of all, from the words he uses. And a lawyer cannot expect a jury to buy his cause if they detect that he does not believe in it completely himself. When a lawyer communicates clearly his passionate and sincere conviction in the merits of his client's case, in a subliminal way he becomes, to the jury, an important *witness* in the case.

My style before the jury in summation is expansive. Leaving my notes at the podium (but not turning the page until I have covered every point), I move freely about the courtroom, raising my voice when in full rhetorical flight, and, some say, on occasion intoning like an itinerant evangelist preacher. And although I try to keep my grammar within shouting distance of Cambridge, I gesture with the energy of a bocce ball player in a Naples piazza.

The following—quoted and paraphrased—is a substantial portion of my final summation in the Jennifer Jenkins murder trial.

"JUDGE KING, Mr. Enoki, Mr. Schroeder, Mr. Weinglass, ladies and gentlemen of the jury.

"This case, of course, has dealt with many issues—among other things, the sea and boats. I don't know about you folks, but I've never had any meaningful, personal experience with either one of them, so I don't know too much about the sea and boats. But I do know a little about the criminal law, having been a prosecutor in the Los Angeles County District Attorney's Office for several years, and more recently, a defense attorney.

"And based on the evidence that came from that witness stand," I said, pointing to the seat where so many witnesses had testified, "I have formed some rather strong opinions about this case and I'm going to share those with you.

"Before I do, however, I want to make a few brief comments about the jury system in America. I view it as perhaps the most priceless legacy we inherited from our legal ancestors, the

British. When you stop to think about it, in America only a jury can cause a fellow human being to end up behind prison bars. For instance, unless a defendant in a criminal case gives up his constitutional right to a jury trial, no judge can find him guilty and place him behind bars. Even the President of the United States cannot put someone behind bars. Law enforcement—the police, the FBI, et cetera—they can put you in the poky, but if you're not convicted in a court of law, they can't keep you there. Only a jury made up of folks like you can cause someone to end up behind prison bars.

"So in a very real sense, the American jury is all that stands between the accused and his loss of liberty. And the realization of this is at once awesome and yet supremely reassuring. I think you can see at a glance the very high and delicate ground you occupy."

I knew the five-inch stack of yellow sheets of paper on the table to the right of the podium might be daunting, if not appalling, to the jury—they might be thinking negatively: *Could there possibly be that much to say? And how long will it take?*

"I know you are all eager to resume your normal daily life, and I don't want to trespass unduly upon your time. However, in the interest of my client, and in the interest of justice, there are a considerable number of points I must go over with you in my effort to help you reach a fair and a just verdict.

"These yellow sheets here constitute my final argument to you. Now that looks like quite a bit," I admitted, waving my hand at the stack, "but this is a *murder* trial, not a drunk-driving case; the lives of two precious human beings have been brutally snuffed out; the first legal proceeding in this case was instituted over eleven years ago; and based on the evidence that came from that witness stand, my client, Jennifer Jenkins, is innocent, yet the rest of her life is hanging in the balance. When you look at it from that perspective, one could almost say: 'Is this all you have to say, Mr. Bugliosi? Is this all you have to say?'

"With respect to a just verdict, justice is the objective of our system of law. In this regard, I want to make what I perceive to be an important observation. I'm going to refer to the opposing side in this case as the prosecution, not the Government.* The very word 'Government' implies that the United States government is out to get Jennifer Jenkins, and it's not going to be satisfied unless she's found guilty. Since we're all citizens of this country, psychologically that puts a certain pressure on you, because you're law-abiding people, and you don't want to do anything that's against your government.

"Because of the potential for this visceral inclination towards the prosecution, I want to provide you with evidence that if this inclination exists, it is unwarranted. That although the prosecution in this case wants a verdict of guilty, which is perfectly proper on their part, the United States government only wants justice, be it a guilty or a not guilty verdict.

"The United States Attorney's Office, which is prosecuting this case, is under the U.S. Department of Justice, and the head of the Department of Justice is the Attorney General of the United States. On the fifth floor of the Department of Justice building in Washington, D.C., in the Attorney General's rotunda, there is this inscription: 'The United States wins its case whenever one of its citizens receives justice in the courts.' The inscription does not say: 'The United States wins only when a defendant is found guilty.'

"Talking about justice and our system of law, in our country, as opposed to most totalitarian nations, under the law a defendant is presumed to be innocent *unless*† the contrary has been proven beyond a reasonable doubt. Now these aren't just fancy, theoretical words. This is a rule of law which has no exceptions to it, a legal jewel that has been cut and polished by the hard experience of centuries, and which has come down through the ages right here into this courtroom.

"And if any judge, or any jury, in any case throughout this land, ignores this strict rule of law, it would be a very serious violation of their respective oaths."

After telling the jury that because of the presumption of innocence the prosecution has the burden of proving guilt, a defendant

---

*Throughout the trial, the judge had referred to the prosecution as "the Government." In fact, the lawsuit was officially *United States of America* v. *Jennifer Jenkins*.
†Not the normally used "until," which implies it's just a matter of time.

no burden to prove his innocence, I told the jurors that Judge King would instruct them before they commenced their deliberations that this burden of proof remains with the prosecution throughout the entire trial; that it never shifts to the defendant. "These are key words," I said. "*The burden of proof never shifts to the defendant.*

"But a very strange—and I say ominous—thing has occurred during this trial. Without directly stating it—they can't state it directly because they know it's contrary to the law—hasn't the prosecution, in a very subtle, clever way, tried to eliminate the presumption of innocence by shifting the burden of proof to Jennifer Jenkins? When all the dust has settled, hasn't the entire thrust of the prosecution's case been—in effect: 'We don't have to prove, Miss Jenkins, that you murdered Muff Graham. We've put you on the island of Palmyra at the time of the murder, and we've put you on the *Sea Wind* after the murder. Now, *you prove that you did not commit the murder.*'

"I say that the prosecution has been forced to try to shift the burden of proof to Miss Jenkins because their case is so devoid of substance that it is the only way they feel they can convince you to convict this woman.

"And I tell them that this is America," I said in a loud voice, pumping my right forefinger into the air, "that the presumption of innocence is a very sacred right in our society, that it is still alive and well and kicking, and you're *not* going to let them get by with it.

"The prosecution in this case did not meet their burden of proof. They didn't even begin to overcome the legal presumption of innocence. In no way did they prove guilt beyond a reasonable doubt. Where is there any evidence, ladies and gentlemen of the jury, either direct or circumstantial, that Jennifer Jenkins participated in any fashion whatsoever in the murder of Mrs. Graham? Where, ladies and gentlemen of the jury? Where?"

I told the jury that before I got into the heart of my argument, I wanted to discuss a number of preliminary matters with them which did not fit comfortably into any of the main areas of my summation.

I urged them to take notes, quoting an old Chinese proverb I always give juries that "the palest ink is better than the best memory."

THE FIRST preliminary matter was the nature of a grand jury indictment. I knew that the jury, being lay people, could very well assume that since a "grand jury" had indicted Jennifer, this previous group of people, carefully considering all the evidence, had already decided she was guilty. And wasn't the *grand jury* "some super investigative body" with access to all types of information a trial jury did not get?

"Actually, just the opposite is true," I explained, reinforcing and elaborating on what I had told the jury during voir dire. "You folks get considerably more evidence than a grand jury. In this case, not only didn't Miss Jenkins nor any other defense witness testify at the grand jury, but the only prosecution witness at this trial who also testified before the grand jury—the *only* witness—was Calvin Shishido.

"I'm not demeaning the grand jury," I said. "I'm simply placing it in its proper perspective for you.

"Next, I want to discuss what arguably could be an extremely important issue; that is, if I wanted to engage in intellectual sophistry with you, which I of course will not do. And that is the issue of whether Muff Graham was murdered, or whether she met an accidental death.

"Mr. Enoki has argued with conviction that Muff Graham was murdered. To which I reply, 'Of course she was.' As Sherlock Holmes used to say to his sidekick, 'That's elementary, my dear Watson.'"

I went on to say, however, that the peculiar facts of this case were such that a defense attorney could at least make the argument, however anemic, that the prosecution had not proved *beyond a reasonable doubt* that a murder had taken place. "In virtually every murder case, you know a murder took place because the autopsy shows the cause of death. In this case, we don't have that. In fact, the prosecution concedes they do not know the cause of death of Muff Graham.

"I'm sure I could come up with several scenarios that point to an accidental death. But I don't think any of them would be sound, logical arguments rich in common sense.

"The evidence, I believe, is very clear that Muff Graham was murdered. That she did not die an accidental death. And I will not argue to the contrary.

"And that leads me to my next point. In my argument, many times I intend to use the plural 'murders,' as opposed to the singular 'murder.' The prosecution only sought an indictment against Miss Jenkins for the murder of Muff Graham, I suppose because Mr. Graham's body has never been found, although there's no requirement under the law that the body be found as a condition precedent to a prosecution for murder.

"In any event, it makes no sense to me that Buck Walker, whom I accuse of being the sole murderer in this case, murdered Mrs. Graham, but spared Mr. Graham. It would stretch credulity to believe that Malcolm Graham did not meet the same horrible fate that befell his wife.

"Another preliminary point, and this is something almost too obvious to mention. We're dealing with certain elementary facts in this case. As you can see, Jennifer is a rather small woman, both in height and weight. And we know from the medical testimony that Muff Graham received several fractures in the region of her head as a result of sledgehammer-type blows.

"Even setting aside the greater problem of Jennifer's dealing with the bigger and heavier Mac Graham, the physical implausibility of Jennifer sledgehammering Muff Graham to death, then somehow managing to carry Muff's heavy dead weight inside the container, or separately, to the dinghy for disposal into the lagoon, all while Buck Walker, the hardened ex-con, is in his tent knitting—the physical implausibility of all this is readily apparent. The very nature of these murders required the physical hand of a strong killer. Buck Walker.

"The only question is whether Jennifer aided and abetted, that is, assisted Buck Walker in these murders." I went on to tell the jury, however, that "even if Jennifer had knowledge of what Buck Walker was doing, even if she were present at the time of these murders—and, of course, our position is that none of these things occurred—under the law, they would not be enough, by themselves, to make her guilty.

"Judge King will give you the following instruction at the conclusion of this case: 'Mere presence at the scene of the crime and knowledge that a crime is being committed are not sufficient to establish that the defendant aided and abetted the crime.'"*

Another preliminary matter was the issue of whether or not the Grahams had kept a *diary* on Palmyra; also, what happened to the *log* of the *Sea Wind*. If the jury believed there had been a diary, and if either the diary or log disappeared because of some action of Jennifer's, it would go in the direction of her having destroyed important evidence, a strong suggestion of guilt. The evidence did not allow me to be on the best footing here, but some response was better than none at all.

"As to a diary, a friend of the Grahams, Herbert Daniels, testified that one time aboard the *Sea Wind* Muff referred to some document to 'recall the name of either a port or a person.' From this, the prosecution infers the document was a diary."

I pointed out that Muff's words could just as well have referred to the *Sea Wind*'s log. 'Moreover, even if it were a diary, Mr. Daniels didn't say when this incident took place. The fact she kept a diary at one time does not mean she was doing so on Palmyra. The prosecution did not clearly establish through any witness that either of the Grahams kept a diary on Palmyra.

"As to the *Sea Wind*'s log, item number 26 on the inventory list reads: 'Navigational logs contained in a five-by-eight-inch plastic folder.'

"Since we know that item number 26 was not the log of the *Iola*—item number 1 was—it stands to reason that this was probably the log of the *Sea Wind*."

*In summation, on key points, I usually cite and read to the jury the exact language of the judge's instruction covering the point. When the jurors later hear the judge repeat the identical words I have quoted, it can subconsciously give my arguments on each point a degree of credibility, almost as if the judge is following me.

The inference was clear: if the log of the *Sea Wind* disappeared, it had to have been lost or misplaced after my client left the *Sea Wind*; that is, while in the hands of the authorities in this case.

"One final point I want to discuss in some depth before I get into the heart of my argument concerns witnesses," I said. "Ideally, witnesses at a trial should be completely impartial. But the reality is that they frequently favor one side or the other in a lawsuit. That's normal and to be expected. However, whatever side they favor, they are only supposed to testify to the facts. They obviously are not supposed to slant their testimony, or take liberties with the truth. And I'm afraid we had that with at least two of the prosecution witnesses. I'm referring to the Leonards.

"When the Leonards learned that their friends, the Grahams, were murdered, I think we can infer they naturally were convinced that Buck Walker committed these murders. And since Jennifer was with him on the island, they assumed she was somehow involved. And I think, further, that because of this they either deliberately or unconsciously slanted certain parts of their testimony against Jennifer. In some instances, I think they flat out invented incidents to coincide with prejudgments they had made.

"But before I get into what appears to be the fabricated testimony of the Leonards, I want to discuss another witness who may or may not be guilty of the same thing. I'm talking about Curt Shoemaker. I have to say I detected none of the deceit and bias in Mr. Shoemaker that was literally bursting out of the pores of the Leonards. However, I am not willing to concede he is telling the truth about the cake-truce incident.

"One thing is very clear, and I think you will agree with me on this. If the incident happened, it would be the type of thing Mr. Shoemaker would never forget, the very first thing that would enter his mind whenever he thought about his last contact with the Grahams. Shoemaker himself, on the witness stand, said this. Therefore, if he never told anyone about it for many years, we can almost automatically assume it never happened."

And the *only* evidence we had, I told the jury, that he ever told anyone anything about either a "cake" or a "truce" was the word of FBI Agent Tom Kilgore, Kilgore testifying that when he interviewed Shoemaker on October 30, 1974, Shoemaker mentioned a cake to him, *but not a truce.*

"Now doesn't it stand to reason that if Shoemaker had told Kilgore about the cake-truce incident he testified to at this trial, Kilgore would have put that in his report?"

I argued that Kilgore's word even as to the cake was suspect because in addition to there being no reference to it in his report, he admitted that when Shoemaker allegedly told him this it had no significance to him.

"When I asked him why, almost twelve years later, he would remember something which was so insignificant to him when he first heard it that he didn't bother putting it in his report, old Tom showed that at the FBI school in Quantico, Virginia, he didn't only learn how to assemble and disassemble a gun, he learned how to tap-dance. He said that the reason he remembered it was that he didn't know you could bake a cake on a boat. I guess Tom felt that things like stoves or ovens, or whatever you bake cakes in, are outlawed on sailboats.

"Since we have to put a substantial query after Tom Kilgore's testimony, we obviously cannot know for sure whether Mr. Shoemaker told the agent about any cake.

"However, we *do* know—because we have a transcript— that when Mr. Shoemaker was specifically asked at Jennifer's theft trial what was said during his last radio contact with Mac Graham, Curt Shoemaker never uttered *one syllable* about any cake-truce incident."

I picked up the transcript of Jennifer's theft trial and read to the jury, word for word, Shoemaker's testimony on this issue, thereby reminding them, once again, of Shoemaker's being asked several times what took place during his *last* contact with the Grahams, and his failure to mention the cake-truce incident even once.

"How do you explain something like that?" I asked rhetorically.

I told the jury there seemed to be three possibilities with respect to Shoemaker. (I was not trying to win outright on the cake-truce incident, knowing I couldn't do it. I was only trying to establish a reasonable doubt on the issue.) The first possibility was that Shoemaker might be telling the truth. The second possibility: "He's mulled this case over so much in his mind, and discussed so many scenarios with people like the Leonards, that by a trick of the mind he's actually come to believe this incident happened, when in point of fact, it did not. And the third possibility is that Mr. *Shoemaker* is Mr. *Storymaker*. For years this case was the great mystery of the Pacific. And perhaps Curt Shoemaker, the ham radio operator and retired phone company employee, decided he was going to be the one to solve this mystery for everyone.

"I must say that Shoemaker's timing is quite convenient, to say the least. He testified that in the month of August he called Mac Graham on the 7th, 14th, 21st, and the 28th. That's only once a week. On the 28th he spoke to Mac for forty minutes. So that's forty minutes out of the entire week. I computed this. There are ten thousand and eighty minutes every week. You divide forty into ten thousand and eighty and you get two hundred and fifty-two.

"That means that if the cake-truce incident took place between the Grahams and Buck and Jennifer, the mathematical probability that it would have taken place while Curt Shoemaker was talking to the Grahams would be one out of two hundred and fifty-two, not the best odds. *One out of two hundred and fifty-two.*

"Andy Warhol said something to the effect that everyone at one time or another during his life will be famous for fifteen minutes. And this case may have been—I'm not accusing Mr. Shoemaker of lying. I'm saying there are three possibilities. I'm trying to be fair, although it's pretty hard to ignore this transcript here—this trial may have been Curt Shoemaker's fifteen minutes.

"Mr. Enoki, in so many words—Elliot usually doesn't say things directly, he's a master of ellipsis—has strongly suggested that the murders took place on August 28th, right after Shoemaker spoke to Mac. But to believe that, you first have to accept as fact that the cake-truce incident did take place. And as we've seen, there's a very substantial question as to that. And even if we accept, for the sake of argument, that it did take place, what evidence does this constitute that a murder took place *at that time?*

"Well, Mr. Enoki says, they were never heard from again. That would be a valid argument if Shoemaker, after he signed off with Mac at 7:50 P.M. on the evening of August 28, 1974, had called back a half hour later and all he got was silence. But he didn't call back until September 4th, seven days later. Seven *days* later. So, the fact that August 28th is the last time Shoemaker spoke to Mac is no evidence at all that the murders occurred at that time.

"Mr. Enoki then argues that Jennifer never made any entry in her diary on August 28th that she and Buck had brought a cake over to the Grahams, and he said this was very suspicious. But again, again, this presupposes that Buck and Jennifer *did* bring a cake over to the Grahams. And we do not know that they did. Jennifer cannot remember one way or the other."

I recalled for the jury Jennifer's acknowledging that bringing a cake to the Grahams was the type of thing she might have done in appreciation for Mac's having loaned her the Fanning chart, and her explanation for not referring to the incident in her diary: lighting on the *Iola* was poor, and by the time she and Buck would have gotten back, it would have been pitch-dark on Palmyra. "Obviously," I acknowledged, "she could have made the entry the next day. There's no question about that. But she may have neglected to do so because she was so busy getting ready for the trip to Fanning."

I mentioned that the one thing that sounded phony to Jennifer about the incident was Mac's supposedly saying there was a truce, since she said there was no feud to settle. "So, Jennifer just doesn't know," I said.

"The point I want to italicize and underline in your mind is that *even if* the cake-truce incident took place, all it would show was that on the evening of August 28th, the Grahams and Buck and Jennifer were in each other's presence. Since we already know there was considerable social interaction between the Grahams and Buck and Jennifer, how can this presence possibly constitute any evidence of murder?"

I offered one final point on this issue. "*If* there was a cake-truce incident, *and if* the prosecution believed that the murders took place *on the Sea Wind* at that time, can we not assume that a multitude of scientific tests would have been conducted on the *Sea Wind* in an effort to secure evidence of the murders, such as blood, or evidence of a struggle?

"At this trial the prosecution called experts in pathology, serology, chemistry, biology, odontology, anthropology, microscopy, metallurgy, and toxicology. And the tests they conducted were highly sophisticated and sensitive. So we know that when the prosecution wanted to prove something through experts, they did so. Yet there was no testimony from any expert witnesses called by the prosecution concerning the *Sea Wind* at this trial.

"Now, only two reasonable conclusions can be drawn from this fact. Not three or four. Just two. And here they are. Either no scientific examination of the *Sea Wind* was ever conducted by law enforcement in this case because they never believed any murders took place on the boat on August 28th or any other time, or the *Sea Wind* was examined with the very finest and most sensitive state-of-the-art equipment and instruments, and absolutely nothing was found. Either conclusion, of course, redounds to the detriment of the prosecution."

On the same issue of whether the murders had taken place *on* the *Sea Wind*, I asked why the prosecution had presented testimony about the swordfish incident and had cross-examined Jennifer at length on the issue. "So far, Mr. Enoki hasn't said. Maybe we'll hear about it in his closing argument. The only thing I can think of is that they were trying to imply that maybe the hole was not a swordfish hole, but a bullet hole."

I pointed out to the jury that we not only had Jennifer's detailed testimony about the swordfish incident, but Robert Mehaffy testified that Buck and Jennifer told him about the incident when they reached Hawaii. Most important, Larry Seibert testified that he actually saw the bill of the swordfish stuck in the hole of the hull.

"If the prosecution sincerely believed that there never was a swordfish attack causing a hole in the hull of the *Sea Wind*, why didn't they call an expert on the behavior of fish to testify that swordfish are not known to do this type of thing? And why didn't they call experts to testify they found no evidence of a *repaired* hole in the *Sea Wind* that gave any indication of having been caused by the bill of a swordfish? Or that they *did* find a repaired hole in the *Sea Wind*, but that it gave evidence—such as the microscopic presence of lead—that it was caused by a bullet? In my opinion, the swordfish issue, ladies and gentlemen, is as dead as the bill in that hole was."

It was time to tell the jury what I felt about the prosecution's star husband-and-wife witness team, the Leonards. I would mince no words.

"I can understand their being very, very upset over the death of their friends, the Grahams," I told the jury. "Anyone who is a decent human being can feel only tremendous sorrow over what happened to the Grahams. But the Leonards, in their unbridled zeal, went too far.

"I think that had to be obvious to you folks. Take the toilet-flushing incident. Both the Leonards were just dying to make you believe that Jennifer was frantically emptying out her purse and flushing down incriminating evidence against herself.

"Yet both of them finally coughed up the fact that although they had spoken to many law enforcement personnel throughout the years, they had never told the toilet-flushing incident to any-one up until one year ago, when they encountered Assistant U.S. Attorney Walt Schroeder and FBI Agent Hal Marshall. There was something irresistible about Walt and Hal that caused the Leonards to break a ten-year period of silence.

"When I asked Mr. Leonard why he never told the FBI agents about the incident when they interviewed him on October 29, 1974, he said he assumed they already knew. Yet he does tell them something they would have a much, much greater reason to know—that just an hour or so earlier, Jennifer was observed row-ing to shore in the Ala Wai yacht harbor and was subsequently apprehended.

"One footnote to this toilet-flushing incident. According to the Leonards, FBI agents were present outside the bathroom, hearing the whole thing. Yet only the Leonards testified at this trial to the suspicious nature of the incident.

"With respect to Jennifer's alleged statement to the Leonards that she would never leave Palmyra on the *Iola*, as with the toilet-flushing incident, though the Leonards had spoken to many law enforcement personnel throughout the years, they never told a soul. They kept it locked in their bosom for ten years. We go through wars and presidencies during ten years. A long, long time. But once again, the Leonards simply could not resist the charm of Walt and Hal, and they finally coughed this up.

"But with *this* statement, they knew they couldn't use the previous argument for their silence that the FBI already knew, since the FBI wasn't on Palmyra. So this is what they came up with. *They never told anyone because no one ever asked them.* Remember that? Never told anyone because no one ever asked them. *Sure*, Mr. and Mrs. Leonard. And yesterday, outside of this courthouse, I saw an alligator doing the polka, and the day before I heard a cow speaking Spanish.

"As I asked them on cross-examination: 'How *could* the agents have asked you about what you say Jennifer told you, Mr. and Mrs. Leonard? How would they have known if you didn't tell them?'"

I asked the jury: "Just how ludicrous can the Leonards get? Here in court, where you *are* only supposed to answer questions, Mr. Leonard, in particular, volunteered all types of information which he perceived to be damaging to Miss Jenkins. But out of court, where you *can* say anything you want, the Leonards are as quiet as a church mouse.

"The Leonards would want you to believe they're the type of people who, if they had seen Nessie, the Loch Ness monster, in the Palmyra lagoon, wouldn't tell a soul unless someone asked them."

I noted that Jennifer had admitted on the witness stand to telling all types of people all types of things. But she said she never told the Leonards she would never leave Palmyra on the *Iola*. I noted further that there was considerable evidence that long after the Leonards left Palmyra, Jennifer and Buck were planning to go to Fanning from Palmyra on the *Iola*.

Lastly, I referred to FBI Agent Kilgore's testimony that the Leonards never told him about this supposed statement.

"Of all people who would have been absolutely certain to mention this alleged remark of Jennifer's to the authorities, surely it would have been the Leonards.

"WITH THESE preliminary matters out of the way, let's get into the heart of the case," I now said. I hoped I had softened the jurors up a bit with my opening comments, rendering them more receptive to the critically important arguments to follow.

"What we're dealing with here, ladies and gentlemen of the jury, is a real murder *mystery*, one that Agatha Christie could have conjured up only on her most inspired of days, the type of murder that rocking-chair sleuths like to ponder into the wee hours beside a crackling fire.

"The only problem is that, unlike an Agatha Christie mystery, this nightmarish story, so tragically for Mac and Muff Graham, happens to be true.

"In this final summation, I'm going to attempt to illuminate, by way of drawing commonsense inferences, the dark, ugly shadows of this mystery. By placing one piece of circumstantial evidence upon another—and Buck Walker was so adept at murder he left precious few pieces of incriminating evidence—I am confident that what will emerge for you are two rather stark mosaics, one of guilt for Buck Walker, and one of innocence for Jennifer Jenkins."

I started by discussing the motive for the murders. "Mr. Enoki, in an effort to fortify his case, tossed your way two motives, the stranded motive, and the severe-shortage-of-food motive, hoping you'll find at least one of them palatable."

I knew it was absolutely crucial that I remove *both* of these motives from the jury's consideration.

Discussing the stranded motive first, which encompassed the issue of the *Iola*'s seaworthiness, I first focused in on prosecution witness Jack Wheeler.

I pointed out that although Wheeler appeared to be a nice enough fellow and was obviously sincere, the jury shouldn't give too much credibility to his statement that the trip to Fanning was almost "impossible." I noted for the jury that Wheeler conceded that he himself never attempted to sail to Fanning. "Don Stevens did," I reminded the jury, and he testified it was possible to sail from Palmyra to Fanning.

"We learned at this trial that tacking against the wind is very common and easy. In fact, by tacking, a boat can proceed without a motor not only against the wind, but also against the current. And we know Jennifer was very familiar with tacking. Not only did she so testify, but her June 21st entry in her diary refers to 'tacking.'

"I might add that Mac Graham himself apparently felt that Buck and Jennifer could make it to Fanning. Jennifer's August 26th diary entry reflects that Mac brought a chart of Fanning over to Buck and Jennifer."

I pointed out that even Wheeler, a prosecution witness, did not feel that Buck and Jennifer were marooned on Palmyra, giving testimony that was diametrically opposed to the prosecution's theory that they were.

"Although Wheeler testified it would have been impossible or very difficult for Buck and Jennifer to make it to Fanning, you'll recall he said they could easily have made it to Samoa, which is fifteen hundred miles away."

With respect to the underlying issue of the *Iola*'s seaworthiness, I argued, "As I perceive it, there are really two issues here. One, was the *Iola* seaworthy or unseaworthy, which to me is not the central issue. And two, whether it was seaworthy or not, did Buck and Jennifer *think* that it was seaworthy, which to me *is* the central issue."

On the first issue, I had to acknowledge that although there was some divergence of opinion, the majority of the witnesses felt the *Iola* was not seaworthy. I went on to point out, however, that witnesses like Leonard and Wolfe, who felt the *Iola* was unseaworthy, never were on the boat, whereas Don Stevens, who believed the *Iola* was seaworthy, was. "So I think this lends a little more weight to his testimony on this point. Furthermore, Stevens, being a naval architect, would be more knowledgeable about such matters than Mr. Leonard and Mr. Wolfe.

"The important point is this: when Buck and Jennifer left Hawaii for Palmyra, although the *Iola* was certainly not a model boat, it obviously was seaworthy. How unseaworthy could the *Iola* be if it could make it a thousand miles on the high seas from Hawaii to Palmyra? Isn't that proof positive that the boat was seaworthy? And there's no evidence that either en route to Palmyra, or while on Palmyra, the *Iola* sustained any *major* damage that would have made it unseaworthy and prevented it from making the trip from Palmyra to Fanning, a short trip.

"But whether or not the *Iola* was seaworthy is not the issue in this case. It's almost irrelevant. The real issue is whether Buck and Jennifer *thought* it was seaworthy. It's their state of mind that's relevant. The *Iola* could be the most unseaworthy boat ever to sail the seven seas, it could be as unseaworthy as a cement block, but if Buck and Jennifer thought it was seaworthy, they would not feel desperate and stranded, would they? Would they?

"Did Buck and Jennifer feel the *Iola* was unseaworthy? Obviously not." I pointed out that in addition to Jennifer's testimony, her diary entries dated August 15th, 23rd, 24th, 25th, 26th, 27th, 28th, 29th, and 30th, all written *after* Wheeler told Jennifer the *Iola* couldn't make it to Fanning, left no room for doubt that she and Buck felt the *Iola* was seaworthy, that they were planning to sail to Fanning, and therefore did not feel stranded. I further noted that Wolfe, the prosecution's own witness, recalled a conversation with Jennifer wherein she told him of her and Buck's plan to sail to Fanning.

"Granted, people like Jack Wheeler and Tom Wolfe said they wouldn't have gone to Fanning on the *Iola*. But their states of mind are not at issue in this case, ladies and gentlemen. Many people would never drive across town in cars that other people wouldn't think twice about traveling cross-country in. Jennifer's state of mind is the issue here, and the evidence is overwhelming that she intended to go on the *Iola* to Fanning.

"Perhaps the very best evidence that Jennifer and Buck never felt stranded is that if they had, they would have sought to hitch a ride on one of the boats leaving Palmyra. But no prosecution witness said that any effort was made by Buck and Jennifer to do so. How stranded could they have felt if they never bothered to ask anyone for a lift off the island?

"Elliot Enoki cannot have it both ways. If they felt stranded enough to commit murder, why didn't they feel stranded enough to ask these people who visited the island if they could leave Palmyra with them?"

I pointed out that even in late August, when all the boats except the *Sea Wind* had left, there was still no problem. "Within a period of a little over two months, seven boats entered the lagoon at

Palmyra. With that type of traffic, Buck and Jennifer would have had every reason to believe that other boats would be coming to and leaving Palmyra within the near future, and they could most likely hitch a ride. At the very latest, they knew their friend, Richard Taylor, would be arriving with his brother on Palmyra in October, only two months away. Ladies and gentlemen of the jury, the stranded motive is just not going to fly. It just doesn't have any wings."

THE DESPERATION-for-food motive, I suggested, was equally "lame and flimsy. Maybe even more so.

"Was there testimony from any witness at this trial that Buck and Jennifer looked like they were suffering from malnutrition? Or that they were losing weight? Or even that they looked weak, or unhealthy, or anything at all like that? I didn't hear any such testimony."

I told the jury that while it was undeniably true that Jennifer and Buck's provisions had dwindled to very little, this didn't connect up to the issue of starvation because they could have lived off the land *indefinitely*. I reminded the jury of the various types of edible food on Palmyra, and the testimony of several witnesses, including that of a *prosecution* witness, Sharon Jordan: "No, you couldn't starve on Palmyra."

I granted that Buck and Jennifer undoubtedly had tired of their limited diet and craved different kinds of foods. That's why they attempted to trade for staples like flour and sugar so she could bake cakes, pies, and bread. "But to want and to prefer different kinds of food for the sake of taste and variety is a far cry from wanting these same foods to forestall starvation.

"I will stipulate that people will kill for self-preservation, such as killing for food to avoid starvation. But do people kill to improve their diet? Have you ever heard of such a thing? I haven't.

"And again, since the Taylor brothers were coming to Palmyra with provisions in October, just two months away, and one could live *indefinitely* off the land on Palmyra, do you mean to tell me that

Buck and Jennifer couldn't live for two more months off the land? *Two more months?*

"In summary, with respect to these motives Mr. Enoki has offered, I'll concede that the *Iola* may not have been the most sea-worthy boat ever to ride the waves, and I'll further concede that Buck and Jennifer obviously were not doing well foodwise on Palmyra. . . . But they weren't stranded, and they weren't starving. Is this just Vince Bugliosi saying this? No, ladies and gentlemen of the jury, *this is the evidence at this trial saying this.*

"So what *was* the motive? We know there's a motive for every murder. What was the motive here?

"It's pretty obvious that Buck Walker, and Buck Walker alone, had the motive. And it was the most commonplace, garden-variety motive you can have: Buck Walker, a twice-convicted robber, wanted the *Sea Wind*, as he must have wanted the other things for which he was previously convicted of robbery. And because he was a hardened criminal, he was willing to murder to get it. The sim-ple motive of wanting something that someone else had, and not having the moral restraint or fundamental humanity most of us possess that serves as a deterrent to committing the act of murder.

"Are we all capable of murder? I don't believe so. Not for a moment. While perhaps all of us are capable of killing in self-defense, and a meaningful percentage of humans are capable of an instantaneous killing in the heat of passion where there's extreme provocation—which is called manslaughter—fortunately, the over-whelming majority of human beings don't have it in their guts, in their system, to commit a cold-blooded, deliberate, premeditated murder. How do we know this? Because statistically the percent-age of such murderers among us is infinitesimal.

"Does the evidence in this case show that Jennifer is the type who could commit a brutal murder?" I asked.

I explained that the crime of murder, by definition, and at its core, reflects on the part of the perpetrator a wanton and utter dis-regard for the life of a fellow human being. "If you're a peaceful, compassionate human being, *you don't commit murder!*" I shouted out. "You don't *do* that. *Nor do you help anyone else do it.*

"The testimony at this trial was not only persuasive, but completely uncontroverted by the prosecution, that Jennifer Jenkins is a very humane, gentle woman who is utterly repulsed by violence. Even by the instrumentalities of violence. You remember in Mountain View, Hawaii, she got Buck Walker to take those guns out of the house? This trial demonstrated that Jennifer Jenkins is one of the very least likely candidates for a murder suspect that one could possibly imagine.

"What about Buck Walker?" I asked, in my effort to separate the two.

I warned that although Jennifer's ex-lover was not present, he must not be considered a "bloodless mannequin."

"The testimony of witnesses at this trial created a very vivid physical and psychological portrait of him. And the portrait that emerged is that Buck Walker, so unfortunately for the Grahams, was tailor-made for what happened on Palmyra. And he was tailor-made to commit these murders *all by himself.*"

I summarized the testimony of defense witness Rick Schulze, the Hawaii lawyer who had described Walker as "rough and coarse . . . paranoid and defensive, and fascinated with weapons." And I reminded the jury that Debbie Noland had testified that Buck had a "firecracker" personality, an explosive and violent temper.

"Mrs. Leonard testified how Buck would row his boat slowly past her boat, and look at her with very hard eyes. She would talk to him, and he wouldn't answer. And she was very afraid of him. Tom Wolfe also said Buck was a scary guy.

"Stop to think about it. How many people have you personally met in your life who were actually scary to you, whom you were afraid of?

"Buck gave every indication of being the precise type of individual who would engage in violent crimes. And we know these indications were accurate ones because Buck Walker, long before he ever set foot on the coral reef of Palmyra, had already been convicted of two armed robberies."

I pointed out to the jury that robbery, of course, is a violent crime, the taking of personal property from the person or immediate presence of another by means of force or fear, such as by a gun or knife, then pressed on with my "prosecution" of Buck Walker: "I submit that it takes a particular type of individual, one whose moral senses are coarse, one who has pronounced antisocial proclivities, to commit an act such as armed robbery."

Because of Walker's two prior robbery convictions, I told the jury, "we have proof positive, not foundationless speculation, that Buck Walker had the instincts coursing through his veins to resort to violence to get what he wanted. And the Grahams had something Buck Walker wanted, the *Sea Wind*.

"This was simply, ladies and gentlemen, a very brutal murder committed *alone* by a cold-blooded human being named Buck Walker for the purpose of acquiring one of the most magnificent boats that anyone has ever seen."

I NEXT DREW bead on what I called the "very core" of the prosecution's case. "Simple arithmetic is all they really have. Four people on an island, two end up dead, and the other two end up with their boat, acting suspiciously. These two must both be guilty, because four minus two leaves two. Basic, simple arithmetic. One of the two, Buck Walker, has already been found guilty. Jennifer is the remaining one, they say.

"In the remainder of my argument to you, I'm not only going to be talking about the evidence in this case, evidence that points irresistibly to Buck Walker's guilt and Jennifer's innocence, I'm also going to be talking about life. Not life as we would perhaps like it to be, but life as it is."

Though it had not come from the witness stand, from the very beginning I knew that human nature would be a part of the evidence in the case I would argue to the jury.

"Some of you, at this juncture, might be saying to yourself: 'Mr. Bugliosi, you're saying that Jennifer Jenkins is a warmhearted, compassionate human being, but you say that Buck Walker is a vicious, cold-blooded robber and murderer. Isn't this somewhat of a contradiction? Because if what you say is true, why would she be with him? Just as water seeks its own level, don't people tend to seek their own kind? The so-called birds-of-a-feather syndrome?'"

Enoki had made the same point. "*What was she doing with him if she was not . . . like him?*"

"That type of question necessarily implies that things in life fall into a predictable pattern. That life proceeds in apple-pie order. But, ladies and gentlemen of the jury, you know as well as I that that's not the way life is. Life is an endless series of inconsistencies, a bewildering mixture of contradictions, where the only thing stranger than fiction is reality.

"For whatever reason, Jennifer loved Buck Walker. Rick Schulze said she saw a spark of goodness in Buck. Jennifer herself testified that though she knew Buck had a bad background, she felt he had a lot of potential and felt she could help him.

"And don't forget that by the time Jennifer found out that Buck Walker had been convicted of robbery, she had already fallen in love with him and started living with him. By that time, she probably had lost the capacity to see Buck Walker for who he really was. Jerome Kern's 'Smoke Gets in Your Eyes' is not just a ballad to dance to, it tells us a lot about life.

"Undoubtedly, most people would not approve of a nice girl loving a guy like Buck Walker. But we don't get to approve of whom people love, do we? We cannot hold it against Jennifer for loving Buck Walker. And, above all, we certainly cannot say that because she was with him, and because she loved him, that it's likely she is also *like* him. That is, that she is also a murderer.

"As an extreme example of what I'm talking about—sometimes extreme examples are good to underscore a point—I'm going to give you a historical one you're familiar with. My example might sound farfetched, but it's relevant because Mr. Enoki's point is that if Buck Walker was vicious and violent, and Jennifer was with him, she was the same type.

"Let me transport you for a moment to the Second World War. While the furnaces were blazing in places like Treblinka, Auschwitz, and Chelmno, the malodorous smell of burning human flesh permeating the countryside, Adolf Hitler, in the rarefied atmosphere of Berchtesgaden high in the Bavarian Alps, was spending pleasurable moments with the woman in his life, Eva Braun.

"Though Hitler was one of the most satanic men ever to walk

the face of this earth, though his monstrous crimes are beyond human calculation—over forty years after his death we're still cleaning up the debris of his Third Reich—Eva Braun apparently loved Adolf Hitler, eventually electing to die with him in that besieged Berlin bunker in April of 1945, rather than escape to safety. Apparently, Eva Braun saw something human in the inhuman Adolf Hitler. Though Eva Braun loved, and on the last day of her life married, Adolf Hitler, whose crimes were of biblical proportions, did that make her the same type of person he was? No historian of this period has even remotely hinted at this, or at her complicity in the horrors of the Third Reich. By virtually all accounts she was a rather uncomplicated, fluffy-headed but decent Bavarian girl of simple tastes.

"If you can conceive of Eva Braun—now, granted, this is an extreme example, but it illustrates the point—if you can conceive of Eva Braun, the woman in Adolf Hitler's life, not being like him, why should you have any difficulty whatsoever conceiving of Jennifer Jenkins, the woman in Buck Walker's life, not being like him at all? Not being capable, like him, of *murder*?"

For whatever reason, I explained, Jennifer was in love with Buck Walker. "And when you love someone, you do things *for* that person. Isn't that what love is all about? Do you do anything, anything at all for the person you love? Well, if you have absolutely no moral fiber you do. You do anything they ask you to do. We know that's *not* the situation with Jennifer, as it's not the situation, fortunately, with most people. But I'll tell you one thing most people will do for their loved ones, and that is protect them when they've done something wrong."

I asked the jury to look at the situation from Jennifer's perspective in the summer of 1974. Why had she and Buck gone to Palmyra in the first place? So Buck could not only escape punishment on the MDA conviction, but, more importantly, avoid being sent back to San Quentin on a violation of his robbery parole.

"He told Jennifer he was terrified of San Quentin, vowing he would never go back. These are the things that were uppermost in Jennifer's mind in the summer of 1974. She loved Buck, and when he told her of his terror of being sent back to San Quentin, what effect do you think that had on her? Well, she told you what effect it had.

"Virtually everything that Jennifer did in this case is traceable to two realities. Number one, that she loved Buck Walker, and number two, she was trying to protect him from apprehension. If you keep these two realities in mind, I say that her conduct will be much more understandable to you."

I added that it was "exceedingly common" for decent, honorable, law-abiding people even to commit crimes to protect a loved one who has gone wrong. "In this case here, Jennifer considered herself Buck Walker's common-law wife. She has never married. Buck was the closest to a husband she has ever had."

As an example of protecting one's loved ones, I asked the jury: "How many times do parents permit their fugitive sons to hide out at home from the authorities, thereby committing the crime of being an accessory after the fact to the crime their son committed?

"In fact, some European nations, by statute, specifically exclude family members from prosecution for harboring a criminal or assisting them in evading apprehension by the law.

"For instance, the family of Dr. Joseph Mengele—you remember him, the notorious Nazi 'Angel of Death' who was responsible for the extermination of about four hundred thousand people, mostly Jews, in Poland during the Second World War—they helped him avoid apprehension from the law for *thirty years*, and the authorities knew this. The family even later admitted it. But West German law protected them from being prosecuted.

"Just like, as they say, you cannot legislate morality, all the laws in the world cannot tear asunder the bond of blood and love that unites human beings to one another. These relationships, of course, are the protoplasm, as it were, of all human existence, without which there would be no laws, without which there would be no civilized society as we know it today.

"What I am saying is that there are laws other than those written in the law books. Laws, emotions, and feelings as indestructible and imperishable as human nature itself, and which no system of jurisprudence has ever yet been able to ignore.

"Can Mr. Enoki come back and say in his rebuttal that I am saying that in defense of your loved ones it's okay to commit any crime you want? Well, he can *say* it, but *I'm* not saying it.

"A parent or spouse of a robber, for instance, might permit him to hide out in their home, but they're not going to go out and commit a robbery or a murder for him. People do things for their loved ones, but they draw lines in the sand. There are limits.

"Lest Mr. Enoki suggest in his rebuttal that since Jennifer loved Buck Walker, and since he was the dominant party in their relationship, he could get Jennifer to go along with him in his plan to murder the Grahams, let me point out that Jennifer Jenkins *did* draw lines in the sand with Buck Walker. True, she testified that she never wanted to create waves with Buck, so she normally let him have his way. But only up to a point. There were limits."

I recalled Jennifer's opposition to having guns in the cabin at Mountain View, and Buck's removing them. I also reminded the jurors of the spaghetti-on-the-wall incident—"Maybe it's a trifle, but it's nonetheless illuminating. Although Buck threw the spaghetti on the wall, he wanted her to clean it up. She said, 'You did it. You clean it up.' And he did.

"On Palmyra, Buck wanted Jennifer to live in his tent with him. She said no, and she did not move to the tent. After they returned to Hawaii, he wanted her to put her name on those registration papers for the *Sea Wind*. She said no, and she did not do it. His name alone appears on those registration papers.

"If Buck Walker couldn't talk Jennifer into letting him keep guns in their home in Mountain View, if he couldn't talk her into living with him in his tent on Palmyra, if he couldn't talk her into putting her name on those boat registration papers, if he couldn't even talk her into cleaning spaghetti from the wall of the cabin, *how in the world could he talk her into committing* two of the most horrendous, brutal, gruesome murders imaginable?"

Allowing this idea to sink in, I paused, sipping from a cup filled with a honey-and-lemon concoction that helps sustain my voice during lengthy summations.

"But Jennifer *was* willing to help Buck avoid being apprehended and sent to prison. She was willing to protect him, which is one of the most natural instincts toward one you love."

I argued that she was continuing to protect Buck right through Shishido's interrogation. "She volunteered virtually everything that happened on Palmyra, but she did not tell him that Roy Allen was Buck Walker, the fugitive. This she did not volunteer to him. In fact, Shishido recalls that the only area where she specifically refused to answer questions was concerning Roy Allen.

"She even took *affirmative steps to prevent* him from learning that Roy Allen was Buck Walker," I said, reminding the jury that to keep the authorities from learning Buck's identity, Jennifer had given Shishido the incorrect date and location she and Buck were first on the *Iola*.

"So right to the very end, she was protecting and covering up for Buck Walker. Not covering up, in her mind, for his being a murderer, but for his being a fugitive from justice on the federal drug charge."

I walked over and stood behind Jennifer at the defense table, placing my right hand on her shoulder. "I say that Jennifer Jenkins is here right now in this courtroom because she loved and wanted to protect Buck Walker, and for no other reason.

"*The prosecution has taken the acts and statements of Jennifer Jenkins resulting from her desire to protect Buck Walker, and tried to convert them into evidence of her guilt for the murder of Muff Graham.* I have every confidence that you folks are not going to let them get by with it.

"Let me ask you this question," I continued, returning to the podium. "If your daughter, or sister, or any young woman you know well, had been in Jennifer's shoes—by that I mean, number one, she's by herself with a fugitive from justice on an almost deserted Pacific island, and also later when they return to Hawaii, and number two, she's in love with this man—if they acted just like Jennifer acted in this case, would you be terribly shocked? To the point where you would say, 'Well, as much as I don't want to believe it, she *must* have been involved in the murders'?

"Now, in asking yourself that question, don't embroider your consideration with the observation that your daughter, or sister, or friend would never have gotten involved with this scoundrel Buck Walker in the first place. Remember, we're talking about life as it is, not life as we would like it to be. Human beings, for whatever reason, often become intimately involved with others who have a background and character completely different from theirs. We know this."

I argued all these points before I got into the key day of August 30, 1974, needing the jury to be much more inclined to believe Jennifer's version of what took place on this day.

"NOW, LET'S try to reconstruct, as best we can, what happened on that tragic day of August 30, 1974. The first question that presents itself, the way I view the evidence, is whether there was in fact a dinner invitation."

I argued it was obvious there was not. For openers, I said, Mac's supposedly telling Buck that if he and Muff weren't back by 6:30 P.M. Buck and Jennifer should come aboard the *Sea Wind* and make themselves at home, made the invitation unbelievable. The Grahams, of course, wouldn't even let their closest friends come aboard the *Sea Wind* in their absence.

"But how was *Jennifer* supposed to have known this particular fact about the Grahams?" I argued. "The prosecution presented no evidence that Jennifer would have had any reason to know this."

Enoki's position was that the relationship between the Grahams and Buck and Jennifer was very poor. Therefore, this increased the likelihood that there was no dinner invitation, and Jennifer would have known this. "But *was* the relationship really that bad?" I now asked. "We're going to have to examine this very closely now, because this is a key issue. The evidence that came from that witness stand simply did not establish that the relationship was that bad."

I told the jury that even the strongest testimony the prosecution offered to prove this important point was somewhat ambiguous and contradictory. With respect to Tom Wolfe's testimony that Jennifer told him both couples, coming to Palmyra expecting to be alone, were irritated with each other, each feeling the other had invaded their privacy, I told the jury that Wolfe may have misconstrued what Jennifer told him. "Jennifer testified she *did* tell Wolfe that the Grahams and she and Buck each had come to Palmyra wanting to be alone, and the Grahams probably still felt that way. But as Jennifer testified, she and Buck no longer did, because as it turned out, the Grahams ended up being very helpful to her and Buck."

I went on to point out a seeming contradiction in Wolfe's testimony: If, as Wolfe said, he was under the impression that the two couples weren't getting along very well and weren't really talking to each other, how, I asked the jury, "do you reconcile that with this testimony by Wolfe on my cross-examination of him?

"'Question: You were aware that on occasion Mac Graham would bring some of the fish he and Muff caught over to Buck and Jennifer, is that correct? Answer: That's correct.'

"If they weren't talking to each other," I asked the jury, "what would Mac do when he would bring fish over to them? Drive his Zodiac past the *Iola* and lob the fish onto the deck of their boat? Moreover, if Party A is not getting along with Party B, does Party A, on his own, bring fish to Party B?"

Wolfe's testimony, I told the jury, did not appear to be clear-cut in its negative import.

"So what *was* the relationship between the Grahams and Buck and Jennifer? Well, although the Grahams came to Palmyra expecting it to be uninhabited, they may not have minded people visiting the island for short periods. But they most likely did not want people who, like Buck and Jennifer, intended to stay there for a long time, the same as they."

There were two other factors involved, I added. The Grahams being decent people, it probably put pressure on them and made them uncomfortable to have Buck and Jennifer not doing well when they themselves were living nearby in relative luxury.

"We also know that Mac and Muff were conservative, middle-of-the-road Americans, and Buck and Jennifer were leading a somewhat unconventional life-style. And we naturally tend to be more distant towards people whose life-style is different from ours. But other than Curt Shoemaker's very questionable testimony about a truce, there certainly was no evidence from that witness stand that there was anything rising to the level of a feud or bad blood between them. In fact, there is substantial evidence to the contrary.

"Jennifer, reading from her diary, recounted many instances for you of friendly interaction. For instance, the Grahams' going to Jennifer's birthday party on July 16th; their exchanging food with each other; Buck and Jennifer giving Mac messages to relay to Hawaii by way of his radio; and so forth.

"You heard all the examples, and I'm not going to go over all of them with you now. You'll have the diary back in the jury room.

"Suffice it to say there was a continuing, ongoing social intercourse between the Grahams and Buck and Jennifer during the summer of 1974 on the island of Palmyra. And we don't just have to rely on Jennifer's testimony and diary to prove this. It was corroborated and confirmed by the testimony of other witnesses." In addition to citing Tom Wolfe's testimony that Mac and Muff would go fishing and give part of their catch to Buck and Jennifer, I read excerpts from the important testimony of Bill Larson that the relationship he had observed between the two couples at the July 25 potluck dinner was very friendly. "You'll note the prosecution didn't call Larson to the stand. They stayed away from him the way the devil stays away from holy water.

"While it is also true that Muff told Larson she did not want Buck and Jennifer on the *Sea Wind*, how much does that mean? I'm sure each of you folks know people you're friendly with whom you might not want to have in your home."

I pointed out that even Bernard Leonard, the quintessential prosecution witness, told the FBI that the Grahams were friendly with Buck and Jennifer, although, because of their different lifestyles, "not extremely" so.

"In fact, even if we accept the prosecution's position that the cake-truce incident did take place—and I think they are light-years away from proving that point—what did Shoemaker say? He testified he heard two women in the background having a conversation, '*and there was laughter.*'"

I went on to tell the jury that since the prosecution had not presented evidence that the Grahams had ever *communicated* any unfriendly feeling they may have had toward Buck and Jennifer, and in fact were outwardly friendly toward them, "when Buck told Jennifer that Mac had invited them to the *Sea Wind* for a bon voyage dinner, there certainly would be no reason for her to believe that no such invitation was made."

I added that Jennifer knew that the Grahams had given bon voyage dinners for others, and that furthermore, she and Buck *had* been on the *Sea Wind* before. "There are references in Jennifer's diary on July 9th, July 28th, August 6th, and August 11th, where either she or Buck, or the two of them, were on the *Sea Wind.*"

I concluded by emphasizing that Jennifer had never vouched for the veracity of the dinner invitation. She simply testified that this was what Buck had told her. "There's an old line in Elizabethan literature: 'I cannot tell how the truth may be. I say the tale as 'twas said to me.'"

Of course, everything I had said thus far presupposed that Buck had told Jennifer, as she claimed, that there was a dinner invitation. But had she concocted the whole dinner-invitation story *with* Buck? I argued that there was evidence, in Buck's own testimony at his *theft* trial, to support the position that he alone had fabricated the dinner-invitation story. ("We don't have his testimony at his *murder* trial because he did not testify," I added, wanting the jury to know a negative circumstance that contrasted with Jennifer.)

I began reading Buck Walker's version of what had happened on August 30. "'*I* saw Mac early in the morning'—notice he said *I*, not *we*—'I guess eight or nine o'clock, and we passed the time of day. We smoked a cigarette or something like that. *I* went aboard his boat and we played a game of chess, a couple games of chess, and he said he was going to help tow us out of the lagoon with his dinghy. So, he invited us over for dinner that night. It was sort of a bon voyage thing. Then *I* went back over to our boat, and Jennifer and I continued getting our boat ready for the next day.'"

Walker's attorney asked Walker if he had seen Mac later that day.

"'*I* saw him about one or two o'clock in the afternoon. He said that he was going fishing that afternoon, and if he wasn't back at the appointed hour of six-thirty, to go ahead and board the boat and help ourselves to a drink . . . and that's the last time *I* talked to him.'

"Note in Buck Walker's testimony there's no reference to Jennifer being present when he had these contacts with Mac Graham on the key date of August 30th. And Jennifer has also testified that on that date she had no contact with the Grahams. Now, I ask you this: if Jennifer had been involved with Buck in the murder of the Grahams, and if they had concocted this dinner-invitation story together, wouldn't it have been natural for them to have said that they *both* saw the Grahams on the 30th?

"Since they would know that if they were ever investigated, the finger of suspicion would naturally point more strongly to the one who did have contact with the Grahams that day, why would Buck take on this additional suspicion all by himself and completely relieve Jennifer of it? Was Buck trying to prove to Jennifer that chivalry was not dead in America?

"That's just pure *moonshine*," I boomed. "If Jennifer had trumped up this phony story with Buck—more importantly, if Jennifer had been involved with Buck in the murders of the Grahams—wouldn't Buck have said that Jennifer was with him on at least one of the occasions he claims to have seen Mac Graham that day? Wouldn't he have insisted on having her available to furnish some support for his story about the dinner invitation?

"Instead, he testified that *all* of his contacts with Mac took place when Jennifer wasn't present. Why did he say this? Because since Jennifer wasn't involved in this sordid and monstrous deed with him, of necessity, he had to say she wasn't present. *If he had said she was, when she knew that she wasn't, he would be revealing his guilt to her,* something he obviously never wanted to do."

I charged that it couldn't be more obvious that Buck alone fabricated the entire story about the dinner invitation.

"As we go along, we will see example after example of Buck Walker's tapestry of lies about the dinner invitation unraveling. Another point in his story that reveals the lie of it all is this: Mac and Muff apparently had ample supplies of frozen meat on the *Sea Wind*, and when they had people for dinner, oftentimes they would serve meat. The Leonards said that. Tom Wolfe said their bon voyage dinner was meat and fish.

"But for Buck and Jennifer, of all people, who had fish literally swimming out of their ears, they were going to serve them *more* fish? Why doesn't it make sense? Because the story was an obvious fabrication. To convince Jennifer of the Grahams' dying acciden-tally *in the lagoon*, Buck Walker had to come up with this story about their going fishing, in the lagoon, for the alleged bon voy-age dinner that night."

I continued my attempted reconstruction of the events (after Buck came by the *Iola* around 9:00 A.M.) of August 30, 1974: per Jennifer's testimony, their making trips from Buck's tent to the *Iola* to bring personal belongings aboard for the trip to Fanning; around 10:30 or 11 A.M., their plan for Jennifer to remain aboard the *Iola* to bake, clean, and stow gear for their trip to Fanning and for Buck to take the furniture from his tent to the Refrigerator House and bring the tent back to the *Iola*; Buck's doing neither (Jennifer's testimony, plus Wheeler's testimony that the 1974 search party found the furniture still inside Buck's tent); et cetera.

"We can infer the real reason why Buck Walker never brought the tent back to the *Iola* that day, or the furniture to the Refriger-ator House, can't we, ladies and gentlemen? He was much too busy on shore and in the lagoon. A grisly, macabre story of terror and cold-blooded murder was taking place on Palmyra that day that would compare favorably with anything seen in a low-budget Hollywood horror film. And Buck Walker had a starring role in it all. He played the part of the human monster."

I stressed it was worth remembering that Buck had been living ashore in his tent since July 15. "The relevance of this, of course, is obvious. Since Buck was by himself on shore, he had much, much more freedom and latitude to do what he did on August 30 than he would have had if Jennifer had been living on shore with him."

I was in a weak position on the next issue: Enoki's argument that if Jennifer weren't involved in the murders, Buck would never have left the dinghy with her, since she might come ashore at any time. In attempting a convincing rebuttal, I once again pointed to Jennifer's testimony that after 10:30 or 11:00 A.M., it had been both Buck's and her plan that she *stay aboard* the *Iola* to swab, store, and bake. "Furthermore, *Buck obviously would know Jennifer's habits*," I said. "He probably had no reason to believe that Jennifer would take the dinghy to shore." I added that it only takes a matter of sec-onds, or a minute, to kill a fellow human being, so even if Jennifer did come ashore, Buck knew it would be highly unlikely she'd catch him in the act. (I didn't add, of course, that if Jennifer had seen anything else—the corpses, or Buck in the process of doing anything with them—it would have been just as bad for Buck.)

I returned to the chronology of that day—from Buck's coming by the *Iola* in the early afternoon and again around 4 P.M., and Jennifer's hearing the Zodiac in the lagoon around 4:30 P.M. ("We can reasonably infer that the operator of that dinghy was Buck Walker, and the cargo was death—the bodies of Mac and Muff Graham"), to Buck's and Jennifer's arriving at the *Sea Wind* around 6:30 P.M.

"There are two things at this point that continue to give the lie to Buck's story," I argued. "Number one, I asked Jennifer if the masthead light of the *Sea Wind* was on when she and Buck arrived for dinner, and she said no.

"Tom Wolfe testified it got dark on Palmyra between 6:00 and 7:00 P.M., and Jennifer also said this. Since we know that Palmyra, at night, was very dark, and since, according to Buck's story, Mac realized he and Muff might get back after 6:30 P.M., and therefore perhaps after dark, not only would common sense dictate he would have left the masthead light on as a beacon for him and Muff, but Wolfe testified that on the one occasion he was with Mac in which Mac thought he might return to the *Sea Wind* after dark, he did leave the masthead light on. So this is further circumstantial evidence that Buck's story was a total fabrication."

The second point I made concerned the apricot brandy. I told the jury it was obvious that Buck Walker had put Jennifer's drink of choice out on the table. To believe otherwise would be to accept the extreme coincidence that the Grahams, who had no way of knowing the unpopular liqueur was one of Jennifer's favorite drinks, *just happened* to set out apricot brandy. Unless, of course, the jury entertained the third possibility—that Jennifer fabricated this story about the apricot brandy to subtly place suspicion on Buck. But if that were so, I reasoned with the jury, "wouldn't she have made sure I knew that apricot brandy was one of her favorite drinks and that the Grahams had no way of knowing this? Wouldn't she have told me this? But she didn't. And she couldn't have assumed I was going to ask her.

"Ladies and gentlemen of the jury, Buck Walker's tale about being invited to the *Sea Wind* for a bon voyage dinner is riddled with holes and implausibilities because it's obvious there never was any such invitation.

"In my attempt to delineate for you, by way of commonsense inferences, the events that took place on the island of Palmyra on August 30, 1974, one reality emerges, and it's compatible with all the other evidence in this case. Namely, that *Buck Walker murdered the Grahams all by himself, and Jennifer Jenkins had absolutely nothing to do with the murders.*

"I believe that only one person alive today knows all of the facts concerning what happened to the Grahams. His name is Buck Walker, and he's been as quiet as a statue. I guess if I were he, my lips would be permanently zippered, too.

"I spoke earlier of the horror and terror that took place on Palmyra on the day of August 30, 1974. Before I continue on with the chronology of events, the question that presents itself at this point is this: If Jennifer is telling a truthful story, why didn't she hear any of this? For instance, if a gun was used, the sound of the gun being fired?*

"Well, to begin with, before we even get into the issue of sounds, although it appears that Buck disposed of the bodies in the lagoon after 4:30 P.M. on August 30th, we don't know *what time of day* the actual murders took place. We also don't even know *where* on Palmyra these murders took place.

"I've thought of several scenarios, but I won't even bother relating them to you since they're just bald, naked speculation on my part. I might add that the prosecution doesn't know any more than we do as to when and where on Palmyra the murders took place.

---

*It may be too obvious to state, but whether or not Jennifer *actually heard* gunshots or screams had nothing to do with the issue of guilt. If she didn't conspire with Buck to murder the Grahams, then of course even if she did hear shots or screams it would be irrelevant. She wouldn't be guilty. But if the jury felt there must have been such sounds, and that Jennifer would have been *capable of hearing* them from the *Iola*, yet she said she didn't, then her story about being on the *Iola* and not hearing anything would be viewed as a lie, and if she was lying, this would point to her guilt for the murders.

"However, I think it's reasonable to assume that Walker would have murdered Mac Graham while Mac was separated from Muff. It's clearly more risky to confront two people when they're together than one at a time. And we know it would not have been difficult for Buck Walker to confront Mac and Muff separately, since there was testimony at this trial that Mac would be by himself often, such as at his workshop, or exploring the island. In other words, Buck would not have needed Jennifer to distract Muff while he murdered Mac.

"More importantly, on the issue of hearing sounds, we don't know for sure *how* Walker murdered the Grahams. However, I believe the circumstantial evidence is that Buck Walker did not use his gun. And that's very, very important."

I summarized that evidence. "Dr. Uberlaker testified that the hole above the left ear in the skull of Muff Graham 'appears to have been made by erosion, not by trauma or projectile.'" Although Dr. Stephens, the medical examiner, testified he could not rule out the possibility the hole was caused by a bullet, I pointed out that he had not reached any conclusion on this issue. "One fact that indicated it was not caused by a gunshot, however, is that Dr. Stephens was unable to find any trace of lead around the hole. So there's no substantive evidence of a gun being used."

I went on to tell the jury that we did, however, have positive medical evidence of multiple fractures, resulting from multiple blows to the region of Muff's head—the fracturing out of the lower jawbone from the skull, as well as fractures to the upper and lower molars, the crown of tooth number 13, and the roots of tooth number 30.

"Dr. Harris testified the fractures were caused by blunt force, a force much greater than that from a human fist. He said something like a sledgehammer would have had to have been used. Muff also had fractures to the radius and ulna bones of the left forearm, and fractures to her left and right tibia, all caused by extreme force. The image that is irresistibly conjured up is that of Walker repeatedly striking Muff Graham, over and over again, with a sledgehammer type of instrument."

I certainly didn't get the image, I told the jury, of Walker shooting Muff to death with his gun, then, as she lay dead on the ground, proceeding to strike her over and over again with a sledgehammer. "That type of overkill would only be the conduct of one who had a prodigious hatred for the victim. There's no evidence that such a situation existed between Buck Walker and Muff Graham."

Perhaps the key piece of circumstantial evidence that Walker did not use his gun, I added, was that when the contents of the *Sea Wind* were inventoried by the FBI at the time of Jennifer's arrest, they *found* his gun.

"It's number 5 on the inventory list," I said. "Obviously, if Buck's gun was the murder weapon, he would not have kept that gun on the *Sea Wind*. He would have disposed of it. If the authorities had his gun, an experienced ex-con like Buck would know—even lay people from watching crime shows on television would know— that if the bodies of the Grahams were discovered, and the bullet or bullets were removed from their bodies, or were found loose in the container after only the skeleton remained, the markings on the bullet or bullets could be matched up with the markings on bullets test-fired from his gun. And that would be the end of the ball game for him. He would have to know this. *The fact that he kept that gun strongly indicates he knew he had nothing like this to fear*, since he didn't use the gun.

"In the absence of any other available evidence, it would appear, not just from the medical and scientific testimony of the prosecution's own experts, but from the circumstantial evidence I've just discussed, that Mrs. Graham was murdered by sledgehammer-type blows to the head, and that no gun was used."

Throughout my argument, the jury was taking notes, an excellent sign. But not my presumed nemesis, the Kansas Rock. He simply sat with arms tightly folded, shooting me a chilly glare that said, "Proceed, Mr. Bugliosi, you have my biased attention."

"The fact that it appears Buck Walker did not use his gun," I went on, "is additional circumstantial evidence that he committed these murders alone. Since a gun is not only much easier to use than an instrument like a sledgehammer, but much more effective, why would he use a sledgehammer?

"Because a weapon like a sledgehammer," I said, continuing in my effort to give the jury missing pieces of the mystery, "would have had one big advantage for Buck Walker over a gun. It wouldn't make any noise. Noise that a gun being fired would make. Noise that Jennifer might hear."

I argued that even if the hole in the skull *was* caused by a bullet— "as it appears it was not"—Dr. Stephens testified that the reverse-coning effect he found around the hole would have meant that it was from a contact gunshot wound.

I referred to Dr. Stephens's testimony that with such a contact-type firing, the gunshot would have sounded like only a "loud pop." And at two hundred yards—the approximate distance between the *Iola* and the *Sea Wind*—he felt the shot might not have been heard at all, "particularly if there were any other sounds on the island. And we'll get into that in a moment," I said.

Reducing the level of my voice, I gripped the rail of the jury box and spoke intimately to the jury. "All of these arguments that I have been making to you folks, all of these inferences I am drawing, where do they all come from? Are they just fanciful ruminations on my part? Did they come from some wishful reverie of mine? Are they the product of tricky and insincere reasoning on my part?

"No, ladies and gentlemen of the jury, they don't come from any of these places. They all come from the evidence in this case that came from that witness stand under oath.

"With the exception of discussing matters of common knowledge, everything I am saying to you is based on the evidence in this case. The evidence is the foundation, the anchor, if you will, upon which everything I am saying to you is based.

"Going on, even if Buck did use a gun, and even if the muzzle of the gun were *not* close to Muff's head, the report of a distant gunshot may not have been audible to Jennifer. There was a cacophony of sounds on Palmyra that in the amalgam would have silenced, or at least considerably muted, the report of a gun.

"As we know from the testimony of several witnesses, there were literally a million birds squawking during the day, and they were loud. And there was the timeless sound of the ocean."

I further reminded the jury that there was a stipulation between the prosecution and the defense that on this particular day at twelve noon, a ship four hundred miles east of Palmyra reported winds of sixteen knots—about eighteen miles an hour. This did not mean, of course, that there were winds of eighteen miles an hour on Palmyra, but it meant "there was a likelihood of some wind, and obviously, this would cause a rustling in the trees that would help to mute sounds.

"And of course, perhaps most of all, the very dense, junglelike foliage on Palmyra muted sound.

"What about screams?" I asked. "Again, we don't know if there were any screams. Buck Walker certainly would have had every reason to try to catch Mac and Muff unawares, such as by striking Mac from behind at his workshop. Mac, having spent a lot of time in Buck's presence, could easily have turned his back on Buck. So chances are there would not be any screams, the first blow to the head from behind rendering Mac unconscious."

There was one additional small point to be made. I noted for the jury that the sixteen-knot wind stipulation included the fact that the winds were coming from the south-southeast, meaning they were going toward the northwest. Since from the *Iola* the location of those places where the murders were likely to have taken place, such as Mac's workshop and the vicinity of the *Sea Wind*, were to the northwest, the wind that day would be carrying any sound farther away from where Jennifer was on the *Iola*, an additional factor muting any loud sound.

"A further question presents itself. If Jennifer would have been unable to hear the gunshots or screams, how could she have heard the sound of the Zodiac?" I had to anticipate, and try to answer, every question that might occur to the jurors during their deliberations.

"Well, number one, we know from the testimony of several witnesses—including Agent Shishido—that the Zodiac had a powerful motor and made a very loud sound when it was operating. Secondly, as opposed to sounds emanating from shore, which would be muffled by the very dense foliage, sounds coming from the lagoon could travel unimpeded by any obstructions. Moreover, it's a known fact that sounds travel faster and retain their decibel level longer over water than on land, even unobstructed land. Therefore, it would not be unlikely that Jennifer would hear the sound of the Zodiac's engine as the dinghy roared away from the vicinity of the *Sea Wind*."

I then reminded the jury that as far as what Jennifer could see from the *Iola*, there was the testimony of Tom Wolfe as well as Jennifer that one couldn't see anything (*Sea Wind*, Mac's workshop, etc.) on the island.

I picked up the chronology of Jennifer's testimony, from her and Buck's first evening on the *Sea Wind*, through their searching for the Grahams in the morning and spotting the Zodiac upside down on the beach.

"We can reasonably infer," I said, "that Buck overturned the dinghy to convince Jennifer that the Grahams had died an accidental death.

"With respect to what took place on Palmyra on the critical day in question, August 30th, Mr. Enoki argued that all I have is the word of Jennifer Jenkins. To which I respond: 'Not quite.'

"We also have the incriminating testimony of Buck Walker at his theft trial back in 1975 that only he, not Jennifer, had contact with the Grahams that day. And I believe I have also drawn some commonsense inferences as to what took place on August 30th. And we don't even have any burden of proof. They do. Judge King will tell you that the burden of proof *never shifts* to the defense," I repeated yet again to the jury.

I went on to point out, on the other hand, that the only arguably commonsense inference the prosecution had as to what happened on August 30 was the old four-minus-two-leaves-two scenario. "I guess it's inconceivable to the prosecution that of the two people left on the island, one could be a vicious, cold-blooded murderer, without the other one also being a murderer."

I realized, I said to the jury, how natural it would be to accept the four-minus-two-leaves-two argument. "This conclusion is simplistic and visceral in origin. Upon contemplation and examination, however, it does not hold any water. It only takes one person, not two people, to kill another. And the fact that these two persons are on a deserted Pacific island does not change that fact."

I told the jury that if, for example, at the time of a robbery, X was seen in the company of the robber, the inference would be that X "was involved in that robbery, because of the millions of other places he could have been at the time of the robbery, he just happened to be with the robber. The argument that it was a coincidence just doesn't wash."

"It's like the fellow who comes home early from work one day and finds his wife in a negligee and a man hiding in the closet. When he asks the man what he is doing there, the man says: 'Well, everyone has to be somewhere.' Likewise, it doesn't wash.

"But here, if Buck Walker murdered the Grahams on Palmyra, as the circumstantial evidence in this case surely shows, *Jennifer Jenkins could not have been somewhere else*. She was living on Palmyra at the time of the murders, not Nome, Alaska, so her presence on Palmyra at the time of these murders means absolutely nothing. Nothing at all.

"Could one ask: 'Shouldn't Jennifer have at least suspected that Buck murdered the Grahams?' Well, *why?* To Jennifer's knowledge, what had Buck done that would have caused her to be suspicious? What had he really done?

"All she knew is that she and Buck, together, had discovered the Grahams' dinghy overturned, and an accidental death seemed apparent to her.

"Let me ask you this. If you were on the island with your loved one—and remember, Jennifer loved Buck—and you and your loved one found the dinghy overturned, would you have suspected your loved one of murder?"

I checked the clock on the wall—it was 4:30 P.M.—and told the judge this was a good stopping place for the day.

After excusing the jury until the following morning, Judge King looked at me and said pleasantly, "You're doing fine, Mr. Bugliosi."

CHAPTER 43

I BEGAN THE FINAL DAY of my summation by telling the jury I would discuss each piece of evidence the prosecutor claimed pointed to Jennifer's guilt.

Jennifer had lied about finding the Zodiac overturned on the beach, Enoki had argued. It was one of the most critical evidentiary issues of the whole trial, and my position was not nearly as strong as I wanted it to be.

"As you know," I began, "there are two high tides and two low tides every day. However, of the two high tides, one is a high high tide, and the other is a low high tide. Likewise, there's a high low tide and a low low tide. There is only one high high tide every twenty-four hours.

"What evidence did Mr. Enoki offer that between 4:30 P.M. on August 30th, when Jennifer heard the Zodiac, and shortly after dawn, when she found it overturned, that there was a *high high* tide? If tides were going to be an issue at this trial, as he is making them, why didn't he secure tidal data for this region of the Pacific and present it to you? Doesn't the prosecution have the burden of proof?

"John Bryden testified that at high tide there would not be any beach in the area where Jennifer testified she found the dinghy. *But there was no attempt to distinguish between a high high tide and a low high tide, where the water would not go up on the beach as far.*"

I pointed out that another prosecution witness, Sharon Jordan, testified that "the coastline was irregular" in the area involved, and there were "parts of the coastline that were close to the water and other parts that were back in, like coves." I produced defense exhibit 25, a color photograph of the area in question, pointing out it "clearly shows the irregularity of the beach in this area."

I next cited the testimony of our strongest witness on this issue, former Assistant U.S. Attorney William Eggers: "Mr. Eggers was on Palmyra within months of the Grahams' disappearance, and therefore was in a much better position than Bryden to observe the effect of tides on the area of beach in question on August 30 and 31, 1974." (Bryden was on Palmyra between 1979 and 1980, more than five years after the time in question. "By his own admission," I argued, "the sand shifts on the beach. And if the sand shifts, the configuration and the dimensions of the beach change.") I reminded the jury that Eggers had flatly contradicted Bryden, testifying there were parts of the beach that were dry some six to eight feet *above* the high-water line—leaving room for the beached Zodiac to have remained *out of the water* between 4:30 P.M. on August 30 and dawn on August 31.

Concluding my argument on this critical point, I said, "With the beach in the area in question as irregular as it is, and without knowing precisely where on this area of the beach Jennifer saw the dinghy, and without even knowing whether there was a high high or a low high tide during the hours in question, we're into a never-never land of speculation and conjecture. Nothing more, nothing less."

Consulting my notes, I went on.

The circumstances under which Jennifer left Palmyra with Buck aboard the *Sea Wind*, their failure to notify authorities, Jennifer's lies, and so forth, were all offered by the prosecution as proof of Jennifer's guilt. I had to counter each one.

After reminding the jury of Jennifer's testimony that she *had* wanted to notify the authorities of the Grahams' disappearance (and was overruled by Buck), and that she did *not* want to take the *Sea Wind* off Palmyra, only yielding to Buck when he told her she could either come with him on the *Sea Wind*, sail off by herself on the *Iola*, or stay alone on Palmyra, I argued:

"Now, perhaps your straitlaced Puritans would pontificate how 'the moral thing' for Jennifer to have done would have been to not go with Buck on the *Sea Wind* because the boat did not belong to them. Ah, Puritans. God invested them with so much morality, although the iconoclast H. L. Mencken once observed that a Puritan is not against bullfighting because of the pain it gives the bull, but because of the pleasure it gives the spectators.

"We're not talking here, ladies and gentlemen of the jury, about rigid, theoretical morality. Nor, as I indicated earlier, are we talking about first-grade arithmetic. The necessity of the situation dictated that Jennifer accompany Buck on the *Sea Wind* back to Hawaii. Wouldn't most people in Jennifer's shoes have done the same, identical thing? You might ask yourself that question back in the jury room.

"I'm not saying that anyone is going to accuse Jennifer Jenkins of being Mother Teresa, but if Mother Teresa had been in Jennifer's shoes, would she have elected to sail off alone on the *Iola*, or stay on Palmyra by herself?"

Jennifer testified that she knew it was very wrong to take the *Sea Wind* from Palmyra, I said. "However, the will of Mac Graham gave her some solace."

I pointed out that even though Jennifer knew the round-the-world trip referred to in the will was an earlier trip Mac had taken with Muff, not the one that brought them to Palmyra, and although she readily acknowledged that Mac, in the "other document" referred to in the will, would never have designated her and Buck to be the ones he would authorize to continue the circumnavigation of the globe with the *Sea Wind*, she nonetheless felt this language at least gave her a glimpse into Mac's desires and feelings concerning the boat. It told her that if anything happened to him, he actually had wanted some other person to complete the circumnavigation as long as the *Sea Wind* was brought back to the mainland within two years. "Clearly, a highly unusual clause," I said, "*but nonetheless, these were Mac Graham's words!*" (I reminded the jury that the prosecution, by their stipulation, was not questioning the authenticity of the will.)

"What we have here, ladies and gentlemen of the jury, was a

young woman who found herself in a highly unusual situation not of her own making, where there were no easy answers, no clear-cut road signs posted, no one to categorically and authoritatively spell out for her the one correct course to follow that would not only be morally beyond reproach, but at the same time protective of the man she loved.

"If any of us feel there were moral lapses on Jennifer's part, strained reasoning and leaps of logic of which Aristotle would not have approved, remember: none of us were in this young woman's shoes on the uninhabited atoll of Palmyra in the deep summer of 1974. And I say that under the circumstances, perhaps we should not be too judgmental. I suggest that only someone who is adept at walking between raindrops could have gone through Jennifer's incredible odyssey and ordeal unblemished and unsullied."

As to Jennifer's lying to Lorraine Wollen about how she and Buck had come into possession of the *Sea Wind*, I argued that it was very clear this did *not* show a consciousness of guilt on Jennifer's part. As she testified, she obviously could not tell Mrs. Wollen the truth and still protect Buck Walker's identity.

What about Jennifer's flight in the Ala Wai harbor? Didn't that clearly point to her guilt? "While it is true," I argued, "that flight can show a consciousness of guilt, the question you have to ask yourself is: *guilt as to what*? If someone had just committed, for instance, a robbery of a liquor store, and when confronted by the police runs away, his flight is pretty obviously tied to that robbery.

"But in this case here, Jennifer had reasons to flee that had nothing to do with being involved in the murders of the Grahams. Number one, her having aided and abetted a fugitive from justice. As she testified, as far as she knew, this made her a criminal, too. Secondly, because of Buck's fugitive status, they hadn't notified the authorities what happened to the Grahams, and she knew this was very wrong. And thirdly, she and Buck were on a boat that did not belong to them.

"We know from the evidence that these three things were uppermost in Jennifer's mind, any one of which by itself could cause her—on the spur of the moment and without calm reflection—to flee. When we put all three of these facts together, it is perfectly understandable that Jennifer's first impulse when that Coast Guard cutter was bearing down on her was to get away.

"The law, which is based on the experience of man, has taken cognizance of the fact that one's flight may be completely unrelated to the charges in the case, and Judge King will give you this instruction: 'In your consideration of the evidence of flight you should consider that there may be reasons for this which are fully consistent with innocence.'

"When we remove these reasons for fleeing in the harbor from Jennifer's mind, we have conclusive proof how she reacted, and it is not by flight. When she learned of her indictment in this case, did she make any effort to flee? No. She called her lawyer and turned herself in.

"Everything I've discussed about why Jennifer fled can be distilled into one fact, and I quote Jennifer's testimony on the witness stand. 'What you have to understand is that Buck's state of mind became my state of mind. Buck was a fugitive on the run, and I was running with him.' 'So his reality became your reality?' I asked. And she answered, 'Right.'

"Can anyone be heard to say that that explanation of why Jennifer fled in the harbor is not eminently reasonable?"

Every prosecutor has a pet argument or example he likes to trot out for the jury to prove his point in a circumstantial-evidence case. I wanted to preempt Enoki by presenting at least two of the popular ones, the second of which I discovered from my research in reading summations he had given in two previous circumstantial-evidence jury trials. This thievery may not be gentlemanly, but a murder trial is not a Sunday-afternoon tea party. Briefly interrupting my response to each item of evidence which Enoki cited as pointing to Jennifer's guilt, I said, "Mr. Enoki will probably argue to you in his rebuttal that I am taking each piece of evidence and examining it alone. He'll probably say that in a case of circumstantial evidence you have to look at all the pieces of evidence together, the entire landscape of the evidence, as opposed to looking at each piece individually.

"This would be a sound argument on his part if each one of these pieces of evidence was clear and unequivocal in the direction it pointed. But each and every one of them is suffering from incurable schizophrenia. Just as any number multiplied by zero still equals zero, the pieces of evidence in this case—each ambiguous and blurry in its own right—do not feed off each other and become clear, robust proof of guilt simply by their marriage to each other.

"Or Mr. Enoki may try to invoke an old prosecutorial argument"—this was Enoki's pet argument—"that went out with high-button shoes—but he might resurrect it—that we're dealing with a jigsaw puzzle here, and although certain pieces of the puzzle are missing, you reach a point where there are enough pieces of the puzzle for you to know the complete picture. And he will claim that that picture is one of guilt. Again, the jigsaw-puzzle metaphor would only be applicable if, despite the missing pieces of the puzzle, there were still a considerable number of other pieces clearly and unequivocally showing guilt. But as we've seen, the pieces of the puzzle which the prosecution is relying on to show guilt are susceptible to interpretations other than guilt.

"And we don't just have one or two missing pieces here, ladies and gentlemen. The prosecution's entire case is full of missing pieces, loose ends, speculations, assumptions. Their entire case is brimming, it is overflowing, with reasonable doubt. 'And yet another yet,' Shakespeare said."

I next addressed the issue of Jennifer's alleged statements to Cal Shishido, as well as certain statements she had made to Bernard Leonard and reporter Bruce Benson.

Concerning Shishido's extremely critical testimony that Jennifer told him she and Buck found the dinghy overturned in the waters of the lagoon, I said, "The decided weight of the evidence shows that Cal Shishido is *wrong* about what he says Jennifer told him. And I think I can demonstrate this.

"When I asked Jennifer at this trial what she told Shishido, she said she could not remember her exact words, but the dinghy was definitely found on the beach, and if she mentioned the word 'lagoon' to him, it would have been to inform him they found the dinghy *on the beach in the lagoon*, as opposed to the beach outside of the lagoon, which would be the beach facing the ocean.

"Not only did Jennifer testify at her theft trial, way back in 1975, that the dinghy was found *on the beach*, but there was a stipulation that if Bruce Benson, a reporter from the *Honolulu Advertiser*, were called as a witness, he would testify that on October 31, 1974—just two days after Shishido spoke to Jennifer—Jennifer told him the dinghy was found overturned *on the beach* about a half mile west from where the *Sea Wind* was moored, exactly as she testified at this trial.

"In fact, within minutes prior to Jennifer talking to Shishido, when Mr. Leonard was rowing Jennifer to the Coast Guard cutter, we have his testimony that she also told him they found the dinghy overturned *on the beach*.

"So, we have Jennifer's testimony, we have Bruce Benson's stipulated testimony, and we have Bernard Leonard's testimony that Jennifer said it was the beach. It appears that Shishido just didn't understand what Jennifer told him, or he neglected to get down her exact words on this point.

"We know he did not tape-record their conversation, he has since destroyed his notes, and he concluded that in his brief two-and-a-half-page report of the two-and-a-half-hour interview he condensed thousands of her words into a small number of his. To compound the problem, it had to be obvious to you folks that Mr. Shishido is anything but a precise, meticulous individual. Compounding the problem even further, Jennifer was speaking very quickly to Shishido when she made her statement. Shishido admitted this on the witness stand. Under all these circumstances, how can Mr. Enoki expect you to treat Mr. Shishido's words that Jennifer told him *the water of the lagoon*, as opposed to *the beach* or *the beach of the lagoon*, as gospel?

"Let me ask you this: if the rest of your life were hanging in the balance, would you feel you could confidently rely on Calvin Shishido's very brief summary of what you told him about an involved series of events?

"I don't accuse Calvin Shishido of a deliberate distortion of what Jennifer told him. I think Shishido was an honest witness. Things like this just happen. And they happen a lot.

"It happened with Mr. Leonard, also Jennifer tells him they

found the dinghy on the beach, and that she thinks it probably capsized *by* Paradise Island." I pointed out that this was corroborated by the stipulated testimony of reporter Bruce Benson. Jennifer told Benson that because of the direction of the wind (from the southeast), she figured that the dinghy had flipped over *around* Paradise Island. Yet, "twelve years later, Mr. Leonard's recollection of what Jennifer told him is that they found the dinghy *on* Paradise Island.

"Jennifer tells Shishido, Benson, and Leonard the same story, and none of them being human tape recorders, they each recall her words slightly differently. And this is just typical. It's common knowledge that even if you tell the same, identical story to five people, you're going to get five slightly different versions of what you said.

"You know," I went on, smiling, "I really loved Cal Shishido's statement, in answer to my question, that he felt it was better for you folks to rely on his recollection of what Jennifer told him than to listen to a tape-recorded conversation of what she told him. You have to like someone who can make a remark like that. Someone who is calculating and duplicitous would not be capable of such a delightful remark.

"One final footnote to the issue of what Jennifer told Shishido. Mr. Enoki argued that Shishido would never have had the Zodiac motor inspected for salt water unless he was told by Jennifer that the Zodiac was found *in* the water.

"But if Jennifer told him the Zodiac was found overturned on the *beach*, why wouldn't he likewise want to have the motor inspected? Being *overturned*, wouldn't the most reasonable inference be that it had capsized in the water and floated to shore, and of course gotten water in the motor in the process? So wouldn't Shishido have still wanted to check that out to see if Jennifer was telling him the truth?"

With respect to Enoki's argument that after Jennifer heard Ken White's testimony at her theft trial that the Zodiac motor had no signs of ever having been exposed to salt water, she changed her story about where the dinghy was found, I argued: "But we know that's not so because *long before* Ken White testified at her theft trial, she told Mr. Leonard and Bruce Benson that the dinghy was found *on the beach*."

Next, there was Jennifer's lie to Shishido that the *Iola* had gone aground on the coral reef in the channel while being towed by the *Sea Wind*. "This, of course, was not true," I said. "But I want you to consider closely the observation I have to make about this untruth."

I reminded the jury of Buck's telling Jennifer that if they told the truth that they had sunk the *Iola*, people would naturally think they had stolen the *Sea Wind*, and that this reasoning appealed to Jennifer because she felt she hadn't stolen the boat. "This is not to excuse the lie. It's only to put it into its proper perspective. I'm not playing word games with you folks, but a lie to cover up the perpetration of a wrong is markedly different from a lie to avoid being accused of something you feel you didn't do.

"I can just hear Mr. Enoki now in his rebuttal. 'Mr. Bugliosi has an explanation for everything Jennifer Jenkins did, and this just isn't realistic.' He'll probably say something like that." (I knew the jury would be thinking the same precise thing.)

I turned toward the prosecution's table.

"Are you going to say that, Elliot?" I asked playfully. The pleasant-faced prosecutor did not return my smile and, of course, said nothing. "You're not going to tell me?" I paused, in a brief moment of levity.

"My response to that allegation is that *the reason* I have an explanation for everything Jennifer did is that based on the evidence she is innocent. And being innocent, there *naturally* is a valid, innocent explanation for everything she did. If she were guilty, there would not be."

There were a few remaining incriminating statements of Jennifer's to Shishido that needed explanation: one being her telling him that Buck and she had rationalized Mac's supposed remark to Buck to "make themselves at home" on the *Sea Wind* to mean that the Grahams wanted Buck and Jennifer to take possession of the boat if anything happened to them.

"Of course, on its face, Jennifer's rationalization, if it had been a serious one on her part, would have been ludicrous beyond words. If she meant what she said, the only defense we could offer in this case would be not guilty by reason of insanity.

"But what she told Shishido was not a rationalization on her part. It was, of course, nothing but a lie. Jennifer testified that when Shishido asked her why she and Roy Allen were on the boat, she could not tell him the truth—that Buck Walker had elected to take the *Sea Wind* instead of the *Iola* in continuing his flight from the law. She said she was trying to answer a question she couldn't answer truthfully and these words just came out.

"And I say that the absurd nature of what she told Shishido is illuminating in that it is not the remark of a shrewd and cunning woman, but rather the remark of an innocent and vulnerable young woman who was scared and confused."

I now met, head-on, Jennifer's perjury at her prior trial. "With respect to Jennifer's lying under oath at her theft trial about the *Iola* going aground while being towed out of the channel, and being left behind, Mr. Enoki argued that this shows Jennifer cannot be trusted to tell the truth now.

"In other words, once a liar, always a liar. The only problem with that type of reasoning is that I don't believe any human being *always* tells the truth. I'll wager every penny I have on that proposition. *No human being always tells the truth,*" I repeated very loudly in the packed but quiet courtroom. My intonation made very clear that I was referring to every single person in the courtroom, including judge and jury, and I was openly challenging the jury to take conscious recognition, for Jennifer's benefit, of this incontrovertible fact.

"They may *say* they always tell the truth, but they don't. And if we were to accept the notion that once a liar, always a liar, then we could never believe anyone.

"But I guess the position of the prosecution is that since Jennifer lied once *under oath*, before another jury, she should never be believed again on that witness stand as long as she lives.

"Charge her with the assassination of President John F. Kennedy," I roared. "If she denies it, don't believe her. Of course she did it. She and Oswald were just like this," I said, thrusting my crossed right index and middle fingers into the air.*

In reminding the jury that Jennifer had lied about the *Iola's* going aground because one of her lawyers had advised her that if she contradicted the statement she had already given the FBI, the theft trial would go badly for her, I noted: "You know, the prosecution didn't call, on rebuttal, this former lawyer to deny this.

"In any event, when a human being is faced with the dilemma of being innocent of the crime they are charged with committing, but if they tell the truth as to a particular matter, chances are they will be wrongfully convicted, so they lie, is that the type of situation where they should never, ever be believed again under oath? Obviously not, ladies and gentlemen."

I sipped my honey-and-lemon blend, pausing for several moments. In having first addressed myself to explaining away all the negative evidence against Jennifer, I hoped I had laid a foundation for the jury to be much more receptive to the next part of my argument.

"LADIES AND GENTLEMEN of the jury, at this time I want to switch gears and discuss with you the many things that point irresistibly to Jennifer's innocence, always bearing in mind that under the law, because of the presumption of innocence, we had no burden of proof whatsoever to prove innocence.

"Firstly, of course, we have Jennifer's testimony. She did not have to testify at all. Many defendants don't. They don't want to have their version of what happened cross-examined by the prosecutor.

"I think it was clear from her demeanor that Jennifer, when she

*Little could I possibly know (or even wildly imagine) that just six months later in London, England, in an exact replica of a Dallas federal courtroom, and after nearly five months of preparation as intense as I've ever done for any murder case in my career, I would be "prosecuting" Lee Harvey Oswald for the assassination of President John F. Kennedy. The twenty-one-hour British television "docutrial" had no script, no actors, a real United States federal judge and Dallas jury, the actual lay and expert witnesses in the case, and a prominent defense attorney (Gerry Spence) representing Oswald.

took that stand, had no hesitation about testifying. In effect, she said to the prosecutor: ask me any question you want. And you can phrase your questions in as artful a way as you know how in your effort to make me look bad. I don't care, because I have nothing to hide. So go ahead and cross-examine me.

"Cross-examination is the principal weapon known to the law for separating truth from falsehood. If a defendant, or any witness, is lying on that stand, cross-examination is the means provided by the law to expose this fact. I don't mean by getting the defendant to confess on the witness stand. Only Hollywood, the chief ped-dler of illusion in our society, portrays that type of thing.

"I mean by making it obvious to the jury, by things such as major discrepancies in the defendant's testimony, the defendant's not having credible answers to many questions, the defendant's demeanor on the witness stand, et cetera, et cetera, that the defen-dant is not telling the truth.

"A perfect example would be to compare Mrs. Leonard on that witness stand with Jennifer. The contrast was dramatic. You were watching Mrs. Leonard, and I think it was pretty apparent she wasn't always telling the truth.

"Let's look at Jennifer. Elliot Enoki is a seasoned and experi-enced prosecutor and cross-examiner. Mr. Enoki cross-examined Jennifer for almost an entire day. His purpose, of course, was to destroy her credibility. But not once did he demonstrate to you folks by his cross-examination that Jennifer Jenkins was not telling the complete truth on that witness stand.

"Jennifer's testimony had the strength of a suit of armor. Why? Because she was telling the truth. And I believe the truth is mighty, and shines by its own light. And that's why it prevailed.

"Jennifer Jenkins's unscathed and undamaged testimony that she had nothing at all to do with the murders of the Grahams is powerful evidence of her innocence. But there was much more evidence at this trial of Jennifer's innocence."

There were the several witnesses testifying to Jennifer's nonvio-lent character. "What's the relevance of character evidence? I think we can look at our own lives for the answer. Do we not conduct our affairs and relate to others on the assumption that people will continue to act as they have in the past? And if they have been of good character in the past, they will continue to be good in the future? That they will not suddenly and without warning act out of character?

"Likewise, I would think that with exceedingly rare exceptions, if someone commits or participates in a vicious, cold-blooded, premeditated murder, somewhere in his or her past, *somewhere*, they will have said or done *something* that gave a hint to those around them that the potential for this type of violence was coursing through their blood. *Something* on the surface would have betrayed the darkness and ugliness that stirred within the recesses of their mind, their soul. In fact, usually, as is the situation with Buck Walker, you don't even have to look very hard. Their background is openly pockmarked with aggressive and oftentimes violent behavior.

"When we look at Jennifer Jenkins, not only isn't there one molecule of evidence that she was a violent or even potentially violent person, but all of the evidence is one hundred and eighty degrees to the contrary. By all accounts, she is a particularly peaceful, nonviolent person. A kind, loving, and very giving person who respects and values the life of her fellow human beings."

Reading from sections of the transcript I had marked and underlined, I reviewed the testimony of our character witnesses: Debbie Noland, Rick Schulze, Leilah Burns, and Lawrence Seltzer.

"Though perhaps most people are nonviolent, if you were to describe them, you wouldn't bother to mention this characteristic, because in a civilized society, people are expected to be nonviolent. If someone were to ask you to describe one of your friends, you wouldn't say: 'Mary? A nice person. One of my best friends. Very nonviolent.' You wouldn't say that. People are expected to be nonviolent.

"But with Jennifer, her peacefulness and abhorrence to violence were *so* obvious and pronounced that it was a personality trait of hers.

"Most people, when they've been visited by any type of scandal, discover that their friends seem to vanish. They become social lepers. Not so with Jennifer's friends. Why? Because these people feel they know Jennifer, and because they feel they know her, they know she couldn't possibly have been involved in this monstrous act.

"The prosecutors, during their cross-examination of our character witnesses, implied by their questions that even if Jennifer was an essentially nonviolent person, in late August 1974 she was in a life-endangering situation, and therefore felt compelled to act in a violent way.

"But there's no evidence of approaching starvation in this case with respect to Buck and Jennifer in late August 1974. We've already discussed that issue *ad nauseam*. I'll close this issue with this quote from the transcript. This is a question by Mr. Enoki of his *own* witness, Mr. Bryden: 'It's also true that if one were on Palmyra, and if one was willing to eat what was there, you wouldn't starve to death on Palmyra?' *That's Mr. Enoki, the prosecutor, talking*. His witness agreed.

"So just what type of life-endangering situation was Jennifer confronted with on Palmyra that would have changed her character for nonviolence?

"What does all this character evidence mean?" I asked. "Well, let me put it this way. What would it have meant to you folks if in their rebuttal the prosecution had called witnesses to that stand who testified that Jennifer was a very aggressive person, prone to violence? Wouldn't that have meant a heck of a lot to you? And if it would have, as I think it surely would, shouldn't the evidence that she is nonviolent mean just as much to you?

"In our case here, although the prosecution was entitled, under the law, to rebut the testimony of the character witnesses for the defense, *they never called one single witness to do so*! And they were placed on notice that we intended to offer a character defense.

"I suggest that the most reasonable inference why they did not call any rebuttal witnesses is that even with the FBI as their investigators, they couldn't find any. None existed. Even Houdini couldn't pull a rabbit out of the hat when there wasn't any rabbit in the hat."

After referring to an instruction on character evidence Judge King would later give, I pressed forward.

"There are degrees of everything in life, ladies and gentlemen of the jury, including murder. Though the result of all homicides is the same—the person is equally dead—this was a *particularly villainous* murder. On a scale of one to ten, this was a ten, and I've prosecuted a lot of murder cases. We presented credible evidence from that witness stand that Jennifer Jenkins is a *particularly peaceful* and nonviolent person. So we're dealing with the outer margins in both the type of crime involved and the type of person accused of committing that crime, making the probability even greater that Jennifer would never commit a crime such as this.

"The murder of poor Muff Graham was not a typical murder. What must have happened to Mrs. Graham when she was mercilessly put to death is so horrible that it's difficult for the average mind to contemplate.

"And as if that ultimate horror were not enough, since the container is really a little too small for a human body—I know this is horrible, but we're talking about murder now, and there's a lot at stake here—maybe a chain saw or the like was used on Mrs. Graham. And then the fire, the attempted incineration of the body.

"What took place is chilling testimony to the capacity for absolute evil in some human beings. Whoever committed this incredibly horrendous murder—and I say Buck Walker and Buck Walker alone did it—had to have been rotten to the core. Rotten and bad and vicious right down to the soles of his feet.

"You've all heard the expression that a tree is known by its fruits. The thorn and the thistle do not bear delicious cherries. And I say that a life of compassion and peacefulness like Jennifer's does not suddenly produce a harvest of unspeakable horror. I submit to you that the strong evidence we offered of Jennifer's character for nonviolence is very meaningful evidence of her innocence.

"I guess one could say at this juncture in my argument, 'If the prosecution's case is as weak as you say it is, Mr. Bugliosi, aren't you belaboring your point? Why continue to argue additional points?'

"That might be a valid conclusion if the rest of Jennifer Jenkins's life were not hanging in the balance, and if there were not two other people in this equation. They sit stoically at the counsel table, taking notes. And when I get through, one of them, Mr. Enoki, is going to get up and tell you why he still feels you should convict Miss Jenkins. They're not about to fold their tent and say, 'Let's go home. We agree with Mr. Bugliosi.' They still intend to go on. And that's why I must.

"In addition to, number one, the unscathed testimony of Jennifer, and number two, the uncontroverted testimony of the character witnesses, there are various pieces of evidence in this case that point to a consciousness of innocence on Jennifer's part. And I want to enumerate them for you.

"Just as guilt leaves the psychological mark which we call consciousness of guilt, innocence leaves a mark we can call consciousness of innocence."

I was about to attempt to turn the tables on the prosecution, using an argument that they (and Len Weinglass) didn't think could possibly be made in this case—that beneath the topsoil indications of guilt in all Jennifer said and did, much of her conduct and many of her statements actually pointed, upon closer scrutiny, in the direction of innocence.

"When a person is guilty of a crime," I began, "he acts the way we would expect a guilty person to act. Guilty. But now and then, even though the person is guilty, there may be one act of his that inexplicably and strangely enough appears to be the act of an innocent person. I'm not referring to a guilty person feigning innocence. That happens all the time. I'm referring to a genuine act that appears to be an act that only an innocent person would do. It's not frequent that you will find this phenomenon, but now and then you might find one such act, and in rare situations, possibly even two or three such acts.

"But ladies and gentlemen, when time and time again, as I will shortly point out to you, a person acts in an innocent way, doesn't it stand to reason that they *are* innocent?

"In our case here, although Jennifer did several regrettable things that were induced by the circumstances in which she found herself, on occasion after occasion she acted in a way that only an innocent person would have acted. Guilty people simply don't do that. If they did, they wouldn't be guilty.

"Some of the points I'm going to mention are not the kind that hit you over the head, as it were, with their obvious nature. However, though they are more subtle, *they nevertheless furnish us with snapshot glimpses of an innocent mind.*

"First, there's Jennifer's diary. If one committed a crime and made entries in their diary, I would think it would be for one of two purposes. Number one, to write to themselves; that is, for their own eyes only. If this were their purpose, chances are they would want to tell the truth. You can't fool your own self.

"Obviously, there's nothing in Jennifer's diary stating or even remotely implying that she was involved in the murder of the Grahams.

"The second purpose would be to write the diary not for your own eyes, but for other people's eyes; that is, to deceive, or to cover up, as Mr. Enoki says. And I say that if Jennifer were involved in these murders and made the entries in her diary for other people's eyes, she obviously would have written them in such a manner as to try to eliminate all suspicion and cast herself in a good light. With that state of mind, if you know, for instance, that you've written whole paragraphs in your diary on common, everyday events, such as baking a cake, or a pie, or reading a book, as Jennifer did in her diary, you're certainly not going to write *less* about the loss of human life!

"Jennifer wrote just one word, 'Tragedy,' about the apparent death of the Grahams. There's simply no attempt by her to deceive, and thereby cover up. Why? Because she had nothing to cover up.

"Another point on this same issue. If Jennifer were involved in these murders and her diary entries were meant for other people's eyes, wouldn't she have dramatized her anguish over the death of the Grahams? Instead, there's no attempt to dramatize in that diary."

I now attempted to explain and possibly even turn to our advantage Jennifer's September 4 entry ("We all grow fatter and fatter on ham and cheese and pancakes and turkey and chili and all the things we hadn't had in so long"). Len felt the entry, just a few days after Mac and Muff's death, was "dreadful. It contradicts everything Jennifer has said. It makes her look terrible."

"The other characteristic we could expect her diary entries to have if she were involved in these murders and these entries were meant for other people's eyes would be a tone of considerable sensitivity. *She never in a million years would have depicted herself as somewhat insensitive, as her entry about eating the Grahams' food arguably comes across as being. Never in a million years."*

But even given the surface insensitivity of Jennifer's September 4 diary entry, I asked the jury to ponder for a moment.

"What was Jennifer supposed to do? Not eat the Grahams' food? Let it rot, and try to live off the fish in the ocean?"

Although, if I had had my druthers, I would have preferred not resorting to it, there was one somewhat indelicate way to force the jury to personalize what Jennifer had done, a reality I felt virtually every juror had experienced.

"If you still feel it was insensitive, what about the rather common phenomenon of even close relatives of one who has just been buried eating the finest foods at family gatherings just an hour, if that, after the funeral? Is that a fact, or is that not a fact? Think about it. This is not to suggest that there is no deep and profound grief. But the eating of fine foods at this seemingly inappropriate time is a fact.

"Looking from a different aspect at that September 4 diary entry about enjoying the Grahams' food, if Mr. Enoki argues that it shows no grief on her part over what happened to the Grahams, then what about the August 30 entry, written by the same person, Jennifer, that says, 'Tragedy'?

"If he argues that the September 4 entry really reflects the essence of Jennifer, the way she felt, then why shouldn't the August 30th entry also really reflect the way she is and the way she viewed the death of the Grahams? And if she viewed their deaths as a 'tragedy,' she wouldn't be likely to be the murderer, would she? In other words, Mr. Enoki cannot pick and choose.

"I say that when we apply common sense and simple logic to our analysis of the diary entries, the very nature of those entries is circumstantial evidence of innocence. If Jennifer Jenkins were guilty, those entries would not read the way they do."

Another point indicating a consciousness of innocence, I observed, was that if Jennifer had been involved in the murders and had fabricated her story about believing that the Grahams had met an accidental death when their Zodiac *capsized in the water* of the lagoon, "even a child would know it would be much more consistent with her fabricated story if she had said they found the capsized dinghy somewhere in the *water* of the lagoon. But Jennifer, from the very beginning, has said that no part of the dinghy was in the water. The fact that she did not say they found the Zodiac in the water shows an unmistakable consciousness of innocence.

"She told you she found the Zodiac on the beach, with no part of it in the water, because that's exactly where she found it. And Jennifer's testimony is corroborated by the prosecution's own witness, boat expert Ken White, who testified that there was no salt in the Zodiac's motor. It was completely clean. The reason for this, of course, is that the dinghy never overturned in the water of the lagoon.

"The most reasonable inference is that Buck Walker overturned the dinghy himself on the shore, after dropping the bodies in the lagoon."

To be extra convincing to Jennifer, why, I asked, didn't Walker overturn the dinghy in the water of the lagoon? "If he had, how was *he* supposed to get to shore? By hitching a ride from a passing shark? Remember, people feared the sharks in that lagoon."

There was further consciousness of innocence, I argued, regarding the Lorraine Wollen incident: "If one had been involved in the murder of the owners of a boat, would one be likely to invite a casual acquaintance—someone you obviously could not expect to protect you from the authorities—on board that boat, as Jennifer did with Mrs. Wollen? Particularly when the pictures of the murder victims are still on the wall, and it's at least possible that the visitor will ask, as Mrs. Wollen did, who they are? I don't think so.

"Also, Jennifer wanting to keep pictures of the Grahams on the boat, and otherwise keep the interior of the boat as they left it, is evidence of how she felt about them. That obviously is not the state of mind a killer would have toward his victims. All of this reflects a consciousness of innocence.

"Some of you might say, 'Well, Buck was also on the boat when Lorraine Wollen came over. We know Buck is guilty, yet he also apparently went along with those pictures of the Grahams being on the wall. Doesn't that dilute the argument?'

"Well, number one, Jennifer, not Buck, invited Lorraine Wollen over. Secondly, Buck had a real problem. As much as he could afford to, he had to appear innocent to Jennifer. He had to maintain the myth that the Grahams had died an accidental death. I think we can assume that if Jennifer had been involved in these murders with Buck, those pictures would have come off that wall.

"Going on, there is more evidence showing a consciousness of innocence on her part. And remember, I believe that other than a guilty person feigning innocence, guilty people don't act innocent. They act the way they are—guilty.

"The act of reregistering the *Sea Wind* was the single most affirmative act to conceal the fact that the *Sea Wind* did not belong to Buck and Jennifer. That was the official change of ownership on that boat."

Buck Walker, guilty of the murders, had every reason to reregister that boat, I added. "Jennifer, being innocent, had no such compelling reason, and she refused Buck's request that she do so.

"These are the registeration papers of the *Sea Wind*," I said, holding them up in front of the jury. "'Owner: Roy Allen. Co-owner . . .' There's nothing there. And the acquisition of this boat was obviously the very reason why these murders were committed. But Jennifer's name *does not appear on these papers*."

I admitted that the next point I was going to argue smacked of high camp. "But it's a major, major point which demonstrates Jennifer's consciousness of innocence," I said.

I went over Jennifer's learning from Joel Peters, on the morning of October 29, that the authorities were looking for Buck and her; their rowing to shore; their hearing Buck's dogs barking on the deck of the *Sea Wind*; Jennifer's suggesting they go back to the *Sea Wind*, put the dogs below, and bring Joel's laundry back to him; and Buck's exclaiming to Jennifer, "Are you crazy? Leave me off at the dock first."

"So, Jennifer drops Buck off, goes back to the *Sea Wind* and puts the dogs below, then takes Joel's laundry back to him. As you know,

Joel Peters testified that Jennifer did, in fact, return his laundry, and shortly thereafter, he became aware of her being pursued in the harbor by the authorities.

"Could this set of circumstances possibly show a stronger consciousness of innocence? If Jennifer had been involved with Buck Walker in the murder of the Grahams, under these circumstances, even returning to the *Sea Wind* to put the dogs below would have been completely out of the question. It would have been preposterous.

"But bringing someone's *laundry* back? As the expression goes, 'Give me a break.' Maybe, *maybe* someone who in their mind is only guilty, like Jennifer, of having aided and abetted a fugitive from justice might do this. But *not* someone who is guilty of having committed two murders.

"There's no clearer, more dramatic, more unequivocal example of the difference between Buck and Jennifer in this case than what happened at this moment. Buck, knowing he had committed murder, did precisely what anyone in his shoes would have done. He had Jennifer drop him off at the dock, and he took off.

"Can there be any question that if Jennifer had also been guilty of these murders, she would have gotten off the dinghy with him?

"We're all aware that the right picture speaks much more eloquently than any words. The Berlin Wall comes to mind because there was a picture of it recently in the newspaper.

"You know, whole forests die every year to feed the printing presses on both sides of the Iron Curtain—trillions of words being written to sell the virtues of democracy vis-à-vis communism and vice versa.

"But the Berlin Wall, which the Communists erected, tells the whole story without one single word being written or uttered. The concrete wall, with barbed wire and armed guards on top, is there not to keep people from getting in, but to keep them from getting out.

"Need anything further really be said?

"Likewise, no words of mine could evoke the picture I ask you to visualize in your mind's eye. The authorities are in pursuit of

Buck and Jennifer, and she knows it, yet there she is, rowing the dinghy to return someone's laundry. Doesn't that say quite a bit, folks? I mean, I think it does. I think it does.

"Jennifer returned that laundry because—isn't it so very obvious?—*she was not running away from any murder.*

"Even if you don't accept that reasoning, which, I submit to you, is inherently sound in its logic, don't you at least have to accept the following:

"Would a human being who has such an exquisite and uncommon concern for a fellow human being that even when her own welfare is in jeopardy, she still finds it within herself to worry about returning another's laundry, of all things, would she be the type of person who would sit down and cold-bloodedly plan the brutal murder of two precious human beings?"

I allowed the question to hang in the air a moment. "The answer is almost too obvious to state. It's a loud, ringing, unequivocal, *no*, ladies and gentlemen of the jury. *The answer is no*," I shouted out.

I charged that the prosecution throughout the trial had sought to portray Buck Walker and Jennifer Jenkins as a Pacific Islands version of the legendary desperado pair of the thirties, Bonnie and Clyde.

"Well, Buck Walker turned out to be a Clyde Barrow, but Jennifer Jenkins ain't no Bonnie. It just didn't work at this trial. It was like trying to rivet a nail into a custard pie. It didn't stick."

I spelled out, slowly, what the charges in this case really meant. "The murders are alleged to be premeditated murders. At a minimum, this means that with cold reflection Jennifer planned, she *planned* to eliminate Mac and Muff Graham. That she helped make the decision on the time they would die, the place, the deadly instruments to be used.

"Premeditation means she knew, in advance, the horrible, ghastly death that Mac and Muff Graham would suffer, and in effect, she said: '*I don't care. Let's do it to them.*' That's what premeditation means.

"This young woman who cared enough to return someone's laundry even though she was being pursued by the authorities didn't care if the lives of Mac and Muff Graham, people she liked and was friendly with, were snuffed out like ants on a sidewalk.

"Can the ineffaceable mark of guilt be placed on the head of Jennifer Jenkins? I say that such a thought is a perversion of all the principles of logic and common sense that we know.

"Let's go on," I said, amplifying on Jennifer's consciousness of innocence.

Her conduct during her interrogation by the FBI on the day of her arrest was that of an innocent person, I maintained. "Not only doesn't she want to talk to a lawyer, not only does she not remain silent, not only is she not closed-lipped and evasive, she can't wait to blurt out what happened on Palmyra. She *wanted* to tell Shishido what happened. She was so eager she even interrupted him when he was advising her of her rights.

"Jennifer not only spoke freely to Shishido, she also gave an interview to the reporter from the *Honolulu Advertiser.* When I asked her on the stand why she talked to the reporter, she said, 'Because he wanted to talk to me.' I'm sure if the League of Women Voters had called her up, she would have talked to them, too.

"Snapshot glimpses, ladies and gentlemen, of an innocent mind.

"Another piece of evidence pointing to Jennifer's innocence is this. Chances are the bodies of the Grahams were disposed of in the lagoon in the same area as where the remains were found. A heavy container would not be likely to be floating in all types of directions in the lagoon. We know there wasn't too much motion or energy in that lagoon, the lagoon being placid even when the surrounding sea was tempestuous.

"Mr. Shishido testified that on October 29, 1974, Jennifer told him the location where the Zodiac was found overturned. And lo and behold, seven years later, Sharon Jordan finds Muff Graham's remains in the same general area.

"Now, if Jennifer knew where the bodies had been disposed of, would she have directed the FBI to the location where the bodies were likely to be found? If someone commits a murder and hides the body, do they turn around and tell the authorities where the body might be?"

I let this argument sink in.

Then went on: "I've been discussing here the many examples of Jennifer's conduct which show a consciousness of innocence, and the fact that guilty people don't act innocent.

"What about the reverse argument Mr. Enoki might make that if Jennifer were innocent, she would not have acted in some instances the way she did? In other words, innocent people don't act guilty.

"Well, ladies and gentlemen of the jury, the reverse argument cannot be fairly or comfortably applied to Jennifer's conduct in this case for the simple reason that, in a real sense, Jennifer *did* have a guilty state of mind, *but not as to the murder in this case*. Rather, it was due to her helping a fugitive from justice escape, her not having reported the disappearance of the Grahams, and the realization that she was on a boat that did not belong to her.

"I say that Jennifer Jenkins's manifestation of a consciousness of innocence has continued right up to the present time in this courtroom. For her to have been guilty of these two hellish murders and testify the way she did on that witness stand for over two days would require the performance and acting virtuosity of a Sarah Bernhardt.

"Jennifer Jenkins is not such an actress. She is a rather vulnerable, decent young woman whose misfortune it was to have gotten mixed up with the wrong man. As we travel this winding and uphill road of life, things like this happen.

"Perhaps Sartre, the French existentialist, might not agree, but I submit to you that Jennifer got caught up in a set of circumstances beyond her control. These circumstances, in a few instances, caused her to act in a manner not compatible with her true nature—acts which, in retrospect, she is not supremely proud of. But again, you know as well as I that things like this happen in life. When you enter that jury room to commence your deliberations, you don't have to leave your human experiences at the portals to that room. You can take them with you, as I know you will.

"Put succinctly, Jennifer Jenkins fell in love with the wrong man, a man on the run. I hate to resort to clichés, but this case is a classic, textbook example of a good, decent person being the victim of circumstances."

"WHAT I WANT to discuss now are three mistakes that Buck Walker made which, because of their nature, point towards Jennifer's innocence. And because there were only four people on Palmyra, and two are dead, since these mistakes point towards Jennifer's innocence, they necessarily point *exclusively* to the guilt of Buck Walker, inasmuch as he is the only one who remains.

"In other words, if the prosecution can play their game of four minus two leaves two, this is a variation thereof: four minus three leaves one.

"One mistake was probably instinctive in nature; the other two, because he committed these murders alone, he was literally forced to make."

I explained that Walker's instinctive mistake (which I said was merely "something for you to consider") was his invariably referring to himself alone with respect to the *Sea Wind*. "He told Larry Seibert and Seibert's boss, Joseph Stuart, '*I* won the boat in a chess game,' and he told Joel Peters not once but twice, 'That's *my* boat.' Not 'That's *our* boat,' but 'That's *my* boat.' Why did Walker find it so natural to say 'I' and 'my' and so unnatural to say 'we' and 'our'? Because he, and he alone, committed the murders in this case. And I think it's a reasonable inference that knowing this he instinctively said 'I,' not 'we.'"

Concerning the second mistake, I told the jury that Enoki wanted them to believe that the burning of the skull and the fire in the container were evidence of the murder of Muff Graham. "Just as war sometimes makes strange bedfellows, trials sometimes do also," I said, explaining that I also wanted them to accept that conclusion, but for different reasons.

"Let's look at that evidence," I said. "On the skull of Muff Graham there is a whitened area—which Dr. Uberlaker called calcinations—over the left eye and extending back about the size of my hand. Uberlaker said this calcination was a localized burning resulting from 'extreme heat being applied to the bone.' Dr. Stephens, the coroner, called it a 'localized burn of high intensity.' Both doctors stated that an acetylene torch could have been the burning agent."

I reminded the jurors that Mac's workshop had an acetylene torch.

"Then there was the testimony of William Tobin, the FBI metallurgist who conducted several tests on the container and concluded there had been a fire *inside* the container fueled by a hydrocarbon accelerant, such as gasoline or kerosene.

"I think we can safely assume that Buck Walker would not have had any reason to start that fire inside the container if Muff Graham's body was not in the container at the time of the fire.

"Now, what's the significance of all this? Winston Churchill once said that at the bottom of every problem, no matter how complex, is common sense.

"This problem isn't even complex. What conceivable reason under the moon would Buck Walker have had to use an acetylene torch and to set an already dead body on fire if it was not to prevent the identification of that body in the event the authorities found it prior to total decomposition? Without the identification of the body, the chances of a prosecution would be considerably diminished. Hopefully, the fire would burn all the flesh, thereby eliminating Muff Graham's fingerprints and other identifying characteristics such as scars and moles, and also consume all the teeth, another mode of identification. Yet we know that this did not happen in this case."

I read the portion of Dr. Uberlaker's testimony in which he stated that other than the burning over the left eye socket and "possible slight evidence of burning" on the right side of the lower jawbone, he found no signs of burning on any of the other bones.

I then read Dr. Stephens's testimony that he would have expected to find evidence of burning on other bones had someone poured gasoline on the entire body and set it afire, as Buck obviously did—but he too had found only the two small areas of localized burning on *part* of the skull.

"Now, if Buck Walker had kept that fire going long enough,

there unquestionably would have been evidence of burning throughout the skeletal remains of Muff Graham.

"We don't know how long Muff Graham's body was on fire. But one thing we do know. *Buck Walker obviously decided not to complete the burning.* We have absolute, conclusive evidence of this. He appears to have started the fire, saw that it was taking too long, so he discontinued his effort.*

"Now I ask you. If Buck Walker had decided to burn the body, why did he, as the physical evidence shows, abort his effort?

"There's only one logical reason that comes to mind. *He must have been rushed for time.* And that begs the question. Why in the world would Buck Walker have any need to feel rushed for time on a deserted Pacific island where there's only one other person on the island with him? I repeat: why would he feel rushed for time? Because this other person on the island, Jennifer Jenkins, was not a party to what he was doing."

I pointed out that in addition to the increased likelihood of Jennifer's smelling and seeing smoke the longer the fire continued, "Buck had to do everything outside of her presence, and he never had unlimited time with which he could justifiably remain outside of her presence. I say that the strong evidence of rushing, which Buck Walker was forced to do, is itself persuasive circumstantial evidence that Buck Walker acted alone in committing the murders in this case.

"The third mistake of Walker's is an extremely strong and powerful piece of circumstantial evidence that points to the innocence of Jennifer Jenkins. It is so strong that even if there were nothing else pointing towards her innocence, this alone, I feel, would be enough to prove her innocence. Let's take it step by step."

My buildup, I could see, had piqued the interest of the jury. I had promised them an explosive inference, and I had better deliver.

"Buck Walker put Mrs. Graham's body in that container," I said, pointing to the aluminum box that had remained in the court-

---

*The jury had heard testimony that it takes heat in excess of 1,000 degrees Fahrenheit for approximately four hours to cremate a human body. Buck Walker most probably did not know this.

room, "and sank it to the bottom of the lagoon for one obvious reason, and another not so obvious reason.

"The obvious reason, of course, is that he wanted to do whatever he could to hide the body from the authorities. Without a body, Buck Walker had to know that the case against him would be much weaker; in his mind, perhaps nonexistent.

"But was the bottom of the lagoon the best place to conceal Muff's body? The answer is unquestionably no. Why? Because Buck Walker had to know that as soon as the Grahams' disappearance became known, the authorities would search for them, as we know they did. And the very first place they would search would be the island and the lagoon, which is again exactly what they did. In fact, he would have to know that the island and lagoon would be the *only* places they would search, since you can't search the ocean.

"Moreover, Buck Walker also had to know that the authorities might find the container, and even if they didn't, he had to know there was always the chance the container and its grisly cargo might someday surface on its own, as it did. So, clearly, the lagoon would not be the best place to bury it.

"Where would the best place be? Just as clearly, far out at sea, where the body—like thousands of other bodies throughout the ages—would be lost forever. An unprotected body in the ocean would normally be consumed by sea life. For eternal secrecy, the sea is the ultimate graveyard. It couldn't possibly be more obvious. Even someone with not too much furniture upstairs would know this.

"What I'm saying, ladies and gentlemen, is that even a simpleminded murderer would know this. All the more so Buck Walker, an exceedingly adept murderer who almost pulled off two perfect murders, leaving very little incriminating evidence behind.

"If Buck Walker committed these murders with Jennifer Jenkins, if they participated together in these murders, doesn't common sense dictate, doesn't common sense tell you, that disposing of the Grahams' bodies far out at sea is the obvious thing they would have done? It would have been so easy for them to have transported the bodies on the *Sea Wind* until they were hundreds of miles out at sea and then thrown the bodies overboard. That way they could have been virtually one hundred percent sure the bodies would never be found.

"But this wasn't done because the perpetrator of these murders was not a 'they,' it was a 'he.' Buck Walker alone committed these murders."

What I said next was an indispensable part of the chain of logic, and therefore *had* to be stated, but it was so self-evident I confessed to the jury it was embarrassing even to utter the words. I explained that Walker obviously couldn't take the murdered bodies out to sea when he and Jennifer left Palmyra on the *Sea Wind* because Jennifer would then know Buck had killed them.

"Buck Walker had no choice but to dispose of Mac and Muff on Palmyra, outside Jennifer's presence, and without her knowledge."

I walked slowly over to the aluminum container. *"I say that this container, being found on Palmyra, speaks out loudly, though it is voiceless. It speaks out against Buck Walker as the one who alone shed the blood of Eleanor Graham.*

"You know, it's not as if Buck Walker buried the bodies in the lagoon because he wasn't even bothering to think about taking steps to avoid being caught. His setting of Muff Graham's body on fire conclusively refutes that notion. The fact that Muff Graham was able to be identified by dental records from San Diego does not negate Buck Walker's obvious intent, as demonstrated by the fire, to prevent the identification of her body.

"So by the fire, we know that Buck Walker was acutely aware of taking all possible available steps to insulate himself from criminal prosecution. Yet he doesn't take the most important and most obvious step of all, disposing of the bodies far out at sea, because without Jennifer's involvement in these murders he could not do this. He was forced, instead, to go through all the trouble of finding a container, putting the body in the container, attempting to incinerate the body, securing the container, and then sinking it in the lagoon.

"When Buck did this, ladies and gentlemen of the jury, he wasn't just hiding the bodies from the authorities. More importantly, and certainly more immediately for him, *he was hiding the bodies from Jennifer*. In the process, he couldn't have made it more obvious that he, and he alone, committed these two nightmarish murders.

"So often, the means a criminal employs to conceal his identity are the precise means that reveal his culpability.

"Can Mr. Enoki make the argument in his rebuttal that if what I say is true about the sea being the best place to hide the bodies, Buck could have *himself* gone out to sea and disposed of the bodies, and the fact that he obviously didn't disproves my argument?

"That argument by the prosecution would not be valid because with the time constraints he was faced with in always appearing to Jennifer that he was on the island, how could he go miles out to sea? Moreover, Bernard Leonard testified that the Zodiac was not the type of boat you would operate out at sea because it would swamp.

"But there was an even better reason why Buck could not bury the bodes out at sea."

I moved to the chart of Palmyra.

"As you can see from this chart, from the dolphins here where the *Iola* was moored, Jennifer had a clear view of the channel, and she could therefore see any boat leaving or entering the lagoon.

"It's true that Jennifer was in the cabin of the *Iola* at the time she heard the dinghy, but Buck would have had no way of knowing this. Furthermore, as Jennifer testified, even from the *Iola's* cabin she could look out the windows or the cabin hatch, both of which faced the channel.

"Buck Walker knew that if Jennifer saw him, by himself, operating the Grahams' Zodiac dinghy and leaving the lagoon, she would know immediately that something was very, very wrong. He'd already told Jennifer, remember, that Mac and Muff went fishing in the Zodiac for the bon voyage dinner.

"And incidentally, as Jennifer testified, there would be no way for her to confuse Buck with Mac. It was daylight when she heard the Zodiac being operated in the lagoon, the lagoon was small, and

there was testimony from Jennifer and Mr. Leonard that if someone were operating a dinghy in it during the day, from the dolphins it was easy to identify the person.

"Note that Buck told Jennifer that Mac *and Muff* had gone
fishing, so even if Buck could have been confused as looking like
Mac, he certainly couldn't have been confused for two people, Mac
and Muff.

"In fact, even if Jennifer couldn't identify who was in the
Zodiac at all, she certainly would know that it *was* the Zodiac
heading out of the channel into the ocean, and Jennifer would
know that Mac and Muff would not be fishing in the ocean. We
had testimony that no one did.

"I said earlier that if Jennifer had been involved in these murders with Buck, they would have buried the bodies far out at sea.
But even in the sea *just outside* the channel would have been much,
much better than burying the bodies in the lagoon.

"But because of the reasons I've stated, Buck couldn't even
bring the Grahams right outside the channel. In fact, because of
Jennifer, Buck Walker couldn't even dispose of the Grahams' bodies in ninety percent of the lagoon."

I directed the jury's attention once again to the Palmyra chart.
I pointed out how only a narrow portion of the lagoon—about a
tenth of it—was blocked from Jennifer's line of vision at the dolphins because of the obstruction on the south end of Cooper
Island that jutted out into the lagoon.

"I say it's no coincidence that Sharon Jordan found the remains
of Muff Graham inside this ten percent strip of area, and Jennifer
found the Zodiac overturned in the same general area—this narrow strip that is not visible from the area of the dolphins. This is
the same area in which Jennifer testified she heard the sound of
the Zodiac being operated about 4:30 P.M. on August 30th.

"Buck could not afford to operate the dinghy or dispose of the
bodies outside this ten percent area," I said, sweeping over the
remaining nine-tenths of the lagoon with my hand, "because of
the likelihood that Jennifer, from the *Iola*, would spot him.

"So we see that Buck Walker was not only forced to bury the

bodies in the lagoon, but even in the lagoon itself he had no choice but to put them in that small area where the Zodiac was found overturned, and Muff's remains were found."

★ ★ ★

I LET THE jury know I was coming to the close of my summation. "But I still have a few more matters to discuss: circumstantial evidence, suspicion, reasonable doubt, then a few closing observations."

I knew I would finish by lunchtime. I had argued about three hours the previous afternoon, and taking time out for this morning's recess, I would end up having argued a little more than two hours today. I was hitting the judge's five-hour limit almost on the button.

"First, circumstantial evidence. To demonstrate the distinction between direct and circumstantial evidence, if the question were whether it's raining outside, and you actually saw the rain falling, that would be direct evidence. Circumstantial evidence of the rain falling would be seeing someone coming into your home with wet clothing. Of course, their clothing could have gotten wet by walking past your neighbor's sprinkler. Or it may have been raining earlier, but it had stopped, and their clothing was still wet. And so on. That's the problem with circumstantial evidence.

"This case is one of circumstantial evidence. Circumstantial evidence is not invalid evidence. It can be good evidence. However, Judge King will give you the following instruction: 'If the jury views the evidence in this case as reasonably permitting either of two conclusions, one of innocence and the other of guilt, the jury should of course adopt the conclusion of innocence.'

"Note that this instruction does not say that the conclusion of innocence has to be *more* reasonable than, or even as reasonable as, the conclusion of guilt. It simply says that if the evidence reasonably permits *a* conclusion of innocence, you should reject the conclusion of guilt. That's the law."

I told the jury that at least *one* reasonable conclusion from the evidence was that Jennifer was innocent, that she was not involved in any way in the murder of Mrs. Graham; and that if they agreed, "under that instruction Judge King will give you, Jennifer is entitled to a not-guilty verdict.

"There's something I want to talk to you about now in a little more depth, because it goes right to the heart of this case. It's the notion of suspicion.

"The prosecution in this case has not offered one single speck of *proof* that Jennifer Jenkins murdered the Grahams, or aided and abetted Buck Walker in any way in doing so. When we subject the prosecution's case to even the weakest of microscopes, one fact is unmistakably clear. Their whole case, their entire case against her, is based on suspicion. Suspicious circumstances. And Judge King will instruct you thusly: 'The jury will remember that a defendant is never to be convicted on mere suspicion or conjecture.'

"Oftentimes in life, as you know, the less we know the more we suspect. And suspicion is a kind of intellectual dye that colors every thought that comes into contact with it. Applied to this case here, as I said earlier, just on the face of it, if four people are on an island, two end up dead, and the other two end up with their boat, making false statements as to how they came into possession of it, we naturally are suspicious because we know virtually none of the facts.

"This trial has focused a penetrating spotlight on a great number of the facts surrounding these murders, and with it, the shadow of suspicion against Jennifer Jenkins has vanished like dew in the morning sun. The more we learned of the facts, the less our suspicion became.

"The prosecution may *call* this case one of guilt beyond a reasonable doubt. But that does not and cannot change the very nature of this case. It's a case of pure, unadulterated suspicion.

"Abraham Lincoln once asked a man how many legs a dog has, and the man said four, whereupon Lincoln said, 'Well, what if we call his tail a leg? How many legs will the dog have then?' 'Five,' was the reply. 'No,' said Lincoln, 'the dog still has four legs, no matter what we call his tail,' thus illustrating that changing the name of something does not change its nature.

"Mr. Enoki will argue to you, of course, that there is more than mere suspicion in this case; that there is evidence. Of course there is evidence. All testimony coming from the witness stand, good or bad, truthful or false, is evidence. But it isn't necessarily proof.

"The prosecution has the burden of *proof*, not the burden of *evidence*. The kind of evidence presented by the prosecution in this case was the kind which, even when viewed in its very best light, only creates a suspicion, not proves guilt beyond a reasonable doubt.

"When Mr. Enoki, in his rebuttal, starts making assertions about Jennifer's guilt, ask him quietly to yourself: 'Where is the proof, Mr. Enoki? Where is your proof?' "

I walked toward the empty witness stand, moving within a couple feet of the perch where so many prosecution and defense witnesses, one by one, had taken the oath and provided additional small pieces of the puzzle. Some of the pieces fit nicely, I thought, while others clearly had not.

"Isn't it a beautiful system of justice we have in this country that no one—not just Jennifer Jenkins, but you and I and every other American citizen—no one can be deprived of their life or liberty without strong, clear proof coming from this witness stand under oath, and subject to cross-examination? Let's hope and pray to God this never changes. Because, among other things, that's what makes this a great country and distinguishes us from totalitarian nations.

"If we only have, at the very best, a case of suspicious circumstances," I continued, "to suggest that Jennifer Jenkins has been proved guilty beyond a reasonable doubt is laughable.

"*Beyond a reasonable doubt*, ladies and gentlemen. By far the most important doctrine in American criminal jurisprudence."

I returned to the podium and paused.

"I'm going to tell you folks something now that's probably going to sound shocking to you, but I assure you, it is the law. The ultimate issue for you to decide at this trial is not: was Jennifer Jenkins involved in the murder of Mrs. Graham, or was she not involved? That is, is she guilty or is she innocent?" A perplexed look swept over the jury, like "What have we been sitting here for, then?" A few jurors looked in the direction of the judge. "Even if that were the ultimate issue," I continued on, "we've presented very, very substantial evidence that she is innocent, that her hands and soul are clean of any involvement in the murder of Mrs. Graham. But that's not the ultimate issue. Under the law, a jury does *not* have to believe a defendant is innocent in order to return a verdict of not guilty.

"The ultimate issue for you to decide is: did the prosecution meet their burden of proving guilt beyond all reasonable doubt, or did they not meet their burden?" I sensed the jury relaxing. Yes, they *had* heard about reasonable doubt before. "That's the issue," I said. "And under that test, *even if a jury believes a defendant is guilty*, if they don't believe it beyond a reasonable doubt, they simply have no choice or discretion. They must, they have a legal duty, to return a verdict of not guilty.

"Is there any person in this entire courtroom," I said, speaking loudly and disdainfully, "who has heard the incredibly weak evidence presented by the prosecution in this case who can say in good conscience that they have *absolutely no reasonable doubt?*"

I then preempted Enoki by making an argument that virtually all prosecutors use: "Mr. Enoki will undoubtedly argue to you that the prosecution only has the burden of proving guilt beyond a *reasonable* doubt, not beyond *all* doubt. And he will be right. If proof had to be beyond all doubt, even the most fanciful, whimsical doubt, then the prosecution would hardly ever get a conviction in any case. But don't let Mr. Enoki fool you with that type of argument. Proof beyond a reasonable doubt is not proof beyond all doubt, but it's about as close to absolute proof as you can get.

"The language is 'beyond a reasonable doubt.' Those are very strong words, and they have been the bedrock of English and American criminal jurisprudence for centuries. Whatever else has changed throughout the years, this rule of law has stood its ground, unmoved and unassailed."

After reading the jurors the instruction Judge King would give on reasonable doubt, I gave them a hypothetical example to make a conceptual connection between the instruction and the evidence in the case.

I then tried to reach the jury at a more elemental level, the level at which I believed many of them might be thinking, or saying, or feeling in their belly, during their deliberations.

"Perhaps the doctrine of reasonable doubt can be illustrated this way. If the state of mind of a juror in a criminal case is 'I *kind of believe* that the defendant is guilty' or 'If I were *forced to bet*, I'd bet he is guilty,' that is not enough. Not enough. Even if the juror's state of mind is 'I believe he is *probably* guilty' or 'I believe he is *most likely* guilty,' again, that is not enough. Not enough. To convict, a jury's belief in guilt has to be greater than this—*beyond a reasonable doubt*," I said firmly.

"The presumption of innocence cannot be overcome by conjecture, by speculation, by vagrant and disjointed circumstances that are suspicious from one vantage point, but innocent from another. It can only be overcome by evidence as clear and powerful as the noonday sun: strong, unequivocal evidence that comes from the witness stand under oath."

Here, I argued, the prosecution clearly had not done that.

I went on to reiterate that although the defense had no burden of proof, "we did present very powerful evidence of Jennifer's innocence: her comprehensive testimony on that witness stand had the unmistakable ring of truth to it; the persuasive and un-rebutted testimony from several witnesses that Jennifer is a peaceful, compassionate person who abhors violence; the many instances where Jennifer's conduct was completely compatible with innocence, not guilt; and finally, the illuminating pieces of evidence that point solely and exclusively to the guilt of Buck Walker, and in the process, exonerate Jennifer, such as Mrs. Graham's body being buried in that lagoon as opposed to out at sea.

"If all of that isn't enough to create a reasonable doubt of guilt, then we should abolish the doctrine of reasonable doubt, because it is just an empty, hollow phrase.

"I ask you, ladies and gentlemen of the jury: if this isn't a reasonable doubt case, what in the world would be?"

I realized, for the first time, that my voice was starting to sound a shade raspy. The honey-lemon mixture had helped, but I was coming to the close of my argument just in time.

"In summary, when you're back in that jury room, consider that there are three separate, independent grounds that justify a verdict of not guilty in this case, each one of which, *all by itself*, justifies such a verdict.

"First, the decided weight of the evidence points towards Jennifer's innocence—that she had nothing to do with the murder of the Grahams.

"Second, the judge's instruction that if there are two reasonable conclusions from the evidence—one of innocence and one of guilt—you should adopt the conclusion of innocence. Certainly, at an absolute minimum, at least *one* reasonable conclusion from the evidence is that Jennifer is innocent.

"And finally, we return, as we must always return, to the doctrine of reasonable doubt. The prosecution unquestionably did not meet their burden of proof. In no way did they prove guilt beyond a reasonable doubt. One could almost say that it is a blasphemy and a sacrilege on the doctrine of reasonable doubt, and all that that doctrine means to our system of justice, to even suggest that they have."

I took out a handkerchief and mopped my brow. I had come to the closing words of my summation.

I lowered my tone a notch. "I think it should be observed, in respectfully anticipating your verdict of not guilty, that even with such a verdict, Jennifer Jenkins has been deeply and irreparably harmed for the rest of her life. The fact that she has been charged with the ultimate crime, murder, will cast a dark shadow over her life for as long as she lives, a grave injustice."

If any jurors still felt Jennifer was guilty, but had a reasonable doubt, I hoped that observation might make it easier for them to vote not guilty.

"As some of you probably know, Clarence Darrow, the great criminal defense attorney of many years ago, used to light up courtrooms with the radiance of his oratory. Darrow was a man of such towering stature that when he represented a defendant in a criminal trial, he always raised his eyesight beyond the perimeters of the particular courtroom in which he found himself. Darrow was known to tell jurors that he was more concerned about the effect of their verdict on the people of this country and the cause he was representing than what the verdict would do to his client.

"Darrow was much more than a trial lawyer. Clarence Darrow was a philosopher, a courageous spokesman for unpopular causes, an unwavering defender of the weak and the oppressed. I view Darrow as one of the moral and intellectual giants of the twentieth century.

"However, Darrow was also a cynic, as intellectuals are prone to be. Oftentimes, his cynicism was warranted by the facts. But Darrow, in an interview with the *New York Times* in 1936, the autumn of his life, said something that I don't really think he meant deep down. It may have been a cold, dank winter day, the old warrior's bones may have been aching. And he said: 'There's no such thing as justice, in or out of a courtroom.'

"Now, if Clarence Darrow really meant that—and I don't think he did—but if he really meant that, this would be something to which I would take exception. I told you much earlier that I believe in the jury system, and I believe that, by and large, juries *do* bring about justice.

"Justice has been described as the ligament which holds civilized beings and civilized societies together.

"There's only one verdict, ladies and gentlemen, only one verdict that would not only be compatible with justice, but would also be in keeping with the evidence in this case, and that, of course, is a verdict of not guilty. *Not guilty.* The facts and the law of this case literally cry out for a verdict of not guilty. The defense has every confidence that you will not let us down, nor will you let down the system of justice you are sworn to uphold.

"My colleague, Mr. Weinglass, and I, and our client, Jennifer Jenkins, want to thank you, each one of you, very, very much for all of the patience and attention you've given us throughout this entire trial.

"Thank you, ladies and gentlemen."

When the judge called a recess, Len and Ted Jenkins came forward. They both were very excited about the summation, and told me so.

Jennifer's mother was close behind.

Sunny, tears filling her eyes, hugged me. "Thank you, Vince. I feel we have a chance now."

It wasn't until an hour or so later that I realized only one person close to the defense had said nothing to me.

Jennifer.

1:30 THAT AFTERNOON

IN REBUTTAL, the prosecution theoretically is only supposed to respond to (rebut) defense arguments. But since I had asserted my client to be not guilty, the door was left open, after responding to my specific arguments, for the prosecutor to go over once again and reemphasize in a new and powerful way all of the evidence against Jennifer Jenkins that, in his view, proved her guilt. Ending his rebuttal on such a strong, affirmative note would have been far better for the prosecution than the route Elliot Enoki took, which was to stay on the defensive for nearly all of his summation, merely responding to my arguments.

"Mr. Bugliosi, went on for some length about a wide variety of subjects in his closing argument," Enoki said as he commenced his rebuttal.

"I believe he spoke for five hours or so. I'm sure you'll all be relieved that I don't intend to stand here and rebut each and every point that he raised or argued. We would probably be here for another five hours."

It was Enoki who looked the most relieved.

"But by not answering every single argument made by defense counsel, I hope you do not get the idea that the prosecution agrees with whatever he did say.

"I'm going to apologize in advance. Obviously, I didn't know everything that Mr. Bugliosi was going to argue. As a result of that, I obviously have not been able to prepare a rebuttal in some logical format."

What Enoki was saying was startling. The prosecutor felt constrained to admit to the jury that he wasn't ready to respond adequately to my summation! He seemed a little confused in what was now the last inning of an important ball game.

"I may be just hitting one subject after another that Mr. Bugliosi has brought up," said Enoki, who proved true to his word and launched into a disorganized and disjointed rebuttal.

"The judge is going to explain that reasonable doubt is not proof beyond all doubt, as Mr. Bugliosi noted. You can still have doubts and uncertainties about the case and still convict.

"In his argument, Mr. Bugliosi said, concerning Bill Larson, something like, here's a person the prosecution never called. He points to this as if this is some sinister thing we did. Well, the prosecution never hid Mr. Larson. You recall that the FBI talked to Mr. Larson. The defense was able to call Mr. Larson. Each side calls its own witnesses. That's our system."

Enoki's next argument addressed Jennifer's claim that her theft-trial lawyer had advised her to commit perjury, but his logic escaped me entirely.

"Mr. Bugliosi made a remark about how the prosecution failed to call Miss Jenkins's former lawyer on rebuttal. Well, first of all, there's no evidence to suggest the prosecution knew of this in advance. Second, there's no evidence in the record to indicate where the lawyer is or what the lawyer may be doing."

Was Enoki telling the jury that the FBI was incapable of finding Jennifer's former lawyer, still a practicing attorney?

"And thirdly, do you really believe that the attorney is going to come in and embarrass himself on that particular question? I don't think that's really a fair thing to suggest that the prosecution do."

Was Enoki saying that the lawyer wouldn't embarrass himself by telling the truth, the truth being he *had* told Jennifer what she said he did? But if Enoki felt this might be the case, then how was it helping him to even make this argument?

"Mr. Bugliosi started out his argument by saying kind of a funny thing. He said he could argue that maybe there was not a murder here, but then he said he wasn't going to do that."

Enoki then went on to spend several minutes arguing why a murder *had* taken place, a point I had already conceded.

"Another thing he mentioned about the log. I'm sorry—about the consciousness of innocence. He said he would have—or she would have had—she would not have made up the story of a Zodiac—of finding the Zodiac up against the beach, because if she was trying to make up a story about drowning, she obviously would have had the Zodiac floating in the lagoon instead. Well, I mean, you have to give some credit to somebody making up a story.

"Mr. Bugliosi argued on in his argument about high high tide, low high tide, high low tide, and low low tide. I don't think there's any dispute that there was a high tide between 4:30 P.M. August 30th and dawn on August 31st. But now he's saying, well, it wasn't the *high* high tide, and why didn't we bring in an expert on tidal conditions? Well, the reason for that is, first of all, that the only evidence in this whole record about *high* high tides and *low* high tides comes actually more from Mr. Bugliosi than from any evidence in the case.

"In a number of things, and a number of points in his closing argument, Mr. Bugliosi relies exclusively on Miss Jenkins's testimony to prove the facts that he's alleging are true.

"And what about Joel Peters and his laundry? I must confess I've never heard of an argument for acquittal based on the return of laundry.

"Now, in this case Miss Jenkins blamed—or at least Mr. Bugliosi has argued that Mr. Walker committed these murders by himself. Now, if Miss Jenkins—or Mr. Bugliosi is going to claim it was Mr. Walker . . ."

Twice, Enoki had to catch himself that it was *I*, not Jennifer, who had put the hat on Buck Walker. Not only had Jennifer not pointed the finger at Walker even to me during our trial preparation, but I knew as a matter of strategy that it would be far more effective for me to accuse Buck than for her to do so.

Enoki went on to make the argument—implausible, at least, to me—that Jennifer had a stronger motive to steal the *Sea Wind* with its food supplies than Buck because he was more accustomed to hardship. "It was she who didn't want to be on Palmyra," Enoki charged, "not Mr. Walker. Remember when she told Tom Wolfe that she was sick and tired of eating fish and coconuts? And who wrote in the diary that they were drooling and dreaming of their next boat? It was Miss Jenkins.

"Mr. Bugliosi argued that for me to argue that food was a motive is nonsensical. That people don't kill to get better food. But people get killed in two-dollar robberies and for cutting somebody off on a freeway.

"It's Miss Jenkins who writes in her diary on September 4th: 'We all grow fatter and fatter on ham and cheese and pancakes and turkey and chili and all the things we hadn't had in so long.' I submit to you that's plenty of motive.

"Mr. Bugliosi also argued that Miss Jenkins would not have aided and abetted Mr. Walker in these murders because she is a peaceful, compassionate person.

"Well, she is simply not a peaceful and compassionate person. Peaceful and compassionate people don't take up with armed robbers dealing drugs, using guns and booby traps. She knew all of that.

"Compassionate people don't leave dead people's relatives no notice. They don't have an attitude of thinking nothing about using the clothes and the money of people who have just died."

Enoki seemed to be regaining his equilibrium.

"And, you know, they don't mug for the camera, as these pictures on the *Sea Wind* headed back to Honolulu attest to, when she is supposedly so distraught over their deaths." Enoki was holding up for the jury several of the photographs taken during the voyage back to Hawaii. It was Jennifer who was smiling broadly, not Buck.

As to my argument that Jennifer was only being protective of Buck, not participating in his crimes, Enoki asked, "How many people are drawn by others into a life of crime? She certainly wouldn't be the first person. Maybe it started out with something small. Then it came to full-scale participation."

Enoki explained that the prosecution hadn't called their own character witnesses to rebut the testimony of the defense's character witnesses because our testimony was not strong enough to cause concern.

"Now, about Mr. Walker keeping the gun. Mr. Bugliosi argued that because the bullets could be matched, Mr. Walker kept the gun because it wasn't used in the murder. Well, I would submit that Mr. Walker, like many other criminals, didn't think he would be caught. So his keeping the gun would not mean anything. After all, Mr. Walker took the risk of being caught with the *Sea Wind* itself, a much bigger thing to be caught with than a gun certainly."

I hoped the jury would see the holes in that argument. Of course Walker stayed with the *Sea Wind*. Securing the boat was the very reason for the murders. Furthermore, being in possession of the *Sea Wind* did not take away his contention that the Grahams had died an accidental death.

Enoki next tried to refute my major argument about the dumping of Muff's body in the lagoon. He was unable, however, to explain away satisfactorily my theory that the body would not have been put there if Jennifer had been involved in the murders. All of his arguments on this point, I was pleased to see, were obvious stretches. Using a buckshot approach, thereby hoping that at least one pellet would strike the jury as making sense, he gamely argued that "criminals make mistakes," that the lagoon, after all, was "a pretty big place" and hence "a pretty safe place to deposit some containers," and that since Buck and Jennifer took eleven days to get ready for departing Palmyra, "you just don't want two bodies, at least one of them partially burned, sitting around in two metal containers, while you get ready to go to sea. It's not a practical alternative." Acknowledging that it would have been the "perfect crime" if the bodies had been dumped at sea, he added, "But you have to look at it from the standpoint of what they thought. They certainly didn't expect anyone to find the containers, or the containers to come up by themselves. For that matter they must have been right. The other one—well, they were partially right. One of them never came up."

If the prosecutor himself had no adequate rebuttal to my argument on this issue, I felt the chances were good that no juror would either.

Enoki next went down a list of his witnesses, defending them and their testimony.

"I believe that for Mr. Bugliosi to suggest that Curt Shoemaker has some reason to fabricate his testimony in this case is absolute speculation. If he made his story up to help the prosecution in some way, why would he put in that he overhears in the background the women laughing? He certainly wouldn't have made that up. And his testimony about Mac talking about the truce was supported by Mr. Wolfe, who testified they were not really getting along. Mr. Bugliosi did some mathematics about the number of minutes in a week, and all this stuff, and you come out with something like one in two hundred and fifty.

"Well, you can do a lot of things with statistics. I suppose I could ask what are the odds of two jurors from Scotland being seated next to each other in San Francisco in a trial where a witness from Scotland, Mr. Bryden, testified. And the odds are probably astronomical. But it's true.

"Now, what is it that Mr. Bugliosi points to as a basis for the Leonards' lying that Miss Jenkins said she would never leave Palmyra on the *Iola*? He points to the fact that they didn't tell FBI Agent Kilgore about this and that the Leonards didn't testify to it in other proceedings. Isn't it likely that they would recollect things in bits and pieces, like most people do, when they try to remember back? And maybe Mr. Eggers should have asked them more questions at the theft trial. But he didn't.

"I would like you to contrast the credibility of the Government witnesses with Miss Jenkins. And the first thing you ought to consider is: who has the real motive to lie in this case? No matter what happens in this case, everyone in this courtroom, all the witnesses, they're going to go their own way. Not Miss Jenkins. She is the one who has the biggest motive to lie in this case. Because it is she who stands to be convicted of murder, not Mr. Leonard, not Mrs. Leonard, and not Mr. Shoemaker."

The temperate prosecutor, in measured tones, pointed out: "She's already admitted to lying under oath to a previous jury. And it's this testimony of an admitted perjurer that Mr. Bugliosi offers to you against the prosecution witnesses. *If she would lie to cover up a theft, she would have all the more motive to lie to cover up a murder."*

Jennifer Jenkins admitted, at this trial, to telling fourteen lies, said Enoki. "I counted them. We also tried to count what happened in that first forty-five minutes of cross-examination. We counted nineteen times that she said she didn't know, or she didn't remember, in answer to questions.

"Miss Jenkins, of course, cried some tears on the stand. But it isn't only due to remorse that a person is brought to tears. One reason, of course, is it could be a performance, a complete performance.

"Or it could be that after all these years she's finally faced with the stark reality of the deaths that she caused. Because there are tears of guilt, too."

After arguing that the reason the prosecution never had any eyewitnesses to the murders was that Buck and Jennifer murdered the only witnesses—Mac and Muff Graham—he went on: "We do have much other evidence of guilt Mr. Bugliosi claims we don't have. We have all of Miss Jenkins's lies, the sinking of the *Iola*, the murder itself. Miss Jenkins fleeing from Palmyra with Mr. Walker. Miss Jenkins fleeing from the Coast Guard in the Ala Wai harbor. The repainting, the reregistration. The use of the *Sea Wind*.

"And we also have Mr. Shoemaker placing them both on the *Sea Wind* unexpected, in the dark, bringing a cake over—in the midst of their running out of flour and all the other ingredients that go into a cake—on August 28th. We also have the absence of diary entries on this visit and no memory from Miss Jenkins for August 28th.

"The question is what the evidence *did* show, not what the evidence did *not* show. And by your verdict in this case, ladies and gentlemen, you can prevent Jennifer Jenkins from pulling off this crime.

"I talked to you about her kind of peeling off layers of lies, or taking off one mask after another. She says one thing, and then: 'No, that's not true. It's really this.'

"I ask each of you to take the rest of those layers off, and expose her for what she really is. It's time, after eleven and a half years, that she accept the responsibility for the murder of Muff Graham. And that's what your verdict would mean.

"Thank you."

CHAPTER 44

FEBRUARY 26, 1986

AFTER INSTRUCTING THE MARSHAL to lock the courtroom doors so there would be no interruptions, Judge King did something I had never seen before. Instead of staying on the bench, he stepped down, went to the podium, and stood before the jury like a lawyer in the case. It was time to instruct the jurors on the law they were to follow during their deliberations.

Much of what he told the jurors they had already heard, in the very same words, from me, but now it was backed by the full force of the legal system.

He paused once, slowly sipping from a cup of water. Then, turning another page, he continued on. In all, it took twenty minutes. When the jury filed out the back door and headed for the jury room to deliberate, it was exactly 10:55 A.M.

I glanced into several of the jurors' faces as they passed before us. There was Linda DeCasper, the forty-four-year-old housewife who enjoyed sightseeing with her family in their motor home. There were the two jurors with Scottish accents, James McGowan and Irene Angeles, both of whom smiled frequently. I had been told that Mrs. Angeles had given Jennifer a few sympathetic looks during the trial, and was therefore perceived possibly to be pro-defense. The oldest member of the jury, Ernest Nelson, the retired Petaluma chicken farmer, had at times seemed impatient with the prosecution. The only one I still feared was the retired engineer Frank Everett—aka the Kansas Rock. I hoped my reasonable doubt argument might help sway him, but as I watched him stride stiffly away, I had no confidence that he would vote anything other than "guilty" on the first ballot.

But there was absolutely nothing more that Len and I could do for Jennifer. Our participation was over. Her fate was now in the jury's hands.

WE WERE told the jury started deliberating right after receiving the case and, following a lunch break, worked the remainder of Wednesday afternoon, not going home until after 5:00 P.M. So far, Jennifer was doing a lot better with her jury than Buck had with his.

Aside from occasional visits to the courthouse, the next day Len and I mostly waited at our hotel; the clerk was to call us if we were needed. Jennifer and her family stayed at Ted Jenkins's home forty minutes away. The clerk was to call them, too, when a verdict came in.

That second day of deliberating, members of the prosecution went back and forth, and at one point in midafternoon, Enoki, Schroeder, and Hal Marshall, all in shirt sleeves, chewed the fat together on the bench seats in the empty spectator section of the courtroom, scoffing at Jennifer's testimony.

For a reporter who stopped by, Marshall, his wit intact, began casting the movie he was sure would someday be done about the case. "Redford will play me," he said, straight-faced. "The *Karate Kid* instructor will play you, Elliot. Dustin Hoffman for Walt Schroeder. Bugliosi will play himself."

Marshall hadn't gotten around to casting Len yet when clerk Kathy Harrell came by to chat. She had been informing all of us lawyers with occasional tidbits. We found out, for instance, that Ernest Nelson had been elected foreman. We also knew when the jury broke for lunch, and when they returned.

At 3:05 P.M., Harrell told us the jurors were taking a break from deliberations. Then, at 3:25, she reported that they were adjourning for the day.

"You know," Harrell whispered to the prosecutors, "I heard arguing in the jury room earlier today."

The next morning the judge told the clerk to contact all of us and have us in court at 11:00 A.M. It seemed the jury had a "question."

We were all there—Len and I with Jennifer, the prosecution team, Ted and Sunny and various Jenkins relatives, and reporters who had covered the trial.

The jury did not appear. What could the question be? we all wondered. It turned out to be far more than just a question.

"I've received a note from the jury," Judge King said, holding a slip of paper in front of him. "The foreman reports, 'We've taken seven votes and we're six and six. What do we do now?'"

I was stunned. The realization that *six* jurors were voting "guilty" jolted me. I could understand the Kansas Rock, but five others had joined him in thinking Jennifer was guilty of first-degree murder! Obviously, the jurors were struggling hard. *They didn't want to let Jennifer walk out the door.*

The judge asked us how we felt about his reading the Allen Instruction to the jury. It urges juries to try to reach a verdict by rethinking whichever position they have taken. Len was very opposed, saying the defense bar throughout the country objected to it. Frankly, I couldn't see how it would hurt us. The Allen Instruction also reminds the jurors, in no uncertain terms, about reasonable doubt.

"I think it might help," I told Len.

"We've got six on our side," he said, "but our people on the jury are the weakest."

How did he know *that*?

"People for conviction are always stronger than those for acquittal," he explained.

"But maybe in this case our six are the strongest," I offered. Judge King ended up giving the jury the Allen Instruction.

It was much more than Len seeing a cup half empty, while I saw it half full. At least in the context of a criminal trial, we had very different ways of looking at things.

Len was very pleased with the six-six split, while I was greatly depressed by it. Len was a career defense attorney, and in his lexicon a "hung jury" was a quasi-victory. For years, he was used to trying to hold back the flood. But since my main background was prosecutorial, as a deputy DA I had been a part of the flood Len had always tried to hold back.

Unlike him, I did not consider a hung jury to be a victory. At this moment, my confidence was ebbing dramatically. I couldn't put aside the chilling thought: *Six jurors believed, beyond a reasonable doubt, that Jennifer had helped Buck Walker kill Muff.*

I went to lunch with Ted and Sunny Jenkins, while Jennifer and Len went off together to eat. As we stepped from the courthouse elevator on the ground floor, we noticed two jurors—telephone company employee Francia Rico, and gray-haired Frances McClung, a retired office worker—heading from the building, obviously on their way to lunch, too.

Two other jurors, Irene Angeles and Kathleen Archer, were also walking together out of the building. Archer was married to a former deputy district attorney. Normally, a defense attorney would not want *anyone* associated with a prosecutor to be on a criminal trial jury. But I had liked Mrs. Archer's thoughtful, fair answers during voir dire and had scribbled "*Good*" under her name.

Since the jury was divided—and keeping in mind the clerk's comment about loud arguing in the jury room—there was a good chance that the jurors who held the same opinion were lunching together. In fact, Jennifer had mentioned noticing McClung giving her "disapproving looks," while Archer had joined Irene Angeles in giving her an occasional pleasant look during the trial. Ted, who had also noticed this, now speculated that Angeles and Archer had to be *our* jurors, with Rico and McClung representing the "guilty" faction.

As we nibbled listlessly at our food, I said I just couldn't believe there were that many jurors against us. "Is there anything I forgot to argue?" I asked Ted and Sunny.

They could only say that it seemed I had covered everything imaginable, and then some.

I shook my head. "A great number of hours went into that summation," I muttered under my breath. "I simply can't believe it failed to convince six people of Jennifer's innocence, or *at least* cause them to have a reasonable doubt."

I asked: "Should we have kept Jennifer off the stand?" Before either of them could answer, I said firmly, "No, she had to testify. If we get a hung jury, I won't be on this case again unless Jennifer also testifies at the next trial."

"Absolutely . . . she had to testify," Ted agreed.

"There's no question," Sunny chimed in. "If we have to go through this terrible ordeal again, she has to tell her story."

After lunch, I decided to walk back to the courthouse by myself, waving off a reporter in search of a quote. Alone with my thoughts and oblivious to the jangle of street sounds, I thought of the terrible reality that Jennifer, whom I believed to be innocent, might be convicted of murder. What could be worse?

I also thought about my career before juries in murder trials. Fortunately, I had yet to lose one. Although I had previously tried only two jury murder cases for the defense, I had won both, and I had prevailed in twenty-one consecutive jury murder trials as a prosecutor. But now there appeared to be a fifty-fifty chance I would lose my first jury murder trial. I wasn't taking it well, although I said to myself that if I lost, it was about time I got my comeuppance. But what about my innocent client?

Where had Len and I gone wrong in this case? What had I failed to argue in my summation? Or was it simply a case of my not being able to see (or my subconsciously averting my eyes from) what was obvious to six of the jurors—that Jennifer was a cold-blooded murderess? Was that really the answer? And did the remaining six jurors also believe Jennifer was involved in Muff's murder and simply temporarily hung up on the issue of reasonable doubt? But if you can't rely on your own conscious judgment anymore, I said to myself, then it's time to cash it all in, and I was still convinced of Jennifer's innocence.

As I was approaching the top of the courthouse steps, the confidence and optimism I always carry throughout a jury trial washed over me once again, and it was a good feeling. I reminded myself that during my summation I had drawn a considerable number of powerful inferences of innocence and reasonable doubt, and the jury had taken far more notes during my argument than they had during Enoki's. This almost automatically meant I was making points with them. The connection between feeling you're making a point in summation and jurors looking down at their pads and writing a note to themselves immediately thereafter is an obvious one. I told myself that when the jurors went back over their notes again, which, being at six-all, they would almost assuredly do, they'd just *have* to go in the direction of not guilty. There just was no way this jury was going to come back with a verdict of guilty, I said to myself. *No way*, I repeated as I pressed the up button for the elevator.

AT THREE o'clock that afternoon, there was another note from the jury, scrawled by Ernest Nelson on a piece of paper ripped from a juror's notebook.

The jury had taken another vote and the judge read it aloud: "The jury is at ten to two. The two are firm.' "

Len whispered to me that he was sure we were on the short end. "Those are our two jurors, Angeles and Archer, holding out for not guilty."

I told him it might be ten to two in favor of not guilty, but Len would have none of it.

"The prosecution looks too happy," he groused. "Maybe the marshal leaked word to them."

Len, without consulting me, stood up with his palms outstretched, beseeching the judge to stop the deliberations now and declare a mistrial. "Your honor," he said, "this has become a war of attrition."

I was in no position to quarrel with him because there was just no way to know what the hell the jury was doing. Enoki asked the judge to let the jury keep deliberating, a sign the prosecution thought things were going their way. Judge King elected to bring in the jury and tell them to decide whether it was worth their deliberating any further. If they decided no, he would declare a mistrial.

As the jurors entered and took their seats, Len brought to my attention the fact that both Kathleen Archer and Irene Angeles, the jurors our side had numbered with us, had reddened eyes and seemed to have been crying. *So Len was right!* These were the two jurors holding out against everyone else! *Unfucking-believable*, I said to myself. The jury apparently was going, inexorably, in the direction of convicting Jennifer of first-degree murder!!

The judge patiently told the jury he wanted them to go back and decide for themselves whether it was worth continuing.

Now I was really down. Randomly, I started asking reporters and others the same question: "Can you think of any conceivable scenario where two jurors who are supposedly on our side could have tears in their eyes if the vote were ten to two for *acquittal*?" I kept getting the answer I already knew. No. Why would they be crying if the verdict was going in the direction they wanted? I was groping aimlessly for some possible favorable twist to the events.

We all kept an eye glued to the clock. Thirty minutes . . . then forty. It was apparent the jury had decided to continue deliberating, trying to persuade the two holdouts to change their vote. Len had become white-faced and grave. If our two teary-eyed women couldn't hold out, he said, this jury was going to return a guilty verdict.

Jennifer was obviously distraught. Like a lost little girl, she went to her big brother in the spectator section, sat down next to him, and leaned her head on his shoulder.

At 4:00 P.M., the judge took the bench. The best we could hope for was a mistrial. To our dismay, the judge said evenly, "*The jury has informed me that they have a verdict.*"

A black gloom came over everyone connected with the defense. Len remained in his chair, too stricken even to try to conceal his disappointment.

I got up and walked over to the gallery, where I leaned down and whispered into Sunny's ear, "I'm . . . sorry." There was a lump in my throat. "I let all of you down. I don't know what I did wrong, but it must have been something."

Sunny, who seemed to have aged ten years since lunch, could say nothing. She just gripped my hand.

I returned to the counsel table and reached out to a dazed Jennifer. She took my hand and stood up. I put an arm around her and we remained standing as the drained jurors entered the courtroom. We would take the verdict, Jennifer and I, standing together.

Even the possibility of a mistrial had evaporated. We had a verdict, and we all knew what it had to be.

The clerk went forward to the jury box and accepted the verdict form from the foreman. She took it back to the judge, who read it silently, then returned it to her. This would be her show, for the judge's poker face gave away nothing. There seemed to be a momentary suspension of breathing in the still courtroom.

I could hear only bits and pieces.

"We the jury . . . as to count . . . murder . . . Eleanor Graham . . . the defendant . . ."

With my arm still tightly held around her shoulder, I tucked Jennifer into my embrace, as if hoping to shield her from what was coming. "I'm sorry, Jen," I said. "I was sure I'd be able to convince the jury that—"

"*. . . not guilty.*"

The courtroom burst alive. The tension broke and people jabbered, shrieked, hugged, and shook hands. Jennifer and I embraced, then turned to exchange hugs with others.

Len was next to me, beaming. He'd made an amazing return from the land of the dead. Color had returned to his cheeks. We shook hands warmly. "Well, Vince, we're undefeated," he crowed. "Maybe we should do this again."

Ted Jenkins, despite his calm outward appearance just minutes earlier, admitted he'd never been more frightened in his life.

Sunny, unable to stop crying, hugged me tightly.

In the midst of this turmoil, Elliot Enoki and Walt Schroeder quietly picked up their briefcases and left, with Hal Marshall following close behind.

The jurors returned to the jury room to gather their handbags, coats, and other belongings. They were greeted privately by Judge King, who shook hands with each one and thanked them warmly.

A few minutes later, we mingled with the jurors in the lobby of the courthouse, eager to figure out just what had gone on during the deliberations.

About some things, we'd been right. The two jurors we had seen going to lunch together *were* for acquittal. Kathleen Archer and Irene Angeles *were* solid not-guilty votes.

"Mrs. Angeles, I have to ask you something," I said. "When the jury was at ten to two, we noticed you had been crying. Why?"

"Mr. Bugliosi, it was the most emotional experience *ever* in my life," she replied, the strain still evident in her voice. "And I was so upset because we just couldn't convince the last two jurors to vote 'not guilty.'" I smiled, outwardly and inwardly. How very deceptive this game of life can be.

Jury foreman Ernest Nelson and Francia Rico had been the last holdouts for guilty. It turned out that the impatience with the prosecution we'd observed in Nelson had stemmed from his frustrated feeling that he had already heard enough. He'd been convinced early on of Jennifer's guilt and voted guilty on every ballot except the last one.

Juror Michael Nevins, one of the engineers on the jury, came up to me. "It was very effective," he commented, "the way you separated Jennifer from Buck, and that you went after Buck."

"Thank you, Mr. Nevins, for letting me know that."

Nevins also said, "I think the jury had the picture of you as a prosecutor, and were surprised to see you on the other side."

About one thing, I'd been dead wrong. Confirming my inability to read jurors, one of the jurors strongest for acquittal was none other than the Kansas Rock. The Rock had actually helped to convince other jurors that not guilty was the only proper verdict. His demeanor during the trial made no sense to me at all.

Irene Angeles had a word of advice for Jennifer.

Softly, but with conviction, she said: "Honey, next time make a better choice of boyfriends."

THE VICTORY party that night was hosted by Ted Jenkins at a downtown San Francisco restaurant named Vincent's—"in your honor," he happily informed me.

Two dozen family members and friends were gathered at one long table. Jennifer sat between Len and me. Appropriately, the first round was champagne, and Ted stood for the toast. "To my innocent sister," he said, smiling.

Everyone sipped the bubbly and gave in to the very festive mood.

Ted wasn't finished. "Innocence doesn't win court cases, good attorneys do." Holding his glass up again, he said: "To Vince Bugliosi and Len Weinglass. Two of the best attorneys in the country."

It soon became apparent that Jennifer was not going to be so giving. Dinner hadn't even arrived when she began criticizing me. I literally could not believe what I was hearing. "You shouldn't have ever called Elliot Enoki by his first name in your summation," she scolded me. "It sounded disrespectful, and patronizing." In our entire time together, four whole years, it was the first time she had ever talked to me in this way. I should have also gotten more sleep during the trial, she said, because I looked tired during my final argument. And, she added, "I didn't like your self-deprecating remarks to the jury, like that La Scala business."

I had very informally begun my summation by jokingly telling the jury that I was standing behind a larger podium than they had seen throughout the trial in order to protect myself in the event they were displeased with what I would be saying and chose to "throw tomatoes" at me as the audience reportedly does at La Scala Opera House in Milan "if they don't like the performance." This kind of occasional self-deprecating remark to the jury is my style. It can also help relax the jurors.

At first, Jennifer's criticism struck me as being funny, I guess because I can sometimes see humor in bizarre behavior. But I soon realized there was something about Jennifer's psychological makeup that I clearly didn't understand. Not one in a hundred thousand defendants would be reacting this way after an acquittal, when everyone else was celebrating and in a congratulatory mood. Of all the happy celebrants, she should have been the most ecstatic, most relieved, and yes, the most grateful. What manner of client was this?

In fact, at no time after the verdict that day did Jennifer say a single word to me indicating any kind of appreciation.

THE NEXT day, a reporter who had covered both murder trials found a downcast Elliot Enoki in a borrowed office on the sixteenth floor of the courthouse, packing boxes for his return home.

They exchanged small talk. Then, out of the blue, the reporter asked: "What would happen if Mac's body were found someday? Would you prosecute Buck Walker and Jennifer Jenkins for *his* murder?"

Enoki stopped what he was doing and looked up. His answer was delivered in a voice firm and resolute. "That's a possibility," the prosecutor said.

MAC GRAHAM, we can speculate with a degree of certainty, lies inside that last missing container. But are his remains still in their watery grave in the Palmyra lagoon, where at any time, like Muff's, they could surface and wash ashore? Or has his makeshift coffin washed out through the channel into the murky depths of the sea that Mac so loved?

Someday, perhaps the sea will tell.

EPILOGUE

BUCK WALKER APPEALED HIS murder conviction. On February 20, 1987, a three-judge panel of the Ninth U.S. Circuit Court of Appeals, noting that "for over a decade, this court and district courts alike have been involved in the unraveling of the mystery surrounding the disappearance of Eleanor and Malcolm Graham in 1974," unanimously upheld Walker's conviction.

Inmate 17950-148 is serving his life sentence at the Federal Correctional Institution at Lompoc, California. Buck Duane Walker will be sixty-eight years old when eligible to apply for parole in 2006. From his cell, Walker types long, soulful letters protesting his innocence to his mother, daughter, one surviving brother, and assorted friends.

Still living in Simi Valley and working as her telecommunications branch office's top salesperson (she earned close to $100,000 in 1990, has her own secretary, and drives a top-of-the-line Toyota equipped with a cellular phone), Jennifer, still single, shares her sprawling two-story home with two old friends from Hawaii and their two children. Like her mother, who lives twenty minutes away, Jennifer tends a rose garden. She enjoys backyard barbecuing on warm summer afternoons and going for walks through a nearby park. When asked if she no longer has any doubt that Buck murdered Mac and Muff, she says, "I guess I'll always have some doubt."

Jennifer's beloved dog, Puffer, died ten days after her nineteenth birthday.

ON MARCH 24, a little over a month after Jennifer's trial ended, I received a thank-you card from Sunny Jenkins: "Vince, you did such a fabulous job! We are forever grateful."

But no word from Jennifer.

Three weeks later, on April 14, I received a letter from Ted Jenkins. "Over the past several years, your confidence in Jennifer's innocence and eventual acquittal gave her strength and courage, and kept her going," her brother wrote. "Without her testimony, for which you unwaveringly fought and tirelessly prepared, the jury's verdict could certainly have been different. If Jennifer's testimony was the turning point of the trial, and I credit you for its superb impact, then your summation was the knockout punch." Without my summation, he wrote, "I dread to think of what the outcome might have been."

Still, I didn't hear from Jennifer.

In late August, six months after the trial, I returned home from the television trial of Lee Harvey Oswald in London. Sifting through a stack of mail, I found a card from Jennifer postmarked August 17.

Jennifer wrote that "words sometimes seem pitifully inadequate to express the deeper feelings in life," and that she had "sat for hours over the last several months trying in vain to adequately convey" her appreciation for what I had done for her. She went on: "Thank you is something one says when someone holds open a door. Are these the only words available when one has one's life saved? Perhaps it's my own limitation. Perhaps more profound words exist. But I don't know them. So, I thank you—for your belief in my innocence—for taking up the lance and shield of my defense—for restoring my life to me. I only wish I knew a bigger word than thanks."

WHILE CONTINUING to practice law but taking only selected cases, I have nearly completed a book on the drug problem in America, perhaps the most serious internal crisis this nation has faced since the Civil War. I am also at work writing an in-depth book on the assassination of President John F. Kennedy, one that I'm confident will shed a different light on the tragedy that altered the course of American history.

The television trial of Lee Harvey Oswald was the closest

thing to a real trial of Oswald that the Kennedy assassination will ever have.

Remarkably, a British television company, through painstaking and dogged effort, managed to round up and persuade most of the original key lay* prosecution and defense witnesses in the Kennedy assassination, many of whom had refused to talk to the media for years, to testify. (Because nearly all of them, fortunately, were relatively young at the time of the assassination, they were still very much alive, although many now live in various parts of the country.) They also secured a jury chosen from the actual rolls of the Dallas federal district by the clerk of the court, and a federal district court judge from Texas. I was the prosecutor. The British production company selected Wyoming's Gerry Spence (of Karen Silkwood and more recently Imelda Marcos fame) to represent Oswald. Reportedly, Spence had not lost a jury trial in seventeen years. I organized and prepared the prosecution of Oswald in virtually the identical fashion I have my many other major murder trials, and worked exclusively on the case for close to five months. In the process, working with the witnesses and the twenty-six volumes of the Warren Commission and twelve volumes of the House Select Committee on Assassinations on a daily basis, I became very familiar with the case.

All of the trial participants were flown to London for the equivalent of about four court days of very concentrated trial. There was absolutely no script, and no actors were used. Spence and I went at it with the same intensity we would have in a real trial. Though only a television trial (five hours of which—out of a total of twenty-one—were shown in the United States, a few additional hours in European countries), the historical importance of it was that when these witnesses testified before the Warren Commission, it was in a nonadversarial context, and therefore they had not been exposed to cross-examination, as they were in London. At the end

*The expert witnesses (in fields such as firearm identification, pathology, photography, handwriting, and neutron activation analysis) were from the House Select Committee on Assassinations that reinvestigated Kennedy's assassination in 1977–79.

of the evidence and Spence's and my final summations to the jury, and after six hours of deliberation, the jury returned a verdict of guilty against Oswald for the November 22, 1963, assassination of President John F. Kennedy.

LEONARD WEINGLASS went back to handling the types of cases that had made him so popular with the political left. He successfully defended Amy Carter, daughter of the former President, and his old friend Abbie Hoffman (since deceased) against charges of trespassing and disorderly conduct stemming from a November 24, 1986, protest against CIA recruitment on the campus of the University of Massachusetts at Amherst.

Elliot Enoki still is the First Assistant U.S. Attorney in Honolulu. Because of a bad back, Walter Schroeder took a medical retirement from the Justice Department in May 1990.

Judge Samuel P. King still sits on the federal bench in Honolulu. Now assigned to "senior status," which for judges means semiretirement, at the age of seventy-four Judge King carries a relatively light caseload. In mid-February 1991, a member of a Northern California water district wrote to Judge King, explaining that his order from the bench during Jennifer's trial for it to cease raining in the Bay Area by February 16, 1986, "worked all too well . . . that was the last real storm to have visited here in the last five years." Now, in the middle of one of the worst dry spells in California history, the water board member pleaded with the judge to set aside his order. In a February 26, 1991, reply to the board member, Judge King, his tongue firmly in cheek, revoked his order and ordered that "rain should fall in California beginning February 27, 1991." That very day the rains came as ordered. What the weather experts described as a "large warm storm coming from Hawaii" deluged drought-stricken Northern California with its heaviest rainfall in five years—more than eleven inches in six days. In retrospect, there was considerably more risk than I had thought in challenging Judge King's authority.

By coincidence, my coauthor, Bruce B. Henderson, crossed

paths on June 26, 1988, with the foreman of Jennifer's jury, the retired chicken farmer Ernest Nelson. They were both in Santa Rosa, California, to see the play *Inherit the Wind*, based on one of Clarence Darrow's most famous cases, the 1925 Scopes "monkey" trial. During intermission, Nelson and Henderson discussed the Jennifer Jenkins trial. "You know, she got away with murder," Nelson said casually. He explained that he'd finally voted "not guilty" only because of the reasonable doubt I'd raised in my summation. "That Eyetalian fellow, Bugliosi, was very clever," he said.

Despite the jury foreman's blunt remark, I'm confident that the jury system returned proper verdicts (for Jennifer Jenkins *and* Buck Walker) in the Palmyra murder case, unquestionably one of the most fascinating and enigmatic true murder mysteries of our time.

In May 1988, at Honolulu's Keehi Marine Center, a sleek new racing yacht with two tanned young men aboard pulled into a slip on a windswept morning. As they went about securing the bow and stern lines to the pier, the men couldn't help but notice the old wooden ketch in the adjacent slip.

The weary old vessel in slip F-3 had once been Mac Graham's pride and joy. It now smelled musty, like rotting wood. Blisters in the wooden finish had been crudely covered with tape that was peeling. Hanging on the side of the cabin was a "For Sale" sign with the name "Alan" and a Honolulu phone number. (In January 1978, Kit Muncey had sold the *Sea Wind* to Ray Millard of Oahu for twenty thousand dollars. Millard, who said it had been his life's dream to own a stately wooden-hulled sailboat, intended to do a major overhaul and refurbishing of the well-traveled *Sea Wind*, but he never got around to it. For years, the boat remained anchored off Millard's seaside home at Pohakea Point in Kaneohe Bay, not being sailed and gradually falling into a state of disrepair. In March 1988, Millard gave Mac's old ketch to Alan Horoschak, a friend from Honolulu. "With the condition she was in, I couldn't have got much for her anyway," Millard explained, "and only from people who wanted to break her up for parts. Alan promised he'd fix her up. He towed her over to Honolulu, hauled her out at a boat-yard, replaced some planks, and did a few other things. At least she stayed in one piece.")

Apparently in an attempt to facilitate the sale of the boat, new paint had recently been slapped on—pea green with brown trim. The quick-fix cosmetics wouldn't fool anybody. The rotten smell told the story. All the galvanized rigging and chain plates were rusted and needed replacing. The wooden hull, which had once cut through the water so majestically, was now laced with long, deep cracks. There was little doubt that this cripple would leak like a sieve at sea.

"Will you look at that garbage scow," said the man who had been at the helm of the racer.

His crewmate stopped what he was doing and stood, arms akimbo, studying a vessel that was considerably older than he, as if trying to peer beyond the obvious. "I don't know," he finally offered. "She has a salty rake to her masts. Looks like an ancient mariner, all right, but in her day, I'll bet she was—something."

AS FOR Palmyra Island, the remote atoll continues to serve up grist for the perpetuation of the belief in the Palmyra Curse for those who are so inclined.

While attempting a trip from San Diego to Hawaii in early June of 1989, a forty-foot sloop hit bad weather and its crew became seasick. Struggling with auxiliary-engine problems while trying to find their way by celestial navigation (most modern oceangoing boats are equipped these days with navigational gear that picks up positional signals from orbiting satellites), the inexperienced crew missed Hawaii and found themselves pushed far to the south . . . ending up at Palmyra Island.

After a brief stay on the atoll, the sloop reportedly departed Palmyra on July 27, 1989, headed for Hawaii. The boat was never seen again, nor were the four people aboard her. Some facts are coincidental enough with the *Sea Wind* mystery for pulp fiction. The missing boat's name: *Sea Dreamer*. Home port: San Diego. Owner: Graham Hughes.

The Coast Guard instituted an extensive search between Palmyra and Hawaii, followed by harbor searches in Hawaii and on the West Coast of the United States for the *Sea Dreamer*, Graham Hughes, his wife, Sheri, and their two sons, Alex, twenty-one, and Ryan, sixteen. Authorities discovered that Alex had—prior to the voyage—registered at San Diego State University. He never showed up for classes. Friends of the San Diego family have not heard from them.

To this day, the *Sea Dreamer* and the Hughes family, last seen on an uninhabited island they didn't even intend to visit, remain unaccounted-for.

WE *do* know the fate of another sailor.

Just before dusk on July 26, 1987, a U.S. Coast Guard C-130 search plane, acting on a tip from a foreign fishing boat, reported spotting a sailboat drifting in dead-calm waters "just southeast of Palmyra."

The plane circled in the darkening skies, its crewmen looking at the boat through binoculars. They could see no signs of life. The sloop's mast was broken off, and the sails were torn. An attempt to contact the boat by radio raised only silence. Visible on the stern of the boat was the name, the *Marara*.

The forty-one-foot sloop and its owner, Manning Eldridge, a forty-three-year-old Garden Grove, California, attorney, had been missing since mid-February 1987, while on the last leg (Tahiti to Hawaii) of a three-year South Pacific cruise.

On August 2, a week after the aerial sighting, a 190-foot cutter intercepted the drifting sailboat, and armed Coast Guardsmen cautiously boarded the *Marara*. Below, in the cabin, they found human skeletal remains.

The Honolulu coroner subsequently identified the deceased as the missing attorney. Owing to the condition of the remains, the cause of death was listed as unknown.

Earlier, when Eldridge had not shown up on schedule in Hawaii, some friends wanted to believe that he had succumbed to the temptations of the tropics and swapped his law practice for life

on a deserted island. For him, the solo cruise had been the fulfill-
ment of a long-held dream to sail through the South Pacific,
far from his job and the inexorable grind of urban living. But
other friends were very worried, and they soon contacted the
authorities.

"Right away, we told the Coast Guard to look in the vicinity of
one small island south of Hawaii," explained his friend and former
secretary Wendi Rothman. "Before leaving for the South Pacific,
Manning talked all the time about wanting to visit a place called
Palmyra Island."

APPENDIX

p. 234: Did Mac kill Muff?

Surprisingly, more than a few have speculated that Mac may have murdered his own wife. They point out that if Mac did it, he would have wanted to place suspicion on others, in this case, Buck and Jennifer. Therefore, he would have had to do it while Buck and Jennifer were still on Palmyra. Is it just a coincidence, they argue, that Mac and Muff's disappearance was on the very last day before Buck and Jennifer were to leave Palmyra? Also, they argue, Mac was much more adventuresome than Muff, and he liked a life on the sea, whereas she was a homebody and didn't even want to go to Palmyra. Did hostility develop between them? And of course, since Mac's body has never been found, how can we be sure he's even dead? Is he living in Tahiti today with a new love, or sailing the seven seas on another boat?

Yes, one can make these theoretical arguments, but to my knowledge, no one intimately associated with the case has ever given a fleeting thought to the possibility that Mac murdered Muff. I know I haven't. The reasons are multifold. All of Mac's and Muff's friends agree that Mac loved Muff dearly, and his doing anything at all to harm her (much less in the exceptionally brutal way Muff met her end) is unthinkable to them. And if there was anyone or anything he loved even close to Muff it was his beloved *Sea Wind*, which, under the circumstances of the case, he would have also had to give up. He also would have thereby been stranded on Palmyra (since we know the *Iola*, the only other boat on the island, was sunk by Buck and Jennifer), with no way to leave except to hitchhike out on a later boat. Not only would this obviously be a highly disagreeable prospect for Mac, but the mysterious disappearance of the Grahams generated considerable publicity throughout the Pacific region, and whoever gave a Caucasian male of Mac's approximate age and description a lift off Palmyra would almost assuredly have notified the authorities. Mac also apparently would have decided and been willing to assume a new identity and literally be on the run the rest of his life, since as of the date of this book, seventeen years after his disappearance, he has not been heard from. Moreover, in addition to giving up Muff and the *Sea Wind*, he also would have to have been willing to give up his sister, Kit, and his then seventy-five-year-old mother. And since there doesn't appear to be any way that Mac could have profited financially from killing Muff (there being no evidence of any insurance policy on her life), Mac would also have to have been willing to give up every cent of his net worth, all of which, under the terms of his 1973 will, he left (in the event Muff did not survive him) to Kit. His assets were subsequently distributed to her in 1975, and Elliot Enoki reported to me that prior to that, all of Mac's accounts had remained untouched, with no activity on them. There is also physical evidence pointing to Mac's own demise and murder: the missing fourth container.

p. 243: Perjury in self-defense is expected and overlooked.
When a defendant who has denied guilt from the witness stand is convicted, the jury obviously believes he committed perjury when he denied his guilt under oath. Yet of the countless defendants convicted of various crimes every year throughout the United States, I personally have never heard of one being prosecuted for perjury following his conviction.

p. 250: The prosecution seeks life imprisonment.
In the Palmyra murder case, the prosecution sought sentences of life imprisonment, not the death penalty. But not by choice. The section of the U.S. Code under which Walker and Jenkins were being prosecuted, Section 1111, provides for the death penalty as an alternative to life imprisonment for a conviction of first-degree murder. However, in the 1972 case of *Furman v. Georgia*, 408 U.S. 238, the United States Supreme Court struck down death-penalty statutes throughout the land, holding that the death penalty was unconstitutional unless the jury was given guidelines by the trial judge to control their discretion in determining whether or not the penalty of death should be imposed. Thereafter, many states enacted new death-penalty legislation to comply with the mandate of *Furman*. But on the federal level, as of the date of the Walker and Jenkins trials, Section 1111 had not been amended to meet that standard, and the Office Manual of the U.S. Attorney's Office instructed federal prosecutors not to seek the death penalty in murder cases because a verdict of death under Section 1111 would be unenforceable.

p. 269: The DeLorean case.
DeLorean was subsequently acquitted. For a defense attorney, the DeLorean case was a "dream entrapment case," said San Francisco criminal defense specialist John Keker.

p. 271: Circumstantial evidence of innocence.

Cases are legion in which certain acts and statements of an accused are deemed admissible circumstantial evidence to show guilt, while the opposite of such acts or statements are *not* admissible to show innocence; e.g., although the prosecution can introduce evidence of escape or attempted escape, the defense generally cannot introduce evidence that the defendant had an opportunity to escape but did not. And while a defendant's incriminating statement comes in under an exception to the hearsay rule, a defendant's exculpatory statement is inadmissible, since the law virtually presumes a self-serving motivation for the latter. Similarly, a suspect's silence in response to being accused of committing a crime is admissible as showing a consciousness of guilt. But if he is not silent, and denies the accusation, the denial is not admissible.

p. 276: My motion that the judge order the prosecution to change the charge to premeditated murder.

At the Walker trial, Robert Hollis, a respected veteran reporter for the *Honolulu Advertiser*, approached me to say that Partington blamed me for the premeditated murder count being added against both defendants in the superseding indictment of January 8, 1985. He said Partington thought my written motion a few weeks earlier on December 12, 1984, had put the idea in the prosecutor's head. I felt this was ridiculous on its face, since Enoki and Schroeder, two experienced federal prosecutors, obviously didn't need me to tell them about the availability and viability of a premeditated murder count. When I confronted Partington, he passionately denied telling Hollis this, but I had no reason whatsoever to disbelieve the reporter. In any event, I reminded Partington that I was representing Jennifer, not Buck, and therefore had to do what I felt was good for her, not Buck. Besides, the felony-murder count could hurt only Jennifer, since only Jennifer's theft conviction had been affirmed on appeal. Walker's conviction had been reversed by an appellate court, so Jennifer alone had to worry about a felony-murder conviction flowing from her theft conviction. Thereafter, Enoki told both Hollis and me that the premeditated murder count was based on Ingman's and Williams's testimony before the grand jury, and that he and Schroeder had contemplated filing it *in addition* to the felony-murder count long before I even raised the issue of substituting it *for* the felony-murder count.

p. 276: The inappropriateness of the felony-murder count.

I also argued that, assuming the Government had furnished us everything we were entitled to receive under discovery, both sides already knew, before the trial, that the prosecution had no evidence the killing took place *during* the perpetration or attempted perpetration of the robbery, a necessary element for the felony-murder rule to apply. Realistically, this legal argument could only be made if there was a premeditated murder count in addition to a felony-murder count in the indictment. With only a felony-murder count, if the jury (or even a judge) believed beyond a reasonable doubt that Buck and Jennifer had murdered the Grahams, there's no way in the world they would return a verdict of not guilty and let Buck and Jennifer walk out of court simply because the Government failed to prove that the murder was "connected" to the robbery. They would automatically (and no doubt correctly) conclude that there was a connection.

p. 278: The duty of a public prosecutor to be fair.

It is often said that the purpose of a criminal trial is to ascertain the truth. But this obviously depends upon the perspective. Certainly the prosecutor, judge, and jury want the truth to come out. Not so with the defense attorney. If his client is guilty, which is usually the case, the very last thing in the world he wants to come out (and that which he attempts to suppress) is the truth. And this verity reflects the very disparate roles of the opposing lawyers in a criminal trial.

The duty of the defense attorney is only to his client, the accused. But the prosecutor has a higher and dual role. He represents "the people" (as in *People of the State of California* v. *Jones*), and in more than a theoretical sense, one of those people is the defendant. So while he can justifiably seek a conviction in cases he believes in, he has the concomitant duty to help insure that the person he is prosecuting receives a fair trial. Saying it another way, the prosecution is the lawyer for the sovereign (state or federal government), and the government's only interest is to see that all of its citizens receive impartial justice. Therefore, as opposed to a defense attorney, it is as much a prosecutor's duty to refrain from improper methods to secure a wrongful conviction as it is to use every legitimate measure to bring about a just one.

In all fairness to the prosecutors in this case, they most likely believed, although erroneously, that they at least had a *legal* right to do what they were seeking to do.

p. 282: Why I did not believe that the prosecution, at Jennifer's murder trial, should be allowed to ask her whether she had been convicted of the theft of the *Sea Wind*.

Under Rule 609(a) of the Federal Rules of Evidence, when a defendant testifies, the prosecution may (for the *ostensibly* limited purpose of impeaching his credibility as a witness) ask him on cross-examination whether he has ever been convicted of a crime if: 1. The crime is a felony, and the probative value of the conviction (that is, the extent to which the fact of the prior conviction tends to indicate guilt in the current case) outweighs the prejudicial effect to the defendant if the jury hears of the conviction. [On the issue of probative value, the thinking goes that an ex-felon is not to be believed in his testimony as much as one who is not an ex-felon. But if a priest or rabbi actually commits a felony, yet pleads not guilty, he is not any more likely to tell the truth on the witness stand than one who has previously been convicted of twenty felonies. If he were going to tell the truth, he would not have pled not guilty.] or 2. Regardless of whether the crime is a felony or a misdemeanor, it involved dishonesty or a false statement.

Among other things, I argued in my brief that the prejudicial effect to Jennifer that would result from the jury's hearing she had already been convicted of stealing the *Sea Wind*, "would be singularly devastating and completely outweigh any probative value. The built-in bias the jury would have against Defendant Jenkins may prove to be insurmountable. If, in the jury's eyes, she has already been judged to be guilty of the theft of the Sea Wind, almost as a necessary corollary they would feel she must also be guilty of Mrs. Graham's murder."

But had Jennifer's theft convictions "involved dishonesty," in which case the above argument could not be considered? In a loose, layman sense, one could say that all thefts involve dishonesty. When I found a split of authority in the cases interpreting the "dishonesty" language in Rule 609(a), I researched the legislative intent behind the language. A Conference Committee Report (H.R. Conf. Rep. No. 93-1597, 93d Congress, 2d Sess. 9) read: "By the phrase 'dishonesty or false statement' the Conference means crimes such as perjury, criminal fraud or false pretenses, or any other crime in the nature of crimen falsi, the commission of which involves some element of deceit, untruthfulness, or falsification bearing on the accused's propensity to testify truthfully."

The legislative intent made it clear, I pointed out to the court, that only those species of theft involving deceit, fraud, or misrepresentation (e.g., obtaining money by false pretenses, larceny by trick) satisfied the dishonesty requirement. The kind of straight theft Jennifer had been convicted of did not. In other words, "dishonesty" required something more than a mere propensity to steal. As expected, Enoki, in his response brief, did not agree.

There had been quite a discussion on the defense team as to whether I should have even made the motion to suppress Jennifer's felony theft conviction. Jennifer's brother, Ted, felt we should openly acknowledge the theft because, he said, the jury would never believe that she did not intend to steal the *Sea Wind*. Len Weinglass's thinking was that it was actually better to let the jury know that Jennifer had been convicted of the theft of the *Sea Wind*. Perhaps, he reasoned, they would not have quite as much motivation to convict her on the murder charge if they knew she had already served hard time for the theft. They could possibly say to themselves that society had already gotten its pound of flesh. I saw some merit in both Ted's and Len's positions, but on balance, I felt that it would be better if the jury never heard that Jennifer had been convicted of the theft of the *Sea Wind*.

p. 289: Interviewing opposing witnesses.

Interviewing the opposition witnesses is essential to proper preparation for cross-examination, though, unaccountably, many lawyers neglect this basic spadework. (For instance, in the Palmyra case, the prosecutors made no effort to interview our witnesses.) When a lawyer attempts to interview the opposition witnesses, there is really no way he can lose. If they give him a statement, he can use it as a basis for impeachment at the trial if it differs from their trial testimony or from any other statement they may have made. Even if they are unwilling to talk to him, as is frequently the case, their refusal can be brought out at the trial to show their bias. I had interviewed some of the Government's witnesses four or five times before Jennifer's trial began.

p. 305: Why J. W. Williams did not testify at the Walker trial.

While Enoki has declined to say why he didn't call Williams to testify, Earle Partington is not reticent about speculating why. He claims that when the FBI first visited Williams in prison on September 27, 1984, the agents *showed* him Ingman's FBI 302 report that outlined Ingman's version of Walker's prison confession, and asked Williams if he could corroborate it. Says Partington: "Williams told them he'd have to think about it. He subsequently wrote to Walker in prison and told him about the FBI's visit. Unbeknownst to me, Walker and Williams then concocted a scheme whereby Williams agreed to fabricate a story for the FBI similar to Ingman's, get himself called as a Government witness, and, on the stand, refute what he'd told the FBI, saying he'd gone along with the FBI because they had offered him such a good deal. Williams would then testify that Walker had made no statements about the Grahams or what had happened to them. Walker and Williams thought this would discredit Ingman's testimony, making it look as if Ingman, too, was most likely going along with what the FBI wanted him too say. Williams, in fact, did tell the FBI a fabricated story on October 9, 1984, but Enoki, I think, suspected an ambush and decided against calling Williams. Ray Findlay and I briefly discussed calling Williams as a defense witness, but decided against it. With Williams telling two different stories—one to the grand jury and FBI, and another to the trial jury—we couldn't count on which story the jury would end up believing."

Plausible, except for the inconvenience of fact. The FBI interviewed Ingman on October 5, 1984, but the 302 report of that interview wasn't transcribed by an agency clerk until October 17, three weeks *after* the FBI's first interview with Williams and even eight days *after* the FBI's second interview with Williams on October 9, 1984, during which he recounted Walker's "walk the plank" story. Therefore, contrary to Partington's assertion, Williams could not have been shown Ingman's report by the FBI at either of their two sessions with him, and therefore could not have based his story on the report. Williams may indeed have decided at a later date to refute his story on the stand, but it seems apparent that his crony Walker *did tell* the sadistic tale; true or not, to both Ingman and Williams at McNeil Island prison.

p. 315: "The average body . . . will float in about ten days."

Mobster Johnny Roselli, involved in the CIA-Mafia plot to assassinate Cuban premier Fidel Castro, was murdered in 1976, stuffed into a fifty-five-gallon oil drum weighted down with heavy chains, and dumped into Miami's Biscayne Bay. Fishermen discovered the drum when decomposition gases produced enough buoyancy to float it to the surface just ten days later. Yet the container holding Muff's bones remained submerged for almost seven years. No witness at Walker's trial was asked why it took so long for Muff's container to surface, but a few of the experts involved shared their theories with Enoki, though there was no consensus. "Obviously, it doesn't take seven years for a body to decompose," Enoki would say later, "so whatever it was that caused the container to rise to the surface, it was something *other* than decomposition gases." He said a small hole or crack in the container might have caused the gases to dissipate, thereby not allowing them to build up to sufficient pressure to float the box to the surface in a timely fashion. (Enoki elicited expert testimony at the Walker trial that the corrosion holes in the container would *not* have prevented the box from eventually floating to the surface.) The longer the container remained on the bottom of the lagoon, Enoki suggested, the more it might have become covered with bottom-growing vegetation.

So what forces caused the box to surface in 1981? One theory advanced is that the Jordans' successful effort (three weeks before Sharon found the box) to raise the submerged rescue boat might have created enough disturbance on the lagoon's bottom to cause the container to break loose and head for the surface. Also, Enoki points to Jordan's mention of a bad storm hitting the island the night before her macabre discovery. Possibly the increased current and wave action had helped free the box. But in the end, Enoki feels, no one will ever know why Government exhibit 28 surfaced precisely when it did, nor why the box that must still hold Mac's remains has apparently never surfaced. "This is just another mystery in the case," Enoki says. Also puzzling is how the heavy wire, which wrapped the lid of Muff's water coffin shut, came loose.

p. 316: Evidence of intense heat inside Muff's aluminum coffin while submerged in water.

Enoki told me, "I could see Walker putting the body in the container, then trying to burn at least the face, possibly to obliterate its features. When he dumped the box in the water, the fire inside must still have been hot and smoldering, which caused the abnormal variation in grain size found by the metallurgist. But whether the fire was started when the box was sitting in the water, or whether the box was still hot from the fire when it hit the water, the FBI expert couldn't tell me. I didn't pursue this forensic evidence as it was just another one of the endless speculative asides to the case."

p. 323: The Walker defense team's search of Palmyra for the second missing container.

Ironically, the defense's search for the missing box was far more complete than the authorities had attempted. Len Weinglass told me that before the second Palmyra trip, Partington had asked Walker if he was sure he wanted them to look for the second container. After all, if they found it, and if the body of Mac Graham was inside, the Government would proceed with a second murder charge against Walker. Walker reportedly said: "Go ahead with your search. *You'll never find him.*" Although Len claimed he had heard this story directly from Partington, the latter would subsequently deny telling Len anything like this, asserting that his client had said nothing of the kind.

p. 343: Len Weinglass's conversation with Dr. Boyd Stephens.

In a telephone conversation with Dr. Stephens after the trial, he said he did not believe he told Weinglass that the ants would have crawled into the bone marrow *only* while the body still had flesh on it.

pp. 355–356: The jury would not receive evidence of the times of the high tides on Palmyra on August 30-31, 1974.

In addition to not learning of the times of the high (and low) tides, the Jenkins murder trial jury never learned the *height* of the tides. The high tide at 4:26 P.M. on August 30 had a height of 2.6 feet above the reference line of "mean lower low"—the average of the lowest low-water height of each tidal day observed over the National Tidal Datum Epoch (nineteen years). The high low tide at 11:08 P.M. on August 30 was 0.1 feet above the reference line. The low high tide at 5:35 A.M. on August 31, was 1.8 feet above the reference line. (It should be noted, of course, that high tides reach—and retreat from—their optimum point gradually.)

Actually, the extremely relevant point of how far up the shore various heights would take the tide was impossible to determine, since it is always influenced by such variables as the direction and velocity of the wind, atmospheric pressure, opposing currents, and the slope at the particular point on the shore. (Here, we never knew the precise point where Jennifer said she and Buck found the overturned dinghy, only the general area.) Also, because of the lack of ocean surge in the lagoon, tides would not carry the water up the lagoon shore nearly as far as they would on the island's shores that fronted the sea.

p. 362: Even Chief Justices of the U.S. Supreme Court are creatures of politics.

Earl Warren was the chairman and keynote speaker at the Republican National Convention in 1944 and the Vice Presidential nominee on the Republican national ticket in 1948. Warren Burger in 1948 was the floor manager for Minnesota Governor Harold Stassen's home-state candidacy at the Republican National Convention, and in 1952 he pledged the Minnesota delegation to Dwight Eisenhower's Presidential bid at the convention. (With no previous judicial experience at all, in 1956 Burger was appointed by Eisenhower to the U.S. Court of Appeals.) Talk about the political vineyards, the nevertheless qualified William Rehnquist (an active political supporter of Barry Goldwater's 1964 bid for the Presidency) provided on-site legal advice in 1962 to Republicans assigned the task of challenging voters' credentials at a Phoenix polling location. The charge by witnesses that he had intimidated black and Hispanic voters on the ground of their inability to read was denied by Rehnquist.

p. 363: "The judge is *killing* me in court."

No lawyer is exempt. For example, only a very few lawyers in the history of the legal profession have practiced law in as grand a fashion or sown more new legal ground (particularly in the area of tort law) than the celebrated San Francisco lawyer Melvin Belli. Yet, despite his considerable legal stature and characteristically gentlemanly behavior in court, he was treated with so much disrespect by a small-town judge in a recent case that he mournfully observed, "The judge is riding me so hard in front of the jury I've got spur marks on my back." Predictably, the judge was a political animal, having run for the office a few years earlier. The judge's campaign theme was to "end the reign of arrogance" of the incumbent judge. Another legal giant, F. Lee Bailey, has from time to time not been treated with the considerable respect he has earned with his sterling courtroom victories.

p. 363: Failure of judges to be impartial.

The prosecution, of course, is not immune; judges can also show preference for the defense. An example was my prosecution of Charles "Tex" Watson for the seven Tate-LaBianca murders. As excerpted from *Helter Skelter* (W. W. Norton, 1974, pp. 465–66): "Judge Alexander not only repeatedly favored the defense in his rulings, he went far beyond that. During voir dire he remarked: 'Many of *us* are opposed to the death penalty.' When prosecution witnesses were testifying, he gave them incredulous, unbelieving looks; when defense witnesses took the stand, he industriously took notes. All this was done right in front of the jury. He also frequently cross-examined the prosecution witnesses. Finally, I'd had it. Asking to approach the bench, I reminded Alexander that this was a jury trial, not a court trial, and that I was immensely concerned that by cross-examining the prosecution witnesses he was giving the jury the impression that he didn't believe the witnesses, and since a judge has substantial stature in the eyes of a jury, this could be extremely harmful to the People. I suggested that if he wanted to have certain questions asked, he write them out and give them to the defense attorneys to ask.

"Thereafter, Alexander cut down on his cross-examination of the prosecution witnesses. However, he still continued to amaze me. When the jury went out to deliberate, he didn't even have the exhibits sent back to the jury room—a virtually automatic act—until after I had demanded that he do so. And once, in chambers and off the record, he referred to the defendant as 'poor Tex.'

"Also off the record was a remark I made to him toward the end of the trial: 'You're the biggest single obstacle to my obtaining a conviction of first-degree murder in this case.'

"Despite the problems presented by Judge Alexander, on October 12, 1971, the jury found Watson guilty of seven counts of first-degree murder and one count of conspiracy to commit murder. And on October 21, after remaining out only six hours, they returned with a verdict of death.

"Judge Alexander remarked, on the day he sentenced Watson, 'If I had tried this case without a jury, I possibly would have arrived at a different verdict.'"

p. 364: Credibility with the jury.

An example of the dynamics involved on this point occurred near the beginning of a major murder trial I prosecuted for the Los Angeles DA's Office. I raised an objection while sitting down. The judge ordered me to stand up when making an objection. I did, after which he told me to sit down. I immediately asked to approach the bench. I was boiling. I told the judge (outside earshot of the jury), "I represent the People of the State of California, twenty million people, and when I stand up in front of the jury in my final summation, I have to have stature and credibility with them. If you tell me to stand up and sit down like a yo-yo, I'm not going to have it. From now on, I'll stand up and sit down in this courtroom when I want to, not when you want me to," whereupon I stalked back to my seat. Thereafter, the judge never again ordered me to stand up or sit down.

pp. 370–371: Reducing everything to writing prior to trial.

I have found that many ideas, thoughts, and concepts do not lend themselves to easy articulation. But they can be mastered if one invests the necessary time. There is a more obvious danger of not reducing virtually everything to a yellow pad. Almost invariably during cross-examination or final summation in a complex case, since a lawyer has virtually no time in court to pause and cogitate, he is simply going to omit many points, some of which may very well have been crucial to his client's cause. How many lawyers walk out of court every day muttering, "Gee, I forgot to ask this question, I forgot to argue that point"? When every point a lawyer wants to make is on his yellow pad, this will not happen, of course.

In my opinion, for whatever it's worth, the majority of lawyers trying cases today have grossly inadequate notes, and therefore are not adequately prepared. There are hundreds of pieces of information in their heads, but because they are human beings, not computers, of necessity the information is disorganized and undigested, and a dangerously high percentage of it is ineffectively presented when it leaves the lawyer's lips in court. The sequence should not be from the lawyer's mind to the jury. It should be from his mind to the yellow pad—for organization, digestion, polishing, and review—and only then to the jury.

p. 382: Effect of an opening statement.

There are distinct advantages to giving an opening statement, perhaps the most important of which is that it gives the lawyer an extra opportunity to sell his case to the jury and predispose them to his side at the beginning of the case. But an opening statement should not automatically always be given, for there are some drawbacks, particularly if one is a defense attorney in a criminal trial, where the prosecution's right to pretrial discovery is very limited. First, the lawyer is divulging to the opposition, right at the start of a case—one that might last weeks or even months—the heart of his case, sometimes even the intricacies of it. And this, of course, gives the opposing lawyer so much more time than he would normally have to work up an effective response. Secondly, when your key witnesses testify to important points, you want their testimony to have maximum dramatic impact. And if the jury has already heard the gist of the story from the lawyer, that impact might be diminished.

In recent years, the opening statement has taken on, in my opinion, inordinate importance in the eyes of trial lawyers, some claiming it's the most important part of the trial. The rationale is that first impressions are usually lasting impressions. Indeed, at least one survey has shown that 70 percent of jurors who formed an opinion in favor of one side at the end of the opening statement voted for that side at the end of the trial. However, no one apparently bothered to consider that maybe the reason was that side simply had the better case, as was apparent even during opening statement.

Implicit in the notion that an opening statement is enormously important is the false assumption that juries are, as one English barrister described them, "twelve people of average ignorance," and that without having yet heard one single solitary word of testimony, they're going to be permanently (or at least substantially) influenced in their view of the case. On grounds of pure logic, this would appear to be very unlikely. Moreover, the jury knows that the lawyers addressing them are taking the positions they are because they are being paid by their clients.

Although I usually elect to make an opening statement, if, in a hypothetical situation, the other side could make one and I couldn't, I'm confident that just these few words would *almost* be adequate to insure that the jury started the trial with an open mind: "You've heard opposing counsel tell you what he *intends* to prove during the trial. Well, as you folks know, there are always two sides to every story, and I would respectfully ask that before you form any judgment, you listen not just to their side, but to the side *we're* going to present during the trial."

Even when jurors *do* form an opinion during the opening statement, it certainly is not etched in marble, and can be overcome by actual evidence and testimony from the witness stand.

Lawyers making opening statements are like two opposing coaches talking on television before a Super Bowl game about what their teams hope to accomplish on the field of play. Jurors, I've long thought, are in the position of TV viewers who tire of prelims and want the game to begin.

If a lawyer does make an opening statement, he should make sure he doesn't bite off more than he can chew, that he doesn't promise the jury he will prove something he may be unable to prove. He must be careful in his statement so he doesn't have to contradict himself or retract by trial's end. It is very effective for opposing counsel to point out to the jury at the conclusion of the case that the lawyer said in his opening statement he was going to prove something and he failed to do so. It hurts his credibility in the eyes of the jury and can adversely affect their perception of his entire case.

p. 396: An alternative to the "why" question.

An alternative to the "why" question is to save for final argument the implications of the witness's testimony, but by that late point in the trial, the witness's reason for his conduct is a matter for competing speculation by the lawyers, not court record. Moreover, the opportunity to make the witness "look like a liar" before the jury's eyes when he is trapped has been lost.

p. 435: Schroeder's line of questions would be calling for hearsay.

When used in a legal sense, "hearsay" has a very specific meaning. Hearsay is a statement made outside of court (i.e., not from the witness stand at the present proceeding) that is offered into evidence to prove not merely that the statement was made, but that it is *true*. If, for example, a witness intended to testify that "Ray told me he saw Michael kill his wife," Ray's statement would be inadmissible hearsay if offered to prove that Michael killed his wife. On the other hand, if a witness testifies at a competency hearing over Grandpa's will that "Grandpa told me the sky was falling," Grandpa's statement would *not* be hearsay, since it would be offered not to prove that the sky was falling, but to prove that the old man had made the statement.

Almost all hearsay consists of oral or written statements, but even conduct, when intended as a substitute for words (e.g., nodding one's head in answer to a question, or identifying a person by pointing), is a hearsay "statement."

It is commonly stated that it is hearsay when a witness relates what someone else said, but an out-of-court statement by the witness himself can also be hearsay. An out-of-court writing by a witness, for example, can be hearsay, and if certain requirements are not met under an exception to the hearsay rule called "past recollection recorded," the writing will not be admissible.

The hearsay "exceptions" apply to situations in which the out-of-court statements carry a likelihood of trustworthiness, such as deathbed declarations and self-incriminating statements of a defendant (people normally do not incriminate themselves falsely). There are, in fact, so many legal exceptions to the hearsay rule (twenty-two, to be exact) that a number of legal scholars feel the tide is running in the direction of eventually abolishing the rule, and like most European countries, allowing hearsay in, to be given whatever weight the jury feels it is entitled to.

Although some of Mac's out-of-court statements to Shoemaker would not be hearsay (e.g., "I guess they've made a truce" was not offered to prove that there was, in fact, a truce), the key statements "There is a dinghy coming over to the boat" and "Let me go up topside and see what's happening" *were* offered to prove that these statements were true; that is, that Buck and Jennifer came to the *Sea Wind* on the evening of August 28, 1974. Although it is unlikely that the spontaneous-declaration exception to the hearsay rule would apply (the precipitating event wasn't so *startling* as to produce an *excited utterance* under stress), the key statements may have been admissible over my objection under the "present sense impression" exception to the hearsay rule—Mac's statements describing what was taking place were contemporaneous with the events he was describing.

p. 441: Prosecution's disbelief that the hole in the *Sea Wind*'s hull was caused by a swordfish.

The prosecution attempt to imply throughout most of Jennifer Jenkins's trial, as well as at the Walker trial, that the hole was probably caused by a bullet was curious. On October 30, 1974, the day after Jennifer's arrest and Buck's escape in the Ala Wai harbor, FBI crime lab experts combed the interior and exterior surfaces of the *Sea Wind* for traces of blood, bullet holes, or any other evidence that a crime had been committed. Nothing was found, but no reference to the search for physical evidence appeared in any of the FBI documents on the case furnished to the defense by the U.S. Attorney's office. This information first surfaced in a telephone conversation with Calvin Shishido on November 28, 1988. "The *Sea Wind* was clean," Shishido said.

p. 476: The need to argue innocence as well as reasonable doubt.

A defense attorney has a serious dilemma when he *only* argues to the jury that the prosecution has not met its legal burden of proving guilt beyond a reasonable doubt. The baggage of such an argument can be that he has thereby, by implication, conceded his client is *not* innocent. In other words, if his client had absolutely nothing to do with the crime, and is completely innocent, it sounds almost inappropriate to only argue that *his guilt* has not been proved beyond a reasonable doubt. Though there is no *legal* implication of guilt in a reasonable doubt argument, as a practical matter it tends to go in that direction, though by analogy, not as conspicuously as a plea of not guilty by reason of insanity. While there is likewise no legal concession of guilt in the insanity plea, that is the precise effect of such a plea. Again, if a defendant had absolutely nothing to do with the commission of a crime, a plea of not guilty by reason of insanity is completely inappropriate. The plea in effect tells the jury, "I'm guilty, but give me a break because I'm crazy."

Suffice it to say that it is advisable, and in fact nearly always essential, for defense counsel to argue his client's innocence. Not only does a jury have to vote not guilty if they believe the defendant is innocent, but a synergism is involved. Even if they don't ultimately conclude he is innocent, the evidence which is presented to prove innocence will normally also go in the direction of helping to establish reasonable doubt. The approach almost necessarily has to be broken down into two levels. At the first level, counsel can argue that the evidence proves, or at least points to, his client's innocence. Defense counsel can then go on to the second level and argue that the prosecution's case against his client was so weak that even if one or more jurors nonetheless believe that he did commit the crime, they certainly should not believe in his guilt beyond a reasonable doubt. And therefore, under the law, they *still* are duty-bound to return a verdict of not guilty.

p. 481: Problems with character defense.

There was a more subtle problem I had. The premise of the character defense is the oft-repeated notion that "people don't change." And originally, the language I had prepared for my summation used these words. But I knew that Enoki, if alert, could argue in his rebuttal that people do change, and cite as one example the also oft-repeated political aphorism that "power corrupts." He could use other, more down-to-earth examples, such as people observing that those who were once their friends "don't know them anymore" once they rise far above them (for instance, a co-worker who becomes a supervisor or president of the company). I had an answer to this, but unless I raised the issue myself, it was one I wouldn't have a chance to use (since after my argument that people don't change, I would not have the opportunity to respond to his rebuttal), to wit: perhaps power doesn't corrupt or change; perhaps it only *reveals*. For instance, the "friend" who becomes the company president and doesn't know his former friends anymore maybe never really was a friend, i.e., people, after all, don't really change. Changed circumstances merely reveal what was latently always there. But since this argument, obviously, could also be used against Jennifer (that is, the claim could be made that the circumstances on Palmyra brought out the latent worst in Jennifer), I decided to take the "people don't change" language out of my summation and leave in language that people don't act out of character. Of course, this *presupposes* that one's character doesn't change, but the "change" issue is disguised and I gambled that Enoki wouldn't be alerted to it.

pp. 503–504: My "prosecution" of Buck Walker.

Regarding my intention to prosecute Walker at Jennifer's trial, not only did I immediately suspect that I would have trouble doing this, but in discussions with Elliot Enoki, he expressly told me he would oppose any such effort of mine. This is why I thoroughly researched the legal defense of "Commission of Crime by Third Person." Curiously, most "third-person" cases are around the turn of the century, many in the mid-nineteenth century in the South. The basic rule is that such third-person evidence is inadmissible on the public policy ground of undue consumption of time—a trial could go on indefinitely if the defendant could accuse one third party after another. However, where it can be shown not only that a third party had a motive (motive alone isn't enough) to commit the crime, but that there is "substantive evidence" connecting him to it, most cases hold that such evidence is admissible. Although Enoki had promised a fight, surprisingly, when the trial started, I was able to get in virtually everything I wanted to without objection. Frequently, Enoki himself offered the evidence, such as Buck's obvious lie that he won the *Sea Wind* gambling. It was as if Enoki, in the absence of my bringing the issue to his attention each time it came up, lost sight of it.

I was unable to get in only two very small matters against Buck, and they were only questionably incriminating. In both situations, among other cases, I cited (unavailingly) the case of *Chambers* v. *Mississippi*, 410 U.S. 284 (1972), for some reason a greatly overlooked case which, in its implications, is one of the very most important *substantive* cases for the defense ever handed down by the U.S. Supreme Court. *Chambers* held that no constitutional right is more important than the right of an accused to present evidence and witnesses in his defense and hence, where "constitutional rights directly affecting the ascertainment of guilt are implicated, the hearsay rule [and therefore, arguably, it would seem, every other established rule excluding evidence] may not be applied mechanistically to defeat the ends of justice."

p. 506: Jennifer had used her real name . . .

Fortunately, Jennifer chose to use her real name on this important occasion. She had used two aliases in her early Hawaiian years, one of which, Susan Mallett, she got a driver's license under when she had too many driving citations. Mallett was the name of the man she was living with at the time.

p. 506: Introducing negative, depreciating evidence on direct examination.

Several years ago, in a celebrated murder case tried in Amarillo, the multimillionaire defendant did not testify or in fact present much of a defense at all. The defense strategy was devoted to making his wife, the star witness for the prosecution, look like the cheapest, most tawdry Jezebel ever to slink down the pike. The defense allegations, though essentially irrelevant legally, were for the most part true, and the uptight Bible Belt jury, aghast at the revelations of immorality on the part of the defendant's wife, in effect convicted her and, almost as an incidental by-product thereof, found her husband not guilty. The defense attorney was later quoted as saying he knew he had won the case "the moment the last redneck was seated on the jury." I cannot help but wonder what the result would have been in this case if the prosecutor had matter-of-factly presented all of this negative, depreciating evidence on direct examination. Maybe, just maybe, they at least would have had a murder trial in Amarillo.

pp. 520—521: Jennifer's recollection of number of times and times of day she saw Buck on August 30, 1974.

Assuming Jennifer's story of what happened on August 30, 1974, is true, as I believe, it's not entirely implausible that Buck had already murdered Mac and Muff by 9:00 A.M. (If so, he most likely hadn't disposed of the bodies at this point; a more time-consuming and laborious task, actually, than killing two human beings. Also, Jennifer said she heard the Zodiac being operated in the lagoon later in the day around 4:30 P.M.) Given Mac's proclivity for getting up and getting out early in the morning, and Muff's for sleeping in, Buck might have killed Mac first, catching him unaware in his workshop or elsewhere, and then gone to the *Sea Wind* to find Muff, who may have still been asleep. Walker could have murdered Muff there or forcibly removed her from the boat before doing so. It should also be borne in mind that if Jennifer had the dinghy throughout the day on August 30 (a point which was never resolved), the safest time for Buck to have murdered Mac and Muff without having to worry about Jennifer coming ashore *would* have been early in the morning.

p. 563: Jennifer thought it was *before* her theft trial that she had drinks with Gordon.

If, in fact, it was *before* her theft trial that Jennifer had drinks with Gordon and if, in fact, she told him what he said she did, by Buck "spilling his guts," Jennifer could have simply been talking about the lies she and Buck had told concerning the *Iola*'s getting hung up on the reef in the Palmyra channel. However, although she didn't learn that the Government had the photographs showing the *Iola* and *Sea Wind* alongside each other on the open sea until later at her theft trial, she did know the authorities left for Palmyra on October 31, 1974, which was just two days after her arrest at Ala Wai harbor. Therefore, she would have known at that time (which was while she was still in custody and hence *before* her conversation with Gordon) that the authorities, not seeing the *Iola* hung up on the reef, would know she had lied. Therefore, it could be argued that she would not have been referring to the reef lie when she spoke to Gordon. On the other hand, since she knew of the authorities' visit to Palmyra, why did she persist in the reef lie at her trial? Is it possible that for some unknown reason, prior to her theft trial it did not register in her mind that the authorities knew of the reef story lie? Or could she have thought that even though the authorities didn't see the *Iola* on the reef, this wouldn't necessarily prove she was lying—that the *Iola* could have sunk before they reached Palmyra, or could have been taken away from Palmyra by visitors to Palmyra after she and Buck left the island on September 11, 1974?

p. 570: ". . . one all-important principle is implicit . . . that a jury does not have to believe in a defendant's innocence in order to return a verdict of not guilty."

Why is it implicit? I make this effort: if the jury were instructed that to convict, they had to be "convinced of the defendant's guilt," the issue for the jury to resolve would seem to be guilt *as opposed to what?* The inference is innocence; i.e., the opposite of guilt. So the issue to be decided would be that of *guilt or innocence*. But this truncated instruction is not given. To the words "convinced of the defendant's guilt" are appended the words "beyond a reasonable doubt." It would seem we have now jettisoned the previously inferential "innocence," at least to the extent that it is no longer a *sine qua non* in the legal equation necessary for a verdict of not guilty. Now the issue seems to be guilt *as opposed to what?* Guilt beyond a reasonable doubt. In other words, when jurors are instructed that to convict, they have to be convinced *not only* of guilt, but of guilt beyond a reasonable doubt, they are clearly being told that *a mere belief in guilt is not enough to convict.* And if a mere belief in guilt is not enough, and has to result in a not-guilty verdict, all the more so *a belief in innocence is not necessary* for there to be a not-guilty verdict.

p. 571: the *ultimate legal* issue for the jury to determine is whether or not the prosecution has met its legal burden of proving guilt beyond a reasonable doubt.

For those who would say that, *as used in court*, there really is no confusion because *guilt or innocence* is understood by everyone to mean whether or not the prosecution proved guilt beyond a reasonable doubt, not "did he do it or did he not do it," see, for example, the 1981 United States Supreme Court case of *Bullington* v. *Missouri*: "Underlying the question of *guilt or innocence* is an objective truth: *the defendant did or did not commit the crime.* From the time an accused is first suspected to the time the *decision on guilt or innocence* is made, our system is designed to enable the trier of fact to discover *that truth*."

It is pure folly to expect a lay jury to be less confused than the U.S. Supreme Court.

See also Felix Frankfurter, *The Case of Sacco and Vanzetti: A Critical Analysis* (1927): "At the trial, *the only issue was—were Sacco and Vanzetti two of the assailants of Parmenter and Berardelli, or were they not? This was the beginning and the end of the inquiry at the trial,* and the end of any judgment now on the *guilt or innocence* of these men. Every other issue is relevant only as it helps to answer *that central question*."

The above is not to suggest that the highest court in the land and legal scholars do not have *any* grasp of the distinction between "proving guilt beyond a reasonable doubt" and "determining guilt or innocence." What it does suggest is that this grasp is fuzzy, unarticulated, visceral, and not sufficiently conceptualized in their minds to enable or compel them to speak or write correctly on the subject.

p. 580: My failure to explore Jennifer's relationship with Joe Buffalo.

Jennifer *had* told me that after her conviction for the theft of the *Sea Wind* in June of 1975 (and while she was on bail pending her appeal) she lived for a few months communally in a large old house in Puako on the Big Island with one Mama Lee (a singer at the Sandbox Bar), Uncle Albert (a seventy-year-old man Mama Lee looked after), a man named Joey who she said had a "criminal background" ("Joey" turned out to be Joe Buffalo, the "friend" she told me she received the letter from before her murder trial), and "others."

p. 612: "[If Shoemaker] never told anyone about it for many years, we can almost . . . assume it never happened."

It seems that Shoemaker *did* tell someone (though it is not known whom) about the cake-truce incident as far back as 1981; still, however, seven years after it allegedly happened. An article on the Palmyra murder case in the *New York Times* on July 13, 1981, titled "Mystery on Pacific Atoll Leads to Murder Charge," stated that Shoemaker testified before the grand jury that indicted Buck and Jennifer that Mac told him, "I guess they're going to declare a truce. They're bringing over a cake tonight." Although Shoemaker did not testify before the grand jury, nor, prior to the Walker trial, in any legal proceeding about the cake-truce incident, the reporter, now retired, obviously got this information from someone, although he no longer recalls who told him.

p. 655: First explaining away the negative evidence.

If a lawyer starts his argument on the positive part of his case without having first attempted to eliminate the negative, at the very moment he is making these arguments the jury is thinking, *But what about this and that?* and the force of his argument will be substantially diluted. Moreover, to end his argument thereafter on the defensive, trying to mitigate or explain away the negative evidence, is very poor strategy. One should always end on an affirmative note.

p. 677: "under that [circumstantial evidence] instruction Judge King will give you, Jennifer is entitled to a not-guilty verdict."

I had pointed out to the jury that even if, in a particular case, the evidence did not reasonably permit *any* conclusion of innocence, and the only reasonable conclusion was that of guilt, by itself even that would not be enough for a guilty verdict. The conclusion of guilt would still have to *also* be beyond a reasonable doubt.

p. 684: "[Enoki] seemed a little confused in what was now the last inning of an important ball game."

I had seen other prosecutors make the same mistake—hastily scratching out their rebuttal while defense counsel is arguing, instead of preparing it well beforehand. Since the prosecutor knows all the weaknesses in his case, he should anticipate every conceivable defense argument attacking those weaknesses and prepare his response long before the defense attorney rises for summation. In fact, the prosecutor's rebuttal should be the most powerful argument he makes in the case.

VINCENT BUGLIOSI received his degree from the UCLA Law School, where he was president of his class. Of 106 felony jury trials, he lost only one case. His most famous trial as a prosecutor for the Los Angeles District Attorney's office was the Charles Manson case, which became the basis of his bestselling book *Helter Skelter*. Both *Helter Skelter* and *Till Death Us Do Part* won Edgar Allan Poe Awards for best true crime book of the year. Mr. Bugliosi lives with his wife, Gail, in Los Angeles, where he is in private practice. He is currently working on a book about the assassination of President John F. Kennedy.

BRUCE B. HENDERSON, who has taught at the USC School of Journalism, is the author and coauthor of many works of nonfiction, including *Empire of Deceit* and his latest, *True North*. Mr. Henderson lives in Sebastopol, California.